W9-AEL-969

# *End of the Affair*

# End of the Affair

THE COLLAPSE OF THE ANGLO-FRENCH

ALLIANCE, 1939-40

## Eleanor M. Gates

UNIVERSITY OF CALIFORNIA PRESS

BERKELEY     LOS ANGELES

University of California Press
Berkeley and Los Angeles, California
© 1981 by Eleanor M. Gates
Printed in the United States of America

1  2  3  4  5  6  7  8  9

Library of Congress Cataloging in Publication Data

Gates, Eleanor M
    End of the affair. The collapse of the Anglo-French
alliance, 1939–40
    Bibliography: p.
    Includes index.
    1.  World War, 1939–1945—Diplomatic history.
2.  Great Britain—Foreign relations—France.
3.  France—Foreign relations—Great Britain.
4.  Great Britain—Foreign relations—1936–1945.
I.  Title.
D750.G37        940.53'22        80-23585
ISBN 0-520-04292-1

*In memory of my father,*
*Payson Grier Gates*
*(1894–1955)*

# Contents

Contents

# Maps and Plans

# *Preface*

THE French decision to surrender in 1940, to opt out of the war and the alliance that proved too much for them, seems far less remarkable today than it did then or even than it might have ten years ago. Separate arrangements following defeat or inconclusive or disadvantageous wars are not that uncommon: England in 1802, Austria in 1809, Russia in 1917, Egypt in 1979 all chose to sever their ties with the coalitions to which they owed formal allegiance.

For a generation the abrupt ending of the alliance linking Great Britain and France seemed an event of cataclysmic importance, an embarrassing, painful, but nonetheless short-term aberration to be condemned and corrected as quickly as possible after 1944. The life of the Entente Cordiale (1904–40) had, after all, virtually coincided with the life of the twentieth century. The passage of time—another forty years—now allows for an altered perspective. In retrospect, the period leading up to and including the two world wars can just as easily be seen as a relatively brief interlude in which the French, by virtue of Germany's meteoric rise to a commanding position, were forced *temporarily* to look to the British and, by extension, to the Americans as the "inevitable" defenders of their security and/or rescuers of their lost territorial integrity. If the ephemeral nature of the relationship was obscured in the immediate aftermath of the second global conflict, when Great Britain together with all the continental powers found their relative power positions so dramatically transformed and curtailed, it became clearer in 1956 during the Suez crisis and especially so from 1958 to 1969, the years of de Gaulle's incumbency, when the Fifth Republic pursued a resolutely anti-Anglo-

Saxon foreign policy designed to free France once and for all from its former subordination to "uncertain" allies.

Some historians have seen in the General's tortuous relations with the British and Americans from 1940 to 1945, coming on top of the Third Republic's unhappy experiences with its cross-Channel and transatlantic neighbors, the basis for his later hostility to NATO and support for an independent French balancing act that would enhance France's international stature. More likely, de Gaulle's wartime frustrations only confirmed a predisposition regarding France's role that at least philosophically links him with some of his worst enemies in 1940. The conception of France itself, associated with the political Right, both antedated and postdated the end of the Anglo-French alliance in 1940.

What seems less likely to change as the result of retrospective analysis is the sheer dramatic impact the story of France's collapse in 1940 and its coming to terms with Nazi Germany has for us. For politically conscious Westerners the fall of France was a tragedy of epic proportions; and this conception is no doubt responsible for the enduring appeal lent the subject of the alliance's breakdown as an essential part of that tragedy. The dissolution of the Anglo-French alliance can still be seen as high drama: The story of divorce on a national scale, the breakup, underlined by great bitterness, of a vital human relationship, it seems to fall naturally into the classic five-act mold of Shakespearean drama, and this is the way I have chosen to present it, complete with prologue and epilogue.

As drama, the subject of the alliance's survival or disintegration understandably owes much to the suspense surrounding the crucial decisions arrived at in 1939 and 1940 and to the high political stakes involved in the alliance for both countries. What gives to the subject a more permanent urgency, however, is the moral dimensions of the decisions made by Britain and France in that these can still be felt and argued about almost as passionately today as they were forty years ago. Knowing the character of the enemy even better than the participants of the 1940 drama did, we continue to be involved in the fall of France in that terrible summer and in Britain's tenuous survival in the months thereafter. This is why we can still be moved by the classic photograph of a weeping Frenchman taken on the day Paris was occupied or by the rousing peroration of a Churchillian speech. Greater knowledge, sophistication, and even cynicism in no way diminish their impact.

It is the moral issues so integral to the falling out between the allies that probably inspired my original and early interest in the alliance as a subject for research, and it is the moral dilemmas facing the leaders of each nation and the interplay or conflict between so-called moral imperatives and national interest as interpreted in the more traditional, worldly sense that I have been at particular pains to recreate. If, finally, "morality" or "moralizing" do not figure in my conclusions, this can be attributed in equal measure to (1) a wholehearted agreement with Anthony Eden's humane statement in the documentary film *The Sorrow and the Pity* that those who did not endure what the French had under German occupation have no right to judge; (2) a commitment to scholarly objectivity combined with a growing willingness to see things from a continental, rather than an Atlantic, point of view; and (3) an increasing absorption in what can probably best be subsumed under the general heading of "esthetic" concerns.

How does an editor whose ties with academic life are peripheral come to be interested in writing such a book? As with most gratuitous acts, the real reasons are probably more poetic, philosophical, or even psychoanalytical than professional or rational. In one sense, nothing in my background compelled me to tackle such a subject; in another, everything was drawing me toward it. And perhaps in this nebulous interplay between free will and determinism lies the emergent theme of *End of the Affair*.

Certainly the inspiration has much to do with a love for intrigue and mystery and the desire to unravel knots and fill in gaps; but equally, or even more so, with a delight in ambivalence, irrationality, and the unruly, elusive nature of truth, in other words, with a preference for the tragic or ironic approach to life over the political or propagandistic. Without in any way wishing to separate myself from the scholarly discipline to which I devoted several years of my life, I would nevertheless identify more with the directors of, say, *Rashomon, Tomorrow Is My Turn* (a French film of which too few people seem to have heard), *The Sorrow and the Pity,* and *Lacombe, Lucien* than with the authors of most of the hundreds of books I have read in preparation for *End of the Affair*.

To reconstruct the past as it was happening; to see with the eyes of those who did not know how the story would end; to refrain from imposing rigid patterns on events that are better understood in terms of fluidities, subtle gradations of change, or, at most, trends; and to appreciate, finally, that the full answers to my most pressing questions would forever remain just out of reach for the reason that the most crucial decisions and thought processes are seldom committed to writing, least of all to government documents: this was the historical task as I conceived it, one requiring analytical, litigious, and archaeological skills in addition to the narrative and dramatic. It is for the reader to judge to what extent I have succeeded.

Many people have helped bring this work to fruition. I should like in particular to thank Professor J. R. Pole of St. Catherine's College, Oxford, for the crucial contacts he facilitated and for his faith and encouragement over a long period of years; Mr. Correlli Barnett, Keeper of the Archives at Churchill College, Cambridge, for his time, interest, advocacy, and innumerable valuable suggestions toward improving the manuscript; Mr. Brian Bond of the Department of War Studies, King's College, University of London, for sharing his thoughts and expertise on matters of mutual interest; Professor Klemens von Klemperer of Smith College for much-needed friendly encouragement and enthusiasm; Professor Philip Bankwitz of Trinity College, Connecticut, for clarifying a number of important points; Dr. Zara Steiner, Director of Historical Studies, New Hall, Cambridge, for her astute questions and criticisms; Professor Edward W. Fox of Cornell University and Professor Patrick Higonnet of Harvard University for giving a sympathetic reading to portions of the manuscript; and John Bright-Holmes at George Allen & Unwin for bearing the major burden of my anxieties over many months and for shepherding this project to completion.Transcripts of Crown-copyright records in the Public Record Office appear by permission of the Controller of H. M. Stationery Office, which is hereby acknowledged. I am also grateful to the staffs of the Public Record Office in London, of the Churchill College Archives in Cambridge, and of the Boston Athenaeum for their helpfulness and efficiency. Last but not least, I should like to thank Professor Marjorie Collins of Mary Washington College, Virginia, Judge R. Ammi Cutter of Cambridge, Massachusetts, and several members of my immediate family for help both material and moral without which this study could never have seen the light of day. Any errors of fact or interpretation as well as any lapses of judgment or taste are of course purely my own responsibility.

June 30, 1980                                              E. M. G.
Princeton, N.J.

# Abbreviations
# Used in Appendices and Notes

### Public Record Office Papers

ADM   Admiralty
CA    Confidential Annex (to War Cabinet Minutes)
CAB   Cabinet papers (broadest heading)
COS   Chiefs of Staff Committee
DO    Defence Committee (Operations)
FO    Foreign Office
JP    Joint Planning Sub-committee
MR    Allied Military Committee
SWC   Supreme War Council
WM    War Cabinet Minutes
WP    War Cabinet Memoranda
WO    War Office

### Published Documents

CE    Testimony or documents gathered by the French National Assembly's postwar Commission d'Enquête Parlementaire and, along with *Rapport*, published as *Les Événements survenus en France de 1933 à 1945*.
DBFP  *Documents on British Foreign Policy, 1919–1939*, 3rd series.
DGFP  *Documents on German Foreign Policy, 1918–1945*, Series D.
FRUS  *Foreign Relations of the United States: Diplomatic Papers*
Procès   Albin Michel edition intended unless *compte rendu in extenso* specified.
Pétain

## BOOK REFERENCES

Kammerer  *La Vérité sur l'Armistice* intended unless other works specified.
Lyet  *La Bataille de France* intended unless otherwise specified.
Michel  *Drôle de Guerre* intended in "Comincia la Commedia";
*Vichy: Année 40* intended in Chapter V.
Reynaud  *In the Thick of the Fight* intended unless other works specified.

# Comincia
# la Commedia

*For they were strange allies, these two peoples: essentially suspicious of each other, perhaps never entirely emotionally convinced by the diplomatic revolution effected in 1904, making the best of it and teetering along in a sentimental mood of music hall jokes and creaking old references to "Mademoiselle from Armentières." As a basis for a war coalition it was a pretty fragile combination. If ever there had been a bloom on the wartime romance of 1914–1918, twenty-five years of varied and sometimes acrimonious relations had largely contrived to take it off.*

> John C. Cairns, "Along the Road Back to France 1940," *The American Historical Review*, Vol. LXIV, No. 3 (April 1959), p. 601.

*Thus we tumbled into Armageddon without heart, without songs, without an ally except France (and she lukewarm), without sufficient aircraft, without tanks, without guns, without rifles, without even a reserve of essential raw commodities and feeding stuffs.*

> Robert Boothby, *I Fight to Live* (London, 1947), p. 194.

# The Separate Slide
# Over the Precipice

THE surprise signing of the Russo-German Non-Aggression Pact on August 23, 1939, abruptly ended any realistic hopes the British and French may have entertained that war could be avoided. It did not end all illusions. Years of appeasement, and especially the previous September's drama at Munich with its last-minute reprieve, were hardly conducive to an unhesitating acceptance of a second European cataclysm within twenty-five years, still less to that total commitment to war which alone makes its waging effective.

Of the two Western allies, Great Britain was undoubtedly better prepared psychologically than was France; war over Poland was, after all, but the logical extension (if not the intended result) of the policy of guaranteeing eastern European states freely embarked on the preceding March in the wake of mass disillusionment over the proven failure of the Munich settlement to appease Hitler. The German entry into Prague was the point of no return, and as such left Parliament and people relatively free from doubt as to where duty lay when Poland was threatened, then finally invaded on September 1.

The position of the government was obviously more complex. The Chamberlain cabinet had not altogether changed its outlook: the Prime Minister was certainly reluctant to cross a Rubicon even of his own choosing, while the subtleties, or ambivalence, of the Foreign Secretary, Halifax, easily led to misunderstanding; no one was absolutely convinced that Britain's permanent interests would best be served by war; to the contrary, an all-out, life and death struggle between the Great Powers pointed to the far greater likelihood of unparalleled disaster. Yet even though their outward show of firmness masked a less than whole-hearted determination and owed as

3

much to fatalism or to concern for British (and their own) dignity and reputation, the final decision of the cabinet to abide by its guarantee was never seriously in doubt.[1] The government *could* at least count on a united nation to support its fearful gamble.

The French Government was in a much less favorable position as it confronted a second world war. Munich and its aftermath demoralized rather more than it stiffened French resolve, being the final failure of a twenty-year effort to contain Germany diplomatically and strategically. It was also a brutal reminder of France's increasing dependence on British support and initiative. Pressured by the British—and their own lack of air preparedness—to abandon a longstanding ally in 1938, they had since been pressured by the British to tighten and even to enlarge their commitments to Poland; understandably, they were less than enthusiastic about honoring these once the pivotal Soviet alliance had eluded their grasp, due, as many believed, to British foot dragging and lack of realism. If the divisions that had plagued the French cabinet during the Czechoslovak crisis were subdued a year later, influential pockets of appeasement remained; and while, after the invasion of Poland, Premier Daladier himself was resigned to another round, his Foreign Minister, Georges Bonnet, did not yet despair of saving the peace. In fact, it was largely owing to his frantic eleventh-hour maneuvers that the Anglo-French alliance almost became unstuck even before it moved into low gear.

The story of how Britain and France delayed declaring war on Germany for some fifty-four and sixty hours respectively after conditions clearly demanded the immediate application of their formal undertakings to assist Poland[2] is familiar but instructive for the differences in outlook between the partners it reveals. These differences—diplomatic, military, and political—revolved around the timing and duration of the ultimatum to be given Germany to evacuate Polish soil. Before Poland's sovereignty was violated, both London and Paris had welcomed the prospect of Italian mediation as possibly the only means of averting war,[3] even though a second Munich would inevitably have resulted in further concessions to Hitler.

Mussolini's offer of August 31 to invite Germany to an international conference, to be held September 5, for the purpose of reviewing the clauses of the Versailles Treaty which had caused the present crisis—provided the Western powers agreed—was thus at issue at the time hostilities began. To the British, the Nazi invasion doomed the proposal, rendering it virtually a dead letter; in any event, no negotiations could take place until the status quo ante was restored.

Bonnet, for his part, was not interested in attaching any prior conditions to a conference other than that the Poles should be present, and after managing to rally the French Council of Ministers to a provisional acceptance of the Italian proposition, even broached the idea to the almost incredulous and totally uninterested Polish Government. Meanwhile, the British had instructed their ambassador in Berlin to warn the German Government formally that unless its forces were promptly withdrawn from Poland, His Majesty's Government would unhesitatingly fulfill its engagements to that country. With this protest the French, somewhat reluctantly, felt required to associate themselves.[4] However, with no time limit imposed on it, the warning lacked teeth. Thus, in communicating Mussolini's (and apparently Bonnet's) proposal for an armistice to be followed by an international conference to Hitler the next day, the Italian Foreign Minister, Count Ciano, was able to assure him that the British and French warnings did not constitute ultimata. The German dictator wanted till noon of September 3 to consider the question.[5]

Because of their unwillingness to negotiate so long as German troops remained in Poland, the British quite logically favored the prompt delivery of an ultimatum with the shortest possible time limit attached to it: naval defense and political considerations alike required a speedy decision. With parliamentary opinion already restive at the thought of any delay in coming to the aid of Poland, the British therefore spent most of September 2 trying to hustle the French out of what seemed almost inexplicable lethargy. The French had a different set of priorities—some electoral—to juggle, so that throughout the day they were urging delay, first on the constitutional grounds that no hostile action leading to war could be taken without the previous consent of Parliament, which was only scheduled to meet at 3 p.m., and second and even more importantly on the grounds that their commander-in-chief, General Gamelin, needed more time to complete the French Army's mobilization and the civilian population's evacuation from the war zone and could not risk enemy air attack while these were under way. And these measures were not expected to be in hand until the night of September 4. Thus the French were willing to wait up to forty-eight hours before any ultimatum they might choose to present on the night of the 2nd took effect, but for diplomatic reasons—due to Bonnet's understanding with Ciano and in the stubborn hope that Italian intervention in Berlin might still be able to save the day—wanted to put off sending their ultimatum altogether until noon of September 3.[6]

Here then, even before the dice were cast, was a distillation of many of the elements that would impinge on the Anglo-French alliance as it developed over the next ten months: in France, factionalism within the cabinet, with the majority oddly subservient to the ploys of a more resourceful minority; abdication of the head of government before the demands of the High Command; and, on the part of some, a desperate faith in the usefulness of Italian mediation and the miracle-working powers of Benito Mussolini; in Britain, readier acceptance of the inevitable; greater responsiveness to a parliamentary opinion in advance of the government; and incomprehension at the slow-moving French political and military machine.

By afternoon of September 2, convinced that there was no hope at all that Hitler would accept their condition for a conference and that procrastination was merely playing into his hands, the British cabinet unanimously resolved on giving him only until midnight to withdraw his troops, after which hostilities would commence, and on sending to Germany an immediate ultimatum to this effect. The Foreign Secretary, concerned at the lack of synchronization between French and British efforts, however, failed to act on the cabinet's decision. This precipitated a first-class political crisis in London in which the needs of the Anglo-French alliance inevitably took a back seat. Following an inconclusive statement by the Prime Minister to the House of Commons that evening, impatient and skeptical members turned both against the French, who were unceremoniously accused of wanting to run out on their responsibilities, and then on their own government for its dilatory and temporizing response to what was clearly naked aggression. Faced by a dangerous rebellion in the ranks which looked as if it might even topple Chamberlain and his associates if they failed to act before Parliament reconvened the next day, the British Government from here on was determined to give the Germans no later than the following morning before its commitment to stand by Poland automatically went into play. With or without France, Great Britain was now compelled to act.[7]

British efforts to get the French to conform to their timetable continued through the night, but the acuteness of Allied disarray on the eve of war is possibly best seen in Winston Churchill's heated words to the French Ambassador, Charles Corbin. Reminding him that he had always championed the Anglo-French alliance and that this was perhaps the last chance for France and England to act together, he warned the Ambassador that if in such grave circumstances they found themselves divided, Britain would then shut herself up in her island from which she would resist fiercely but thereafter would not concern herself further in continental affairs.[8] It was a prophetic warning, but failed in its immediate object of screwing French courage to the sticking place.

Daladier stubbornly refused to alter the French Government's schedule for the opening of hostilities unless British bomber support were sent over immediately, though ultimately, after the British agreed to retard their time limit, he was amenable to advancing his by a half day—a compromise that still fell short of full synchronization. Bonnet, for his part, would not give up the impossible dream; using Anatole de Monzie for the task, he was until dawn of September 3 still attempting to obtain a conference through the offices of Count Ciano on the basis simply of a symbolic retirement of German forces in Poland—a proposal so forlorn that Ciano himself promptly consigned it to the waste basket. French and British could not finally agree to act in concert. The British duly presented their ultimatum to the German Government at 9 a.m. on September 3, a state of war to become effective two hours later, the French theirs at noon, to go into effect at 5 p.m. the same day.[9]

In this way the British and French lumbered into war, half-hearted or uncertain, quarreling amongst themselves, distrustful, and out of step as usual. Significantly, the German Foreign Minister could blame the failure of Mussolini's last-minute efforts to save the peace on "British intransigence."[10] It was hardly the most auspicious start for an alliance, but then fortunately, for the time being, it was to be a funny kind of war.

# The Reluctant Allies

THE lack of synchronization ruffling the surface of Allied unity as Britain and France slid into war served to underscore one inescapable fact: that the needs and interests of the two partners were not ipso facto identical. Close cooperation between them, as a French foreign minister had observed some years earlier, may have been "commanded by geography, by history, by a common ideal, and by the gravity of present circumstances."[1] The realities of the relationship since its inception presented a somewhat different picture.

Fear of imperial Germany and, for Great Britain especially, the dangers of the naval race had brought the two together in 1904 in that diplomatic revolution known as the Entente Cordiale. Yet the convergence of French and British colonial interests in Africa and their growing naval interdependence in the Mediterranean had still not sufficed to bring England into the war at the side of France in 1914. For that, the violation of Belgian neutrality was necessary.[2] Great Britain would, in the final analysis, fight only for her traditional concern, the maintenance of the European balance of power: to prevent one great military power from dominating the continent and, at the same time, the coasts of the Channel and ports of the Low Countries in such a way as to menace her own security.

The common struggle to defeat Germany in World War I did not prevent the emergence of disparate concerns once victory was attained. For Britain, these could be and were met by the liquidation of Germany's fleet and colonial empire. France's preeminent concern, by contrast, remained a very specific fear of her intrinsically more powerful neighbor—only temporarily disarmed—and the need to build up strategic security against the recurrence of that threat. In

8

short, the French recognized what the prestige of their army in 1918–19 tended to obscure: the essential weakness of a poorer, less populous, and insufficiently industrialized France vis-à-vis Germany in the absence of more tenable frontiers, dependable allies, and the imposition of economic measures designed permanently to reduce the German giant's capacity to cause trouble in the future.

Few of France's long-term requirements were satisfied by the Treaty of Versailles. In place of the autonomous Rhineland state under permanent Allied control demanded by the French, there was to be only a demilitarized zone on the left bank of the Rhine subject to Allied occupation for fifteen years; instead of the outright annexation of the Saar, only the ownership of the region's coal mines was transferred. For their future security, the French were forced to make do with the promise of the Anglo-Saxon powers to come to their aid if attacked by Germany, a poor substitute in any case for the strategic advantages that the permanent stationing of their own troops on the Rhine would have conferred. As it turned out, they were to lose even this, for when the United States Senate repudiated the guarantee of June 28, 1919, given France by Woodrow Wilson, the British too allowed their undertaking to lapse. Thus, in the years to come, all would depend on the willingness of the Allied powers forcibly to prevent the Germans from violating the demilitarized zone and reconstituting it as an offensive springboard for the invasion of their western neighbors. But for Britain there was to be no automatic commitment to render military assistance to France—a fact of decisive importance in the history of Anglo-French relations between the wars. This was a wound that could only be salved, not wholly healed, by the Locarno agreements of 1925 in which the British offered impartially to guarantee the frontiers of Belgium, France, and Germany against aggression, while simultaneously disinteresting themselves in the security of Germany's eastern neighbors and without moreover having the military forces or plans to back up their paper guarantee affecting western Europe.[3]

Britain's fear of involvement versus France's relentless search for security thus set the stage for twenty years of opposition between the allies in what nevertheless purported to be a common endeavor: to keep the peace in Europe, and, more specifically, to prevent Germany from breaking it. Their very different attitudes toward Germany— and answers to the question of how strong their former enemy might be allowed to become without menacing the vital interests of either— determined the nature of the conflict. For France, this meant trying to keep German strength, economic as well as military, at the level set by the Treaty; for Britain, concerned with finding a counterweight to French power on the continent and also convinced that British trade depended on a healthy German economy, it meant wanting to restore Germany to much of its prewar power. Thus, France pitted its attempts to coerce Germany, and to build up a system of alliances in the east (with Poland and the Little Entente powers) to contain her, against Britain's attempts to conciliate Germany by redressing what appeared to be the worst grievances; its insistence on maintaining the status quo as an indivisible whole against Britain's more flexible approach to revisionist aims; its hardbitten realism against Britain's lapses into sentimental idealism or shortsightedness.[4]

Since, as Arnold Wolfers has pointed out, "the British objected even in principle to the idea of preserving peace by the preponderance of any country or group of countries on the Continent," believing that this could only lead to a renewed Franco-German conflict in the west, almost inevitably they threw their energies into subverting French policy. "Both to prevent any provocative encirclement of Germany and to diminish the risks of entanglement, the British policy attempted to draw France back from Central and Eastern Europe, or, if that were impossible, at least to make it difficult for her to give military assistance there."[5] The British were determined to limit their own commitments to the Rhine, but here too kept the French guessing so as to exercise greater leverage over them. And because the French knew from experience that they could not do without British support in any future conflict with Germany, they were in a poor position to resist British pressures. In this way, the French allowed their policies to be eroded without however completely relinquishing them, while the British, charging themselves equally with the manipulation of Germany *and* France, consistently weakened the one continental power with whom they were ever likely to be in alliance again.

France's essential isolation with respect to Germany was revealed in 1923 when the British refused to support the French over the question of reparations and denounced their invasion of the Ruhr to collect them. They also disapproved of the encouragement given by France to German separatist movements. This falling out sealed the collapse of the Entente that had been in course since the wrangles of the peace conference. The upshot was that even though the French continued to enjoy unquestioned military superiority over the Ger-

mans, they lost the psychological initiative and little by little the will
for whatever aggressive action might prove necessary to enforce the
Treaty and keep Germany from regaining the preeminent position it
was always her potential to achieve. The reflexes of the gendarme
gradually gave way to a defensive outlook, later known as the Maginot mentality, at the same time as the system of eastern alliances that
France had constructed clearly demanded a willingness to take the
offensive in any future war.[6]

Aside from reparations, France's trump card with Germany remained the presence of French forces in the Rhineland and its bridgeheads, poised, if need be, to strike at the industrial heart of the
country. In 1929, the British forced the French to give way on both
counts: to accept a substantial scaling down in the amount of reparations, and the evacuation of all occupation troops by June 1930, five
years before their scheduled departure. France was once again
thrown back on her own borders, her safety now dependent on the
Germans' fidelity to a hated treaty, or on their own willingness to
mount a major operation of war against the Germans should they
decide to remilitarize the zone after all.[7]

Britain's more benign view of Germany and continuing dislike of
French hegemony, her greater faith in internationalism as represented
by the League of Nations, and ever-present concern for abstract justice regardless of strategic imperatives inevitably led to Anglo-French
clashes over disarmament. Britain's own defense spending was at
rock bottom by the late 1920s, being geared to the ten-year rule,
adopted in 1919 and continued thereafter, and based on the assumption that there would be no major war for the next ten years. British
and French strength was still superior to German strength by the
early 1930s, though clandestine German rearmament and the progressive dismantling of Britain's onetime naval and air preeminence
had narrowed the gap. Instead, however, of recognizing realities,
which precluded any dilution in France's relative standing, the British
were committed to universal disarmament, under the auspices of the
League, as the solution to the world's ills. At the Disarmament Conference of 1932, they therefore adopted the policy of pressuring the
French to relinquish their precarious military superiority in order to
conciliate Germany by acceding to its demand for equality of status.
The dilemma for the British lay in the fact that because they could
not really afford rearmament they had a huge stake in the League's
success, while the government's own military advisers were at the
same time urging rearmament on the grounds that the country was

unable to fulfill its commitments either in Europe or the Far East. Hitler's accession to power thus found Britain and France at odds on a fundamental issue (for the French of course would not disarm in the absence of additional security), Britain's armed forces weaker than ever, and the British public pacifist to the core while simultaneously committed to a League of Nations whose effectiveness in the final analysis depended entirely on British and French power and their will to use it.[8]

The advent of Nazism in Germany clearly called for an end to Anglo-French friction and a concerted effort to block Hitler from breaking the shackles of Versailles, with the help of whatever additional allies could be mustered. However, even after the Germans in March 1935 announced the illegal existence of an air force and the introduction of conscription, in direct repudiation of the Treaty, the British persisted in believing that Germany could be appeased by further concessions. They therefore aimed for a freely negotiated general settlement among the powers rather than the erection of a common front against Germany, such as it seemed France had in mind in signing the Franco-Soviet mutual assistance pact in May. And, far from cooperating with the French, the British quickly signed what was virtually a German-dictated naval agreement behind their backs. The total disarray and flabbiness of the former allies were in this way exposed to a Germany now openly on the march. France and England together might still be stronger than Nazi Germany, but the crucial fact was that they could not or would not get together— nor adapt themselves to the worsening strategic balance.

Their failure was demonstrated afresh in their handling of the Italo-Ethiopian crisis of 1935–36. For France, concerned above all with Germany's rapidly growing strength in Europe, it was necessary to ensure Mussolini's continuing interest in the independence of Austria and, at the very least, the safety of its own southeastern flank by Italy's benevolent neutrality; for England, already confronted by the nightmare contingency of a future war against two major powers stronger than herself—Germany and Japan—and with an imperial lifeline spanning the Mediterranean, Italy's friendship was equally essential. The French frankly preferred an old-fashioned deal with this neighbor they had only recently been reconciled with as a result of their mutual anxieties over Hitler. The British Government also would have been content to see Mussolini take most of what he wanted. Strong pro-League and pacifist sentiment among an ill-informed British public, however, forced on the government a policy that fell between two stools: economic sanctions that were insufficiently severe to deter or defeat Italy but quite strong enough to produce lasting enmity. France was the biggest loser when, as the result of Anglo-French initiatives, the Italian dictator aligned himself with his counterpart to the north. Furthermore, while at the prompting of Britain the French had reluctantly fulfilled their obligations to the League on behalf of Ethiopia, they still had no assurance that the British would do likewise in the face of more dangerous German transgressions.

That they would not was proven, even before the liquidation of the Abyssinian affair, by their reaction to Germany's reoccupation of the Rhineland on March 7, 1936. Here was the crucial test—a clear-cut breach of the treaty which, if tolerated, would cut France's strategic position out from under her by making it impossible henceforth for her to go to the aid of any central European allies—of whether French and British could at last act together to retrieve what was left of their costly victory only eighteen years before. The demoralized French, despite the impeccability of their legal and moral position, could not bring themselves to mobilize their large, unwieldy army in response to the violation, certainly not without British assistance or encouragement, and this the British, notwithstanding the obligations assumed at Locarno to uphold the integrity of the demilitarized zone and to take action in the event of the agreement's violation, refused to give. Yet the unhindered remilitarization of the Rhineland was not only a direct threat to France; it also brought England within easy range of German bombers. The balance of power from here on began to tilt unmistakably in Germany's favor. But by this time, France's foreign policy, as the American Ambassador would wryly report the following year, seemed to have been reduced to registering "German violations of the Treaty of Versailles in order to prepare a beautiful White Book to be published at the outbreak of the next war."[9]

Theoretically, the British still recognized, as they had at Locarno, that their frontier too lay on the Rhine. And in April 1936 they agreed to the staff talks for which the French had pressed all along, though even at this date they refused to discuss operational matters. In the event of an attack on France or Belgium, the British contribution to protect their "common" frontier was to be two divisions, which meant for all practical purposes that any continental campaign would be left to the French.[10] Over the next two and a half years this was the limit of British aid contemplated, the defense of the Empire and home defense requirements taking priority over any continental commitment for the British Army. A realistic recognition of the possibility of war against Germany, however, did not alter the direction of British diplomacy: appeasement, it was thought, could still avert that threat, and this was not to be achieved by the lineup of Europe into opposing blocs. An old-fashioned balance of power strategy the British now saw as more likely to spark a general conflagration.

In any event, the British did not commit themselves to a large-scale rearmament program until 1936, a program that took a year to get off the ground, by which time Germany had far outdistanced them both in industrial capacity and air preparedness. Britain's principal rearmament efforts were invested in the Royal Navy, which was counted on to repel any attempt at invasion, and especially the Royal Air Force, whose task would be to deter the anticipated and much-feared knockout blow from the air or retaliate against an enemy bombing campaign. From 1934 to 1938 a strategic counteroffensive against Germany was held to be the main contribution Britain could make to the outcome of the war on land, and for this purpose the building of a powerful bomber force was concentrated on—the concomitant being the neglect of the army and the acceptance of a role of "limited liability" for this poor relation among the services. Only when it was realized in early 1938 that Bomber Command could do little in the early stages of a war either to achieve its strategic aims or to protect Britain from enemy attack was the emphasis shifted to the defensive needs of the country and to the fighter force that would be required to meet them.[11] But whether the stress was on the offensive or defensive in the air, the potential of a land battle such as the French were preparing for to play a determining role in warfare continued to be soft-pedaled, if not altogether ignored, in British thinking.

The changing emphases of British air strategy impinged doubly on Anglo-French relations to the extent that control over the Low Countries and northern France was felt to be necessary to implement Britain's offensive and defensive plans. As the official historians of Britain's strategic air offensive against Germany note, so long as the doctrine of the air counteroffensive held sway, "the alliance with France and her role in preventing the Germans from acquiring bases nearer Britain and providing bases for the medium and light bombers of the Royal Air Force was . . . regarded as fundamental." But by early 1938 the Low Countries figured less prominently in the strategies opted for by the government. Not only was Bomber Command being equipped with an all-heavy bomber force capable of reaching

Germany from United Kingdom bases, but with the acceleration of the fighter program and the installation of early warning (radar) stations, the chances of Fighter Command's being able to cope with a German air attack at home had substantially improved. In short, as Michael Howard remarks, British weapons systems "were beginning to make a foothold on the continent of Europe . . . expendable." Thus, a policy that was insular to begin with had by the time of Munich become even more strongly isolationist, with Britain's traditional concern for the balance of power on the continent the chief casualty of this new fixation on air power and the preeminent part it was expected to play.[12]

Not surprisingly, then, it was the relative weakness of the RAF which determined British policy throughout the Czechoslovak crisis, though appeasement of Germany with respect to her eastern European grievances had proven congenial long before the 1938 assessment of comparative strengths as between France and Britain on the one hand and Germany on the other made the dangers of war quite so formidable. March 1936 was probably the last occasion on which the French might have acted independently against the Germans with a good chance of success had they but had the requisite determination; by September 1938, their strategic isolation in western Europe, growing passivity and pessimism, and conviction that they could risk nothing without British support made it almost a foregone conclusion that they would allow themselves to be maneuvered by the secret warning that "Britain was not automatically obliged to go to war if France resisted German aggression against Czechoslovakia" into sacrificing their strongest eastern ally.[13] But though France and Britain were thereby spared a war they felt they could not win, it was at the cost of France's strategic position, which depended on the possibility of forcing upon Germany a two-front war, being totally undermined.

It was the dawning recognition of this in late 1938 and early 1939—and the implications it had for France's presumed willingness and ability to sustain a contest with Germany virtually alone—that led to Britain's abandonment of "limited liability" and belated acceptance of a projected British Expeditionary Force of sizable proportions. Reckoning with the possibility that "France might give up the unequal struggle unless supported with the assurance that we should assist them to the utmost," and admitting that "If France were forced to her knees, the further prosecution of the war would be compromised," the Chiefs of Staff at last spelled out that connection, so often underplayed in the past, between the land defense of France and the security of the United Kingdom itself.[14] A month later, on March 29, Anglo-French staff conversations got under way. At the same time, in answer to the German takeover in Czechoslovakia, the British Government precipitously guaranteed Poland and Romania in a last-ditch attempt to deter Hitler in the east. But the British issued their guarantees before assuring themselves of the one thing which really would have frightened Hitler—an alliance with Russia—and which therefore should have been considered a sine qua non. This was a total reversal of the policy the government had so stubbornly maintained for twenty years, a development not without irony, as Arnold Wolfers has observed, in that "Britain turned to the one-time French point of view just at the moment when some prominent French statesmen were recommending its abandonment, and after France had lost most of the defenses which she had sought to build up for the purpose of pressing this policy effectively."[15]

In addition to the incompleteness of their defense preparations, it had been largely geographic and economic considerations—Britain's relative invulnerability as an island, its more widely scattered imperial interests compared with France's colonial concentration in Africa and the Levant, and the conviction that any war against Germany was bound to turn into a world war with Italy and Japan as well, which they didn't have the resources to win—that in 1938 had led to Britain's military advisers recommending against involvement in a European war. Only a few months later, while still not optimistic about the prospects, their emphasis had swung round to the "moral and other repercussions" on Great Britain's world position of a refusal to intervene and to the fear that the "failure to take up such a challenge would place Germany in a predominant position in Europe." In other words, the situation could only worsen with waiting.[16]

Thus, in the spring of 1939, in the least propitious circumstances, the British Government rediscovered the importance of the European balance of power and set out diplomatically to win for itself and France the eastern allies it had for two decades eschewed or already lost. And if the French—or at least the majority of Frenchmen—showed themselves willing partners in this new policy of firmness, it was because France, no more than England—and for similar political and moral reasons—could not run indefinitely from the worsening situation. Not only did they now have the close military alignment with Britain they had always sought, they could also assume that if they were to abandon their allies—England or Poland—they would soon be left completely alone to face a head-on German move directed against themselves. And in a choice between Hitler and Britain, no matter what the provocations over the past twenty years had been, there could be only one outcome.[17] It was Armageddon sooner or later in any event.

# *Slouching into War:*
# *Poland*

THE first hesitant steps taken by the British and French could hardly have inspired an enemy, let alone their eastern ally Poland, to believe their intentions were serious. Indeed the Anglo-French declaration on bombing policy immediately served notice to the Germans that the Allies wished to keep the war within bounds and that they would not retaliate in kind for enemy action known to be taking place in Poland. It was, of course, only humane to limit themselves to "strictly military objectives in the narrowest sense of the word," to leave to the enemy the onus for initiating "aerial atrocities."[1] Yet, as applied, the policy struck many as ludicrous; for while the Luftwaffe was uninhibitedly scattering bombs over Polish cities, civilians, and military installations alike, Bomber Command set itself the task of blanketing northern and western Germany with 10 million propaganda leaflets—the opening gambit in what soon became known as the confetti war.[2]

Perhaps nowhere is the mood of the phoney war period better illustrated than in Sir Kingsley Wood's celebrated response to Leo Amery's suggestion, on 5 September, that incendiary bombs be dropped on the Black Forest munitions stores: it was unthinkable, he said, and furthermore "there was no question of our bombing even the munition works at Essen, which were private property, or lines of communication, and that doing so would alienate American opinion." The Air Minister argued that "the Service Departments considered no good whatever could be achieved by air intervention and that the Poles would not be helped by it."[3] This interpretation of Britain's pledge to support Poland immediately and to the limit of its forces took even the government's worst critics by surprise. However, the Air Staff had already concluded that in view of the enemy's preponderance in striking power a strategic air offensive against German industry—though potentially decisive in the long run—was for the present too risky an undertaking and that they and the French had more to gain from a period of severely restricted air warfare in which, for all practical purposes, only the German fleet would be considered fair game. Thus Britain's bomber force, which was seen primarily as an investment for the future in need of conservation and expansion, played no useful role during the Polish campaign or for many months to come.[4]

Nor did the French, for all practical purposes, show any greater desire to aid the Poles. Mesmerized by the threat of retaliation on France, General Gamelin fully agreed that the Allied air forces should not launch any air attacks against Germany or Poland.[5] He was also unwilling to assault the Siegfried Line at a time when French forces outnumbered German troops in the west by two and a half or three to one.[6] By the terms of the military accord negotiated between France and Poland four months before, the French were obliged not only to take immediate air action in accordance with a prearranged plan but on the third day following the announcement of mobilization to undertake local diversionary operations and from the fifteenth day to launch a general offensive against Germany with their main striking forces. However, although the necessary political protocol confirming their old alliance and bringing into effect the recent military convention was signed September 4, no large-scale offensive ever materialized. General Gamelin instead contented himself with "fiddling about with [the] Siegfried line" (as Sir Alexander Cadogan put it)—small operations that served primarily to improve the French defensive position by erasing an awkward enemy salient here and there. Even these minor advances were stopped on September 12, with British concurrence, then forfeited altogether at the close of the Polish campaign, when the French C-in-C decided to withdraw the bulk of his forces behind the Maginot Line.[7]

No one, of course, had expected that the Allies would be able to save the Poles from annihilation, though originally it was hoped that Polish resistance would last through the winter. The entry of Russia into the strategic picture on September 17 had also not been foreseen. Yet only a few were sufficiently knowledgeable about the critical Allied defense picture to be able to say, as did Halifax's Principal Private Secretary, Oliver Harvey, that he could quite see that it was wrong "to dash off against the Germans, either by land or air, merely to relieve the Poles, when by conserving our effort we should be able to deal a much shrewder blow later." For these hard-headed "realists," Poland "must go down now to rise again as a result of allied victory in the west, perhaps not till two years' time."[8]

The rationale behind Anglo-French passivity toward their Polish ally was neatly summed up by General Gamelin's statement on September 4 that "to break or discourage the French Army, Navy, or Air Force [in their initial battles] would in no way advance matters but would weigh heavily on subsequent events and on the final outcome of the struggle." In fact, this was the policy accepted by both British and French military planners a full six months before the war. As Sir John Slessor reveals, "The French [then] made it clear that they had no intention of attacking at all in the opening phase. They said their strategy would be to form a firm defensive front and preserve the integrity of their territory." Where the British guarantee to Poland was concerned, he comments, "the vague term, 'all support in our power,' really meant nothing because it was not in our power to give them any support . . . as opposed to eventually liberating and avenging them." In September, therefore, "the immediate problem . . . was what we could do, not so much to relieve pressure on the Poles (we never believed that would be practicable to any significant degree), as at least to do something, if only as a gesture, to sustain their morale and 'show willing.' " In other words, Anglo-French obligations were simply converted into a public relations campaign; making Poland a *casus belli* was thus not to be taken advantage of to force Germany to fight a two-front war from the outset. Her fate would depend on the Allies' ability to bring about Germany's eventual defeat.[9]

# The Politics
## of Pessimism

GENERAL Beaufre's description of the entire phoney war as "a sort of giant charade acted out by mutual consent from which nothing serious could emerge if we played our part right"[1] is particularly apt when applied to the first few weeks of World War II. In short, as Laurence Lafore wittily comments, if September 3 looked like a turning point to the participants, in retrospect it can be seen that war for the British and French governments more closely resembled von Clausewitz's definition of the belligerent art as politics continued by other means. Refusing to wage war on land or in the air, their declarations for all practical purposes amounted to little more than formal protests against Hitler's aggressive policy, one more way station on a diplomatic road whose final direction was still uncertain.[2]

Of France it was commonly said that "the nation went to war looking over its shoulder, its eyes seeking for peace."[3] Even an American observer in Paris more attuned to cultural events than to taking the political pulse of the country could detect as early as September 10 that efforts were still being made to hold up the war, to prevent its starting in earnest: the *New Yorker*'s Janet Flanner saw it as "the first war that millions of people on both sides continued to think could be avoided even after it had officially been declared."[4]

True, the French press did not question the necessity for going to war, while Parliament seemingly without dissent had promptly voted the requisite war credits when called into session on 2 September.[5] In France, as in England, the government might well have fallen had it succumbed to another Munich. Yet these official gestures somewhat obscured the shakiness of the overall political structure, which had been profoundly affected both by the fierce domestic debates grip-

21

ping France since 1934 and by international developments following Hitler's rise to power. From 1936 on, traditional party affiliations had tended to give way to a more polarized lineup on the issue of resistance to or appeasement of Nazi Germany, and the appeasement elements lingered just below the surface of national unity. Thus, with both the extreme right and the Communist Party officially dedicated to subverting the regime, there was by September 1939 also no party either in the center or on the moderate left or right which stood wholeheartedly behind the government's war policy or in which the partisans of diplomatic compromise did not play a prominent role. The French Assembly, probably with some exaggeration, was said to be dominated by defeatism; but at least forty-five parliamentarians, grouping themselves around either Bergéry and Déat in the Chamber or Laval in the Senate, were actively working toward an understanding with Hitler, and their influence was disproportionate to their small numbers. In any event, Daladier was the subject of bitter criticism both inside and outside Parliament for his policy. On the basis of statements made before various parliamentary commissions and other witnesses, it would appear that the Premier himself never completely ruled out the idea of a compromise peace. Certainly he had inner doubts and reservations.[6] As revealed to one military confidant, these revolved around the inequality of effort between French and British, whom Daladier, taking a leaf out of Bonnet's book, accused of having engaged France in the war at a time pleasing to themselves, when in actuality it was probably either too early or too late. In this connection, he did not preclude the possibility of making peace if powerful reinforcements, particularly in aviation, did not put real life into the alliance. It was merely a threat, of course, not government policy, but nevertheless reflective of France's more general malaise over the war.[7]

In these circumstances, it is not surprising that the peace feelers sent out by Germany—starting September 28 in the wake of Poland's collapse and formalized by Hitler's Reichstag proposal of October 6—should have intensified French doubts as to the purpose and usefulness of the war.[8] In fact, so great was the pressure for immediate withdrawal in the Chamber of Deputies at this time that the American Ambassador, for one, was not sure Daladier would be able to resist it.[9] Yet in spite of Daladier's hesitations and ambivalence, it was typical of his stolidity—and immobilism—that no favorable reply was contemplated. Publicly he stated on October 10 that the French had "taken up arms against aggression; we shall not lay them down until we have sure guarantees of security—a security which cannot be called in question every six months."[10] In short, *il faut en finir*. Privately he argued, with more resignation than appetite: "We have got to go on to the end, and if the house falls, let it fall on us."[11] To this end, he had earlier shifted Bonnet—whom the British feared would intrigue to get France out of the war—from his key post at the Ministry of Foreign Affairs.

In Britain too, a lack of enthusiasm for the war among the circles that counted most belied the relatively solid front put up by the public at large. As early as September 6, Harold Nicolson noted in his diary that "Chamberlain did not want this war, and is continually thinking of getting out of it. He may be right." Certainly the Prime Minister was not likely to be spurred on to a more forceful policy by his mail, a substantial percentage of which contained appeals to stop the war. Another MP, Leo Amery, writes that from mid-September to mid-October there was a veritable wave of defeatism throughout the country. This passive sort of pessimism was confirmed by the American Ambassador, Joseph P. Kennedy, in conversations not only with three cabinet members—Sir Samuel Hoare, Mr. Hore-Belisha, and Lord Halifax—but also with the King, to all of whom Kennedy attributed the belief that if the government had to be maintained on a war footing for long it would mean the "complete economic, financial and social collapse" of England, to say nothing of the bolshevization of all Europe.[12]

Probably the most prescient and certainly the most prominent defeatist was Britain's former Prime Minister and World War I stalwart, Lloyd George, who, unable to see any real possibilities of winning the war, urged his colleagues in the House of Commons to insist upon a secret session of Parliament at which the government would be forced to estimate exactly what the prospects of victory were. "But if the chances are really against us," he told Nicolson on September 20, "then we should certainly make peace at the earliest opportunity, possibly with Roosevelt's assistance." While refraining from spelling out these views in an open session, Lloyd George on October 3 nevertheless asked the government not to reject casually or precipitously any proposals for peace which might be offered. These he felt should be discussed by the House in private. Though this surprising interpellation was not approved by the Commons in general, it was welcomed in that quarter of the House which from the beginning had opposed war and which now wanted it brought to an immediate conclusion.[13]

Ironically, the Lloyd George speech and the passionate echoes it found in at least some supporters came in response to one of the strongest and most positive statements on the war situation Mr. Chamberlain had made to date. In this he made light of the Russo-German Declaration of September 28 and of the peace proposals that were expected to follow it. "The reason for which this country entered the war . . . ," he stated, "was to put an end to the successive acts of German aggression which menaced the freedom and the very security of all the nations of Europe." The invasion of Poland was the immediate cause of the war, but it was not the fundamental cause. "That cause was the overwhelming sense in this country and in France of the intolerable nature of a state of affairs in which the nations of Europe were faced with the alternative of jeopardising their freedom or of mobilising their forces at regular intervals to defend it." Whatever the nature of any peace proposal, he concluded, "no threat would ever induce this country or France to abandon the purpose for which we have entered upon this struggle."[14] This presaged Chamberlain's firm rejection of Hitler's offer on October 12, which, as has been seen, was matched by an identical French reaction.[15]

The statement addressed to the Russian Ambassador by Lord Halifax's parliamentary under-secretary, Mr. R. A. Butler, on 18 October that the British Government was "ready to make peace even tomorrow" if only the agreement reached were lasting is often cited as evidence of the Chamberlain government's lack of wholeheartedness in the pursuit of objectives publicly proclaimed.[16] Certainly the Foreign Secretary and others in the Foreign Office kept alive their prewar ties—as well as establishing new ones via the Vatican—both with the secret German opposition and with Goering throughout the fall and winter and on into April of 1940. From the records of these exchanges it is clear that Chamberlain and Halifax did not demand (though they would have preferred) the complete dismantling of the National Socialist edifice as a precondition to possible peace negotiations with Germany. What they were concerned with primarily was the installation of a government—of almost any configuration—that was capable of negotiating, in other words, whose word could be trusted. This did not preclude doing business with Goering, who might have had some role to play in a transitional government; nor did it preclude a generous peace in which Germany would have been allowed to keep a good share of the ethnic enclaves it had thus far absorbed, provided Czechoslavakia and Poland were reconstituted as independent states. What *was* an essential precondition was the removal of Hitler and Ribbentrop—the two worst offenders on the international scene—and naturally the continued quiescence of the Wehrmacht in the west; Halifax also stipulated that where negotiations were concerned the British and French must act together.[17] Modest as these demands were, they in no way contradicted what the Prime Minister had stated in the House of Commons on October 12 about the unacceptability of peace conditions which began by condoning aggression and the impossibility of relying upon the promises of the "present German Government."[18]

Even so, cabinet members were suspicious when on November 1 they were told of the Foreign Office's contacts with the "Generals"; while Harold Nicolson, who first got wind of these sub rosa contacts on January 17, concluded that there was "still a group in the War Cabinet working for appeasement."[19] However, because even the minimal conditions necessary before direct negotiations could begin were so unlikely, the Foreign Office, despite its coven of intermediaries and despite Halifax's sporadic hankerings, had few illusions as to the possibility of peace suddenly descending. Hitler himself was no longer interested in any peace initiatives after mid-October.

Clandestine contacts and dissident voices notwithstanding, the war went on, most realizing, as the Marquess of Crewe phrased it on October 12, that any offer put forth by Hitler could only be "an olive branch shot out of a catapult."[20] Churchill, who on September 3 had taken his place in Chamberlain's War Cabinet as First Lord of the Admiralty, was in any case not suspicious of his colleagues who had been prominent appeasers, only reserved as to their tactics. According to Hugh Dalton, he was satisfied that they were now determined to see the war through to the end. Though giving robust leadership to the Royal Navy, Churchill, like his colleagues, was opposed to Britain's taking the initiative in air warfare.[21] There were, after all, eminently good reasons for continued caution and delay.

# Disparities, Divisions, and the Search for Diversions

THE phoney war—the twilight war, the *drôle de guerre,* the "Bore War," the *sitzkrieg*—was so called because for seven months on the western front the belligerents sat facing each other across their respective lines, seldom exchanging shots, limiting themselves to routine patrols and air reconnaissance, sometimes even engaging in playful signals, all apparently waiting for something definitive to happen. Whether this would turn out to be peace or a new hot war was not known, but in the interim the front on which all eyes were trained produced fewer casualties than did the hazards of the London blackout. With good reason, neither side wanted a replay of the 1914–18 holocaust. Such a pacific philosophy could reach ridiculous heights, as when Alfred Duff Cooper, a former First Lord, shortly before the Germans' spring offensive, told an American audience in Paris that the Allies had "found a new way to make war—without sacrificing human lives."[1]

France and Britain may have been temperamentally incapable of fighting unless attacked, as some have thought, but there were also sound reasons why the Allies adopted a defensive strategy. Believing that no armed victory was possible in the near future because their armed forces, except at sea, were inferior to what the enemy could bring to bear, the Allies accepted the inevitability of a protracted war and used the reprieve granted them to improve their defenses and to make good their deficiencies on land and in the air. Placing their overall faith in the efficacy of a naval blockade and their ability to call on the financial and economic resources of the USA, France and Britain looked upon any delay as militarily advantageous because it was only in a long war that their full industrial productive capacity—

26

together with America's—would come into play to offset Germany's head start. This made for a waiting game and placed an automatic limitation on any major effort that would lead Germany to unleash its superior forces before the Allies were better prepared. In that from September 1939 to May 1940 no offensive plan against Germany's western front was even considered, this left Hitler completely free to strike when and where he chose. There were differences in emphasis between French and British thinking, but by and large both countries shared a bias for peripheral planning and too often indulged themselves in the fancy that Nazi Germany might collapse from within as the result of economic or political pressures. Chamberlain even had a "hunch" that the war might be over by spring. Both also had an almost mystic belief in the French Army's ability to withstand anything the enemy might throw against it.[2]

In fact, of the two powers, the British appeared to have an even greater faith in the French Army than did the French themselves. It was Churchill's opinion, expressed in 1938, that France's army represented "the most perfectly trained and faithful mobile force in Europe," and this evaluation probably better mirrored British military opinion in 1939 and early 1940 than did any indictments that were rendered retrospectively.[3] Insofar as the British Army at the time of the war's outbreak existed largely on paper, it was a convenient faith to have.

True, the British had promised to send to France's assistance thirty-two divisions by the end of the second year of the war, while on September 8 the cabinet had determined on an objective of fifty-five Imperial divisions by the earliest possible date. Nevertheless, for most of the phoney war period, the British Expeditionary Force in France amounted to no more than a handful of divisions. If the Secretary of State for War, Mr. Leslie Hore-Belisha, could take pride in the fact that Britain's flow of troops to France, which had been settled before the war, was by autumn running ahead of schedule and that the BEF of 1939 was larger than that of 1914, Anthony Eden, for his part, visiting General Gamelin's map room at Vincennes in November, "was not proud of the minute British contribution represented by two small Union Jacks on pins amidst a forest of Tricolours."[4] By May the BEF would still not exceed ten divisions of fighting capacity, or only about half the British forces in action by the spring of 1915. The French were understandably disquieted; in fact, the disparity in numbers between the German and Franco-British forces haunted them constantly; but what, after all, could be expected from an ally that had not introduced conscription until May 1939, and then only hesitatingly and largely for the sake of countering German propaganda? British policy with respect to its land contribution was based on one unchanging assumption: that the French Army could be relied on to hold the line until Britain had mobilized and trained its manpower. No one, as Sir Samuel Hoare (Lord Privy Seal) points out, "either in London or Paris ever expressed a doubt as to the French ability to resist."[5]

However, though the French were confident that they could fight a defensive war when and if one were forced on them, they were nevertheless not about to undertake any action which might provoke the Germans in the Western theater into taking the offensive. The French General Staff's quietist approach and the feebleness of British assistance led inevitably to differences between the Allies, many of which were exploited by German propaganda. For instance, some British saw in the French reluctance to permit Bomber Command to inaugurate offensive operations once the western front opened up an unwillingness to fight, which they contrasted with their own eagerness to put the doctrine of strategic bombing to a test. But inasmuch as the initiation of aerial warfare over Germany would most probably have inspired enemy reprisals against French rather than British territory, which the French with their much smaller air force, ill-prepared antiaircraft defenses, and vulnerable war industries felt unable to cope with, the concept of strategic bombing found no favor in France during the phoney war and would prove even less popular in the spring once long-term strategic aims came into conflict with the immediate tactical needs of the French Army.

To the French the whole idea seemed to exemplify their fear that the British were content to fight the war by remote control and to allow the principal burden to fall on their ally: *les Anglais fournissaient les machines, les Français leur poitrines,* as the popular slogan summarized it. With so few British divisions in line, it was all too easy to resuscitate the World War I jibe that the British were willing to fight the war down to the last Frenchman. The fact that in the first seven months of the war British losses in men and matériel ran considerably higher than comparable French losses (e.g., 4,000 British sailors lost at sea, as opposed to 1,500 deaths among French soldiers in the Maginot Line)[6] was either unknown or ineffective in the face of the Goebbels contention that Britain had selfishly dragged France into a meaningless war for which she was prepared to shed vast quantities of French blood without making any important sacrifices herself.

What French politicians were principally concerned with was that judged by the prolongation of peacetime conditions in England, the British did not appear to be taking the war very seriously. There had been ample preparation for air warfare, as the evacuation of children from large cities, the issuance of gas masks, and the strict observance of blackouts showed, but the changeover to a wartime economy was painfully slow: food rationing did not go into effect until the beginning of the new year, while unemployment, despite the expected needs of war industries, actually increased by 200,000 in the first three months of the war to a high of 1,430,000 and was still at the one million mark in May 1940.[7]

Worst of all, from the French point of view, conscription in England was only partial, with classes under the Military Service Act being called up gradually, due to the lack of equipment, both the youngest and older age categories being exempt from risk in the early stages of Britain's mobilization. By spring British conscription still only affected men up to 27 or 28, while in France all able-bodied men between 20 and 50 were mobilized.[8] According to French statistics, one Frenchman in eight had been mobilized, whereas in England it was only one Englishman in forty—or so the French Finance Minister, Paul Reynaud, complained to British officials during a mid-November visit. The British claimed that Reynaud had included in his mobilization figures French police, railway and dock workers, etc. whose opposite numbers were not included in the British figures, and that when these were eliminated the proportions were much the same. The Chief of the Imperial General Staff, in fact, felt compelled to ask Reynaud "not to repeat such obvious rot."[9] The British had drawn up a scheme of reserved occupations before the war which enabled manpower to be kept in the essential war industries rather than wantonly mobilized into the army. There was no such system in force in France, and war industries did suffer fairly severe dislocations as a result. In fact, for the sake of fattening their battalions, the French General Staff sometimes allowed aircraft specialists to be employed as carrot peelers in the army, as the Armaments Minister discovered to his disgust. As a result, 130,000 of these specialists later had to be released.[10]

Even if French statistics were slanted to emphasize their national sacrifices, it was nevertheless apparent to observers from both countries that France had been affected by the war to a much greater extent than England. According to a Ministry of Information report in January, there was no French citizen whose life had not been turned upside down. "As a result of the war," it stated, "the standard of living in France has fallen very sharply, and working hours have been lengthened, while in England conditions are practically untouched."[11] And this difference in living standards between the two countries was most noticeable where it could hurt most—in the food, equipment, comforts, and pay scales of armed forces personnel. Where the British soldier earned 17 francs a day, his French counterpart had to make do with a paltry 75 centimes (or a rate of 2 shillings to 1½d). Though not a new problem, it was just the sort of annoyance which provided grist for the Nazi propaganda mill as well as confirmation for traditional French Anglophobia.[12]

If the French feared the British were changing too slowly in response to the war, many Englishmen were concerned that the French were changing too fast and that in the process the democratic basis of French governmental life was being thrown overboard. In a note to Lord Halifax in October 1939, Sir Stafford Cripps complained that "The closing down of one of the largest political parties in France and the suppression of a large section of the press are not the acts of a Government that is seeking to preserve democracy and freedom. The fact that it is the Communist party that is being attacked and not the pro-German reactionaries makes the situation all the worse."[13]

Using the Russo-German Non-Aggression Pact as a convenient handle, the French Government had in fact not lost a minute in mounting a campaign against its most powerful enemy on the left. On August 26, a week before the war began, *L'Humanité* was banned, though at this stage it still served as a mouthpiece for French unity in the face of Nazi aggression. A month later, on September 26, in spite of the solid support for war credits the Communists in both Chamber and Senate had given on September 2, the Communist Party was declared illegal and dissolved, though many of its members promptly reconstituted themselves under the name of the Worker and Peasant Group. On October 5, municipal councils which were Communist were suppressed, while two days later the first wholesale arrests of Communist deputies began. A further repressive decree, the "loi des suspects" passed on November 18, facilitated the government's task by suspending individual civil liberties and granting prefects the right to intern by force persons considered dangerous; it was used largely against Communist workers. On November 30, the same day the chambers granted full powers to the government for the duration, eleven other Communist deputies were formally deprived of their parliamentary immunity. Then, by the law of January 20, 1940, sixty-one elected Communists who had failed to repudiate the Comintern prior to October 26 were additionally deprived of their seats in the Chamber or Senate and placed in jeopardy, the law being put into effect during the following month. Forty-three such ex-deputies and one senator were indicted before a military court in February, placed on trial on March 20, and found guilty on April 3 of spreading propaganda emanating from the Third International. All were deprived of their civil rights and most sentenced to long prison terms. Finally, on April 9, the government passed a decree, obviously aimed at the Communists, which assimilated to treason acts by individuals who demoralized the army or nation with a view to damaging national defense.[14]

The British Ambassador may have been naive enough to accept at face value the French Government's line that the Communists were not being imprisoned and punished because they were Communists but because they had been acting as traitors and saboteurs. However, it took little political savvy for others to realize that the French forces which had been traumatized by the Popular Front's victory in 1936 were in large part using the war and the party's Moscow-jaundiced interpretation of it conveniently and expeditiously to liquidate their worst enemies. Not surprisingly, those who had most ardently defended appeasing Hitler at the time of Munich became the most implacable partisans of proscription once the Communists switched to a policy of "revolutionary defeatism" and began peddling their own brand of pacifist propaganda. Though the anti-Communist measures were initiated by Daladier, they were continued and even reinforced by the succeeding Reynaud government, which did not get around to arresting the French pro-Nazis for *their* activities against the internal and external security of the state until June 6. Even then the really big fish were not pulled into the net. It was, as libertarian British critics noted, a peculiar way for a democracy to be conducting a war against Germany. Meanwhile, throughout 1939 and 1940, French concentration camps were filling up with resident aliens from all over Europe, but predominantly with anti-Nazi or leftist refugees from countries already overrun by Hitler or in the hands of his totalitarian allies.[15]

These measures, together with the French Government's increasing reliance since the spring of 1938 on ruling by decree at the expense of Parliament's traditional functions and prerogatives, as well as its reliance on a misguided censorship which so deprived the public of real news that out of sheer boredom it turned to the Traitor of Stuttgart, Ferdonnet, to counteract the high-sounding and dangerously overoptimistic handouts of official propaganda,[16] were disquieting signs in a country which, like England, was presumably pledged to the championship of democratic institutions everywhere.

France's concern with the domestic threat posed by Communists was, naturally enough, reflected in the generally anti-Soviet bias of French foreign policy and military planning. This new wrinkle to what had started out as a fairly intelligible war against Germany, even if ambivalently undertaken, came to the fore not only with the Russian attack on Poland, September 17, but particularly after the Soviets invaded neutral Finland at the end of November 1939. This provided a new jolt to Allied moralists, ever conscious of their role as sole defenders of the old League of Nations principles. It also served as a springboard for new tensions between France and Britain.

As Alexander Werth points out, a "lunatic fringe" in both countries had managed to convince itself that it would be "strategically advantageous" to take on both Russia *and* Germany—its usual premise being that the Soviets constituted an even greater threat and were therefore at least as suitable an enemy as Germany. Certainly this applied to those sections of the French Right who had always opposed a Franco-Soviet pact and who in many instances would have preferred a joint front *with* Germany against the Bolshevik menace. It apparently applied to some quarters in England too, for, on Christmas Eve 1939, Oliver Harvey thought that if only Hitler disappeared and Goering and Co. took over in Germany, there would be many in England foolish enough to accept a German offer of peace "conditional on a joint crusade against Russia."[17]

For all such ideologues Finland was a bonanza—the thin end of the wedge towards a patched-up peace. According to the journalist André Simone, French newspapers at this time, excepting the few which had opposed the Munich settlement, began openly to treat the Soviets as Public Enemy Number 1—so much so that a visiting British MP told Simone that "Reading the French press one has the impression that France is at war with Russia and merely on very unfriendly terms with the Nazis."[18] *The Times,* though more measured in tone, was not far from the same outlook.[19] In any event, for lack of excitement on the western front, the Finnish campaign soon became the focus of attention in France and England, with aid to gallant Finland—the symbol of successful resistance to oppression—arousing as much enthusiasm as the war against Germany.[20] (It even served temporarily to align Allied and Italian policy—with assistance to Finland also being favored by certain elements in Germany itself!)

It was not only popular sentiments that were aroused, however. French and British observers of the Winter War in the north, as Paul Marie de la Gorce points out, were impressed by the early defensive victories of the Finns and by the poor showing of the Russians despite their numerical superiority. Some of them, at least, allowed themselves to be persuaded of Soviet impotence and demoralization. As a result, serious consideration was given the idea of Allied intervention in Finland as well as the possibility of more direct operations against Russian oilfields, all of which measures implied the acceptance of open warfare with the Soviet Union.[21]

But if the British were able to contemplate such risky moves, at least they did so free from ideological animosity. The war against Germany remained uppermost in their strategic conception. Chamberlain, according to his biographer, was motivated only by military interests with respect to the Finnish war: he did his best to help Field-Marshal Mannerheim, but was also aware that a Soviet conquest of Finland would be of no help to Germany.[22] While neither Halifax nor the Permanent Under-Secretary at the Foreign Office wanted war with Russia over Finland, they were nevertheless concerned to "keep our moral position intact." This meant, as Cadogan minuted on December 6, that they might "have to go a long way in reprobating what Russia has done, in condemning her aggression and even . . . of affording such assistance to Finland as we can, while making it plain that our effort must necessarily be directed against Germany—the real originator of all these disturbances."[23]

All this made for a pragmatic, somewhat contradictory, and at times even ingeniously laissez-faire approach to Russia. For instance, with the question of the Soviet action against Finland coming up before the League, Britain's delegate "was instructed to resist the imposition of sanctions on Russia if this was proposed and to try to get a Resolution condemning Russian aggression which would leave everyone free to do what they could. He was to try to avoid the question of the expulsion of Russia [from the League], but if this were raised should vote for it as if we like it, in the hope that we should not lose very much with Russia, and would gain with Spain, Italy and the U.S.A."[24]

Without wishing to complicate their affairs unduly, the British hoped nevertheless to damage Soviet interests by prolonging the Finnish war, in the belief that its continuation would automatically reduce the help the Russians could bring Germany while simultaneously limiting their mischief-making capacity in the Balkans. But, like the French, the British were inclined to underestimate the Soviet military machine so that, as Lord Halifax told the Labour Opposition on February 10, while the government "had no intention of declaring war on Russia, we were disposed to think that the fear of Russia declaring war on us ought not to deter us from any course of action that would certainly seem wise."[25] This was the negative side of British pragmatism, or muddling through.

Other Englishmen, as early as September 20, immediately following Russia's invasion of Poland, had been both more analytical and more farsighted. In the House of Commons, Mr. Robert Boothby advised against taking "too tragic a view of the situation" or of succumbing to the "national temptation to indulge in flights of morality." "We do not want to go about the whole world today finding enemies and declaring war on them," he stated. "We want all the support we can get; and I hope and believe that one day we shall get the support of Soviet Russia." Likewise, Mr. Price noted that "Russia has no interest in seeing the German *Drang nach Osten* going down the shores of the Black Sea" and thought that Britain had "a community of interest with her in that matter."[26]

Other more powerful voices were also aware that Russia's use of some 100 divisions in Poland and her generally westward advances could bring no satisfaction to the Germans. Winston Churchill, among others, was always convinced of the fundamentally anti-German orientation of Soviet policy and by October 1 was obliquely predicting the Grand Alliance which eventually did come into being after June 1941.[27] Four weeks later—and one month before the Russo-Finnish war broke out—he was to advise the cabinet to try "to persuade the Finns to make concessions" to "Russian claims for naval bases in the Baltic" on the grounds that these bases were needed only against Germany and that in the process of taking them a sharp antagonism between Russian and German interests would become apparent.[28] General Ironside, Chief of the Imperial General Staff, also "never lost sight of the fact that Russia might one day become our ally, and he warned the Government against antagonizing the Soviets too much."[29] The Chiefs of Staff on the whole thought that the aim of Allied diplomacy should be the dissolution of the Russo-German coalition and therefore were inclined to be dubious about the usefulness of any measure which might bring Russia into the war at the side of the Germans.[30]

There were, of course, those in France—especially the professional diplomats at the Quai d'Orsay (though the Secretary-General of the Ministry of Foreign Affairs was not conspicuous among them)—who were also aware of the defensive and anti-German character of Soviet moves since the signing of the August 23 agreement. Yet this apparent paradox was more readily understood, and even gleefully accepted, in England, where domestic ideological divisions had never gotten out of hand and where foreign policy could therefore be approached with a greater objectivity. French cabinets, by contrast, constantly enmeshed in internal politics, tended to be at the mercy of public opinion. Thus, even General Gamelin, who alone among France's most prominent military chiefs still looked to the future formation of an anti-Hitler coalition, was led to subordinate his own personal perceptions to governmental expediency.[31]

France's domestic bias projected outward was not the only factor in French military planning, nor was Britain's greater cautiousness more than relative. General Gamelin had from the beginning felt the need to divert German attention from the western front, a policy in which the British acquiesced, sometimes readily, as with General Ironside and Winston Churchill, sometimes only reluctantly or under protest. It was a testament to the continuing shadow cast by the Great War over Allied thinking that throughout the phoney war period Anglo-French planners devoted their principal energies to projects that they hoped would recreate the conditions of the earlier conflict by drawing others into the maelstrom to assist them. French and British strategists casting their eyes over the map of Europe, the Mediterranean, and the Middle East came up with a veritable Cook's tour of possibilities involving the Balkans, the Aegean islands, the Caucasus, the Balearics, the Arctic, and Scandinavia. General Beaufre has described this extravaganza as "real lunacy"; Liddel Hart called it "a wonderful collection of fantasies—the vain imaginings of Allied leaders, living in a dream-world until the cold douche of Hitler's own offensive awoke them."[32]

Certainly in their desire to open up new theaters of war as far away from home as possible, there was insufficient recognition that at this point in time Germany, by virtue of her central location and superiority of means, was in a better position to respond to Allied initiatives than were the Allies to hers and that it was therefore in Germany's interest, much more than it was in the Allies', to see the enemy's forces dispersed. If General Pownall, Chief of Staff to the BEF, realized that the enemy could well afford to run two shows at once and therefore warned of the unpleasant implications for the western front of any reduction in Anglo-French forces there, his was a voice crying pretty much in the wilderness. Even the Chiefs of Staff, at the insistence of the CIGS, had in the spring of 1940 expressed the view that Germany would be unable to take the offensive simultaneously in both the Balkans and Scandinavia (though, according to Sir John Slessor, neither the Air nor Naval staffs really believed this). That practically none of the Allied proposals, so hotly debated for months on end, survived the discussion stage is no doubt fortunate considering what their probable consequences would have been. Indeed, it is hard to dispute the harsh judgment that Hitler meted out in July 1940, after the Germans had captured a fair proportion of the French General Staff's and Foreign Ministry's archives: "When I compare the facts with the documents which have been seized in the archives of our enemies," he said incredulously, "I ask myself whether these have been drafted by blind men, idiots, or agents of bad faith."[33] At the very least, the quarrels or divergences in opinion evoked by these plans subtracted from the energy and unity of purpose which the Allies would soon need in a far more crucial sphere.

# Finland:
# The Alliance Makes
# Its Debut

THE different vantage point from which British and French viewed the strategic options available to them was revealed in the first weeks of the war when the possibility of opening up an eastern front was discussed. The French clearly favored the establishment of an Allied force at either Salonika or Constantinople as a means of strengthening the will of the Balkan states (Turkey, Greece, Yugoslavia, and Romania), with their 100-odd divisions, to resist any German (or Russian) move towards the Mediterranean or the Straits. They expected this new front to flare up by spring, an eventuality they contemplated hopefully and for which purpose three divisions in the Levant, under General Weygand, were being readied. But from the start the British doubted whether such a policy was within the limit of their resources or could be accomplished without provoking Italian intervention in the war. It was the Chiefs of Staff's opinion that they were in no position to undertake "adventures" in the Balkans and that "any diversion of force to the Middle East must result in a corresponding diminution of our military effort in France." Their main object in the area was simply to implement the Allies' treaty obligations towards Turkey, not to turn the Balkans into a tinderbox. Thus, in spite of continuing French pressure for a Balkan expeditionary force, the British refused to commit themselves beyond diplomatic efforts to build up a benevolently neutral Balkan bloc, with the contrary intention of keeping the war away from the Balkans for as long as possible.[1]

In any event, the Balkans no longer seemed quite so inviting to the French once the Russian invasion of Finland on November 30 opened up the even more exciting prospect of action in the frozen wastes of northern Scandinavia. It was over aid to Finland that some of the more fundamental differences between the Allies began to harden into a pattern of mutual opposition and disenchantment. For the French, the Russo-Finnish War was a welcome development because it appeared to answer a multiplicity of needs both political and strategic: as part of the war against Germany, it offered the possibility of large-scale operations directed against the Soviet Union which would weaken or destroy its ability to supply Germany with vital raw materials such as oil and grain; it would also, and not just incidentally, keep the fighting far from France's frontiers; but above and beyond these uses, it was hoped that the widening of the original anti-German conflict into something approaching a holy war against both totalitarian powers would serve to bring in on the French side a host of new anti-Communist allies. From this basic conception sprang the impossible (and barely articulated) dream of a French pincer movement that would cross the European continent from the Baltic to the Black Sea, with Allied forces in Scandinavia sallying forth to meet General Weygand's troops pressing forward from Syria to the Caucasus.[2]

For the British, aid to Finland was of interest largely because it could serve as a springboard for stopping the flow of Swedish iron ore to Germany via the northern Norwegian port of Narvik or, better still, as a means of embroiling both these neutrals in the war against Germany as a result of provoking German retaliation in Scandinavia. The mining of Norwegian territorial waters, through which the Germans were transporting the ore during the winter months, might have accomplished the same purpose, but this would have been an obvious infringement of Norway's neutrality. The advantage of offering aid to Finland was that the only possible route into that country for either men or munitions lay directly through Narvik and over its mountain railway to the Swedish mines at Gällivare; thus, if their "generous" impulse on behalf of Finland found favor with Norway and Sweden, and Narvik were allowed to be set up as an Allied supply base, they could easily control the iron traffic at its source and in this way kill two birds with one stone.[3] Finnish resistance per se, though considered desirable, was of much less concern to the British than to the French, whose anti-Soviet bias consistently impelled them in idiosyncratic directions.

The Scandinavian question, as an interallied problem, first came up at the Supreme War Council on December 19 when Daladier urged the sending of an Allied relief force to assist Finland and the breaking off of diplomatic relations with the Soviets. Inasmuch as the Chiefs of Staff had already concluded that no real advantages could be derived from declaring war on the USSR, the British, while not opposed to forwarding military equipment, hedged at any action that might evoke an adverse response on the part of Russia. However, from this point on they began giving serious consideration to a variety of plans which could be tied in with help to Finland. But Narvik and the iron ore shipped from that port remained the focus of their attention whether it was a question of dispatching an expeditionary force or merely of naval action to intercept the traffic.[4]

The French, by contrast, continued to give priority to assisting Finland. To this end, in January, they advocated an Allied landing at the Finnish Arctic port of Petsamo, then in Soviet hands, combined with the sending of 30,000–40,000 "volunteers" disguised as civilians through the neutral countries for the purpose of reinforcing a Finnish operation against the Russians. For the French, even a definite risk of open hostilities with the Soviets was worth taking if it enabled Finland to hold out for months instead of merely for weeks: for, unlike the British, the French entertained virtually no hope that the Russians would one day be in their corner. From the British point of view, however, the sole advantage of this scheme was that technically it avoided infringing the neutrality of Norway and Sweden and therefore did not depend for its success on their cooperation, which was uncertain at best. Otherwise, the British were quite unsettled by the apparent appetite of the French for taking on a fresh enemy, and especially for the chance it would afford the Allies of bombing the oil center of Baku. That Russia's entry into the war might adversely affect Britain's imperial interests in the east, in India or Persia, was not considered. Furthermore, the French plan contributed nothing to stopping the iron ore flow to Germany.[5]

If, at the Supreme War Council on February 5, the British were able to ride the French "off their silly Petsamo scheme," as Sir Alexander Cadogan phrased it, it was only in exchange for a formal British commitment to save Finland. The British plan accepted by Daladier combined assistance to the Finns with the capture of the Swedish ore fields, and for this a strong Anglo-French expeditionary force of 100,000 men, due to set forth in mid-March, was envisaged. In addition, the Allies agreed to make military preparations for supporting Norway and Sweden if a German threat against southern Scandinavia materialized. Command in the new theater and responsibility for coordinating the necessary arrangements was assigned to the British. The chief difficulty of the plan was that putting it into operation depended on the consent of the Norwegian and Swedish governments, when neither heretofore had shown any inclination to risk its neutrality in such a dubious cause. Daladier, however, was opposed to allowing the reluctance of the neutrals to nullify the plan.[6]

February, with its large-scale planning for a complex, multipurpose operation, brought Anglo-French solidarity to a short-lived high, for it was not long before the whole scheme started to come unstuck. With Norway and Sweden refusing to play the roles assigned them in this "mid-winter madness," the British cabinet vacillated, French complaints over British slowness and indecisiveness mounted, while old plans, previously discarded, were dredged up in despair only to be discarded once more. Churchill again pressed for the mining of Norwegian territorial waters as a means of provoking the Germans to violate Scandinavian neutrality and of thereby giving the Allies their chance of getting to Narvik; while the French Government plugged for the outright occupation of Norwegian ports since Norway refused (or was unable) to protect the neutrality of the Leads herself. Yet, however urgently the French pleaded with the British to override Norwegian and Swedish objections, the British could not quite bring themselves—at least in time—to force Scandinavian neutrality because their whole Narvik to Finland odyssey depended on the use of an intact railway.[7]

By early March, as the plight of the Finns became ever more desperate, the frustrations and fears of the French rose proportionately, leading them to warn the British of the serious consequences for the Allies—including a strain on their own relationship—that would result if nothing were done to prevent a Finnish collapse.[8] The greater importance of Finland in French domestic calculations was shown by the willingness of the French Government to take an independent line with the Finns that could not but disconcert the more conservative and less interested British. General Ironside thought the French "absolutely unscrupulous in everything." Among other things, they were encouraging the Finns not to make their appeal for Allied intervention dependent on Norway and Sweden granting them transit rights because, they inferred, the French Government was prepared to override the objections of the Scandinavian governments in order to meet Finland's requests. Because of some evidence that the Norwegians contemplated only token resistance to a British landing, the French Prime Minister persisted in believing that both the Norwegian and Swedish governments really wanted to have their neutrality violated. On March 1, without consulting the British Government, Daladier promised, and the next day publicly announced, that if the Finnish government formally appealed to them the French were ready to send 50,000 volunteers by the end of March and 100 bombers immediately. All this was most embarrassing to the British who did not in any case wish to promise what could not be performed but who also did not want to appear as pikers by comparison, still less as patsies when the whole project collapsed, and the French did seem, almost, to be setting them up.[9]

Despite news from Helsinki on March 6 indicating that the Finns were close to "throwing up the sponge" (the Finnish negotiators left for Moscow that day), the British still favored going ahead with the Scandinavian expedition, though the maintenance of Finnish resistance formed only a subsidiary motive. On March 11 the French Ambassador remonstrated over British backwardness and obstructionism: If the British did not do more to save Finland, he stated, M. Daladier would be forced to resign—a disquieting prospect to the British, who preferred Daladier with all his faults to any unknown quantity who might replace him. Sir Alexander Cadogan countered by accusing the French of telling fairy stories to the Finns about the amount of aid forthcoming, when in reality the Allies could only offer 13,000 men by the second half of April. Nevertheless, to placate their ally, Chamberlain on the 11th publicly announced the British Government's readiness, "in response to an appeal from them for further aid, to proceed immediately and jointly, to the help of Finland, using all available resources at their disposal"; while on the same and following days the cabinet decided to go ahead with the Narvik operation (as well as with preparations for landings at Trondheim, Bergen, and Stavanger), even if it were to meet with minor resistance from the Norwegians, so that they could respond to a Finnish appeal regardless of the attitude of the two neutrals. It was a useless gesture, however, for on the night of March 12 the Finns quietly came to terms with the Russians, thus depriving the Allies of their main excuse for action in the Scandinavian theater.[10]

Daladier, of course, was the most prominent casualty of Finland's collapse. Having publicly identified himself with those Frenchmen who had most warmly embraced the Finnish cause—for whatever reason, realist, idealist, or anti-Bolshevik—he was bound to be blamed when the policy failed. Blind to the greater calamities the country had possibly been spared in Finland, Parliament could see in the outcome of the affair only that the government's taste for action was lacking, its ability to plan and risk deficient. The defeatists, among other of his critics, now seized their chance and, on the very day after the Treaty of Moscow was announced, Pierre Laval attacked the Premier in a secret session of the Senate both for his irresponsibility in declaring war and for his indecisiveness in conducting it. His enemies in the Chamber also closed in: "Those who have known neither how to avoid war or to prepare for it are also not qualified either to end it or to win it," was Gaston Bergéry's chilling summation.[11]

Therefore, it was hardly a surprise when on March 20 Daladier did not survive a vote of confidence, being brought down not by the no votes cast, of which there was only one as against 239 yes votes, but by the 300 deputies who chose to abstain. Daladier himself felt that his defeat was due in good measure to British ineptitude and diplomatic fence-straddling. At any rate, he had defended himself in the Chamber of Deputies on March 19 by claiming that "The reason which prevents the French Government . . . from being able to go to the limit of its help lies in the fact that neither Britain nor Turkey wish to take the slightest responsibility for a military or diplomatic rupture with Russia." He also confided to the Secretary-General of the Foreign Ministry, Alexis Léger, that "what had really taken the stuffing out of him was his loss of faith in his ability ever to induce the British Government to take prompt action or a strong line."[12]

There was no doubt that the French were considerably more disturbed than were the British by the débâcle in Finland and even more demoralized over the do-nothingism that had characterized the first six months of the war. British backwardness seemed incurable, their refusal to act, as Anthony Eden saw it, perhaps even "menacing to those who were keeping an army of many millions in the field, with nothing to show for it but the dislocation of a nation's life."[13] Thus there *were* dangers in the continued stalemate. The British recognized this, as the Foreign Office had already been warned by sources inside France that "the failure to seize the initiative would mean a strengthening of the movement in favour of a compromise peace."[14] Yet, from the British point of view, there was an equally great danger in going out on a limb considering the present state of Allied resources.

The immediate consequences of the loss of Finland vis-à-vis Anglo-French policy making was that the French could now be counted on to renew their pressure for dramatic changes elsewhere—the Balkans, for instance—as well as for some definitive act in Scandinavia that would serve to convince public opinion that a war was indeed being waged. This was made clear even before Daladier's fall or the advent of M. Paul Reynaud on the international scene.[15]

# Dress Rehearsal
# in Norway

THE new Premier came to power on March 21 with the reputation for being both a *belliciste* and a man of great ambition. In fact, the British Ambassador thought him insatiably ambitious and would, at one time or another, describe him as high-strung, a lightweight in his thinking, and with "pocket-Napoleon proclivities," though he also gave him credit for "his courage and his resolution to go through to the bitter end." If Churchill was delighted to see Reynaud replace Daladier, because of the latter's role at Munich, the Foreign Office on the whole was suspicious of his activist approach, seeing personal motives behind it and, like Mr. F. K. Roberts, feeling that Daladier was "not only much more representative of the real France, but also in the long run a much more reliable figure, and one likely to return to power."[1] Not surprisingly, Reynaud immediately appropriated as his own all the projects that had been rattling around in French closets in order to fulfill Parliament's mandate "that the war should be prosecuted with increasing energy"—and to fulfill it quickly in view of the bare majority of one his government had received from a badly disunited and skeptical Chamber on March 22.[2]

On March 25 Reynaud passed on to the British an important memo setting forth the French Government's views on the future conduct of the war. This summed up a number of programs previously raised with the British in March and concerning which there was already a decided difference in outlook. M. Reynaud now proposed that the Allies seize control of navigation in Norwegian territorial waters immediately with the object of provoking a German retaliation which would then give them (the Allies) the chance to occupy certain strategic points on the coast of Norway and ultimately to

43

gain control of the Swedish ore fields. He also suggested bombing the
oil centers of the Caucasus in order to restrict the supply of petrol to
Germany and to paralyze the economy of the USSR before the Reich
could mobilize it to its own advantage. To further reduce Germany's
supplies in Russian oil he advocated the immediate dispatch of British and French submarines to the Black Sea to intercept this seaborne
traffic. The memo made it quite clear that the French Government
was more than willing to break off diplomatic relations with Russia
and indeed wanted to examine with their ally a good justification for
doing precisely this.[3]

The substance of all this was, of course, familiar to the British
from earlier French notes and approaches; only the form was new—
and apparently off-putting—for General Ironside confided to his diary on 26 March that "M. Reynaud has issued the most extraordinary paper stating how he proposes to win the war. He says that so
far nobody has done anything and he proposes to do it . . . . when
the P.M. read the paper he went through the ceiling." In fact, the
memo gave Chamberlain "the impression of a man who was rattled
and who wished to make a splash to justify his position. He thought
the projects put forward by him were of the crudest kind. That he
should mention submarines going into the Black Sea without mentioning Turkey seemed fantastic." Chamberlain was no doubt a little
harsh on Reynaud personally, for the Premier was merely putting
forth projects which had long been contemplated at the Quai
d'Orsay or by Gamelin, Weygand, or Darlan—France's defense establishment—while working under the aegis of Daladier. All in all,
Ironside concluded after conferring with the French Chiefs of Staff
who had arrived in London on March 27, "The French had thought
out nothing and put up the very vaguest things. *All of them to be
executed by us with a little vague help from the French.*" The most
troublesome point that emerged, he thought, was that "the French
had not grasped the question of baiting Russia and Italy into war
unnecessarily." Whether or not this was a somewhat exaggerated
interpretation of the French position presented that day, it was certainly true that the desire "to break the back of Russia" had become
almost obsessive in certain French milieux, civilian and military, and
that Finland was no longer even considered necessary as a convenient
cover. The interest in bombing Russian oil reserves would not finally
be abandoned until April 23.[4]

Since the liquidation of the Finnish imbroglio, however, the British
had retreated from their March 12 position even further into do-

nothingism. They had always been skeptical of any "Balkan adventure" that might complicate their relations with the Soviets or with neutral Turkey. But they rejected the Caucasian bombing scheme not for this reason but because the Chiefs of Staff thought that while bombing *could* bring about a *Russian* economic and military collapse, there was no action they could take against the USSR that would effect an early *German* defeat.[5] The COS, recognizing that the Allies had "embarked upon this war incompletely prepared and in a position of dangerous weakness relative to the enemy on land and in the air," were quite content to remain on the defensive except at sea and in the economic sphere during the first phase of the war. They did not wish to prejudice any change in attitude that might come over Russia or Italy or to take action against other neutral powers unless it was balanced by direct action against Germany herself. In short, as Lord Halifax summed it up, for the Allies there was the "desirability of our preserving a position of static warfare as long as possible."[6]

Boiled down, this meant that where Scandinavia was concerned, the British (Churchill of course excepted) were no longer prepared to occupy strategic points in Norway and were not much more enthusiastic than they had been about mining Norwegian territorial waters. From the point of view of the criticism they could expect to receive from the neutrals if they took action, Lord Halifax doubted whether the German violations of Norway's neutrality were sufficiently numerous or recent to justify the retaliatory steps proposed by the French Government; furthermore, the interception of the Swedish iron ore coming down from Narvik would at this time of year have only a limited effect on Germany because the main Baltic port of Lulea in the Gulf of Bothnia, heretofore frozen, would shortly be opening up.[7] What the British preferred was that further pressure be put on Stockholm and Oslo for the Swedes and Norwegians themselves to stop the traffic, and, in place of the mining of Norwegian waters, that fluvial mines be activated in the Rhine—the last a pet project of Mr. Churchill's known as Royal Marine which the British cabinet had accepted on March 6 but about which the French Government had already expressed reservations.[8]

By the time of the Inter-Allied Council held March 28 to discuss the war's future course, the British were nevertheless prepared to offer something better than their old preference for standing still in order to meet what was felt to be M. Reynaud's pressing need for "striking events" to dissipate the demoralization and uncertainty in

France resulting from the Finnish fiasco. For this purpose, they were ready to compromise: as a quid pro quo for the new front in Norway they expected the French to insist on, they would demand the fluvial mines scheme. Mr. Chamberlain therefore took the initiative by proposing the Royal Marine operation, the sending of a warning to the Scandinavian governments, and the mining of Norwegian territorial waters if the results of their démarche proved unsuccessful.

M. Reynaud was also adept at haggling. Referring to the openness of French opinion to Nazi propaganda that the French had been dragged unwillingly into the war, following the blank check given Poland by the British, he stated that the Germans appeared to count on the discouragement felt by millions of Frenchmen under arms as a result of their long months of inactivity and on the emergence of a government ready to reach a compromise peace with the Germans at the expense of Great Britain. As for Royal Marine, the French War Committee had previously rejected it on the grounds that the weight of the inevitable German reprisals would fall on France; however, they might agree to the operation if the British accepted the French proposals. Reynaud accepted the British plan for mining Norwegian waters but wanted it to be set in motion immediately and to be followed by the interruption of the Lulea traffic in the spring. In addition, he wanted a rapid resolution of the question of whether Baku was to be bombed or not and thought that the necessary bombs should be sent to Syria beforehand. To Chamberlain's argument that an attack on the Caucasus would mean war with the Soviet Union, that such "might be popular in France, but it would not be popular in England," and that Russia could take counteraction by interfering with the Allies' own oil supplies in Iran, Reynaud agreed that the operation would only be worthwhile if it led to decisive results against Russia and constituted a serious blow to Germany, but he nevertheless believed it did hold out these possibilities.

A compromise agreement was then worked out, with action planned for the immediate future according to a precise time schedule. Warnings were to be sent to Norway and Sweden on April 1; mines sown in the Rhine on April 4—subject to the agreement of the French War Committee; mines laid in Norwegian territorial waters to stop the traffic from Narvik on April 5; and magnetic mines dropped by air on the rivers and inland waterways of Germany on April 15. The landing of troops in Norway was to be undertaken if the Germans invaded the country or seemed on the point of doing so.[9]

There was, of course, a hitch. The Rhine project, which was intended not only to divert German attention away from the Norwegian theater but also to deflect world opinion from the Allies' "brutal" violation of Norway's neutrality, was rejected by the French War Committee on March 30, at the instance of both the President of the Republic, who feared reprisals against French war industries in the east, and the Minister of Defense, Daladier, who, it was suspected, out of hatred for his successor wished "to put a spoke in Reynaud's wheel."[10] (General Gamelin, Admiral Darlan, and Reynaud reputedly had all supported the project.) French "ratting" over the fluvial mines naturally infuriated the British, leading the Prime Minister to threaten the French Ambassador with the alternative of "No mines, no Narvik" and Sir Alexander Cadogan to complain that the French "talk about 'vigorous prosecution of the war,' which means that *we* should do it, provided we remove the war as far as possible from France!" In fact, when Corbin observed that the abandonment of both projects would leave the Allies in the position of "doing exactly nothing," neither Chamberlain nor Cadogan had scrupled to employ some ready-to-hand blackmail, their argument being that such barren results from the recent Supreme War Council would indeed be very embarrassing for M. Reynaud.[11]

Winston Churchill was duly dispatched to Paris (April 4–5) to plead for his project and to frighten the French into acquiescence. Daladier, however, remained unmoved, demanding at least a three-month postponement, while Churchill, not wishing any more than the French to lose out on the fruits of the Norwegian operation, was ultimately forced to accept the setback and to advise the British cabinet to make do with a one-sided deal. He was by this time convinced that if they forced the French to fall in with their wishes on Royal Marine, in consequence of which French interests did in fact suffer serious damage, it might well prove a mortal blow to the alliance; while contrarily, a failure to carry out the Norwegian operation would probably topple Reynaud.[12]

All this inevitably delayed the unfolding of the time schedule agreed to on March 28. The warnings to the Scandinavian governments were not sent until April 5, while the mining of Norwegian waters off Narvik was put off to April 8. The next day, of course, the Germans invaded Denmark and Norway, proceeding to the capture of the most strategic points in the latter with a speed, daring, and efficiency that astonished the world. A new theater had at last opened up, the Germans had indeed taken the proffered bait, but, although conditions now offered precisely the opportunity the Allies had hoped for, the campaign was to prove anything but what the British or French had bargained on.

If Finland brought about Daladier's undoing, Norway within the month was to prove Chamberlain's own personal Waterloo—as well, incidentally, as an unpromising testing ground for Anglo-French relations under stress. The British War Cabinet had on April 1 accepted the proposal of the Chiefs of Staff—in the event the Germans invaded Scandinavia or were on the point of doing so after the mining of Norwegian territorial waters—to send forces to Narvik to secure the port and railroad up to the Swedish border, to Stavanger to destroy the airfield, and to Bergen and Trondheim to keep these ports out of enemy hands.[13] The Germans, as it turned out, forestalled the Allies in every instance. The Supreme War Council meeting hurriedly in London on the afternoon of April 9 resolved to send strong forces to recapture the chief Norwegian ports, with the concentration on Narvik, but in the weeks that had elapsed since Finnish resistance ended most of the units and shipping earmarked for Scandinavia had been dispersed, so that much had to be improvised.[14]

In the days that followed, despite some significant successes scored by the British Navy at sea, almost everything that could go wrong did.[15] In northern Norway, the investment of Narvik proved such a formidable undertaking that it could not be mounted for six weeks after the British arrived in the area. To the south, Allied troops were landed at Namsos and Andalsnes, April 16–19, for the purpose of supporting a direct naval assault on Trondheim, which the French now saw as the quickest route to the Swedish ore fields and the Foreign Office favored for political reasons. By April 20 these two widely separated subsidiary landings north and south of the ancient Norwegian capital had been converted into the main attack, to be carried out by means of a pincer movement. At the Supreme War Council held in Paris on April 22 and 23 the Allies agreed to stand fast in Norway and that Trondheim and Narvik were still their prime military objectives; yet already at this date the talk in London was of desperate situations, the need to cut losses, and evacuation.[16] By 26 April, the situation in southern and central Norway had deteriorated to the point where the Chiefs of Staff and cabinet were decided on the need to clear out.

When British and French again met at a Supreme War Council that evening, Churchill therefore proposed, in view of the Germans' overwhelming air superiority in Norway and the impossibility of mounting an operation on Trondheim or of maintaining themselves there even if the port were taken, that the whole area be evacuated. General Gamelin duly protested against the British decision, while the French Ambassador, M. Corbin, was also much exercised by the political repercussions a withdrawal would have on Sweden, the Balkans, and Italy—and "not least in respect of public opinion in France itself, where there would be bitter criticism." By the next day, when Reynaud and Daladier had joined them, British and French were still far from complete accord on how to handle their forces in Norway. Mr. Chamberlain thought the main "question was how best to put a favourable complexion upon the situation." But the French Premier was unhappy at the prospect of evacuation and desperately supported such measures as might serve to save appearances—for instance, Gamelin's proposal for gradually withdrawing the Namsos contingent northwards along the coast so that it might continue to cover Narvik and to protect Allied communications. This was accepted in principle, but with considerable reticence, by the British, and there was finally general agreement that the attack on Trondheim would have to be abandoned and the forces at Namsos and Andalsnes withdrawn "as soon as it became militarily necessary." Two days later Reynaud tried to have the Council's decision rescinded, but evacuation of all but a small detachment shipped north to Mosjoen from Namsos was nevertheless effected during the first three days of May, and with it the campaign in central Norway came to a close.[17]

The battle for Narvik still remained to be fought, but by May 28 when the Allies finally won the prize they had coveted so long it was purely for purposes of prestige that they were fighting at all, the decision to evacuate having already been made. Completely overshadowed by the events of May 10, the Northern theater was in any case by this time merely a backwater, its significance almost as faded as that of the forgotten Caucasian oil wells.

Recriminations over the bungling of the campaign were not lacking. Because it was primarily a British show, it was naturally the British who received most of the blame. To begin with, the French could not understand why British intelligence units had failed to interpret correctly the German naval buildup and moves northward or to prevent their lightning blow. They were also unpleasantly surprised to find that the Royal Navy was not always mistress even in its own element. They were more than dissatisfied with the British conduct of operations. General Ironside on April 26 thought it nat-

ural for the French to "feel that we have not carried out the orders of
the Supreme War Council" and feared, as a result, that they might
withhold the French contingent from Narvik (though they did not).
Both Reynaud and Daladier, as Ambassador Bullitt reported on April
28, were "bitter about the manner in which the Norwegian affair has
been handled." In fact, Reynaud was "violent on the subject of lack
of brains in the British Government and the British High Command." The confusion resulting from the dispersal of command between the Admiralty, Air Ministry and War Office, the Chiefs of
Staff and Military Co-ordination Committee, London and assorted
sectors in Norway seemed particularly appalling, and Reynaud told
the British Ambassador on May 13 that he was "forced to the conclusion that our failure in Norway was due in large part to the
dispersal of command; there seemed to be no one man responsible
for the operations as a whole either in London or on the spot. Minor
operational decisions seemed to be taken by the War Cabinet in
London, a body which he would have thought totally unsuitable,
although it was of course the right one to take big decisions such as
the general conduct of the campaign . . . . "[18] Reynaud, who had
hoped for so much from Norway and who had, somewhat prema-
turely, announced to the Senate on April 10 that the permanent road
to the iron supplies had been cut, was most of all disappointed in the
lethargy and lack of leadership provided by the Chamberlain government. For him, they were "all old men who do not know how to take
a risk."[19]

This did not prevent the French Premier from attempting to saddle
General Gamelin with responsibility for the disaster. "Have you
given the British leave to have us defeated?" he had asked the Generalissimo at the beginning of the campaign in a pointed reference to
the latter's passivity and abnegation of control. A month later, determined to replace Gamelin with either Georges or the more dynamic
and imaginative Weygand, Reynaud opened up a massively documented and brutal indictment of him in the cabinet council, though
Daladier protested that it was "totally indecent" to make Gamelin
the scapegoat for the Norwegian check, which in his opinion was a
purely British failure, the result of the Admiralty's "stupidities."
Faced with the impasse, Reynaud attempted to submit the resignation of the whole government, thus bringing on a ministerial crisis.
This was May 9, and the problem of the High Command remained
unresolved.[20] But Norway had contributed to the fact, as Gordon
Wright points out, that France faced invasion with "a patched-up

cabinet whose two strongest members had just fought each other to the ground, and a commander who had just been openly repudiated by his premier."[21]

In England, of course, Norway brought about equally dramatic results. If public opinion as represented by Parliament could put up with the relative inactivity that had marked the first seven months of twilight war, including the government's failure to save Finland, it was not prepared to accept without protest the fumbled attempt to expel the Germans from Norway. The campaign raging just across the North Sea being in large part a naval affair touched Englishmen in the one element where they were least prepared for failure and most ready to demand not only explanations but heads. On May 2 Chamberlain announced to the Commons the Allies' withdrawal from central Norway, and a major debate on the issue was scheduled for May 7 and 8.

The debate, probably the most important and certainly the most passionate in British history, as it turned out, ranged far wider than Norway to encompass everything from Munich and the government's prewar appeasement policy to its lackluster, inept, and equivocal performance ever since September 3. Furthermore, many were unkind enough to remind the Prime Minister of what he had said on April 4 about Hitler's missing the bus.[22] The blows that rained down on the government were deadly, and all the more devastating in that many of the most pointed attacks originated not with the Opposition but from within the frustrated, fed-up (and frequently influential) ranks of Chamberlain's own Conservative Party. Thirty-three such Tories were angry enough to vote against the government when it came to a division, while almost twice as many abstained from giving their leader a vote of confidence.[23]

The government, if it still held a majority of 81—down from 200[24]—could hardly survive unchanged, and, in the event, Mr. Chamberlain resigned during the afternoon of May 10. This opened the way to Winston Churchill, who ironically, as First Lord of the Admiralty, had contributed as much as anyone (and probably more) to the fiasco which was ultimately to bring him to power. For England it was the end of an era, for Churchill the start of the most stirring chapter in his or his country's life.

# *All Quiet on the Western Front*

DURING the first eight months of war, despite a few false alarms, the western front had remained the quiet sector Gamelin hoped it would, with the result that the Allies probably devoted more of their verbal energies to discussions of far-away fronts that were not expected to be decisive than to the one theater that was from the start recognized as crucial. But here, in contrast to the peripheral regions where British sea power was the predominant factor, the French were fully in command by virtue not only of their numerical preponderance but also because of their greater vulnerability to attack and their presumed superiority in all matters strictly military. Considering the relative weight the two powers could bring to bear on this front, the principle of French direction was in fact more readily accepted by the British in 1939 than it had ever been during the first four years of the 1914–18 conflict. As a consequence, the British tended to go along with the strategy mapped out by the French, despite misgivings or differences of view, their chief leverage being a larger and more modern air force than that possessed by the French.

The British, for instance, were originally rather leery of Gamelin's proposal to move into Belgium, either to the Scheldt or the Dyle, in the event that the Germans attacked there and the Allies were invited in in time. They wished to avoid any encounter battles of the World War I type, which, in the absence of staff planning with the Belgians, seemed inevitable if an advance into Belgium were adopted. Because the neutral Belgians refused to concert plans with the Allies, the British favored meeting the Germans from their prepared positions on the Franco-Belgian frontier. At any rate, General Ironside, unlike Gamelin, expected the main German thrust to come through Luxembourg and the Ardennes rather than through Belgium. The Secretary of State for War, Mr. Hore-Belisha, also felt strongly about this in September, when he made it "quite clear to Daladier and Gamelin in Paris that in no circumstances would the British Government agree to the B.E.F. leaving their prepared positions and advancing into Belgium." But, although the cabinet was reluctant, it nevertheless concluded that whether or not British troops could safely advance to a forward position was a technical matter falling within the competence of the Supreme Commander in consultation with the British Chiefs.

Gamelin could marshal a number of arguments in favor of adopting the boldest of the alternatives then under consideration—meeting the enemy as far east as possible, on the Dyle River (in front of Brussels) and on the Meuse. For instance, by comparison with either the French frontier or Scheldt solutions, the Dyle-Meuse constituted a better natural obstacle; it would shorten the total Allied line by some 70-80 kilometers, thus conserving divisions for other purposes; it would also help to redress the unfavorable balance of forces by making available to the Allies an additional 22 Belgian divisions; France's northern industries could more easily be protected from an advanced line; for the future, the position definitely offered superior offensive possibilities; finally, Gamelin thought that the loss of Belgium, together with that of Holland, by making the British more apprehensive about their own security, would deprive the French of their fullest cooperation in the battle to come.

Sir Henry Pownall, the BEF's Chief of Staff, also regarded the prospective move as excellent, superior to both the other positions that had been discussed. In any event, the British Air Ministry had its own reasons for wanting the Allies to occupy as much of Belgium as possible: it would prevent the Germans from establishing air bases from which their bombers together with fighter cover could attack England, while at the same time it would bring the RAF that much closer to the Ruhr. This factor ultimately proved decisive with the British. (Indeed, according to some French critics, from October Chamberlain was actually *pressuring* Gamelin to run the risk of an encounter battle in case of aggression against Belgium.) Thus, by November 9, both Ironside and Lord Gort, Commander of the BEF, in spite of their initial hesitancy, had agreed to Gamelin's plan to advance to the Antwerp-Namur (Dyle) line if the Germans invaded Belgium. This policy was formally endorsed by the Allies at the Supreme War Council of 17 November. Meanwhile the Belgians had secretly agreed to organize the Dyle line. In fact, so won over to the move into Belgium had the British Chiefs of Staff become that by April 8 they were urging Gamelin to carry it out even if the Germans attacked Holland alone and regardless of whether the Belgians wished to maintain their neutrality in these circumstances. This was eventually agreed to by the French High Command on 23 April.[1]

Much harder to reconcile were the different approaches to air power. On September 12 the Allies had agreed for the present not to use their air forces against land targets in Germany, though they would retaliate if the Germans began bombing. Air policy was further delineated on November 17 when it was decided that only if the Germans bombed aircraft factories or similar objectives in France or Great Britain would Britain's heavy bomber force be authorized to retaliate immediately against the Ruhr without further reference to the French Government. However, in the event of a German invasion of Holland or Belgium, air attacks were still to be limited to strictly military objectives in the narrowest sense of the term. But the RAF had long been dissatisfied with this passive policy, and wished to test out its strategic bombing concepts by a full-scale assault on the Ruhr as soon as enemy action against France or Britain looked as if it might be decisive. The French, however, were adamantly opposed to initiating action of this kind, even in the event that Belgium was in danger of being overrun. Daladier not only considered that the risks of retaliation from a superior German air force were too great but he did not believe that bombing the Ruhr would prevent the Germans from invading or occupying Belgium. For this purpose he advocated bombing the enemy's motorized divisions, supplies, lines of communication, and aerodromes—all air attacks to be undertaken in close liaison with French and British military operations. These targets were thought by the British to be unprofitable.[2]

It was the start of a long-lasting and important quarrel, in which, oddly, the French General Staff had the support of the British Army and War Office, who seemed almost as suspicious as were their allies of an independent air force with its own independent policy. But for better or for worse, the British Air Ministry was in a position to make its voice heard; not only did it have the planes, each type with its specific advantages and limitations, but, perhaps more to the point, it also had the technical expertise with which to browbeat the layman and ultimately to alter or to determine policy.

Six months before the war the French and British staffs had agreed that if the main German attack was directed on France the primary task of their bomber forces would be to stop the invasion and to contribute to the success of the battle on land. Yet this policy, from which the French never veered, had not taken into consideration the functional differences between the medium and heavy bombers of Bomber Command or the fact that neither had been designed for tactical operations in support of ground forces. Only in the autumn of 1939 did it become clear how these technical considerations would impinge on the strategy and tactics favored by the British. Thus, on 9 November Sir Cyril Newall, Chief of the Air Staff, was forced to tell General Gamelin that the British lacked appropriate aircraft with which to bomb German ground forces, and instead proposed a concentrated attack on the Ruhr, which he claimed would have a much greater effect on the war in the long run. Gamelin, however, was not interested in the long run; what he wanted was direct effects on the battle at hand which might otherwise be lost for lack of air support. But, aside from this consideration, the French were to remain reticent about bombing the Ruhr because, unlike the British, they did not feel their air force could effectively protect either their cities or their aircraft installations against German retaliation. Thus the November 17 compromise was as far as they were prepared to go for at least another six months.[3]

By mid-April Gamelin was still reluctant to initiate any bombing against German industry or urban areas except by way of reply to similar action on the part of the enemy. More specifically, the British found him equivocal as regards the air action to be undertaken by the Allies if the Low Countries were invaded—in spite of the fact that they had sweetened the pill of their Ruhr proposal somewhat since November. The British now proposed using the full offensive strength of the RAF in the area of the enemy's advance in the Low Countries as well as in the area east of the Rhine through which the Germans' line of communications and supplies ran: their medium bombers would be used directly against the advancing German columns, as previously arranged; a small proportion of their heavy bomber squadrons would be used against German concentration areas and communications between the Rhine and the Dutch and Belgian frontiers; while the balance of the heavies would be directed against enemy communications through the Ruhr and other important installations in the Ruhr, including marshaling yards and oil refineries. Because the heavy bombers could operate only by night, except in the direst emergency, so the British argued, the Ruhr operation in itself would constitute no diversion of strength from their

primary aim, which was to establish the Allied armies in a forward
position in Belgium. However, Gamelin and the French still did not
like the plan and it was probably only because the British threatened
to reserve to themselves the right to take independent action if Holland were invaded that at the April 23 Supreme War Council it was
finally agreed that in the event of a German invasion of either Holland or Belgium, or both, the RAF would be authorized, without
further consultation between the Allied governments or high commands, to immediately carry out bombing attacks against marshaling
yards and oil refineries in the Ruhr.[4]

Even so, the French were still not prepared to authorize a general
air offensive against German military targets; they remained unen-
thused by "the new possibilities of long-distance air action"; and, as
Sir Samuel Hoare, who replaced Sir Kingsley Wood as Air Minister
on April l, points out, "Between them and our Air Staff was a gulf of
opinion that was never fully bridged and that continually impeded
sound decisions [in the Air Ministry's opinion] until the French collapse ended the chapter of argument."[5]

# The Allied
# Balance Sheet

THEIR doubts and differences notwithstanding, the Allies in the late spring of 1940 remained cautiously optimistic and stubbornly confident of ultimate victory. Finland had been a frustration, while Norway was not only a strategic setback but a blow to Allied pride and prestige as well. Yet there were grounds for comfort, if not complacency. No one had expected the war to be a walkover or without its quota of reverses. The British, according to their half-deprecatory, half-hubristic maxim, were accustomed to losing every battle but the last, while Reynaud's Minister for the Colonies, Georges Mandel, could mordantly intone "We shall go on from catastrophe to catastrophe towards final victory"[1] with the confidence of one who had witnessed at close hand the Allies' snatching victory from the jaws of defeat twenty-two years before. Reynaud, at least, had introduced a note of optimism and energy into French governmental life that contrasted favorably with Daladier's incurable pessimism.

Though it was later to be thrown back at him in the same way that "Hitler missed the bus" was contemptuously thrown back at Chamberlain, the French Premier's assertion that "We shall win because we are the stronger"[2] had much that was solid to support it. The British and French *did* possess command of the seas; their empires, the first and second in the world respectively, *could* ensure them access to the resources required for waging and surviving a long war, if only they were willing to accept the drain on their finances; the blockade of enemy-controlled territory *would* in time be effective;[3] while Allied war production, coming up from behind, was now attaining a healthy rhythm. By spring French fighter production had at last entered the modern era. Not only that but French and British financing of the American aircraft industry's expansion and the orders and options placed in the United States in March were expected to give the Allies complete control of the situation in the air by September 1940 or spring 1941 through the development of an annual production rate of 12,000 planes and 20,000 engines.[4]

All depended on the Allies' ability to prevent the Germans from winning a quick contest, and this aim, it was believed, would be foiled by the superior power of the defense over the offense in modern warfare. If this was a faulty conception of war, at least it was a shared misconception, the British no more than the French having learned anything much from their military innovators to cause them to question or abandon doctrines that seemingly had been validated by success against the same foe in the Great War. In any case, in view of their tardy preparations for war and what was considered "a position of dangerous weakness relative to the enemy on land and in the air,"[5] the Allies had little choice but to adopt a defensive posture on the western front until they had further built up their strength. Both French and British were geared to the idea of a war of at least three years' duration, which in their mind's eye they saw unfolding according to the slow-motion tempo of 1914–18.

General Gamelin was fairly certain that the Germans would launch a major offensive in 1940, that it would come through Holland and Belgium, and that the enemy would no doubt enjoy an initial superiority. Yet he also believed that in the showdown he would be able to fight a successful defensive engagement. He was confident that by May the French Army would be ready to face a prolonged battle, so that looking to this date he had asked Daladier in mid-March to find some way "to incite Germany to bring matters to a head, and to compel her to invade Holland and Belgium." He had also wanted to march into Belgium on April 9 in response to the German invasion of Denmark, but was once again forestalled by the Belgians' reluctance to relinquish their neutrality.[6] He was not alone in surveying future prospects with a certain equanimity; possibly the one faith common to all Frenchmen, no matter how fearful or faction-ridden in other respects, was their belief in the French Army. Even if it should fail at the start, so popular reasoning went, it could always be counted on to pull off another "miracle of the Marne."

Nor could the British really fault this view despite their irritation with some of the wilder schemes dreamt up in Paris or their suspicion of the disconcerting French mix of overzealousness abroad and convoluted cautiousness at home. In a sense, the British were forced to believe in the French Army. As General Ironside freely admitted: "It is the only thing in which we can have confidence. Our own Army is just a little one, and we are dependent upon the French." But, from direct observation in January, he had seen nothing amiss with the state of the French Army, nor did Lord Gort report anything wrong. British liaison officers found French morale good, and when Gamelin told the CIGS on March 31 that the French Army, despite its deficiencies, would fight, Ironside was confident that the long "peace in war" had not adversely affected their soldierly spirit. Formidable as the Nazi Wehrmacht was known to be, it was still thought by the British that a German offensive against France could be halted, and even as late as May 4 the Chiefs of Staff estimated that there were "sufficient land forces to maintain the security of French territory against both Germany and Italy, if adequate air protection and support [were] provided." Thus it was not only Francophiles such as Winston Churchill who accorded high marks to the French Army. Faith in the underlying military virtues of the heirs of Napoleon, or at the least in the recuperative powers and plain doggedness of the sons of Foch and Pétain, was the received professional opinion of the day. And in Ironside's view even Chamberlain (who could certainly not be accused of overfriendliness to the French) was banking on the French Army to give time to the British to get ready.[7]

In part, Allied confidence stemmed from a concerted effort to avoid some of the difficulties that had plagued Anglo-French relations during the last war. For instance, in September 1939 France and Great Britain were at least able to begin the war on land under a unified command, whereas in World War I this had not been established until April 1918. (Command at sea was exercised either by a Briton or a Frenchman according to the zones in which Allied ships were operating, while in the air no unity of command had been envisaged.) For the coordination of Allied policy, the two governments had agreed in August 1939 to set up a Supreme War Council that would meet alternately in London and Paris once war broke out, a step not taken in the previous war before November 1917. This body, of course, had no executive authority, whatever decisions were taken at its sporadic meetings requiring the prior approval of each government to become effective. It had no common secretariat. Nor was there a combined general staff, such as the Americans and British developed later in the war, to assist the Council; this had been proposed by Chamberlain only to be turned down by the French, who feared it might be used to advance Britain's imperial interests.

The Allied Military Committee nevertheless brought the two staffs together for periodic exchanges of views, which fed into the compromises reached at the top when the heads of government met at the Supreme War Council. This collaboration was in turn supplemented on a day-to-day level by the plethora of military missions exchanged between the two countries.[8] All in all, if the machinery for the higher direction of the war still had some kinks in it, the framework for a closer integration of effort at least existed.

Likewise, economic unity, which had only been achieved in the fourth year of the first war, was well on the way to realization by the third month of the second. By December, a major financial agreement had been hammered out by which the financial contributions of the two governments to the war were fixed on the basis of the national wealth of each—France to contribute 40 per cent, the United Kingdom 60 per cent. Especially important was the establishment, on 17 November, of the Anglo-French Coordinating Committee under the direction of Jean Monnet (who had headed the Inter-Allied Maritime Transport Council in World War I) to ensure the most efficient use of the economic resources of both countries and to avoid insofar as possible competition in the procurement of war materials abroad. Of the nine interallied agencies working under his aegis, none proved more successful than the Allied Purchasing Commission, chaired by Arthur Purvis, whose French and British members worked in closest harmony and loyalty once British opposition to Daladier's plan for the large-scale purchase of American planes was dropped in late January. Raoul Dautry has also testified to the collaboration on industrial and scientific matters that developed between the two countries.[9] Both sides were justifiably proud of their advances in cooperation and understanding and inclined to sentimentalize, largely for propaganda purposes, about the successes achieved.[10]

# Tightening the Knot

THE question of war aims could not be so readily disposed of, and, because even informal discussions of how Germany ought to be treated after the war were ticklish and often productive of controversy, the whole topic was generally avoided by mutual consent.[1] French insecurity vis-à-vis their German neighbors had, after all, been the slippery rock on which Anglo-French relations had foundered after 1919. In November Lord Halifax admitted to the Marquess of Lothian, British Ambassador to the United States, that

any overt discussion of War Aims might at this moment lead us into disastrous controversy with the French . . . . They have only a vague idea that war has come upon them again owing to our having taken the teeth out of the Versailles settlement, and having ever since shown a sentimental spinelessness in dealing with Germany. If they have any definite idea, it appears to be the dismemberment of Germany.

(The French did indeed want a divided Germany, possibly the Rhineland, and the "liberation" of Austria.) Nevertheless, in reply to a request from Daladier on October 23 that Allied war aims be studied in common, the British did set forth their general views on the subject in a long memorandum that was not submitted to the French until December 22. The French were concerned primarily with obtaining effective material guarantees that would protect them against any possibility of future German aggression. The British, however, while agreed on the need to prevent Germany from again building up such a preponderance of armed might that it could menace the peace of Europe, wanted to postpone considering the actual methods (e.g., territorial adjustments, reparations, arms limitations) by which such a guarantee would be established until after the defeat of Germany had been secured. They therefore advised against any public statement of war aims that was cast in too precise terms and suggested that the two governments limit their official declarations to general principles on which they were already agreed.[2]

Indeed, the larger issue of war and peace aims constituted such a can of worms that both governments would have preferred to keep the lid clamped over it even with their own peoples. When on October 9, for instance, the Prime Minister was asked for a specific statement regarding the country's war aims, he hedged, replying only that "His Majesty's Government and the French Government are in complete accord as to the purposes for which we entered the war and these purposes have more than once been already stated by both Governments." However, the issue could not be ducked that easily and it figured prominently in the House of Commons debate held three days later. In this, Sir Stafford Cripps rightly accused the government of having expressed aims that were "excellently vague in their definition," aims which "when examined, amount to nothing more than a determination to try and revert to the *status quo* before the war, and a determination on the part of this country and of France to preserve untouched as far as possible their domination over world affairs." Again on 30 November, when there was another major debate on peace aims, the Prime Minister was accused (by Hugh Dalton) of still showing "a certain timidity and some fear that further discussion of this subject in this country would somehow militate against the successful prosecution of the war." But the reason for the government's timidity was obvious. Mr. Strauss summed it up: "If we cannot agree among ourselves, it seems fairly safe to assume that we are not likely to reach agreement with France. . . ."[3]

The French Government too had trouble defining its war aims, though here the problem was less the difference between what was preached (democracy) and what was practiced as what ideology was to be preached to begin with. As François Fonvieille-Alquier points out, the pragmatic solution was simply to adapt French war aims to the circumstances:

So [that] a neutral, looking with detachment at the Phoney War, would have understood that France was fighting (1) for Poland from 3 September to October 1939; (2) in a crusade of the democracies against the totalitarian countries in the month which followed; (3) after 13 December for the defence of Christian civilization against the atheistic and impious barbarism, with the emphasis on that which came from the Asiatic steppes; (4) and, when the attitude of Italy began to inspire some momentary confidence in French governments, for the defence of Latinity.[4]

But the fact that differences as to aims—which could be subsumed under the heading of French realism versus British idealism—were potentially open to exploitation by the enemy had seemed cause for concern from October on, and it was hoped by the British that they could be dealt with at least to the extent of the Allies' formally undertaking not to sign a separate peace. General Spears, a former high-ranking liaison officer with the French, MP, and trusted friend of Winston Churchill, was a prime mover in pressing for the speedy conclusion of such an agreement. In November he told the Foreign Secretary that "if German propaganda got hold of the fact that there was no such agreement and started proclaiming to the French that England was keeping a back door open to slink out of the war when she had made her own terms, leaving France in the lurch, it would be far more difficult to conclude, as it would then appear to have been forced upon us by the enemy. French distrust would be thoroughly aroused, and it was after all to our advantage to bind the French, as they had been uncertain starters and their hearts were certainly not as yet in the war."[5]

It was for much the same reasons—to bind the French and to shut the door firmly against the possibility of any future negotiations— that Élie Bois had as early as September 11, in the *Petit Parisien,* launched a press campaign for a no-separate-peace agreement, having in mind an agreement similar to that signed in the previous war by M. Delcassé and Sir Edward Grey. On October 11, in answer to Hitler's speech, and again on October 26, in response to a recent attempt by Ribbentrop to drive a wedge between the Allies, Bois renewed his demand for a "solemn public declaration between France and Great Britain that neither one nor the other would conclude a separate peace." Though Allied diplomats and statesmen subsequently played down the political, as opposed to the propaganda, value of such an agreement, Bois—like Spears— makes clear the dominating motive of the original proponents of the pact: "the necessity for bolting, as it were, and padlocking the alliance of the two countries."[6]

The French Ambassador in London had not been particularly enthusiastic when the matter was first broached but had nevertheless agreed to get the ball rolling. Nor was the British Government especially enthusiastic about the proposed Anglo-French agreement. According to Lord Halifax's summary of a meeting held at the Foreign Office on December 14, it was "felt that the matter was largely academic, as it was obvious that neither country could conclude peace separately." Therefore, when the Prime Minister put the suggestion to the French Ambassador, he had told him that "we did not feel strongly either way about it."[7]

Differences in approach to the problem delayed its resolution, the British Government looking upon a no-separate-peace declaration largely as a propaganda tool, Daladier, on the other hand, hoping to profit from the exchange of views on the subject to wrest some specific guarantees from the British on the shape of the postwar settlement. The subject was informally discussed at the December 19 meeting of the Supreme War Council, its complications where war and peace aims were concerned being recognized, and during the winter the Foreign Office and the Quai d'Orsay applied themselves to working up draft agreements that would pledge both countries to full cooperation during and after the war and to the exclusion of any consideration of proposals for a separate peace. At the February 5 meeting between the Allies Daladier evidently agreed to a no-separate-peace declaration being made. In the meantime, however, the British had run into a snag, in that not all their dominions were willing to go along with the agreement, which caused them to suggest postponing the declaration. By February 21 Sir Alexander Cadogan, Permanent Under-Secretary at the Foreign Office, was ready to drop the whole idea of any Anglo-French declaration if his opposite number in Paris, Alexis Léger, thought it wise.[8]

As the British Ambassador, Sir Ronald Campbell, reported on February 27, Léger was emphatically in favor of going ahead with the proposal, dominions or no, while Georges Mandel also urged the early conclusion and publication of a no-separate-peace agreement.

The reason he [Mandel] gave, couched in suitably camouflaged words [Campbell wrote], was that, whilst a government of which Daladier was the head (and incidentally himself a member) was perfectly sound as regards no separate peace, he would not put his hand in the fire for any other. When I asked him whether he felt sure that any government here [in France] which could be so foolish as to contemplate a separate peace would consider itself bound by an act of its predecessor, he said it would be virtually impossible for it publically to repudiate a binding instrument of the kind.

Mandel's purpose, the Ambassador thought, was to "take the heart out of those who are working to undermine Daladier with the thought in their minds, if they succeed in ousting him, of seeking an accommodation with Germany."[9] Thus, Campbell too favored the publication of an Anglo-French agreement at an early date, considering "that it would impose a solemn and binding obligation upon all future French Governments." However, the Ambassador hoped the proposed text might be expanded so as to give some contractual form to the continuance of Anglo-French economic and military collaboration after the war. He wanted something that would both encourage the French and assist understanding between the two countries when the time came to arrange peace terms by dissipating French suspicions as to the attitude the British Government would adopt upon the defeat of Germany.[10]

In the event, it was not Daladier at all but Paul Reynaud who on March 28 signed the declaration on behalf of the French Republic— one of his first acts as Premier—and a French draft, in place of the British, that was substituted and accepted by the British without discussion.[11] The declaration read simply:

The Government of the French Republic and His Majesty's Government in the United Kingdom of Great Britain and Northern Ireland mutually undertake that during the present war they will neither negotiate nor conclude an armistice or treaty of peace except by mutual agreement.

They undertake not to discuss peace terms before reaching complete agreement on the conditions necessary to ensure to each of them an effective and lasting guarantee of their security.

Finally, they undertake to maintain, after the conclusion of peace, a community of action in all spheres for so long as may be necessary to safeguard their security, and to effect the reconstruction, with the assistance of other nations, of an international order which will ensure the liberty of peoples, respect for law, and the maintenance of peace in Europe.[12]

The only difference between this agreement and a similar pact that had been negotiated by the two governments and Russia on September 5, 1914, was that the 1940 accord prohibited a separate armistice as well as a separate peace—a novelty the French had introduced.[13] Because of its brevity and apparent innocuousness, it was accepted primarily as a formality, and with some military officers at the conference "it passed almost unnoticed." Probably few among the French delegation had the impression that they were sealing the destiny of their country by a solemn or considered contract.[14] Yet in a sense, the Anglo-French agreement of March 28 marked a sort of triumph for the "sounder" elements in French politics as opposed to the peace party headed by Bonnet and was certainly a feather in the cap of all those on both sides of the Channel who had worked so to cement the alliance.

If the agreement did not win universal approval in France, it did nevertheless command the enthusiastic backing of many groups and was favorably received by all sections of the French press with the exception of the *Action Française*.[15] True, it might have been more precise regarding the peace procedure to come, the material guarantees that French security demanded, and the military contributions to the common cause that could be expected from each country.[16] But, had this specificity been demanded, there would, of course, have been no agreement whatsoever. Besides which, at the time of its signing, the declaration was seen largely as a manifestation of solidarity and purpose, a pact that would come into play only when Germany was forced to sue for peace. It was not until after circumstances had changed completely that it was more fully analyzed and then found wanting.

After the war, Reynaud would claim that his motivation in signing the accord had been "to burn his bridges in case things turned out badly and thus to prevent France from making a separate peace,"[17] but it is quite unlikely that such dire premonitions or long-range political aims were in the forefront of his consciousness at the time. More probably, Reynaud had no idea that by entering into such an agreement he was compromising France's future freedom of action or placing the French Government in a disadvantageous position; on the contrary, he believed he was placing France in a better position to wage war effectively because Britain would be obliged by this instrument to reach full agreement with France before any peace terms could be discussed with Germany. In any case, it was not primarily due to his efforts that the declaration had been signed, and Daladier was supposedly jealous of his success in bringing it off.[18]

Covered by the President of the Republic, according to Laurent-Eynac, who accompanied him, Reynaud had gone to London with the mandate of his war cabinet to sign the accord (though if possible to introduce into it provisions relating to French security), and the text of the agreement had been approved by this body on his return. Furthermore, when in mid-April he discussed the pact together with his war policy before secret sessions of the Senate and the Chamber, he had received an ovation in the upper house and a unanimous vote of confidence from the deputies.[19] Only sixteen deputies had abstained from this unanimity and, as Louis Marin was later to testify, they had done so not out of hostility to the pact, which they favored, but simply because they thought the Reynaud ministry incapable of conducting the war.[20] All in all, as his Minister of Blockade, Georges Monnet, put it, Reynaud's increased standing in the Chamber could actually be considered a tribute to the negotiations he had conducted in London.[21]

And so, with the installation of Reynaud in France, and of Churchill in England, Anglo-French relations appeared to be in peculiarly congenial and secure hands. Yet the question troubling at least a few Frenchmen in 1940 remains valid today: had the war and the no-separate-peace agreement imposed on the two allies risks and obligations that were commensurate?

Certainly in the months since September the war had been fought largely at sea, where the British bore the brunt of whatever effort and losses were required. Yet it was on land that the Germans with their much-vaunted Wehrmacht were expected to make their big move. Here, France was exposed to the enemy over much of its frontier, whereas the British Isles were conveniently sheltered from the enemy by a protective channel. And by spring 1940 it was not seriously thought that the Germans would attempt a cross-Channel invasion or the air offensive that would precede it so long as France remained unbeaten.

The advent of air warfare, nevertheless, had made for a fundamental change in Britain's position. The country *could* now be directly threatened as it had not been before. Thus, the potential for competition between the defense requirements of France and Great Britain was built into the situation. Back in 1909, when the Anglo-French entente was still in its infancy, a cabinet subcommittee reporting on the military needs of the Empire had concluded that "a military *entente* between Great Britain and France can only be of value so long as it rests upon an understanding that, in the event of war in which both are involved alike on land and sea, the whole of the available naval and military strength of the two countries will be brought to bear at the decisive point."[22] That was the crux of the matter: the decisive point. Where indeed was it? The French never doubted for a moment where it lay; the British, on the other hand, were not so sure.

To meet the coming storm, France counted, as always, on the protection afforded by a large army; England, on her fleet and air force; on the continent the British depended primarily on the French shield. To the British, as a maritime nation, time and space could never have quite the same meaning they had for the French; to the French, on whose territory the war would be fought, they were of the essence. The policies best suited to the continental and maritime interests of each nation were intended to be complementary and, in spite of the predictable conflicts and competing claims, might have been crowned with success. But a successful partnership demanded one thing as a minimum: the French Army had to be at least strong enough to maintain the integrity of French soil until British forces could supplement it in might and numbers. The smallness of the British contribution to the armed forces in line in France—on the ground as in the air—was still only a potential threat to Allied unity in May 1940. The German offensive launched against Belgium, Luxembourg, and the Netherlands on May 10, however, provided a wedge that was to shake the alliance to its foundations.

*I*

# *Trial by Fire*
# *in the North*

*May 10 – June 4*

*When there are no oats in the stable, all the horses will fight. In battle it's the same way. So long as all goes well, everyone is euphoric; but as soon as things become difficult, we begin to glance at our neighbor and say: "He's not making progress! He's slow!"*

General Weygand, testifying May 24, 1949, before the Parliamentary Commission of Inquiry, in *Les Événements Survenus en France de 1933 à 1945: Annexes: Témoignages et Documents Recueillis par la Commission d'Enquête Parlementaire* (CE), VI, p. 1692.

*If our Expeditionary Force is cut down, then "goodbye" to the Entente Cordiale with France . . . the only alternative is a selfish isolation which would lead to a combination of all Europe against us under the dictatorship of Germany.*

Col. Spencer Ewart, Director of Military Operations, commenting in his diary, 1908, quoted in Michael Howard, *The Continental Commitment* (London, 1972), p. 36.

# Breakthrough
# on the Meuse

PLAN D, the "Dyle solution," had been jointly endorsed by the French and British governments on November 17, 1939, as the most probable maneuver to follow in the event of a German invasion of the Low Countries, and it was in conformity with this prearranged operation that Allied troops marched into Belgium on May 10. By pivoting on Mézières, more than 30 of the 40-odd divisions of the French First Army Group, including 9 divisions of the British Expeditionary Force, were to swing around from their prepared defenses along the French frontier to an advanced position inside Belgium along the Dyle and Meuse rivers. Here they hoped to support the 20-division-strong Belgian Army commanded by King Leopold and also to connect with the small Dutch force under General Winkelman. Roughly, the Allied defense, involving the 102 French, British, and Polish divisions allotted to the North-East front,[1] was to be conducted along a line running from above Antwerp in the north, south through Namur to Mézières, then southeast along the French border to its junction with the heavily fortified Maginot Line.

Determined to avoid a repetition of the 1914 disaster in which they had been caught off guard by a strong German wheeling movement on the right, the French were sending their most powerful elements forward to come to grips with the enemy along an advanced linear front.[2] Yet in effecting this maneuver the Allies were playing directly into the enemy's hands, for this time, in a reversal of the World War I Schlieffen plan, the Germans had decided to deliver their knockout blow on the left—to the south. By a massive thrust in the Sedan area at the hinge of the frontier fortifications and the Maginot Line, precisely where the French were weakest, the Germans planned

71

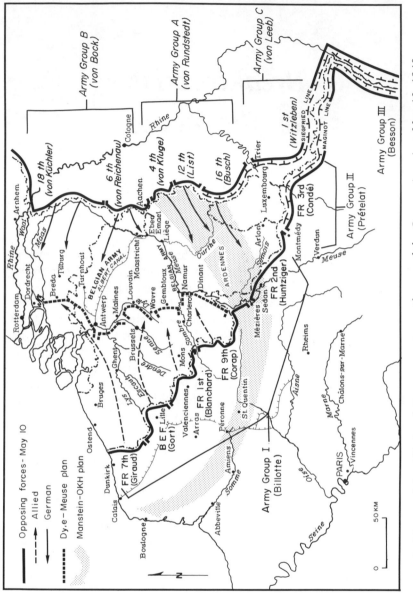

1. *Lineup of the Allied and German armies on the eve of the German invasion, May 10, 1940.*

to cut the French forces in two, then encircle and annihilate the Allied armies in the north before going on to destroy the remainder of the French Army in a second phase of the campaign.[3] The success of the German plan depended on the Anglo-French advance into Belgium and on the Allies' continuing to believe that the Belgian plain would be the main battlefield, even though the German drives across northern Belgium and southern Holland were largely of a diversionary character.

Thus, four days into the campaign, disaster struck the French from an unexpected quarter. Having first penetrated the Ardennes, the Germans next proceeded to break through the French lines on the Meuse along a 50-mile front from Dinant to Sedan. Between May 13 and 14 three German bridgeheads across the Meuse were secured, so that by May 15 seven panzer divisions were free to head for the coast or for anywhere else in France. Not only had the Germans succeeded in shattering the left wing of Huntziger's 2nd Army and the whole of Corap's 9th, but they were well on their way to realizing their principal objective—the outflanking of the Allied armies in Belgium.

The breakthrough at Sedan, which was to decide the fate of the French Army, elicited from the French High Command neither an immediate order to the northern armies to withdraw from Belgium nor for a coordinated counteroffensive to deal with the spreading bulge. That the main weight of the German attack was concentrated on the southern Meuse was recognized at French GHQ by May 15; however, its direction following the breakthrough remained uncertain a while longer. In fact, whether the Germans intended to take the Maginot Line from the rear, drive towards Paris, or advance westwards to the coast was not finally clear to General Gamelin until May 18.[4] By this time his armored reserves had been squandered piecemeal, while General Billotte's First Army Group above the breach was struggling with the German vise fast tightening about it. In short, in the first week of blitzkrieg, every assumption the British had made about the French Army was to be invalidated, as well as every assumption they had made about their own role as ally.

# The Battle
# for Air Support

WINSTON Churchill, who had succeeded Neville Chamberlain as Prime Minister on May 10, first heard of the breakthrough at Sedan when Paul Reynaud telephoned him at 5:45 p.m. on May 14, immediately after the French themselves had learned the catastrophic news. The French Premier immediately requested ten additional squadrons of fighter aircraft to stop what was then thought to be a German drive on Paris. This request for further British air support, to be repeated ever more insistently throughout the following weeks, was to prove the single greatest irritant between the Allies. What was plain from the outset was that, despite eight months of talks on how the British air forces would operate once the Germans struck in the west, no clear-cut agreement on air policy had ever emerged. Chamberlain's written promise, dating from October 1939, that all British aviation, whether stationed in France or in England, would be thrown into the battle at the decisive moment in full accordance with the French[1] might be invoked. But the controversy, involving not only the tactical uses the air force should be put to but the basic strategy to be followed, remained.

Had Britain's and France's air forces been combined, they could have opposed some 2,700 modern aircraft in line to the approximately 3,200 employed by the two German air fleets operating on the western front in May. German bomber strength would still have outnumbered Allied capacity by at least 2½ to 1, but Allied fighters, according to most estimates, may actually have had the edge, while in reconnaissance planes Germany was only slightly better off. However, the total Allied strength was not combined, the bulk of Britain's fighter force having been preassigned a defensive role in the United Kingdom, and the bulk of its heavy bomber force being reserved for long-distance strategic targets within Germany that were expected to affect the enemy's basic war potential. Thus, to the 1,200 aircraft available to the French in the North-East theater Britain contributed about 630 planes (of which, on May 10, 130 were fighters and 160 bombers), a figure which was to vary considerably from day to day as squadrons were added, then withdrawn or depleted. England's strategy therefore combined with the maldistribution of French aircraft between the armies and the interior and the further dispersal of French fighters to points outside the battle zone (the Italian frontier in particular) to accentuate greatly the Luftwaffe's initial superiority.[2]

On May 10, the British had in France, ready to participate in the coming battle, an Advanced Air Striking Force (AASF) composed of 10 squadrons of medium bombers and 6 of fighters (with preparations for the reception of 4 more fighter squadrons) and an Air Component attached to the BEF composed of 13 squadrons, 4 of which were fighters. Air Marshal A. S. Barratt was in overall command of the two units, which together formed British Air Forces in France (BAFF), although the uses to which they would be put were ultimately determined by Bomber and Fighter Commands in the United Kingdom subject only to the agreement of the War Cabinet. There was no unity of command with French air forces, which for all practical purposes were subordinate to French land forces. According to the rough division of labor accepted by General Gamelin before the war, the French were to provide the fighter force, the British the bomber force. Where fighter support was concerned, England had in fact already gone far beyond the prewar engagements entered into.

The divergent air strategies favored by Britain and France had already occasioned what was close to a running battle between the Allies in the eight months prior to the German attack, not to speak of continuous friction between the RAF and the British Army, which, like the French, favored tactical, as opposed to strategic, bombing and the use of Britain's entire metropolitan air force, not just a portion, in the struggle to stop a German onslaught. The Air Ministry's established policy, so the official historian J. R. M. Butler explains, was not to "fritter away" British bomber strength on "minor objectives" such as the French had in mind but instead to husband it for major targets like the Ruhr, which promised to be "decisive." The French had hated this project all along, believing that bombers could always be more usefully employed elsewhere; in addition, they remained highly skeptical of British claims that the Ruhr bombing could so dislocate German industry as to impose an appreciable delay on the advancing German Army. A tentative compromise seemed to have been reached by spring when the British Government accepted a more prominent role in the main battle for the heavy bombers than that proposed by the Air Ministry, and the French reluctantly agreed that in case of German aggression against Holland or Belgium the RAF should be automatically authorized to bomb oil plants and marshaling yards in the Ruhr.[3]

Yet neither the organizational setup of British air forces in France nor the patchwork compromise reached by the Allies were quite satisfactory to anyone. The BEF still did not have the air arm it felt it required to compete successfully with the tactics used by the German Army working in closest harmony with the Luftwaffe. Lord Gort furthermore believed that all British air forces cooperating with the armies in the field—not just the Air Component—should be under the operational control of the man responsible for the conduct of operations, namely himself. Moreover, both he and Ironside agreed with the French that no air force operating in France could possibly be run from England. Thus, the army remained at odds with the Air Ministry, with whose forces in France it had only indirect communications via the War Office even during the most critical days in May. Air Marshal Sir Charles Portal of Bomber Command, for his part, continued to oppose the commitment of over half the British bomber force to the land battle, even to the point of predicting disaster for the war in the air on the very eve of battle. And the French could never really accept the British policy of withholding anything from the big battle, which to their minds would be *the* decisive one. Thus, a fundamental conflict of interests was in the making when Reynaud's requests started pouring in in the wake of the disasters to the north.[4]

British losses in the air during the first week of battle were undeniably formidable, amounting to 248 aircraft. On May 14, for instance, of the 71 bombers which took off for Sedan, 40 failed to return, the worst loss ever sustained by the RAF for an operation of comparable size. On May 10 the Advanced Air Striking Force had possessed 135 serviceable bombers, by May 12, only 72. In fact, in the first five days the AASF lost one aircraft in every two sorties. Statistics such as these convinced Churchill, at least, that "the continuance of fighting on this scale would soon completely consume the British Air Force in spite of its individual ascendancy."[5] British production simply could not replace the downed aircraft at anywhere near the rate of loss suffered when bombers and their fighter escorts participated directly in the battle according to the French prescription. This entailed a limit on the help that could be sent the French, a limit Churchill claimed was based on Air Chief Marshal Sir Hugh Dowding's solemn warning that "with twenty-five squadrons of fighters he could defend the island against the whole might of the German Air Force, but that with less he would be overpowered." (Actually, Dowding was laying claim to thirty-six fighter squadrons as his last-ditch minimum.)[6] In any event, as the official RAF historian puts it, Dowding had "determined to fight his battle—in his opinion the one decisive battle—over England, not France; and this he could do only if the Germans attacked England before Fighter Command had been offered up on the altar of Anglo-French solidarity."[7]

A desperate call from Reynaud at 7:30 in the morning on May 15 announced that the French were beaten, that they had lost the battle; he therefore begged for all the aircraft and troops the British could send.[8] Incredulous that the situation could be quite as bad as described, Churchill nevertheless volunteered to fly to Paris the next day. In the meantime, buoyed by the surface optimism and calm still radiated by the French High Command, which nevertheless knew that the Battle of the Meuse was lost, Churchill allowed the Chiefs of Staff and cabinet secretariat, under strong pressure from Dowding who appeared that day before them, to turn down the French request for more fighters.[9] Twenty-four hours later, the gravity of the crisis had become more apparent to the Prime Minister, though a still greater shock lay in store for him in the French capital.

Accompanied by Sir John Dill, Vice-Chief of the Imperial General Staff, General Ismay, his deputy as Defence Minister, and Air Marshal Joubert de la Ferté, Deputy Chief of the Air Staff, Churchill arrived in Paris on the afternoon of May 16 to find the French Government in an almost paralyzed state. It was from this date that British doubts as to their ally's capacity for leading the coalition crystallized in almost definitive fashion. General Dill would conclude immediately after the Anglo-French meeting, in view of Daladier's and Gamelin's demoralization, that "the French Higher Direction of the War [was] within measurable distance of being beaten."[10]

That the French Government was already preparing to evacuate the capital was made clear by the clouds of smoke arising from the large bonfires set in the gardens of the Ministry of Foreign Affairs and into which state documents were continuously tossed from the windows of the building as the Anglo-French discussions progressed.

In this bizarre atmosphere Gamelin explained to the British that the Germans had broken through on a front 50 kilometers wide and had already penetrated over 60 kilometers inward from Sedan. They were now believed to be advancing rapidly either towards Amiens and Arras or on Paris. To Churchill's question, "Where is the strategic reserve?" Gamelin replied simply that there was no more.[11] Dumbfounded that the French High Command, with a 500-mile front to defend, had not provided itself with a "mass of manoeuvre," Churchill could only belatedly mourn that the British Government had not insisted on knowing the dispositions of the French Army. When he next asked Gamelin when and where he proposed to attack the flanks of the German bulge, Churchill received an even more devastating reply: "Inferiority of numbers, inferiority of equipment, inferiority of method," followed by a hopeless shrug of the shoulders.[12] In this way the magnitude of the disaster and the extent of French despair were brought home to the English for the first time.

Inevitably, Gamelin renewed the appeal for the support of the British Air Force in stopping the gap leading to Paris. With respect to French needs, General Bergeret, Deputy Chief of the French Air Staff, and Reynaud both pointed out that up to then the French and British had concentrated their aircraft on different objectives, that indeed they seemed almost to be fighting separate wars. In combination, they might successfully launch a counterattack against the German armored thrust.[13]

That morning the British cabinet had authorized Churchill to move four additional fighter squadrons to France.[14] The French now asked for the dispatch of six more, a request which, if complied with, the Prime Minister thought would leave Britain with only twenty-five fighter squadrons at home—the final limit. Mr. Churchill explained why the maintenance of thirty-nine fighter squadrons was absolutely vital to the country.[15] This was the force that kept the German Air Force away from British war industries, whose production was essential for the continuance of the war. So long as British fighters were there, the Germans would have to rely on night raids, the results of which were necessarily uncertain. By contrast, daylight raids, which would become possible if the defense of the United Kingdom were weakened, would certainly have disastrous results for the final outcome of the war. Churchill also argued that bomber aircraft should be used to strike at "essential" targets, like the Ruhr, the destruction of which affected Germany's war potential, rather than to fight tanks, a job he felt could be better done on the ground.[16]

Nevertheless, the French appeal did not fall on deaf ears, and at 9 p.m. Churchill wired the War Cabinet to warn that, unless their ally's demand were met, French resistance might be broken up as rapidly as that of Poland. He therefore advocated that for the next two or three days all available French and British aviation, including Britain's heavy bomber force, should be concentrated over the German bulge so as to give a last chance to the French Army to rally its bravery and strength. "It would not be good historically if their requests were denied and their ruin resulted," he stated, adding that if all else failed the British air striking force could still be shifted to assist the BEF should it be forced to withdraw.[17] Late that same evening Churchill was able to announce the cabinet's affirmative reply to Reynaud and Daladier.

At least the Prime Minister allowed the French to believe that the RAF was placing ten additional squadrons (or twenty fighter squadrons in all) at their disposal. Temporarily, this boosted the morale of the French leaders, but actually the War Cabinet's decision on the night of May 16 involving the six extra squadrons requested by the French was considerably less generous than had been represented. First of all, the squadrons were to be concentrated in Kent, operating from French bases only during the day. Second, three squadrons were to operate in the mornings, the other three to take over in the afternoons. Thus the cabinet was not actually committing itself fully in case catastrophe ensued—the result of the strongest pressure exerted on it that night by Air Minister Sir Archibald Sinclair and Chief of the Air Staff Newall, both of whom shared Dowding's point of view. Moreover, of the additional squadrons dispatched to France after the fighting began, at least three had come at Lord Gort's expense, having previously been promised to the hard-pressed Air Component. And in the course of the next three or four days the fighter strength of the AASF would be reduced to three squadrons, its bomber strength to six, while the Air Component, which in ten days had lost 195 Hurricanes, was withdrawn to England starting on 19 May. This was the same day on which Churchill would decide that no more fighter squadrons should leave the country, no matter what the cost to France, a decision confirmed by the War Cabinet on the 20th.[18]

# The Looming
# Contingency

THUS, if the trip to Paris heightened Churchill's consciousness of French needs, it also made him aware that French strategy and planning had placed British forces in a most precarious position. As a result, upon his return the next day, he asked his colleagues to examine "the problems which would arise if it were necessary to withdraw the B.E.F. from France, either along its communications or by the Belgian and Channel ports." At the same time, General Ironside, Chief of the Imperial General Staff, proposed to the Admiralty that all small vessels should be collected and organized with a view to evacuating the men of the BEF through Dunkirk, Calais, and Boulogne if the worst should happen.[1]

At this stage, however, both Churchill and Ironside considered these measures merely as precautions against the possibility of a disaster which still seemed relatively remote. The War Office on 17 May viewed the idea even more negatively, believing that a total withdrawal of the BEF from France would be impossible owing to: (1) the scale of air attacks that could be expected, (2) the weakness of their antiaircraft resources, (3) the fact that no plan had ever been prepared to meet such an eventuality, and (4) the presumption that if they were to move the BEF across from France at the same leisurely pace at which they had landed contingents during the autumn, any evacuation would take up to nine weeks.[2] Nevertheless, such drawbacks notwithstanding, only a week after the British had advanced into Belgium in the expectation of fighting a long war, the possibility of a total evacuation was being reckoned with.

While in England Churchill was preparing to meet the direst eventualities, Reynaud, in an effort to stiffen the resistance and morale of the

80

French, was making some important changes in the chain of command. First of all, he decided to replace Gamelin as Supreme Allied Commander with General Weygand, Foch's Chief of Staff in World War I and, since 1939, Commander-in-Chief of French forces in the Middle East. Weygand was summoned to Paris from Beirut on May 16. Then, on May 18, Reynaud brought Marshal Pétain, heretofore France's Ambassador to Spain, into the government as Vice-President of the Council and shifted Georges Mandel, Clemenceau's formidable deputy who had dealt with defeatism in the earlier war, to the Ministry of the Interior. The Premier himself took over the Ministry of War, shunting his rival Daladier over to the Quai d'Orsay. But, while Weygand was en route from his post in Syria and before he could assume command on the 20th, the Germans were racing to the sea virtually unopposed. When on May 20 they captured Albert and Amiens and in the evening reached Abbeville and the coast, the encirclement of the Allied armies in Belgium was complete.

South of the breach, two new armies struggled to organize themselves and to build up a front on the Somme and the Aisne. Meanwhile the Allied divisions still intact in Belgium were also attempting to form a second front north of the gap to protect themselves against an upward swing by the German armies. This could be done only by siphoning off forces from the line of the Escaut (Scheldt), to which the Franco-British forces had now retreated, stretching from Terneuzen in the north to Arras in the south, which in turn increased Allied vulnerability to a breakthrough from the east. On 17 May, on orders from General Georges, the BEF had prolonged its defensive flank by occupying certain points on the Canal du Nord from Douai to Péronne, at the same time attempting to cover Arras, British GHQ and a road center vital to any southward offensive or retreat. Because General Blanchard's 1st Army had experienced the heaviest fighting and the heaviest casualties so far, it was incumbent on Lord Gort to accept the principal burden of forming the new front to the south and with it a new role in the overall Allied scheme. This unexpected transformation of the BEF's role was responsible for much of the tension that soon arose between the French and British commands.

Even before the outset of hostilities the British had accepted the principle of a unified command; yet they had insisted on the BEF being directly under the orders of the French Supreme Commander, or of the C-in-C on the North-East front, General Georges, rather than subordinate to the commander of an army group. Gort's relations with the French Command were regulated anew on May 12 at an Allied conference held near Mons. Here, King Leopold of the Belgians and Gort's Chief of Staff, Lieutenant-General H. R. Pownall, agreed to accept coordination in the field by General Billotte as the representative of General Georges—in a sort of apostolic succession deriving from Gamelin. In this way Billotte could direct operations for the whole Allied left wing.[3] As General Ironside describes it, Gort "had the right of appeal against any orders he received. But matters were not simple if he wished to exercise such a right. In theory he was under the direct command of the French Generalissimo, but in actual fact he was . . . far beneath the authority to which any appeal could be made and have any effect."[4] With the northern armies surrounded and communications cut, any direct appeal to French General Headquarters would soon be out of the question. Yet during the next few days Gort's confidence in the French Command was to weaken progressively and his reliance on his own judgment increase proportionately—a situation that could only presage trouble for Allied rapport.

Gort had his first doubts about the French during the withdrawal to the Escaut. First, although Billotte had decided on May 15 to retreat, Gort was not informed of this until a half day later; second, during the withdrawal, he had received contradictory orders from Billotte and Georges; and third, upon reaching the Escaut he found that it no longer constituted an effective barrier because the French 1st Army had inundated the ground in the Valenciennes area by decreasing the water level on the front occupied by the BEF (from Oudenarde to Maulde). But, as his biographer makes clear, Lord Gort started experiencing more general misgivings as to the French Army's fighting qualities from 15 May on—misgivings to which the reports of his liaison officers with neighboring French units must have contributed in no small measure. For it was from them that he learned of the general administrative chaos prevailing as well as of the demoralization and "malignant inaction" gripping Billotte's and Blanchard's headquarters; at the former, many of the staff had broken down and wept upon hearing the worsening news from the 9th Army front, while at the latter, according to Gort's informant, "Blanchard was every day losing the respect of his officers," who, "with one or two exceptions," also did not deserve his.[5] The French liaison mission at Gort's headquarters was not slow to detect or to report on the British Command's growing lack of confidence in the French and, for its part, also noted as a harbinger that Lord Gort had shipped home his personal luggage as early as May 18.[6]

Lack of effective communication in the field accounted for much of Gort's anxiety. For one thing, there was no wireless communication within the First Army Group due to French insistence on wireless silence,[7] and, for another, telephone communication among the various commands virtually ceased seven days after the battle opened. As explained by General Montgomery:

From the 16th May onwards the German advance began to cut the land lines, and telephone communication ceased on that day between Supreme H.G. (Gamelin) and H.Q. North-East Front (Georges). From the same date all direct communications ceased between General Georges and Army Group No. 1 (Billotte). Also, from the 17th May Gort had no land telephone lines to Belgain H.Q. on his left, the First French Army on his right, and H.Q. North-East Front (Georges) behind.[8]

Therefore, coordination of operations was difficult, depending as it did on a cumbersome system of staff visits and liaison postings. Gort was not kept properly informed of general developments respecting either French or enemy movements, not even of the 9th Army's collapse, and was therefore forced to rely on his own intelligence network. Only after the French began to call on the BEF for reserves to close the gap to the Somme and after they began to realize that they were to a great extent dependent on the British to save the Allies in northern France and Belgium did they stop ignoring them altogether.

At midnight on May 18–19, just after reaching the Escaut, Gort had his first conference with Billotte since the start of the campaign. Only after Billotte had reported the full extent of the crisis and admitted that "he had no plan, no reserves and little hope" did Gort realize that "there was an imminent danger of the forces in the north-eastern area ... being irretrievably cut off from the main French forces in the south."[9] Logically, there were three possible solutions to the situation: 1) the closing of the gap by means of simultaneous counterattacks from both north and south of the Somme; 2) a fighting withdrawal by the Allied armies north of the gap to cut their way through to the Somme; or 3) a withdrawal to the sea followed by evacuation.

As no one could verify whether the French had sufficient reserves south of the gap capable of staging a counterattack strong enough to close it, the first alternative was discarded. A single-handed attack by the northern armies also appeared most problematical, especially in view of the fact that seven armored divisions were operating on their flank, and was not considered very seriously by the two commanders. Gort writes that "the French High Command had never suggested such a movement up to that date and it is doubtful whether even had they decided on immediate withdrawal as soon as the French 9th Army front on the Meuse had been penetrated, there would ever have been sufficient time for the troops in the north to conform." Gort clearly favored evacuation as the only practical scheme. To this end he discussed the possibility of withdrawing towards the Channel ports and of holding a defensive perimeter there long enough to enable the BEF to embark, "preferably in concert with the French and Belgians." But Billotte did not commit himself to this option.[10]

Yet Gort, conscious of the necessity of saving the BEF at all costs— and equally conscious that his lines of communication were on the brink of being severed, that the 1st Armoured Division, which would only begin landing at Cherbourg on May 20, would not now be able to reinforce him, that the BEF's Air Component was in process of returning to England, and that 85 miles of his rear were covered by only the thinnest of screens—quite naturally felt it "only prudent to consider what the adoption of such a plan might entail." Therefore, on the 19th Gort had his Chief of Staff, Pownall, telephone the Director of Military Operations at the War Office to discuss the situation with him.[11]

As reported in his diary, in his first conversation with the DMO (Major-General R. H. Dewing) at 11:30 a.m., Pownall

explained to him in camouflaged language that the B.E.F. might be forced to withdraw. The position on our right was very bad, if it deteriorated our right would be in the air and we could not stay where we were. We were therefore examining the possibility of a withdrawal in the direction of Dunkirk whence it might be possible to get some shipping to get some troops home. . . . we felt that Georges should realize that the situation, as we knew it, was such that withdrawal might become inevitable if French operations further south, to close the gap, did not meet with success.

Then, following a corps commanders' conference at which General Brooke "hatched" an alternative plan for saving the BEF should it be cut off, Pownall told Dewing at 1:30 p.m. that they were also studying "a possible withdrawal towards Bruges and Ostend." But in response to these developments, the Chief of Staff found Dewing "singularly stupid and unhelpful," wanting to know why the BEF could not withdraw instead to Boulogne, which Pownall realized the Germans would reach long before the British could. In the face of obvious objections, Pownall ended by assuring the War Office that the BEF "definitely were not going to withdraw at present, but only if the necessity were forced upon us by the failure of the French to fill the gap."[12] Yet in anticipation of the worst, as Brooke's diary entry for May 19 makes clear, "G.H.Q. [now] had a scheme for a move in such an eventuality towards Dunkirk, establishing a defended area around this place and embarking all we could of the personnel of the B.E.F., abandoning stores and equipment."[13]

And on this date, despite its defective understanding of the situation, the War Office immediately opened discussions with the Admiralty on the possibility of maintaining the BEF through Dunkirk, Calais, and Boulogne, as well as on the question of evacuating non-combatants, and on the contingency, then considered unlikely, of evacuating the main body of troops through these ports. Though the War Cabinet hoped Gort would find a way of cutting his way south to the Somme, they also felt, as Churchill puts it, that "there was no reason why all possible precautions and preparations should not be taken for the sea evacuation if the southern plan failed."[14] Therefore, on May 20 the Prime Minister ordered Vice-Admiral Sir Bertram Ramsay to assemble a large number of small vessels that would be ready to proceed to ports and inlets on the French coast; and that day a conference was held at Dover to consider "the emergency evacuation across the Channel of very large Forces."[15]

As of 19 May London was not at all attracted by the idea of evacuation. Encirclement was still not complete and the prospects of Boulogne, Calais, and Dunkirk holding out long enough to permit such an operation seemed dubious at best. It seemed quite possible that if a plan of evacuation were adopted it would end in catastrophe, with most of the BEF, to say nothing of the British evacuation fleet, at the bottom of the Channel. When informed that Gort was examining a possible withdrawal towards Dunkirk, General Ironside, for one, could not accept such a proposal. Concerned above all with preventing a break in the British line of communications, Ironside immediately ordered Gort to get a large proportion of his reserves down into the Douai-Béthune-Arras area, so that if the worst came the BEF would be prepared to turn south and cut its way through to the Abbeville-Amiens line and eventually to the Seine to cover Le Havre. Ironside was in fact delegated by the cabinet to go to Flanders to see that Gort forced his way through to the south, while

Sir John Dill, at General Georges's headquarters in France, was ordered to help coordinate a joint Franco-British offensive.[16]

Yet the precise character of British thinking on May 19 was probably lost on the French. For even as Dill was assuring General Gamelin of Ironside's promise that the French Generalissimo's orders, whatever they were, would be carried out by British troops, disquieting news arrived via Billotte and Georges that the British were now thinking of retreating on Dunkirk or Calais, a possibility that continued to haunt the French Command for the next week in spite of British assurances to the contrary. The seeds of suspicion were thus laid on this date, and all too easily kept alive by memories of the Haig-Nivelle clash of 1917, when the British had looked to the Belgian ports while the French insisted they extend their lines southward. Furthermore, the CIGS's offer to meet Gamelin in the north so that the two of them together could oversee the direction of events could not be fulfilled inasmuch as Gamelin's career came to an abrupt end that very night.[17]

The British, however, were intent on doing something. At 8:15 on the morning of May 20 Ironside arrived at Gort's command post at Wahagnies with instructions for Gort to strike in force southwards towards Amiens with a view to taking up a position on the Somme on the left of the French Army. This maneuver was to be carried out in conjunction with the French 1st Army. But even before Ironside produced his "sensational" order, it was "perfectly obvious" to Sir John Slessor of the Air Staff, who had accompanied the CIGS from London, from conversations held earlier at British GHQ, "that it was too late to carry out the movement suggested by the Prime Minister" and that the C-in-C's thoughts were principally fixed on evacuation—if even that were possible.[18]

Gort maintained that the proposed "withdrawal to the south-westwards, however desirable in principle, was not in the circumstances practicable." He argued that seven of his nine divisions were then in close contact with the enemy on the Escaut and that their withdrawal would open a gap between the British and Belgian lines through which the Germans would immediately penetrate. Furthermore, the area to be attacked was strongly occupied by the enemy, the BEF's communications with its bases were on the point of being interrupted, and the supply of ammunition was precarious. Finally, Gort believed that the French 1st Army and the Belgians would not go along wth the maneuver. Nevertheless, after considerable prompting, and even though "realizing that the order bore no relation to the situation as it existed," Gort conceded to the extent of proposing a limited counterattack—one he had already planned—to be launched the following day to the south of Arras. If he could not break through to the Somme, he might at least narrow the gap.[19]

Ironside and General Pownall then left for French 1st Army head-quarters near Lens to arrange for French participation in the operation. Here, according to the exasperated CIGS, they found Billotte and Blanchard depressed, defeated, and utterly without plans, "quivering behind the water-line north of Cambrai while the fate of France hung in the balance." Only after Ironside lost his temper and "shook Billotte by the button of his tunic" did the French commanders agree to attack towards Cambrai the next day with two divisions. Nevertheless, Gort warned Ironside on his return to British headquarters that the French "would never attack." Ironside thereupon telephoned General Weygand, who had assumed formal command that day, that there was no coordination in the north and that Billotte should be relieved—advice the new French Generalissimo did not at all appreciate. Ironside also sent a threatening telegram to General Georges to the effect that, unless the French 1st Army made an immediate move on Cambrai or unless Georges himself launched a counterattack northwards from Péronne, Billotte's Army Group would be completely and finally cut off. General Dill also exerted pressure on Georges, and Gort's liaison officers with Billotte and Blanchard conveyed similar messages.[20]

Ironside then returned to London to report to the cabinet on 21 May that confusion reigned in the French High Command and that Gort had received no orders for the past eight days. He was by this time convinced that any large-scale operation to effect a junction with the French armies south of the Somme must be principally dependent on the action of the French. (Indeed, according to Pownall, Ironside was very rapidly converted to all Gort's ideas.) But, in the light of his and Dill's investigations into French capabilities, any "bold stroke southwards" by Billotte or any concomitant move northwards by the French Third Army Group seemed very unlikely. Gort himself informed the Secretary of State for War, Anthony Eden, on May 21 that unless the situation on the French 1st Army front was reestablished, the BEF's withdrawal to the southwest was impossible.[21]

Gort nevertheless pressed on with his plan for a limited counterattack to the south of Arras on the 21st in spite of learning from Blanchard that the two divisions of the French 1st Army (Altmayer's

V Corps) scheduled to make a concerted effort southwards from Douai that afternoon would not be able to start before May 22. Only a part of one light mechanized division belonging to General Prioux's Cavalry Corps could cooperate. Major-General H. E. Franklyn, in overall charge of the operation and of British troops (of the 5th and 50th divisions) in the area, was led to believe that his task on 21 May was a relatively minor one—mainly to block the east-west roads to the south of Arras and to secure the town itself. Yet the French, under the impression that the British attack had a larger purpose, hoped that the British would forge on to Bapaume, which was only 20 miles from the Somme at Péronne; the British, equally unrealistically, hoped that the French 7th Army would advance northwards from the Somme to help pinch off the German armored units in the Channel area from the more slow-moving infantry following behind. And, though Franklyn had not even been warned by Gort that a large counterattack was under discussion or that it was to be undertaken *with* the French, both French and British headquarters in the north began to think of the operation as the first stage in a projected attempt to reestablish an unbroken front. The attack, launched at 2:30 p.m. by the tank expert Major-General Sir Giffard Martel, did have an initial success and, as it turned out, produced a disquieting effect on the Germans quite disproportionate to its size and real potential. However, the whole affair lasted only a few hours: two British columns advanced some 10 miles into enemy-held territory, then, after being subjected to intensive dive-bombing and a vigorous counterattack by Rommel's 7th Panzer Division, were compelled to halt their promising drive and eventually to pull back to the west of Arras and along the River Scarpe.[22] The French attack launched the next day in the direction of Cambrai fared no better; and on the night of May 23 both retreated northward to positions that were at least 50 miles from the Somme.

# Paper Tiger:
# The Counterattack Manqué

BFORE he was superseded Gamelin had outlined a plan (his Secret and Personal Instruction No. 12 of May 19) for resoldering the nearly encircled First Army Group in the north to the rest of the French armies south of the breach. This was to be accomplished by means of counterattacks launched from both north and south of the gap, the object being to cut off the overextended panzers from their infantry support and thus to open up the route of the Somme. Weygand did not cancel the order—in fact, according to Gamelin, Weygand was in complete agreement with it—but neither did he confirm it in toto. On May 20 Weygand asked Billotte to attack to the south and ordered the Third Army Group to move on the Somme. But before issuing more specific orders he wanted to investigate the situation in the north for himself.[1]

Weygand's first attempt to make contact with the northern armies was enough to indicate how desperate their plight had become. Because all road communications had been cut by the night of May 20, the new Generalissimo was able to reach Flanders only by a circuitous and dangerous plane trip on the 21st. At Ypres Weygand conferred first with King Leopold and his military adviser General van Overstraeten, then with Billotte, and suggested a plan for reuniting the two segments of the Allied armies through attacking the German salient at its narrowest point. Differing somewhat from Gamelin's scheme in that its axis was farther to the west, Weygand's envisaged a large-scale attack to be launched as soon as possible by the French and British in the north towards Bapaume and Péronne simultaneous with one mounted by Frère's 7th Army in the south. It also comprehended the cooperation of the Belgians, who were to protect the left and rear of the Allies by falling back progressively from the Escaut to the Yser.

This sacrifice move by the Belgians Leopold was most reluctant to make and in fact refused to accept for the time being. Not only were the Belgian Army's stores and munitions all to the east of the Yser, but the King believed that the only real hope for the Allies lay in the three armies immediately swinging northwest and there forming a giant bridgehead behind the Lys that would cover Dunkirk and the Belgian ports from Gravelines to Ostend. However, not wishing to undermine Weygand's "offensive spirit," Leopold failed to make his position crystal clear. Billotte, who was more than dubious about the idea of an offensive towards the Somme, gave the appearance of being even more amenable, while the British Commander, completely negative on this score, was unaccountably absent from this important meeting and therefore unable to argue his case at all. Thus Weygand left Ypres at 6:30 p.m. not only with an inaccurate picture of the capabilities of the Belgians and French but also with the disturbing impression that the British were unwilling to cooperate or to take orders. Actually, Gort had not been notified of the time and place of the conference until the last moment.[2]

The failure of the two commanders to meet undoubtedly contributed to the growing estrangement and lack of trust between French and British—because as of this point their relations rested on an equivocation: official British support for Weygand's ideas offset by the BEF's unofficial resistance, which was never openly admitted or explained. Weygand, in fact, would thereafter be unable to give Gort any direct orders, for by this time, with the last telephone cable at Abbeville cut, all important communications with Army Group I had to pass first through the French Embassy in London, or French naval headquarters at Dunkirk, before being transmitted to the commanders in the field.

At 8 p.m. Gort, accompanied by Pownall, finally reached Ypres and there, along with King Leopold and General van Overstraeten, received a briefing from Billotte concerning Weygand's plan, the execution of which was left to his discretion. The first requirement was to create the necessary reserve. Gort, however, explained that because his available reserves were already committed to the counterattack east of Arras then in progress he could not join with the French in a further offensive until some of his divisions on the Escaut had been relieved. To achieve this, it was ultimately agreed that on the following night the Belgians would withdraw to the Lys and the

British to their old fortified position on the French frontier between Maulde and Halluin, their sector temporarily prolonged northwards to Courtrai. The French and Belgians would then relieve three British divisions by the night of May 23–24. But none of the participants in the conference had much faith in their ability to carry out the Weygand plan. The Belgians considered their position practically hopeless; Gort conceived the counteroffensive as an effort that would emanate largely from the south, although this was the antithesis of Weygand's conception; and Billotte, as Sir Arthur Bryant reports, admitted that "though a counterattack had been ordered, his troops were in a state of such confusion that they were not only incapable of an offensive but could barely defend themselves."[3] It was probably as a direct result of this depressing conference that later that night Gort's Chief of Staff ordered work begun on a contingency plan for the evacuation of the BEF—the first concrete planning undertaken by headquarters with regard to this possibility, although a general scheme had already been outlined on May 19.[4]

Thus, Weygand's plans were at odds with the facts—either because he had been deprived of the necessary information and down-to-earth evaluations of his subordinates in the field or because he failed to take into account the pessimistic implications of what he had witnessed in the north. Still worse, Billotte, the general charged with executing the maneuver and the only French commander in the north to have firsthand knowledge of both Weygand's plan for a counteroffensive and the subsidiary arrangements made with the British and Belgians, was to be fatally injured that night in a motor accident on his way back to headquarters. After this, there was no one to coordinate the movements of the three armies. General Blanchard immediately replaced him as acting commander of the First Army Group, but his succession as coordinator in the north was not officially confirmed for some days.

Neither London nor Paris yet knew of the results of Franklyn's abortive southward push when on May 22 Churchill, General Ismay, and Air Vice-Marshal Sir Richard Peirse flew to Paris to meet with Weygand, Reynaud, and Sir John Dill and the British Ambassador at a special session of the Allied Supreme War Council. At French General Staff headquarters at Vincennes Weygand outlined his plan for reuniting the northern and southern armies. From the north, the French and British forces were to strike out to the southeast from around Cambrai and Arras with the purpose of falling on the enemy's flank in the St.-Quentin-Amiens pocket; from the south, General Frère's army was to push northwards from the Beauvais area in order to increase the pressure on the German armored elements in the vicinity of Amiens, Abbeville, and Arras. The Belgians were to shorten the Allied line by withdrawing in two stages behind the flooded Yser, stopping first on the Lys, thus enabling reserve forces to be built up further south. At least General Weygand now *believed* that the Belgians were ready to play the covering role he had assigned them and to conform to the program about which they had expressed such reservations the previous day—though his conclusions on this score probably resulted from misreading intelligence he had just received from the French Mission at Belgian headquarters regarding the final arrangements made at Ypres after his departure on May 21.[5]

Churchill and Dill, without informing Weygand that Gort thought it impossible, although the CIGS and the War Office knew his thoughts on the subject, gave the plan their enthusiastic approval. Churchill, in fact, stressed that "it was indispensable to reopen communications between the armies of the north and those of the south by way of Arras"; the BEF, he explained, had only four days' provisions left and all their supplies and war matériel were in ports from Calais to St.-Nazaire, which therefore made the opening of these lines of communication vital to Lord Gort.[6]

Agreement would have been complete had not Air Vice-Marshal Peirse turned down Weygand's demands for the closer cooperation of all British air units at the front during the impending offensive. But Peirse refused to abandon completely long-distance bombing in favor of working by day on precise objectives, which he said British bombers were too slow to deal with, while he also insisted on the bulk of the RAF fighter force remaining based on England, which meant that fighter squadrons could spend only twenty minutes per flight over the theater of operations. "This first exchange of views on the employment of the British air forces," Weygand writes, "gave a foretaste of the disappointments we were to suffer in that matter."[7] Yet despite this the atmosphere of the conference was cordial and confident.

The British Prime Minister then dictated a résumé of the decisions reached (which according to Churchill and Reynaud had Weygand's approval, but which according to the latter was dictated in London and contained references to dates and numbers of units involved that he had not specified at the Supreme War Council). These "conclusions" were then telegrammed to Lord Gort, after Churchill had conferred with the War Cabinet at home. The gist of the plan as transmitted was that, supported by the Belgian Cavalry Corps, the British and French in the north were to attack towards Bapaume and Cambrai *the next day* with about *eight* divisions. Integral to the plan was the assumption that the Belgians would or could conform to Allied movements by retreating farther to the west than they had previously told Weygand they were willing to and that the French divisions on the Somme would play an important role in the operation.[8] It was, at best, a hopelessly unreal summary, whether or not the Supreme Commander had given it his stamp of approval. In fact, when Pownall came across this "extraordinary telegram from Winston" on May 23, he was to characterize its author—Churchill—as a madman so unbelievable did its contents seem.[9]

Whatever the nature of the plans dreamt up in Paris, Lord Gort felt it was impossible to obey any orders to attack straight away. Such an offensive, he thought, could not conceivably be launched before 26 May at the earliest. He advised Blanchard of this on May 23, explaining that his 5th and 50th divisions were still engaged with the enemy around Arras, while his 2nd, 44th, and 48th divisions could not be relieved for another forty-eight hours. To implement their part of the Weygand plan he proposed that two British divisions together with the French Cavalry Corps and a third French division should stage an attack to the south on 26 May. But he emphasized to Blanchard that "the principal effort must come from the south, and that the operation of the northern forces could be nothing more than a sortie."[10] Gort suggests that Blanchard was in fundamental agreement with the delay suggested. For the present, Gort saw his most urgent task as guarding against enemy incursions from the rear. On the night of 22–23 May the BEF had retired from the Escaut to its winter defenses along the French border. But though its eastern line was thus shortened, the BEF had immediately to strengthen its southwestern flank along a 40-mile canal line running from La Bassée to the Channel to stave off destruction from that quarter.

The discrepancy between the high-sounding orders he was receiving from home and the reality of the Allies' deteriorating position also led Gort on May 23 to ask Sir John Dill to fly over because he "was not sure whether the situation which was developing for the Allied armies in the north could be accurately appreciated except on the spot."[11] Skeptical of the government's ability to judge the merits of Weygand's plan from afar, Gort was hoping to enlist the support of Britain's most respected military authority for his own point of view. In this he was backed up the next day by Sir Roger Keyes, the Prime Minister's personal representative with the King of the Belgians, who also begged Churchill to send Dill out at once in the hope that he would be able to stop the offensive before the BEF was committed to it; Keyes felt that was what Gort wanted.[12] In fact, already on May 22 Gort had told one of his liaison officers, Major Archdale, that "he believed the time was approaching when his responsibility for the safety of the B.E.F. was going to outweigh his obligations to the French High Command."[13] For his failure to align himself with the thinking of the French High Command, Weygand would not forgive him—or the British.

# A Chill Descends

As of May 23 and through the next forty-eight hours, the Allies entered a tortuous and critical period. Given the fact that direct communications between French General Headquarters and the First Army Group had been cut and that messages coming from either direction were inevitably delayed by the necessity of passing through England, and that, furthermore, the British were receiving contradictory information from their commander in the field and the British liaison officer with Weygand, confusion and strain were only to be expected. If communication on the psychological level broke down at this point, it was to some degree because communications on the technical level had already failed. It was impossible to know what was going on in the field at the moment it was happening, and by the time various reports could be pieced together to form an even moderately coherent picture, events had moved on so rapidly that any decision based on such information was already out of date. In these circumstances it is not surprising that relations between the French and British prime ministers began to assume a more disagreeable character. But in the spate of telegrams that now began to flow between London and Paris can also be detected a new defensive note, an earnest of each ally's desire to establish its position historically.

Churchill's was the opening gambit. Mindful that the BEF had been put on half rations that day, making time all the more vital, and also fearing that the French were dragging their feet, Churchill on the morning of 23 May telegrammed Reynaud to urge "immediate execution of Weygand's plan" and to demand "the issue to the French commanders in north and south and Belgian G.H.Q. of the most stringent orders to carry this out and turn defeat into victory."[1]

However, despite his apparent enthusiasm for the offensive, at 4:50 that afternoon Churchill telephoned Reynaud to ask whether a withdrawal to the ports should not be considered in view of the fact that the movement of enemy armored divisions northwards was threatening the BEF from the rear. Reynaud replied that Weygand was fully aware of the situation but was insistent that the offensive go on.[2]

In actual fact, Weygand was not fully informed as to events or capabilities on either side of the Allied front. Furthermore, his report over the phone to Churchill of the recapture of Péronne, Albert, and Amiens by the French 7th Army was to prove wildly inaccurate.[3] The British, if momentarily elated by this news, nevertheless remained skeptical and while still not abandoning all hope in the Weygand plan, in Ironside's words, gave Gort "complete discretion" to move the BEF as he liked "to try to save it." Specifically, the Secretary of State's telegram (sent off at 8 p.m. and received the next day) gave the Commander-in-Chief "latitude to withdraw to the Channel ports if the attacks on his communications compelled him to do so." He should endeavor to cooperate in the plan, but if this proved impossible he was to inform the War Office so that the French could be notified and suitable naval and air arrangements made.[4]

A still later telegram sent by Churchill to Reynaud (at 5 a.m., May 24) registered British impatience and loss of confidence in the French Command. In this Churchill communicated Lord Gort's complaints concerning the lack of coordination among the three armies in the north, thereby calling into question Blanchard's competence. He also repeated Gort's warning that any advance by him could only be in the nature of a sortie and that relief would have to come from the south inasmuch as he did not have sufficient ammunition for a serious attack. The Prime Minister concluded by stating that they were nevertheless instructing Gort to persevere in carrying out the Weygand plan, but requested a copy of the French directive for the plan and the details of the French Army's northern operations, a strong hint that the British believed their ally was doing little.[5]

On the 24th the French returned the fire. That Lord Gort had declared his intention of waiting for the principal effort to be made by troops of the French 7th Army from south of the Somme was in itself enough to upset all Weygand's calculations, but when the Commander-in-Chief learned through Blanchard of the British Army's "unauthorized" withdrawal on the night of May 23–24 to the Haute Deule Canal (that is, the retreat of Frankforce), his anger reached boiling point. After this, the hope of reuniting the severed armies could no longer be seriously entertained, the northern armies' base for an attack having disappeared. Reluctantly forced to abandon his plan, he would not do so before first placing the blame squarely on the British.

In a telegram to Churchill sent at noon, Reynaud conveyed Weygand's surprise and indignation at the withdrawal of British troops from Arras the night before. But inasmuch as the French were still unaware of the extent of the British retreat, Reynaud made a point of declaring France's determination to hold to the decisions reached jointly two days earlier by the Supreme War Council and concluded by stating the necessity of conforming to the orders of the High Command.[6] The bad feeling at this time was heightened by the High Command's not completely unfounded suspicion that Gort was receiving from London different orders from those issued by Weygand. In fact, that very day Weygand told Baudouin, Secretary of the War Committee, that after his telephone conversation with Ironside the evening before he could "have boxed his ears" and that it was "impossible to command an army which remains dependent on London in the matter of military operations."[7]

In a second telegram sent after receiving additional information from Weygand, Reynaud informed Churchill that the British Army had, "contrary to formal orders . . . decided on and carried out a withdrawal of forty kilometres towards the ports," at a time when French troops, moving up from the south, were gaining ground towards the north in their advance to meet the Allied armies in the north. "This withdrawal," he continued, "has naturally compelled General Weygand to modify his arrangements. He believes that he must, as a result, give up any idea of closing the gap and of re-establishing a continuous front."[8] At this point it was easy to picture the British as culprits, for neither side as yet knew the details of the British retreat northwards; however, Weygand *did* know that General Besson, in command of all troops of the Third Army Group on the Somme and the Aisne, had found it prudent to abandon his share in the maneuver—the attack from the south—using the British retreat from Arras as cover.[9]

That same evening Reynaud received Churchill's reply to his earlier telegram. Churchill made it clear that he still supported the Weygand plan and had as yet received no word of the evacuation of Arras. A second message sent during the night acknowledged that Gort had been "forced by the pressure on his western flank, and to keep communication with Dunkirk for indispensable supplies, to place parts of two divisions between himself and the increasing pressure of the German armoured forces," which had taken St.-Omer and were menacing Calais and Dunkirk. Churchill believed, however, that Gort was still persevering in his southward move. "Nothing in the movements of the B.E.F. of which we are aware," he continued, "can be any excuse for the abandonment of the strong pressure of your northward move across the Somme, which we trust will develop." A bit waspishly, the Prime Minister pointed out that "having waited for the southward move for a week after it became obvious[ly necessary]," they now found themselves "ripped from the coast by the mass of the enemy's armoured vehicles" and that therefore there was "no choice but to continue the southward move."[10]

The last round in this telegraphic cycle came to a close when, at 1 p.m. on May 25, Reynaud wired Churchill that as a result of the British retreat from Arras General Weygand had at 4 p.m. [actually 4:35] on 24 May given leeway to General Blanchard to abandon the offensive to the south and had alternatively ordered him to form as extensive a bridgehead as possible covering Dunkirk, which was essential for supplying the First Army Group. But Reynaud further informed Churchill that, in view of the latest telegram from Blanchard available to the French High Command, Weygand had approved Blanchard's stated intention of attacking towards Bapaume as scheduled. What he did not tell the British was that a senior officer of Blanchard's staff received by him and Weygand at noon that day (the 25th) had reported that there was no longer any hope of Blanchard's being able to attack, that, in fact, the 1st Army had only three divisions left in a fit state to fight and that these had only a day's ammunition and provisions left. Major Fauvelle had also reported that the British Army seemed to be preparing to reembark and that the Belgian Army was slipping away. Yet it was in the light of *this* news that Weygand telegraphed Blanchard at 3:30 p.m. on May 25 that he was now "the sole judge of the decisions to be taken, and that the honour of the Army was in his hands."[11]

The period May 23–25 marked a turning point in Anglo-French relations. Until then there had been differences over tactics, timings, and personnel, but outwardly there was still general agreement on the objective sought. Lord Gort appeared to be the only exception to this consensus and it was on him that Weygand focused his wrath. Weygand, mistakenly, as he was to admit after the war, condemned Gort for the withdrawal from Arras; but probably Gort's principal sin in the eyes of Weygand was that he saw more clearly and at an earlier date what eventually would have to be done. It was not until his political superiors fell in with his plans, however, that a conflict in strategy between the two governments arose.

Faced by a disaster that might easily have led to the loss of their entire army, the British felt they had a right to press on with their plans for evacuation regardless of what the French Command wanted. But, faced by a disaster that threatened to engulf the whole of France, the French were equally determined to hold out for as long as possible in the north in order to give themselves more time to prepare for the second German offensive soon to be launched against the Somme. After the projected Allied attack to the south came to nothing, it would seem, in Marc Bloch's words, that "the two General Staffs, under the influence of mutual disenchantment, gave up almost entirely any further pretence of collaboration." The British had already lost their faith in the French military's strategic capacity; the slowness and ineffectiveness of French movements completed their disillusionment. The French, on the other hand, were embittered as they watched their partner growing more high-handed and selfish with each new threat to their mutual safety. Under the circumstances, it was inevitable that "the thermometer of the alliance" would shortly "register a heavy fall."[12]

Events at Boulogne and Calais were to contribute further to this rapid lowering of temperature. At Boulogne, the British garrison, which had been reinforced with two Guards battalions from England only the day before, was ordered to reembark on the night of 23 May, and did so (4,368 were evacuated) apparently without informing the local French commander of its intentions. With most of the town in enemy hands by the next day, the isolated defenders of the citadel nevertheless held out until morning of May 25, when they were allowed to surrender with the honors of war.

At Calais, which the British reinforced on May 22 and 23 with Queen Victoria's Rifles, a tank regiment, and two regular battalions, the story was also strained. Here the British again prepared to evacuate, only to be deflected by new orders from General Ironside on 24 May explaining that General Fagalde, the French officer who had just been placed in command of all Allied troops in the Channel ports area, forbade evacuation from Calais. They were now ordered to carry out its defense "in an active not a passive manner." But, lest the defenders think they were being sacrificed merely "for the sake of Allied solidarity" (an impression given by the War Office), Churchill had to make sure they understood that the "hold to the last" stand being asked of them was principally to keep the enemy away from the BEF at Dunkirk. This the 3,800-man garrison under Brigadier Nicholson did quite heroically, holding on until completely overwhelmed late on May 26. In the process, however, there had been inter-Allied clashes: large numbers of French and Belgian troops had tried to force their way onto British naval vessels sent to evacuate noncombatants; while, according to General Guderian, of the 20,000 prisoners taken by the Germans in Calais "the majority had not wanted to go on fighting" and had therefore been locked up in cellars by the English—an exaggeration, but only in that most were simply hiding out in cellars by their own choice.[13]

# Giving Up the Ghost

As of May 24, the Franco-British-Belgian forces were packed into a triangular area bounded to the north by the mouth of the Escaut, to the southeast by Valenciennes, and to the west by the Channel port of Gravelines. The canal line on their southern flank was being reinforced, but already the Germans had established bridgeheads only 15 miles west of Dunkirk. It was on this day that von Rundstedt, backed by Hitler, ordered the tanks of the Hoth and Kleist groups to stop their advance and to leave to von Bock's Army Group and the Luftwaffe the task of finishing off the encircled Allies. In this way the Allies gained a reprieve of three days. In the east the Belgians had retreated to the Lys, but refused to fall back on the Yser. The British manned the frontier line from Halluin to Bourghelles, while farther south still the French were strung out in a narrow pocket running through Maulde, Condé, Valenciennes, and Douai. Notwithstanding the retreat of Frankforce, the French and British were still making efforts to bring off the projected counterattack southwards. But it was on their eastern front that the Germans next concentrated their pressure by attacking the hinge between the Belgian Army and the BEF.[1]

When late on 24 May the enemy broke through the Belgian line, creating a gap between the Belgian right wing and the British left, Gort was presented with an immediate risk of the two armies becoming separated and of the Belgians falling back in a northerly, rather than a westerly, direction. Since any German penetration towards Ypres would have turned both flanks of the BEF and threatened its line of communications to the coast, he therefore considered it "vitally urgent to prolong the British front without delay northwards to

Ypres, along the old Ypres-Comines Canal . . . and around Ypres itself to the line of the Yser canal." In support, Sir John Dill, who was about to replace General Ironside as Chief of the Imperial General Staff, and who had arrived at Gort's headquarters on the morning of May 25, now telegraphed the Prime Minister and the Secretary for War that "there could be no disguising the seriousness of the situation" and that "in his opinion the proposed counter-attack to the south could not be an important affair in view of the enemy attacks which had penetrated the Belgian defenses" on the Lys.[2]

That evening Gort made his "fateful" decision. Having learned during the afternoon that the French would be able to spare only one division for the attack planned for 26 May, he was convinced that there was no longer any hope of a breakthrough to the south. Moreover, he believed that the crumbling of the Belgian defenses had created a peril of overriding importance, a belief corroborated by the capture that day of German 6th Army orders for a large-scale attack on the Ypres-Comines front to be launched on the 26th. Thus, on his own responsibility, Lord Gort, in Churchill's phrase, "resolved to abandon the attack to the southward, to plug the gap which a Belgian capitulation was about to open in the north, and to march to the sea."[3]

Just when Gort made this decision cannot be precisely determined. General Franklyn claims that when he saw Gort at 4 p.m. the Commander-in-Chief had already "made the bold decision to contract out of the counter-attack and to use 5th and 50th Divisions to deal with the extremely menacing approach of a German Corps through Belgium"; while General Pownall speaks of the decisions canceling the move down south of the two divisions as having been made at 5 p.m., also at 6 p.m.[4] But events of the day before are also relevant here. According to Gort's biographer, the C-in-C on 24 May had given "instructions that his staff should again examine the arrangements for a withdrawal to the coast which he had first considered a wise precaution five days previously."[5] This is borne out by Pownall's diary entry for May 24, where the Chief of Staff adds that to go southwest was now impossible. However, independent action was apparently not being contemplated, for Pownall writes: "But of course we can't withdraw on our own, for when we do go it means the Belgians pack up and probably also the French." Yet in the same entry Pownall also speaks half-optimistically of the preparations being made that day for the attack on the 26th, "which it is hoped will go down between the Lys canal and the Canal du Nord—past Cambrai—to the line of railway at Havrincourt and join up, please God, with the French from the south. If that can be done, and an encouraging telegram has come from Weygand, the gap will be closed." Thus, no final decision appears to have been made before May 25.[6]

Brooke's biographer says simply that having felt since May 19 that the only hope of saving his troops lay in retreating to the one port still left them, the British Commander-in-Chief "decided to stake everything, including his own honour, on keeping open the road to Dunkirk and withdrawing along it while there was still time."[7] With this end in mind, Gort therefore sent the two British divisions (first the 5th and the next day the 50th) scheduled to take part in the Weygand plan to the north to restore the line between General Brooke's II Corps and the Belgians on his left.

Gort immediately communicated his decision to French Army Group headquarters, where it was initially received badly, probably because General Weygand's latest telegrams had not yet arrived, and early the next morning (May 26) conferred with General Blanchard at Attiches. By then Blanchard too felt that the time for a counterattack to the south was past and had already decided during the night on a retreat to the northwest as well as on sending one of his light mechanized divisions to reinforce the Belgians. Together they arrived at a plan for withdrawing the main body of the BEF and the French 1st Army behind the line of the Lys west of Lille, with a view to forming a defensive bridgehead around Dunkirk. Gort did not discuss with Blanchard a further withdrawal to the sea—and, by implication, the question of an eventual British embarkation—though he felt that "the possibility could not have been absent from his mind."[8]

Although up to now Gort had been given no instructions specifically authorizing him to undertake such an operation, at 10:30 a.m. he received a telegram from the War Office indicating that London had at last come around to his conclusions.

The government's final decision was taken only a few hours after Gort's. At a Defence Committee meeting held at 5:30 p.m. on May 25, Churchill was still inquiring "whether it would not be possible for the combined Armies in the Northern area to march Southward together, breaking away through the enemy's Armoured Divisions by force of numbers, and covering their march by flank guards and rear guards." However, General Dewing of the War Office doubted this, replying laconically that "It was very hard for an Army to move when subject to attack on three sides simultaneously." When the committee met again at 10 p.m., all the information received pointed in but one direction. Major-General Sir Henry Karslake, who had visited French GHQ that morning, reported that Brigadier Swayne, chief liaison officer with General Georges, was pessimistic concerning the chances of any effective attack being launched from south of the Somme in the next few days. A letter from General Spears stated that there was no chance of disengaging the Blanchard Group and that "General Weygand's opinion was that attacks to the South by the group of armies in the North, including the British Army, could serve no other purpose than to gain breathing-space before falling back to a line covering the harbours." Finally, General Dill, who had just returned from the BEF that day, gave it as his opinion that if the projected drive to the south were tried and failed, then Lord Gort would be in a much worse position than he was at present and would not have sufficient strength left to try the only other course open to him, namely to cut his way north to the coast. "If this alternative were also to fail, he would be surrounded and would have to capitulate." This proved conclusive, and the committee thereupon expressed itself in favor of an immediate march to the coast and the reinforcement of Dunkirk. Instructions were sent by the War Office to this effect later that night and approved by the War Cabinet the next morning.[9]

Thus, the Secretary of State now reported to Gort that he was able to hold out no hope that the French offensive from the Somme could be made in sufficient strength to effect a junction with the northern armies. "Should this prove to be the case," Eden wrote, "you will be faced with a situation in which the safety of the B.E.F. will predominate. In such conditions [the] only course open to you may be to fight your way back to [the] West where all beaches and ports east of Gravelines will be used for embarkation." Gort was assured that the Navy would provide a fleet of ships and small boats and that the RAF would give full support. In the meantime, however, he was expressly ordered not to mention the possibility of such a move either to the French or the Belgians—at least until the Prime Minister had first had a chance to clarify the situation with Reynaud.[10] A still later telegram from the War Office approved Gort's conduct and authorized him "to operate towards [the] coast forthwith in conjunction with [the] French and Belgian Armies." He was also told that General Weygand would no doubt issue orders in the same sense.[11]

In the interim, Churchill (or so he claims) had informed Reynaud, in London that afternoon on a flying visit, that British policy was to evacuate the BEF and had requested him to issue corresponding orders.[12] Whether he was as explicit as he might have been regarding their evacuation intentions remains in some doubt, however. Reynaud does not mention the subject in his memoirs. Nor do the War Cabinet minutes for the afternoon of May 26 make any mention of the Prime Minister's specifically disclosing British evacuation plans to the French. When the cabinet met at 2 p.m., Churchill, who had already seen but not yet settled the matter with Reynaud, was primarily interested in getting Weygand to "issue orders for the B.E.F. [*sic;* French 1st Army is apparently meant] to march to the coast. It was important to make sure that the French had no complaint against us on the score that, by cutting our way to the coast, we were letting them down militarily." The Secretary of State for War was asked to prepare a telegram for dispatch which could then be brought over to Reynaud in mid-afternoon. Yet the message sent Weygand merely asked the Supreme Commander to give Blanchard formal authority to order a withdrawal to the ports.[13] Thus, it is quite possible that the touchy subject of a wholesale evacuation was soft-pedaled,[14] and the French left to infer it from the marching orders given Gort—in spite of the fact that a policy of embarkation had already been decided on that morning,[15] that it was referred to in the afternoon, and that it would be put into effect that evening at 7 o'clock. In any case, notwithstanding its importance, the topic did not have priority in the Anglo-French discussions on 26 May, particularly for Paul Reynaud.

By giving Blanchard permission to withdraw in the direction of the coast, it would seem that Weygand had tacitly accepted the inevitability of evacuation; yet for some days the Supreme Commander remained unreconciled to this course. Although recognizing that "the creation of a vast bridgehead covering the French ports corresponded better to the existing resources and circumstances than a southward offensive,"[16] this did not mean that he was willing to countenance Gort's moves towards reembarkation. But, by persisting in holding out hope for schemes that had not the slimmest chance of success (e.g., the preservation of the country around Dunkirk and its prolonged defense as a beleaguered fortress supplied by sea) and by insisting on the primacy of the French Command in the north long after it had ceased to exercise the initiative or control required by the situation, Weygand succeeded only in further exacerbating the strained relations between British and French.

The contradiction between British and French policies was exemplified on May 27: Gort was told by the Secretary of State that his sole task now was to evacuate to England the maximum British force

possible,[17] whereas General Prioux, who had assumed command of
the French 1st Army on May 25, was still acting on out-of-date
orders from Weygand that the battle would be fought on the position
of the Lys without thought of retreat.

Early that morning Lieutenant-General Sir Ronald Adam (representing Lord Gort and charged by the C-in-C with arranging for the
embarkation of British troops) had met in Cassel with General Blanchard, General Prioux, General Fagalde, Admiral Abrial (the French
commander in overall charge of Dunkirk since May 21), and General
Koeltz (representing General Weygand) to draw up plans for the
defense of the Dunkirk perimeter and to discuss how the bridgehead
was to be organized for the reception of retiring troops. Yet even
here the British policy of evacuation was not discussed, although
embarkation of troops had already begun, nor was the possibility of
a French evacuation brought up. Instead considerable time and energy were spent on a vain scheme to disengage Calais, in conformity
with the aggressive spirit of Weygand's order of 26 May, which
Koeltz had come specifically to disseminate. Certainly the British
were reprehensible in not informing the French earlier of their plans
to embark: General Koeltz was to learn only late that night (May
27)—and then rather by accident—from Lord Gort of a plan to
reembark 30,000 men per day, and had the distinct and correct
impression that the British were executing this plan without having
discussed it with either General Weygand (who certainly did not
know of it at the time of Koeltz's departure) or General Blanchard.[18]
But General Weygand's failure to inform either Abrial or Blanchard
of the British Government's intentions, once known, or of the fact
that the French High Command was even considering evacuation
was not only to cause additional bad feeling between the British and
the French but was to have fatal consequences, for the French commanders in the north were thereby unable to make the necessary
decisions to save their troops in time.

That it *was* considering this possibility is shown by the fact that
Darlan, who had witnessed Major Fauvelle's exposition on the 25th,
had met with Weygand later that day to discuss the French Admiralty's forthcoming role and to announce his intention of sending his
Chief of Operations, Captain Auphan, to England to gather information and to work out a common plan. Moreover, after learning of
Blanchard's withdrawal order on the 26th, Weygand had telephoned
Darlan that it was now necessary to examine with the British Admiralty the possibility of evacuating the Flanders forces through Dun-

kirk. Captain Auphan had left for Dover on the morning of May 27.[19] Weygand would later claim to have abandoned both his plans—the defense of a solid bridgehead around Dunkirk as well as the big offensive to the south—by the night of May 27, and from the 28th to have concerned himself primarily with reembarkation.[20] But, even allowing for the incompleteness of information available to him at any one time, such a claim does not seem to be borne out by the character or timing of the orders he issued thereafter. Rather, Weygand appears to have acted with a dangerous and almost inexplicable slowness throughout this crucial period.

The collapse of the Belgian front, followed by King Leopold's acceptance of unconditional surrender terms at midnight on May 27,* ushered in the final trials of the northern armies. The Belgian capitulation made it imperative for Gort to come to an understanding with Blanchard. But when the two met at Houtkerque (British GHQ) at 11 a.m. on 28 May, Blanchard was horrified to hear of British orders to reembark. His orders, reconfirmed only that morning, encompassed no more than a retreat to the Lys and the formation of a wide bridgehead around Dunkirk for the purpose of saving everything that could be saved. Gort wanted Blanchard to retire his troops on the Lys another 15 miles closer to the coast that night. As it was, their corridor to the sea was less than 15 miles wide at its narrowest point. Even more pressing was the withdrawal of some five divisions of the French 1st Army still fighting in and around Lille, which were in imminent danger of being totally cut off by the narrowing pincer movement of the enemy between Armentières and Halluin.

In a scene charged with emotion, Gort entreated Blanchard to retire his troops immediately. Now that the Germans were striking in force from the southwest, center, and northeast, the only alternatives were evacuation or surrender. It was essential to prevent the Germans from getting behind them on the southwest that very night. To make matters worse, a liaison officer from the French 1st Army arrived at this point to report that General Prioux considered his troops incapable of retreating farther that night and therefore intended to remain in the sector between Lille and Béthune. Yet Gort was convinced that any units still south of the Ypres-Cassel line by the next morning would be irretrievably lost. In a final effort to win him over, Gort "begged General Blanchard for the sake of France, the French Army and the Allied Cause to order General Prioux

---

*See Appendix A, Leopold's Surrender.

back."[21] But Blanchard remained unshakable in his determination to uphold Weygand's orders and in his belief that evacuation was impossible and hardly worth the effort involved. He wanted the British to delay their retreat another twenty-four hours so as not to expose the French further to the enemy's assaults. Nevertheless, in spite of the inevitably unflattering light cast on the BEF's movement by the French decision to stand fast, Gort affirmed his intention of carrying out his government's orders by withdrawing all his forces to the Ypres-Poperinghe-Cassel line that night. It was only at 10 p.m. on 28 May that Blanchard finally brought himself to ask Weygand to authorize and prepare for the embarkation of as many French troops as possible—General de la Laurencie in the meantime having secured Prioux's permission to withdraw III Corps, together with the remains of the Cavalry Corps, into the Dunkirk perimeter and to share in the evacuation.[22]

As a further complication, Gort received a personal appeal from Weygand on this date (May 28) "to ensure that the British Army took a vigorous part in any counter-attacks necessary." Presumably, Weygand had in mind Calais, which had fallen on the 26th but which on the 27th (when he wrote to the BEF commander) still formed a key element in his plan for the reoccupation of the coast between Dunkirk and Cap Gris Nez. Gort now dismissed this order out of hand, claiming in his *Despatches* that "When he sent this message, he [Weygand] could have had no accurate information of the real position or of the powers of counter-attack remaining to either the French or the British." General Koeltz, whom Weygand had sent on May 27 to coordinate the situation in the north, "had not, as yet, had time to return to G.Q.G. with a first-hand report on the situation, and in any case the time for such action in the northern theatre was long past."[23]

Weygand, on learning the next morning (May 29) from Blanchard that Gort was independently regulating the withdrawal of his troops towards Dunkirk, with the result that the flank of the French 1st Army was uncovered, was quick to have Reynaud lodge a protest with the War Office against the "too selfish attitude of General Gort."[24] Fresh orders were, in fact, issued to the 1st Army, but they did not come soon enough to save the 50,000 French soldiers of IV and V Corps who were completely trapped near Lille by the afternoon of May 28 and forced to surrender on the night of May 31.[25]

# *Dunkirk*

IN SPITE of Weygand's refusal to come to grips with it and in spite of the French Navy's reservations about participating in it, the evacuation was by this time in full swing. Originally, the odds against the success of any evacuation seemed almost insuperable; with luck, it was thought, perhaps some 45,000 could be rescued. The British Government had given its consent to the operation only because the alternatives appeared even riskier. The French, however, initially regarded a large-scale embarkation as so unfeasible as to be virtually out of the question. They were also well aware that, even if an evacuation could be achieved, it would merely free the German armies in Belgium and northern France for an offensive towards Paris. A short reprieve gained at the expense of the armies in the north seemed the best they could hope for. For these reasons the French would not fall in with British plans until the eleventh hour, and even then their attitude remained ambiguous. Weygand was prejudiced against the operation to begin with because it resulted from British initiative, not his own, and beyond that because the British had been preparing for the contingency of evacuation since May 19—when Lord Gort had first counseled reembarking—without bothering to consult the French. The improvisation forced upon the French therefore remained to handicap their efforts.[1]

Having taken the preliminary steps during the preceding week to meet just such an emergency, the British Admiralty was fully prepared to commence "Operation Dynamo" at 6:57 p.m. on May 26. By this date, in fact, the Navy had already evacuated 27,936—administrative units and other noncombatant personnel—under the policy of partial evacuation adopted on May 21. By the night of the

109

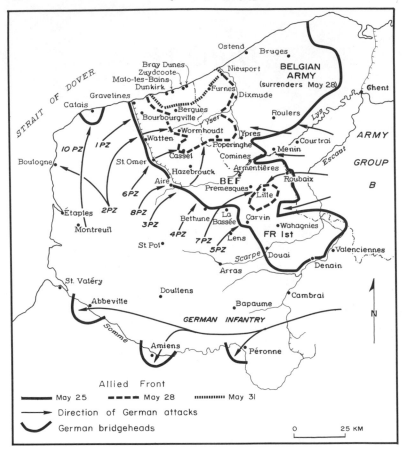

2. *Encirclement of the Allied armies in the north, end of May 1940.*

28th a substantial part of the French 1st Army was en route to Dunkirk, while by the next evening most of the BEF had arrived within the limits of the perimeter, which now ran along the line Mardyck-Bergues-Furnes-Nieuport. As of May 30, French troops, accompanied by a mass of motorized and horse transport that added to the congestion on the already clogged roads, were also beginning to appear in numbers. Some of La Laurencie's units would cover 160 kilometers in less than seventy-two hours.

Amidst the chaos of Dunkirk Lord Gort once again clashed with the French authorities. "Admiral Abrial," according to Gort's account of 29 May, "had apparently received no orders from his Gov-

ernment that the whole of the British troops were to be embarked,"
and therefore "professed great surprise" when he heard Gort's intentions. "He had, it seems, imagined that only rearward elements were
to be withdrawn, and that British troops would stay and defend the
perimeter to the last, side by side with the French." On the afternoon
of May 29 Weygand did authorize the "progressive" evacuation of
the 1st Army, but Abrial seemed to think that the Dunkirk perimeter
could hold out indefinitely. Gort, on the other hand, was convinced
that he had only about forty-eight hours left in which to evacuate the
BEF and was in no mood to brook delay. Meanwhile, the French
troops pouring in "were expecting to embark along with their British
comrades, notwithstanding that no French ships had so far been
provided." Gort urged the War Office to exert pressure on the
French to establish once and for all a clear policy on embarkation
and also to take their full share in providing naval facilities. Nevertheless, for the night of the 29th, Gort allotted two British ships to
the French and also put the beach at Malo-les-Bains at their disposal.[2] In fact, though Gort may not have realized it, French ships
were beginning to arrive on May 29 and would be working to capacity by the following day.

A mixture of faulty liaison and obscurantism on the part of both
governments was to blame here. At a naval conference held at Dover
on May 27, attended by Vice-Admirals Ramsay and Somerville on
the British side and by Captain Auphan, Admiral Odend'hal, Chief
of the French Naval Mission in London, and Rear Admiral Leclerc,
Admiral Abrial's Chief of Staff, on the French, it had been decided
that both nations should pool their shipping resources during the
evacuation. Auphan had worked out a plan with the British whereby
the French could join the evacuation operation without delay, and
this plan had been approved by the French Admiralty the next day
on his return to France. Yet neither Gort nor Blanchard was informed of the results of this meeting. Furthermore, it was only by
way of Auphan's report that the French High Command, so Weygand and Darlan were to claim, first learned *officially* of the British
decision to evacuate and of their advance preparations.[3] May 29
would make clear to the French just how massive and rapid the
British operation was.

Churchill was as much exercised by the potentially explosive diplomatic situation on hand at Dunkirk as by his anxiety for the ultimate
success of the operation. Gort, although he provided for the evacuation of about 5,000 Frenchmen on the 29th, had not disguised his

own negative feelings concerning this policy in the telegram he sent off to the CIGS at 2:48 p.m. "Small parties of French have already been embarked," he wrote, "but every Frenchman embarked is at [the] cost of one Englishman . . . . Remains of 1st French Army on arrival will deserve embarkation but by no means all those now in this area."[4]

Nevertheless, in orders to Eden and Dill that day (May 29), the Prime Minister emphasized that it was essential that the French should share in the evacuation and insisted that they must not be dependent only upon their own resources. And in a message to Major-General Sir Edward Spears, now in Paris attached to Reynaud, Churchill declared Britain's desire for French troops to share in the evacuation to the fullest possible extent, and stated that the Admiralty had been instructed to aid the French Navy as required. "We do not know how many will be forced to capitulate," he wrote, "but we must share this loss together as best we can, and above all, bear it without reproaches arising from inevitable confusion, stresses, and strains." Whether the spirit of Churchill's directives was accurately translated can perhaps best be judged by the orders sent Gort that evening by the new CIGS: Gort was informed that the Vice-Admiral, Dover, and the French Admiralty were now agreed that the means of evacuation should be shared. "In these circumstances and in view of [the] necessity for maintaining French solidarity," he was ordered, "you should make what arrangements you can in cooperation with British Naval and French authorities to evacuate a proportion of French troops." Nothing yet was said about equal proportions. Furthermore, Gort was told that his instructions that the safety of the BEF was his primary consideration still stood. By May 30, with all British troops within the perimeter, 120,000 men had already been evacuated. Of this total only 6,000 were French, which caused Churchill again to emphasize the urgent need to get off more French troops in order to avoid irreparable damage to relations between England and France.[5]

Whatever Churchill's wishes and concerns may have been, they do not seem to have been executed either promptly or enthusiastically. For instance, from a War Office appreciation of Operation Dynamo written eleven months after the event, it would appear that a policy enabling equal numbers of Frenchmen to be embarked was at work from the night of May 30–31—a day and a half after the Prime Minister's initial instructions had been issued; while Vice-Admiral Ramsay claims to have received formal orders to the effect that soldiers of both countries were to be given an equal opportunity of being evacuated on British ships and boats only on the morning of May 31. This order was received by the Senior Naval Officer, Dunkirk, at 10:44. General Pownall, for his part, finding that there was still some confusion at BEF headquarters on the 31st as to what the government's policy was, made sure that the fifty-fifty policy adopted vis-à-vis the French would *not* be understood as applying "retrospectively" [*sic*].[6] At any rate, by noon of 31 May, out of a cumulative total of 165,000 embarked, the French still accounted for only 15,000.

This disparity in numbers was the first question raised by Reynaud at the meeting of the Supreme War Council held in Paris during the afternoon of May 31, and attended by Churchill, Attlee (Deputy Prime Minister), Ismay, Dill, Spears, and the British Ambassador on the British side, and by the French Premier, Pétain, Weygand, Admiral Darlan, Paul Baudouin (of the war cabinet secretariat), and Captain Roland de Margerie (head of Reynaud's private office) on the French. Churchill tried to explain that many of the British evacuated were administrative units on hand before any fighting groups reached the perimeter; in addition, the disposition of the two armies in Flanders gave the British an inevitable, if fortuitous, advantage because they were closer to Dunkirk. Reynaud nevertheless stressed the fact that out of 220,000 British soldiers encircled in Dunkirk, 150,000 had already been evacuated, whereas of 200,000 Frenchmen only 15,000 had found ships thus far. Such a marked British preponderance in embarkation proceedings, he felt, "might entail grave consequences in the political field."[7]

Churchill took this opportunity to point out that up to the present the French had had no orders to evacuate and that one of his principal reasons for coming to Paris was to ensure that the same orders were given the French troops as the British. The CIGS had already spelled out British evacuation policy to Weygand in a telegram sent the previous evening which made it clear that they had no intention of holding on indefinitely at Dunkirk—the essence of Weygand's original scheme—and which asked the Generalissimo to coordinate his orders to the senior French commander at Dunkirk with those already given Lord Gort.[8]

Weygand now finally agreed that Admiral Abrial should be issued orders to this effect, but to his request that everything should be done to evacuate the eight French divisions farthest from the coast,[9] Churchill, backed by General Dill, replied that it would not be possible to

keep Dunkirk open longer than another forty-eight hours. The losses
in shipping and aircraft were too great to be endured much longer. It
was finally agreed that the bridgehead around Dunkirk should be
held jointly by the French and British for as long as possible so as to
evacuate the maximum number of men. French units entrusted with
Dunkirk's defense were authorized to embark once it had been established that no more troops outside the perimeter could reach the
points of embarkation. Churchill had gallantly insisted that it should
be the three British divisions which would form the rearguard of the
perimeter defense. The British Admiralty was to be responsible for
blocking the harbor once the evacuation was complete. The British,
however, agreed only reluctantly that Abrial should be in charge of
evacuation proceedings. And they evinced even less enthusiasm when
Reynaud asked for the full support of the RAF to be transferred to
the new front when Dunkirk was finished[10] and for the return of all
evacuated troops to France as soon as possible. Churchill ended the
meeting with a general survey of the Allied position in which he
proclaimed his faith in ultimate victory and the necessity for holding
out no matter how great the odds.

Even as formal agreement was being reached in Paris, however, a
new storm between the Allies was breaking in the north. Gort himself
relinquished control of the BEF that afternoon and prepared to sail for
England. The remaining 40,000 British troops were entrusted to Major-General Harold Alexander, who was, according to Gort, instructed "to operate under the orders of Admiral Abrial, and to assist
the French in the defense of Dunkirk." However, he was also told that
if any of the French Admiral's orders seemed likely to him to imperil
the safety of the BEF, he should immediately appeal to the Secretary of
State for War; again, that while he was to collaborate with Abrial in
arranging for the evacuation of the force under his command, he
should do this "also in accordance with the policy which may be laid
down from time to time by H. M. Government."[11]

Alexander, at any rate, was determined to finish his job as quickly
as possible, being convinced that the Germans would break through
the defensive perimeter at any moment. His decision to withdraw the
last British corps in line that very night (May 31–June1) inaugurated
a new and ugly debate with the French. General Fagalde had already
incorporated the three British divisions of I Corps into his plan of
defense; without them the French would be left to fight a rearguard
action against ever-increasing odds. In a bitter exchange with Alexander and Captain Tennant, the Senior Naval Officer at Dunkirk, on

the afternoon of 31 May, both Abrial and Fagalde demanded that the perimeter be held until all troops, French and British, were embarked and insisted that both share in the defense. This is what Lord Gort, in his last letter to Admiral Abrial, had led the French commanders to believe would be the British plan of action. But Alexander refused to comply with this order, claiming that his mission was not that of holding a bridgehead but of embarking the entirety of the BEF.[12]

This was the sense not only of Gort's most recent oral instructions to him but of orders just received from the War Office which emphasized that the safety of the BEF was to be his prime responsibility. Alexander immediately referred the problem to the Secretary of State, who as yet had no idea of the conditions subscribed to by Churchill at the Supreme War Council only two hours earlier. After being warned by Alexander (via the last telephone communication between La Panne and England) that the BEF was in extreme danger of being wiped out unless evacuated immediately, Eden agreed to the withdrawal of the remaining British forces as rapidly as possible, on condition that evacuation facilities were shared with the French on a fifty-fifty basis. He instructed Alexander to aim for completion by the night of June 1–2. Alexander then reported to Abrial that he was willing to hold his sector of the perimeter another twenty-four hours and to delay the departure of his corps until the following night. He would agree to nothing more. This was the plan adhered to, a slight modification arranged early the next morning allowing only for detachments of the 4,000-strong British rearguard to lend support to the French on the intermediate line through June 2.[13]

When Abrial informed the French High Command on June 1 of the approaching departure of the last British elements, Weygand telegraphed Sir John Dill, demanding in the name of Allied solidarity that "General Alexander should be kept at the side of the French troops to enable their embarkation to be terminated, in accordance with the assurance given by the British Prime Minister" the day before.[14] Churchill himself wired Weygand on June 1 to urge the completion of evacuation that night and to inform him that he had ordered Alexander to judge, in consultation with Abrial, whether it was possible to stay on until the next day.[15] A second message, to Reynaud, warned against prolonging embarkation procedures and maintained that Abrial was not in a position to judge the situation because he was controlling operations from a casemate. These messages prompted Reynaud to note icily to Spears that "the decision to have a united command only lasted twenty-four hours" and provoked Weygand's attack on Churchill the next day as "a producer of fine speeches" but "a maker of promises which he did not keep."[16] And in the British decision to pull out on June 1–2 there did seem to be, as Baudouin noted, "a painful discrepancy with the declaration of Mr. Winston Churchill at the Supreme War Council on Friday when he claimed for the English the honour of composing the rearguard."[17]

Most of the remaining British troops embarked on the night of June 1–2, but the last of the rearguard pulled out at midnight on the 2nd, with General Alexander following in the early hours of June 3. Weygand successfully intervened in London on the 2nd to secure the prolongation of British naval and air support so that the French rearguard, which, by holding on, had "enabled the last British contingents to sail," would not be sacrificed.[18] Over 50,000 French soldiers were rescued on the nights of June 2 and 3; the senior French officers departed at 2 a.m. on June 4, the last ship pulling away from the shores of Dunkirk at 3:40. After the blockage of the harbor, the operation was officially declared ended the next day at 2:23 p.m. During the last two days the Royal Navy had continued its efforts almost exclusively for the benefit of the French, but then during the last forty-eight hours the French were virtually alone in manning the defenses of an extended perimeter. Along with the port of Dunkirk, 30,000–40,000 Frenchmen were to fall into the hands of the Germans on the morning of June 4.

Why this should have happened later became the subject of some pointed speculation. If the reason is not as simple as that cited by General Alexander, who claims that the nonevacuated "as good Frenchmen . . . didn't want to leave France, but preferred to remain in their own country—even as prisoners of war," the evidence does suggest that French failures, rather than any unwillingness on the part of the British Navy, were principally to blame. Certainly there were breakdowns in liaison, which could account for the failure of waiting French soldiers and waiting British ships to have made contact at Dunkirk mole the night of June 2–3 and which led to Rear Admiral Wake-Walker's frustrated signal at 1:15 a.m.: "Plenty of ships, cannot get troops." Places for 10,000 were lost in this fashion. But, above and beyond these perhaps inevitable mix-ups, the French, as David Divine points out, failed "to produce a logical plan for the movement of units, to make certain that orders reached the units, that the organisation existed to guide them to the proper points, and that the necessary discipline was enforced."[19]

Then, too, French estimates as to the number of troops within the bridgehead varied from day to day. For instance, although the number of French remaining as of the evening of June 1 was given as 25,000, by the next day this figure had spiraled, the French Admiralty reporting 47,000 troops still within the perimeter, while Admiral Abrial was requesting facilities for the evacuation of some 65,000 over the next two nights. By nightfall of June 3, the French estimated that 30,000 remained. Sufficient ships were sent to lift this number provided the men could reach the embarkation points while it was still dark, but here British naval personnel ran into terrible problems with the landlubbing French, who, in spite of the desperate circumstances, often had to be begged and bullied aboard the rescuing small craft allotted them. Even so, 27,000, or almost all those believed to be in Dunkirk, were taken from the piers and inner harbor during the course of this final effort.[20] And yet it was not a mere 3,000 but nearly 40,000 who were rounded up by the Germans the next day.

According to Auphan and Mordal, this happened because French plans to embark General Barthélémy's rearguard were defeated at the last minute by the sudden appearance of thousands of disarmed men—noncombatants and riffraff chiefly—who converged on the jetty and thus prevented the escape of the disciplined soldiers who had fought till the end. Thus it would seem that a breakdown in French Army organization, discipline, and morale (borne out, moreover, by Robert Merle's depressing novelistic description of French soldiers at Dunkirk) probably had more to do with this final tragedy—in which the real last-ditch defenders were left behind— than the peremptoriness often ascribed to the British.[21]

Thus ended the epic nine days of Dunkirk and with it the first phase of Anglo-French relations during Germany's blitzkrieg campaign in the west. Technically, the achievement of the evacuation under the most adverse circumstances was one of the most remarkable feats in modern history. Under constant bombardment from a numerically superior air force, under increasing pressure from a victorious army converging from all directions, and under conditions of almost unimaginable chaos and misunderstanding in which small boats were often rushed and capsized by panicky men and order sometimes regained only with the aid of revolvers and machine guns, the Allies had somehow managed to perform a miracle. In spite of cruel losses,[22] the Royal Navy, aided by the French Navy after May 29, had successfully embarked 338,226 soldiers—198,315 of whom were British, 139,911 of whom were Allied (mostly French).[23] The

British had contributed over 700 ships and boats of all sizes and classes, the French about 160.[24] The French Navy alone had probably taken off at least 35,000 Frenchmen.[25]

Yet, in spite of the heroic contributions made by both sides, Dunkirk and the three-week campaign leading up to it left a legacy of rancor and estrangement between the two allies. The French were all too conscious of the contempt felt by the British for their strategy and conduct of the crisis and especially for the collapsed figures who failed to rise to the occasion. They were resentful that the British had acted on their own militarily, first in secrecy, then in direct violation of orders from the French Command. They had resisted the whole idea of evacuation from the beginning, but then, once having accepted it, felt cheated out of an equal share. Finally, they believed that it was they who had borne the brunt of the fighting to cover an evacuation from which they could not expect to benefit. Thus, in thinking it all over, many, like General Weygand, could not help feeling that "since May 16th Churchill had played a double game, and had abandoned France to herself."[26]

The BEF, after being caught up in one of the worst defeats in history in which it lost 68,111 in killed, wounded, or missing and virtually all its equipment, was given a hero's welcome in England by a grateful and deeply moved public.[27] Dunkirk united the British as never before, inspiring an optimistic determination to fight on no matter what the cost. But if in a sense Dunkirk constituted a victory for the British, or at least a deliverance that occasioned solemn rejoicing, it could not but spell something very different to the French. England could take refuge in its splendid isolation and feel exhilarated by the threat from without; France, with the threat on its doorstep, could only feel divided and bowed under.

If, for the British, the Dunkirk disaster could be accepted as the end of a bad beginning, for France it marked the beginning of the end. Between May 10 and June 4 the French Army had lost over a quarter of its numerical strength—and this qualitatively its best. The northern armies had been virtually annihilated. All 20 Belgian divisions naturally had to be written off as well as 9 out of the 10 British divisions that had been present at the start of the campaign; with the loss of 24 French infantry divisions, including 6 of the 7 motorized divisions they possessed, of 2 light cavalry divisions, 3 light mechanized divisions, and 1 armored division, the French could now depend on only about half the effective strength they and their allies had been able to muster less than a month before.[28] The better part of their mechanized forces had been wiped out in Flanders and their air force—unimpressive in any event—badly mauled.

British air power operating out of Kentish airfields had participated actively while the evacuation was in progress but, with Fighter Command's loss of 106 aircraft during that eventful week set against a total loss of 432 Hurricanes and Spitfires from May 10 to 31,[29] there was justifiable concern in France as to the amount of help that henceforth could be expected from this quarter. As of June 4, the British had based in France only the 3 fighter squadrons of the Advanced Air Striking Force. Thus to face the Germans there now remained in France only 49 incompletely formed and badly equipped Allied divisions (including 3 under-strength armored and 3 cavalry divisions) between Longuyon and the sea, in addition to 13 divisions immobilized in the fortified sector or on the Alpine front.[30] To this meager array of ground forces in the line Britain could contribute only 1 infantry division and a portion of 1 armored division. Thus, for the French, the whole drama of Dunkirk—and especially the British departure—was a foretaste of total disaster and tangible evidence of their essential isolation. With a sense of shock and despair, therefore, they prepared to meet the new German offensive alone. They had not long to wait. It started the next day.

# II

## *The Growing Rift Between the Allies*

*May 15 – June 12*

*. . . a time might come when the French would cease to be enthusiastic about their relations with Great Britain if they were left with the impression that it was they who must bear the brunt of the fighting and slaughter on land.*

Lord Halifax at a meeting of the Committee of Imperial Defence, December 15, 1938, quoted in Michael Howard, *The Continental Commitment* (London, 1972), p. 126.

*The French are pushing us for a larger Army in France, and if we do not have it, the French Army may collapse and then all our Navies and Air Forces will not be of much good to us. We may think that we can retreat inside Great Britain and fight in the air, but we cannot do this. Our first line is in France and we must fight in France. We cannot escape that.*

General Sir Edmund Ironside, December 13, 1939, in *The Ironside Diaries, 1937–1940,* edited by Col. Roderick Macleod and Denis Kelly (London, 1962), p. 172.

# "A Certain Eventuality"

WAS General Weygand right in concluding at the time of Dunkirk that since May 16 Churchill had been playing a double game, that he had in fact already abandoned France to herself? The answer to this question is of course related to the answers evoked by a number of subsidiary questions: Was there a point at which a French defeat was definitely assumed? Did the possibility or expectation of French military collapse substantially affect the assistance Britain was willing to give? Or should contingency planning carried out in utmost secrecy be construed as duplicity?

Churchill's policy during this period seems relatively simple and consistent: to give the French the maximum support possible short of ruining his country's capacity to continue the war. He would state as much at every opportunity, though perhaps with less emphasis on the caveat than there should have been—because that of course was the rub. How much aid *could* the British afford? General Weygand always believed that what the British sent over to France was far inferior to their means; certainly it was less than what they had been able to deliver in May 1915, a comparable period in the previous war. And Churchill remained ever conscious of the debit. Nevertheless, as he had strongly hinted to the French Ambassador on the eve of the war, he had never believed that England's fate was automatically tied to that of France, and his primary obligation was, obviously, to see to his own nation's survival, a concern which allowed for considerable latitude in dealing with the French. But the diplomatic terms in which his day-to-day policy was dressed hardly concealed the direction it was unambiguously assuming. Whatever ambiguities can be read into Churchill's position in the second half of

May appear to stem less from any basic uncertainty on his part than from a tendency to impulsiveness combined with a personality in which the most hard-headed realism—to the point of ruthlessness—vied constantly with an ineradicable romanticism and a somewhat childish sentimentalism. The two strains did not preclude each other and should not have confused any Frenchman determined to avoid wishful thinking.

That the British Prime Minister was also to a large extent dependent on his military experts—none of whom was even slightly sentimental—for the course his country pursued should also have been obvious. Churchill's fertile imagination and dynamic—not to say overbearing—personality notwithstanding, the Chiefs of Staff could put up a formidable front, before which even the great man was often obliged to defer.[1] Churchill's deference to the military was not always to be as marked as it was in late May and early June, but it is interesting to note that on both sides of the Channel, as the disaster spread, decision making tended increasingly to escape control by the two prime ministers involved—perhaps, in the final analysis, to the relief of both. But it is clear that just as the French were traumatized by the depth of their defeat as it bore down on them in mid-May, the British too, instinctively realizing that this time their customary stiff-upper-lip response would not suffice, suffered a massive loss of faith in their ally, which was both awkward and inexpedient to articulate, but a loss of faith nonetheless from which neither partner could really recover.

Recognition that the French might be defeated—and Mr. Churchill's reaction to such a prospect—had come as early as the morning of May 15 when "he had found it necessary to point out to M. Reynaud [over the phone] that whatever the French might do, we should continue the fight—if necessary alone." Reynaud, according to the minutes taken at a Chiefs of Staff meeting held two hours later, "had then pulled himself together, and had said that the French too would fight to the end." Nevertheless, as a result of the disastrous news relayed to him, the Prime Minister asked his Chiefs of Staff to study the possible effects of a German breakthrough.[2] This study would surface shortly under the title "British Strategy in a Certain Eventuality."

Air Marshal Sir Hugh Dowding, as has been seen, had all along opposed sending his fighter force out of the country, but from 15 May on, with the situation on the Meuse worsening fast, he could claim that if more fighters were taken from him not only would they fail to achieve decisive results in France, but, in their absence, he would be left too weak to carry on at home. In a letter addressed to the Air Ministry, he warned that the possibility of defeat in France must now be faced and concluded with one of the most ominous predictions ever made:

I believe that, if an adequate fighter force is kept in this country, if the fleet remains in being, and if Home Forces are suitably organised to resist invasion, we should be able to carry on the war single-handed for some time, if not indefinitely. But if the Home Defence Force is drained away in desperate attempts to remedy the situation in France, defeat in France will involve the final, complete and irremediable defeat of this country.[3]

Solemn as this warning was, however, it did not as yet represent the viewpoint of either the Prime Minister or of all the Chiefs of Staff, Ironside in particular. Furthermore, Barratt in France, as of May 16, still "thought that he would be able to stop the 'rot' if he could be sent four additional fighter squadrons at once"; while Sir Cyril Newall, Chief of the Air Staff, believed the Germans were not yet in a position to attack Britain in very great strength unless they first diverted their bomber force from the battle in progress. Therefore, with Churchill's encouragement, the Chiefs of Staff agreed to part with at least four of the precious squadrons that had been demanded and would, before the day was out, agree to the employment in France of a total of ten above and beyond what the AASF already had. "The Committee felt, however, that fighter assistance to the French Army would be valueless if the troops were not going to fight" and that "it was essential to find out as soon as possible what action was being taken on the ground to counter the German thrust."[4]

That afternoon in Paris Churchill did indeed find out, but chivalrously, in spite of his reservations, had backed the French request for reinforcements anyway. But the possibility of his ally's defeat had definitely penetrated and this presentiment was in no way disguised when he met with Reynaud and Daladier at the former's flat late that night. There, according to Baudouin, who was also present, "crowned like a volcano by the smoke of his cigars, he told his French colleague that even if France was invaded and vanquished England would go on fighting until the United States came to her aid, which she would soon do in no half-hearted manner. . . . Until one in the morning he conjured up an apocalyptic vision of the war. He saw himself in the heart of Canada directing, over an England razed to the ground by high explosive bombs and over a France whose ruins were already cold, the air war of the New World against the Old dominated by Germany."[5]

That was Churchill in one of his apocalyptic moods. For the present, however, the Prime Minister had no intention of retreating to Canada,[6] and on May 17, back in England, contingency planning got under way quite realistically and methodically. That day Churchill asked Chamberlain, Lord President of the Council, to examine the consequences of the French Government withdrawing from Paris, "as well as the problems which would arise if it were necessary to withdraw the B.E.F. from France, either along its communications or by the Belgian and Channel ports."[7] This did not mean that Churchill and the cabinet were convinced on this date that it *would* be necessary to withdraw the BEF; on the contrary, for another week they continued to hope that Lord Gort would be able to fight his way through to the south, though the hope became dimmer as the days progressed. Nevertheless, a total French collapse was considered quite possible as of the 17th.

For instance, Sir Alexander Cadogan wrote in his diary that night that the Foreign Secretary had gone "to a meeting of a Ministerial Committee to consider how we proceed when France has capitulated and we are left alone,"[8] while General Ironside, noting in his diary that they now stood "faced by a completely Nazified Europe," asked himself the searching questions the Chiefs of Staff would henceforth have to grapple with:

What chance have we in reality of continuing the struggle by ourselves with the French knocked out? Could we maintain the Air struggle? . . . Could we keep our industry going under Nazi bombardment from so close as Holland and the Channel ports? Could we get enough of the B.E.F. men and equipment back to England to ensure security against air invasion?

This, as he admitted, marked the end of the "fool's paradise" in which the British had lived, depending largely upon the strength of the French Army. Unlike some of his colleagues, however, the CIGS at this point still believed that there was "no use holding anything up for a problematical continuance of the war" if France collapsed.[9] Churchill was evidently not sold on this line of reasoning, and the next day, in recognition that "the French may be offered very advantageous terms of peace, and the whole weight be thrown on us," he suggested to the Chiefs of Staff that it might be well to send over to France only half of the armored division then embarking.[10]

On May 18 the Chiefs of Staff Committee presented to the War Cabinet a report on "The Air Defence of Great Britain" which indicated that they now endorsed Dowding's views. They considered fifty-three fighter squadrons the minimum necessary to defend the country, and they were currently reduced to thirty-seven, of which six were operating daily in France. Their conclusion was that they had reached the absolute limit of air assistance to France compatible with any chance of defending the United Kingdom, the fleet, Britain's aircraft industry and seaborne trade. While fully recognizing that if further fighter assistance to France was denied it was "not beyond the bounds of possibility" that the French Army might give up the struggle, they nevertheless did not think that throwing in a few more squadrons, "whose loss might vitally weaken the fighter line at home, would make the difference between victory and defeat in France." Most important for its strategic implications was their "absolute certainty that while the collapse of France would not necessarily mean the ultimate victory of Germany, the collapse of Great Britain would inevitably do so." They were all agreed that even if the French were overwhelmed England should fight on.[11] It was in the light of this report that the next day Churchill ruled that no more fighter squadrons should leave the country, no matter what happened across the Channel, a decision confirmed by the War Cabinet on May 20.[12]

By May 24, the restriction on further air support for France was extended to a ban on the sending of more troops as well. The Prime Minister, at a meeting of the Defence Committee that day, held that the danger of an invasion of the United Kingdom was now too great, and that "M. Reynaud was being informed accordingly."[13] This position was maintained by General Ironside once he became Commander-in-Chief of Home Forces; anxious not to dissipate the paltry resources at his disposal in a vain attempt to postpone defeat in France, he too, like Dowding, thereafter disclaimed responsibility for the security of the British Isles unless all available land forces were given over to him.[14]

The major decisions taken by the British Government from May 16 on represent a growing realization of the near inevitability of defeat in France and, above all, of the utter precariousness of their own position. This awareness was to culminate on May 25 with the completion of the Chiefs of Staff paper "British Strategy in a Certain Eventuality," on which the Joint Planning Subcommittee had already submitted several drafts since May 19. The paper dealt with the means whereby Britain could continue the fight single-handed if French resistance collapsed entirely, involving the loss of a substantial proportion of the BEF, and the French Government then came to terms with the Germans. It was assumed that in this eventuality all French forces in both Europe and North Africa would cease to fight and that both continental France and French North Africa would be accessible to the enemy in due time. It was thought that perhaps parts of the French fleet and portions of the land and air forces of outlying regions of the French Empire would continue to lend assistance. The other basic assumptions of the study were that Italy would have intervened on the side of the Germans and that the United States would be willing to give the British full economic and financial support, "without which we do not think we could continue the war with any chance of success."[15] Considering the strength of isolationist sentiment in America, the latter assumption was indeed problematic at this stage.

Their conclusions were pessimistic. The immediate effect of a French collapse on the situation in the Mediterranean, they predicted, would be the loss of naval control in the western half of that sea. As for the United Kingdom, whether it could hold out against a concentrated German attack depended on three things: (1) the morale of the people; (2) their continuing ability to import the minimum commodities necessary to sustain life and to keep British war industries going; and (3) their capacity to resist an invasion by sea or air. All these in turn depended primarily on whether their fighter defenses would be able to reduce the scale of attack to reasonable bounds, and on whether they would have the capacity to replace wastage, both in fighter pilots and aircraft. The Royal Navy, it was thought, was strong enough to ensure their overseas supplies, but whether it would have the ability to defeat a seaborne landing in the face of heavy enemy air attacks on both ships and bases was less certain. The navy's maintenance of effective forces on the east and south coasts of England and their operation in strength in the Channel could no longer be counted on. For an invasion of Great Britain the Germans would have available at least 70 divisions, as opposed to only 3½ British divisions that were trained, equipped, and mobilized, 3 partly trained divisions, 5 untrained divisions, and 2 armored divisions. Under these conditions, the Chiefs of Staff reasoned, "Should the Germans succeed in establishing a force with its vehicles in this country, our army forces have not got the offensive power to drive it out."[16] The prospect presented was grim in the extreme.

Under slightly different and somewhat tendentious terms of reference remitted to them by the Prime Minister (namely, in the event of peace terms being offered Britain which would place the country entirely at the mercy of Germany through disarmament, cession of naval bases, etc.), the Chiefs of Staff on May 26 again tackled the prospects of continuing the war alone against Germany and Italy: Could the navy and air force hold out reasonable hopes of preventing a serious invasion and cope with the expected air raids? Once again they arrived at the same grim conclusions: "If with our Navy unable to prevent it and our air force gone, Germany attempted an invasion, our coast and beach defences could not prevent German tanks and infantry getting a firm footing on our shores. In the circumstances envisaged above our land forces would be insufficient to deal with a serious invasion." The crux of the matter was still air superiority, to attain which Germany would first have to knock out the RAF and the British aircraft industry. But there was no way to guarantee the protection of industrial centers against night bombing. Ultimately, they thought, the survival of the aircraft industry would depend on how the work force stood up to attack. In the one comfort allowed Churchill, whose leanings were well known, the Chiefs of Staff professed that the real test would lie in the morale of Britain's fighting personnel and civilian population; this, they claimed, would counterbalance the numerical and material advantages enjoyed by Germany.[17] But, for the rest, as David Divine points out, the report read "perilously like an admission of defeat."[18]

This then was the opinion of Britain's highest military authorities on the eve of Dunkirk, the day Lord Gort, with the backing of the cabinet, began his march to the sea, the day—significantly designated a Day of National Prayer, and by Chamberlain "the blackest day of all"[19]—Operation Dynamo was put into motion, and the day Winston Churchill was scheduled to meet with the French Premier in what can possibly be considered the most crucial encounter of the war.

# The French Temptation

IF THE British Government, unknown to the French, was preparing as early as May 17 for the eventual withdrawal of the BEF from the continent, should developments require it, a significant segment of French opinion had begun from that date on to envisage an even more drastic withdrawal—withdrawal from the war itself. Paul Reynaud states that during the great anxiety of May 16, following the German breakthrough at Sedan, "an armistice was already being talked about at General Headquarters."[1] Whether the word "armistice" itself was used is not particularly relevant; what is important to the drift of French thinking at this time is that by the evening of May 15 General Gamelin was agreeing with a stunned Daladier, still Minister of Defense—in a telephone conversation witnessed by the American Ambassador—that the French Army was doomed.[2] But the generals did not constitute the government, and though defeatism was rife in some political circles it did not yet have the upper hand. Reynaud himself, realizing that the military situation was probably irreparable, informed his colleagues on the 16th that the government might find it necessary to go to North Africa and carry on the war from there.

The British, although they could not fully appreciate the degree of defeatism that prevailed in Paris, had at least been shocked enough by the disorder and planlessness they found in the French capital at the meeting of the Supreme War Council on May 16 to recognize the possibility that France might be tempted if advantageous peace terms were offered. The underlying fear that French resistance could end soon and that the French might then be willing to negotiate with the Germans, accompanied by the threat that the full weight of the enemy's might would then fall on Great Britain, certainly influenced many of Britain's military decisions. These in turn further discouraged the French High Command and made the realization of British fears all the more probable.

Reynaud's political and military reorganization of May 18–19 might have caused the British more anxiety than it apparently did. Under the circumstances, however, the inclusion of Pétain and Weygand in French governmental councils could only seem a step of obvious wisdom, while the promotion of Mandel, long a trusted friend of Churchill on whom the latter relied for much of his information about French politics, aroused even greater enthusiasm in London. Mr. Churchill in fact congratulated Reynaud on the strong compact government he had formed.

The substitution of Charles-Roux for Léger, who since 1933 had been permanent head of the Ministry of Foreign Affairs, was puzzling, however, and caused some consternation in English diplomatic circles—if not elsewhere. Oliver Harvey, from his vantage as Minister at the British Embassy in Paris, thought Reynaud's sacking of Léger "monstrous and quite indefensible from every point of view. . . . The Entente had no greater or better friend. For years and years he worked for it."[3] Indeed, Alexis Léger was well known as the Quai d'Orsay's leading spokesman for Anglo-French solidarity, the very policy Reynaud was pledged to defend and claimed to personify. Léger had been one of the principal architects of the March 28 agreement forbidding any separate peace or armistice negotiations and, along with Georges Mandel and Colonel Charles de Gaulle, was considered one of the "intransigents" around Reynaud. For this very reason he had won the enmity of the French appeasers, who accused him of having wrecked any possibility of agreement with Italy (he had certainly dismissed the idea of Italian mediation on August 31, 1939) and of being the "willing vassal" of England, and who hoped by his removal to weaken the Franco-British alliance. What was ominous about his dismissal, aside from the inconsistency on Reynaud's part that it seemed to reveal, was that it could be interpreted as a harbinger of a more "realistic," or opportunistic, French foreign policy in the future, and Mandel had warned Reynaud of this danger.[4]

Charles-Roux had been French Ambassador at the Vatican and was thought to be, at least by Lord Perth, former British Ambassador in Rome, "not much of a friend" to England.[5] Perhaps even more unsettling to those in the know was that the change strongly suggested that the less savory elements—at least from the British point of view—of

Reynaud's entourage (e.g., his mistress, Comtesse Hélène de Portes, the banker Paul Baudouin, since March 30 Under-Secretary of State to the President of the Council as well as Secretary of the War Cabinet and of the War Committee, and Lieutenant-Colonel de Villelume, who on May 19 became director of Reynaud's Office of National Defense) were gaining in influence over the Premier—for they had, after all, engineered Léger's fall—and that henceforth considerations of political expediency, in short, Reynaud's desire to improve his standing in the Chamber of Deputies, which from the beginning of the war had been a volatile and somewhat untrustworthy body, must be reckoned with as integral elements in Reynaud's direction of the war.

As it turned out, Reynaud's other appointments proved far more troublesome, for the two men on whom he had counted to stiffen the resistance of the nation quickly showed themselves of fragile mettle. Not only were Weygand and Pétain unable to restore the military situation or effectively rally the morale of the country, except momentarily, but they actively used their tremendous power and prestige to strengthen and even to lead the defeatist elements within the government.[6] Both, in fact, had been convinced either before or shortly after their arrival in France that the war was lost and that a reasonable armistice ought to be accepted.[7] The growing disaster was to play into their hands.

Upon assuming command, Weygand had but one hope, that of gathering the full force of the French and British armies behind the Somme to oppose a numerically and materially superior enemy. The loss of the northern armies, the best trained and best equipped he had, would render any hope of standing firm unreasonable. Therefore, the success of the Weygand plan was essential. When it became apparent on May 24 and 25 that this was collapsing, Weygand knew that the battle was lost. He himself had nothing else to offer militarily, being disinclined to see the war in global or long-range terms. For the present, his immediate need was to find a scapegoat, and the British provided a convenient one, readily acceptable to traditionally Anglophobic sentiment. At the daily War Council on 24 May Weygand accused Lord Gort of having abandoned Arras without being compelled by the Germans to do so, and complained of the impossibility of commanding an army which remained dependent on London for military operations. Gort's "refusal to fight," the "defection of the English," and the implication that "the British could never resist the call of the harbors" would hereafter be constant themes in Weygand's discussions with members of the French cabinet.[8] That his opinion, carrying the weight it did, could not but have a poisonous effect on all who listened is obvious. By placing the blame for the French disaster on the British, and by making it appear that the English had already failed to live up to their part of the bargain, Weygand, it would seem, was preparing the way for questioning those obligations which tied France to Britain and which were the basis of the alliance.

Anglophobia, ripening at the time of Dunkirk and in the days leading up to it, was not confined to government circles. Clare Boothe Luce, whose contacts in France ranged widely, "watched with fear the hatred of the French for the English growing by giant leaps and bounds." "Many people," she noted, "now quite openly blamed the whole horrible fiasco on the English High Command, or on some rumoured counter-order of Churchill's, which had marred Weygand's last attempt to get through." That these negative sentiments were paralleled in England during the month of May is well documented. Harold Nicolson, MP, comments in his diary entry of May 24 on "the rather dangerous anti-French feeling and the belief that the French Army has lost its morale"; and, again on May 29, on the public complaint made by the French Ambassador "that our Press is putting all the blame on the French Army." As early as May 16, according to Oliver Harvey, Winston Churchill, who had arrived in Paris that day "full of fire and fury," was "saying the French were lily-livered and must fight." Increasing skepticism as to the French ability or will to fight is also plentifully recorded in the diary kept by Sir Alexander Cadogan, Permanent Under-Secretary at the Foreign Office, whose summation of Gort's report to the cabinet on June 1 was that the "French—with [the] exception of Laurencie's party— [were] evidently worse than useless!" The appraisal was shared by Neville Chamberlain, who, in a letter written to his sister the same day, characterized French generalship as "beneath contempt," chauvinistically (and quite inaccurately) going on to declare that "as usual the brunt of all the hard fighting and the hard work fell upon the British."[9]

Indeed, in the *private* papers of British policy makers during this anxious period, it is hard to find a kind word expressed for the French military, except perhaps by General Ironside, whose tone is more one of despair and sorrow than of anger or bitterness—and he was replaced as CIGS on May 27. The French Army had been the linchpin of England's continental policy, and when it faltered, the reaction was inevitably harsh, sweeping along even so stalwart a champion as Winston Churchill in the quickening tide of disillusionment. The publicist Alfred Fabre-Luce, whose own Anglophobia and Vichyite inclinations do not necessarily invalidate his perceptions, perhaps puts his finger on the cause of the mutual antipathies developing at this time when he characterizes Churchill's attitude towards the French Army as a "sincere but interested love, that of a knight for his mount."[10] It helps explain the recurrent themes in this underground war of recriminations: on the part of the British, accusations of French failure, cowardice, incompetence, and senility; on the part of the French, accusations of British perfidy, dishonor, and selfishness. This whole dark side of Anglo-French relations must of course be kept in mind in tracing developments on the official level, where frankness to this uninhibited degree could hardly be expected to displace the time-honored formulae and sinuosities of traditional diplomatic exchange. Yet its effect must of necessity have been powerful.

According to Reynaud, it was from the moment that Weygand realized the impossibility of rescuing the northern armies that he conceived the idea that France ought to lay down its arms. Indeed, according to Baudouin's account of a meeting between himself and the General on the evening of May 24, Weygand shared Baudouin's belief that there was now only one object—"to get France out of the ordeal which she is undergoing so as to allow her, even if defeated in the field, to rise again." Amongst his intimates, Lieutenant-Colonel de Villelume tells us, Weygand, almost from the time he took command, ceaselessly and violently attacked the government because it did not wish to hear of an armistice—though the General would publicly refrain from using the taboo word until a more opportune moment arose.[11]

Reynaud himself had little doubt that the battle was lost—the obvious, after all, could hardly be denied. In fact, to the American Ambassador on May 18 Reynaud had admitted the possibility of the "absolute defeat of [both] France and England in less than two months." The only real hope, he seemed to feel, lay in action by the United States.[12] Certainly for the space of a few days, at least, especially after the hopes engendered by the Weygand plan collapsed, the French Premier wavered in the course he was to follow, although he would later seek to obliterate the record of his tangled thoughts during this murky period, preferring instead to emphasize his differences with the General and the Marshal rather than admit for a moment that there had ever been common ground. This must be borne in mind when following his very tendentious though valuable account. Yet, if Reynaud did not at first take any practical steps towards meeting a radical deterioration in the situation, he would shortly recover sufficiently to affirm his determination to fight on to the end and, above all, to struggle to keep the Anglo-French alliance alive.

His arguments, however, that France's only hope of independence lay in close collaboration with the two great Anglo-Saxon democracies; that France still retained intact the second empire in the world and the second-largest fleet in Europe; and, finally, that honor forbade France to break its pledged word to its ally not to enter into a separate armistice fell on deaf ears. Pétain refused to see things from an "international" point of view, believing that a universal armistice was inevitable in any case and that the national interest would best be served by coming to terms with the new masters of Europe and not by abandoning the French people to the enemy. "This thesis," writes Reynaud, "was supported by Weygand, but with a characteristic twist." Obsessed by fear of internal revolution, he was determined to preserve the army intact so that it could maintain order. Furthermore, Weygand believed that should the enemy enter Paris the duty of the government was to await him there, just as the Roman senators had formerly awaited the barbarians, calmly seated in their curule chairs.[13] Reynaud therefore claims to have known from this time on (May 24–25) that if the battle about to be waged on the Somme were lost Weygand and Pétain would form a coalition to *demand* an armistice.[14] What was not suspected at this date was that Weygand and Pétain, in conjunction with Rightist elements, might associate a cessation of hostilities with the disappearance of the regime itself or that their efforts to obtain an armistice would be simultaneous with their attempts to discredit the Third Republic.[15]

Reynaud, according to his own account, refrained from forcing the resignations of Weygand and Pétain out of fear that the Army could not afford still another commander-in-chief—its third in two weeks—at such a crucial stage and in recognition that France would be totally demoralized by the removal of its two greatest military heroes. Hoping to avoid a rupture which he believed would cut France in two, Reynaud preferred to postpone any discussion on an armistice; meanwhile he would prepare to continue the war from North Africa and would set about reconstructing his cabinet in order to get rid of those members he feared would come down in favor of an armistice on the day the question arose. In this way Reynaud hoped that if the battle of France were lost, Pétain and Weygand would be won over by the unanimous decision of the reorganized government.[16] But in this expectation Reynaud was to be sadly disillusioned, for his measures to combat the influence of Weygand and Pétain were to prove as ineffectual and as capable of backfiring as had his original steps to bolster the government. In effect, the Prime Minister soon found himself in the embarrassing position of having strapped two national monuments to his back, under whose weight he was doomed to collapse.

# The Problem Posed

THE stark realities of the situation and the options remaining to the French Government were brutally outlined before the War Committee at noon on May 25. This was the session at which Major Fauvelle, fresh from the holocaust in the north, made it clear that any counterattack was now out of the question, and as a consequence predicted an early capitulation. In his opinion, the Battle of France was already lost—the campaign at least, if not the whole war. This meant that there were but three possibilities left: (1) the evacuation of the 1st Army and the transfer of the armies of the east to North Africa; (2) the continuation of the struggle within the confines of metropolitan France, in the Breton and Cotentin peninsulas; or (3) a demand for an armistice. To Reynaud privately he emphasized that it would be necessary to evacuate troops to England and Algeria if one wished to continue the war. As has been seen, it was in the light of this interview that General Weygand gave Blanchard carte blanche to fall back in the direction of Dunkirk.[1]

However, the Generalissimo's strategic conception of the war, as evidenced by his decision on May 25 to deliver battle on the position of the Somme, the Aisne, and the Maginot, and that this line was to be held at all costs, "without thought of retreat,"[2] was hardly in conformity with the suggestions made above and in effect precluded all but the last possibility—final defeat in the Battle of France to be followed, inevitably, by an armistice. The truth was that in the disadvantageous conditions in which they would now have to face a major German offensive there was *no* solid line of resistance left in France. Weygand knew it, but nevertheless could not admit the alternative—the necessity of abandoning the national territory—a decision which

137

after only two weeks of real war would admittedly have tested the heroism of all but the most rugged of French generals. "Weygand's response," as Philip Bankwitz points out, "was an extraordinary and fateful step by which, five days after assuming command, he confined the battle within the traditional continental sector, and within a restricted part of that sector as well." By this decision, and corollary decisions taken in the next two weeks which were to straitjacket the government still further, Weygand "dismissed once and for all any possibility that the non-European world could maintain or defend an operational bridgehead in North Africa, let alone effect an early reconquest of the French homeland."[3]

Whether Weygand's strategy was the correct one to adopt in the circumstances or whether an alternative military policy might have been better suited to French interests or have had any practical chance of succeeding were issues that should, logically, have been openly discussed both within the French Government and between the French and British. But the implications of the General's operational order (promulgated May 26) were never rejected outright, possibly because not fully appreciated at the time, and would be attacked only in the most lackadaisical fashion when they were. The plain fact was that Weygand's supreme authority in military matters, that is, his statutory responsibility for the conduct of operations as opposed to the government's constitutional responsibility for the general direction of the war, placed the head of government in an ever-tightening bind because the military and political could no longer be separated; the one impinged on the other at every turn. This was becoming the major reality even before the new battle was joined, and the British no more than the French dealt with the problem squarely or decisively. The particular vantage point of each partner to the alliance was in fact becoming something of an irrelevancy to the other.

The question of a possible cessation of hostilities was first raised formally within the French Government at a second meeting of the War Committee held at 7 p.m. on May 25. Many accounts of this meeting exist, each containing valuable insights and partial truths, but inasmuch as most are tendentious they must be approached with caution. What now seems clear is that the question of an armistice, not yet having become a political "hot potato," was approached in a pragmatic spirit, rather than defensively or dogmatically, in which some semblance of a dialogue between proponents and opponents was still possible. This would not be possible once a politically orthodox line had been established; and after the war witnesses would naturally seek to justify their own words while at the same time incriminating those of their enemies. At the time, however, there was no orthodoxy and, as a consequence, no heresy: there were merely a few puzzled and apprehensive people in something of a state of shock, mulling over possible solutions to a most unpromising situation, quite unconscious that their words would one day be enshrined in history—or used in briefs drawn up against them. In short, the political decisions confronting the government as a result of France's military setback were at least adumbrated here, although they were by no means thrashed out.

General Weygand opened the proceedings by painting a gloomy picture of what could be expected from the coming battle, in which the French armies, minus those in the north, would have to hold the line of the Somme and the Aisne against three times their own strength and with only a fifth of their armored forces left.[4] To save honor it would be necessary to fight on until the line had been completely broken, but from this "struggle to the death" he anticipated the worst. An orderly retreat from the Somme-Aisne position to the lower Seine and the Marne, Weygand thought, would not be possible under conditions of such numerical inferiority.

Reynaud then asked General Weygand's advice concerning the position the government should adopt if the Germans approached Paris, but Weygand—to the President of the Republic's horror—pronounced against the government's departure from the capital, even though by remaining it would risk imprisonment. "Thus, what Weygand was asking for," claims Reynaud, "was an armistice, and, as a corollary, the capture of the Government."[5] Reynaud pointed out: "In the hypothesis that we lose the armies of the north . . . it is not inevitable that our adversary will accord us an immediate armistice and is it not indispensable to avoid the capture of the government if the enemy enters Paris?"[6] Reynaud undoubtedly hoped by this observation to indicate that for the moment the decision incumbent upon them had nothing to do with an armistice but only with the independence and security of the French Government. The seat of the government if the capital were threatened was the issue. However, M. Albert Lebrun, President of the Republic, entered more slippery ground by asking General Weygand what the situation of the government would be if the French armies were dispersed and destroyed. "What freedom of examination would the French government have if any peace offers were addressed to it? Would not the government's freedom of examination be greater before the destruction of the French armies?" He then went on to say that the government had, of course, signed engagements which forbade a separate peace, but if Germany, after her initial successes in France, should propose to end hostilities on relatively advantageous terms, the government must at least be in a position to examine them closely and to deliberate at leisure—in other words, outside the enemy's reach, outside Paris if necessary. Reynaud, in response to both Weygand and Lebrun, commented that if peace offers were made to them they would in any case be obliged to inform England and ask her advice. But, he recalled, they were bound by a formal agreement; in addition, Churchill had already indicated that he favored a desperate resistance regardless of what happened to France. These observations, so he claims, were intended to eliminate the topic from debate, not to prolong it.[7]

General Weygand's point of view was this: he recognized that a cessation of hostilities was an interallied problem, that one could not adopt the extreme solution of pursuing a hopeless struggle for the sake of honor without first examining the consequences of such a policy with England. Because England was now threatened by the loss of its entire army and a possible German invasion, he thought that an immediate exchange of views between the French and British governments as to future policy would be most useful. Weygand, it would seem, though allowing others to make the first direct references to peace proposals and armistice accords, thought that the time was ripe for discussing the possibility of an armistice with England and believed moreover that the British would be ready to initiate or to receive such overtures. Lebrun and Reynaud, on the other hand, were apparently thinking less in terms of soliciting an armistice than of the best course to follow should the Germans approach the French with offers.[8]

Reynaud, in fact, had already discussed this contingency with Jules Jeanneney, President of the Senate, earlier that day, when he had asked the elder statesman whether it would be appropriate to submit to the chambers any German peace offers, direct or indirect, that might be received once the Germans became masters of the coast. Jeanneney had advised that "it could only be a question if the government itself judged them acceptable or, at the least, worthy of examination"; but he thought it necessary to hope that they would prove unacceptable because otherwise they would only mask Germany's design of crushing France in two steps, much as Czechoslovakia had been crushed first by Munich, then by Prague. Lebrun too, as he told the presidents of the two assemblies the next day, thought that "the government would have to consult the chambers only if the propositions to be submitted appeared to it to conform with the honor and interests of the country." But in none of these discussions was the possibility of soliciting peace proposals raised.[9]

Pétain, for his part, in apparent indifference to the obligations entailed by the Anglo-French agreement of March 28, asked whether there was a complete reciprocity of duties between France and England. He felt that the duty of each nation towards the other should be in proportion to the military aid the other had extended as well as proportionate to the sufferings experienced by each. Inasmuch as England had thrown into the struggle only ten divisions, as compared with the eighty French divisions then engaged, and had not as yet felt the full brunt of the war, his conclusions were obvious[10]—France owed virtually nothing to Britain.

The Minister of the Navy, César Campinchi, according to Baudouin, whose *procès-verbal* is the principal source for the War Committee meeting of May 25, declared himself in full agreement with Weygand on the utility of immediate discussions with the British and suggested that Reynaud have a meeting *à deux* with Mr. Churchill in order to explain to him the seriousness of the French military situation. But he stated he could not agree with the Marshal's remarks on England: "It was not so much a question of aid as of risks. And the problem before them was that of the risk France was running." It was up to the military chiefs to advise the government to cede if it was not possible to go on. He believed that the loyalty of France should not be placed in question and that "a treaty of peace ought never to be signed by France without England's previous consent." Yet, still according to Baudouin, Campinchi also declared that "if the present Government had given its word to England, another Government would feel less constraint in signing a treaty of peace without that country's previous agreement. The present Government would have only to resign."[11] However, loyalty required setting forth their unhappy plight before their ally, and this was a matter of urgency.

Pétain's observations, together with some of General Vuillemin's complaints regarding the RAF's meager contributions, were the only anti-English notes introduced. No one had suggested *asking* for an armistice, although the general idea was obviously charging the atmosphere. A cessation of hostilities was envisaged primarily as a question to be taken up *jointly* with the British. Discussion seems to have been based on what was then felt to be a strong likelihood that the Germans, flushed with an easy victory in the north, might offer peace on relatively favorable terms[12] and, because France was bound by an agreement with England not to conclude a separate peace or armistice, London would have to be consulted. There was general recognition that France's bargaining position with Germany would not improve with time, that it would be greater before the final destruction of the French armies. With the Battle of France written off in advance as a probable failure, the moment was appropriate for the French Government to take stock of its policy.

Although the committee was in agreement as to the necessity for immediate consultations with the British Government, there was somewhat less agreement as to what questions should be raised in London. Reynaud "thought that an exchange of views with England could be justified, even if only because it would provide an opportunity of asking her whether she was ready to agree to important sacrifices to prevent the entry of Italy into the war."[13] Weygand and General Vuillemin also urged talks concerning the military aid France could expect from Great Britain in the coming weeks, and Weygand again pressed for an immediate examination with England of the peril France would run if the army, because it had been sacrificed to save the national honor, was not strong enough to ensure the maintenance of public order. Baudouin believed the War Committee had charged Reynaud to find out what the British Government's attitude would be should the French be driven to ending hostilities. In other words, under what conditions would they liberate the French from their engagement not to sign a separate armistice? In any event, Reynaud promised to go to London the next day to explain to the English the inequality of the struggle to be waged and to explore with them the possible steps to be taken if Paris were captured; but he recognized that England was entitled to say that France was bound by her signature to continue the struggle—even without hope.[14]

# May 26:
# The Crisis Contained

THE Anglo-French discussions in London on May 26 and their sequel over the next few days represented a sharp departure from any Allied conversations of the recent past. Highly secret, and, as a result, little known, they reveal the sense of desperation felt by both governments at this critical juncture—as evidenced in their willingness to entertain measures that would have been rejected as repugnant only days before. They also bear witness to certain differences in method and attitude that can be seen in retrospect to have marked something of a watershed in the history of the alliance.

Though both Churchill and Reynaud deal with this meeting in their memoirs, neither elaborates on its significance. Indeed, Reynaud has at times falsified both the letter and the spirit of what transpired in London on May 26. According to Churchill, who first lunched with the French Premier privately, "M. Reynaud dwelt not obscurely upon the possible French withdrawal from the war. He himself would fight on, but there was always the possibility that he might soon be replaced by others of a different temper."[1] Whether, as Professor Langer theorizes, Reynaud went so far as to explore whether, "if the British were unable to furnish greater air support, it might not be in the common interest for France to conclude an armistice before the Germans seized the entire Channel coast area"[2] cannot be proven; but the Premier assuredly did all in his power to let the British know how desperately serious the situation was—for both partners. For instance, he warned them of the danger to Britain should the Germans gain control of the French coast from Dunkirk to Brest. Furthermore, if the Battle of France were lost and the Germans reached the Seine, Pétain, he confided, would throw all his weight on the side of an armistice.[3] The French had not up to now received any peace overtures from Germany, he said in reply to a question on this point from the Prime Minister, but "they knew they could get an offer if they wanted one."[4] Reynaud made it clear that his ministers agreed with General Weygand that the French means of resistance would soon be exhausted and that they therefore considered the struggle on land hopeless. With Germany virtually in command of all continental resources from the Atlantic to the Pacific, he could not expect much from the Allied blockade. In addition, if the Germans took Paris, they would gain control of the French aircraft industry as well. Finally, he thought that for the present little hope could be placed in help from the United States.[5] The drift of Reynaud's somber recital was obvious. However, in spite of this, the French Premier apparently did not ask the British to relieve the French Government of its promise not to enter into a separate armistice, for on his return to Paris that evening, he admitted to Baudouin, who had met him at Le Bourget, that he "was not able to put the question." Baudouin in fact criticized him for not having fulfilled "the mission with which the War Committee had entrusted him."[6]

Whether Reynaud failed to "put the question" of a separate peace out of loyalty to his principles or because tactics suggested a more profitable approach or because Mr. Churchill was simply too formidable an opponent cannot be known. In any case, the British Prime Minister, as he had told the Defence Committee the evening before, had a pretty good idea as to why Reynaud wished to meet with him alone on the 26th[7] and was therefore fully prepared to deal with such an issue, having armed himself with an *aide-mémoire* he had asked the Chiefs of Staff to prepare on the assumption that the object of Reynaud's visit would be to say that the French now wished to make a separate peace. This contained a host of arguments calculated to keep France from capitulating.[8]

But that Churchill had need of such heavy artillery seems unlikely because somewhere along the line Reynaud made it clear that the primary purpose of his visit was to obtain the support of the British Government "for concessions to Mussolini in the hope of keeping Italy out of the war, and to explore the larger possibility of securing mediation in some form by the Italian Government."[9] In short, Reynaud was willing to buy off the Italian dictator if only he could be induced to pull their chestnuts out of the fire as he had done so obligingly back in September 1938 and had been half prepared to do again in September 1939. This was the only solution he could see to a seemingly impossible situation.

Ten years later, Reynaud would tell the Parliamentary Commission of Inquiry investigating these matters that he had said nothing to the British of what had gone on at the War Committee the day before, that he had spoken exclusively of Italy on May 26, and that he did not feel he had been charged with any other mission by the committee. He also denied that in London a diplomatic solution via an international conference had been considered.[10] All this, of course, is far from what M. Reynaud actually discussed on the date in question. A rather piercing light is thrown on what was probably Reynaud's state of mind on 26 May by the testimony given the Parliamentary Commission in 1951 by Colonel de Villelume, who as *directeur* of Reynaud's *cabinet de Défense Nationale* had considerable influence on him at this time. Along with Captain de Margerie, he had accompanied the Premier to London, though he was not present at his meetings with the English. Villelume claims that on the 26th Reynaud was in favor of an armistice and had gone to London especially to speak about it. The day before, the Colonel had advised Reynaud to draw certain conclusions from the military situation, respecting which no reestablishment was possible: "So long as we parley before our fate is sealed [he had said], we can still hope to save something. But if we present ourselves around an empty table, our last cards having been played, the conditions which will be imposed on us will obviously be a lot worse. I believe that it is necessary to sound Italy with a view to a mediation." This then was the real purpose of Reynaud's trip: to propose that the Allies *jointly* ask the Italians for their intervention on behalf of an armistice.[11]

Churchill's point of view, predictably enough, was that the British were not ready to give in on any account and that they would rather go down fighting than be enslaved to Hitler; furthermore, they were confident that they had a good chance of surviving a German onslaught.[12] Therefore France must stay in the war. Such, at any rate, was the interpretation placed by the Prime Minister on the first of the Chiefs of Staff reports he had received dealing with "a certain eventuality" (the situation that would arise if the French dropped out of the war); the War Cabinet had not yet had a chance to study this paper (it was being circulated), although they *had* been given the COS memo on Reynaud's visit, a possibly significant bit of shuffling which no doubt helped Churchill to control his cabinet.[13]

While the French Premier waited at Admiralty House, Churchill conveyed the gist of their discussion to his colleagues, who met in the early afternoon. He himself "doubted whether anything would come of an approach to Italy, but said that the matter was one which the War Cabinet would have to consider."[14] The subject had actually come up earlier when the War Cabinet met in the morning. At that time Lord Halifax reported on the conversation he had had the preceding day with the Italian Ambassador. This had been initiated by Halifax, the ultimate purpose of the exchange being not only a projected (though still undefined) bribe to Italy but also an indirect peace feeler towards Germany, and had been undertaken simultaneously with an urgent appeal to President Roosevelt asking him to use his influence with Mussolini in order to induce the latter to organize an international conference.[15] To Signor Bastianini's fatuous claim on this occasion that "Mussolini's principal wish was to secure peace in Europe" the Foreign Secretary had replied that peace and security were the Allies' main objects too and that they would "be prepared to consider any proposals which might lead to this," provided their liberty and independence were assured. However, Churchill's feeling at this morning meeting was that peace and security could be achieved only at the unacceptable price of German domination of Europe; furthermore, he was opposed to any negotiations which might lead to a derogation of British rights and power.[16] Nevertheless, in the afternoon he suggested that Lord Halifax should see Reynaud to go over the specifics the French had in mind.

The substance of Reynaud's plan of approach to Mussolini, as summarized by Halifax, was that the Allies should give an undertaking to Signor Mussolini that if he would cooperate in obtaining a settlement of all European questions, which would safeguard the independence and security of the Allies and serve as a basis for a just and durable peace in Europe, Britain and France would at once discuss with him, and attempt to solve, those problems in which Mussolini was primarily interested; further, that the Allies should request Mussolini to state in secret just what these interests were. If Italy remained neutral and the desired peace conference was arranged, Great Britain and France would then do their best to meet Mussolini's wishes.[17] More precisely, as Reynaud states directly, their offers "should deal with the status of Gibraltar, Malta and the Suez as regards Britain, and Djibouti and Tunisia as regards France."[18] In the opinion of the French, British agreement to the internationalization of the three Mediterranean possessions in question was a sine qua non for the opening of such negotiations.

Before leaving, Reynaud also met with Churchill (again), Chamberlain, Attlee (Lord Privy Seal), and Eden. According to Reynaud, Lord Halifax, without committing his government to precise offers, had "expressed his willingness to suggest to Mussolini that, if Italy would agree to collaborate with France and Britain in establishing a peace which would safeguard the independence of these two countries . . . the Allies would be prepared to discuss with him the claims of Italy in the Mediterranean and, in particular, those which concerned the outlets of this sea."[19] However, the other members of the War Cabinet, Churchill intimates, were in principle opposed to any concessions, feeling that such offers would be useless because Mussolini would imagine that he could win more for himself by entering the war on the side of a victorious Germany than he could possibly acquire by peaceful negotiations. They were inclined to believe that Mussolini would only understand a policy of strength and therefore thought more in terms of bringing the war home to the Italian people by means of bombing as soon as Mussolini opened hostilities.[20]

Thus, although Halifax appeared to be sympathetic, Reynaud did not succeed in wresting any promises from the British. He was to be given an answer the next day, after the War Cabinet had had a chance to discuss the matter. But he was under no illusions as to what he might expect. On his return to Paris that evening Reynaud told Baudouin: "The only one who understands is Halifax, who is clearly worried about the future, and realizes that some European solution must be reached. [But] Churchill is always hectoring, and Chamberlain undecided." Concerning the specifics of the projected approach to Mussolini, Reynaud claimed that "Halifax agreed, but Churchill took refuge behind the War Cabinet."[21] Reynaud also reported his sense of failure respecting his mission to London to the Vice-President of the Council, Camille Chautemps, the next day. According to the latter, Reynaud "had spoken without reticence [to the British] and had exposed all aspects of the problem. But he had found no echo in the thought of the Prime Minister and concluded by saying that we would have 'to drink the cup to the dregs.' " The British Ambassador, who also saw Reynaud on May 27, "found him very depressed and saying that he would now soon be swept away and his place taken by those who had wished to make peace."[22]

In the informal discussions that followed Reynaud's departure on the 26th, the two options open to the British Government were outlined and defended respectively by Mr. Churchill and Lord Halifax. The Prime Minister thought that the British were not in the same position as the French, as they still had certain powers of resistance and attack available to them; besides, the French were more likely to be offered decent conditions by Germany than were the British. "If France could not defend herself, it was better that she should get out of the war rather than that she should drag us into a settlement which involved intolerable terms." There might even be certain advantages to France's bowing out before being broken up, if only she could retain the position of a strong neutral. Nevertheless, Churchill hoped that France would hang on. He was afraid of being maneuvered into a position of weakness in which, before having fought seriously, they invited Mussolini "to go to Herr Hitler and ask him to treat us nicely." He thought there was no real possibility of getting out of their present difficulties, for any German terms would certainly stipulate an end to their rearmament efforts. However, the Prime Minister did not altogether reject the idea of an approach to Mussolini. Much would depend on what proportion of the BEF could be brought back from France; therefore it was best to decide nothing for the present.[23]

The Foreign Secretary's argument was based on his belief that considerations of the worsening balance of power on the continent could not but be alarming to Mussolini. Therefore, he thought it desirable to allow France "to try out the possibilities of European equilibrium." There would in any case be no harm in making the attempt, as they could always refuse to consider any outrageous terms. Finally, Lord Halifax "thought that if we got to the point of discussing the terms of a general settlement and found that we could obtain terms which did not postulate the destruction of our independence, we should be foolish not to accept them."[24] Both men were agreed, however, that an approach along the lines proposed by Reynaud would have little chance of succeeding.

Overnight the Prime Minister's position hardened. When the War Cabinet met the next morning (May 27) to consider the reports the Chiefs of Staff had submitted earlier, Churchill challenged these as exaggerating the dangers before the country. Their conclusions had been based on an estimate of German air strength which gave the enemy an advantage of 4:1. Mr. Churchill thought the true proportion closer to $2\frac{1}{2}$:1.[25] Thus, when the War Cabinet reassembled during the afternoon of the 27th to discuss the French proposal, the divergence between the Prime Minister and the Foreign Secretary was even greater. Of this meeting, Halifax wrote in his diary:

At the 4.30 Cabinet, we had a long and rather confused discussion about, nominally, the approach to Italy, but also largely about general policy in the event of things going really badly in France. I thought Winston talked the most frightful rot, also Greenwood, and after bearing it for some time I said exactly what I thought of them, adding that, if that was really their view, and if it came to the point, our ways must separate. . . . But it does drive me to despair when he [Churchill] works himself up into a passion of emotion when he ought to make his brain think and reason.[26]

What the Foreign Secretary was referring to was that Churchill now expressed himself adamantly against an approach which Mussolini was sure to view with contempt and which moreover ran the risk of ruining the integrity of their moral position on the home front. "The approach proposed was not only futile, but involved . . . a deadly danger." If the French would not go on with the war, let them give up. The British could best help Reynaud by letting him know that whatever happened in France *they* would fight on to the end. Even if they were beaten, they would be no worse off than if they were to abandon the struggle while their prestige was at its nadir. Mr. Churchill thought the whole maneuver was intended to so mire them down in negotiations that they would not be able to turn back.[27]

Lord Halifax disagreed. He could not recognize any resemblance between what he had proposed and the suggestion, made by Attlee, that an approach to Mussolini would be tantamount to suing for terms. He reminded the Prime Minister that on the previous day he had shown himself not unwilling to discuss terms provided they did not affect matters vital to the independence and essential strength of the country, that he had even admitted "he would be thankful to get out of our present difficulties on such terms," but that he now seemed to suggest that under no conditions would he contemplate any course except fighting to a finish. To the Foreign Secretary's mind, the future of the country turned on whether enemy bombing succeeded in knocking out their aircraft factories. Halifax was prepared to take that risk if their independence was at stake but, if it was not, "he would think it right to accept an offer which would save the country from avoidable disaster." He had previously conceded that the whole issue was probably academic in that they were unlikely to receive any offer which would not come up against their fundamental conditions. Churchill's response was that he "thought it unnecessary to widen the discussion by including an issue which was unreal and unlikely to arise." The most Halifax could get from Churchill was an admission that—in the event of France collapsing and Hitler offering terms to both Allied powers—though he would not join the French in asking for such, "if he were told what the terms offered were, he would be prepared to consider them."[28]

The War Cabinet as a whole agreed that they should not solicit terms from Germany. Most also believed that an approach to Mussolini "would be positively damaging to the interests of Great Britain" and, further, that it "was most unlikely to have any practical effect." Nevertheless, for diplomatic reasons, it seemed advisable not to give the French an outright refusal. Therefore, for the moment, delay appeared to be the best policy, and Sir Ronald Campbell in Paris was instructed accordingly.[29]

In the meantime the French Ambassador had told Lord Halifax that Reynaud regarded it as "a matter of great urgency" to give "geographical precision" to the terms of the approach to Mussolini. To Halifax's statement that the War Cabinet would oppose this suggestion, M. Corbin had replied none too subtly that "he would not like it to be thought that, if certain action had been taken, France might have been able to continue the struggle."[30] The pressure was on.

In fact, in its anxiety to leave no stone unturned to prevent Italy's entry into the war, the French Council of Ministers on the night of May 27 decided to make Rome some concrete offers of its own, without subordinating these proposals to corresponding British offers, though the French were to keep the British informed of their negotiations. The Foreign Ministry's projected offer to the Italian Government envisaged concessions relating to the coast of French Somaliland—the port of Djibouti and the Addis Ababa railway; possible rectification of the Tuniso-Libyan frontier; cession of a large stretch of territory between the Libyan hinterland and the Gulf of Guinea; or alternatively some sort of Franco-Italian condominium in Tunisia. M. Charles-Roux, Secretary-General of the Ministry of Foreign Affairs, who believed these offers far too generous and hoped the British would object to them, not only warned against alienating England by isolated diplomatic initiatives but insisted that London be consulted before Rome was approached. Therefore, on the 28th, the Quai d'Orsay sounded out the British on the opportuneness of the French proposition. But some ministers, especially de Monzie, who thought that with the surrender of the Belgians the time for treating had arrived, had questioned the need to align French policy with British, and, as Reynaud later told Jeanneney, a rupture had only narrowly been averted.[31]

Opposition to the French proposal, both to the general idea of calling upon Mussolini to mediate and to any specific concessions that might be involved, seems to have crystallized within the British Government, or at least within the mind of Winston Churchill, by May 28. That afternoon, after giving a frank account of the situation in France to all ministers of cabinet rank outside the War Cabinet, Churchill told his assembled colleagues: "I have thought carefully in these last days whether it was part of my duty to consider entering into negotiations with That Man." But, he concluded, after evoking what a Pax Germanica would mean for British sovereignty, "I am convinced that every man of you would rise up and tear me down from my place if I were for one moment to contemplate parley or surrender. If this long island story of ours is to end at last, let it end only when each one of us lies choking in his own blood upon the ground." According to Hugh Dalton, who recorded the scene, upon this ringing call to arms "there were loud cries of approval all round the table" and "no one expressed even the faintest flicker of dissent."[32]

Thus strengthened, Churchill telegraphed Reynaud that night that the War Cabinet did not feel that this was the right moment for an approach to the Italian dictator. With the rescue of their northern armies most problematical, not only were they bereft of any bargaining position with Hitler, but the effect of such an offer on the morale of the British public would be very dangerous and the French proposal could serve only to confirm Mussolini in his aggressive designs by persuading him that the Allies were on their last legs. Furthermore, President Roosevelt's attempts to intervene on their behalf had been rudely rebuffed by Rome and as yet there was no response to the approach made by Lord Halifax to the Italian Ambassador on May 25.[33] Thus, without denying the French Government the right to formulate a proposal of its own, the British indicated that they desired not to be associated with it.[34]

Reynaud at this juncture—May 29—favored abandoning negotiations with the Italians, but Daladier, now Minister of Foreign Affairs, together with Anatole de Monzie, Camille Chautemps, and Paul Baudouin (who felt that England should be forced to accept the proposal to internationalize the entrances to the Mediterranean in a way that would satisfy the demands of Italy), persisted in their desperate efforts to placate Mussolini (and, where de Monzie and Baudouin were concerned, to obtain a conference through Italian mediation that would result in peace). Ignoring the warning of Sir Ronald Campbell concerning the danger of unilateral action, Daladier and his associates pressed for the immediate opening of direct negotiations with Italy and even managed to concoct a note which, by its hints concerning the Mediterranean and the impression it gave of France's willingness to disregard the ties binding her to England, alarmed French Foreign Ministry officials.[35]

Of this first draft of the note that was ultimately to be submitted to the Italian Ambassador, Charles-Roux, who now strongly opposed a démarche, commented that "it revealed too much of a tendency to promise what did not lie within our own power to carry out." He therefore called attention to the fact that France "had no jurisdiction over Malta or Gibraltar and that, if it were not completely forbidden in diplomacy to dispose of another's property, at least it was necessary that the third party should not be an ally whose aid one was invoking at the very same time."[36] Charles-Roux succeeded in having the terms of the text modified, as well as in having it sent to London for approval, especially after General Weygand had agreed that France's need of England's help was so great that "nothing must be done that might result in the least weakening in Franco-British collaboration."[37] And inasmuch as the Foreign Office raised no objections, the French note, which in its final form avoided concrete offers, was delivered to Signor Guariglia on May 30.[38] Thus France, whose ambassador in Rome had already warned that any offer would now be ill-received, did not spare itself one further humiliation; as could have been predicted, the French proposal to Mussolini was insultingly ignored, Count Ciano commenting to François-Poncet on June 1 that they had "no answer to make" because they considered themselves "to all intents and purposes at war with you."[39] Apparently Daladier and Co. did not recognize the futility of their gesture or, as Alfred Fabre-Luce points out, that there could be "no Munich after a Sedan!"[40]

# Stiffening the French

THE Anglo-French negotiations respecting Italy, if they did not actually impair relations between the Allies, certainly served to distance them further by accentuating England's growing self-confidence and readiness to "go it alone" compared with France's increasing tendency to clutch at straws.

What Reynaud had said on 26 May of course caused grave concern in London, for it meant not only that the British were faced with the prospect of the Battle of France being lost, but that they must also consider as a strong possibility France's neutralization and the shift in the balance of power this would entail. This put them in more of a quandary then ever. The problem up to this point had been primarily a military calculation: how to balance the needs of the battle in progress against the minimal requirements of defense at home. A diplomatic, or public relations, factor now had to be added to the equation: how little could be given the French while still allowing the British Government to maintain some sort of hold or influence over French policy in the future? And this calculus was in turn complicated by the fact that the British did not at first seem to know exactly what would be in their best interests.

According to Sir Alexander Cadogan, Churchill, after talking with Reynaud on the 26th, "seemed to think we might almost be better off if France *did* pull out and we could concentrate on defence here." Cadogan himself came round to this view a few days later when he noted that, by keeping the French in the fight and continuing air protection at the expense of their own, they were forced to fall between two stools. They should give them a token perhaps, but since that would still not prevent the French from reviling them, all in all he preferred to "cut loose and concentrate on [the] defence of these islands—come the 4 quarters of the world in arms!"[1] But this was not Churchill's considered opinion—though a certain ambivalence would remain. However vital the defense of the United Kingdom was, there were other things at stake as well and therefore it was necessary to prolong French resistance as long as possible and to keep them officially in the war.

With this in mind, Churchill tried to make it quite clear that Britain would fight on in any case, and this unshakable determination was to become the keynote of all Anglo-French negotiations in the next three weeks. Because few Frenchmen believed that England had the capacity to withstand German arms alone, it was vital to make the French realize Britain's resolve, for it could affect their own decision. To this end, Major-General Edward Spears, whom Churchill had appointed his personal representative with Reynaud, was instructed to assure one and all in France that Britain was going on and that the Prime Minister had been advised by his experts that the country had the power to do so. Spears was also instructed to resist all suggestions by Reynaud of "cutting out" and to remind him of France's duty to continue the war and of his own personal duty not to hand over responsibility to those who intended to give up the struggle, which would have been a roundabout way of betraying England as well as France. But, if Reynaud's personal courage and resolution were bolstered by these daily pep talks, it was increasingly difficult for others not to be engulfed by Pétain's pessimistic belief that the war was lost, that resistance was futile, and that peace terms should be sought as soon as possible, or to counter his claim that Great Britain's contribution to the war was so small that it was not entitled to a say in the matter.[2]

Churchill always had the highest regard for his chosen emissary, not only because of his fluency in the French language—which some Foreign Office critics accused Spears of speaking "rather better than English"—but because Spears could be trusted more than anyone else to press Churchill's personal policy. Spears saw himself as a great Francophile, though it is hard to reconcile this self-image with the belief he expressed to the British Ambassador in Paris, shortly after Munich, that France had thereby been "so completely disgraced that no right-thinking Englishman should shake a Frenchman's hand." In any event, the qualities of sympathy or understanding are seldom apparent in the account he has left of his mission, which at times reads almost like a primer in British chauvinism and self-righteousness. The one thing the unsubtle Spears most assuredly was not was a diplomat. Pierre Varillon writes of him as a "disquieting person who, ever since 1914, could be seen to surface each time the shadow of misfortune fell across France." During World War I (when Spears was a high-ranking liaison officer) Marshal Foch had not liked him, while Paul Cambon, France's Ambassador to London, had denounced him as a dangerous intriguer who insinuated himself everywhere and who spent his time sending off bales of reports to the War Office.[3] Reputedly an agent of the Intelligence Service, his role in 1939–40 was not essentially different. But since someone who *would* intervene in French politics in an attempt to influence French policy was precisely what Mr. Churchill wanted, presumably Spears's knack for irritating people would not have been considered a liability. In a sense, Spears served as an alter ego to the Prime Minister, allowing Churchill to play the compassionate statesman while *he* busied himself with the rough and tumble of international politics.

Reynaud was in something of a dilemma from which there appeared to be no convenient exit. Camille Chautemps is probably correct in saying that from May 27 on Reynaud "considered the indefinite prolongation of hostilities as chimerical."[4] But with the failure of his attempt to embroil the British and French jointly in negotiations with Italy, to say nothing of Mussolini's lack of interest, his options were dwindling. He was publicly committed to the prosecution of the war against Hitler and both politically and personally committed to the Anglo-French alliance, which he did not wish to jeopardize in any way. Yet in late May, as reported by Ambassador Bullitt, he had no great faith in his ally's capacity and felt that "Britain would be unable to survive a separate peace for more than a few weeks."[5] In conformity with Mr. Churchill, he was willing to drop the Italian maneuver as inopportune, but apparently thought that the time might be ripe for another approach after the Somme-Aisne front collapsed.[6] Certainly he was quite explicit in letting the British know that if the new front were broken the continued assistance of the French Army would be most difficult, if not impossible. In fact, hints of this nature abounded, but precisely for what purpose—whether to warn the British of what he thought was inevitable and thereby to gain their understanding in advance, or in order to extort as much help from them as possible so as to avoid such an outcome—is not altogether clear. It is quite possible that M. Reynaud's purposes fluctuated with his moods; they certainly seemed to fluctuate according to his interlocutor.[7]

The British Ambassador, at any rate, thought that Reynaud was "hardly up to the herculean task of galvanising his rather flabby team (always excepting M. Mandel, Dautry, and perhaps Campinchi) into activity." Amongst those who were aware of the gravity of the situation, the Ambassador believed that there was not a single Frenchman who did not feel, even if he would not admit it, that France was beaten. Yet Campbell could not make up his mind whether Reynaud was "wholly sincere" when he expressed his inflexible resolve to fight on to the bitter end, "or whether at some moment he would allow himself to be set aside and a Government installed that would be ready to make a separate peace." Campbell sensed that Reynaud's stout-hearted professions came "from the head rather than from the heart" and therefore was not entirely convinced by them, but even then he did not know whether he was doing the French Premier an injustice.[8]

If Baudouin's minutes are to be trusted, then the French Premier, at least towards the end of May, was not so much opposed to an armistice per se as to the *kind* of terms he expected the Germans to propose. On May 29, for instance, he told Baudouin that if the French Army were completely defeated, he was not opposed to a request for a suspension of hostilities, but that he was "convinced that the enemy would impose dishonourable conditions . . . and it would then be necessary to fight in the Breton redoubt." If anything, his conviction that it would be impossible for the government to negotiate with the Germans, either because they would refuse to treat or because they would put forward unacceptable conditions, incompatible with the honor and vital interests of France, grew stronger with time, as did his belief that it would be imprudent for the French to cut themselves off from their allies.[9] In fact, all things considered, it looks very much as if, with every other option virtually sealed off, Reynaud had by the time the battle commenced talked himself round to his original position—war to the bitter end. But to combat the pressure he was up against daily he needed all the support he could get from the British, and this he did not feel was always forthcoming.

For instance, quite apart from the important material aid he was requesting and not receiving, Reynaud felt let down by Britain's phlegmatic response to the Belgian capitulation on the night of May 27, an event which could not but have a stunning effect on the French, adding to their sense of isolation and intensifying the defeatist sentiment among them. To counteract this, to inspire anger in the place of hopelessness, the French Premier on 28 May had vigorously and publicly condemned the action of King Leopold, and he believed he had a right to expect no less from the British Prime Minister. Churchill, on the other hand, initially suspended his judgment on the responsibility of the King, the British press and BBC being asked to steer clear of the subject, and this difference in attitude towards Belgium's retirement from the war was to rankle for days until on June 4 the question was finally settled by Churchill's speech in the House of Commons.[10] It was obvious, as General Spears, the British Ambassador, and many others realized, that the French Government hoped to gain something from the Belgian defection—a scapegoat and the chance to distract popular attention from the shortcomings of the French High Command, as well perhaps as a convenient explanation for the Allied evacuation then under way.[11] But, in addition, it was essential for the sake of the Anglo-French alliance to have the public, both British and French, brand Leopold's withdrawal from battle and his refusal to head a government in exile as a shameful betrayal of his allies and as a political surrender to the enemy. Thus, by characterizing the Belgian capitulation in the blackest possible terms, Paul Reynaud must have hoped in some measure to embarrass Weygand's and Pétain's efforts towards the same end.

Weygand, however, was not to be deterred. At their morning meeting on May 29 Weygand handed Reynaud a note in which he advised the French Government to plan in advance the vital decisions it would have to take if the French Army's present defense positions along the Somme and the Aisne were finally broken. He warned that the French Army might be powerless to stop an enemy thrust against the Paris region, where 70 per cent of the nation's war industries were concentrated. "In this case," he stated, "France would be incapable of continuing a struggle which ensured a co-ordinated defence of her territory." Pointing to the necessity of getting from the British all the assistance in their power, Weygand added that "the British Government should know that a moment might come after which France would find herself, against her will, unable to put up a fight which would be of any military use in the protection of her soil. This moment would be marked by the final breakthrough of the positions, in which the French Armies have been ordered to fight without thought of retreat."[12] According to Reynaud, this memorandum was accompanied by commentaries from Pétain and Weygand on the need for soliciting an armistice in this likelihood.

To this Reynaud replied in a memo on the 29th: "Because, in the eventuality previously mentioned, the whole of the national territory could no longer be defended does not necessarily mean that we would be able to suspend hostilities in circumstances which would be compatible with the honour and vital interests of France."[13] Instead, he asked Weygand to examine the possibility of constructing a national defensive redoubt on the Breton peninsula which could be used as a seat of government[14] in the event that the enemy was making rapid thrusts throughout France; he also informed Weygand of his intention to raise two classes of conscripts which could be sent to continue the war in North Africa.

Reynaud and Weygand were not yet at odds—this would occur only *after* the battle—but the polar positions associated with each *were* by late May in process of formation. Reynaud, of course, recognized that as Supreme Commander Weygand, with Pétain's powerful support, was in a position to influence political decisions that were outside his realm of authority and accordingly tried to limit this authority to strictly military matters. It was not easy to separate these areas of competence, however, as Reynaud discovered when seeking to implement his decisions to prepare Brittany as a stronghold and to send half a million young men to be trained and kept in North Africa. The generals and admirals could sabotage his policies at every turn and thereby transform the government's efforts into futile gestures.

Although the British, as a result of Reynaud's representations on May 26 and of General Spears's intelligence work, were aware of the forces developing in France, and were themselves considering decisions to be made in the event of France's withdrawal from the war, officially relations between the two countries revolved about the immediate problems at hand—the deliverance of the Anglo-French forces in Flanders and the implementation of the French line on the Somme in preparation for the coming battle. Before the decisive battle, the political machinations of Weygand, Pétain, and their coterie were confined largely to private conversations and could not intrude into formal discussions between the Allies. Bitterness, recriminations, and disillusionment there certainly were, but for the present the dissolution of the alliance was still only a contingent possibility—depending on the capacity of the French to resist the German attack. The Supreme Council that met on May 31 dealt only with practical differences between the two nations. The common aim was still to stop the enemy—not to stop the war. As Weygand notes, it did not give rise to a sincere and realistic discussion on the essential questions, which, after the events in Flanders, were threatening to impair the solidarity of the alliance. Or, as Baudouin puts it, rather more bluntly, whether France was to continue the struggle regardless of the cost, even if useless and expensive in both lives and money, was a problem that did not find its way onto the agenda.[15]

That the British took cognizance of the precariousness of the alliance, however, is revealed by Churchill's plea on this occasion for the maintenance of "the closest, the most trustful, the most complete unity." Churchill's vow that the British Government and people would go on to the end, whatever the issue of the battle in France or however great the hardships, was in reality an attempt to convince the French of Britain's confidence in the ultimate outcome of the war and to dissipate all thought they might have of abandoning the struggle. But, as General Spears reports, Churchill's moving declaration was heard only "by a tiny audience of men who, with one or two exceptions, were already half enemies."[16] In fact, Baudouin became convinced during the Prime Minister's closing remarks that the British were even then coolly assuming that the French would succumb in the struggle and that they had already put on mourning in preparation.[17]

Though, of course, the word "armistice" was not mentioned at the May 31 conference, in an informal discussion following the meeting, one Frenchman, unidentified by Churchill, ventured that "a continuance of military reverses might in certain eventualities enforce a modification of foreign policy upon France." To this thinly veiled hint that France might embrace neutrality, General Spears, lent authority by Churchill's presence, bluntly warned Pétain that such a policy "would not only mean blockade, but *bombardment* of all French ports in German hands."[18] In this way, Spears hoped to make Pétain come to grips with the terrible consequences that would result from the surrender and separate peace he was contemplating. The British realized that only by warning the French of their unshakable resolve to fight on, no matter who fell by the way, and of their capacity for ruthlessness in pursuit of victory was there any chance of jogging the defeatists out of their simple-minded dream of quietly laying down their arms and finding themselves at peace.

# Always Hungry,
# Always Asking for More

THE first few days of June were spent in frantic attempts to put the French defenses in order. With only 62 divisions in line bolstered by a few light armored units to face the 138 divisions disposed of by the enemy, and little by way of an air force, the French were forced to rely on the British to help redress the balance. Constantly goaded by Weygand, Reynaud did not let a day pass without pressing Churchill for an increase in assistance by British forces, especially that of the RAF. Although Reynaud was to write after the war that "Churchill would have committed the gravest of faults if he had sacrificed all his air strength in the Battle of France, when this was going to be indispensable to him several weeks later in order to defend Britain against German aerial attack," at the time he was entirely preoccupied by the battle which was being waged to cover Paris.[1]

The real strength of the French Air Force at this time was somewhat problematic, depending on which sources one credits, but was undoubtedly not fully appreciated by the British, whose complaints centered largely on its "lethargy," its disorganization, its refusal to make use of whatever aircraft *were* immediately to hand, and its overdependence on the RAF. Testimony introduced by Daladier at the Riom trial, held under Vichy auspices to discredit the post-1936 governments of the Third Republic, subsequently revealed that on July 28, 1940, the French Air Force had more than 2,000 first-line aircraft available in either unoccupied France or North Africa, the implication being that they could have been used in action earlier. Yet, as Pierre Cot, Air Minister from 1936 to 1938, points out, less than 1,000 planes (at any one time) were actually used during the Battle of France; thus, he claims, the High Command was employing only 45 per cent of its first-line strength in the battle that was to decide France's fate.[2] But obviously, the High Command did not include reserves in its day-to-day calculations.

On June 3 Weygand reported to the War Committee that the French were losing 33 planes a day, of which only half were being replaced. Yet, as of May 30, General Vuillemin's statistics showed that since the start of the battle on 10 May 660 aircraft had been lost, while new deliveries during the same period amounted to 571. Laurent-Eynac, Minister for Air, told the War Committee the same day that there had even been an increase in French air strength since early May, except for fighters, which had declined by 150 machines to a current total of 350; bombers now numbered 186, training planes 166. The need for fighter protection was clearly urgent, but otherwise the French may even have been better off at the front than earlier.[3]

Vuillemin claimed that at the end of May the British possessed 650 fighters and 240 bombers. Basil Collier, in *The Defence of the United Kingdom,* puts Britain's first-line fighter strength even higher: at over 700 fighters, of which some 600 were Hurricanes or Spitfires. The official historian of the RAF, however, claims that on June 4 Fighter Command had only 466 operationally serviceable aircraft, of which 331 were Hurricanes and Spitfires. Yet Churchill told the War Cabinet on June 4 that they now had about 45 fighter squadrons—which was the equivalent of some 720 machines.[4] If the higher figures are accepted, this would mean that in combination the British and French forces, *if* deployed, could have met the Luftwaffe's fighter strength during the second phase of the campaign with a slight numerical advantage, and, if the lower figures are accepted, at only slightly under parity. Both French and British at this time were claiming higher kill rates than the enemy. Furthermore, British output was rising so fast that of the nearly 500 fighters that were lost in France during May and June all would be replaced by the end of June.[5] What was not known at this stage were the terrible wastage rates suffered by the German Air Force, which in many units ranged as high as 50 per cent, and the fact that Allied aircraft production had started outdistancing German production in April 1940.[6]

Without benefit of statistical hindsight, however, both British and French had to arrive at their decisions on a different basis. The overestimation of German air strength and capacity had inspired in both partners an initial unwillingness to make use of their reserves— a strategy the French especially might profitably have reevaluated during the course of the battle. The British had already made their basic decisions regarding their own minimal needs back in mid-May. Now, in early June, the decision as to how much assistance could be made available depended on three things: (1) the orientation of the coming German attack; (2) the distance from the new battlefield of English air bases; and (3) the security British air forces could count on once in France. Already on May 31 the Prime Minister had told the French that "if the English fighters had been able to take part with ease in the battle of Dunkirk, it did not follow that the same would be the case when fighting began on the Somme. In fact the Somme was the limit for home-based planes."[7] And the knowledge that of the 660 French aircraft lost up until June 1, over half had been destroyed either on the ground or by accident[8] could hardly have reassured the British as to the wisdom of transferring their squadrons to French airfields. If an amalgamation of British and French air power had failed of achievement in May, by June, with the Germans in control of the Channel coast and the French faltering politically, such a hope was quite out of the question.

On June 2, in a telegram to Churchill, Reynaud drew attention to the necessity for powerful and immediate British assistance in the common cause. Observing that the BEF was supposed to be brought to a strength of fourteen divisions by this date, he requested the immediate dispatch of the three available divisions and, in addition, the reshipment as soon as possible of re-formed units of tried fighting value rescued from Dunkirk. Second, he asked that British bomber aircraft supply, before and during the battle about to be engaged, an assistance at least as powerful as that which they contributed during the battle in northern France. This collaboration, he stated, could be given without the bombers being based on France. Third, he asked that British fighter aircraft give even greater help than what they had supplied before and demanded that they should be based on French airfields for the duration of the battle.[9]

On June 5, at their daily conference, Weygand was quick to place on record that the battle had begun without France's having received from her ally the reinforcements asked for. That same morning Reynaud received Churchill's reply to his message of 2 June. In this note Churchill emphasized (1) that the elements of the BEF saved from the northern front could be sent back into battle only after being fully reequipped and reorganized; but that two divisions were ready to be sent over within the next fortnight and a third lacked only artillery; (2) that the fighter force had suffered greatly in the last battle, particularly in terms of pilots lost, and that this factor should be considered with regard to the scale of help Britain could lend in the immediate future; but that nevertheless, the three squadrons of fighter aircraft then in France would immediately be brought up to full strength; and (3) that the six squadrons of bomber aircraft in France would also be brought up to strength, and that the rest of British bomber strength, though remaining based on England, would continue to participate as in the past, priority being given to intervention in the battle itself and to attacks on objectives chosen by the French High Command.[10]

Fundamentally, according to Sir Alexander Cadogan, the decision "*not* to fall between two stools and not to send [British] fighter protection over to France" had been made by the War Cabinet on June 3. Again Air Marshal Dowding had been in attendance, graphs of wastage rates in hand, to press his point of view when the reply to the French appeal was up for consideration. He insisted that their fighter operations must be regulated in accordance with industry's rate of output so as to ensure that they did not squander the capital of their fighter aircraft. This time he was assured that his squadrons would not be further depleted, even though he expected to be as strong as ever within the month. Churchill, however, would persist in his efforts to do more.[11]

The Chiefs of Staff in their June 3 report to the War Cabinet had produced some powerful arguments against sending further support of any kind to the French: (1) the defeatism of the French leadership; (2) the improbability of the French holding the Somme-Aisne line; (3) the small difference the transfer of a few British forces would make; (4) the need at home of both the BEF and a strengthened fighter defense; and (5) the expectation that any forces dispatched to France could be written off in advance. Against the putative advantages of taking a toll of German bombers while they were still engaged in France and thereby proportionately reducing the threat to their own security had to be placed the definite disadvantage of the heavier wastage rates incurred by fighters operating out of French bases compared with those operating from England. And together with their own imperative defense needs had to be considered whatever military, geographical, and political assistance the French by staying in the war could still render them opposed to the very real damage they could do by bowing out. It was this last consideration which ultimately determined a recommendation of some very limited reinforcements in spite of the view of the Chiefs of Staff that "the despatch of any forces to France at this juncture must further increase these risks [to the United Kingdom] to a dangerous degree. Nevertheless," they concluded, "the military disadvantages of the consequences of a flat negative to the request of the French Prime Minister leads us to the conclusion that we must accept the additional risks involved in assisting our Ally." Significantly, the Joint Planners in their preliminary study had recognized that Germany might "achieve her aim of separating the Allies as it must be well known that France will claim a greater measure of help than we are either capable of giving or prepared to provide."[12]

In his disappointment with Churchill's summation of this Reynaud could not resist remarking to General Spears, the bearer of the bad tidings, that "if it had been necessary to prolong the air battle over Dunkirk to save British troops, the RAF would have continued fighting in spite of its losses."[13] He also bitterly criticized Churchill's declaration to the Commons the previous day that "before all else the territorial defence of Great Britain must be organized."[14]

Reynaud at once replied to Churchill to urge him to speed up the dispatch of the British divisions, especially in view of the German offensive launched that morning, and also to note his rejection of General Vuillemin's urgent request for the immediate dispatch to France of ten fighter squadrons, to be followed as soon as possible by ten additional squadrons, in other words, half the fighter aircraft based in England. Reynaud stressed the fact that if British fighter aircraft did not give the French Army the assistance demanded by Vuillemin the battle would be lost and Paris occupied by the enemy. "The British Government," he concluded, "is aware what the consequences of the loss of this battle and the capture of the capital will be."[15] This dark hint was inserted at the suggestion of Pétain who, along with many others, felt that resistance should not be continued if Paris fell. In fact, on hearing how little the British would do to help, the Marshal had said to Reynaud: "Then there is nothing left but to make peace, and if you don't want to do it, you can leave it to me."[16]

Pétain already nurtured the liveliest misgivings regarding British intentions; he thought that with all their troops back on home soil, most of their planes stationed in England, and a still dominant fleet, Britain must now be preparing to make a compromise peace with Hitler.[17] The fact that England was "selfishly" withholding its air force and reserve divisions from the great battle about to be waged was only proof, as the Marshal told Ambassador Bullitt, that "the

French government would do its utmost to come to terms immediately with Germany, whatever might happen to England."[18]

On June 5 all minds dwelt on the possible consequences the loss of the battle would have. Weygand bluntly told Reynaud that if the battle were lost and France overrun the most courageous course would be to open negotiations with the enemy. Reynaud denied that this was a realistic alternative and insisted that, if necessary, the government should leave France. In spite of Weygand's belief that a "redoubt" in Brittany would have no military value, the Premier nevertheless ordered General Colson to continue with preparations for its construction. This idea together with his plan for sending two new classes of recruits to North Africa, which he had raised several times since May 29 and which the generals objected to on the grounds of a lack of arms, of equipment, and of transport, constituted Reynaud's stab at a strategic alternative to Weygand's traditional conception of the war. However, at this turning point, Reynaud also believed he could still accomplish something by political reconstruction—his third try in four weeks—and it was to this that he devoted his principal energies on June 5.[19]

That evening Reynaud's reshuffled cabinet was complete. Intended ostensibly to consolidate the government and to strengthen the Premier's hand in the political battles he saw coming, the new lineup actually contained a little something for everyone. Defeatists such as de Monzie and Lamoureux were dropped, but so also were two ministers personally displeasing to Marshal Pétain, Sarraut and Daladier, the latter after the Foreign Affairs Committee of the Senate on May 24 had unanimously decided that the former prime minister's continued presence at the Quai d'Orsay would, in Baudouin's words, be an "insult to French diplomacy."[20] Thus Reynaud assumed the additional burden of the Ministry of Foreign Affairs. General Charles de Gaulle, fresh from his front-line command of the 4th Armored Division, was appointed Under-Secretary of State for National Defense and immediately charged with building up France's capacity to continue resistance whether on metropolitan soil or from North Africa, for which purpose he would shortly be sent to England to procure as much aid—in the air and on the ground—as was possible and to make the appropriate shipping arrangements should an evacuation overseas prove necessary.[21]

In his retention of Camille Chautemps as Vice-President of the Council and in his other appointments, however, Reynaud revealed a talent for picking disastrously; Paul Baudouin, who now became

Under-Secretary for Foreign Affairs, as well as remaining Secretary to the Presidency of the Council and to the War Cabinet; Yves Bouthillier, appointed Secretary of Finance; and Jean Prouvost, the new Minister of Information, were to be the first to desert Reynaud when the time came and were to figure among those who intrigued most actively against him. As protégés of Mme de Portes (Reynaud's powerful mistress), they were members of the "Royal Household"; and many observers, even then, wondered what *they* were doing "in this *lutte à outrance* Cabinet." All in all, though the British Ambassador thought it an improvement, the new cabinet was probably not much more "firm," or anti-Munich, than the one Reynaud had started with back in March.[22] True, it largely conformed to one prescription Jules Jeanneney had given Reynaud—that their attitude towards Italy should be the touchstone for cabinet members; yet the "new" team could hardly have diminished his fears over rumors that Reynaud's firmness was specious, masking an underlying fragility, as the result of his entourage's influence (particularly that of the "financiers"). But the President of the Senate had given fair warning: the cabinet reorganization *would* be watched.[23]

In the early evening of June 5 Churchill sent his first reply to Reynaud. He complained that the British had been given no precise information (as to the nature of the assistance required or where it was needed) with which to meet a request of the French Air Force made that morning. Four bomber squadrons and two fighter squadrons were ready to strike from England, if only they were directed where. These operations were to supplement those undertaken by British forces stationed in France.[24] A later and much sharper telegram contained Churchill's reply to Reynaud's approach of the day before. In it he observed that the French divisions brought back from Dunkirk would not be fit to enter the line before the month was out,[25] whereas the British were trying to send over one of their reequipped divisions within a fortnight. He also castigated Vuillemin's letter of request as completely unreasonable and insulting, stating that it had created the worst possible impression on everyone in London and considerably increased his difficulties in securing aid for the French. Churchill again stressed that British fighter aircraft had been strained to the breaking point over Dunkirk and that their formations were still terribly mixed up. As for the French suggestion put forward earlier that day (June 5) that the air strengths of both countries be placed under a single command: it was not possible at all with regard to fighter aircraft, and only possible for the bomber forces if command were exercised by a Briton.[26] British lack of confidence in the French Command was barely concealed here.

Pent-up hostilities exploded into the open at an exceptionally stormy meeting of the War Committee the following morning. Weygand again accused the British Army of refusing to fight and of having acted on secret orders from London prior to Dunkirk, then hysterically supported the undiplomatic Vuillemin who had cast aspersions on the contributions of the RAF. Spears retaliated by insulting the French Air Force and the competence of its commander. The one beneficial result of these fireworks was the revelation that Weygand had heretofore not met Air Marshal Barratt, commanding all British air units in France, and the establishment that afternoon of liaison between the British and French with regard to the use of British aviation placed at the disposal of France. Henceforth, all British bombers, whether based in France or England, were to be employed for the purpose of the Battle of France, though nothing definite was as yet settled concerning fighter aircraft.[27]

At 5:30 p.m. on June 6 Churchill telegrammed to report that the British 52nd Division would embark for France the next day, followed by the Canadian division on June 11, and that a third division would follow as soon as possible if the French could provide artillery. He also stated that British fighters intervening that day in the battle on the Somme were refueling in France, thus enabling them to undertake sorties of longer duration.[28] For a brief moment things looked brighter, and the French leaders expressed satisfaction.

On June 7 both ambassadors added their voices in support of the French Premier, Sir Ronald Campbell suggesting in a statement intended for the Prime Minister that every German plane and pilot destroyed in France meant one less which could be used against the British Isles later—and also calling attention to the difficulties of M. Reynaud's position now that the Foreign Affairs committees in both houses of the Assembly were clamoring to be told the exact proportion of the RAF cooperating in France. M. Corbin, for his part, argued before Lord Halifax that for lack of assistance the French Air Force was kept in almost constant action and that the army was forced to abandon ground it would otherwise have held. In his view, the Germans would attack only one enemy at a time; therefore, for the sake of their collective security, both the British and French air forces should be concentrated at the point of greatest risk—France.[29]

During the day Churchill informed Reynaud that by the following day British support would amount to five full-strength fighter squadrons in France plus four fighter squadrons based on England but operating from advanced refueling stations south of the Somme.[30] He also reminded Reynaud that during the last two nights enemy aircraft had attacked England. But to Reynaud's request on the 8th for the British to throw all their forces—not just a quarter—into the battle, as the French were doing, Churchill replied firmly that the British were giving all the support they could, "short of ruining the capacity of this country to continue the war."[31]

Churchill's views on the Battle of France seem in fact to have reached definitive form by June 8. Before the Defence Committee that evening, he argued that there were two alternatives. They could regard the present battle as decisive for both France and Britain and throw in the whole of their fighter resources in an attempt to save the situation. If they failed, they should have to surrender. Or they could recognize that the present land battle, while important, would not be decisive one way or another for Great Britain. If it were lost and France was forced to submit, they could continue the struggle with good hopes of ultimate victory, provided their fighter defenses were not impaired. But if they cast them away the war would be lost, even if the front in France were stabilized, because Germany would then be free to turn its air force against England, which would be at its mercy. The Prime Minister therefore felt it would be fatal to yield to the French demands and jeopardize their own safety. The Chiefs of Staff, of course, had been convinced of this all along, but up until this point Churchill had usually argued on the other side.[32]

Thereafter, Reynaud suspended his importunate requests (eleven telegrams and seven personal phone conversations by his own reckoning), leaving General de Gaulle to pursue the subject in London. But on the results of this mission de Gaulle was obliged to report to his French colleagues on June 10, so Baudouin writes, that although the British agreed to do more than they had up to the present (by allowing eight squadrons based on England to patrol the French front every day), "Mr. Churchill had [nevertheless] flatly refused to empty England of fighters, for the battle of France was no longer of great importance in his eyes."[33] To Churchill himself de Gaulle had admitted that "it was the only decision Britain could take."[34]

# The Battle Lost

As GENERAL Weygand had feared, the Germans quickly proved their superiority over the French forces organized along the 600-kilometer line that bore his name. In spite of some attempt to develop a defense in depth, the Third Army Group could not long withstand the German armored assault launched against the length of the Somme June 5. A bad breach in the 10th Army sector on June 7, which permitted a huge mass of tanks to pour through to Forges-les-Eaux, split that army in half and thus seriously imperiled the whole Allied left wing. The consequent separation of the 51st Highland Division—Britain's only division in line—together with the French IX Corps from the rest of the 10th Army and the threat of encirclement hanging over them provided the French and British with one more occasion for dispute.

By June 7, the French were again (and unjustly) accusing the British of withdrawing on their own initiative and of refusing to obey the orders of General Robert Altmayer. Weygand, moreover, now openly referred to the British commander in question, Major-General Victor Fortune, as General "Misfortune." In actuality, the enemy breach was increased by the movement of 10th Army headquarters towards the Oise, when its own left was retiring in the opposite direction, parallel to the coast.[1]

Churchill blames the ruin of General Ihler's IX Corps and the British 51st on the French Command's dogged refusal to face facts. In spite of repeated British representations, the High Command would not allow Fortune to retreat on Rouen in time. Only after the Germans had reached the Seine (June 9), and two panzer divisions were heading for the coast to bar IX Corps' escape by way of evacua-

169

tion, were orders finally given to withdraw to Le Havre. They were too late, so that by June 10 this group was completely cut off in the Rouen-Dieppe cul-de-sac. Though the Royal Navy was able to rescue a portion of the British and French troops on the nights of June 11 and 12, 8,000 British were nevertheless compelled to surrender to Rommel in Saint-Valéry-en-Caux after French forces under Ihler's command hoisted the white flag early on the 12th. Churchill did not conceal his bitterness; on a smaller scale, it was Dunkirk all over again—only this time without the "deliverance."[2]

Meanwhile the Germans had broken both wings of the Third Army Group and on 9 June expanded their offensive eastwards into Champagne so that the battle raged from the Channel to the Argonne. On the morning of June 10, the day the French Government evacuated Paris for its temporary stopover in Touraine and the day Italy declared war, General Weygand submitted his second memorandum to Reynaud. In this he noted that the armies were now reestablishing themselves on the lower Seine, on the position guarding Paris, and along the Marne, and that this was the last line on which any effective resistance could be hoped for. Weygand warned the Prime Minister that, though the armies were still fighting and their maneuvers still coordinated, the final rupture of the French lines of defense might occur at any moment. If this should happen, he concluded, "our armies would continue to fight until their strength and means were exhausted. But their disintegration would only be a matter of time."[3] The implications of this formal memo, if not explicitly set forth, were obvious. Indeed from 7 June Weygand believed the military situation to be irreparable, had stated as much, and with the strong backing of the Marshal had insisted that the government demand an armistice.[4] But for the time being Reynaud persisted in placing his trust in the Breton redoubt and in an appeal to the United States to enter the war.

Fearing the effects of continued reverses on French morale and not wishing to leave Reynaud at the mercy of his defeatist colleagues, the British on June 10 pressed for another meeting of the Supreme War Council. Because direct telegraph and telephone lines to Paris were no longer functioning and because the British were unaware of the exact whereabouts of the French Government, such a rendezvous was arranged only with difficulty, possibly with the help of General Weygand, who welcomed an opportunity to inform Churchill of the "real situation."[5] The news reaching Weygand on the 11th was undeniably grave. In the west Paris was threatened with a double envel-

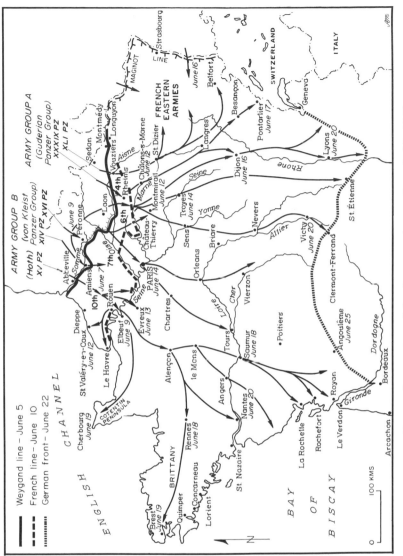

3. *France: Progression of the German advance, June 5–22, 1940.*

171

opment; in Champagne the Fourth Army Group was retreating southwards beyond Rheims; while still farther east the French units in the fortified sector were in their turn faced with encirclement. To hold the line between the sea and Longuyon the French could now muster only thirty standard divisions.

The Château de Muguet at Briare, on the Loire, where Weygand had reestablished general headquarters after leaving Vincennes, was the seat of the Anglo-French meeting which got under way the night of June 11. In this somewhat ramshackle setting, the British were represented by Churchill, Eden, Generals Dill, Ismay, and Spears; the French by Reynaud, Pétain, Generals Weygand, Georges, and de Gaulle, with Admiral Darlan and others joining the conference the next day. Little was accomplished here, but the pervasive hopelessness of the leading French spokesmen was an indicator of how far things had fallen since their last joint meeting ten days before.

Churchill wasted no time in stating his purpose in coming: it was to consider with the French "how best to carry on with the struggle which nothing could prevent the British from pursuing." This had been his position consistently, but the Prime Minister must have felt doubly justified by his knowledge that the Joint Planners believed that the British would be signing their own death warrant if they were to accept any peace proposals the Germans might make in the wake of France's collapse which resulted in a lessening of their ability to maintain the United Kingdom as a secure naval and air base or to apply economic pressure against Germany. Their conclusions, submitted only that day, were quite categorical: they could "conceive of no peace offer which Germany might make in the near future and which would be acceptable to us while our armed forces remained in being."[6]

Churchill expressed the hope that the Germans would soon turn on the United Kingdom, not only so as to gain a breathing space for the French front but also to give the RAF a chance to smash German air power. "If the French Army could hold out until the spring of 1941," he went on, "between twenty and twenty-five British divisions would once more be placed at its disposal."[7] Weygand's exposition of the military situation, however, left little hope that the French could hold out for another two weeks, much less for another year. All his forces were engaged in the battle—not a single battalion remained in reserve. Over a part of the front there was only a thin curtain of troops. The armies were falling back to the last line of defense envisaged by the High Command, and this had already been breached on the lower Seine in several places and was now threatened on the Marne. There was nothing to prevent the enemy from reaching Paris. In short, the Generalissimo could not guarantee that the lines would still hold the next day; and should that happen he would be unable to assure a coordinated defense of French territory.[8]

General Georges, C-in-C on the North-East front, only confirmed the main points of Weygand's account, adding that in Flanders the Allies had lost a minimum of 35 divisions out of 103 as well as all their mechanized cavalry and a substantial proportion of their armored divisions. Of the effectives engaged in the present battle, between 20 and 25 divisions were completely dislocated, giving the Germans a preponderance of three to one. Georges's conclusion was that the French were at the end of their tether.[9]

Churchill's attempts to instill optimism and the will to fight on thereafter met with little enthusiasm. To his talk of holding the front for another three or four weeks, Weygand replied that it was a question of hours, not of days or weeks; at his suggestion that Paris be stubbornly defended on a house-to-house basis in order to absorb the invading army, the French froze perceptibly; and when he recalled the spring of 1918 and the Allied recovery from a situation which all had thought lost, Marshal Pétain recalled that in the World War I battle to which Churchill alluded, he, as Commander-in-Chief of the French Army, had been in a position to send not three or four but 20 divisions immediately and ultimately 40 divisions to set matters right on the front of General Gough's army. Furthermore, 60 British divisions were then in line, and he also had a reserve of 60 divisions. Pétain ended by expressing the feeling of every Frenchman present, whether defeatist or not, that turning Paris into a ruin would not affect the final event.[10]

That the gulf between British and French thinking would be further aggravated by the question of additional air support seemed almost inevitable in the circumstances. The responses were by this time predictable. Weygand now requested that every British fighter plane be sent to France and thrown into the battle, arguing: "Here is the decisive point. Now is the decisive moment. It is therefore wrong to keep any squadrons back in England." But Churchill maintained that this was neither the decisive point nor the decisive moment. That moment would come when Hitler hurled his Luftwaffe against Great Britain. If the British could only keep command of the air over their own island and keep the seas open, as they definitely expected to, they would win back for the French all that had been lost. But a

minimum of fighter squadrons had to be maintained at all costs for
the defense of Britain and the Channel and nothing would induce
him to surrender these. The air arm was the instrument on which US
intervention depended. Furthermore, it was not at all certain that a
contrary decision would reverse the situation in France. The subject
was temporarily closed by Reynaud's dryly remarking that "nothing
was less desirable than the break-up of the British Air Force except
that of the western front" and by his reiteration that history would
undoubtedly record that the Battle of France had been lost through
lack of aviation.[11]

Weygand declared that once the defensive battle then in progress
was lost, he saw no means of preventing the invasion of the whole of
the national territory. If the worst happened, if all of metropolitan
France were occupied, he found it difficult to imagine how France
could carry on with the war. Here, Reynaud quickly interrupted to
state that "in his capacity as Supreme Commander, he had just given
extremely competent advice about the military sphere, but that 'the
question of continuing the war was a political matter, and depended
on the decision of the Government.' " But Reynaud did admit that
"if the last line of defence broke, a political question would arise."[12]

When Churchill then asked about the possibility of establishing a
bridgehead on the Atlantic, Weygand explained that he did not expect much benefit from the Breton redoubt* as Brittany presented
both strategic and logistical problems: it had neither fortifications
nor resources and could not be defended for long. Furthermore, it
would be difficult to withdraw troops into the peninsula while at the
same time they were engaged in fighting to the last on another position.[13] When the Prime Minister next urged that guerrilla warfare be
waged in various regions of France to disperse the enemy's efforts
once coordinated warfare became impossible, Pétain replied that this
would mean "the destruction of the country," and it was obvious
that none of the Frenchmen present wished to risk the physical devastation of France. Churchill contended that falling a helpless prey
to the enemy was worse than the destruction of the towns. In a more
hopeful vein he remarked that "the Allies were not far from reaping
the harvest as concerned the manufacture of arms and munitions,"
but Reynaud quickly answered that that was "like talking of rain to
a man who is in the middle of the Sahara."[14]

It was clear that in the presence of such pessimism little was to be

---

*See Appendix B, Churchill, Weygand, and the Breton Redoubt.

gained from prolonging the discussion that evening. No one had brought up the question of continuing the war from North Africa. In fact, no one had brought up any of the practical problems on whose solution the survival of the coalition depended. Moving towards a conclusion, Churchill said that if the French Army was forced to suspend the struggle, Britain would fight on until Hitlerism was crushed. With its air force and fleet, the Empire would be able to hold out for years and to impose the severest blockade on Europe. "The Nazis might succeed in dominating Europe, but it would be a Europe in revolt, and all this could only end in the downfall of a régime supported above all by the victory of its machines." The "nightmarish" question of what the French Navy would do if the Army suspended fighting in France was tentatively broached by Churchill, but then dropped as Reynaud brought the meeting to a close by stating that the French Government was no less determined to carry on the war than the British. For his part, Churchill said diplomatically that "Great Britain had the utmost confidence in the French High Command" and reiterated England's regret that she could not help France more in such a tragic hour.[15]

One other jarring episode occurred that evening. At the Supreme War Council of May 31 Reynaud had agreed to a joint air and naval operation against northwest Italy once Italy was at war, though the French air command had never approved the measure and though Reynaud himself had opposed it when the idea was first broached by Chamberlain on April 27. Arrangements had been made with French concurrence to move a force of British heavy bombers to French airfields near Marseilles for this purpose. Before the start of the conference Reynaud had asked that this mission, scheduled to take place that night, be put off, but, as part of the striking force had already left England, the subject was dropped. During dinner, however, Air Marshal Barratt called with the news that the local French air command was objecting to the departure of British aircraft from the Marseilles airfields on the grounds that the British would not be able to resist Italian reprisals on southern France. Although Reynaud agreed that the French authorities should be ordered to withdraw their objections, the British bombers never did take off: trucks and carts driven onto the airfield prevented them from leaving the ground. Reynaud could only apologize the following day when Churchill and Eden reproached the French for having sabotaged the policy of hitting hard at Italy, originally accepted by both powers.[16]

The only new factor introduced the next morning was Weygand's report that "an order had been given, should the external defences of Paris be broken, to declare the city an open one in order to avoid a useless shedding of blood and the destruction of the city." The General—with the acquiescence of Reynaud—had actually made this decision on June 10,[17] on the grounds that if the line of the lower Seine, the advanced position before Paris, and the Marne were held the capital would automatically be defended, but if the armies gave way there, the defense of Paris would be militarily useless. But, more than anything else, the decision to abandon Paris was symbolically a harbinger of the end.[18] To conclude the conference, Churchill formally requested that if a fundamental change in the situation occurred "the French Government would let the British Government know at once, in order that they might come over and see them at any convenient spot, before they [the French] took any final decisions which would govern their action in the second phase of the war."[19]

Before leaving, Churchill had a last private talk with General Georges, who told him that "the French Army's capacity for resistance was coming to an end, and that before long an honourable armistice would be the only possible outcome." Then, indicating what was soon to become the principal preoccupation of the British Government, Churchill took Admiral Darlan aside to express his hope that he would never surrender the French fleet. Darlan promised that, whatever happened, the fleet would not fall into German hands, and that in the last resort he would send it over to Canada.[20]

That afternoon Churchill was forced to report to the War Cabinet in London that "Weygand . . . saw no prospect of the French going on fighting" and that "Marshal Pétain had quite made up his mind that peace must be made. He believed that France was being systematically destroyed by the Germans, and that it was his duty to save the rest of the country from this fate." It was clear that a chapter in the war was closing and that England and France were, in the words of General Spears, "within sight of a cross-roads at which the destinies of the two nations might divide." Churchill at this time thought that there might be two French governments, one which made peace, and one which organized resistance from the French colonies; but one thing was sure: although for a while England might still have to send some support to France, they must now concentrate their main efforts on the defense of the island.[21]

In France, as the French Army's last line of defense on the Seine and the Marne was cracking everywhere, Weygand, at 1:15 p.m. on June 12, ordered a general retreat. The Battle of France was lost.

Already Weygand had told Reynaud: "The country will not forgive you if, in order to remain faithful to Britain, you reject any possibility of peace."[22] In a few hours the Supreme Commander would formally ask his government to conclude an armistice. Thus, a quarter of a century after it was first attempted, the Schlieffen plan, 1940s style, had at last achieved its object. As General de Gaulle noted, the Germans had not only broken strategic unity between London and Paris; they had also succeeded in dividing England and France.[23]

# III

# *Crisis Over the Armistice*

## *June 12 – June 16*

*The theatrical aspect, always considerable in political life, increases all the more to the degree that reality disconcerts the tempers that it subdues. One upholds a cause, but one plays a role, the implications of which cannot appear before the end of the play; in other words, one plays it passionately, but blindly: one chooses, but at the very moment one is choosing one guards against a future that one cannot foresee, any more than one's adversary can.*

Emmanuel Berl, on the French Council's deliberations in Touraine, in *La fin de la III<sup>e</sup> République* (Paris, 1968), p. 29.

*M. Marin is right in saying that we were violent against each other. In fact it was similar to that meeting of the Committee of Public Safety where Carnot and Saint-Just hurled abuse at each other and where Carnot then said to Saint-Just: "What are you doing?" And Saint-Just answered: "I am making an indictment so as to have your head." It was this way with us, except that we lacked their nobility.*

Raoul Dautry, testifying on the last meeting of the Reynaud cabinet, before the Parliamentary Commission of Inquiry in January 1949, in CE, VII, p. 2034.

# *The Opening Phase:*
# *June 12*

ALTHOUGH the question of an armistice had been touched on only obliquely while the British Prime Minister was still in France, Marshal Pétain did not hesitate to tell his old friend General Spears shortly after the Briare conference that an armistice was inevitable and that it was "sheer pusillanimity to shirk the issue." Belittling the scheme for sending recruits to Africa, Pétain stated: "There are no rifles there to arm them with. In any case, the disorganisation of the Ministry of War is such that they could never get the men to the harbours, still less to sea, and if they could, Italian submarines would undoubtedly drown them." When Spears suggested that the French could not leave the British to fight on alone in what would still be their common struggle, Pétain countered with: "You have left us to fight alone." From his point of view, "as France could not continue the struggle, wisdom dictated that England too should seek peace, for she certainly could not carry on alone." He thought the British Government would quite calmly allow France to be destroyed under the pretense that it could defy Germany and even beat her, and would then sue for peace too late. Meanwhile, it would have been the end of France. The indifference of the British Government was proved by the fact that it was withholding the greater part of its air force in the decisive battle.[1]

The truth was that Pétain knew the only battle he considered decisive to be already over and done with; but just as the British, in their anxiety since the crisis of May, would seem to have forgotten France, England too for the Marshal and General Weygand now no longer existed in any real sense. The inability of France's two greatest military leaders to look beyond their own defeat to future developments

181

on a possibly global scale together with their firm belief that "within three weeks England would have her neck wrung like that of a chicken"[2] were to be the determining influences in the ongoing political and moral drama that unfolded over the next four days and that finally ended, on June 16, with France's request for an armistice.

However, it was not the octogenarian Marshal but General Weygand who at this point took command of the pro-armistice forces. According to Gamelin, his successor had the reputation for being the "born adversary of Republican ideas"; during the 1920s Georges Clemenceau had even predicted that Maxime Weygand might one day bring down the Republic.[3] Whether intended literally or not, the remark showed an appreciation not only of the General's lifelong contempt for Republican institutions and politicians (as contrasted with his attachment to the aristocratic past) but also of his quasi-fanatical devotion to the army, which he chose to see as the symbol and natural leader of the nation. In Weygand, a violent temper and a rather archaic romanticism, combined with a passionate conviction that the traditional social order in both its civil and military manifestations must be maintained at all costs, inevitably led to a direct confrontation with the government once defeat in metropolitan France was assured and anarchy or other radical social change threatened to undo everything he had championed throughout his seventy-three years.[4] If he did not actually plot against the government in the sense of organizing or condoning a coup d'état—and this is not altogether clear—he nevertheless went far beyond the limits of the constitutional authority granted him, ultimately preferring the role of rebel to relinquishing the possibility of an armistice, which an indecisive cabinet made somewhat problematical. In the contest of wills with Reynaud that was fast approaching its climax, ruthless determination and absolute consistency of purpose, and ironically even his worst defects, were to be his greatest assets, qualities that gave him an initial, if incomplete, advantage over his adversary.

General Weygand had already determined upon his course of action even before the British ministers had left Briare. Now, a few hours later, towards 7 p.m. on June 12, General Weygand explained to the Council of Ministers assembled at the Château de Cangé, provisional seat of the President of the Republic, that to prevent the complete breakdown of civil and military order and the invasion of the entire country it was essential for the government to address an immediate request for an armistice to the German Government. The war, in his opinion, was irretrievably lost. This was the first time that the question of the armistice had been brought out for open discussion in a ministerial council. On the solution to this problem depended the survival of the Anglo-French alliance and the future of Anglo-French relations. And it was here within a group of two dozen men, who, because Parliament was scattered and no longer able to meet, now took on the burden of both executive and representative functions, that the problem was ultimately resolved not by thorough rational discussion but by procrastination and default.

The picture Weygand painted of a headlong flight of soldiers and refugees inextricably mixed, often uncontrolled and unfed, with anarchy threatening to engulf the country, was indeed grim. But, although Weygand was backed by virtually all the senior army commanders and although an armistice had been clandestinely promoted by the defeatist clique for nearly three weeks, his proposal within the Council was strongly opposed by Reynaud and a large number of ministers. Only Pétain and the new Minister of Information, Jean Prouvost, openly supported the General's request.

Weygand contended that if the armistice conditions proved too severe all they had to do was to reject them. But the idea of asking for Germany's terms "on approval" was ridiculed by Reynaud, who insisted that the German conditions were already fixed and would certainly include the occupation of all French ports and the use of the French fleet against England. They would have committed a cowardly action to no purpose. The Premier recalled that in signing the agreement of March 28 with Great Britain the French Government had undertaken not to enter into separate armistice or peace negotiations with the enemy and that France was obligated to honor her pledged word. The national interest also dictated respecting this pact, for a future without the friendship and support of the Anglo-Saxon world was inconceivable. César Campinchi, Minister of the Navy, pointed out that, inasmuch as the fleet was inevitably involved in the question of an armistice, that consideration alone should rule out Weygand's proposal, because to let the fleet fall into German hands to be used against England would be the height of dishonor. Others, among them Raoul Dautry, Minister of Armaments, Georges Monnet, Minister of Blockade, Louis Rollin, Minister of Colonies, Laurent-Eynac, Air Minister, and Louis Marin, Minister of State, cited as arguments against an armistice the fact that France still had a navy and an air force which could continue the fight alongside Britain; the fact that the French Empire was untouched and could serve as a base for carrying on the war; and the possibility of increasing aid from

America. Lastly, Reynaud stressed that the government could withdraw to the Breton redoubt in order to direct the battle from there in
conjunction with the British Government, before finally retiring to
North Africa.[5]

To these arguments, which struck Weygand as cheap heroics and
Baudouin as parliamentary speechifying, Weygand opposed the impossibility of holding out either in the Breton redoubt, "which only
existed in the imagination of the President of the Council, and still
had not troops available for its defence," or in North Africa, which
he claimed was totally unprepared for sustained resistance. In any
event, whatever the government decided, he refused to go "chez les
nègres."[6]

Most of Reynaud's ministers were also opposed to the Brittany
scheme, though the vague possibility of a governmental move to
Quimper still hung fire for another twenty-four hours.[7] Brittany, in
fact, was as yet organized only rudimentarily, and militarily the project had never commanded the support of anyone but Reynaud and
General de Gaulle. The shelving of the Breton move, however, did
not preclude a decision in favor of the more crucial move to North
Africa. But there was no real discussion as to the technical feasibility
of this larger plan, which was, after all, the essence of the problem
before the Council. Indeed, as Weygand later pointed out, no statistics were called for regarding the resources still available to the government (in men and matériel) or the means and time by which they
could be transferred to Africa or their chances, once there, of successfully resisting the forces that the enemy could marshal against them.[8]
The question of an armistice was seen and thus dealt with largely in
political and emotional terms by all participants.

Because on this date "the idea of resistance to the end, even in
exile, was so profoundly rooted in the thought of the great majority
of ministers," as Camille Chautemps and most other witnesses
agree,[9] it would seem that the Premier had carried the day. However,
this victory was only partial at best, especially considering that a
number of ministers—Chautemps in particular—had rejected the
idea of an armistice only because public opinion was not yet prepared for it,[10] while still others definitely came out against the government's eventual transfer to Algeria, Prouvost on the spurious
grounds that he refused to become an émigré. In addition, this minister advocated seeking "a national solution" to their problems, declaring that France had been under foreign influence too long.[11]

Reynaud also allowed himself to be tripped up on a motion that was introduced by his vice-premier just as the meeting was coming to a close at 11 p.m. From Reynaud's point of view the most dangerous aspect of a demand for an armistice was that it would separate France from England, and at Briare he had promised Churchill to take no serious decision before consulting with him again. Therefore, when Chautemps, ostensibly to mollify Weygand and to preserve the appearance of unanimity within the Council, suggested that Churchill return to France, it was agreed that the British Prime Minister should be invited to attend the Council the next day to lay his views before the French ministers and to discuss with them the problems arising from the General's request. Even more significant, it would appear that Chautemps also managed to wrest from Reynaud, immediately after the meeting's adjournment, the promise that he would "examine with Churchill what would happen between France and England if we were compelled to sue for an armistice."[12] In any event, few ministers wanted to commit themselves finally before hearing what the British leader had to say.

Thus, though Reynaud still disposed of a large majority who thought it the duty of France to resist, in many ways he had lost ground during the course of the evening. He had certainly not used his authority to best advantage. First of all, he had granted Weygand entrée into the Council, whereas the General had previously been limited to expressing his views before the much smaller War Committee. Second, he had failed to confine him to a purely technical or advisory capacity but had instead permitted his violence and considerable theatrical talents free rein—without, moreover, first preparing his colleagues for such an onslaught, although he *had* attempted to guide the outcome of the debate by emphasizing the gravity of the Anglo-French agreement even before giving the floor to his opponent. Third, he had refrained from forcing Weygand to admit that the cabinet had overwhelmingly decided against him, but instead, largely as the result of Chautemps's seemingly innocuous maneuver, had allowed the question to remain open.

For his actions at Cangé Reynaud has been harshly criticized, especially by Chautemps, who claims that the Premier "would not have proceeded otherwise if he had been resigned in advance to the check of his own policy."[13] Quite likely, however, Reynaud reasoned that the foremost proponent of an armistice might as well be heard in person by the government sitting formally inasmuch as the question was sure to be raised by Pétain in any case. It was certainly not an issue one man alone could decide. Furthermore, in the chaotic setup of the administration throughout Touraine, with ministers and ministries widely scattered, telephone communications reduced to a rudimentary level, and daily travel seriously impeded by refugee traffic, it would not have been practical to have continued the routine of separate and frequent meetings that had prevailed in Paris. The government was virtually forced to meet as a whole.

Reynaud believed that Weygand's intrusions into governmental deliberations could be limited if necessary. If the General got too far out of hand, Reynaud evidently hoped to eliminate him altogether as a factor, for on the previous day at Briare he had authorized de Gaulle to interview General Huntziger to determine whether the latter was willing to assume the Supreme Command for the express purpose of continuing the war from North Africa. De Gaulle, or so he claims, had indeed found the commander of the Fourth Army Group willing and had told him that he would shortly be receiving the government's instructions. However, by the evening of June 11 it was clear to him that the Premier no longer looked upon Weygand's replacement as an immediate problem, and so the idea was dropped for the time being. Reynaud apparently had hopes of winning over the Generalissimo and the Marshal by a show of strength in the Council.[14]

Whatever Reynaud's plans for dealing with his opponents and managing his colleagues, the fact that the issue of the armistice had finally been aired in the Council meant that henceforth it would remain central to the government's business, with no possibility of being shunted aside. The inconclusiveness of the Council's deliberations on the night of the 12th was an indication of the momentum the idea of capitulation had already gathered.

# Paul Reynaud
# at Tours:
# June 13

JUNE 12 marked the opening stages of the French cabinet crisis. The problems dividing the French Government were difficult, but they could be formulated quite clearly. Was France to go on fighting a hopeless struggle, or should the country lay down its arms? If the latter, was this to be achieved by an armistice or by a purely military surrender? If France opted for an armistice, how was this to be reconciled with the March 28 agreement with Great Britain? And, if France continued the war, how, where, and under what circumstances was this to be done? The Supreme War Council held in Tours on June 13 to discuss the problems arising from General Weygand's demand for an armistice, however, failed signally to clarify the situation. Instead, by the misunderstandings engendered there, it inaugurated a period characterized by confusion, counterorders, and cross-purpose endeavors. The last Supreme Council to be held, it should have been devoted to an exhaustive appraisal of France's capacity to contribute further to the alliance. But because both prime ministers chose to play a waiting game, and were less than open about what they wanted from each other, the most important issues were dodged altogether and other embarrassing topics only hinted at. From such a meeting it is not surprising that the most various accounts have emerged, accounts which in turn were to provide rationales for the totally divergent paths taken by both nations.

As Paul Reynaud was to play the key role in this stage of Anglo-French relations, some insight into the man's background and character is necessary in order to assess the motives prompting him and to appreciate better the meaning of what he said and did. Ironically, had Reynaud in the years after the war defended himself less vigorously and less copiously he would today stand as a more credible witness. But the fact—as one critic points out—that for nearly twenty years he tried, by continuously retouching and remodeling the texts, "to eliminate every trace of human weakness, [and] to erect for posterity a statue of bronze"[1] initially arouses in the critical reader that very skepticism which Reynaud apparently hoped by his exculpatory explanations to suppress. Yet, if the desire to conceal feet of clay or to rewrite history in a flattering light is to invalidate *his* testimony, then the testimony of most of his critics must stand equally condemned.

On the credit side, Reynaud was indisputably a man of talent and ability, innovative, farsighted in his conception of finance and foreign policy, impressive in his grasp of the nature of modern warfare, a genuine patriot who had consistently opposed Hitler's aggression and even considered resigning from the Daladier cabinet at the time of Munich. Clearheaded to a fault, *l'homme raisonnable raisonnant* par excellence, he was clever, witty, like Churchill a brilliant speech-maker—and not without guile. However, neither prudence nor profundity were among his virtues, and his temperament under stress often appeared at odds with his professed doctrine. Self-confident and even arrogant to all appearances, he yet lacked that inner core of confidence akin to religious fervor or mystical faith which alone enables a Churchill, a de Gaulle, a Clemenceau, or a Robespierre to inspire, to convert, to impose, and finally to triumph. If his intelligence permitted him to predict the reverses that did actually befall France, his character and his heart, as one sympathetic observer suggests, were perhaps less prepared for the sufferings and sacrifices that these reverses logically implied.[2] These human vagaries notwithstanding, Reynaud's ambition to lead, his never-failing combativeness, his very lucidity might still have carried the day had the hurdles to be overcome not been so high, so frequent, and so frightening. On the purely mundane level, his greatest weakness was his political isolation: as an independent man of the Right, he enjoyed no party following and was therefore forced to rely on the same dreary combinations and political compromises that had so weakened every French government that had come to power in the decade preceding the war. Under the circumstances his consistency sometimes suffered lapses.

Just how much control over the developing situation or what degree of freedom in his choice of tactics Reynaud actually had is hard to assess. His most hostile critics—generally, though not exclusively, those who favored an armistice—claim that he enjoyed quite a lot but that he failed (deliberately, they imply) to make use of it. In contrast, analysts of the relationship between the civilian and military powers, in stressing the restrictions under which the head of government operates during a period of crisis, suggest that Reynaud was struggling against insuperable odds and that his freedom to act was in fact illusory. Still others, looking to psychology rather than to politics for understanding, portray Reynaud as a Gallic Hamlet who was torn by inner conflicts, paralyzed by passivity, weakened in will; or alternately see in him the jurist who was trapped by a text of his own making (the Anglo-French agreement) from which he was reluctant, out of embarrassment, to liberate himself.[3] Not surprisingly, Reynaud himself supports none of these interpretations.

Officially, Reynaud based his policy on the Anglo-French alliance and *résistance à outrance*. To what degree his personal sympathies were engaged in this direction after mid-May is less clear. Not surprisingly, his political advisers and cabinet colleagues included some of the most unimpeachable stalwarts the country could boast. However, his public policy had not prevented him from socializing with and retaining or recruiting into his cabinet a number of men who were known defeatists, or at best doubtful teammates; nor did it immunize him from the constant and debilitating pressure exerted on him by his mistress, Mme Hélène de Portes, to end the war and come to terms with Germany.* Some degree of self-contradiction—above and beyond the lawyer's ability to see both sides of an issue—must inevitably be assumed from these contrary impulses and preferences. It is also reasonable to assume that the strain of crushing defeat and of his multiple offices, coupled with the continuous intriguing around him, had taken their toll, and that Reynaud, who knew as well as anyone that the Battle of France was lost, in his heart might have been relieved to lay aside his responsibilities, especially before some terrible and irreparable rupture both within the cabinet and the country at large took place. Certainly the chief American observers in Bordeaux, along with many others, believed so. Charles de Gaulle has observed sympathetically that "Only those who were eye-witnesses of it can measure what the ordeal of being in power meant during that terrible period"; yet, concludes the General, rather contradictorily, Reynaud "faced the storm with a steadfastness which did not waver."[4]

---

*See Appendix C, Mme Hélène de Portes.

By his enemies it was said that he believed an armistice to be inevitable and that the stands he took, the speeches he made, the orders he gave were all for the record—mere posturings intended for public consumption which were, however, quite divorced from reality. And when one juxtaposes Reynaud's actual accomplishments against his stated intentions one is at least forced to give his accusers a fair hearing. Certainly his own labored, often abstruse explanations as to his actions and motivations are not always reliable guides to events which need above all to be separated from the polemics and myths that have subsequently surrounded them. Yet if his account, in its multiple permutations, is flawed both by gaps and distortions, it can still be profitably followed—and even credited—so long as it is supplemented and corrected by less partisan witnesses and so long as it is recognized that the Premier was above all ambivalent, that his tactics were often questionable or mistaken, and that he had much to conceal, which, for the sake of history, his own reputation, and ultimately the Franco-British partnership whose survival was his most genuine concern, he had done better to reveal. For all that, his British allies, at any rate, were finally to conclude that Reynaud had fought for the alliance to the best of his ability, against men who were stronger than he, that he had never "double-crossed" them, and that "France having no Churchill, he was probably the best political leader she had."[5]

As of June 13 Reynaud was ostensibly proceeding with his program, though possibly with less decision than he might have mustered. In a note for Weygand he outlined the Supreme Command's task: to hold out for as long as possible in the Massif Central and to constitute and defend the Breton redoubt; while General de Gaulle was ordered to prepare, with General Colson, for the transfer of French forces to North Africa. Reynaud also informed Sir Ronald Campbell and General Spears, who were impressed by the Premier's confident air, of his intention to fight on in Africa. However, he did not hide from his colleagues Mandel and Jeanneney that the Command had not been executing the orders previously given to it and that the Breton redoubt was not at all ready. Therefore, in conformity with the wishes expressed by the cabinet the night before, he—and they—decided to move the provisional seat of government to Bordeaux rather than to Brittany.[6]

En route to Tours in the afternoon to meet Churchill, as he has explained it retrospectively, Reynaud had second thoughts about the opportuneness of permitting what Camille Chautemps, Vice-President of the Council, had called a sort of "Supreme Council held in the heart of the French Council of Ministers." Reynaud feared that the "understanding" words expressed by the Prime Minister two days before at Briare (which he perhaps interpreted too generously) might be used by the pro-armistice faction against those who favored continuing the war. According to General Ismay, Churchill had then said: "If it is thought best for France in her agony that her Army should capitulate, let there be no hesitation on our account, because whatever you may do we shall fight on forever and ever and ever."[7] With these words possibly lingering in his mind, Reynaud reasoned that for the Council to consult Churchill before taking a definitive stand would be to admit that the continuation of the war was not the only possible solution.[8] Whether this train of thought had any effect on Reynaud's willingness to bring Churchill together with his colleagues *after* the conference remains somewhat unclear.

Meanwhile, in the confusion no arrangements had been made for receiving the British contingent at the airfield so that Churchill and his party had to make their way unattended to Tours, where they were then subjected to the unctuous defeatist chatter of Baudouin, who joined them for lunch. Baudouin, as Churchill remarks disapprovingly, was later to spread the idea that the British Prime Minister had agreed with him "that France should surrender unless the United States came in."[9]

Finally, at 3:30 p.m., the Supreme War Council got under way at the Tours Prefecture. Representing the English, besides Churchill, were the Secretary of State for Foreign Affairs, Lord Halifax; Lord Beaverbrook, the canny and efficient Minister of Aircraft Production; General Ismay; Sir Alexander Cadogan, Permanent Under-Secretary at the Foreign Office; Sir Ronald Campbell; and General Spears. Reynaud was accompanied only by Paul Baudouin, Under-Secretary of State to the Presidency of the Council and for Foreign Affairs, though they were joined later in the conference by General de Gaulle. The official English transcription was made by Captain Berkeley, the official French *procès-verbal* by Captain Roland de Margerie, then *chef de cabinet* of Reynaud in his capacity as Minister of Foreign Affairs. Both Baudouin and Spears also took notes during the session, the latter providing a necessary corrective to Baudouin's account, set down in what he later called a "style télégraphique," which in several important respects is unreliable.

Reynaud immediately informed the British of the position adopted by Weygand and Pétain the preceding evening in favor of an armistice. The majority of the Council had not endorsed this view, he said, but, if Paris were taken, the question would inevitably be raised again. Reynaud felt that if the French Army could fight on a while longer help would soon be forthcoming from Great Britain and the United States. As he had been heartened by Roosevelt's permission to publish his appeal of June 10, he proposed sending another message to the American President informing him that the fate of the Allied cause now lay in his hands. His government "would not continue the struggle unless Roosevelt's reply conveyed a firm assurance of immediate aid."[10] According to Reynaud, he "intended to act as a loyal but exacting ally." In so doing he was to paint the blackest picture of events and even to adopt the arguments of his adversaries, devil's advocate fashion. But, at the same time he was warning Churchill, he was to reaffirm his own personal determination to resist. Reynaud claims that he used threats only to obtain the maximum support from Churchill as regards Roosevelt.[11] This mode of operation naturally provoked some confusion in the British, who were aware of the French Premier's rather different professions only two days before.

Reynaud declared that, while he himself was well aware of the solemn pledge to Britain that no separate peace would be entered into, he could not ignore the possibility of an opposition forming against him in the cabinet in favor of an armistice. He begged them, in this case, to remember that France had sacrificed everything in the common cause and to take account of her sufferings. It would be a shock if the British Government failed to concede that France was physically incapable of carrying on or if it expected France to continue the war "with the only result of delivering up her people to German despotism and Nazi corruption. . . . Would Great Britain realise the hard facts now facing France?"[12]

Mr. Churchill replied that Great Britain realized how much France had suffered. "She grieved to find that her contribution to the land struggle was at present so small, owing to the reverses which had been met with as a result of applying an agreed strategy in the North." The British nevertheless had but one thought, to win the war, and everything was subordinate to that aim; no difficulties or regrets could stand in the way. As he was well-assured of Britain's capacity for enduring until Germany was beaten,

they would therefore hope that France would carry on fighting south of Paris down to the sea, and if need be from North Africa. At all costs time must be gained. The period of waiting was not limitless: a pledge from the United

States would make it quite short. The alternative course meant destruction for France quite as certainly. Hitler would abide by no pledges. If, on the other hand, France remained in the struggle, with her fine Navy, her great Empire, her Army still able to carry on guerrilla warfare on a gigantic scale, and if Germany failed to destroy England . . . if then Germany's might in the air was broken, then the whole hateful edifice of Nazism would topple over. . . . At all events England would fight on. She had not and would not alter her resolve: no terms, no surrender.[13]

A declaration of faith, however, did not answer Reynaud's question and momentarily the Frenchman relied on irony to make his point when "he said he was personally convinced that Great Britain would not give way until she had known sufferings equal to those now endured by the French people."[14] Reynaud was anxious to know how the British Government would react in a certain contingency. He asked Churchill to suppose that a French government might say to the British Government:

"We know that you will continue the war. We also would continue it if we had any hope of a sufficiently early victory that would re-establish France as she deserves to be re-established. In such a case we would be at your side to continue the struggle, if need be in North Africa. But we see no sufficient hope of an early victory. There is no chance of the United States joining in the conflict in the months before the Presidential election. . . . It is quite natural that Great Britain should go on with the war . . . but we, the French Government, do not think we can abandon our people without their being able to perceive a light at the end of the tunnel. We cannot abandon our people to German domination. We must come to terms. We have no choice. . . . Our problem is this. Should we persist in a war without hope and should we leave the land of France? It is now too late to organise the *Réduit Breton,* and the French Government could not remain there; nor is there a hope of finding any place in France where a genuine French government might escape capture. If we left, the position would then be that Hitler would in all probability set up a puppet Government with so-called legal powers which would at once set about its task of corruption." In the hypothetical case of a French Government reasoning as I have just done, and coming to the conclusion that it had not got the right thus to abandon France to Germany, would not the British Government then agree that France, having sacrificed what was finest and best of her youth, could do no more? Would Great Britain not agree that, France having nothing further to contribute to the common cause, she would release her from the agreement concluded three months ago and allow her to conclude a separate peace? Could this not be conceded whilst maintaining Anglo-French solidarity?[15]

Reynaud claims that in speaking thus it was not his intention to ask Churchill to free France from its pledge of March 28, that, on the contrary, he was thinking in terms of what some other government, one to which he would not belong, might feel constrained to do.[16] However, these nuances were lost on his listeners. Baudouin interpreted his words as a request for authorization to sign a separate armistice.[17] And Churchill together with most of the Englishmen present certainly believed that Reynaud was asking that France be released from its treaty obligations.[18] Whether the question was, strictly speaking, hypothetical or not could have been of little importance to them because under the circumstances they would not have distinguished between the conjectural and the actual—or the personal and the collective; the problem remained the same in any case.

In response to the question posed, Mr. Churchill answered that "in no case would Great Britain waste time and energy in reproaches and recriminations. That did not mean that she would consent to action contrary to the recent agreement." Churchill urged that before posing decisive questions the first step ought to be M. Reynaud's further message to President Roosevelt, putting the present position squarely before him. Churchill himself would send a telegram to Roosevelt supporting Reynaud's plea for American intervention. He went on to say that England would always cherish the cause of France and that, if England won the war, France would be restored in all her dignity and greatness. But that was a very different thing "from asking Great Britain to consent to a departure from the solemn undertaking binding the two countries."[19]

In the course of his following comments on the development the war would take in its next phase, undoubtedly made to disabuse Reynaud of any notion that France might bow out while maintaining easy relations with England, Churchill recalled that France could not hope to elude the consequences of the coming duel between Britain and Germany. The English blockade of Europe and the bombing of German-held territory would cause suffering in France, as a result of which a bitter antagonism between the French and English might arise. To this Reynaud replied that it was just such a separation of England and France and the possiblity of lasting antagonism between them that he wished to avoid. That was why he was asking England to recognize what France had suffered for the common cause, and why, failing a free and solemn declaration along these lines, he would be very preoccupied for the future. It could result in a new and very grave situation in Europe. General Spears saw in these last words a veiled threat that if England did not promise not to injure France, France would consider joining the enemy.[20] But Churchill again deferred the answer to this question: "We will have to consider all that after the arrival of the American response.... if this response is unfavorable and if, then, you announce to us your resolution to treat separately, we will have a whole mass of problems to examine."[21]

Churchill nevertheless thought the seriousness of the question warranted a private discussion with his colleagues before it could be disposed of definitively. The Englishmen therefore withdrew briefly to the Prefecture garden, where they decided against committing themselves to anything for the time being.[22] According to Spears, Churchill on returning then recapitulated their position: Lord Halifax and Lord Beaverbrook had approved what he had said earlier and it could be assumed that the rest of the British cabinet would also agree. President Roosevelt should be approached at once by identical appeals from both England and France. And a little later: "As regards what M. Reynaud had said concerning a separate peace, no reply to that question could be given until the President's answer had been received."[23] Churchill himself, in his memoirs, claims to have summarized the British position in even less equivocal terms:

We could not agree to a separate peace however it might come. Our war aim remained the total defeat of Hitler, and we felt that we could still bring this about. We were therefore not in a position to release France from her obligation. Whatever happened, we would level no reproaches against France; but that was a different matter from consenting to release her from her pledge.[24]

However, although the official British minutes show that this clear-cut position was articulated earlier in the conference, after the adjournment it would appear on the basis of this transcript that Mr. Churchill limited himself to saying only that "discussion with his colleagues had not altered his views, which were certainly shared by the whole British Government."[25]

Because Reynaud has treated Churchill's words of June 13 in rather different ways at different points in his career, it is difficult to say exactly how he interpreted them on the occasion in question. Yet how Churchill's pronouncements were "heard" or understood by the French at this conference—and here the British Prime Minister's intonations and facial expressions must have carried a weight that no official document can properly register—naturally bears on the important question of whether or not the British statesmen had implicitly released France from the agreement of March 28, or at least whether such an inference might reasonably have been drawn.

Testifying before the Supreme Court on July 24, 1945, long before he had had the opportunity to read either Churchill's memoirs or the British minutes of the meeting, which the Foreign Office sent him in 1947, or even the French *procès-verbal,* which only came to light in 1949, Reynaud clearly remembered Churchill's manifestation of sympathy for France and his promise for the future: whatever happened, England did not intend to overburden an unfortunate ally, and if the British emerged from the war victorious, they would not forget their fallen comrade; France would be restored in its power and grandeur. But Reynaud implied in his testimony that Churchill's and his colleagues' statements at Tours were unofficial, that they had been speaking only in their own behalf. Significantly, none of the "Churchillian" words remembered by Reynaud in 1945 relate to France's obligation to honor its pledge. Nevertheless, Reynaud stated on several occasions during the Pétain trial that Churchill's words did not have the character of an assent to an armistice, that they did not disengage France from its commitments.[26] Yet in his memoirs, first published in France in 1947 and again, in a somewhat different guise, in 1951, Reynaud writes that Churchill had added that "there could be no question of absolving France from the pledge which she had given." This time, rather at variance with what he had formerly testified, Reynaud claims that Churchill had said that his words, having been approved by Halifax and Beaverbrook, could be considered as expressing the views of the British Government.[27]

It is difficult to follow the confused peregrinations of M. Reynaud's memory—there would be still further wrinkles during the Vichy period—but it seems probable that on the date in question (June 13) the French Premier was somewhat uncertain as to what had been said or intended but was definitely more impressed by the generous sentiments expressed by Mr. Churchill than by his insistence on holding France to its word. This seems borne out by President Albert Lebrun's recollection of what Reynaud told the Council upon his return from Tours. Paraphrasing Reynaud, he writes that the British ministers, after promising further reinforcements, had added "that if France was forced to sign a separate peace . . . England would not overwhelm her unhappy ally. With victory, she would reestablish France in her integrity and independence. Such at least was their personal opinion, to be ratified by the British cabinet."[28] At any rate, within the next two to three days Reynaud had apparently forgotten the exact tenor of Churchill's remarks, and this probably accounts for his later insistence on the personal and conditional character of the three English cabinet members' declarations.

Paul Baudouin's accounts, if more internally consistent, are also more blatantly tendentious, an example of the ability to hear only what one desires to hear. In his version, Churchill answers Reynaud's question in this way:

In any case there shall be no recriminations. In such an assumption recriminations would be vain, and one does not address them to an ally who has been unfortunate. . . . France has been sacrificed in the struggle against the common enemy, and whatever may be her attitude after her defeat, Great Britain will in any event restore her to her power and greatness. Great Britain will always cling to France.

From these words Baudouin derived France's "moral authority" to ask for an armistice. Baudouin also claims that, after conferring with Halifax and Beaverbrook, Churchill reported that what he had just said about Great Britain's promise in any event to restore France to her power and greatness could now be considered as confirmed by the British Government.[29] But here Baudouin had clearly misunderstood *which* words were being confirmed. Whether deliberately or merely conveniently, Baudouin somewhere along the line had ignored what to English ears was obviously a key phrase. Yet nine years after the event, before the Commission of Inquiry, Baudouin was to stick to this interpretation of Churchill's response. There had been no explicit authorization given the French to ask for a separate armistice, he admitted, but the British Prime Minister *had* assured them that if they did so there would be for France no serious consequences. Churchill, he claims, was primarily concerned with *when* the armistice request would be made—whether in ten or fifteen days—and specified only that no action be taken before Roosevelt's reply was known. In short, while Churchill did not approve an armistice request, he expected it, and anticipated no trouble about it later.[30]

Baudouin's account would not have such significance if it were not for the fact that it was his version of the conference that was most actively propagated in the next few days and his version that was generally credited.[31] Certainly the idea that the British no longer expected or required the French to go on fighting provided welcome grist for the defeatists' mill. Indeed, by the next night, Oliver Harvey had cause to note the harm being done by the "idea encouraged by

[the] P.M.'s generous words . . . that even if France did fall out, it would make no difference and we would set her up again."[32] This obviously was Baudouin's handiwork.

There is an additional dispute connected with the June 13 Supreme War Council. According to the official minutes and the lengthy accounts of the meeting given by Churchill, General Spears, Reynaud, and Baudouin, at no time during the conference was the subject of the French fleet brought up. Reynaud, in fact, cites this as proof that he neither requested nor received Churchill's authorization for an armistice, for, he argues, had he done so, Churchill would surely have subordinated his agreement to guarantees concerning the fleet. And, as he told the Parliamentary Commission in 1950, Churchill "did not raise the issue for the simple reason that I did not tell him that I intended to ask for an armistice."[33]

Yet General de Gaulle, who was present at the Tours conference only for its last few minutes, offers dissenting evidence. Of Churchill's remarks to Reynaud after the French and British had reconvened he writes:

Coming to the prospect of an armistice between French and Germans, which I expected would provoke an explosion from him, he expressed, on the contrary, a compassionate understanding. But suddenly, moving on to the question of the fleet, he became very precise and firm. Obviously the British government was so afraid of seeing the French fleet handed over to the Germans that it was inclined, while there was still time, to barter its renunciation of the March 28 agreement for guarantees about the fate of our ships. This was, in fact, the conclusion which emerged from that abominable conference.[34]

One might be inclined to dismiss this passage as a monumental piece of confusion based on a telescoping of events taking place over several days. Yet it receives some backing from a statement made by Baudouin on July 4, 1940: contradicting the evidence of his own notes on the conference, Baudouin on this date claimed that "Mr. Churchill himself declared during the Supreme Council of June 13 that, if France did not deliver her war fleet to the enemy, Great Britain, even in case of a separate peace, would remain faithful to her."[35] Therefore, it is just possible, as Albert Kammerer suggests, that the question of the fleet may have formed the object of at least semi-official conversations at some point during the afternoon.[36] But if, in fact, a conversation regarding the fleet did take place, no Englishman has ever admitted its existence, much less the implications the French Under-Secretary of

State for Defense and the Under-Secretary of State for Foreign Affairs (at least in 1940) assigned to it.[37]

It is, however, agreed by all sources that Churchill urged Reynaud to send a new appeal to President Roosevelt, which would be supported by telegram from London, and that Reynaud promised that the French Government would postpone giving its reply to the proposals of General Weygand until the President's answer had been received. There was little other official business. The two leaders made a tentative appointment to meet a day or so later, after they had heard from Roosevelt, at which time Reynaud hoped he would be able to come to some agreement with the British Government concerning the circumstances in which France could continue the war. Churchill requested and Reynaud agreed to order the transfer to England of the more than 400 German pilots who were prisoners of war in France, many of whom had been shot down by the RAF. Churchill announced that while they were awaiting the President's answer British reinforcements would continue to disembark in France. Reynaud, possibly as the result of prodding from more vigorous colleagues such as Marin or General de Gaulle, whom he had seen during the conference's recess, concluded by stating that the point of view he had put forward earlier in the conference was purely hypothetical. His personal convictions were embodied in the message he was addressing to Roosevelt. "The case would only arise if the President's answer was unfavourable. In that eventuality, however, a new situation would have arisen which would involve grave consequences."[38]

The Englishmen met MM. Jeanneney and Herriot, presidents of the Senate and Chamber of Deputies respectively, as well as Georges Mandel and Louis Marin, in a lugubrious and rather pathetic interview, then departed for the airport about 5:30. They were apparently not invited to attend the Council of Ministers, though Churchill later wrote that they would have been very willing to do so. In fact, they did not even know there was to be a meeting of the French Government that evening.

Thus, the Supreme Council had not really accomplished anything except to stall for time, a detailed discussion of all basic issues having been shelved until Roosevelt's response was known. The only decision had been to charge Reynaud with making a new and more impassioned appeal to the American President either to enter the war immediately or to declare in no uncertain terms that he would do so in the foreseeable future. In short, the weight of the United States was counted on to provide that "light at the end of the tunnel" otherwise so conspicuously lacking. Retrospectively, encouraging this would appear to have been a great tactical error on Churchill's part. But that Churchill did not believe an American about-face to be unlikely is shown by his and his colleagues' reaction to President Roosevelt's answer to Reynaud's message of June 10, which they discussed at the War Cabinet meeting in London later that night (June 13). Indeed, Churchill was every bit as anxious as Reynaud to send off the appeal and had in fact been advised by his Chiefs of Staff that very day to support such a move. They had written: "We consider that the moment has come when France should make a direct appeal to the United States of America for immediate military aid and suggest that steps should be taken forthwith for this appeal to be made."[39] Thus, in a manner of speaking, the blind were leading the blind.

Still worse, even before Churchill had left Tours, Baudouin was bruiting it about that Churchill had shown complete comprehension of the situation and "would understand if France concluded an armistice and a separate peace." As Spears points out, Baudouin's tendency to misinterpret may have derived from Churchill's habit of saying "Je comprends" to Reynaud, indicating his understanding of the French words spoken before they were translated. At any rate, Spears was shaken enough to extricate from the departing Churchill, for his own personal knowledge, a "categorical confirmation that at no time had he given to anyone the least indication of his consenting to the French concluding a separate armistice." And in his message to Roosevelt late that night Churchill wrote that he "did not hesitate in the name of the British Government to refuse consent to an armistice or separate peace."[40]

# Cangé II:
# June 13

AT THE second meeting of the Council of Ministers at Cangé, which followed at 6 p.m., the proponents of an armistice made crucial gains. For this reverse, Reynaud was in large part responsible. The ministers, summoned especially to hear Churchill's opinions on the subjects raised the previous evening and impatiently awaiting the English party since mid-afternoon, were stunned and angered to find that Churchill would not be present. Chautemps interpreted Churchill's absence as a lack of regard for the French Government in its distress, but most simply felt with considerable justification that they had been deceived by their premier. The bad atmosphere in which the meeting began only increased when Reynaud informed his colleagues that at the Supreme War Council just held in Tours (about which they had not been consulted) he had announced the decision taken by the French Government to continue the struggle and to reject the advice of General Weygand, after which the Allies had left, taking with them evidence of the complete agreement between the two governments.

This of course was not what Reynaud had just told the British (his remarks to Mandel, Marin, Jeanneney, and Herriot during the conference's recess about what he was discussing with the British had been much franker), but then the picture he *had* painted of his cabinet's attitude—in being overpessimistic—was equally inaccurate. By these duplicate deceptions, Reynaud was apparently trying to maneuver both the British Government and his own—in the case of the British, by preparing them for the worst, in the case of the French, by conning them into accepting a *fait accompli*, which at the very least would help to gain time. In this way he no doubt hoped to keep control of a volatile situation, but not surprisingly his peremptoriness had quite the opposite effect: the defeatists were instead roused to open hostility, while the waverers, their confidence eroded by the credibility gap thus exposed, became more receptive than ever to the promptings of Weygand and Pétain. Yves Bouthillier, Minister of Finance, protested violently against the Premier's statement: not only had Reynaud broken his promise to let Churchill be heard, but he had communicated to the head of a foreign government a decision of the French Council of Ministers (to continue the prosecution of the war) which in reality had not been taken—the only decision the previous day having been to take no decision before asking the advice of the British Government on the question. Chautemps also accused Reynaud of committing the French Government to a decision on his own responsibility. Reynaud's only defense against these charges was that Mr. Churchill had been in a hurry to return to England (or, alternatively, as others remember it, that Churchill did not think it appropriate for a foreigner to participate in a meeting of the French cabinet), and that the day before a large majority had expressed themselves against an armistice. President Lebrun upheld him on this last point.[1] At any rate, Reynaud was again going to address President Roosevelt to ask for the immediate entry of the United States into the war, and the decision of the government would only be taken after examining this response.*

General Weygand then reported on the military situation, reiterating his demand of the previous day for an immediate cessation of hostilities. When Campinchi, supported by Monnet and Marin, again raised the subject of the fleet and argued that "there was no point in asking for an armistice unless the Government was prepared to hand over the Fleet to the enemy," Weygand suggested that the French Navy be put out of the enemy's reach by directing it to North African ports while the government was waiting for the American reply and before any armistice negotiations had begun. No decision was reached on this point, however, because so many were opposed to the very principle of an armistice. Weygand also stated that he would reject the armistice if delivering the fleet were a condition.[2]

Somewhere about this time General Weygand made the sensational announcement that the Communists had seized power in Paris, where the police and Republican Guard had been disarmed, and that telephone communications with the capital were cut. Mandel quickly

---

*See Appendix D, Reynaud's Last Appeal to Roosevelt.

foiled what he suspected was an attempt to panic the cabinet (and thus hasten a decision in favor of an armistice) by telephoning M. Langeron, the Prefect of Police, who denied that Maurice Thorez, the Communist Party chieftain, was in the Elysée and confirmed that Paris was orderly and quietly awaiting the arrival of the Germans the next day.[3]

Ruffled by the strong opposition he was meeting from the *résistants,* Weygand then returned to his curious thesis that the government had been cowardly to abandon Paris, that it should have awaited the Germans there as the Roman Senate had awaited the barbarians when they invaded Rome. Having lacked the courage to stay in Paris, he argued, at least it should have the courage to remain in France, if only because the people would not otherwise accept the sacrifices demanded of them and because the government could not otherwise retain its authority over the country. The idea of remaining outside the country for several years—presuming that the colonies were disposed to receive a defeated government in the first place—then of reconquering France by bombing its cities and population was to his way of thinking an absurd and odious program. He personally would never leave metropolitan soil under any conditions—not even if he were put in irons. On this sour note, the Generalissimo stormed out of the meeting, expostulating that the ministers were crazy (Mandel's smiling had especially galled him) and ought to be arrested. He had previously threatened to arrest General de Gaulle for having taken measures on Reynaud's orders to continue the war in North Africa.[4]

In support of Weygand's view that the government would have no authority over France if it went to the colonies, Pétain, in a prepared statement, declared that it was impossible for the French Government, without deserting, to abandon French territory. The duty of the government was to stay in the country whatever might happen, under penalty of no longer being recognized as such. To deprive France of her natural defenders during a time of general disorder was to deliver her over to the enemy. It was necessary to wait for a French renaissance by remaining on the spot, rather than by abetting an Allied conquest of French territory in circumstances and after a delay impossible to foresee. Outside the government if necessary, Pétain vowed to stay among the French people to share their trials and miseries. An armistice was to his mind the necessary condition for perpetuating an eternal France.[5]

Thus began the campaign of intimidation waged by the Commander-in-Chief and the most prestigious member of the cabinet to link a cessation of hostilities on French soil with the much profounder decision to retain the government in France. In effect, in an attempt to impose their wills, Weygand now refused to obey the government should it command the continuation of the struggle from North Africa and Pétain threatened to resign rather than leave metropolitan soil.

In opposition to their demagogic appeal to feelings of loyalty to the motherland, Reynaud evoked the honor of France. The war would go on and, whether France signed an armistice or not, the blockade of France by Britain and the seizure of France by Germany were inevitable. The French people would be captive for a long time, and if France broke with Britain it would be left without hope. "To ask for an armistice would, therefore, be to lose both honour and hope."[6] Besides driving a fatal wedge between France and Britain, it would also alienate the United States, on whom final recovery depended.

Reynaud's reasoned appeals to honor and the long-term interests of France, however, were less influential with many in the cabinet than the violent insistence Weygand could bring to bear or the cold determination of Pétain. There were, of course, the "irreconcilables," or "durs"—Marin, Campinchi, Monnet, Dautry, Rio, Rollin, and, chief among them, the coolly detached but ferocious Mandel, who, as Baudouin describes him, sat "silent and contemptuous today as yesterday, with his stony eyes amused to record among his colleagues a fear and a mediocrity greater than even he had imagined."[7] But Bouthillier with unexpected passion and insolence, Baudouin and Chautemps with considerably greater suavity, had come out more or less openly in favor of an armistice, and to these could now be added Ybarnegaray and Pomaret. Still others were wavering.[8] However, a decision either for or against an armistice was again postponed and no conclusion was reached other than to await Roosevelt's reply to Reynaud before taking any further action.

If Reynaud was serious about continuing the war, then the mistake in not inviting Churchill was obvious. The day before, the current of opinion had been strongly in favor of going on with it, but as of the 13th the pendulum began to swing unmistakably towards surrender.[9] The prestige of Pétain had weighed heavily on the ministers and there had been no counterbalance such as the British Prime Minister would have provided. In the opinion of General Spears, "only Churchill could have persuaded them that Britain not only had a chance but genuinely believed in ultimate victory."[10] Only he could have convinced them that France's interests did not lie in abandoning the struggle. But Reynaud had apparently miscalculated both his own position and the psychology of his colleagues. He may also have been sufficiently confused by Churchill's statements at Tours that he did not honestly know whether the British leader's presence would have acted as a bracing tonic or merely as a cathartic on the cabinet. But certainly his absence could only aggravate Anglo-French misunderstandings at this stage; at a Council of Ministers there would at least have been many witnesses, and of necessity some greater clarity and comprehension must have emerged which could then not later have been called into question. As it was, by the night of June 13 the possibilities of France remaining in the war were disappearing fast. Spears writes:

The British ministers had left Tours with no great hopes. The subsequent meeting of the French Cabinet had made more tenuous an already slender chance. Reynaud's authority over his colleagues had been greatly diminished. Weygand had been openly rude to him and had insulted the whole Cabinet without being called to book, and, as a result of it all, the question that affected the history of France for all time, the question which if wrongly resolved might tarnish her past as well as cast a shadow over her future for centuries, was made to depend not upon her own will and determination, but upon the decision of another nation, the United States, and the final word rested not with her own leaders, her Cabinet, her Prime Minister or her President, but with President Roosevelt.[11]

# June 14:
# Dangerous Moves

ON JUNE 14, as calm temporarily descended on the diplomatic front during the French Government's move to Bordeaux, the last unhappy scene between British and French was, predictably, being played out in the military arena. In the morning, Lieutenant-General Alan Brooke, who had been sent back to France to reconstitute the BEF as part of the British effort to bolster the morale of the French Government and to maintain France in the war, met with General Weygand at Supreme Headquarters at Briare to arrange the deployment of British troops already landed or about to disembark.

According to Brooke, Weygand told him frankly "that the French Army had ceased to be able to offer organised resistance and was disintegrating into disconnected groups." Nevertheless, Weygand let it be understood that the previous day their respective governments had decided to defend Brittany by holding a position in front of Rennes. Brooke was therefore to concentrate the Canadian division at that point while British forces already engaged with the French 10th Army would continue their task until they could be collected around Le Mans. Though Brooke thought the plan had no hope of success and though Weygand and General Georges both saw it as "romantic" or even "idiotic," the three drew up an agreement prescribing the role of the BEF in the maneuver—Brooke under the impression that it was an order previously agreed to by his own government, though the Breton plan had never been mentioned to him before his departure. Yet even while the document was being prepared Brooke instructed Major-General Sir Richard Howard-Vyse, head of No. 1 Military Mission at French GHQ, to fly to England to advise Sir John Dill that the only course left open to the

British was to stop sending further troops and to evacuate the rest (some 150,000 men). The military missions attached to Weygand and Georges he also thought should now be withdrawn. At the same time, Air Marshal Barratt, Commander-in-Chief of British Air Forces in France, also recommended the immediate evacuation of his squadrons, French dispositions for a southward withdrawal having deprived him of the protection he felt was required.[1]

In the afternoon Brooke appealed personally to Dill to stop the flow of troops and equipment and to order the reembarkation of the BEF at once because the position was hopeless. Shortly thereafter, having first referred the matter to Churchill, who claimed there was no such agreement between the two governments on the Brittany scheme,* Dill ordered Brooke to evacuate immediately all military stores, lines of communication troops, and all other units not needed for operational purposes—in short, everyone not already under the orders of the French 10th Army. In the evening, however, Churchill balked at reembarking the 52nd Division, telling Brooke in a heated telephone conversation that he had been sent to France precisely to make the French feel that the British were supporting them; but he was finally won over by Brooke's argument that remaining longer in France would only result in throwing away good troops to no avail. (However, for political reasons, it was subsequently decided at least to delay the departure of the two brigades in question.) Then at 10:20 p.m., the Secretary of State for War formally released Brooke from French command, though he was instructed to continue cooperating with French forces fighting in his vicinity. He was to prepare for the evacuation of the whole of his force, yet, somewhat ambiguously, was told that this decision could only be taken by agreement between the two governments—an agreement that was never to come from the French. Early on June 15 partial evacuation commenced. However, the British units under General Marshall-Cornwall cooperating with the French 10th Army (including the Evans armored division, the heterogeneous Beauman "division," and a brigade of the 52nd), by express order of the government, continued to fight on until June 17. The evacuation of British troops was completed at 4 p.m. on June 18. Barratt's bomber force also returned to England on the 15th, though five fighter squadrons remained longer in France to cover the withdrawal of British and Allied troops from ports all along the coast.[2]

---

*See Appendix B, Churchill, Weygand, and the Breton Redoubt.

In his message to Weygand (sent the night of June 14–15) explaining why British forces were resuming their liberty in relation to the French Command, Dill wrote that Brooke could no longer count on receiving orders from the High Command due to the difficulty of communications, but neglected to mention that Brooke had only signed the June 14 agreement on the assumption that both Allied governments had agreed that Brittany should be held. The rather peremptory and condescending terms in which this message and the companion message to the French Premier were couched, together with the news that British reinforcements had ceased and that the two main British military missions were packing up for home, could only cap Weygand's hostility to the British, for as yet he had no intention of releasing Brooke from French command. But, in view of British decisions to the contrary, Weygand warned his allies early on June 16 that he now considered himself relieved of all responsibility with regard to British troops; and, in fact, French headquarters did not bother to inform Brooke a day later that the French Government had requested an armistice.[3]

Here, starting on June 14, was the final liquidation of Anglo-French coordination in the military sphere which had been pretty clearly foreseen even before Dunkirk; not surprisingly, the same bitterness and self-righteousness on both sides marked its passing. Theoretically, the political alliance could have survived this latest blow, but as a backdrop against which the most critical decisions had to be made it surely contributed its mite. June 14, however, witnessed more than this particular casualty: that morning Paris was occupied by the Germans, while the French Government itself, sharing in the rout of its armies, was once again in flight, strung out along the long road to Bordeaux. The British too were moving—in an altogether different direction—closer to a resolution of how they would confront the French.

While Reynaud drafted his final appeal to President Roosevelt, emphasizing the responsibility America would bear if she did not exert the maximum effort and stating that henceforth France could only continue the fight if American intervention reversed the situation by making victory for the Allies certain, Churchill in a formal message to the French Government did what he could to strengthen French resolution to fight on. Proclaiming the "indissoluble union" of the two peoples, Churchill pledged to the French Republic Britain's determination never to turn from the conflict until France stood erect in all its grandeur. But by renewing Britain's undertaking to France he was obviously anticipating a reciprocal assurance from the French Government. Lest there be any misunderstanding about this, Campbell, in reading Churchill's telegram to Reynaud on the evening of June 14, after both had reached Bordeaux, informed Reynaud that the British Government would not willingly permit France to abandon the struggle and that it intended to insist that France abide by the terms of the March 28 agreement.[4]

Reynaud stated that it was still his intention to continue the struggle from North Africa, that in fact he was sending General de Gaulle to London to obtain the necessary shipping for troops and war matériel,[5] but he was nevertheless discouraged by President Roosevelt's answer to his earlier message of June 10, which he had received that morning, for it contained no promise of a declaration of war. It was clear that he did not share Churchill's very inflated view of the President's message, either his belief that it was "decisive in favour of the continued resistance of France" or that the document implied that the United States was now "committed beyond recall to take the only remaining step, namely, becoming a belligerent in form as she already has constituted herself in fact."[6]

Churchill was not being unscrupulous in taking this tack with Reynaud, as might otherwise be assumed, for he had told the War Cabinet on the night of 13 June that he felt the President's message meant that Roosevelt intended to enter the war in the near future. "The President could hardly urge the French to continue the struggle, and to undergo further torture, if he did not intend to enter the war to support them." Lord Beaverbrook also thought it now inevitable that the United States would declare war. Churchill furthermore believed that the message was "quite sufficient as an answer to M. Reynaud's final appeal, but it would be observed that it had come in advance of it, which made the effect even more striking." In fact, the whole cabinet, noting that the message contained both a promise of all material aid and an invitation to France to continue fighting even if the government were driven overseas, concluded that the implications of the message were perfectly clear to the Anglo-Saxon mind.[7]

However, the Gallic mind quite rightly did not see matters in this optimistic light, and the Premier's apparent indecisiveness and fatigue led Campbell and Spears to wire later that night that at this point the best way to strengthen Reynaud against his defeatist colleagues was for the British Government to declare unequivocally that it would in no way condone a separate peace by France. This was the path being urged on them by their friend Georges Mandel, who was convinced that only a hard line could arrest the drift towards an armistice.[8]

The city of Bordeaux, as it turned out, was by mid-June probably the worst place in France for a government wanting to continue the struggle to have come. If the physical dispersal of ministers and ministries in Touraine had made it impossible for Reynaud to cleanse his government of unwelcome elements, at least it had also prevented them from actively "conspiring" against him and had permitted him some measure of control over subordinates still far removed from the pressures of a volatile public. In short, what might yet have been possible in the cloistered surroundings of Cangé became that much more remote once the atmosphere of rout, panic, and moral decomposition that prevailed in the capital of the Gironde began to spread its virus throughout cabinet and parliamentary circles, an infection obviously less conducive than ever to firmness, rational thought, or difficult decisions of any kind. The crowds, the refugees, the chaos, discomforts, and fears all played into the hands of those who wanted to liquidate the war as quickly as possible; in these congenial conditions, the masses were theirs almost by default to be led in a pro-armistice direction, and efforts towards this end began now to take on the appearance of being orchestrated. Anti-Semitism, among other evils, was rife, while Anglophobia, heretofore relatively restrained and restricted to private outbursts, rose unmistakably to the surface. As a token of the low esteem in which the British were held in some French circles, Sir Ronald Campbell found on his arrival in the city that he and the Embassy had been relegated to quarters a full 50 kilometers from Bordeaux, a distance that would have rendered their task impossible. Only with the help of the Minister of the Interior—Mandel—were they finally accommodated in a local hotel. Even then they were to have trouble not only in finding people but in getting them to listen to them over the next few days.

# The Slide Downhill:
# June 15

As OF the next morning (June 15), Reynaud still hoped to induce the government to depart for North Africa. The plan, so the British Ambassador reported, envisaged the bulk of the government going to Algiers while Marshal Pétain would remain in France to head a governmental administrative commission to negotiate.[1] However, Reynaud was fast losing control of events and was on this day faced with reverses of major proportions.

In the morning Admiral Darlan announced that the French Navy could not execute de Gaulle's plan for transporting large numbers of troops (870,000 was the figure given) and equipment to North Africa—he thought the demand "preposterous"[2]; the Marshal, for his part, affirmed his intention of resigning that night unless an armistice was requested or the United States declared war; in the afternoon—convoked by the Marshal—Weygand, Darlan, Baudouin, and Bouthillier met with Pétain—unknown to Reynaud and contrary to ministerial etiquette, which frowned on such extraconciliar conclaves—in what, most probably, was an effort to coordinate their next moves;[3] finally, Weygand rebelled openly against both Reynaud's and President Lebrun's authority.

During the course of the day it became obvious to the British Ambassador and Spears that France's decision to fight on virtually depended on an assurance by Roosevelt that America would enter the lists and that, failing such an assurance, a decision for an armistice would follow rapidly. Things were slipping fast, they noted, and it was becoming "more and more difficult to obtain a straight answer or a definite expression of opinion" from anyone, though they continued to put pressure on as many ministers as they could reach. Even in the event that the French Government decided to split in two, they telegraphed London, the plan to continue the war from Africa seemed unlikely to materialize because Pétain and Weygand would still control the armed forces. Reynaud himself told Campbell and Spears that he planned to resign if he could not obtain sufficient support for continuing the war. If, on the other hand, the cabinet as a whole backed him, he would accept the resignations of the defeatists, including Pétain, and would dismiss Weygand. He personally would never go back on England and would never be a party to surrendering the French fleet and allowing it to be used against a loyal ally.[4] As an indication of the importance attached by the British Government to the fate of the French fleet, Sir Ronald Campbell in the morning had told both Charles-Roux and Reynaud that if France's warships were not put into safekeeping, Churchill and Halifax "would consider as a veritable defection any soundings . . . of the Germans with a view towards an armistice."[5]

As for Reynaud himself, the Englishmen felt that he was definitely weakening and showing signs of lassitude notwithstanding his still firm intellectual stance against an armistice. In Spears's opinion, he was terrified at the prospect of Pétain's resigning and of having to govern in the face of the Marshal's and Weygand's combined opposition. "He had put up and was still putting up a brave fight, using against the defeatists, a little intermittently perhaps, the total strength God had given him. . . . He had made and was making mistakes, but they were not dictated by self-interest or fear. He was . . . doing the very best he could according to his lights and powers."[6]

In a bitter dispute with Weygand shortly before the Council of Ministers convened that afternoon Reynaud tried to convince the General that a cease-fire, such as the Dutch Commander-in-Chief had ordered, rather than an armistice, which the government wished to avoid in order to maintain solidarity with the Allies, was the best solution to France's military defeat. Weygand should settle the time when the struggle was to end, allowing the government, the fleet, and the remainder of the air force sufficient time to reach North Africa; if he did not wish to take such a responsibility on himself, he would be covered by a written order from the government. But Weygand again objected that the government could not leave France and indignantly refused to obey such a "shameful" order.[7] It was the government that must take the responsibility for ending hostilities.

Refusing to understand the somewhat dubious distinction Reynaud was making between a capitulation and a cease-fire sanctioned by the government,[8] Weygand, for the sake of preserving the honor of the army, instead advocated an armistice, which in his opinion would at the very least involve mutually binding conditions serving to limit the rights of the enemy, whereas a capitulation (or cease-fire) would be unconditional. Reynaud, on the contrary, believed that an armistice would have as its effect not only the capitulation of all the armed services in France and the Empire but the capitulation of the honor of the entire country as well. By giving any contractual sanction to defeat, as the British frequently reminded Reynaud, the French Government would be acting in a way contrary to the practice followed by all the governments of countries thus far occupied by the Germans, which had remained in the war by establishing governments in exile.[9] Reynaud, for his own survival, should have summarily fired Weygand for his flagrant insubordination, but although he had at last decided on the necessity of this move he again deferred actually doing so in the hope of first gaining the support of the Council.

Ironically, Reynaud almost succeeded in his efforts to keep France in the war. Only determined leadership was lacking. At the Council of Ministers which met between 4 and 7:55 p.m. Reynaud apparently managed to convince all his ministers, including even Pétain, that the most appropriate way to stop the "horrible and useless massacre" just described by Weygand in his report to the Council and piteously echoed by Camille Chautemps was by a cease-fire order to be given when the Command deemed it necessary and which would take effect immediately—unlike an armistice, which would take several days to conclude. In this way the government could still carry on the war from the Empire, with its substantial resources, and preserve its honor. Thus, in spite of the growing defeatism in the Council, the waning popularity of the Premier, and the intensified efforts of Weygand, Pétain, and Pierre Laval (now operating out of the Bordeaux City Hall through the courtesy of the Mayor, Adrien Marquet) to effect an armistice, at least for the space of a few minutes on June 15, Reynaud had the support of his colleagues for the "Dutch solution."

Taking advantage of such support, however ephemeral, Reynaud at this point, if he were ever going to do so, should have relieved Weygand of his command and replaced him with any general willing simply to obey orders. But Reynaud feared a military coup in this event which Pétain would back.* Furthermore, he did not believe

---

*See Appendix E, The Possibility of a Coup in Bordeaux.

that any government could survive in the face of Pétain's opposition. Above all, he felt he needed Pétain on his side and, if possible, a neutralized Weygand as well. Therefore, he hit on the unfortunate expedient of asking the Marshal, momentarily amenable to the cease-fire solution, to persuade Weygand of the rightness of the cabinet's view. This of course was fatal. As might have been foreseen, Pétain soon returned from the adjoining room in which the Supreme Commander was waiting (after his performance on June 13, Weygand had been excluded from full attendance at Council meetings by Reynaud), having been reconverted to his original idea.[10] He now threatened to resign if the Council did not decide on an armistice. Thus, the Council once more found itself at an impasse.

Having failed first of all to resolve the problem by audacity, having then been foiled by the backfiring of a false maneuver, Reynaud now demanded an immediate settlement of the question but quickly lost control in a sensational turn of events. "At this serious juncture," writes Churchill, "M. Chautemps . . . slid in an insidious proposal which wore the aspect of a compromise and was attractive to the waverers."[11] Chautemps had been preceded by Frossard, who spoke in favor of a compromise in order to maintain the unity of the government, which was fast dividing into two hostile camps: he wanted proof one way or the other that an armistice would (or would not) involve dishonorable conditions. But it was the so-called Chautemps maneuver that actually paved the way to an armistice, just as it had been the Vice-Premier's suggestion on the night of June 12 that in a sense had inaugurated the cabinet crisis.

Refraining from openly supporting Pétain and Weygand, Chautemps, according to Reynaud's summary, stated that if the ministers were to follow Reynaud to North Africa they should at least be protected against an adverse public reaction, which would interpret the government's departure as desertion. He himself was convinced that the enemy's conditions would be unacceptable, but the only way to establish this beyond doubt was to ask the Reich what conditions it would attach to a cessation of hostilities; the French Government, of course, would remain entirely free to reject the armistice terms if they proved dishonorable. Once this inquiry had been made, every Frenchman would understand that the government's only choice lay in continuing the war, a decision that implied the transfer of public authority outside metropolitan territory. With public opinion satisfied, there would then be no further difficulties in uniting the cabinet and rallying the nation to greater resistance. "It was, therefore, only a matter of getting Britain's consent to such a step, the object of which was to place the Government in a position to carry on the war."[12]

Chautemps, who was famous for his *nègre-blanc* solutions to seemingly irreconcilable differences between opposing factions and who, according to Pertinax, "even on the brink of the precipice ... could no more be kept from bargaining for middle terms than an apple tree from bearing apples," always claimed that he was sincere in seeking a way out of the impasse at which the Council had arrived and that he introduced his motion primarily for the purpose of preserving unity and preventing the government from falling. He wished also, so he has explained, to avoid a direct confrontation with the High Command, whose growing influence he feared. If the German conditions were unacceptable, and here Chautemps himself had in mind the *peace* conditions Germany would propose, to be elicited via a discreet sounding of the enemy by a neutral authority, the French would continue the struggle by transferring the government overseas. But "if, contrary to expectation, these conditions appeared moderate, our English friends undoubtedly would be in agreement with us to study them."[13]

Seduced by the subtlety of Chautemps's suggestion and tempted as usual by the opportunity to avoid coming to a definite decision and thereby confronting the divisions which in fact existed, the majority of the Council (13 for, 6 opposed, according to Reynaud's count) showed its approval of this step.[14] Even some who actually opposed an armistice were now lured from their stance because the proposal, by attacking the problem from an unexpected angle, succeeded in thoroughly confusing the issue. They did not realize, as Churchill had on a similar occasion, that one could not play with the idea of an armistice, that "it was not ... possible to embark on this slippery slope and stop," that "the mere announcement that the French Government were asking the Germans on what terms an armistice would be granted was sufficient in itself to destroy what remained of the morale of the French Army."[15]

In fact, one of the worst features of the proposal was its chameleonlike nature: it enabled each minister, except the most straight-thinking, to see in it what was personally congenial to him. Few at the time (or later) appeared to have a clear idea whether it was peace or armistice conditions that were to be inquired about or which neutral government might be selected to sound out the Germans. Moreover, there was no practical recognition of the fact—though

Marin pointed it out—that the Germans could hardly be expected to divulge their peace terms, contrary to custom in these matters, before an armistice had been agreed to; or, that for all intents and purposes, an inquiry concerning the enemy's conditions made by a third party was the same thing as demanding an armistice outright. But the confusion surrounding the Chautemps proposal, together with the reprieve from personal responsibility it granted, no doubt contributed to its success.[16] It also made it impossible henceforth for either Reynaud or President Lebrun to know precisely where many of the Council members stood.

Having fought a losing battle against the proposal,* so that he now found himself in the minority in his own government, Reynaud declared his intention to resign. The effect of the proposal, he stated, would be to separate France from its allies. However, he was soon dissuaded by President Lebrun, who insisted that Reynaud give way to the majority and agree to ask the British Government's consent to an inquiry concerning the German terms. This was made easier for him by Ybarnegaray's having previously demanded that the Council unanimously resolve never to deliver the fleet, an engagement, it was felt, that would make the French appeal more attractive to the British. Reynaud later justified his acquiescence to this step by reflecting that such an inquiry amounted "to an implicit recognition that France had not the right without Britain's consent to ask for armistice terms," which "was equivalent to acknowledging that, if Britain refused, France could not persist without forfeiting her honour." Lacking British authorization, he could then return before the Council strengthened in his argument on the inviolability of France's given word. He also recognized that if he did resign he would only be playing into the hands of the opposition, that it would open the way to Pétain or Chautemps succeeding him, which would *surely* mean an armistice. Reynaud therefore agreed to transmit the request on condition that he specify that it emanated not from him but from a majority of the Council.[17]

Following the adjournment of the Council and a second fiery scene with Weygand, now more intractable than ever, Reynaud summoned the British Ambassador and Spears to communicate the Council's decision to ask leave of the British Government to inquire through the United States what armistice conditions Germany and Italy would offer France. The President of the Council added that, if Britain agreed

---

*See Appendix F, Behind the Chautemps Proposal.

to France's taking this step, he was authorized by the Council to declare that the surrender of the French fleet to Germany would be an unacceptable condition. Should the British Government withhold its consent, however, he would probably have no choice but to resign. He could not, in this case, guarantee that his successor would maintain the cabinet's decision not to deliver the fleet. Furthermore, inasmuch as Roosevelt's reply to Reynaud's last appeal—bringing the painful news that the American President's declarations implied no military commitments—arrived at this moment, Reynaud also reminded Churchill in a written message that at their last meeting he had agreed to reconsider the question of authorizing a request for an armistice if President Roosevelt's reply was negative. That eventuality having materialized, Reynaud now felt obliged to put the question afresh. An answer was requested for early the next morning.[18]

All in all, though Reynaud had reiterated that "he would in no circumstances repudiate a document to which he had put his signature," his disquieting remark about what a successor government might do with the fleet and his insistence on resigning *unless* His Majesty's Government authorized the French Government to ask for armistice terms understandably led Campbell and Spears to see in his maneuver an attempt to *force* the British to condone France's repudiation of the Anglo-French agreement.[19] Their suspicions would appear to have been well founded, for the Premier's words in effect held out no palatable alternative to the British. Had Reynaud really wished to provoke Britain's refusal, as he would subsequently maintain, he could easily have stated as much or qualified his communication in a way that would not have been inconsistent with the reasons he later gave for agreeing to make the démarche. Reynaud's presentation of the situation moreover seems doubly inconsistent because, considering that he himself was not prepared to make this inquiry of Germany under any circumstances, he would also have had to resign even if the British agreed to his request. All Reynaud's ingenious explications to the contrary notwithstanding, it looks very much as if on the night of June 15 he believed that he was near the end of his rope and that it would probably be advisable for him to step down. This analysis is strengthened by what he reported to Jeanneney and Herriot the following day about the results of the June 15 Council. He then recalled that "ceding to the current, he had opened up conversations with Churchill with a view towards finding an honorable basis for a separate peace, if they were driven to it." He would not consent to charge himself with the task of interrogating the Germans on their intentions because that would be to contradict everything that he had done and said up to this point. He would instead withdraw. But he did not doubt that when Germany made known its conditions they would arouse such a furor in the country that the will to resist would reassert itself among the hesitants. It therefore appeared to him "tactical" to go along with this inquiry if the Council was of that mind. He looked upon it as "an abscess to be drained."[20]

Thus, though Reynaud had fought it, he appears to have quickly adapted himself to the logic or illogic of the Chautemps proposition and, not sensing the dangers of the "slippery slope," even to have hoped to derive some future advantages from it—for he was to admit to the deputy American Ambassador, Anthony Drexel Biddle, at midnight on the 15th that "only by such a move could he show the French people . . . the severity of the German terms, and [thereby] justify a flight of the Government to Africa or England."[21] In the light of these conversations, it is hard to conclude other than that Reynaud was now on the brink of abandoning the fight to make his views prevail,[22] although at the same time he apparently believed that his departure from the scene might well be of short duration and that he would inevitably be called back to power to lead a resistance government overseas once Germany's terms had been ascertained and found unacceptable. But, to his mind, it was first of all necessary to get France off the hook with the British—no matter what happened later.

# June 16:
# Britain's Conditional
# Acceptance

ON JUNE 16, a day that witnessed the most dramatic and confusing sequence of events perhaps ever recorded in the history of either nation, the survival of the Anglo-French alliance hung by the slenderest of threads. Faced with the crisis that Reynaud's request of the previous evening rendered unavoidable, the British Government now had three options: (1) to accede to the French Government's ascertaining the German conditions in the hope that their severity would force the French to reject them and to reorganize the government with a view to all-out resistance; (2) to follow Mandel's advice—which was that any manifestation of sympathy, or even of understanding, on Britain's part would only encourage the waverers and that for England to tolerate a French inquiry regarding Germany's conditions would be to make an abject surrender inevitable[1]—and categorically refuse their consent in the belief that the French cabinet would then be shocked into recognizing the realities of the situation; or (3) to give the French Government permission to negotiate on a conditional basis that would offer the British at least minimal security for a future in which any further French assistance would probably be out of the question. To have accepted the first option would have meant falling into the same trap the French ministers had, although temporarily it would have preserved Anglo-French unity. On the other hand, to have demanded their pound of flesh by requiring France to live up to the letter of the law would have run the risk of alienating the majority of ministers and might have served only to lessen that sense of responsibility to treaty obligations which they wished to foster.

Yet initially, during the night of June 15–16, it looked as if the

British position was hardening in exactly this direction. At 12:50 a.m. Mr. Hopkinson of the War Cabinet Office relayed to Sir Ronald in Bordeaux a message from Lord Halifax regarding Reynaud's request, the gist of which Campbell had telephoned at 11:50 p.m. This advised: "You must resist this proposal as strongly as possible. . . . They [the French] should be reminded of the understanding on which the last conversation [Tours] ended and they should be told that they must on no account take any final decision before a personal exchange of views has taken place. If these arguments prove unavailing they should be strongly urged to follow the Dutch model and leave France with you, but they must on no account take any decision hostile to H. M. Government before their departure." Campbell stated at this time that the " 'brutal question' was to some extent accompanied by safeguards." By this he was undoubtedly referring to the French cabinet's decision that in return for Britain's authorization to sound the Germans they would consider the surrender of the fleet an unacceptable condition.

Further phone calls at 2 a.m. and 3:40 a.m. related to the possibility of arranging a meeting between Churchill and Reynaud. The essence of London's anxiety throughout the night was that the telegram (No. 362 DIPP) embodying their hardest line to date had not yet arrived, though Campbell stated that he had already made use of many of the arguments contained therein. This earlier message indicated that the British wanted the French Government to avoid any formal negotiations with the enemy with a view towards peace or surrender, though a purely military capitulation was acceptable to them, and were angling now for the French Government to set itself up in exile in England. That way the French could keep all their resources, particularly their fleet and air force, in the service of the Allies.[2]

By morning the whole position was seen in a different light—events had, after all, moved on rapidly since the previous afternoon. Given the sentiment of the French Council, insofar as they understood it, the British War Cabinet was inclined to feel that the safest policy would be to grant the French permission to initiate negotiations on a conditional basis. It was this course, as the lesser of many evils, that the British Government therefore decided on; however, before the day was out the British were to abandon their original objective and, in a complete misunderstanding of the circumstances, gamble everything on a grandiose scheme which, instead of gaining them the maximum of what they wanted, resulted in their losing even what they considered minimal.

The inconsistencies of British policy were paralleled by the mistakes, ambivalencies, and deviousness of Reynaud's own politics. First of all, he did not correctly appreciate the strength of the anti-armistice sentiment still obtaining in the cabinet and therefore could not use it to his or the alliance's advantage. Second, he did not confide his tactics to the British, who were therefore unable either to talk him out of the dangerous game he was playing or to throw their support elsewhere. Third, and most serious, he concealed Britain's policy from his own government after it had become absolutely essential to make it known. Churchill had naturally interpreted Reynaud's communication of the night before as a sign that he had weakened. Reynaud, on the contrary, in what must surely be his bravest though most hazardous attempt to justify himself before history, has always claimed that he wanted his démarche to fail: that he hoped that the British would refuse their consent, that the Council would then recognize France's moral obligation to continue in the alliance, and, as a corollary, that the President of the Republic would entrust him with the formation of a new and viable government. As questionable as this claim is, and as unlikely as the sequence of events pictured may be, there is no denying that had such a scenario been played out it would have rescued Reynaud from his most immediate difficulties. A simple yes or a simple no were therefore from his point of view the most desirable responses he could have received from the British. The one thing he could not have wanted, considering the probable adverse effect on his colleagues, was something in between, iffy, ambiguous, and smacking of that old French bugbear, *la tutelle anglaise*. Thus, Reynaud and Churchill would find themselves working in opposite directions during most of the 16th, their efforts joining in a last desperate move only at the eleventh hour.

While the British cabinet considered Reynaud's request to be released from the Anglo-French agreement, Reynaud himself at 10 a.m. was conferring with the presidents of the two assemblies, MM. Jeanneney and Herriot, to obtain their consent to the eventual removal of the government to North Africa. Brought before the assembled ministers (the cabinet), which met at 11, they here formally confirmed their opinion that the public powers must be transferred outside of Bordeaux to safeguard national sovereignty and to make possible the continuation of resistance.[3]

In the Council of Ministers itself, Reynaud stated that he was not yet able to make known to them the results of his representations to the British Government the previous evening, as he was still awaiting

Churchill's reply, but that (in Baudouin's words) "the British Cabinet considered that France was bound by her promise not to treat with Germany separately, and that she could not be relieved of the promise."[4] This no doubt reflected his meeting "early in the morning" with the British Ambassador and General Spears, at which time they had told the Premier that they had not yet received the British cabinet's answer but that "he need be in no doubt as to the impression it [his request of the night before] had made." They also bluntly pointed out that "the agreement not to make a separate peace had been concluded to meet just such a contingency as had now arisen."[5]

Baudouin, however, seized on this opportunity to declare publicly his surprise and regret "that the British Cabinet should have gone back on the undertaking not to crush an unlucky ally such as France," repeating at this psychologically advantageous moment what he had already told many of his colleagues in private: that "this undertaking had been given by Mr. Churchill at Tours, and had then been confirmed by his two colleagues in the War Cabinet, Lord Halifax and Lord Beaverbrook."[6] At this point, and almost as if on cue, Pétain read his long-threatened letter of resignation, in which he scored the government's delay in asking for an armistice and refused any longer to be associated with maneuvers whose sole purpose was to play for time. Only on the insistence of President Lebrun, who promised that an answer would be given him during the day, and on Reynaud's interjection that, since France had asked Britain to absolve her from the pledge she had signed, the least they could do was to await their ally's reply, was Pétain stalled and the Council able to be adjourned until 5. Reynaud also mentioned the possibility of still another meeting with Churchill to be held that afternoon in Nantes.

At midday, summoned by President Lebrun, who was conferring with Weygand, Reynaud had his third and last dispute with the General, who still refused to obey the government. Reynaud, again as on the day before, planned to remove him from his command at the afternoon meeting of the Council, for it was obvious that his obstructionism was making it impossible to govern.

Thus, it would appear that Reynaud to all intents and purposes was proceeding with his official policy—if not very effectively—when a remarkable series of communications began. Sometime in the afternoon, Sir Ronald Campbell and General Spears brought Reynaud the British Government's reply to the question he had posed the previous evening in the name of the French cabinet. In a telegram dispatched at 12:35 p.m. and incorporating the War Cabinet's decision, Churchill had written:

Our agreement forbidding separate negotiations, whether for armistice or peace, was made with the French Republic, and not with any particular French administration or statesman. It therefore involves the honour of France. Nevertheless, *provided, but only provided, that the French Fleet is sailed forthwith for British harbours pending negotiations,* His Majesty's Government give their full consent to an inquiry by the French Government to ascertain the terms of an armistice for France. His Majesty's Government, being resolved to continue the war, wholly exclude themselves from all part in the above-mentioned inquiry concerning an armistice.[7]

This decision, so different from the approach the British had seemed bent on only the night before, when they were leaning towards Mandel's solution, resulted from three major points considered by the War Cabinet on June 16, although none were analyzed very carefully. Concerning Reynaud's request, the Lord President of the Council had argued that, if the British refused, "it was clear from Sir Ronald Campbell's telegrams that the present French Government would probably resign and their successors might be very much worse from our point of view. M. Reynaud had told the Ambassador that he could not guarantee that his successor would maintain the decision reached by the Council of Ministers that the surrender of the Fleet would be considered an unacceptable condition." Chamberlain's conclusion was that "This was an argument which was very difficult to resist, and it seemed therefore that we had no choice but to consent to the French making enquiries." In short, it would be expedient, because they could not stop the French from pursuing this course in any event, and it was far preferable to keep Reynaud, a known quantity, at the helm than to risk an unfriendly politician coming to power. Clement Attlee, for his part, seemed to suggest that a French armistice would not make all that much difference; he doubted whether, even if the French Government moved out of the country, it could take an active part in the war as it would be susceptible to German blackmail in the form of pressure exerted on those who remained in France. However, the Prime Minister, who backed by the Chiefs of Staff insisted on conditions regarding the fleet being attached, was more legalistic: it was important not to give any impression that by the mere resignation of M. Reynaud the French Government would be clear of its obligations, which had been contracted by a solemn treaty.[8] And his was the decisive voice.

There was no discussion as to the probable interpretation any Frenchman might place upon their conditional agreement.

Reynaud's immediate reaction to the British proposal, as it turned out, was wholly unfavorable, and he made no attempt to conceal that he thought the conditions posed quite absurd. The British were asking that the French fleet be sent to British waters at the very moment it was engaged in protecting Algeria and the western Mediterranean and also at the same time the British were urging the French Government to leave for North Africa. Reynaud argued that acceptance of such conditions would mean laying all of French North Africa open to attack by the Italian fleet. Reynaud in his memoirs implies that his reaction was motivated by an unwillingness to admit that France was leaving the coalition (though on the basis of their message it was obvious that the British Government despaired of any further French contributions and hoped only to salvage what was most precious to them—the fleet). Spears, too, notwithstanding his suspicions of the night before, thought that Britain's consent was unwelcome to Reynaud because his opposition to an armistice had been based on France's pledged word to Great Britain and, of course, this argument would become valueless once the French cabinet knew that the British were in principle willing to concede that France might ask for one.[9]

Clearly, the real explanation is a lot more complex. Although Reynaud refrained from mentioning it, he must also have been well aware that the posing of such conditions not only constituted an infringement on French sovereignty but that their acceptance would negate beforehand the value of any inquiry vis-à-vis the Germans by placing in English hands the principal trump on which subsequent negotiations—if there were any—would rest. Chautemps's belief that Reynaud was using the danger to French North African possessions merely as a pretext to get the English to withdraw their conditional agreement to the Chautemps proposal is more than possible but incomplete as an explanation; because the pertinent question to ask is whether it was the consent or the condition that Reynaud wanted to see withdrawn. In this respect, it is noteworthy that the President of the Senate, Jeanneney, before whom Sir Ronald Campbell had put the British condition, rather as a trial balloon, before communicating it to Reynaud, also "did not commit himself to advocating it." In fact, his reaction was identical to Reynaud's, namely that the condition posed "would have the immediate result of delivering the Mediterranean to the Italian fleet." And, contrary to

Spears's belief that he did not find the proposal offensive, Jeanneney himself writes that he was struck by the "unfriendly tone" of Mr. Churchill's message.[10] Thus it can be assumed that Reynaud had several reasons for finding the British answer ill-advised: conforming to the conditions laid down would not have helped the French no matter what course they adopted, and he realized that any attempt to "sell" them would almost certainly be doomed in advance.

But there is still another factor. Reynaud's response may also be interpreted as a delaying tactic rather than as an exhibition of confidence in his ability to convince the cabinet of its obligation to honor France's pledged word or as an outright rejection of Britain's conditions for releasing the French Government from the Anglo-French agreement. Something seems to have happened before the arrival of Campbell and Spears which could have renewed Reynaud's faith in his official policy, something which provided him with a new argument for keeping France in the alliance. However, Reynaud did not inform Campbell and Spears of what was afoot, other than that Churchill had telephoned him regarding a meeting; nor did the Foreign Office enlighten them either. Spears only knew that he felt Churchill's message to be a serious mistake, not only because it robbed Reynaud of his moral armor but because the stipulation concerning the fleet laid down by the British would probably not be accepted by the French cabinet, which would see in it a proof of distrust (which it was) and would interpret it as an attempt to hold the fleet hostage (which was, naturally, the whole purpose of the demand).[11]

London nevertheless seemed determined upon this course and at 3:10 the Foreign Office dispatched a second message to Campbell, who communicated it sometime before 4 p.m. to the French Premier. Amplifying the earlier telegram, it stated that the British Government expected to be consulted as soon as any armistice terms were received, not only by virtue of the treaty forbidding a separate peace or armistice but also because of the consequences of an armistice to Great Britain, whose troops were still fighting with the French Army. The message also pointed out that in stipulating the removal of the French fleet to British ports the British had in mind French interests as well as their own and were convinced that the hand of the French Government would be strengthened in any armistice discussions if it could show that the French Navy was out of the reach of German forces. In conclusion, the French Government was reminded that the British expected it to make every effort to fly the French Air Force to North Africa (or England) and to extricate the Polish, Belgian, and Czech troops still in France.[12] The tenor of the message clearly indicated that the War Cabinet already looked upon the armistice as a *fait accompli* and that its sole concern henceforth was to pick up the pieces and to protect British interests as best it could. By now Campbell and Spears realized that their most important task was simply to prevent the French fleet from falling into the clutches of the Germans.

# June 16:
# The Proposal of Union

ALMOST at the very moment this message was being delivered to
Reynaud and while Campbell and Spears were still at his side,[1] General de Gaulle telephoned from London with the startling news, unprecedented in diplomatic history, that the British Government had
decided to offer France a proposal of union, by which the Anglo-
French alliance would be reinforced and transformed into a political
union within which the interests of the two nations would be amal-
gamated. De Gaulle then dictated the text of the proposal, which the
British War Cabinet had just approved, henceforth to be known as
the Declaration of Union.

By the terms of this document, the governments of the United
Kingdom and the French Republic were to declare that France and
Great Britain were no longer two nations, but one indissoluble
Franco-British Union. Joint organs of defense, foreign, financial, and
economic policies were to be provided for by the constitution. Every
citizen of France was to enjoy immediate citizenship of Great Britain,
every British subject to become a citizen of France. Both countries
would share equal responsibility for repairing the devastation caused
by the war, wherever it occurred. During the war a single war cabinet was to govern from wherever it best could, and all the forces of
Britain and France, whether on land, sea, or in the air, were to be
placed under its direction. Both parliaments would be formally associated. France was to keep its available forces in the field, on the sea,
and in the air, and the Union was to concentrate its whole energy
against the power of the enemy.[2]

This extraordinary document, communicated under such dramatic
circumstances only an hour before the Council of Ministers was to

meet, had an equally remarkable background. For its history we must turn to events on the other side of the Channel. According to Churchill, the idea of a Franco-British union had first taken shape on June 14 at a meeting attended by Sir Robert Vansittart (the government's first diplomatic adviser), Major Desmond Morton (Churchill's private secretary), and Jean Monnet and René Pleven (both members of the French Economic Mission in London). With the object of providing Paul Reynaud with "some new fact of a vivid and stimulating nature with which to carry a majority of his Cabinet into the move to Africa and the continuance of the war," this group had evolved the outline of a declaration of indissoluble union.[3]

The idea for the union did not arise quite so parthenogenically as Churchill suggests. It had actually been kicking around in somewhat inchoate form since the early part of the year, often in connection with the related proposal for a "no separate peace" agreement. Sir Ronald Campbell had suggested in early March that the proposed text for that agreement be expanded so as to give some contractual form to the continuance of Anglo-French economic and military collaboration after the war. The Ambassador thought that such a declaration would serve to encourage the French and to allay their suspicions regarding future British intentions when the time came to arrange peace terms with a defeated Germany.

Even as far back as November 1939, however, the question of some sort of permanent union between the two countries had been jointly taken up by the Royal Institute of International Affairs and the Centre d' Études de Politique Étrangère—at the suggestion of the Institute's director, Arnold J. Toynbee, who believed that unless such an entity were formed the unification of Europe would inevitably be produced by Germany, whether during or after the war. The idea gained greater impetus as the result of a short visit to France in March by Professor Toynbee and Sir Alfred Zimmern, during which they had heard the French Senator Honorat, an ex-Minister of Education, make a proposal outlining such a Franco-British union before the Centre d'Études de Politique Étrangère on March 11. The Senator had proposed the adoption of a treaty of perpetual association between France and Great Britain that would have provided, among other things, for the pooling of defense, for the common conduct of foreign policy, for the joint control of the economic resources of both powers, and for the enjoyment of passive rights of citizenship as between the nationals of each country. These ideas had been made known to the Foreign Office by way of reports submitted by Toynbee and Zimmern on March 13 and 26 respectively. Apparently, at this early date, the idea aroused some enthusiasm in France, where it was felt that it would simultaneously stimulate French morale, impress neutral opinion, and discourage the Nazis.

By April the question of union was being dealt with in Britain by three bodies: (1) the Ministry of Information, with a view to educating public opinion; (2) Chatham House, on a professorial level; and (3) Lord Hankey's committee on postwar unity, which was examining the administrative and practical problems involved. Although its only practical expression was in the Supreme War Council and the Anglo-French Co-ordinating Committee, this did not dampen verbal adhesion to the idea of Anglo-French unity, or prevent Churchill from referring to an "indissoluble union" between the British Empire and the French Republic as if it already existed. "In fact," one of its earliest proponents, Orme Sargent, noted in a letter to Oliver Harvey on April 14, "it may be said that no Minister opens his mouth now without making some allusion to this subject." Thus, by mid-June, the necessary groundwork had already been laid. For it to spring to life, only total catastrophe was required. As will be seen, its relationship to the Anglo-French agreement of March 28 was still, on the part of the British, its principal attraction.[4]

Churchill, whose initial reaction to any concrete realization of Anglo-French union was unfavorable, states that he first heard of the plan on June 15 at the Carlton Club while lunching with Lord Halifax, the French Ambassador Charles Corbin, Vansittart, and others. Raising the subject at his afternoon War Cabinet, Churchill goes on to say, he was surprised to find that this "immense design whose implications and consequences were not in any way thought out" actually evoked an enthusiastic response.[5]

Churchill appears to be somewhat confused in his time sequence here. The subject of an indissoluble union had first been broached in his presence at a meeting of the War Cabinet on the morning of the 15th, at which time the Prime Minister was primarily concerned about consulting with the French Government as soon as possible on the question of the fleet. There was no afternoon cabinet meeting that day. Furthermore, discussion that morning had revolved around a June 14 memo from Leo Amery (similar in content, but not identical, to the Vansittart project), which had left the cabinet feeling dubious. Whether Churchill discussed the matter at lunch on the 15th at the Carlton Club is doubtful. Harold Macmillan, MP, states that the same group of people mentioned by Churchill (with the addition of Leo

Amery and himself) discussed the plan for a Franco-British Union at dinner at the Reform Club on June 15. However, Churchill *did* lunch the following day with de Gaulle and other Frenchmen at the Carlton. The cabinet enthusiasm he attributes to the afternoon of 15 June most probably belongs to the afternoon of 16 June.[6] In any event, the project was temporarily laid aside on the morning of the 16th while the War Cabinet first addressed itself to answering Reynaud's request of the night before for the formal release of France from its treaty obligations. The morning's deliberations were embodied in the two telegrams sent to Sir Ronald for delivery to Reynaud.

In the meantime, General de Gaulle had arrived in London early that day to arrange for British tonnage to carry French troops, arms, and equipment to North Africa (or England) after their evacuation from French ports. Informed of the crisis in Bordeaux by Corbin and Monnet, he had immediately agreed to back the Vansittart project already under way and soon became its most active advocate. The exact schedule of events connected with the progress of the Franco-British project throughout the day remains unclear (no two accounts agreeing in detail, and General de Gaulle's in particular being as confused as is Churchill's). According to René Pleven, a key participant in the affair, the General (apparently during the British Government's morning session) telephoned Bordeaux to warn Reynaud that an event of great importance was being prepared in London. He therefore asked that no decision regarding a cessation of hostilities or negotiations with the Germans be taken before further details were sent to him. A second phone call seems to have been made after de Gaulle discussed the project with Churchill—either at 12:30 p.m. or at 3:15. According to the French Premier, de Gaulle outlined the idea of the political union he believed the British intended to offer France and also held out the possibility that Reynaud would be asked to head the new Franco-British war cabinet. At this time Reynaud accepted the principle of the union, but insisted that the Allies let him have the text of the proposal in time for a Council of Ministers at 5. Such a *coup de théâtre*, he felt, might well alter the entire situation.[7]

It was while lunching that day with the Prime Minister and M. Corbin that de Gaulle succeeded in convincing Churchill that "some dramatic move was essential to give M. Reynaud the support which he needed to keep his Government in the war" and urged the acceptance of the proposal of indissoluble union to meet this purpose. De Gaulle no doubt reasoned that at the very least it would gain time by encouraging the French Government to adjourn all decision and would augment the chances of the public powers being safely transferred outside France. Both de Gaulle and the French Ambassador had disapproved of the decision reached by the War Cabinet that morning, the substance of which had already been transmitted. Since there were now plans afoot for a meeting the next day between Reynaud and Churchill in Brittany, de Gaulle wanted Churchill to use this opportunity "to make a further attempt to dissuade the French Government from asking for an armistice" and with that end in view to join with Reynaud in issuing "a declaration announcing [the] immediate constitution of [the] closest Anglo-French Union in all spheres in order to carry on the war." As a result of de Gaulle's pressure Churchill decided to suspend action on the decision previously reached and accordingly telegrammed Sir Ronald instructing him to postpone delivery of the two earlier messages.[8]

The draft proclamation that Vansittart (at Halifax's request) and Morton in consultation with Monnet and Pleven had previously labored over was now ready. It was this document that was presented for consideration when the War Cabinet reassembled at 3 p.m. Its difficulties were obvious, as was readily agreed, but Churchill felt that under the circumstances they should not allow themselves to be "accused of a lack of imagination." At 3:55, on hearing from de Gaulle that Reynaud believed he could hold his position if only he received the proposed proclamation of unity in time, the War Cabinet approved an amended version and authorized General de Gaulle to fly with it to Bordeaux that evening. It was immediately telephoned to Reynaud. In addition, the cabinet proposed that Mr. Churchill, Mr. Attlee, and Sir Archibald Sinclair, representing Britain's three political parties, as well as the three Chiefs of Staff and Sir Alexander Cadogan, should meet Reynaud at sea off Concarneau in Brittany at noon the following day to discuss the draft proclamation and related matters. Then, not long after de Gaulle's historic call, Churchill himself telephoned Reynaud to receive the Premier's agreement in principle to the declaration and to make final arrangements for the next day's meeting.[9]

In the opinion of Campbell and Spears, Reynaud appeared to be quite transfigured by the news, for he believed that with this proposal he could carry the day and keep France in the war. He now declared that for such a document he would fight to the last. Reynaud quickly concluded that the proposal of union put the two earlier messages of the British Government in a completely different light: "Instead of resigning itself to the rupture taking place, it had decided to try and keep France at Britain's side by reinforcing the alliance. . . . Thus was born the conception of a general proposal . . . which, taking the place of the conditional acceptance which the two telegrams had given me, was *ipso facto,* to render such an acceptance null and void." And Spears immediately noted that "the proposal, if accepted, meant that France would go on in the war united with Great Britain. The disposal of the Fleet would then be a question of strategy to be settled by the joint staffs." Reynaud therefore presumed, with the enthusiastic agreement of Campbell and Spears, that Britain's new offer superseded the two telegrams on the subject of the fleet.[10]

Reynaud's reasoning was correct up to a point: certainly the proposal of union was intended to supersede the previous telegrams; however, it was not intended to render Britain's conditional consent "null and void" if the proposal of union was not favorably received by the French cabinet. Churchill points out: "The War Cabinet had not altered its position in any respect. We felt, however, that it would be better to give the Declaration of Union its full chance under the most favourable conditions. If the French Council of Ministers were rallied by it, the greater would carry the less, and the removal of the Fleet from German power would follow automatically. If our offer did not find favour, our rights and claims would revive in their full force."[11]

However, this aim, vital from the point of view of the British, who were determined not to watch the French fleet go down the drain whatever else might happen, was not made clear in the excitement. Churchill's telegrams instructing Campbell to have Reynaud delay action on, and himself to suspend action on, the previous messages were received by Campbell and Spears only upon returning to their hotel, after Reynaud had left them to read the proposal of union to President Lebrun. A message was thereupon sent Reynaud at the Council to inform him that "the two telegrams should be considered as cancelled." In an understatement, Churchill remarks that " 'suspended' would have been a better word."[12] It appears that Campbell and Spears, in their hurry to paraphrase the text of the telegram, may unwittingly have undermined the British cabinet's strategy. This mistake, moreover, was compounded either by their rush to withdraw or by Reynaud's overwillingness to hand back the two documents* and

---

*See Appendix G, The Case of the Elusive Telegrams.

by his eagerness to interpret the British Government's latest move as a revocation of its consent (and of its condition) and as a change in policy, rather than merely as a change in tactics.[13]

This could have been, as Reynaud himself claims and General Spears also believed, because he wished to be able to oppose, in the name of France's pledged word, any demand for an armistice, and still "hoped that, by playing the card of British intransigence, he could sway the Cabinet to his thesis." Or it could equally well have been, as his words to Jeanneney and Herriot later that evening suggest, because "the formula that [Mr. Churchill] had presented first could not be entertained."[14] A combination of both these motives seems a strong possibility—the long-term advantages of the Anglo-French Union together with its diplomatic packaging having not only revived his combative spirit but obscured the fact that in British eyes both proposals, where the fleet was concerned, amounted to the same thing.

# The Government's Collapse

WHATEVER hopes Reynaud may have nurtured regarding the British proposal, they were not destined to last long once the Council of Ministers got under way at 5 p.m. Before broaching what he considered the main business of the day, the Premier made two preliminary communications. He first read out Roosevelt's telegram,[1] with its depressing conclusion, then acquainted the Council with Great Britain's refusal to annul without conditions the Franco-British declaration of March 28 or to authorize a demand for an armistice. He apparently had some idea that the British refusal would tend to nullify the negative effects of the President's reply, an initial misreading of his colleagues' sensibilities. In his memoirs Reynaud reports that he indicated that the British Government "had at first given its consent and then withdrawn it," and on July 24, 1945, before the High Court, he testified that, though he had not read the two telegrams to his colleagues, he had summarized their contents. He claimed also to have mentioned the British demand that French ships be sent to English ports. However, all these statements appear to stretch the truth considerably, for Reynaud did not disclose the existence of the two telegrams, he furthermore concealed what from the Council's point of view was their substance (Britain's conditional release), and left the ministers with the impression that the British Government had adopted a wholly intransigent attitude—a presentation quite in keeping with his assertions before the Commission of Inquiry in 1947 and again in 1950 that he had "maneuvered" to have Britain's authorization withdrawn.[2]

According to Chautemps, Reynaud stated that the British Ambassador had given him a brief note which declared that the proposed

234

démarche (the Chautemps proposal) engaged the honor of France. "As he should have been able to foresee," writes Chautemps, "such a lesson, administered in a disobliging manner to the government of a friendly people who had just submitted to an unmerited disaster for the common cause, produced a painful impression." If this was in fact the tenor of Reynaud's digest, it would explain the "chilling" effect reported by Lebrun.[3] However, as the conditional British response *did* evoke France's honor, Reynaud was certainly within his rights in alluding to it.

By the time Reynaud got around to reading the proposal of union a pall had already descended. Reynaud read the British declaration twice, stressing the importance it held for the future and announcing Churchill's impending visit the following day for talks on the subject. However, the proposal fell flat; it won the oblique support of perhaps two or three,[4] but in the majority inspired mainly skepticism or outright hostility—not to speak of a sense of irrelevance. There was some unenthusiastic academic discussion, but those who had been waiting impatiently for the past five days for armistice proceedings to begin were not prepared to examine the proposal with even a show of seriousness. Some, such as Pomaret, simply had no taste for becoming a subject of His Majesty. Ybarnegaray, however, thought that the union would relegate France to the status of a dominion (as did Chautemps) and that even being a Nazi province was preferable to the probability of seeing the French Empire subordinated to Great Britain. In any case, France's sovereignty overseas and over its other resources seemed to be jeopardized by the plan. Pétain, for his part, saw in the proposal just another attempt to retard an armistice, an astute political trick that was incapable of changing the military facts. Convinced by Weygand that England was lost, he felt that to make a union with Great Britain at this point would be tantamount to fusing with a corpse.[5]

Undoubtedly, as a number of critics have pointed out, the surprise—or last-minute—element associated with the scheme, far from evoking the enthusiastic response hoped for, had actually contributed to the plan's overwhelming rejection.[6] The idea was first of all too big to be rapidly digested by minds cast in a traditional nationalist mold. Even to its avid supporter General de Gaulle, it seemed "obvious that one could not, by an exchange of notes, even in principle fuse England and France together, including their institutions, their interests, and their Empires, supposing this were desirable."[7] More to the point, by June 16, with everything collapsing and Anglophobia gathering force in France, the proposal was very much too late. Whatever its intrinsic merits and prospects, had it been submitted several days earlier it would at least have received serious attention because then it could have been considered before the question of an armistice took center stage. For the offer to have had any *real* chance of success, Léon Noël believes, it should have been formulated before the disaster at Dunkirk; but then before Dunkirk, or indeed at any time before June 16, there was not the remotest possibility that the British cabinet would have rallied unanimously to such a revolutionary notion. Only in extremities were the British willing to take this step.

The trouble was that the French Council of Ministers recognized this—not only that a genuine and equal union of the two nations was impossible in the circumstances of France's defeat, but that the only purpose behind the proposal was to keep France and French resources, particularly the fleet, formally committed to the war. The British hoped that their offer of union would strengthen Reynaud and thus prevent an armistice. But, as Charles-Roux has pointed out, "the offer could hardly strengthen the position of the President of the Council at the very moment when, *sotto-voce,* the declaration of March 28, 1940, was being held against him as an imprudence." Any project that proposed to tighten the bonds between France and England, he thought, was doomed to failure at a time when many ministers, quite to the contrary, were straining to loosen them. In Chautemps's opinion, at a moment when to save France only the most powerful and immediate material aid would have done, the offer seemed not only inadequate to the situation but indeed almost laughable; while, according to Bouthillier, there was between the grandiose project put forward and the immediate cares of the French ministers a cruel discrepancy. The offer of union was considered not to have answered the question posed by the French Government. This sentiment is echoed by Baudouin, who had earlier told Reynaud that at any other time the offer would merit careful examination, but that what the Council had to decide that evening was simply whether or not they were going to ask Germany her terms for an armistice. Others apparently agreed with this assessment, and thus the debate on the question of an armistice versus the pursuit of the war from North Africa resumed.[8]

Hereafter Reynaud had little control over his colleagues or the situation generally. He again picked up the old points—the necessity for the government to go to North Africa to pursue the struggle and the obligation to honor the Anglo-French agreement—but by this time his much-used arguments had ceased to be effective. Mandel would later tell Campbell and Spears that Reynaud, having shot his bolt, "had spoken without heat or fire, like a lawyer defending a cause he did not believe in and for which he had been promised an inadequate fee."[9] Then, in the midst of the Council's wranglings, President Lebrun had read out an alarming telegram from General Georges stating that the Germans had now reached Dijon and the Saône front, that armored columns were advancing on La Charité-sur-Loire, and that it was absolutely essential to come to a decision. This message Weygand had had delivered directly to Lebrun, on whom it had the desired effect, rather than to the President of the Council, as was customary.[10]

At this point Frossard, sensing the Council's desire at last to be done with the business, returned to the proposal made by Chautemps the previous day to sound the Germans as to their conditions for an armistice. Reynaud's argument that the question no longer obtained because the approach to Britain had come to nothing was futile (as well as incorrect) and was undercut by Baudouin's dogged (and equally incorrect) insistence that at Tours Churchill had already authorized France to seek an armistice. This Reynaud denied unequivocally, and in answer to a question put by Marin he stated that France's honor was irretrievably pledged "up to the hilt." But, with the discussion now turning into a quarrel between "capitulards" and "deserters" in which accusations of cowardice were bandied about, it was clear that the cabinet was in a state of decomposition. Unable to make his point of view prevail, Reynaud had either to step down as Premier or to reform his government immediately. He therefore brought the debate to a close by affirming his wish to confer with President Lebrun. The ministers were asked to reassemble at 10 p.m.[11]

Reynaud apparently believed at the time that had a vote been taken the majority would have cast their votes against him, if not on the question of the armistice itself, at least on that of the government's departure overseas. He states that the opposition had increased from two on the night of June 12 to thirteen by the evening of June 15.* He therefore opposed a vote being taken, not only because it was contrary to the rule that prevailed in the Council of Ministers, but because he wished to avoid formally putting himself in the minority on a vital question and consequently compromising his chances of being called to power again for the express purpose of

---

*See Appendix H, Reynaud's Cabinet: Rundown on the Armistice.

forming a government dedicated to resistance. Before any modification of the government could be made, however, the President of the Republic's agreement was necessary. It is possible that Reynaud took an unduly pessimistic view of the situation at this point and somewhat misjudged his standing in the Council. But, as his colleague Dautry has pointed out, hovering over all of them was a sense of urgency induced by defeat, by bombardment, and by the knowledge that tumultuous antiwar meetings were springing up around Bordeaux. In the irrational and spent atmosphere of this last crucial Council, in which all issues had become rather hopelessly confused—the Franco-British Union with departure for North Africa and both with the continuation of the war, an inquiry concerning the enemy's conditions with an armistice per se—in which improvised proposals were batted about like ping-pong balls, in which insults but not sustained arguments were exchanged, and in which the only ministers who attempted to reason dispassionately were those who showed themselves hesitant or who raised objections or introduced qualifying comments, it is entirely understandable that Reynaud might well have felt he was in the minority. In any case, he knew he could no longer govern with the Council such as it was. Because if there was a majority it was no longer possible to say what it corresponded to—or even which of the intimately related issues might have been judged of such overriding importance as to warrant a vote.[12]

Around 7:30 p.m. the British Ambassador and General Spears were summoned to the Prefecture, only to learn that Reynaud had failed and was about to resign. They begged him to postpone this irretrievable step and to get rid of the "evil influences" in his cabinet, but left the Premier feeling that little hope remained. They were only just in time to get a message through to London announcing the opening of a ministerial crisis and warning Churchill that the meeting arranged for the next day must therefore be held up.[13] The Prime Minister and his party, in fact, were at that moment seated in the train at Waterloo, ready to set forth on the first leg of their overnight journey to France, when Campbell's message from Bordeaux reached them.

Campbell and Spears had but one hope left; as Reynaud had not yet officially resigned, it was still possible that the President of the Republic might entrust him with the formation of a new government. With this in mind, they sought out the President of the Senate to urge him to use his influence with President Lebrun to reappoint Reynaud, who could then form an administration from which the defeatists would be excluded.[14]

Meanwhile Reynaud had consulted informally with Albert Lebrun. With the cabinet now approximately evenly divided between pro- and anti-armistice factions, power to shape the direction of events lay primarily with the President. As Parliament was not assembled to make a choice between factions, it was up to Lebrun to exercise his constitutional rights as arbiter. Theoretically, as Henri Becquart points out, since under the circumstances Parliament was not in a position to sanction the acts of a new government by a vote of confidence, he would have been well within his rights to have left power in the hands of a man whose war policy had been unanimously approved by the Chamber on April 19 and again acclaimed by that body on May 16 and by the Senate on May 21.[15]

This was no doubt asking too much of Albert Lebrun. Not only had the situation changed dramatically since May, but by neither character nor temperament was he fitted for so trying a role in a period of crisis. For instance, Jules Jeanneney thought the President conscientious and correct but lacking in the critical spirit and still more in the taste for exercising the authority vested in him. "To deplore, to offer no resistance, to submit: it is his nature. The times require something else," he had written of Lebrun as far back as September 5, 1939. Pertinax's assessment is even more devastating: "That through the interplay of political rivalry, and thanks to the principle 'Let the most insignificant among us come up on top,' the republic of Poincaré, Clemenceau, or even Fallières . . . should have had this silly creature to lead it through the most serious hour of its history is enough to make one believe that it stood judged and condemned by Providence."[16]

The President was not actually pro-armistice; on the contrary, he had favored the so-called Dutch solution and the removal of the government to North Africa. But he was not a stalwart, he too had been seduced by the convenience of the Chautemps proposal, and he was not impervious to the military's pressure for an immediate decision. Nor was he unmindful of the effect on public opinion that the resignation of Pétain and the replacement of Weygand by still another general presumably would have had. Furthermore, France's obligation to honor its pledge to England did not weigh heavily on him, as was brought out years later in evidence presented at the Pétain trial, wherein Lebrun stated:

... from the moment when one of the two countries signatory to a convention such as that of March 28 retains a part of its forces for its own defense instead of risking all in the common struggle, which is just what the British Empire did, it can always make use of this document to recall the obligations inscribed therein, but it no longer has the necessary moral authority to say: I cannot release you from your engagement.

Finally, Lebrun believed that Reynaud represented a minority and that a consensus of opinion had at last crystallized in favor of an armistice, or at least in favor of an inquiry. The President of the Republic therefore pronounced in favor of ascertaining what armistice conditions would be offered.[17] A strict parliamentarian, Lebrun felt that if Reynaud retained power it must be to exercise it in conformity with the opinion of the majority.

As on the day before, he asked Reynaud to abide by the Chautemps proposal and to stay in power to put it into effect. This Reynaud refused to do, stating that he was the last person qualified to make an approach to Germany in that he had based his whole policy on the Franco-British alliance. Acceptance of Lebrun's entreaties the previous day had offered Reynaud a last chance to maneuver within the framework of the alliance—either to get British permission or to find an alternative solution that would make an armistice unnecessary—but to give way on the 16th meant, for all intents and purposes, actually asking for an armistice, which the British had explicitly refused to admit. The Premier therefore replied: "If you want such a policy carried out, go and ask Marshal Pétain." Only in this sense did Reynaud "counsel" Lebrun to charge Pétain, the principal opponent of his policy, with forming a new government.[18]

A short while later at 9 p.m., Lebrun formally consulted the presidents of the two chambers, in the presence of Reynaud, before making a final decision. Given a rundown of the situation by the Premier—including Britain's offer of union and its refusal to consent to an armistice—and apprised of the President's intention of giving effect to the Chautemps proposal, both Jeanneney and Herriot expressed their opposition to the idea of making inquiries of Germany and their preference for reinforcing the alliance with England. Jeanneney believed that any inquiry into armistice conditions could only hamstring the country's resistance. But because Reynaud now felt it "tactical" to submit to the inquiry if that was the Council's opinion, and because he refused to carry out such a mission himself, they agreed that in these circumstances Reynaud could only resign. Yet, when asked by Lebrun to designate Reynaud's successor if the Council imposed the Chautemps proposition, they advised the President to retain Reynaud—obviously for the purpose of carrying on with his original policy.[19]

Taking advantage of his constitutional prerogative, however, Lebrun set aside their advice and decided on Pétain as the new head of government. Reynaud did not bother with the formality of handing in the resignation of his cabinet at another session of the Council.* Before 10 o'clock the formation of the Pétain government was under way. The long struggle was over.

Was this the inevitable outcome of the cabinet crisis? Could Reynaud really have acted differently? Did he make use of all the powers available to a head of government? Georges Bonnet, among others, has placed the responsibility squarely on Reynaud, a conclusion shared—from an anti-armistice angle—by Louis Marin.

One thing is certain [Bonnet writes], Paul Reynaud did not *have* to resign—the constitution is quite clear on this point. Until there had been a vote in the chamber the Prime Minister was free to replace his ministers as and when he wished. Even had the President of the Republic refused to sign the necessary decrees, Reynaud was still free to reduce the number of portfolios and thus surround himself with a homogeneous group, determined on continuing the war from North Africa. . . . It is a hard fact of the constitution as it then stood that an invested Prime Minister could not be overthrown by a vote of his Cabinet. Reynaud could have continued in power had he wished.[20]

Such a position, however correct it may be technically, nevertheless overlooks a good deal. First of all, it ignores what would have been considered feasible in 1940, what would have been deemed compatible with contemporary parliamentary practice. Second, it ignores the time factor: what might just have been possible on June 12, to wit, a radical reorganization of the government, could have been accomplished on June 16 only under the aspect of a ministerial coup; and this might well have served as an invitation to civil war. At this point Reynaud could hardly have afforded to add to his already formidable list of enemies the President of the Republic, who would have been completely alienated by such an unorthodox bid for power. There is also the question of what countereffort Reynaud might have evoked on the part of his opponents had he tried to get rid of such powerful personalities as Pétain, Weygand, Chautemps, etc. They were, after all, backed by physical force, which Reynaud believed they would not hesitate to employ. The truth of the matter seems to be that

---

*See Appendix I, Reynaud's Resignation.

without a functioning Parliament the Prime Minister felt himself more dependent, not less so, on traditional parliamentary usages, and could not have bypassed President Lebrun unless he had been willing to jettison the whole democratic tradition as understood both by him and his colleagues. As Reynaud himself points out, what his critics actually reproach him for is that he did not violate the constitution. Lebrun had supported him on June 5 when he reorganized his government, but would no longer go along with such a policy on June 16. The President of the Republic, he reminds us, "only took his decision after consulting the Presidents of the two Chambers."[21]

M. Louis Marin's ironic comment is of course haunting, and expressed by such a principled critic must carry weight: "One continues to ask by what mystery or by what aberration the President of the Republic together with the President of the Council, both of them hostile to an armistice, after having consulted the President of the Senate and the President of the Chamber, who were equally opposed, called to power the man whose very first act they knew would be to demand an armistice."[22] But, vital as the question is, it tends to ignore the realities of the situation as they were felt by most of the participants at the time: the popularity of and adulation accorded Pétain and Weygand, the personal hostility shown *belliciste* ministers, the threat of riots among the Bordeaux populace, and the feeling that a continuation of the war would not be supported by the country at large. These factors had to be taken into consideration in a country purporting to be a democracy. In after years neither Rollin nor Dautry believed Reynaud could have remade his government in the conditions then prevailing; it was just not possible to constitute a ministry from which Pétain and Weygand would have been excluded. Indeed, Dautry concludes that the only way in which Reynaud could have coped with the situation was by recourse to revolutionary methods, namely, by interning Pétain and Weygand and then bundling the rest of his cabinet onto a plane and heading straight for Algeria. He did not think that the minority in the Council, feeling themselves backed by public opinion, would have bowed to the will of the majority. Therefore, it would have been necessary to arrest the opponents of the government, but for this the government needed troops, which were not then available to it, plus the belief that the country would have upheld its decision. This, of course, was the crux of the matter. There was good reason to believe that Parliament and the people would not have done so. Revolutionary sentiment, for the most part, was just not there in these sons of the Third Republic.

Even Mandel, according to Georges Monnet, believed "everything depended on Lebrun." Therefore, Reynaud's perceptions of the situation were probably correct.[23]

The defeated Premier met with Campbell and Spears for the last time at 10:30 p.m. to inform them of his resignation. He had been beaten, he said, by the "combination of Marshal Pétain and General Weygand, who were living in another world and imagined they could sit round a green table discussing armistice terms in [the] old manner." This "had proved too much for [the] weaker members of the Government on whom they worked by waving [the] spectre of revolution." Reynaud stated that, while he had not informed his colleagues of the British Government's two earlier messages, he had said that "he assumed they still held that [the] surrender of [the] Fleet . . . would be regarded as an unacceptable condition"—to which there had been general assent.[24]

Reynaud believed that President Lebrun intended to return to a policy of resistance if the Pétain cabinet did not succeed in obtaining an armistice. Because he felt sure that the Germans would offer only unacceptable conditions, he expected that the new government formed expressly to receive them would inevitably fall. So convinced was he that in this case Lebrun would again call him to power that he asked to keep the appointment with Churchill arranged for June 17. But Spears abruptly indicated that on the next day there would be a new government and that Reynaud then would no longer speak for anyone.[25] A chapter had ended and already Spears was looking to the future. His original mission at an end with the fall of Reynaud, he was now more concerned with seeing to the safety of General de Gaulle, who had arrived shortly before to discuss the application of the British offer, than with the political hopes of the ex-Premier.

The British had failed rather spectacularly either to keep France at war or to wrest from the French Government any sensible guarantee regarding the fleet. The War Cabinet's decision to change policy horses in mid-stream may or may not have been wise, but certainly the fact that their original demand, which was to have been revived in the event of the second's failure, was not even communicated to the Reynaud cabinet or to the French President can only be attributed to ineptitude. It would be easy to make a scapegoat of Reynaud for having concealed from the Council the contents of the two telegrams even after the proposal of union was rejected; but then he had never been asked by Campbell and Spears to reveal the British Government's demand for the French fleet as a quid pro quo for allowing armistice inquiries, either during the Council's evening session as an alternative to the Franco-British Union or later when he conferred with Albert Lebrun. Added to which, even after the commencement of the ministerial crisis was known, neither Churchill nor the Foreign Office bothered to instruct Sir Ronald to deliver to the new French Government, from the moment it was formed, the important messages concerning the fleet which had been withdrawn under such mysterious circumstances earlier that day.[26] Both British and French were to pay dearly for this oversight.

# IV

# *The Question of the French Fleet*

## *June 17 – June 22*

*When the military apply themselves to making war, they do not always win it, but when they get mixed up in politics, that is really a catastrophe.*

Pierre Laval, testifying on October 4, 1945, at his own trial, in *Procès Laval* (Paris, 1946), p. 51.

# The Telegrams Resurface

THE Pétain government was quickly organized. Camille Chautemps, whose ingenious proposal had brought down the Reynaud cabinet, again became Deputy Premier. General Weygand took over the reins of the Ministry of National Defense, and two other high-ranking military men, Generals Colson and Pujo, were entrusted with the ministries of War and Air respectively. Most significant for the future was Admiral Darlan's acceptance of the post of Minister of the Navy, a fairly clear indication that the independent-minded Commander-in-Chief of the undefeated French Navy was now ready to align himself with the point of view advocated by Pétain and Weygand.[1] Other ministers, eleven of whom were retained from the Reynaud cabinet, included Bouthillier, Ybarnegaray, Frossard, Pomaret, Rivière, and Chichery.[2]

There had been only one rough spot in the otherwise smooth transition. Pierre Laval had refused the Justice portfolio when offered it, demanding instead the Ministry of Foreign Affairs already promised to Baudouin. Pétain had given in, but then on the repeated objections of Weygand, who feared that Laval's appointment would "throw France into the arms of Germany," and of Charles-Roux, who threatened to resign as Secretary-General if Laval came to power,[3] the Marshal backed down, ultimately rewarding with the post Paul Baudouin, whose tireless efforts on behalf of an armistice had done so much to bring Pétain to power. President Lebrun and Admiral Darlan, believing that there were already sufficient complications with England, had also counseled Pétain against giving such leverage over foreign policy to the wily Auvergnat.[4] The nomination of Laval, France's most vociferous critic against everything English and now

247

the advocate of *rapprochement* with Germany, if not actually a reversal of alliances, a man whose very name had been anathema in England since the Italo-Ethiopian imbroglio of 1935–36, could only have been interpreted in London as the prelude to more hostile moves. His exclusion from the new government represented a victory for those who wished to preserve at least some semblance of continuity in foreign relations in spite of bringing the military alliance with Great Britain to an end.

By 11:30 p.m. President Lebrun had signed the documents appointing the new ministers, and within a half hour after the Council had held its first session it was decided unanimously to ask Germany its conditions for an armistice. The Spanish Government was chosen to act as France's intermediary with Berlin. In the confusion of the hour France's promise to Great Britain not to negotiate separately was either forgotten or dismissed altogether. Equally forgotten was the spirit of the Chautemps proposal—at least as it had been understood by some of its supporters; in the context of a cabinet come to power for the express purpose of ending the war, it was now no longer a question of simply soliciting information from Germany, though representations to this effect would continue to be made. In fact, it was on Weygand's proposal that the Council had deliberated, and this time M. Chautemps in no way intervened to recall the words of his own. The rush to get on with the business of negotiating took precedence over all other considerations. The enemy's peace conditions, according to the General, were not alluded to.[5]

Yet something of the character of the new Foreign Minister and of the direction the Pétain government was prepared to take can be deduced from the conversation Baudouin had with the Spanish Ambassador, Señor de Lequerica, at 12:30. In this Baudouin made it quite clear that the French Government was interested in more than just an immediate cessation of hostilities; the Spanish Government was also requested to find out what *peace* conditions Germany would propose. In fact, responding to a precise question on the point put by Lequerica, Baudouin admitted that the "armistice terms were, of course, always a temporary expedient": it was the kind of peace they could obtain that was of ultimate interest. This double-headed request was quickly speeded across the border.[6] And at 9 a.m. the next day Baudouin handed a similar request to the Papal Nuncio for presentation to the Italian Government.

In a far more trying interview, held in the presence of Charles-Roux, the new Minister of Foreign Affairs next faced Sir Ronald

Campbell at 1 a.m. Informing him of the decision taken by the French Government and of the request just transmitted, Baudouin attempted to allay the fears of the British Ambassador by insisting that an inquiry concerning the conditions under which an armistice might be arranged was not equivalent to accepting them whatever they might be; it was not to conclude an armistice at any price. He had no doubt that the terms offered would be unacceptable, but in any case the government would never subscribe to conditions contrary to French honor; it would not accept any naval clause prejudicial to England or any measures which would make a French force fight against its former ally. Admiral Darlan, Baudouin asserted, had taken the necessary measures to ensure that no part of the fleet would ever be handed over to the enemy. To a rigid and increasingly icy Campbell, Baudouin insisted that "nothing would be changed in the end in the close relations between France and England." He "asked England to look at the French decision, not in the narrow spirit of a jurist, but with the sympathy of a friend who sees another weak and trodden underfoot without having the power to help him."[7]

The Foreign Minister then recalled the generous sentiments expressed by Mr. Churchill at Tours, which encouraged him "to hope that although His Majesty's Government could not approve of the French Government's action they would at least understand it." Sir Ronald, who was openly skeptical, limited himself, each time Baudouin repeated his assurance that the fleet would never be surrendered, to taking formal note of his words, "apart from expressing great distress that a French Government should have gone back on the signature of an agreement expressly designed to prevent such a thing happening." As he reported later that night to the Foreign Office, he thought it well to refrain "from indulging in any severe recrimination, such as might create an impression that His Majesty's Government would henceforward wash their hands of France and thereby give any who would be ready to grasp at it the shameless pretext to claim that the Government was released from its understanding about the fleet, to which it was essential to hold them."[8]

Baudouin evidently found this hour-long interview with Campbell something of an ordeal—both embarrassing and sterile.

During the course of the last few weeks when our troops were being beaten down under the hammer-blows of Germany [he was to write], I have never on any day or at any moment felt that behind the icy manner of Sir Ronald

Campbell there beat the heart of a friend. I have always had before me the faultless representative of England, the very aloof high official who was opposed to any display of personal feeling and who was devoid of any real initiative. The stiffness of our nocturnal conversation was terrible, and his reserve was not to be explained by the normal British rigidity, for his looks hardly concealed his extreme caution.[9]

It is quite likely, of course, that Campbell's coldness was accentuated by proximity to Baudouin; certainly there was no love lost between the two. If anything, the Ambassador's opinion of the French Foreign Minister was even less flattering, for he was later to describe him as "voluble, specious and unreliable," as a man whose "dominating motives were fear and the desire to stand in well with the conqueror after the inevitable defeat."[10] These then were the conflicting personalities on whom the principal burden of Anglo-French relations would rest during the crucial six days to follow.[11]

Campbell apparently did not on this occasion mention the conditions relative to the fleet that the British Government had insisted on earlier that day as a prelude to France's negotiating with the enemy. And when he saw Baudouin during the afternoon of June 17 it was merely to stipulate that the British Government must be consulted before any armistice terms were accepted, a condition the Foreign Minister readily agreed to. However, Campbell was doubtful whether he would obtain satisfaction on this point. Inasmuch as the French Government had already broken its word by violating the March 28 agreement, he thought it unlikely that it would hesitate to violate the obligation to consult the British once the German terms were received.[12]

It was no doubt an error on Sir Ronald's part not to have mentioned in his initial interview with Baudouin the conditions previously posed by the British War Cabinet, but it is quite likely that he was not altogether clear at this moment as to what use, if any, his government wished to make of the two telegrams sent on June 16. It was only late the next morning (of the 17th) that Lord Halifax informed the Ambassador that, if he had not already done so, he "should at once make to [the] new French Government the communication contained in my telegram No. 369 and inform them of the contents of my telegram 368" and still later in the day that the Foreign Secretary spelled out for him that the "necessary pre-condition to [the] assent of His Majesty's Government to [a] French application for [an] armistice was that [the] French fleet should be sailed for British ports." Campbell was told that the French Government must understand that this vital condition had not yet been fulfilled and that he "should not cease to urge [the] French Government, if they persist in seeking [an] armistice, to sail the fleet at once."[13]

However, even before these instructions reached Bordeaux, Campbell had insisted to Pétain, when he saw him first thing in the morning, that when the German demand for it was presented it was absolutely essential for the French fleet to be in British control and no longer in the power of the French Government to dispose of; this, he added, was the least the British could expect. But the Marshal declined to agree that the fleet should be handed over to England; his idea was that in these circumstances the fleet should be scuttled. Sir Ronald also tried to discover at this time what the French Government intended to do if, as was to be presumed, the German conditions proved unacceptable. Would it move to North Africa? But on this point, as on a number of others, the Ambassador "failed to elicit any satisfactory response." In fact, Campbell found conversations with Pétain rather fruitless.[14]

Lord Halifax nevertheless thought it worthwhile for Campbell to remind the new head of the French Government that "though we take it for granted that Marshal Pétain would wish to be scrupulous on any point of honour, we do not yet know that this express and vitally important stipulation has been fulfilled." Campbell was to recall to the French Government that "this agreement [of March 28] was not concluded on behalf of any particular French government, but on behalf of the French Republic."[15]

"In order to make absolutely certain that no member of the present government should be in any doubt as to the attitude of His Majesty's Government," Sir Ronald, during the afternoon of June 17, brought to Charles-Roux the text of the two telegrams from Lord Halifax that he had delivered the day before to Reynaud and had then withdrawn on instructions from London. Campbell writes that he asked the Secretary-General to see to it that the contents of these messages were "brought formally to the notice of the Council of Ministers in writing," after which Charles-Roux had "left for to do so."[16] According to Baudouin, this meeting between the two men took place at 4:45, whereas *he* only learned of the existence of the telegrams at 7 or 8 that evening.[17]

The Secretary-General's account of his meeting with Sir Ronald is equally brief. According to his recollection, Campbell, when asked why the two telegrams had been withdrawn, had stated that he believed it was because they had been replaced by the offer of union. But as this project had not followed up, he judged it necessary that they be brought to the attention of the French Government.[18] Neither Charles-Roux nor Campbell elaborates on whether any further hint was given regarding how these documents were now to be interpreted, although the Ambassador may have felt that their meaning was obvious. Whether Campbell had been crystal-clear on this first day in the life of the new administration cannot be known. But whether or not the recommunication of the two telegrams conferred on them a new validity, as Bouthillier points out, was a problem that had to be solved, for the question would affect the attitude the French Government would have to take on the subject of the fleet before the departure of its plenipotentiaries.[19]

Baudouin's initial puzzlement over the telegrams is perhaps understandable. It was only late that night that Churchill sent off what Sir Alexander Cadogan considered a "scorching" personal message to Marshal Pétain and General Weygand, copies of which were to be furnished to President Lebrun and Admiral Darlan, stating his conviction that they would not injure their ally by delivering the fleet to the enemy ("Such an act would scarify their names for a thousand years of history") and urging them not to fritter away precious hours during which the fleet could be safely sailed to British or American ports.[20] Baudouin also did not yet know that in discussing the question of the fleet with Charles Corbin in London on the 17th, Churchill had expressed his fears that by virtue of the disorganization produced by defeat French warships might be taken by surprise if the Germans suddenly occupied the ports, thereby rendering their escape impossible. This was why he thought it in France's "essential interest to decide the question in advance by sending the fleet to England or to the United States, as we ourselves should do if we found ourselves at the worst extremity."[21] But unless liaison between various members of the French Government was totally lacking—or unless a conspiracy of purposeful dumbness surrounded the question—it is difficult to see why this "mystery" was not properly cleared up by the following day.

Asked by Baudouin to throw light on the situation the next morning, Paul Reynaud explained that the two telegrams had actually been taken away by the English Ambassador and replaced by the offer of union. Under these circumstances he had not thought it fit to mention them to the Council of Ministers on June 16, because in his eyes they no longer existed.[22]

Later that morning (June 18) Baudouin asked the Ambassador himself what significance he was to attach to the delivery of the telegrams to Charles-Roux the day before, whether restitution of the documents "proceeded solely from a desire to clear up completely the successive phases of the Franco-British negotiation of June 16th, or if it gave fresh life to these proposals on the part of the British Government." Campbell stated that he understood the question very well, but that before responding he would like to consult his instructions again. Returning from the British Embassy an hour later, Campbell, according to Baudouin's account, reported that he did not consider that the fact of having delivered these proposals to M. Charles-Roux revived them, and he begged Baudouin to treat these two documents solely as the principal elements of a negotiation which had ended on June 16 in the only British proposition that was definitive, namely, the offer of union made by Mr. Churchill. They had now simply to be filed in the archives. From this explanation, for which there is no corroborative evidence from Campbell, Baudouin concluded that he was not obliged to take account of the two telegrams or to inform the Council of Ministers. Consequently he communicated them only to the Marshal and to Admiral Darlan.[23]

Yet Sir Ronald had previously asked Charles-Roux to see that the messages contained therein were brought to the attention of the French Council of Ministers in writing! If it is assumed that the Secretary-General would not have mishandled this request in transmitting it, then Baudouin's ingenuousness becomes more than a little suspect. As Sir Lewis Namier suggests, he must have realized that this was no mere diplomatic formality and that the British Government had more on its mind at this juncture than the completeness of the French Foreign Ministry's archives. In view of the fact that Sir Ronald had, during the course of their conversation, insisted on his government's concern in the matter of the fleet, it is difficult to understand how Baudouin could have failed to see that his simplistic explanation was completely at variance with British interests or that "the demand contained in these two messages was merged in the proposal of union, and that it re-emerged when union was rejected."[24] One is tempted to conclude that if Baudouin did not understand Campbell it was because he did not want to.

Baudouin claims to have learned only about August 10, 1940, following the return to France of the Marquis de Castellane, Chargé d'Affaires in London throughout July, that in the view of the British Government the proposal of union "did not annul the two telegraphic messages of June 16th." That had been made clear in a memorandum sent on July 12 to Castellane by Lord Halifax, who stated that the return of the telegrams signified that at any moment France could be released from its engagement to Great Britain provided that it first sent its fleet to British ports. Baudouin therefore blames the ensuing misunderstanding between the two governments on Sir Ronald's misinterpretation of his instructions, which, he claims, "largely depended on the construction put by London on the progress of events."[25]

If Baudouin is guilty of insincerity, however, the British Government can also be charged with perpetuating its original tactical error—either through ambiguousness or slowness. Although Baudouin was undoubtedly exercising his talent for misinterpretation, it is likely that, a plethora of instructions notwithstanding, Sir Ronald had bungled matters unintentionally. The least that can be said is that he did not make it altogether clear that the telegrams were operative as of that moment and that he also seemed rather unsure as to the significance of what he was doing.

At least two very well qualified diplomats thought there had been bungling involved. For instance, Charles-Roux has written:

The only certain conclusion that one can draw from this important episode is that it involved a false maneuver on the part of England. In its own interest as well as in the common interest, it would have been better if the two telegrams of June 16 had not been withdrawn, but that having been, they should have been communicated the same day to our Council of Ministers. Their comings and goings between the British Embassy in Bordeaux and the French government could only weaken their import. Reappearing the day after the armistice demand, restored to French authorities who had not even suspected their existence the day before, produced under an unclear title on which there probably subsisted some ambiguity, they could no longer be as operative as their author undoubtedly intended them to be.[26]

Sir Robert Vansittart, Chief Diplomatic Advisor to His Majesty's Government, for his part, feared "that an expensive error was made when the French were authorised to seek terms of the Germans." He believed that it had "set us on a downward path up which we have never been able to climb again." He had not known that "such a telegram was in contemplation . . . until after it had gone"— the clear implication being that he would never have approved it had he been previously consulted.[27] This viewpoint, shared incidentally by General Spears, could well have influenced Campbell on June 17 and 18.

For this mix-up three possibly interrelated explanations occur: (1) Baudouin's account may simply be untrustworthy, in spite of Charles-Roux's insistence that the Minister for Foreign Affairs was acting in good faith when he recorded his June 18 interview with Campbell; (2) the British Ambassador, while insisting always on the substance of his government's demand, that is, on the safety of the French fleet, preferably by means of its being sent to England, nevertheless may have separated the question of the fleet from the question of the telegrams' validity in the belief that the rush of events rendered such a concern obsolete or unnecessary;[28] (3) the Ambassador may have deliberatively refrained from legalistically reactivating his government's demand of the 16th out of fear of offending Admiral Darlan and other members of the French Government by an obvious manifestation of distrust. By 18 June he may well have felt that it would be wiser to proceed on an ad hoc basis, reevaluating the situation day by day. He was no doubt also aware that in the final analysis the British were entirely dependent on the decision the French Government itself would arrive at concerning the fleet—regardless of any prompting on their part.

# Promises, Promises

GROWING awareness on the part of the British of their inability to control the French did not mean that threats were not efficacious, or that the British refrained from making them—though they did so only obliquely. Just before the Council of Ministers met at 11 on the morning of June 18 the American Ambassador, Anthony Drexel Biddle, had handed Admiral Darlan the text of a sharply worded note sent by Cordell Hull the previous day. (A copy was subsequently given to Baudouin during the course of the meeting.) This warned that unless the French Government, *before* concluding any armistice, took steps to guarantee that its fleet did not fall into enemy hands, it would be pursuing a policy that would fatally impair the preservation of the French Empire and the eventual restoration of France's independence and autonomy; furthermore, if the fleet *were* surrendered, the French Government would permanently forfeit the friendship and good will of the United States.[1] The uncompromising tenor of this message, which had actually been instigated by the British, could hardly be overlooked.[2] Despite its peremptory tone, the Council there and then "decided unanimously against handing over a single warship to Germany or Italy," however grave the consequences of such a refusal might be. If the surrender of the fleet formed part of the conditions, armistice negotiations would be broken off.[3] However, the Council did not discuss the practical means by which the French Government might have proved to Britain and America not only its determination never to deliver the fleet but its actual capacity for protecting the fleet from capture.

The British Ambassador thought that he had been promised rather more than this when he talked with Pétain and Baudouin prior to the Council's meeting. Armed not only with the Prime Minister's strong message for Pétain and Weygand but with new instructions from his government concerning the "shame" France would incur by accepting dishonoring armistice conditions, along with a British invitation to the French Government to take refuge in England, Campbell once again begged the Marshal to place the French fleet beyond the enemy's control "within the few hours that remained." Pétain limited himself to generalities, but Baudouin, somewhat surprisingly, "said that the decision as regards the fleet had already been taken and only remained to be confirmed by the Council of Ministers that morning." As Campbell later reported, the Foreign Minister "had no doubt that this would be done and was absolutely categorical on this point."[4] Campbell, while hopeful, waited for the proof of the pudding—that is, for definite orders to materialize.

At this point, the Ambassador certainly believed that the decision of which the Foreign Minister had spoken had to do with sending the fleet to British ports, but Baudouin denies ever saying that a decision in this sense had been taken. At the end of the Council's meeting, Baudouin duly informed Campbell of the decision that *had* just been reached and asked him to send Churchill the most solemn assurances that no part of the French fleet would be used by the Germans; the pledge which the French Government had given England was unqualified and final.[5]

Although Campbell deeply regretted that the earlier "decision" had not been ratified, he was somewhat mollified by Baudouin's explanations. The Council's attitude, the Foreign Minister told him, was that "it was a point of honour for France to receive the armistice terms with her armies and fleet still fighting." If the armistice had to be rejected because it included the surrender of the fleet, French forces would continue the struggle for as long as they could. Before capitulating on land, "the fleet would go to join up with the British navy, or, in the last resort, would carry out pre-arranged orders to scuttle itself." Campbell was also "assured that orders to that effect had been made out and would be issued immediately if this had not already been done." In reporting these developments, the Ambassador stated his belief, for the moment, that "the French were playing straight with us." Marshal Pétain, General Weygand, and Admiral Darlan, he thought, "were all men of honour." The Council's change of mind since the morning he attributed to "Admiral Darlan's reluctance to part with his fleet while [it was] still fighting and to a rather stiffer attitude on the part of the Government as a whole. To that extent it was a healthy sign."[6]

Thus Campbell on 18 June seems to have set aside his initial pessimism regarding the character and intentions of the new French Government in favor of a qualified optimism. The key to this new-found equanimity, as Oliver Harvey's diary entry for June 18 makes doubly clear, was that on the question of the fleet the Ambassador had found Baudouin "fairly satisfactory": The "Fleet could not be handed over now because [the] war was still continuing, but orders had been given for its ultimate departure for [the] U.K. or for scuttling."[7] That all these suavely phrased, self-confident-sounding assurances of Baudouin's were somewhat hasty and insincere, or at the very least misleading, now seems fairly certain. Hasty because they appear to have been motivated more by a momentary desire to placate a troublesome ambassador than by the need to deal with the matter substantively. Insincere because Baudouin had told the American Ambassador shortly *before* he met with Campbell at 1 p.m. that "he could not . . . say that the French Fleet would join the British Fleet; it might be sent overseas or it might be sunk."[8] And misleading because the context in which the assurances were offered (that is, that they would come into operation *only* if the fleet's surrender were demanded by the Germans) was not stressed. Of course, the British may have been so convinced that the surrender of the fleet *would* be required that the contingent nature of Baudouin's pledges escaped them.[9] In any case, they undoubtedly influenced how the Ambassador interpreted his instructions, specifically what Campbell said to Baudouin regarding the meaning to be attached to the two telegrams in question as well as the nature of the demands he thought were required at this point.

In addition to mollifying Campbell, Baudouin likewise charged Corbin in London with notifying Churchill of the "definitive" position taken by the Council on the subject of the fleet. He also took this occasion to thank the Prime Minister for the words of good will he had pronounced in favor of France and to acknowledge the assurances given the French Ambassador the day before that with victory England would reestablish France in her integrity and power. Baudouin, however, was not pleased with the distinctions the British leader was beginning to draw between the French people and the Pétain cabinet, and it was for this reason perhaps that he expressed the hope that the British Government would never invoke "the cruel necessity in which our country is placed today to loosen the solemn engagements already cemented by so much blood spilled in common." Corbin, for his part, warned Baudouin that it was especially according to the fate of the French fleet that the Anglo-Saxon world would judge whether or not France had been false to her engagements to Great Britain.[10]

If the British did not immediately resort to direct threats but instead relied on registering their anxiety concerning the fleet and on reiterating that France was not relieved of its treaty obligations to continue the war (as in Churchill's speech to the Commons on the afternoon of June 18),[11] it was no doubt because they still hoped that a semiconciliatory attitude would pay higher dividends. The political power structure in Bordeaux was as yet only indistinctly understood; therefore, for the present the British preferred to wait for the Pétain government to sort itself out and clarify its policy before taking any irrevocable steps. Although their soundings and approaches were to take different forms, the goal remained the same: to make certain that the French fleet would not fall into German hands under any circumstances. From their point of view, the only way to ensure its safety was by having it sent to British or American waters or, failing that, by having it attached to a French Government established in North Africa. The French had formally declared their determination never to deliver the fleet to the enemy, but for the British simple promises were not enough.

For Great Britain, survival itself was at stake. With a minute and badly disorganized army and a numerically inferior air force, England's major bulwark against an expected German invasion lay in the superiority of the Royal Navy. The British believed that if the French fleet joined their own it could make a vital contribution to the Allied war effort. Its total tonnage was about 40 per cent of that of the Royal Navy and, in addition, the French fleet could boast some of the world's fastest and most modern ships. Particularly strong in destroyers (of which the Allies had lost 32 since the start of the war, leaving the British with only 68, out of some 133 commissioned, fit for service in home waters in mid-June), the French could have vastly improved the effectiveness of Britain's convoy system while proportionately reducing the German submarine threat. On the other hand, if England's advantage in sea power were lost or substantially reduced by the addition of any part of the French Navy to Germany's already overwhelming resources, the chances of holding out would be desperately slim. Specifically, according to a US Office of Naval Intelligence report issued on June 17, "the combined naval power of Germany, Italy and France would be about one third greater than that of Britain, and greater also than that of the United States even if the American Fleet were to be brought back from the Pacific." As for France's seven completed capital ships, about which the British were especially fearful, their addition to the arsenals of Germany and Italy would have given the Axis equality with the British in this decisive category.[12] Therefore, at all costs, naval supremacy had to be maintained.

From the French Government's point of view, the picture looked very different. Convinced that all would soon be over in England and that their ally would also be forced to sue for an armistice, the French Government did not think primarily in terms of the merit it would store up for itself by heeding British pleas and admonitions. The possibility of an ultimate British victory seemed too remote to put much faith in the promise of future favors. The needs of the present were far too pressing. France's own survival as a sovereign nation was also at stake. The French cabinet therefore could not think that England's opinion of France's conduct in the matter of the fleet was of overriding importance. To be sure, the continuation of Great Britain's friendship was desirable, for no one could be absolutely certain about the ultimate outcome of the war, especially if the United States were to join in, and undoubtedly France stood to gain by an Anglo-American victory, but for the immediate future and probably for a considerable time to come Germany held all the winning cards.[13]

Because in their weakened position the French would have but one real bargaining weapon in the forthcoming negotiations with the Germans—an undefeated fleet—it seemed ill advised either to prejudice these negotiations beforehand by an act of hostility sure to rouse the ire of the Germans or to deprive themselves of the capacity for striking back at the Germans at some later date if conditions warranted it. Without the fleet they would be at the enemy's mercy. Furthermore, if, after the French had directed the fleet to England for safekeeping, the English then decided to use it against Germany, there would be nothing to prevent the Germans from imposing the harshest terms on France, including the occupation of the entire country and the taking over of North Africa. Again, if the British were defeated, what would prevent them from using the possession of the French fleet to bargain with the Germans for their own advantage at the expense of French interests? What the French apparently did not consider was the paradox that if the British *were* defeated—which the absence of French naval assistance of course made more possible—or chose to use their *own* first-class navy to wrest tolerable terms from Hitler, then the French fleet would immediately lose most of the diplomatic importance they attached to it. But this equation, that the value of their precious fleet was in large measure a function of continuing British resistance, was too subtle—or remote—to weigh in the balance.[14] Consequently, the French cabinet was inclined to regard the fleet as a trump card to be retained at all costs, whether as a weapon if France had to fight on or as a means of exerting pressure on the Axis powers to grant more lenient armistice terms or a more generous peace. Seen as the "means by which the prisoner could blackmail his jailer,"[15] the fleet was a counterweight that could never be given up if France hoped to exercise any control over its destiny or carry any influence in the future.

The British, still hopefully cherishing illusions as to the identity of interests existing between the two nations, or at any rate pretending to, remained ignorant of the views held by the most influential members of the French cabinet. Indeed, one can almost say, they were deliberately misled as to French intentions by an elaborate series of subterfuges and equivocations. The most far-reaching of these centered on the French Government's "decision" to leave for North Africa. The question had reasserted itself due to the rapid advance of German forces towards the Bordeaux area and the consequent threat to national sovereignty posed by the possible capture of the government.

# *To Leave*
# *or Not to Leave*

THE Marshal himself was determined to remain in France in any event, but under pressure from MM. Jeanneney and Herriot, supported by President Lebrun, Pétain on June 18—almost casually, it appears, and probably without realizing its full implications—half accepted the idea of dividing the government in two. According to the formula presented to him, he would stay on in France, together with some departments, but to permit the government to function and to negotiate freely—that is, outside the enemy's reach—he would delegate his powers as chief of government to the Vice-President of the Council, Camille Chautemps. The President of the Republic, the Vice-President of the Council, the leaders of the two representative assemblies, and the essential ministers would then leave for North Africa. Both Jeanneney and Herriot, on the basis of this discussion, believed that full agreement had been reached and that the question was now decided—though President Lebrun remained rather more skeptical.[1]

Regardless of whether the matter had ever been "settled," the Marshal in the course of the next day or so was to become distinctly unsettled by all those who agreed with Laval that the government could not leave France under any circumstances and that the idea of having two governments was the worst possible solution: under such an arrangement, they argued, Pétain would be stripped of any real power; moreover, the government in Algiers would be subjected to British pressure, as a result of which the armistice would surely fall through. In this way, the Reynaud policy, so recently rejected, would be revived. Baudouin, for his part, when he heard of the plan (on 18 June), urged Pétain to play for time, and this course was undoubtedly

262

far more to the Marshal's liking.[2] Pétain, either through old age, fatigue, or cunning, was subject to being swayed by whomever he had talked to last, but fundamentally he was opposed to all schemes that suggested adventurism or demanded great energy. The acceptance of suffering and the admission of past mistakes were still, to his mind, the best means by which France would be regenerated. There was also his ambition to remain master in his own house to be reckoned with.

What the French Government would do hung in some suspense throughout June 19. Whether it should leave Bordeaux and, if so, where it should go next was discussed, but the Council of Ministers seemed unable to make up its mind definitively, though certain arrangements indicating an imminent departure for Perpignan were put in motion. The Council did decide that when the time came the Marshal should give the necessary order for the President and a certain number of ministers to leave. Much of the day was devoted to selecting and instructing the plenipotentiaries who were to receive the enemy's conditions. These were General Huntziger, heading the delegation, the career diplomat Léon Noël, Vice-Admiral Le Luc, Deputy Chief of the Naval Staff, General Parisot, former Military Attaché in Rome, General Bergeret, Deputy Chief of Staff of the French Air Force, and M. Charles Rochat, Deputy Director of Political Affairs at the Ministry of Foreign Affairs—their instructions being to break off negotiations at once if Germany asked for the surrender of the fleet or for the occupation of any part of France's colonial empire.

An armistice appeared near at hand, yet, at the same time, if the Germans approached much closer to the provisional capital, the government would have to move to avoid being captured. In the hope of preventing this, Pétain urgently requested the German Government to halt the advance of its troops in the direction of Bordeaux "so that the French Government could deliberate in complete liberty."[3] That this request, transmitted by Baudouin via the Spanish Ambassador, was a thinly veiled attempt on the part of the pro-armistice faction to bargain collaboratively with the enemy, for the mutual benefit of both, is shown by what Lequerica told his government: if the German troops continued to advance on Bordeaux and if the opening of armistice negotiations was delayed much longer, the Reynaud faction might well regain the upper hand. The German Ambassador in Madrid accordingly telegraphed Berlin: "The [Pétain] Government would not be able to survive a threat to Bordeaux by German troops."[4] Likewise, Ambassador Biddle wired Secretary of State Hull on the 19th that the French had informed the Germans that negotiations must be contingent on a cessation of the German advance southward; otherwise, a majority of the government would go to North Africa to continue the war from there.[5] Hitler's only answer was to bomb Bordeaux that night, although this did not prevent Pétain from addressing similar requests to the German Chancellor again on June 20 and 21.[6]

Nevertheless, by evening of 19 June his anxieties concerning the rapidity of the German advance were such that Pétain in principle authorized Chautemps, accompanied by the ministers of his choice, to leave for North Africa, where he would be furnished with the necessary authority to direct the government. The government's departure for Perpignan, preparatory to its embarkation for Algiers, was projected for the next day. The plan was then represented by Pétain to the British ministers in Bordeaux as virtually resolved, though in reality it was still tentative and had yet to be ratified by the Council.[7]

After a stormy meeting on the morning of June 20, at which Weygand, Baudouin, and Bouthillier had vehemently protested against the proposal to give Chautemps a delegation of powers, the majority of the Council of Ministers, in a surprising show of civilian strength, pronounced in favor of transferring the seat of public authority to Perpignan, whence the government would embark from nearby Port-Vendres. Departure was fixed for 2:30 that afternoon, with the next Council slated to take place at 9 a.m. (June 21) in Perpignan.

According to Chautemps, this ministerial Council was more divided than the crucial one that had met on June 16. With the Marshal unexpectedly acquiescing in the idea, or appearing to, he writes, many ministers now decided to support the move to North Africa, and thus the departure thesis carried. Chautemps therefore considers the Council's decision on this date one of the most important acts of the period and defends its genuineness against accusations that it was only a pretense "intended to gain time and to lull the vigilance of the partisans of resistance" by pointing out that if Baudouin had been involved in a plot to prevent the departure of the government, he would not have fought against the proposition with such insistence on the 20th but instead would simply have played at going along.[8]

The Council's deliberations were undoubtedly genuine, but, far from proving the absence of a plot, the Council's firmness on the 20th would seem to have inspired one. Whether or not Baudouin was one of the principals in the plot to keep the government grounded in

France is not completely clear. He himself describes the Council's decision to go to Perpignan as a compromise between immediate flight to North Africa and staying on in Bordeaux. Though he too prepared to leave, he nevertheless remained confident that the departure would not actually take place.[9] At the same time, the Council also decided that those members of the assemblies wishing to accompany the government to North Africa were to be provided with transportation on the steamer *Massilia,* which was scheduled to sail that evening from Le Verdon, at the mouth of the Gironde.[10] This time the decision *appeared* to be irrevocable.

But Weygand and Darlan together with Laval, all mutually determined to keep the government in France at all costs, were able to convince Pétain during the course of the day that a new displacement of the seat of government (followed by the embarkation of the highest authorities of state) at the very moment the French plenipotentiaries were leaving for the German lines would be disastrous and that departure must therefore be postponed. The necessity for having but a single government and keeping it in France, as they saw it, was twofold: (1) not only would the Germans refuse to grant an armistice to any government that had left the country or to any rump government remaining on French soil that lacked full authority; but (2) an overseas government meant the almost certain continuation of the war and, with that, a German-Italian (and probably Spanish) attack upon North Africa, which they believed themselves impotent to repel. Thus, a flight to Algiers would both scuttle the negotiations about to begin and deprive them of any effective bargaining counter for the future.

Chautemps, on the contrary, taking a very different line from the one he had propagated in the days preceding the fall of the Reynaud government, argued (at least retrospectively) that the failure to move overseas carried quite the opposite meaning: "... in preventing my departure and that of the President of the Republic, after having first decided it, and in this way revealing to the enemy his final resignation to defeat, the Marshal, in one stroke, both encouraged the conqueror's exigencies and forbade himself to resist them. In fact, the decision to remain at Bordeaux was equivalent to an unconditional surrender."[11] This, of course, was the position officially adopted by the British, and therefore somewhat surprising coming from one who had argued so forcefully on earlier occasions that the departure of the government was impossible until *after* the terms of the armistice were known.

There was some sort of backtracking by the cabinet's inner circle even before 2 p.m. Then, in mid-afternoon, finding a convenient pretext, the Marshal in effect countermanded the Council's decision by asking Chautemps and the President of the Republic, who were completely packed and on the verge of leaving, to postpone their departure till 6 p.m.; a little later, to the relief of a deputation led by Laval, he also revoked the delegation of powers previously signed. Raphael Alibert (Under-Secretary of State to the Presidency of the Council), on his own authority and without Pétain's knowledge, completed the delaying maneuver by "officially" ordering each minister to remain in his residence until 8 a.m. the next day while awaiting further instructions from the Marshal.[12] The British were first told simply "that departure [was] no longer urgent" and later that the "French Government had decided to stay another night so as to enable them to learn [the German] terms," expected shortly, in Bordeaux.[13] Pétain, his mind at last firmly made up, now planned to arrest President Lebrun if he attempted to leave the city.[14]

Lebrun, having already postponed his departure for two days, was still anxious to leave on June 21. Had he done so, and been followed by a sufficient number of ministers to form a viable government, it is quite possible that the distance between Algiers and metropolitan France would then have encouraged a rejection of the armistice. But, profiting by the President's hesitation, the Laval clique made one last bid to prevent the dissolution of all their schemes and succeeded in intimidating Lebrun (though the President would later deny it) by a mixture of threats, imprecations, and guile, to the point where he once again suspended his departure—this time until after the armistice conditions, expected that very evening, had been examined.[15] Furthermore, shortly after his meeting with the Laval deputation, Baudouin warned Lebrun that if the Pétain government left Bordeaux, a de facto government, with M. Laval at its head, would immediately be formed in the city, and that this government would soon have a big following.[16] By the 22nd, Laval was able to denounce the President's intended departure as a sure way of preventing the conclusion of the armistice. After this there was no more talk of going to North Africa, but for four days it had loomed as a distinct possibility and the British had been encouraged to believe that the move was definite. It is in this light then that relations between the French and British governments in the last few days before the armistice was signed must be viewed.

# The Bordeaux
# Conversations

ALTHOUGH the reports emanating from Campbell on June 18 and 19 were moderately optimistic, the British Government did not relax its vigilance. Fully prepared though it was to give the Pétain administration a fair trial, it frankly distrusted its defeatist makeup and felt that it had ample reason to do so, especially inasmuch as France's own representatives in London were disquietingly skeptical. Roger Cambon, Chargé d'Affaires at the French Embassy, had told Orme Sargent at the Foreign Office on 17 June that "the new French Government would behave worse than King Leopold" and that the British Government "should not put too much trust in Admiral Darlan"; while Ambassador Corbin, in talking with Lord Halifax, professed little faith in the strength of the Bordeaux government to take even the most obvious or necessary precautions to protect itself from German capture. Sir Ronald Campbell also revealed that Camille Chautemps, while telling him that his own resolution to reject dishonorable conditions remained as strong as ever, had "added rather ominously that the present government contained new elements whose opinions he could not guarantee beyond all manner of doubt." In short, as the Foreign Secretary flatly put it to the British Ambassador in Madrid, the British simply could not rely upon French promises not to hand over their fleet to the Germans. Minuting on 18 June, Orme Sargent had suggested sending a cabinet minister to Bordeaux "to strenghthen Sir R. Campbell's hand in resisting the forces of treachery which I fear are rampant among Bordeaux French politicians and generals now in power."[1]

The government was already thinking along these lines; in the end it did even better than this. To reinforce the many appeals transmitted through ordinary diplomatic channels, Churchill, in the hopes of obtaining more positive guarantees from the French, decided to send not only the First Sea Lord, Admiral Sir Dudley Pound, but the First Lord of the Admiralty, Mr. A. V. Alexander, and the Secretary of State for the Colonies, Lord Lloyd, as well. All were to make contact with the appropriate authorities of the new government in Bordeaux with the object of securing the French fleet. What emerged from these conversations held over a period of forty-eight hours, however, was viewed rather differently by the French and British participating in them.

Arriving in the late afternoon of June 18, Pound and Alexander immediately sought reassurance as to the future of the fleet from Admiral Darlan himself.[2] Rear Admiral Auphan, Under Chief of Staff of the French Admiralty, the only other Frenchman present at this discussion, relates that Darlan clearly told them that "if the armistice convention . . . exacted the delivery of the fleet . . . the French government was unanimously decided to reject that clause and, if need be, to renounce the whole armistice." He explicitly promised them that in no case would French warships be put at the disposal of the Germans to be used against the British. He then gave his word of honor that whatever happened French warships would never be utilized by anyone but the French themselves; "they would remain French or they would be destroyed." Auphan states that the British authorities posed no conditions on the subject of the armistice and never demanded that the fleet pass into British ports as a preliminary to negotiations. The question simply did not come up. In his opinion, the British left "moved, cordial, and, to all appearances, satisfied."[3]

The same scene viewed from the British angle shows a somewhat more complex situation. It is true that the British made no direct demand that the French fleet be sent to England; and certainly the issue of the fleet's removal was not tied by the First Lord or First Sea Lord to the War Cabinet's condition for acquiescence in an armistice. But the question of the fleet's departure for England most certainly did arise. According to notes taken by the Deputy Director of Plans, who, together with the British Naval Attaché, was also present, Admiral Darlan was in fact "somewhat hurt at the idea that the French Fleet should be sent to British or friendly ports whilst it was still fighting." Moreover, he seemed anxious to head off the topic: in explaining "that the *Richelieu* should have left that day for Dakar and that all other ships that could steam and were in danger, by reason of the enemy advance, of falling into their hands would go to Dakar . . . he suggested America or Canada ultimately for the *Richelieu* on account of working up and final fitting out which, if done in England, would subject her to a heavy scale of bombing attack." Perhaps as a sop to the British, "Darlan stated that he had arranged that all French merchant ships lying in those ports likely to fall shortly into the hands of the Germans, especially those ships carrying war material, should clear from French ports . . . and sail to Great Britain." On the other hand, he requested that all French mine-sweepers evacuated to British ports now be sent back to Atlantic harbors still in French hands. Thus, contrary to what Auphan suggests, the British desire to see the French war fleet on their shores was made perfectly clear to Darlan but was simply parried. Nevertheless, the British had reason to feel moderately satisfied. Mr. Alexander expressed himself happy with the discussions that had recently taken place in the French Council of Ministers and congratulated Darlan on the French Navy's recent successful attack on the Italian coast. Agreement was also reached on technical matters. Finally, there was the Admiral's repeated assurances that "he would on no account ever surrender the French Fleet, that the French Navy would go on fighting until an armistice was called . . . but if the armistice terms were dishonourable to France, the Fleet would fight to the end and anything that escaped would go to a friendly country or would be destroyed."[4]

The positive nature of the interview is also attested by Oliver Harvey, who wrote in his diary that night that Alexander and Pound had found Darlan "satisfactory." The First Sea Lord, both in the message he sent to the Prime Minister during the night of June 18–19 and in his report to the War Cabinet the following day, expressed the view that the situation was completely different from what they had expected. It would not be possible at present to send the French fleet to British ports, he explained, as French troops were still fighting, but, if the armistice terms contained a demand for the fleet's surrender, before the armies capitulated the French fleet would be sailed to friendly ports if practicable or, in the last resort, they would be destroyed. Steps had already been taken to protect France's capital ships; French merchant vessels were sailing for British ports, oil stocks in French harbors were being destroyed, and plans had been laid between Admiral Darlan and the First Lord for the demolition of French ports to prevent their falling intact into enemy hands. As the British Ambassador later reported, both envoys had found Darlan friendly and determined and were impressed by the Admiral's consistency and sincerity.[5]

On June 19 at 11 a.m. Baudouin in his turn assured Mr. Alexander and Sir Ronald Campbell that armistice negotiations would be broken off if the Germans or Italians asked for a single ship or demanded occupation of any part of France's colonial empire. He furthermore swore that the most definite and permanent orders would be given to prevent any French warships from ever falling into enemy hands to be used by them. According to Baudouin, Alexander then went on to Darlan to get the details of these precautionary measures. Again at 10 p.m. that evening Campbell and Alexander, now joined by Lord Lloyd, received further reassurances in conversations with Pétain, Baudouin, and Darlan. The Marshal was quite categorical about the fleet's not being handed over to Germany, but said that it might have to be scuttled. This, as Baudouin explained to Sir Ronald and as Campbell later reported, meant that "in the highly improbable event that the armistice terms proved acceptable apart from the question of the fleet, the latter would be scuttled rather than handed over to us [the British], whilst in the contrary event it would go on fighting." Mr. Alexander, according to the Ambassador, continued to press the fleet question "with the utmost vigor and with obvious effect." His main concern was to get the French to turn their destroyers over to the British rather than to scuttle them.[6]

Then, the following morning (June 20), after seeing Darlan, Lord Lloyd told Baudouin that "as a whole the precautions taken by Admiral Darlan to prevent the fleet from falling into the hands of the Germans should . . . be effective, but he was frightened all the same that the ships lying in French harbours might be taken by surprise." Baudouin assured him that "from that very moment no ship would be stationed in any part of the country which was in German occupation," but Lord Lloyd persisted and asked him to send the fleet to North Africa. "He had already made this request on the previous day to Admiral Darlan who had rejected the suggestion of anchoring the ships near Oran since the roadstead was not, as was the case at Toulon, defended by shore batteries." Baudouin nevertheless promised Lloyd that he would press the Admiral to give the British every possible satisfaction in the matter, following which the Colonial Secretary left "in good humor and fully satisfied."[7] Lloyd also confirmed to Ambassador Corbin later that day that the measures being taken by the French Admiralty (towards sheltering the fleet at Mers-el-Kébir and Dakar) satisfied him and that he had no further demands to make.[8]

Lord Lloyd himself writes that eventually he obtained "agreement as to the move to Africa and also most definite undertakings as regards the fleet." He was apparently congratulated by Churchill and Halifax on the success of his mission upon returning to London, but the glow of success was short-lived, for on June 21 he woke up to find that "Brown [Lebrun] and Pétain had ratted again and had decided to stay on in Bordeaux."[9]

Baudouin also claims that in the course of these extended discussions the British never posed any conditions concerning the fleet's being sent to England. "Everything passed, in these conversations, as if the telegrams of June 16 had never existed. The two lords confirmed by their silence the declaration that the English ambassador had made June 18."[10] But, if the British did not *press* their demand that the French fleet be sent to British waters, it was obviously because by this time they realized that it would definitely be turned down and would possibly do more harm than good. (Darlan had quickly intimated this.) Reynaud had, after all, refused to do so, and now that an armistice had been asked for it would be all the more difficult for the French to agree to the measure. Furthermore, in the light of what they had been told, it no longer seemed quite so necessary on the date in question (June 19–20) as it had only two or three days before. For instance, in a moderately optimistic mood, Lord Halifax wrote Sir Samuel Hoare on June 19:

Alexander and Pound went over to Bordeaux yesterday and have sent an encouraging report about the prospects of the French playing the game as to the fleet. Darlan seems at present quite firm but, after the experiences of recent days, I do not feel happy in placing over-much confidence on any verbal professions from any body.... George Lloyd went out there this morning to assist in the task of holding up their hands, and there seems more possibility than there did 48 hours ago of their taking a stiff line if, as I anticipate, the German terms are such that any normal government would immediately reject them.[11]

Although the members of the British party left with few tangible guarantees, they had received Darlan's promise that the armistice would not be signed unless ships were allowed to be concentrated in ports of nonoccupied territory, and had been told of the "irrevocable" orders supposedly issued by Darlan to scuttle any ship that the Germans might attempt to lay hold of. The fact that the bulk of the French war fleet which was still in Atlantic ports had made good its escape on the 18th and 19th of June (with the remainder being destroyed or scuttled) must also have cheered them, even though the destination of the most important units was Africa, not England.[12] But, these developments notwithstanding, the major satisfaction they derived from these meetings must have rested primarily on what they were led to believe was the direction the new government was about to take.

In fact, the chief purpose of Lord Lloyd's visit was to hurry the French along this path by offering to put at their disposal the transport necessary to evacuate to North Africa the maximum of men and matériel, plus British military assistance, provided the French Government left at once to set up a fresh seat of power overseas.[13] Lord Lloyd and Sir Ronald had even been authorized by the War Cabinet to renew the offer of Franco-British Union in this eventuality.[14] Lloyd had duly extended the offer of transport both to President Lebrun and the Foreign Minister and had even dispensed with the detailed arguments he had come armed with to induce the French Government to establish itself outside France, having been advised by Campbell and Alexander that this would be unnecessary as the government had already so decided.[15]

All with whom the British representatives had come in contact— Pétain, Baudouin, Darlan, Lebrun, Jeanneney and Herriot—had affirmed that the government would depart the next day (June 20) for Perpignan, and from there embark for North Africa. From evasiveness on 18 June as to the intentions of the French Government—that is, whether or not it would leave for one of the French colonies—Sir Ronald Campbell and the British party then in Bordeaux had from the morning of 19 June onwards been treated to a series of assurances as to the imminence of the government's departure from the threatened city.

On that date the Ambassador reported that the Council of Ministers had decided that on the approach of the enemy to Bordeaux the President of the Republic, the presidents of both houses of Parliament, and three or four ministers would proceed overseas to carry on the government. These ministers would be nominated by President Lebrun and leave with a written order from him countersigned by Marshal Pétain. General Weygand, it was thought, would probably go too in order to coordinate the further French war effort. The Minister for Foreign Affairs, when conveying the Council's decision, had at the same time spoken to the First Lord of the Admiralty of the measures being taken to enable a continuance of the defense of the French Empire from North Africa. Later that night, when Pétain appeared to express some hesitancy on the question, Baudouin, as Campbell recorded it, had been quick to explain that "departure had been decided in principle and would be finally settled (including [the] time of departure) tomorrow morning. When reminded that he had said this morning that the matter had been settled, he replied that was so in principle, but that it remained to be finally ratified tomorrow." The Foreign Minister had ended by saying "he hoped that the party might be got off in the early afternoon." Things looked even brighter the next morning (June 20) and the Ambassador was able to inform London of the Council's "decision to move at once to Perpignan," where it would hold another meeting for the purpose of taking cognizance of the armistice terms, "after which members of the Government will move with the Presidential party to North Africa." It was now the intention of the government, so Campbell reported, "to send a larger number than previously contemplated." The Ambassador was now convinced that the British Embassy would be leaving that evening to accompany the French Government in its peregrinations and therefore requested transport to be sent immediately to Port-Vendres, as "departure for North Africa might take place any time after tomorrow night." It was only at this point that the government reversed itself by a last-minute change of plans, deciding to stay on in Bordeaux to receive the German terms (the "Germans having offered to reinstate [the] telephone line between Tours and Bordeaux") and thereby knocking into a cocked hat all the assurances the British had so painfully wrested from them over the past forty-eight hours.[16]

Considering what a world of difference the establishment of a French government in Africa would have made, for in this case the fleet almost certainly would have followed the government, it is easy to see why the British had earlier felt some satisfaction. And in this matter the most senior members of the French Government—excepting the presidents of the assemblies and the President of the Republic, who were themselves duped*—can be charged with deliberate duplicity, for they had no intention of letting power slip out of their hands by permitting such an exodus and in fact plotted to prevent it. But the English ministers had already left before the illusion as to the firmness of the Bordeaux government's intentions was dissipated by Pétain's turn-about on the afternoon of the 20th. From this time on, however, Campbell was to remain more than ever suspicious and on guard.

---

*See Appendix K, The Republic's Three Presidents.

# Hitler's Terms

Seeing the efforts made to prevent (or at least to delay) the government's departure, the British Ambassador now prepared a note for delivery to Baudouin early the next morning (June 21) reminding him that his government "expected to be consulted as soon as any armistice terms were received." To this the Minister for Foreign Affairs replied in writing that "he did not think it necessary to inform [Campbell] afresh that it had always been the intention of the French Government to have an exchange of views with His Majesty's Government as soon as the armistice conditions were known."[1] Despite this promise, Campbell nevertheless felt that if the German conditions were subject to a short time limit, "no effective consultation, if any at all, would be feasible." Yet even though his anxieties were increasing rapidly, the Ambassador had by no means given up hope. As he informed his government, he believed the question of the fleet to have been safeguarded by the instructions issued by Darlan on June 20; he proposed now "to insist on the despatch of a nucleus Government overseas" as the minimal British requirement, "this step being . . . the only thing which would encourage His Majesty's Government to stand by France to the end." As yet he had no reason to suppose that the government had weakened in its resolve to leave. But although he had "impressed this point on him in the bluntest language a dozen times, Marshal Pétain seem[ed] unable to grasp the significance of it."[2]

By midday on June 21 Campbell was afraid that, the decision to move to Perpignan having been canceled, even the idea of sending a small government overseas would now be thrown overboard too. In this event he intended to "try to persuade the President and the Presidents of the Chambers and any other right minded Parliamentarians on whom we could lay our hands to come away on H. M. S. *Galatea*." He reported M. Herriot's opinion that there was still a majority among the civilians in the cabinet in favor of resistance, but thought it significant that there was no longer unanimity and anticipated that such a majority might dwindle yet further. "M. Laval and company," he disclosed, were "active." Conscious that his message might seem confused and conflicting, the Ambassador claimed that the situation was likewise, changing as it did from hour to hour. At this point he could no longer believe anything he was told, "except by Marshal Pétain, who was evasive or silent about the things I wanted to know, and by the Presidents of the two Houses, who were not kept informed by the Government."[3] And had Campbell had more insight into the Marshal, who by every intimate account ever written of him, even by his most ardent supporters, was thoroughly unreliable, he would not have expressed even this degree of equanimity.

A few hours later the Ambassador wired that the situation was not improving: a German armored division was well on its way to Marseilles [or farther west along the Mediterranean coast] with the obvious intention of cutting off the government's retreat to Perpignan; furthermore, the French were again warning the Germans that if Bordeaux were not free from aerial bombardment the government "might have to move elsewhere," which struck Campbell "as a bad sign, as implying the reverse in the opposite case." In addition, the French censorship was suppressing war news favorable to the Allies such as might have inspired public opinion to support continued resistance. This, as Oliver Harvey points out, was Prouvost's doing.[4]

Despite signs to the contrary, when Campbell again saw Baudouin at 4 p.m. he was assured that the government's plans remained unchanged. The Foreign Minister "was quite categorical that the intention was still to send the President and a small Government overseas," proof of which was that "Admiral Darlan had been instructed to provide a warship at St. Jean de Luz." But it was now clear to Campbell that "even if that were true at the moment evil influences were at work." His darkening pessimism was not dissipated by a talk shortly thereafter with M. Chautemps, who "confirmed the intrigues and kaleidoscopic character of the situation" and described the "lamentable influence" General Weygand's "mystic mood" had exercised on the thinking of the government.[5]

On top of these concerns, Campbell had also to worry about the fate of the German air crews captured in France, which the Reynaud government had promised to turn over to the British but which, despite their constantly renewed inquiries, had still not been produced. Campbell now feared that their prisoner-of-war camp had been overrun by the German advance.[6]

The Ambassador had previously been told by Baudouin that he did not expect to receive the armistice conditions until some time that evening. With mounting anxiety, Campbell continued to fear that there would not be sufficient time for the intergovernmental consultations promised him. From Compiègne—in the very clearing and identical railway coach made famous by the events of November 11, 1918—to which the Germans had fittingly brought the hapless French delegation, General Huntziger finally telephoned the text of the German terms, together with some German commentaries on them, around 9 p.m. As soon as copies were transcribed, Marshal Pétain, the Foreign Minister, General Weygand, Admiral Darlan, Secretary-General Charles-Roux, together with Bouthillier and Alibert, began a preliminary examination of the German demands to determine their general tenor. It was during this night of June 21–22 that all the misunderstandings and conflicts that had plagued relations between the British and French governments during the past week came to a head. The arrival of the armistice terms acted as the catalyst.

Though few would have guessed it, Hitler—for the sake of a cheap and quick victory—had decided to offer the French relatively moderate armistice conditions. Using the time-honored formula "divide and conquer," he was astute enough to realize that if he hoped to bring England to terms in the near future he could not afford to antagonize the already defeated French to the extent of driving them back into cooperation with the British. Their national interests must be made to seem distinct. In short, a break with England would have to look like a bargain. The occupation of all of France would be a mistake because that would only encourage the French to set up a government in England or North Africa, from which they could then continue the war in partnership with the British. It was preferable to permit the existence of a genuine French government in metropolitan France, where it could be persuaded into a policy of collaboration. With French sovereignty thus assured, the French Empire would also remain under French domination and, by remote control, subject to German influence as well. As for the fleet, the best thing from the German point of view would be for the French to scuttle it, the worst, for it to unite with the British Navy; in the latter case, a combined Franco-British force would be able to develop a convoy system that would allow Great Britain to supply itself without difficulty and to transport large numbers of troops to the Mediterranean and Africa, thereby creating new theaters of war. Therefore, it would be unwise to demand the outright surrender of the fleet. France would not agree in any event, and against the slight possibility of the French sinking their fleet there was the much greater probability of its joining the British fleet. Its neutralization was the obvious answer. Hitler felt that the best plan would be to require the French to assemble their fleet in such a way that it could not be moved or dispersed, either in French ports under German or Italian control or in neutral ports.[7]

Certainly the British Chiefs of Staff had not been able to fathom what conditions Hitler would come up with. Indeed they were convinced that any terms offered would include a demand for the surrender of the fleet and that no armistice would be granted until after it had been turned over. They also assumed that the Germans and Italians would demand the use of French bases for operations against the British.[8] Why it never occurred to the British that the Germans might *not* demand the French fleet remains a mystery, especially inasmuch as there were a number of good minds in London working constantly on just such hypothetical questions. Emmanuel Berl suggests that Pétain, by contrast, through his contacts abroad, may have had serious reasons for thinking that an acceptable armistice was not only possible but likely, in short, that Hitler by virtue of his own needs would refrain from exacting the one thing that would have been deemed inadmissible. "That Hitler wanted an armistice, it appears then probable that Pétain believed it, and even, given his intimate relations with Madrid, that he knew it."[9]

In the opinion of Baudouin and Weygand, the armistice, though harsh and a diktat, offered several advantages that could not be considered lightly. It avoided the total occupation of the country by preserving for France an unoccupied zone equaling about two-fifths of the metropolitan territory. It authorized the maintenance of the French Government and permitted it to function administratively throughout the entire country as well as diplomatically abroad. It left to France the custody of its overseas empire and its fleet, and allowed for the maintenance of an army of 100,000 men in France and for military forces sufficient to keep order and maintain French sovereignty in North Africa and the other French colonies. Finally, the armistice provided for the restoration of order by the return to their homes of several million refugees and for the future of the economy by the rapid demobilization of some 2 million men.[10] A capitulation, by contrast, would most probably have involved the loss of French sovereignty, the total occupation of France's metropolitan territory, including its Mediterranean ports (which could then have been set up as German submarine and air bases, with all that would have implied for Allied communications with the East), and of course the capture of the entire French Army together with its war matériel. This was not only Weygand's point of view; it was also the opinion of Léon Noël, perhaps the armistice delegation's most cautious member.[11]

Although Charles-Roux found the armistice terms unacceptable, thinking that to leave for North Africa would be preferable,[12] Weygand and the others in the Privy Council, which undertook the first examination of the convention, were inclined to be relieved by them. It was chiefly in detail that the conditions were found objectionable. However, in the Council of Ministers that followed this preliminary survey, there was apparently more opposition to the convention. According to Baudouin, MM. Chautemps, Frossard, Rivière, and Février, together with the President of the Republic, were all negatively inclined, while Admiral Darlan too had an emotional moment in which he declared the necessity of fighting on. Pomaret says simply that they were *all* relieved because the terms were less harsh than they had feared, and President Lebrun later admitted that, though they found the terms of the convention painful, they had not contemplated going so far as to refuse the armistice as a whole. In any case, a spirit of resignation would prevail by the next morning.[13]

This may have been, as former Prime Minister Pierre-Étienne Flandin points out, because the armistice terms were not especially harsher than those formerly imposed on the Germans by the Allies—the clauses concerning demilitarization, disarmament, and control being based on the convention of 1918. What made the 1940 armistice tolerable—including the substantial extent of French territory to be occupied—was the assumption that it was only temporary because the war with Britain would soon be terminated.[14] Flandin does not mention that the Allies in 1918 had demanded the surrender of the German fleet.

The clauses most relevant to France's relations with Great Britain included the following:

*Article VIII.* The French war fleet—with the exception of that part left at the disposal of the French Government for the protection of French interests in its colonial empire—will be assembled in ports to be specified and there demobilized and disarmed under German or Italian control.

The designation of these ports will be made according to the home bases of the ships in time of peace. The German Government solemnly declares to the French Government that it has no intention of using for its own purposes during the war the French war fleet stationed in ports under German control, apart from those units necessary for coast surveillance and minesweeping.

It further declares, solemnly and categorically, that it has no intention of formulating claims with regard to the French war fleet at the time peace is concluded. Excepting that part of the French war fleet, still to be determined, which will be assigned to the safeguarding of French interests in the colonial empire, all warships outside French territorial waters are to be recalled to France.

*Article IX.* The French High Command shall furnish the German High Command with detailed information concerning all mines laid by France, as well as concerning all harbor and coastal barriers and installations of a defensive and protective character. The sweeping of minefields is to be carried out by French units to the extent required by the German High Command.

*Article X.* . . . The French Government will likewise prevent members of the French armed forces from leaving French territory, and will see to it that no arms, equipment of any kind, ships, planes, etc. are transferred to England or elsewhere abroad.

The French Government will prohibit French subjects from fighting against Germany in the service of states with which Germany is still at war. French subjects who do not comply with this condition will be treated by German troops as *franc-tireurs.*

*Article XI.* Until further orders, French merchant vessels of every kind, including coastal and harbor craft, will be prohibited from leaving port. . . . French merchant ships outside French ports will be recalled to France by the French Government or, where that is not possible, directed to neutral ports.

*Article XIX.* . . . The French Government undertakes to prevent the transfer of German prisoners of war or civilian prisoners from France either to French possessions or to foreign countries. . . .

*Article XXIV.* The present Armistice Convention will remain in force until the conclusion of the peace treaty. It can be denounced by the German Government at any time and instantly rescinded if the French Government does not fulfill the obligations assumed by it in the present agreement.[15]

As to the peace conditions that Germany might ultimately offer, and concerning which the French delegation had been instructed to inquire, no hint whatsoever was given the French. General Huntziger was apparently encouraged to believe that the Germans would not long defer the conclusion of a definitive peace—certainly a principal goal of the Pétain government, however it might interpret its quest for an armistice to the British. What the Germans (or Italians) would have claimed at the time of a peace treaty was not of course fixed, but inasmuch as their dreams were not modest any information along these lines could only have disquieted the French.[16] For the moment, therefore, it was simply a question of the acceptability of the first step, the armistice.

# Sir Ronald's Vigil:
# Diplomatic Confusion

WHEN the Coucil of Ministers did meet in full session at 1 a.m. on the night of June 21–22 to study the terms of the convention, members applied themselves principally to discussing and drafting amendments to the more onerous provisions; these were to be telephoned by General Weygand to General Huntziger in Rethondes before 9 a.m., as prescribed, and there proposed to the Germans. Charles-Roux had previously warned that the naval clauses would not suffice to reassure England; that the British would think that a French warship, disarmed in an occupied port, would be at the mercy of the enemy. Darlan too expressed serious misgivings on this point. The Council therefore decided to demand of the Germans that France's warships be stationed and disarmed in North or West African ports rather than in their home bases, two-thirds of which would fall in the occupied zone. It was decided not to leave a single ship in any port to be occupied by the Germans, and, at Baudouin's suggestion, Admiral Darlan agreed to send the greater part of the fleet to Oran.[1]

Sir Ronald Campbell meanwhile was impatiently waiting at the Prefecture to be informed of the armistice conditions. Whether or not Baudouin kept his promise to the British Ambassador to communicate these conditions as soon as they arrived has been a source of controversy and confusion—the result largely of the rather exaggerated claims put forth by both British and French authorities during the heat of war, to apparently unintentional inaccuracies perpetrated by Charles-Roux, and to the lacunae in factual information occasioned by the secrecy surrounding firsthand British accounts for a thirty-year period after the events in question. At least some of this confusion can be dispelled. What remains must be attributed to the

281

trauma of the occasion and to the serious assaults on ordinary human memory and emotions that this inevitably entailed.

The reliability or unreliability of Baudouin's account of the night of June 21–22 has been the principal bone of contention. In opposition to claims that he broke his promise to Campbell to communicate the German conditions as soon as they arrived, Baudouin contends that as soon as he became cognizant of the armistice terms at 10:30 p.m. he asked Charles-Roux to maintain contact with Campbell to inform him of them. He believed this had been done because at midnight, when Charles-Roux emerged from the preliminary meeting, he had conversed for several minutes with the Ambassador. As proof, Baudouin cites the fact that at 1:30 a.m. Campbell sent into the Council of Ministers a note drawing their attention to the "insidious character of the conditions concerning the fleet" and emphasizing that no reliance could be placed on the word of the Germans, as they only made promises to break them. From this Baudouin concluded that the Secretary-General must have given Campbell at least a summary of the armistice conditions.[2]

Not until 3 a.m. did the Ambassador finally see Baudouin, and then only briefly. A painful scene ensued. According to Baudouin, Sir Ronald rushed up to him and, abandoning his customary imperturbability, bitterly complained of the cavalier manner in which the French Government was treating him. He then insisted that the British Government ought to be represented at any discussion at which the French Government decided its policy. Baudouin, fatigued and with still more work ahead of him that night, "observed that the representative of the British Government could not be present at the deliberations of the Council of Ministers, but, on the other hand, if the British Government would have the goodness to obtain from the German Government an extension of the short time allowed the French Government to go into the matter," he "would willingly hear his views at length." Baudouin claims to have given Campbell a copy of the German conditions (his own) and of the general line of modifications to be suggested by the French, then to have arranged to meet the Ambassador at 7:30 in the morning to give him more detailed information. However, Campbell failed to appear for this appointment, and instead went to complain to Pétain of the Foreign Minister's cursory reception of him the previous night. As the Council of Ministers was due to meet again at 8 for a last reading of the armistice text and the proposed amendments, Baudouin still did not have the time to meet with Campbell even after learning of his dissatisfaction. But, he claims, Charles-Roux received him at 9:30 and at that time told him of the amendments the French were requesting. As the Council was in almost continuous session throughout June 22 (meeting 8–12, 2–4, and again at 5:15), Baudouin implies that he did not have time to talk with the British Ambassador until late that night; at least, he mentions no meeting between them; to the contrary, he specifically states that he was unable to see Sir Ronald in the afternoon, though he says M. Charles-Roux did receive him to give him the German explanations as to why they had refused to modify the article concerning the fleet.[3]

Charles-Roux's account is at odds with Baudouin's on several critical points. First of all, he says nothing about communicating the armistice terms to Campbell at midnight. He claims only to have chatted momentarily with the Ambassador at 1, never having been instructed to do otherwise and furthermore unaware that Campbell was awaiting any communication from him. As for the meeting between the Ambassador and Baudouin following the adjournment of the Council, Charles-Roux learned (from others) the next day that Campbell had recalled Baudouin's promise to contact the British Government as soon as possible after receiving Germany's conditions and had demanded to know what they were. But Baudouin, "arguing that the ministers had not yet finished deliberating, had refused to part with the text of the convention, the first consideration of which, he felt, was due the French government." Charles-Roux implies that it was not until the afternoon of June 22 that the armistice conditions in their entirety were made known to the Ambassador; furthermore, that it was only at some point during the day, and not the preceding evening, that Baudouin first ordered him to meet with Campbell, and even then it was not for the purpose of communicating the armistice conditions. Baudouin asked only that the Secretary-General receive the British Ambassador that day and communicate to him the French demands for amendments and the German replies. But the Foreign Minister indicated to Charles-Roux at this time that he had already sent the terms to Campbell. However, in going over the proposed French modifications and the reasons for the German refusals later that day, Charles-Roux sensed that Campbell was not following his explanations, that he appeared quite unfamiliar with the substance of what was being discussed. Therefore, interpreting his instructions broadly, he at this time placed before the Ambassador the text of the convention together with the French proposals and the German responses. From this incident apparently sprang the Secretary-General's belief that this was Campbell's first real knowledge of the enemy's terms.[4]

Sir Ronald Campbell's telegrams and final report throw considerable light on many of the murkier aspects of this complex twenty-four-hour period, though a few points remain obscure and some discrepancies inexplicable. One thing is certain: Campbell had the armistice conditions in writing by 3 a.m. and was able to send London the full contents of the enemy's terms in a message that was dispatched at 9:30 a.m. on June 22, and received at 5:50 p.m. Summaries of the German conditions were received even earlier, those concerning the fleet at 2:40 p.m.[5]

Campbell's version of the events described earlier by Baudouin and Charles-Roux is as follows:

I was informed by the Ministry of Foreign Affairs about midnight by telephone that the armistice conditions had been received by telephone and would be considered by the Council of Ministers at 1 a.m., after which the Minister for Foreign Affairs would receive me. I went at once to the Presidency of the Council, where the Secretary-General of the Ministry of Foreign Affairs told me broadly the main conditions. On hearing the condition about the fleet (Article 8) I hastily wrote a note calling attention to its insidious character and the folly of placing any reliance on the German word so many times broken, and demanded that the note should be taken into the Council which by that time was sitting at the Presidency of the Republic nearby, whither I then went, accompanied by the Canadian and South African Ministers, whom I had asked to join me there. We sat in a darkened hall, where people talked in whispers and gloomy officers flitted backwards and forwards until about 3 a.m., when on the termination of the Ministerial Council, I asked the Minister for Foreign Affairs, as he came out, to inform me of the nature of the conditions and of the result of the Council's deliberations. He said that he was going away to draft the reply which had to reach the Germans by 9 a.m. and that he had not time to speak to me. I said that I and the Dominion Ministers must be received and informed of the conditions and of the reply which it was proposed to send. M. Baudouin replied that what interested us was the condition about the fleet, of which he gave us a hasty outline, adding that, on the suggestion of Admiral Darlan, it had been decided to make a counter-proposal by which the fleet would be sent to French North African ports where it would be dismantled. I said that it ought to be sent further away. If sent to a Mediterranean port, it would risk falling into Italian hands. M. Baudouin said that in that case it would be scuttled in accordance with the decision already taken. He then moved away, saying, in response to my demand, that he had not got a spare copy of the German conditions. On my continuing to insist, he eventually gave me one. I then said that I must protest formally against this procedure and insisted on being received somewhere where we could talk quietly. With bad grace M. Baudouin showed us into the Council room, where we found the President of the Republic. Much the same scene occurred and I renewed my protest in the presence of the President, who merely made some irrelevant remark. It proved impossible further to detain M. Baudouin, whose attitude throughout was, to say the least, discourteous. When I reminded him of the letter which he had written to me that very morning admitting the intention of the French Government to consult H. M. Government on receipt of the armistice conditions, he confined himself to saying that the French reply would not be definitive but would "put questions." When I finally said that I must formally insist on being received before the draft reply to the German terms was submitted to the Council of Ministers, he agreed with bad grace to see me at 8 a.m.[6]

The Ambassador concluded from "this shameful scene, [which was] witnessed by Ministers and their secretaries who were standing round," that "the French had completely lost their heads" and would henceforth be totally "unmanageable." Nevertheless, Baudouin's rudeness notwithstanding, Campbell did telegraph Halifax the long-awaited news shortly thereafter.[7]

Baudouin's behavior on the night of June 21–22, although explicable on the grounds of extreme preoccupation and irritation, was a serious diplomatic blunder in that it poisoned for all time Campbell's opinion of him (which in turn influenced Churchill) and made further trust next to impossible. It would certainly have been feasible, and well worth his while, despite the need for speed, to have given a few minutes to Sir Ronald before 1 o'clock, when the second (and less important) Council of Ministers began its deliberations. Because, as Emmanuel Berl cleverly paraphrases Baudouin's remarks to the Ambassador when he did finally see him at 3 a.m., after having first kept him waiting for three hours, what he then said amounted to: "Up to the present I have not had the time, now I have no more and, in a short while, everything will be consummated." This degree of disagreeableness was hardly calculated to disarm someone who already suspected that the French might be subscribing to secret clauses in their negotiations with the enemy. Berl further analyzes the unhappy confrontation: "It is probable that if he [the British Ambassador] had been a better psychologist, if his lucidity had not been clouded by anxiety, fatigue, and anger, Sir [Ronald] Campbell would have understood that had the French, beginning with Baudouin, been less resolved not to betray England, they would have been far more adroit and hypocritical towards him." "More of a psychologist, Sir Ronald Campbell would have understood that Baudouin was all the more ill-natured in that he sensed himself quite innocent."[8] All of which does not make Baudouin's conduct any the more astute or praiseworthy, especially inasmuch as foreign ambassadors are not required, or expected, to be either geniuses or mind readers.

Nevertheless, it is clear that at least to the extent of handing over the relevant document, Baudouin—albeit grudgingly and apparently under protest—did after a fashion keep his word, and that Charles-Roux and others were quite wrong in thinking that the Ambassador had to wait till the next day for this all-important communication. Charles-Roux is also misleading as to the nature of his midnight talk with Sir Ronald: it may not have been lengthy, but what he did disclose about the fleet was enough to let the Ambassador know that, from the British point of view, it would never do.

# Diplomatic Conclusions

CAMPBELL'S first appreciation of the German terms, as reported by telegram, was that they were "diabolically clever" and had "destroyed the last remnants of French courage." "If, as I presume to be certain, [the] Germans reject [the] French counter-proposal as regards the fleet under threat of continuing their advance, I do not believe for a moment that the French in their present state of collapse will hold out against [the] original German condition to recall the fleet to French ports and might even reverse [the] scuttling order. They could still square their conscience by saying [that the] ships could not be used against us." The British would then be "thrown back on Admiral Darlan's pathetic assurances to [the] First Lord of the Admiralty."[1]

Baudouin claims that he waited in vain for the Ambassador to keep his appointment at 7:30 a.m. on June 22. Campbell, according to his report, thought the meeting was for 8. Whether Baudouin was at this time playing a game of hide-and-seek precisely so as to avoid Campbell cannot be known. What is even stranger is that, though Baudouin fails to mention it, Campbell apparently *did* see him just before the Council of Ministers met at 8 to consider the final draft of the French reply. The Ambassador had insisted on seeing Marshal Pétain, which, he writes, he did "with great difficulty in the company of the Minister for Foreign Affairs." The Ambassador at this time begged the Marshal

to see to it that France kept a solemn engagement binding the honour of France, and renewed more than once in recent days, not to allow the fleet to fall into German hands and thus strike a mortal blow at an ally who had

287

always been loyal and with whom France had had a no-separate-peace obligation. If France was no longer in a position to hold to that obligation, she could
still hold to the one to which I was referring. To recall the fleet to French ports
to be disarmed under German control was equivalent to surrender.

The Marshal said only that His Majesty's Government need have no
qualms: "The French Government hoped to get the fleet away to
African ports, such as Dakar and Madagascar. It would sink itself if
ever in danger of falling into enemy hands." Campbell was unable to
reconcile the discrepancy between this statement and what the Foreign Minister had told him at 4 a.m. as to the fleet's being sent to
North African ports. It might be the result of what he had said to M.
Baudouin "as to the danger of sending it to be disarmed in Mediterranean ports under Italian supervision or, more probably, to confusion." But he was sure that he was now "being kept more and more
at arms length" and that he was "becoming [the] object of hostile
looks from the rank and file of Ministers."[2]

In the meantime, Campbell had sent his naval attaché to see Admiral Auphan, the French Naval Chief of Staff, who also said that the
French Government "hoped to arrange for the internment of the fleet
away from French metropolitan ports"—for instance, at Dakar,
French Congo, or Madagascar. "Admiral Auphan stated categorically that the ships would remain under the French flag and with
orders that should the Germans or Italians attempt to interfere with
them in any way or at any time their crews would sink them at
once."[3]

According to Oliver Harvey, "H. E. [His Excellency the
Ambassador] went before lunch again to see Charles-Roux and obtained with great difficulty [the] text of [the] French reply."[4] The
French Government's revision of the clause applying to the fleet ran
as follows: "The French fleet (with the exception of that part which
is left at the disposal of the French Government in order to safeguard
French interests in the Colonial Empire), after having been demobi-
lised and after having disembarked ammunition under German or
Italian control, will be based on French African ports. The crew of
each ship shall not exceed half the normal peacetime crew." But this
the Ambassador found "wholly unsatisfactory—indeed little if any
better than [the] German version."[5]

As soon as he had secured the text, as he explained in a long
telegram to Halifax, Campbell forced his way into the house of the
Minister for Foreign Affairs and demanded to be received at once.

(Baudouin says nothing of this episode.) Here he argued that "once in German hands for [the] purpose of control, no ship would be allowed to leave German hands. [The] Minister for Foreign Affairs argued that in the case of ships absent from their base ports (the very large majority) [the] Germans would be invited to send Control Commissions. As regards [the] others (if any), [the] scuttling order would be carried out if there were any attempt to remove, or otherwise interfere with, French crews." The Ambassador replied "vehemently and at length that all this was totally unsatisfactory and would lead, as he must realise, to [a] breach of faith by France." But Baudouin continued to assert that the key to the whole situation was the scuttling order and offered to instruct Admiral Darlan to tell Campbell exactly how it would be applied in practice.[6]

Campbell thought there was still some chance that Darlan could be worked on or that the ships absent from their home ports might "take the law into their own hands whether on Darlan's instructions or spontaneously." For the most part, however, he had "little remaining doubt" that he was "confronted with deliberate bad faith on the part of [the] politicians" and that there was an "organised conspiracy to keep [him] from ascertaining the facts." As he put it, in a most uncharacteristic burst of plain speaking, he had "to deal mainly with a crook [i.e., Baudouin] who is now the leading spirit in the Government and an old dotard whose word of honour nevertheless remains our only hope." He was doing everything humanly possible but felt that from the moment the Germans set a short time limit the scales had been weighted against him.[7]

Furthermore, when Campbell tried to set up an appointment with Admiral Darlan that afternoon, he was told that the Admiral was "too busy" to receive him but that he "need have no anxiety." The Ambassador thought this an "obvious prevarication" and was forced to the conclusion, although he had previously had faith in Darlan, that henceforth "it would be inadvisable to rely implicitly on Admiral Darlan doing the right thing."[8]

Campbell's subsequent messages to Halifax, some in response to instructions that had been more than overtaken by events, merely registered the downward trend in the Bordeaux atmosphere. There was no fight left in anyone, he reported, and French soldiers back from the front were selling their arms. Though he could not get a straight answer, he took it for granted that "in the altered circumstances (now approaching a land-slide) there was no longer any question of setting up a Government overseas." All the arguments that they were accustomed to using had "long since ceased to make any appeal whatever except to the very rare die-hards." The Minister for Foreign Affairs was becoming ever more elusive and evasive, and it was in vain that he pointed out to him that after their exchange of letters about consultation "he was under an obligation to keep me promptly and fully informed of each stage and step." To this "M. Baudouin merely replied that he was doing so."[9]

The Ambassador made his last stand that day when Charles-Roux sent for him at 6 p.m. to inform him of the reply the Germans had made to the French counterpropositions. With respect to Article 8 (the clause dealing with the fleet), although the Germans would not agree to insert the French modification (the proposal to station their warships in African ports) into the convention, they did not refuse to "contemplate" acceptance of the suggestion made: they simply considered it "a measure of application falling within the competence of the Armistice Commission."[10]

Besides communicating the text of the German reply, the Secretary-General stated that he was also authorized to make the following confidential statement: "The dispositions taken by Admiral Darlan are such that no ship would be utilisable were an attempt to use it to be made." This, he thought, should give the British "complete satisfaction." But the Ambassador "repudiated this with contumely and said that this lamentable clause might well make just the difference . . . between victory and defeat, and therefore jeopardise also all hope of a future for France." He could not but "regret that the Anglo-French Alliance, on which such confident hopes had been founded, should have dissolved in such circumstances."[11]

According to Charles-Roux and Albert Kammerer, Campbell also said a good many other things at this crucial interview. In sum, he accused the French Government of having agreed to deliver the fleet in spite of its promises. He claimed that the execution of Darlan's orders might always be prevented by the sudden irruption of German troops onto a French ship; that it was not just a question of knowing that the French Government was determined not to let its fleet be taken, but, more to the point, whether it could be sure of success in its efforts. Stating that the guarantee exacted of France by Great Britain (the sending of French warships into English waters) had now been replaced simply by Hitler's word of honor, he formally protested against the disarmament of French ships in their home ports, most of which would fall under German occupation, and emphasized that in accepting Hitler's promise the French Government would bear responsibility for the countermeasures England would be obliged to take. He recalled the conditions Churchill had posed six days before for authorizing an armistice and repeated that the only efficacious guarantee would be the transfer of the fleet either to English ports or to ports in the United States. Finally, Campbell let it be known that England would never forgive France for accepting the armistice and that putting her signature to it would in effect constitute a falling out between them. France would never rise from such a fall.[12] So dramatic and frightening was the confrontation, in fact, that Ambassador François-Poncet, who happened to be present at this meeting, was later to describe its effects thus: "The scene became so poignant, and I had such a keen awareness of what it signified, so shortly after the visits exchanged by the heads of the two nations, amidst the enthusiastic acclamation of both peoples, that I abruptly left the room so as to conceal the tears which rushed to my eyes."[13]

At the close of this interview Campbell told the Secretary-General of his intention to leave for England as soon as the armistice was signed. As he could be of no further use (and as the French Government would, within a few hours, be under the control of the enemy), he thought it his duty "to return home for report and consultation after which His Majesty's Government would no doubt review the situation in the light of further developments." As he reported later to Lord Halifax, he "thought it well to add that rider in order not to give the impression that His Majesty's Government might abandon France altogether and thereby encourage the French Government to consider themselves released from any further obligation, notably the undertaking to scuttle the fleet rather than allow it to be used against us."[14]

During the afternoon, despite the Germans' somewhat dubious response on this point, the Council of Ministers had confirmed its earlier decision to station French ships only in ports not under German control, or in North Africa. A little before 4 it decided unanimously to accept the armistice conditions, provided that their own countersuggestions side by side with the German replies were appended to the convention by means of a protocol. But this the French delegation did not feel up to demanding, fearing thereby either to weaken the force of what verbal concessions they had obtained or lest the Germans break off negotiations altogether. A last perfunctory Council of Ministers therefore merely ratified their inevitable acceptance. The armistice was duly signed at 6:50 p.m.—German summer time.[15]

The French did not bother to inform the British Embassy of this officially, but since the outcome was predictable that hardly mattered. This last disservice was merely the culmination of a week during which the Ambassador had felt himself deceived on several counts by Baudouin and Pétain, insulted and put off as a tiresome bore, and finally, insofar as it was possible, ignored altogether. British efforts over the past week had come to naught. From their point of view, the French fleet had not sailed away to safety, and in spite of repeated French promises to the contrary, Campbell thought it might easily be seized by the Germans. The French Government, notwithstanding its "decision" to move to North Africa, was remaining on metropolitan soil, where it would be continually subjected to the pressures of the occupation authorities. And the chasm between French and British thinking and interests had grown ever wider. Chagrined by the "disastrous and shabby ending" of his mission, Campbell nevertheless thought it would be futile to attempt anything more. If the French wished him to stay on, as they did, he believed it could only be that "the French Government hoped by detaining me to give the French public and outside world the impression that His Majesty's Government had condoned their actions." The Ambassador therefore felt perfectly justified in terminating his mission on his own initiative.[16]

Taking leave of Baudouin at 11:30 that night, the Ambassador admitted that he was not going by express order of his government but that he was anticipating its wishes in returning quickly to inform the Foreign Office of recent developments. Inasmuch as the entire staff of the British Embassy was leaving, leading in its train the diplomatic representatives of Canada and South Africa, the implications of Campbell's decision were obvious. By his departure a unilateral rupture of diplomatic relations between London and Bordeaux was being effected. Genuinely alarmed by this move, Baudouin made one last effort to persuade Campbell that France's warships would be disarmed in their African bases, that no naval force would ever be stationed in an Atlantic port, and that the sojourn of large units at Toulon was only provisional. But these assurances, "whose very reiteration tended to shake my confidence" and which Campbell had finally come to believe were but "the expression of a pious hope rather than a sacred pledge," had now lost whatever power they may once have possessed either to tranquilize or to deflect. By this time the Ambassador had had more than enough.[17]

Although absence is frequently considered an error in diplomacy, and the departure of the British Naval Mission is here especially questionable, there is nothing to indicate that Campbell's superiors would have wished him to remain (he was praised for the conduct of his mission while en route to Plymouth) and even less to suggest that London appraised the situation in a more sanguine fashion. Lord Halifax told Charles Corbin during the evening of June 22 that it was with extreme emotion that the British Government had learned of the German exactions concerning the fleet, which it considered equivalent to an actual seizure. He added that even the French delegation's counterproposal (to Article 8), which had been rejected by the Germans, did not offer any guarantee and would not prevent the French fleet from being used against Great Britain by the Germans for the reason that France would simply no longer be in a position to make Hitler respect his promises.[18]

That night Churchill prepared a statement for broadcast the next day which violently attacked the French Government in words that sought to dissociate the French people from those of its leaders who had signed the armistice and who had therefore presumably fallen under Nazi domination. His Majesty's Government, he stated, could not believe

that such or similar terms could have been submitted to by any French Government which possessed freedom, independence and constitutional authority. Such terms if accepted by all Frenchmen would place not only France but the French Empire entirely at the mercy and in the power of the German and Italian dictators. Not only would the French people be held down and forced to work against their Ally, not only would the soil of France be used with the approval of the Bordeaux Government as the means of attacking their Ally, but the whole resources of the French Empire and of the French Navy would speedily pass into the hands of the adversary for the fulfillment of his purpose.

When Great Britain was victorious, she would take to heart the cause of the French people, in spite of the action of the Bordeaux government; but a British victory constituted the only hope for the restoration of France's greatness and liberty. Therefore the British Government appealed to all Frenchmen, wherever they might be, to render the accomplishment of this task more sure and more swift by aiding to the utmost of their strength the forces of liberation.[19]

In calling upon French citizens to continue the fight alongside Great Britain, Churchill, like General de Gaulle, who on June 18 and again on the evening of June 22 had been permitted the use of the BBC to broadcast appeals to France not to surrender,[20] was, in effect, inviting French nationals to dissidence, to rebel against the government that would henceforth be obliged to observe a scrupulous neutrality. A new and forbidding era in Anglo-French relations was beginning. With the signing of the armistice the alliance had been shattered. French and British interests once again assumed clearly disparate shapes. Whether in these profoundly altered circumstances the two governments could achieve some sort of modus vivendi or whether, propelled by their separate fears and anxieties, they would race headlong into hostilities was the stark reality that now had to be faced.

# V

# *Towards a Final Break*

*June 17– July 4*

*We put all our forces in line and because we don't win a second battle of the Marne they call us traitors and cowards.*

> General Weygand, testifying April 7, 1949, on the attitude of England and America, before the Parliamentary Commission of Inquiry, in *CE,* VI, p. 1618.

*There was nothing vainer or more dangerous for the two countries than to fly at each other's throat after a defeat for which they had been jointly responsible. To whom could their recriminations be helpful except to those whose whole propaganda had been calculated to produce just such a break? I understood very well that England had been painfully surprised by some of the clauses of the armistice . . . but the only attitudes that seemed to me appropriate to the extent of our common misfortune were, on the part of England, the affectionate deference of a warrior to the wounded comrade he must leave behind and, on the part of France, the sorrow of a soldier disarmed, his silent exhortation to his happier fellows able to continue the strife, and the hope of rejoining it one day at their side.*

> André Maurois, *Memoirs, 1885–1967* (New York, 1970), p. 260.

# The Politics
# of Intimidation

WITHIN less than twenty-four hours of the signing of the Franco-German armistice the situation between England and France was completely transformed. The British Ambassador had retired; now, on June 23, Charles Corbin, in protest against the armistice and the collapse of the "policy of close collaboration between the two countries" he had worked for since 1933, resigned in London, leaving the management of the French Embassy to Roger Cambon.[1] It was also on the 23rd that Pierre Laval entered Pétain's cabinet as Minister of State, a decisive fact signaling the end of Anglo-French cooperation and the beginnings of a policy of *rapprochement* with Germany.

But, if Paul Baudouin was willing to jettison the alliance with Britain, he was apparently most unwilling to sanction the movement towards an actual reversal of alliances that crystallized about Laval. Confronted by an almost insoluble problem—the necessity of finding favor in Germany's eyes while simultaneously maintaining England's friendship—Baudouin hoped to ride the horns of his dilemma by steering a steady course between extremes. Baudouin's task was complicated not only by the violently Anglophobic sentiments to which some of the most prestigious members of the French Government gave vent but also by mounting disaffection within the Diplomatic Corps and the threat of dissidence in the colonies. What militated most actively against his success, however, was Britain's refusal to be mollified or to accept the brand of friendship offered.

In the wake of Campbell's abrupt departure, Churchill's menacing speech, and General de Gaulle's call to rebellion, Baudouin warned against heeding Laval's demand for an immediate break with England and urged Pétain to maintain a policy of friendship with

Britain in all weathers. Pétain, however, was not inclined to friendly gestures, and in a speech broadcast that evening added fuel to the fire by personally denouncing Churchill for intervening in the affairs of France, for presuming to judge the honor and interests of France, and for attempting to divide the people of France by idle talk and empty schemes.[2]

In a lengthy telegram to the French Embassy (for communication to Lord Halifax) explaining the French Government's position, Baudouin nevertheless adopted a predominantly conciliatory tone in spite of protesting against Churchill's offensive statements and "absolute lack of sang-froid." Expressing his astonishment at the "completely changed attitude of the Prime Minister," Baudouin harked back to the "friendly understanding of France's need to end hostilities" that Churchill had shown at Briare and Tours.

In these circumstances [he asserted], surprise cannot be the excuse for a violence of word and an intemperance of phrase which go so far as to call in question the constitutional authority of the French Government. . . . its main preoccupation has been to avoid any action which could make of France or any element of French activity a weapon that could be used directly against Great Britain. The French Government believes that none of the conditions of the armistice to which it has subscribed implies the abandonment of this concern. In particular it knows for certain that in no case will the French fleet be able to be used in operations against England.

Baudouin deplored the fact that the solemn declarations of the French Government had not been received with the confidence to which they were entitled and emphasized that there was no distinction between the "Bordeaux government" and the French nation. There was "only the French Government, supported by the affection and approval of the French people." He concluded by stating his confidence, or hope, that the British Government did not wish an unfortunate construction to be put upon the departure of its ambassador.[3]

Paul Reynaud himself, fearing that Churchill's broadcast portended a move towards hostilities, sought to allay the Prime Minister's fears concerning the fleet in a personal message (which was, however, sent at the Marshal's request) that appealed for faith in the French Navy and for the continuance of friendship between the two countries. But this appeal remained unanswered, Churchill concluding from it only that "M. Reynaud could be no more relied on than any of the other members of the Bordeaux Government."[4]

The British were, in fact, abandoning conventional diplomatic niceties in order to make it quite clear that they would not accept the armistice. Churchill's speech late on June 22 constituted the opening shot in a carefully calculated campaign of intimidation. It was followed up on June 23 by the delivery of a sharply worded message from George VI to the President of the Republic. Expressing dismay that the French Government was contemplating sending the fleet to North Africa, where it would be disarmed and where it would be in evident danger of falling into enemy hands, the King sternly recalled the solemn pledge given by the French Government that in no case would it accept conditions which risked ending in such a result. The significance of this warning lay in the fact that it made clear that even if the French Government succeeded in having Article 8 modified and obtained permission to dismantle the fleet in North Africa rather than in metropolitan ports (a modification the Germans had not yet agreed to), the British Government would not accept this as a satisfactory alternative to sending the fleet to British or American waters.[5]

In the evening, immediately following General de Gaulle's dramatic announcement of the formation of a French National Committee, which called into question the very legality of the Pétain regime, the BBC issued even more disquieting news. "The British Government," it announced, "find that the terms of the armistice just signed, in contravention of agreements solemnly made between the Allied governments, reduce the Bordeaux government to a state of complete subjection to the enemy and deprive it of all liberty and of all right to represent free French citizens. H.M. Government therefore now declare that they can no longer regard the Bordeaux government as the government of an independent country."[6] Without ceasing to recognize the Pétain government, the British Government had decided to recognize the Provisional French National Committee, set up that day by General de Gaulle in opposition to the Marshal's government; henceforth, the British Government would deal with the Committee on all matters relating to the prosecution of the war so long as it continued to represent all French elements resolved to fight the common enemy.[7]

Recognition of a French National Committee was especially significant at this juncture in that it directly countered the advice given by two pro-British Frenchmen. Ambassador Corbin together with Alexis Léger, the recently ousted Secretary-General of the Ministry of Foreign Affairs, then in London, had already expressed their opposition to the budding Gaullist movement and asked the Foreign Office to suppress the General's broadcast on June 23. They were particularly alarmed by the support the British Government seemed willing to extend to it. Corbin thought the British were adopting the wrong approach if they wanted to see French resistance continued. The establishment of a French government in North Africa would have a chance of rallying public opinion behind it, but a shadowy committee set up on foreign soil under British tutelage, he believed, would not appear to French eyes to be any more independent than the Bordeaux government.[8] That their advice was rejected was proof that by this date the British were no longer interested in subtlety or sensitivity: all approaches would be used simultaneously and indiscriminately.

More insults were heaped on the French Government with the publication of an official communiqué on June 24. Not only was the armistice characterized as a violation of sworn faith but Baudouin was singled out for having broken his word that France would not accept conditions that were ignominious or dishonorable. "His Majesty's Government," the statement read, "can not imagine conditions more humiliating than those consisting of consigning the greater part of its territory and the totality of its war matériel [to the enemy] for the conduct of a war against an ally bound to France by a solemn reciprocal accord not to subscribe to a separate peace or armistice."[9]

Finally, on June 25, following France's armistice with Italy (signed at 7:45 p.m. on June 24) and the coming into effect of both agreements, Churchill returned to the charge in an important speech to the Commons that defined Britain's position in unequivocal terms. In it the relations between the two countries over the past six weeks were recapitulated and, for those who cared to understand, the future was foreshadowed with extraordinary frankness.

At the outset, Churchill expressed his government's hope that the French Empire, protected by the French Navy, would continue the struggle at the side of its allies; in addition, he hoped that the Empire might become the seat of a French government that would rally to the forces of freedom and organize armies of liberation. The British Government, he stated, could not believe that the highest interests of France were faithfully represented in the melancholy solutions adopted by the Bordeaux government. In the meantime support would be given to any French movement outside the power of the enemy that would work for the defeat of Nazism and for the restoration of France. At that moment Churchill could not define the exact nature of Britain's relations with the Bordeaux government. But he thought that the influence of the enemy, the collaboration of pro-German ministers, and the propaganda efforts directed against England would certainly render Anglo-French relations difficult in the future. He did not know whether Great Britain would have any representative in "unoccupied France";[10] but the British would endeavor to maintain contact with the French people "through the bars of their prison." Meanwhile all attention would be focused on the defense of Great Britain. The security of Great Britain and of the British Empire would be powerfully, though not decisively, affected by what happened to the French fleet.

Returning then to the question that had engendered so much confusion, Churchill claimed that concerning his conversations with Paul Reynaud at Tours, the Bordeaux government had published information quite inconsistent with the truth. He had told M. Reynaud at that time that he could not release France from its engagement not to make a separate peace or armistice; nevertheless, on June 16, the British Government had given its assent to an inquiry by the French Government as to the conditions of an armistice provided the French fleet were dispatched to British ports and remained there throughout negotiations. The British Government had reminded the Pétain government, after it came to power, that it had not fulfilled the one condition necessary to relieve it of its obligations. To support their views they had sent the First Lord of the Admiralty, the First Sea Lord, and Lord Lloyd to establish contact with the new ministers, and this delegation had received the most solemn assurances that the fleet would never be allowed to fall into the hands of the Germans. Churchill then turned to the naval clause to which the French Government had subscribed:

This Article ... says that the French Fleet, excepting that part left free for the safeguarding of French interests in the Colonial Empire, shall be collected in ports to be specified and there demobilized and disarmed under German or Italian control. From this text it is clear that the French war vessels under this Armistice pass into German and Italian control while fully armed. We note, of course, in the same Article the solemn declaration of the German Government that they have no intention of using them for their own purposes during the war. What is the value of that? Ask half a dozen countries what is the value of such a solemn assurance. Furthermore, the same Article 8 of the Armistice excepts from the operation of such assurances and solemn declarations those units necessary for coast surveillance and mine-sweeping. Under this provision it would be possible for the German Government to reserve, ostensibly for coast surveillance, any existing units of the French

Fleet. Finally, the Armistice can at any time be voided on any pretext of non-observance, and the terms of the Armistice explicitly provide for further German claims when any peace between Germany and France comes to be signed.[11]

In short, Churchill held that the signing of the armistice in itself was a violation of the March 28 agreement; further, that the French Government had broken the promises given the British ministers on June 18 and 19 not only not to deliver the fleet but never to let it fall into the hands of the enemy; and, finally, that Hitler's assurances were worthless and constituted no guarantee whatsoever. He served notice to all that the British Government had finished with words and fruitless negotiations and would thereafter act however, whenever, and wherever necessary to defend Great Britain and to further British interests. In addition, Churchill was taking up a position vis-à-vis history and justifying in advance whatever stern measures his government might decide to take. "At all costs, at all risks, in one way or another," they had to "make sure that the Navy of France did not fall into wrong hands," and thus bring England and others to ruin.[12]

Churchill's address to the Commons on June 25 was official notification that from the British point of view understanding was no longer possible and indeed not even desirable. The severe public declarations of the Prime Minister, together with the alarmed protestations of Lord Halifax and other official pronouncements of the government, should have left no doubt as to the direction British policy was taking. But, if the British Government's ultimate intentions were still a mystery, it was quite clear that Britain's immediate goals were in direct conflict with those of Bordeaux. Even before the armistice terms were known the British had to some extent cast caution aside in a determined effort to salvage what they could from the wreck of France. As early as June 18 they had taken initiatives in North Africa and elsewhere in the French Empire that could only antagonize the Pétain government and complicate an already delicate situation. Their purpose was none other than to swing over all of France's overseas possessions to a policy of continued resistance.

# North Africa:
# Its Role in British Policy

CHURCHILL'S opinion, expressed retrospectively in terms of global strategy, was that with a French government established in North Africa the British and French fleets together would have enjoyed complete mastery of the Mediterranean and free passage through it for all troops and supplies. Nourished by American production, the British and French air forces based on North Africa could then have taken the offensive by bombing the Italian mainland and by severing Italy's communications with its armies in Libya. In this way, by concentrating on the weakest link in the Axis, the entire North African shore might have been cleared of Italian forces by 1941, and France would have remained a principal power throughout the war. Pursuing such a policy, France would have been spared the internal schisms that tore the country apart not only in 1940 but throughout the war and for many years thereafter; furthermore, the sufferings imposed on the French people by direct German rule would probably not have much exceeded those they were eventually subjected to anyway. As for what the enemy would have done in these conditions, Churchill argues that Hitler could not have invaded North Africa and fought the Battle of Britain at the same time. He would have had to choose, and if he had opted for Africa the British could have moved troops and air forces to Morocco and Algeria more quickly than he and in greater strength. But, given his need to crush England and to launch this attack as soon as possible, Hitler might *not* have followed the French across the Mediterranean for the simple reason that any major operation through Spain to Morocco would inevitably have prejudiced his coming campaign against Great Britain as well as his perennial dream of conquering Russia.[1]

General Weygand's view, also expressed retrospectively, was that with but eight badly armed divisions available for the defense of North Africa, with the low reserves of munitions and almost total lack of war industry present, the limited or nonexistent means of replenishing the supplies needed, and the inability of the French Navy and mercantile marine to transport the required men and matériel in time, a prolonged struggle in this part of the world was not possible and that to have transferred the war here in June 1940 would simply have been to lose North Africa. He believed that French North Africa could have been attacked in southern Tunisia from Tripolitania by an easily reinforceable Italian army or through Spanish Morocco either by Spanish troops if Spain declared war or by German troops permitted passage through friendly territory if Spain remained nonbelligerent. These were the enemy's two bridgeheads. Gibraltar's defenses, he thought, were too weak at this time to have long held up an enemy landing. Furthermore, Italy's bases on Sicily and Sardinia offered many possibilities of joint air and naval action against the French naval bases at Bizerte and Mers-el-Kébir; and France's enemies could have coordinated their attacks so as to split up the French defense along 2,000 kilometers of land and sea frontiers. In short, though the French and British naval forces in the Mediterranean together with French fighter squadrons escaping from metropolitan France "would have made the enemy pay dearly for his crossing to Africa," they would not have been able to stop it. And with this pessimistic estimate of French chances of resisting overseas, the other preeminent military figure in the Pétain cabinet was in complete agreement: "Admiral Darlan would not answer for it that they would be able to prevent the crossing of the Sicilian channel or the Straits of Gibraltar."[2]

North Africa's capacity to continue the struggle had not been studied or discussed in any coherent fashion by the Reynaud cabinet. Campinchi, Minister of the Navy, believed that it would be impossible for the enemy to pursue a French government settled in North Africa if only the French fleet passed to the other side of the Mediterranean, while Laurent-Eynac later stated that the modern planes transferred to North Africa in the third week of June would also have constituted an important defensive resource. But, although in mid-June of 1940 the Minister of the Merchant Marine, Alphonse Rio, had told the Council of Ministers that he had 400–500 ships at his disposal should the government decide to go there, he later testified before the postwar Commission of Inquiry that the evacuation of sizable forces by that date, in the conditions then prevailing, was no longer a practical proposition: much more time would have been necessary. And, significantly, Raoul Dautry, Minister of Armaments, though a veritable Jacobin on the subject of continuing the war, did not see fit to present his important memo to this effect before the Council at Cangé—most probably because he realized that its depressing implications regarding North Africa (though by no means hopeless for the distant future) would have aroused even more opposition to the government's proposed departure among his colleagues than had been shown already.[3]

Furthermore, any departure for North Africa for the purpose of continuing the struggle was inescapably tied to the prolongation of a desperate resistance in metropolitan France, which by presenting major obstacles for the enemy to reduce would have served to slow down the German advance and thus have allowed time for a proper evacuation. It was precisely this courageous program, however, that the High Command had all along refused to countenance, and in this the Reynaud ministry would seem in part to have acquiesced, first by its acceptance of Weygand's strategy as outlined on May 25 and again by its acceptance on June 15 of the Premier's unrealistic argument in favor of a Dutch-style cease-fire, as a measure capable of putting an end to the useless massacre more quickly, more humanely, and less destructively than could the armistice his opponents were demanding. The truth of course was that a decision in favor of North Africa, to be effective, entailed a greater, not a lesser, sacrifice from metropolitan France even in the short run.

Whether the French could have or should have continued the war from North Africa in 1940 is a question lying beyond the scope of this book. Certainly Weygand's thesis has found ample support amongst English and American historians, diplomats, and military analysts in the postwar period,[4] just as Churchill's convictions were shared by at least some knowledgeable Frenchmen at the time.[5] Retrospectively, good arguments have been advanced by both sides on the basis of information that has subsequently come to light concerning German, Spanish, Italian, and American intentions or capabilities. Even with the support of statistics and hindsight, however, all such conclusions regarding the final outcome had this or that course been followed remain purely speculative. What is important is the basis on which decisions were arrived at in 1940. And most of the evidence suggests that technical considerations played but a minor role in the French Government's decision; that while the shortages and deficiencies in manpower and matériel and the unquestioned difficulties of undertaking continued resistance evoked by members of the Pétain cabinet were real enough, minds nevertheless had been made up long before the requisite information was gathered and that social and political considerations—that is, the desire to maintain order both within France and the Empire together with the conviction that Germany had already won the war and that Britain's surrender was only a matter of time—weighed more heavily in the scales than any optimistic advice (or pessimistic evaluations) tendered by military personnel on the spot. That a French North Africa loyal to Vichy may ultimately have proved beneficial to the Allied cause is therefore in a sense irrelevant in "judging" the decisions reached.

On the other hand, was the British decision to push for continued resistance in France's colonial empire any more disinterested? Had France's ability to hang on been appraised differently in Whitehall than it had been at Bordeaux? In short, what were Britain's motives in advising the French Government to embark on such a hazardous and unprecedented venture?

Whatever Mr. Churchill may have thought about French prospects of continuing the war from North Africa, it seems fairly clear that his chief military advisers hardly concerned themselves with the question—at least in any detailed fashion—for the angle from which they tackled strategic problems, that is, Britain's ability to continue the war alone, virtually precluded this concern. From the time the Chiefs of Staff first faced the possibility of a French military collapse their constant assumption was that the collapse would be quasi-total and that it would involve political surrender as well, premised on the neutralization of France and its empire, or worse. The immediate effect of a French collapse, they stated in their initial report on "British Strategy in a Certain Eventuality" (issued on May 25), would be the loss of naval control in the western Mediterranean, with all French European and North African territories becoming accessible to the enemy in the course of time, as a result of which they would have to be treated as hostile territory. Their concern throughout the three weeks preceding Reynaud's resignation was directed not so much to spreading the war to new theaters of operation as simply to keeping the French in the fight for as long as possible and in default of this, or simultaneous with this, to salvaging whatever could be rescued from France in the way of military hardware and economic goods.[6]

Briefly, what the British wanted was no less than the French Navy and mercantile marine, the remains of the French Air Force, the removal of French gold and securities to the United States, the transfer of as much military equipment as possible, certain industrial raw materials, machine tools, diamond dies, military and civilian specialists and technicians, and, as a negative requirement, the destruction of all war matériel, factories, and oil supplies that would otherwise fall into enemy hands, in addition to the destruction of certain highly secret British technical equipment and documents.[7] Making headway through this lengthy shopping list was, as the British were well aware, a delicate matter requiring proper timing and diplomatic finesse, and Sir Ronald Campbell had to devote considerable energy to the task during his last ten days in France.

Planning, however, had gotten under way in late May when Lord Hankey was charged with responsibility for arranging the acquisition of these assets. Believing that compliance with these demands was "the least the French should do for us if ever we are to live with them again on reasonably good terms," Hankey also thought that the transfers should be made *before* the French entered into negotiations with the Germans. Sir Alexander Cadogan, conscious of the delicacy of the situation, however, had minuted to the effect that they could not "ask the French to do this before the event. It would sap the last of their morale." In a more practical vein, William Strang had commented that it was "doubtful whether the French would accede, since to do so would merely rouse the Germans to make the armistice and peace terms even more severe than they might otherwise be." He believed the French were unlikely "to be governed by the long-range view that by strengthening us they increase the chance of our victory and their restoration. They would not ask for an armistice unless they had lost all hope of that."[8]

When Sir Ronald Campbell in turn was asked by Cadogan for his opinion regarding the "best way of setting about trying to secure these objects," the Ambassador replied that, if the Somme-Aisne line were broken through and if the French *did* fall for a German offer, "the pickings left over which we might rescue will, with the exception of the fleet, not be very substantial." What troubled him was how and when to broach the matter with the French. He would "be very reluctant to breathe any word to them at present" [June 4] as "the effect would be deplorable." Furthermore, he thought the German terms "would almost certainly include a threat of being more severe if all military material, stocks, etc. were not left in situ. And if the French committed the shame of falling for a separate peace they would not boggle at that condition." As for the possibility of the fleet's being surrendered, Campbell concluded, "If the French *were* to let us down, they would presumably go the whole hog."[9] In the event, pessimistic prognostications notwithstanding, the British did rather better than expected, although the principal prizes—the fleet and the air force—continued to elude their grasp.

As can readily be seen, however, the flow of goods that most interested the British from this time on was the one towards Britain, not the desperate trickle towards France, because by late May British military planners had for all practical purposes written off French efforts in advance. Indeed, the main reason advanced by the Chiefs of Staff on June 3 for continuing even a low level of aid to the French was a negative one. It was true that if France continued the war with British support the French Army would be able to serve as a drain on Germany, that the French fleet would remain active, and that French North Africa could contain some Italian forces; but the argument that appeared overriding to them was that a France that had capitulated might be a France ruled by a pro-German government prepared to join the ranks of the enemy, with all the grave military consequences this would imply. Thus, they felt driven to recommending the acceptance of still further risks in meeting their ally's demands not for strictly military reasons but for reasons of political strategy.[10]

France's African empire did not figure in this strategic planning in any positive sense. If it was necessary to keep certain key bases out of enemy hands, the actual removal of the war to this front was not at first seen as a serious possibility or even as an advantage. The British Ambassador on June 5 thought that once Paris was taken French resistance would be as good as broken and that, though the continuation of the French war effort from overseas would be a good idea from the point of view of French morale, it would be "extremely impractical" from other points of view—that is, the distance between North Africa and England and the lack of contact a French government installed there would have with His Majesty's Government. Sir Ronald was certainly not alone in preferring to see a French government in exile established in Great Britain. An independent French war strategy was definitely not seen as desirable.[11]

When the Chiefs of Staff and Joint Planners started applying themselves to the question of France's colonial empire, as they had to in mid-June, with French resistance on the point of collapse and the government's resolve hourly weakening, the only role granted North Africa was strictly subordinated to Britain's immediate needs. As made clear in instructions transmitted to British consular representatives, attachés, missions, and liaison officers stationed either in France proper or the French Empire, in the event of a French collapse they were to make every effort to prolong the resistance of French units even after the capitulation of the French Government. The policy was what it had been all along: "to prevent as far as possible French naval, military and air equipment from falling into enemy hands and to encourage all elements we can to join our own forces." The removal or destruction of French air resources and factories was to be prepared for, and French pilots, mechanics, and even whole squadrons induced to come to British territory. The same was to apply to selected individuals and technicians in the army, as well as to weapons and war matériel. As for the navy, French ships were to be persuaded to join the British fleet or, failing this (and here the British did not expect success), to sink themselves. If possible, arrangements were to be made for the destruction of valuable naval equipment, the blocking of certain bases, and the use by Britain of French colonial ports such as Casablanca and Dakar. Finally, all three services were to be offered the inducement of British pay in return for service under the British flag. In short, an attempt was to be made to have all French assets useful to Britain's war effort transferred lock, stock, and barrel to British control.[12]

On June 14 and 15 the Chiefs of Staff spelled out the policy to be adopted towards French colonial possessions in greater detail. That their basic assumptions were wrong (that is, that the German conditions would include not only a demand for the French fleet but also the use of any French bases by German or Italian forces for operations against Britain) in no way affects the basic strategy involved and, in the event, had no real effect on the tactics employed. "Our ability to defeat Germany," they reported, "will depend upon our being able to control at source Europe's essential external supplies . . . and upon the retention of key strategic positions from which we can exert what will virtually be a blockage of the whole of Europe." France was to be cut off from her colonies and treated as part of Greater Germany.[13]

Since without the French fleet the British would not be able to control sea communications in the western Mediterranean, they could not expect for long to prevent the enemy from making use of French North African bases and the economic resources of the area. They would therefore have to rely on a policy of sabotage, subversion, tribal unrest, and winning the assistance of individual French officers to accomplish their ends. There could be no question of the British themselves taking over French possessions, as their aim was simply to try to control colonial produce at source and to deny the use of French colonial bases to their enemies. Where French territories—like Morocco—whose sea communications were already under British control were concerned, there was no need to attempt to occupy them. As soon as the French Government came to terms with the enemy, they recommended, an appeal should be made to the local administrations of all French colonial and mandated territories to continue cooperating with the British, in return for which the British would do all in their power to assist these territories to defend themselves.[14]

It was a perfectly rational policy from the British perspective, but in it French North Africa played the part of a pawn, not that of a principal. (At this stage, the possibility of the area's being genuinely neutralized seemed too remote even to take into consideration.) But without being able to count on the French fleet, and the British never did, their scenario could hardly have read otherwise. When for a few days in June, between the 19th and 21st, the French will to resistance appeared to be reasserting itself, British planning was momentarily jolted. Fundamentally, however, there was never more than one policy. The British simply did not have the wherewithal for any other. The prolongation of French resistance, no matter where it might lead, was the policy best calculated to serve British interests during Britain's period of unpreparedness.[15]

With this goal in mind, and conscious also that public opinion in the French colonies was strongly opposed to an armistice and wholeheartedly in favor of continuing the war from the Empire, the British Government did not hesitate to throw its weight behind a scheme to set up in North Africa a separatist government that would cast in its lot with the Allies. On June 17, the day Pétain publicly announced that it was necessary to cease the fight, Sir Ronald Campbell was authorized to approach certain individuals, such as the stalwart Georges Mandel, for the purpose of encouraging them to go overseas where they could exhort local authorities to continue resistance. At the same time, British consular representatives and liaison officers in Rabat, Tunis, Algiers, Beirut, Dakar, Djibouti, and elsewhere were instructed to concert their efforts along the same lines. On June 18 and 19 approaches were made to General Auguste Noguès, Resident-General in Morocco and Commander-in-Chief of all French forces in North Africa, to Governor-General Le Beau of Algeria, Marcel Peyrouton, Resident-General in Tunisia, Gabriel Puaux, High Commissioner in Syria, and

Pierre Boisson, Governor-General of French Equatorial Africa (who on June 25 was named High Commissioner for all French West Africa), in an attempt to induce them to declare for the continuation of the struggle at the side of the British Empire. Simultaneously, approaches were also made to the chief French naval commanders in North Africa and the Near East as well as to high-ranking air force personnel and army commanders. General Noguès, singled out for special attention by virtue of his prestige and authority over the fate of the French Empire, was worked on by General Dillon, chief of the British mission in Algiers, and by General Liddell, Governor of Gibraltar, who by letter offered military and economic aid, while from London came appeals from General de Gaulle proposing to consider Noguès as chief of the resistance forces and offering to put him in touch with the British Government. Because of his political leanings and family connections (his wife was a daughter of Delcassé), it was thought that Noguès would be naturally inclined toward the preservation of the Anglo-French alliance.[16]

Because the British still hoped to do business with the Bordeaux government, especially with regard to securing the French fleet, these initial soundings were hedged about by a certain reserve and diplomatic nicety. Even so, they constituted at least an oblique call to dissidence, for in the consular directives activated on June 17 the government in Bordeaux was to be represented to the French authorities overseas as without force or popular backing and as acting only under duress. Consuls were authorized to offer Britain's military assistance (the nature of which was not specified, however) to French territories that wished to defend themselves as well as economic and financial help where this was deemed advisable.[17] Though the offer of financial assistance on 17 June was not meant to sound like bribery, it is clear both from later instructions transmitted and a Chiefs of Staff memo on the subject, as well as from information sent the French Minister of Foreign Affairs by French colonial officials immediately after the British approaches, that this was what was intended. The creation of a free French government prepared to resist was also alluded to.[18]

As was to be expected, and as Sir Ronald Campbell quickly informed the Foreign Office, these approaches could only occasion outrage in Bordeaux. "Monsieur Charles Roux deplored the effect which these instructions had produced at a time when the French forces still held the field and it had been decided that if [the] German terms were excessive [the] war would be continued." The Secretary-

General begged that the British Government "would not render more difficult the task of those here [in Bordeaux] who were working in the direction we would wish them to go." Lord Halifax's answer to Campbell was that he should remind the French Government that these instructions had been sent only after Marshal Pétain's formal declaration that French resistance had ceased and that an armistice had been asked for. "It could not then be foreseen that [the] French Government would once more rally and there was of course no intention of interfering with [the] French Government's authority or causing it any embarrassment."[19]

Actually, it was the British who were embarrassed and temporarily thrown into confusion by the apparent readiness of the French Government (manifested the 19th and 20th of June and still a vague possibility on the 21st and 22nd) to go to North Africa to pursue the war if the German terms proved inadmissible.[20] Equally embarrassing was the "magnificent response" from French authorities in the colonies who were not only eager to fight on side by side with the British but insistent on the military aid their allies had apparently been so willing to offer. The call to fight on, with or without the Bordeaux government's authority, had already been sounded and could not be taken back. But there was a certain amount of backing and filling on the diplomatic front due to the unexpected turn of events in Bordeaux. Discussions in the colonies continued discreetly, but for the time being Lord Halifax forbade consular officials to give any publicity to the undertakings set forth in his circular telegram No. 18 (which consuls had acted upon on June 18). "To do so even unofficially," the Foreign Secretary wrote, "might have [an] adverse effect on [the] French Government at a moment when their future action is still undecided." Even as late as June 22, when the Pétain cabinet had already made up its mind to accept the armistice, Halifax was still telling the consular corps that, while they "should continue to promote a spirit of resolution among the French authorities" with whom they came in contact, they "should be careful pending further instructions not to do anything to encourage dissident or independent action."[21]

# North Africa:
# The French View

THIS resolution was by no means lacking in many parts of France's colonial empire, so that for close to a week after the Pétain government came to power the overseas French and the British attached to them enjoyed something of a honeymoon of mutual hopes and expectations. The responses varied widely, ranging from the solid determination of individual French officers to join their British allies by whatever means necessary and the tremendous enthusiasm shown by virtually the entire population of Morocco—Muslim as well as French, civilian as well as military—to the lukewarmness of certain anti-British naval circles and the understandable hesitancy of most governors either to disobey the home government or to act alone failing the establishment of some sort of centralized, directing authority in North Africa which would serve to justify their stance. Firm leadership and a coordination of efforts were the most obvious ingredients necessary to the continuation of the war in Overseas France.[1]

Of the principal colonial officials involved, M. Puaux and General Mittelhauser, Commander-in-Chief of operations in the Near East, were definitely prepared to resist the demands of Bordeaux and to join hands with British forces in Palestine and Egypt. They thought that the French Army in Syria could hold on even without the aid of metropolitan France, so long as they had British support, though they were not prepared to go into dissidence alone. General Legentilhomme in French Somaliland was even more adamant about the need for continuing cooperation with General Wavell regardless of what either Bordeaux or the governor of the colony decided; in fact, he planned to use force to prevent the capitulation of the local governor.[2] On the other hand, Le Beau in Algeria was somewhat noncommittal, while Peyrouton in Tunisia, though anxious to resist any threat from Italy, nevertheless ruled out an attempt at separatism. M. Boisson was also hesitant, waiting to see what other African territories would do.[3]

However, it was General Noguès whose influence would be decisive. At the outset he had announced his readiness to take direct responsibility for conducting resistance from North Africa and had in fact begged the government either to come itself to North Africa to continue the struggle or, at the least, to allow it to be pursued from there. General Weygand on June 21 had requested Noguès's presence in Bordeaux, no doubt to impress on him the thoughts of the home government on the need for an armistice. Noguès, fearing arrest and also the agitation in the colonies that his absence might produce, had refused and instead sent a statement on June 22 defining North Africa's capacity for defending itself in the event of intervention by the Axis powers.[4]

In response to specific questions posed by General Weygand, Noguès had telegraphed: "North Africa, with its present resources, the reinforcements in aviation now in progress, which have a capital importance, and with the support of the fleet, is capable of resisting the enemy's enterprises for a long time." The threat from Spanish Morocco he judged to be the principal danger: this must be taken care of by a preventive action to be launched from the moment Italian or German forces entered Spanish territory. Although he could undertake this operation with the forces of which he disposed, Noguès nevertheless asked for immediate reinforcements in armored units, antitank guns, and antiaircraft weapons. Land operations against the Italians in Tripolitania were ready to be mounted and, although they could not have a very vigorous character during the hot season, commando raids on the enemy's rear could be launched, while in September or October major offensive operations could be undertaken with North African means reinforced by the new units that would have been created thanks to British and American cooperation. Such operations could be coordinated with a British attack on Cyrenaica. Furthermore, with the 600 planes now at his disposal, North Africa was capable not only of supporting land and naval operations but of intervening effectively against vital points in Libya and Italy. His stocks of motor fuel and munitions corresponded to around two months of operations.[5]

This basically optimistic report, however, was interpreted in a very pessimistic light by Weygand, who, as he admits, found nothing in it to modify his previous views. Weygand always made much of the fact that on June 2, when faced by the prospect of handling the enormous contingent of 500,000 men Reynaud was proposing to send to North Africa, Noguès, in a telegram enumerating the difficulties of installing, clothing, equipping, instructing, and assuring the health of this number, had stated that he could receive no more than 20,000 recruits and then only provided all their matériel was furnished by metropolitan France. Noguès, according to Weygand or Weygand's spokesmen, also claimed that the climate of North Africa during the hot season was very bad for young soldiers, who, as a consequence, died like flies. It was also known that Noguès had signaled the serious deficiencies of his army to the government, though these had been aggravated in May and June, first by Gamelin, then by Weygand's levying two of his divisions as well as reinforcements in tanks and planes to meet the crisis in France; Noguès had protested against losing a third division in this way.[6]

Because on June 17 Noguès had sent three of his staff officers to France to expedite the shipment of all available men and matériel to North Africa, some of these deficiencies were in course of being remedied—despite the inertia and bad will of both the Ministry of War and Ministry of the Navy. (These officers were arrested on June 23, while others sent by Noguès were arrested on the 25th.) Even so, as André Truchet and Commandant Lyet both point out, the evacuations effected up to June 27–28 were not entirely negligible and included some 10,000 soldiers and officers, more than 600 air officers, a large proportion of France's remaining aviation, and thousands of tons of arms, munitions, and supplies. The Admiralty in mid-June had evaluated its transport capacity at some 100,000 men without matériel, yet Weygand was aware that Darlan had originally thought an evacuation from Dunkirk would be impossible and was therefore inclined to underestimate what could be accomplished. He also knew that the French contracts with the United States for planes, motors, weapons, etc. ($600 million worth), which had been transferred *en bloc* to England on June 17, would have been available to North Africa if the French Empire had continued to fight. The first cargoes from America were due in late June, though only 125 first-line combat planes were scheduled for delivery over the next three months. Finally, Weygand knew that Noguès was well known for his prudence, and that despite deficiencies he had judged it possible to defend North Africa even with the limited means at his disposal.[7]

Of course by mid-June it *was* terribly late in the game to attempt such a monumental task, a risky undertaking at best, but what was accomplished bears no comparison to what might have been accomplished had Weygand given the transfer his blessing and put his organizing force behind it from the beginning—and had the armistice not intervened while the effort was in full swing. The fact that the Pétain government made no attempt to examine the problem formally before June 22 and 23 shows that the question was not an open one at this date (indeed the Marshal admitted to Charles-Roux on the night of June 21 that it was closed) but rather an attempt to justify a course that had already been decided on by Weygand as early as May 29, when Reynaud first broached the subject.[8]

Significantly, the first real investigation into the technical possibilities of continued resistance from North Africa was undertaken by the Council of Ministers only on the morning of June 22, by which time the acceptance of the Franco-German armistice was almost a foregone conclusion. To have additional information at its disposal the Council on this date sent General Koeltz to Algiers, where on the 22nd and 23rd, according to what Noguès told Senator Tony-Révillon a week later, he and his staff sought to convince Koeltz of the "great chances of success" a policy of resistance would have; although, according to Koeltz himself, the two did not discuss questions of policy at all, since Noguès had already sent in his formal reply to Weygand, but merely examined Noguès's technical needs, which were great; Koeltz nevertheless found Noguès calm, determined, not pessimistic, and ready to assume responsibility for continuing the struggle in North Africa if the government so decided.[9]

What exactly Koeltz reported to the Council at its afternoon session on June 23 remains unclear;[10] however, it appears that General Noguès's overall point of view was never communicated directly to the Council of Ministers before the armistice, but rather a much-doctored version of his report along with earlier telegrams that better conformed to the preconceptions of Weygand and the other pro-armistice members of the government. Certainly the references to Noguès's report made by Baudouin and Bouthillier, whose emphasis is always on the defective state of North Africa's military resources, on the impossibility of opposing a German invasion, and on the imminent risk of becoming involved in war with Spain, bear only a tenuous resemblance to what the Commander-in-Chief had actually written or advised. However, on the basis of this tendentious interpretation, the Council apparently concluded that "the idea of continuing the struggle in North Africa was only a chimera of which the immediate effect would be its conquest by the Germans. North Africa could only be saved by the armistice."[11] At any rate, on the night of June 23–24 the transport of men and matériel from France, upon which Noguès had counted, was abruptly stopped by the Ministry of the Navy on orders from Darlan.

# Caution Cast Off

JUST as June 23 marked the end of a deliberately ambiguous policy towards North Africa on the part of the Bordeaux government, so too on this date did the British Government cast off the scruples and restraint which up to this time had inhibited its representatives in their dealings with the French colonial administration. Early on June 23, British representatives were instructed to make the following communication to the appropriate French authorities:

The present French Government in accepting under duress the enemy's conditions for an armistice have been prevented from making good the solemn pledge of France to her British allies. They have resigned themselves to the accomplished fact of the German occupation of metropolitan France. But this occupation does not extend to the vast territories of the French Overseas Empire, which remains with its frontiers, its defences and its huge economic resources intact.

The French Overseas Empire has still a vital part to play in the struggle for civilisation, the successful outcome of which alone can restore the liberty of France. We, the British Government and British people, are resolved to continue this struggle to the end, and our victory will mean the restoration of the greatness of France. We call upon the civil and military authorities of all French overseas territories to stand by our side and fight hand in hand with us until victory is reached, and thus redeem the pledge of the French Republic.

We appeal to them to do this even if they receive orders from the Government in France to surrender to the enemy, for that Government are already under the control of the enemy and can no longer be regarded as representatives of France. Moreover the Government have no constitutional mandate to surrender French territory.

Until such time as a free, independent, and constitutional authority has been re-established on free French soil we shall do everything in our power

to maintain the integrity and economic stability of all French overseas territories provided they stand by us. We further guarantee that these territories
will be provided with funds to cover the payment of the salaries and pen-
sions of all civil and military officials throughout the French Overseas Empire who are prepared to co-operate with us.[1]

This was the straightforward call to dissidence that the cabinet had
all along determined to sound just as soon as the armistice was
signed. Less clear—at least to British officials who were attempting
to win converts to the cause of continued resistance—was what, if
anything, lay behind such an ambitious policy. It soon became apparent to those who were urgently requesting aid on behalf of the
French that there was absolutely nothing. General Noguès needed
practically everything—trained cadres, arms of all kinds, especially
antitank and antiaircraft guns, tanks, trucks, and one or two additional divisions—but when General Dillon tried to get some of this
for him from England, he was told by the War Office on June 21 that
"it was impossible at the moment to provide an expeditionary force
for North Africa" as the result of the British having lost so much
equipment in France and the extent of their present commitments.[2]
It was a crushing blow to those of His Majesty's consuls and
liaison officers who during this period were thinking in terms of an
Allied offensive to be launched from North Africa or even of more
modest ventures requiring only a Lawrence of Arabia-like imagination and investment.[3] But the decision, imposed by the army, apparently evoked no opposition in the cabinet committee coordinating
French colonial matters, which was told simply that "with reference
to the several proposals and requests that British assistance should be
provided to the North African colonies in the way of troops, aircraft
and equipment generally, it was quite out of the question to despatch
any sort of expeditionary force both on account of the urgent requirements of home defence and the absence of the equipment which
would be necessary for any such expedition." However, this important decision in no way altered British aims. General Liddell and
General Dillon, to whom the above information was conveyed, were
to be told "that at the same time everything should be done to
encourage French resistance in North Africa while avoiding any promise that direct military assistance would be forthcoming."[4] Britain's
total inability to help and the general lack of confidence, as made
clear in Foreign Office comments on the subject, in any possibility of
an offensive or even North Africa's ability to defend itself indicates

that if on nothing else the French and British General Staffs had reached identical conclusions with respect to the real strength of overseas France. But these disquieting prospects were "naturally not for communication to the French."[5]

General Dillon in his brief but colorful account of his mission to General Noguès says nothing as to how the latter was affected by this disappointing news. Yet British insolvency must certainly be borne in mind as we look at the fairly rapid guttering of resistance attitudes throughout French North Africa and the Levant along with the quasi-total alignment of the *grands chefs* behind the government in Bordeaux. There were definite signs of weakening in Algeria, Tunisia, and West Africa on June 23 and 24. Not only had Britain's "financial inducements" produced an "unfortunate reaction" among proud naval officers, who protested that if Frenchmen continued to fight on it would be solely in support of principle, but British promises of help were received with something less than full confidence: the Resident-General in Tunisia thought that any help would be too little and too late. It was evident that with the signing of the Franco-German armistice the French Government's grip was tightening, not loosening.[6]

For Noguès, on whom the others depended, British bankruptcy would seem to have been an important, if not *the* most important, concern. For instance, in explaining himself to a Moroccan group on June 27, he claimed that General Dillon had left him no hope of substantial or speedy help. And this—that is, his lack of arms and munitions and the impossibility of procuring them—together with the unexpected default of the fleet and the Spanish (and German) threat hanging over French Morocco he listed as the three reasons for the course he was taking. To others he claimed that the two conditions essential for the continuation of the war, especially an aeronaval offensive against Italy, were the support of the French Government to render it legal and the support of the French fleet to make it effective. And by all accounts, though he might in a pinch have done without the first, he could never have done without the second because the navy was absolutely indispensable. In addition, as his *chef de cabinet*, General Bertrand, would later testify, at the same time (June 24) Noguès learned of Darlan's defection—in short, that "La Marine ne marche pas"—he also received a pessimistic appraisal from the commander of French aviation in North Africa, the burden of whose complaint was that, in the absence of maintenance crews for the planes he had received and because of technical defects in many of these machines and a lack of spare parts, it would be very difficult to make use of the aircraft that *were* available.[7]

According to Dillon, who was in touch with Noguès throughout June 24, the General finally showed his hand that night at a midnight conference. The armistice with Italy had just been signed and Noguès was now in possession of a telegram from Baudouin informing him that no military occupation was foreseen for either North Africa or the Levant and suggesting that the armed forces permitted would be sufficient to maintain order and French prestige in the colonies. Noguès was afraid, Dillon writes,

of the attitude of the fleet, owing to its allegiance to Darlan, and he had doubts which way Darlan was going to move. He told me that he would keep his troops on a war footing as long as he was able. Then I asked him straight out if he would start a separate government for North Africa. I assured him that all classes would be behind him. It was then I realised that I was dealing with a man who was weak, and who would not disobey any orders issued by a Marshal of France. He told me he could not do without arms and without the Navy. The Navy would follow Darlan—and Darlan had 'ratted'. . . . I asked him again to form an independent government for the French Empire, but to no effect. In the end I realised that the chances of the fight being carried on in North Africa were remote.[8]

By the next day (June 25) Noguès was reluctantly ready to bow to the formal orders of his government to execute the armistice (though he allowed himself the luxury of reaffirming his point of view in one last forceful message to Bordeaux;[9] General Weygand in the meantime recalled Noguès to a strict sense of duty and discipline, at the same time reminding him that the elements of appreciation of which he disposed did not permit him to judge the situation that the government had had to confront—and whose decisions, he insisted, were in no way contrary to honor).[10] In the wake of Noguès the others were brought round to submission as well. In the important territories, M. Puaux and General Mittelhauser held out the longest, until June 27, then they too regretfully fell in line.[11] Thus, by June 25 all real hope of seeing a dissident government established in North Africa by the colonial officials themselves had collapsed. Thereafter, British overtures would be summarily rebuffed. And, as resistance attitudes ebbed, Anglophobic sentiments quickly swelled to fill the vacuum.

The British Government, however, did not abandon its efforts. Its attempts to foment rebellion in North Africa had already provoked the greatest irritation and anxiety in Bordeaux, especially while the government was still negotiating the conditions of an armistice with Italy. On June 24, on instructions from Baudouin, Roger Cambon had demanded the immediate recall of the British consuls in Tunis, Algiers, and Rabat. He also protested against the support the British were giving to General de Gaulle by lending him the use of the BBC with which to appeal to the French people over the head of their government. As he told the Foreign Office, he "hoped that His Majesty's Government would not make it necessary for the French Government to recall the Embassy from London," as "this embassy was the sole link now existing between the two Governments and it would be disastrous if that link were broken." To all these complaints the British Government responded only on June 28, and then negatively and rudely.[12]

In the meantime, to supplement the activities of the British consuls, Churchill had decided to send Lord Gort, former chief of the BEF, and Alfred Duff Cooper, Minister of Information, to North Africa for the purpose of entering into contact both with General Noguès and with Georges Mandel and other members of Reynaud's cabinet who had sailed on the *Massilia*.[13] Mandel, it was thought, had both the capacity and the will to organize a separatist movement dedicated to resistance.

The *Massilia*, whose final party included twenty-six deputies (of whom Mandel, Campinchi, Daladier, Delbos, and Jean Zay were the best known) and one senator (Tony-Révillon), had finally weighed anchor at 1:30 p.m. on June 21. Sailing at a time when all the members of the government had been forbidden to leave Bordeaux, the ship's political passengers had only been permitted to depart through the connivance of Darlan and Pétain, who found it a convenient way to disembarrass themselves of their principal critics. The British should have been, but apparently were not, fully aware of the low status this group enjoyed in the eyes of the Pétain "regime" and of what this portended; for on one occasion, in the days immediately preceding Sir Ronald Campbell's departure from Bordeaux, the Marshal, in a wildly indiscreet remark to the Ambassador, "after admitting that there was a question of sending a government overseas, [had] added that if the British navy torpedoed their ship on the way he personally would have no regrets."[14]

The whole affair, in fact, had many of the earmarks of an ambush. Some of the passengers, having left in the belief that the government itself would depart shortly thereafter for North Africa, had received the news of the signing of the armistice while on board with surprise and indignation and had immediately demanded to be returned to Bordeaux to avoid being branded as "fugitives." Others, more cynical about the Pétain government, had apparently already given up on Bordeaux and now looked to North Africa—or, alternatively, to England—for the nation's salvation. In any event, the *Massilia* had continued its journey, and passing by Rabat, which British intelligence believed to be its destination, had landed at Casablanca on the morning of June 24. With the permission of the Moroccan authorities, Daladier and Mandel immediately set about their business. That afternoon, while Daladier visited Mme Noguès (General Dillon would also call on her the following day), Mandel met openly with the British Consul-General in Rabat; the next day he visited the British Consul in Casablanca as well. Also on the 24th Mandel tried unsuccessfully by telephone to persuade General Noguès (in Algiers) to act immediately towards forming a resistance government in North Africa. This, together with Mandel's contacts with the consular officials and the impending arrival of the British Government's representatives, not to mention the simultaneous coming into effect of the two armistices on June 25, was enough for Noguès to order Mandel's confinement on the *Massilia,* which from that evening was placed under strict control, then temporarily moored outside the harbor. Campinchi's attempt on the 25th to persuade the captain and crew to take off for England was equally unsuccessful.[15]

Thus the arrival of Lord Gort and Duff Cooper in Rabat on the evening of June 25 coincided with the turning of the tide against all efforts to establish an independent French government in North Africa in conjunction with the British. Already orders had been given to airfields and seaports to prevent the landing of any Englishmen, and, although Gort and Duff Cooper surmounted this obstacle, they were nevertheless forbidden to continue by air to Casablanca or to communicate with Mandel there by telephone. General Noguès in Algiers also refused to receive them, on the grounds that such a meeting would embarrass his government. Begged by M. Morize, Secretary-General to the Residency, to make no more attempts to contact the former French ministers and deputies, now under suspicion of subversion, Gort and Duff Cooper, realizing that their mission was a total failure, flew off to Gibraltar the following morning.[16]

This was not quite the end of the matter, however. Possibly inspired by the very frustrations he had met with in Rabat, Duff Cooper on June 28 advocated the landing of an expeditionary force on Moroccan shores as the only way of preventing the establishment of Italian and Spanish hegemony over the whole North African coast. Not surprisingly, the Prime Minister was an avid backer of the scheme, the purpose of which was to form a rallying point around which a French administration sympathetic to the Allied cause could be built up and also to secure the use of the port of Casablanca. For this operation, which was given the code name Catapult II, the Chiefs of Staff estimated that an expeditionary force of 25,000 would be required. However, in submitting their views on July 1, the Chiefs of Staff pronounced the project unfeasible and strongly advised against it. Their report nicely summarized British policy towards North Africa:

In our view, the despatch of an expedition to North Africa is based upon a false strategical conception. It would, of course, be to our advantage that the French should be re-established in North Africa, so that they should continue the fight in all possible theatres of war. The French effort in North Africa, however, must necessarily be a wasting one since without the support of Metropolitan France, they could not hope to prolong the fight for any length of time unless we are prepared to maintain their effort. We cannot recommend that we should divert, at this critical moment, forces essential for the defence of the United Kingdom in order to keep alive a French resistance which we know must very soon collapse.

In short, it was a restatement of their continuing belief that the reestablishment of the French in North Africa was not essential to the prosecution of the war. This clear-cut decision notwithstanding, Churchill on July 1 directed the Chiefs of Staff to work out plans for the operation regardless of its implications. He thought that the expedition should sail in the last half of July. However, the Chiefs refused to modify their previous views on the unsoundness of Catapult II, and Mr. Churchill thereafter was forced to let the matter drop.[17]

# Straws in the Wind

THE proceedings of the British consuls, the abortive mission led by Gort and Duff Cooper with a view to inciting rebellion in North Africa, together with the violent charges leveled by Churchill against the "Bordeaux government," were sufficient in themselves to justify an immediate rupture of all diplomatic relations. As it was, the recall of certain consuls had already been asked for, while British liaison officers in North Africa were simply ordered out of the country and told to discontinue their intrigues. General Dillon himself was sent packing from Algiers on June 29 after being given minimal notice.[1]

In addition, the French Government harbored other grievances against the British. The French division recently evacuated from Norway was still in Great Britain and the British were showing no haste in repatriating it despite the demands of the French General Staff. (On the 29th General de Gaulle succeeded in winning over a small proportion of these men to the Free French cause.) Then, since the night of June 24 a French squadron of cruisers, Force X, which up till then had been actively cooperating in the Mediterranean, had been blocked in its base at Alexandria by a powerful British naval force.

All these affronts to French sovereignty evoked protestations from Paul Baudouin in due course. His policy, as stated to the press on June 25, was that with the conclusion of the armistice France must adopt the attitude of a neutral country; his efforts therefore would be directed towards defending French neutrality "as much against the pressure of Germany as against the entreaties of England." But, if Baudouin was required to protest against Churchill's polemics and the belligerent movements of the British Government, he was also in no mood to make matters worse. Any intemperance in the public statements of the Foreign Minister could only strengthen Laval's hand and might soon lead to a situation over which Baudouin would be able to exercise no control.

In his attempts to restrain British reactions Baudouin applied himself particularly to refuting British grievances, which in his eyes were either imaginary or only hypothetical. The armistice sought by France, he insisted, was not, as the British thought, equivalent to the Belgian capitulation (which the French themselves had so bitterly condemned), because France had treated only after the exhaustion of all its resources and military resistance. As for the fleet, the principal bone of contention between England and France, he could do no more than President Lebrun had already done when responding (on June 24) to King George's message—that is, to recall the repeated assurances his government had given that the French war fleet would never be used against Great Britain. Baudouin was ever solicitous in stating his desire and determination to maintain friendly relations with the British Government. But, in explaining the circumstances which had led to the signing of the armistice and the reasons for the French Government's decision to remain in France rather than pursue the war from the Empire, Baudouin refrained from alluding to any of the basic differences in opinion separating the two governments.

No explanation, for instance, was offered as to why the German aviators shot down in France, and promised by the Reynaud government to England for safekeeping, had been surrendered to the Germans (in execution of the armistice clause demanding the restoration of German prisoners of war) when presumably the avoidance of this dishonorable retrocession would have been so simple. The agreement of March 28, whose violation was invoked so often by the British, was barely mentioned; in its place there were only tendentious references to Churchill's "understanding attitude," self-serving interpretations of the telegram affair, an embarrassing reminder of Lord Halifax's leaning towards a "diplomatic solution" in May, and somewhat maudlin evocations of martyred France's sacrifices on behalf of England. And, while England's major complaints concerning the fleet were skillfully evaded, Hitler's promise not to touch the fleet, joined with Darlan's vague affirmations that every precaution would be taken, were held up as unquestionable guarantees.

This was certainly that "deliberate obtuseness on the part of M. Baudouin and his colleagues" that L. B. Namier credits with causing the final break between Britain and France. True, Baudouin had no desire to alienate England, but underlying all his attempts at patching up the differences between the two governments was the unspoken conviction that events would soon vindicate those who had sought an armistice, that France would shortly find justifications unnecessary when England too concluded an armistice or, if the British continued to fight, failed in their effort. In other words, as Albert Kammerer paraphrases the thought, there was no point in adhering to an engagement that no longer corresponded to the circumstances, especially when the beneficiary of the engagement would no longer be in a position to demand its execution.[2]

Under the circumstances it is not surprising that Baudouin's efforts to put Anglo-French relations back on a normal diplomatic footing met with total failure. On June 27 Baudouin had dispatched a semi-official mission to London both to test the ground and to "enlighten" Lord Halifax on the French situation and the real intentions of the French Government. However, the former appeasers Messieurs Bressy and Chastenet, whose forthcoming arrival Roger Cambon announced to the Foreign Office, were refused the necessary entrance visas on instructions from the Foreign Office and left high and dry in Lisbon.[3] Equally unsuccessful were Baudouin's efforts to get the British to send a chargé d'affaires to represent them in Bordeaux.

If the French had at first thought that the immunity left by the armistice convention to the entire French colonial empire and the Mediterranean coast of metropolitan France, plus the efforts the French Admiralty was making to have the fleet disarmed in North Africa, would suffice to appease the British, they were beginning to be less confident of this idea during the last days the government remained in Bordeaux. A plethora of explanations and assurances had failed to produce any relaxation of British fears or any détente in provocative actions.

On June 28 Churchill recognized General de Gaulle as the leader of all Free Frenchmen, wherever they might be, who would rally to him in support of the Allied cause. Then, on June 29, Count René de Saint-Quentin, the French Ambassador to the United States, telegraphed from Washington that an article by the French journalist Pertinax (André Géraud) appearing in the Baltimore *Sun* had warned that the British were on the point of employing brutal methods to secure the French fleet. Although an act of force by the British Navy against the French still appeared an unlikely eventuality, the French did not hesitate to appeal to President Roosevelt to use his influence in London to lead the British Government back to an amicable understanding. However, Cordell Hull and Sumner Welles made it quite clear to M. Saint-Quentin that they greatly regretted that the French Government had not sent the French fleet to England; and, as they would not exonerate the French from wrong in this matter, they would not serve as official mediaries between London and Bordeaux or make themselves the advocates of the French position with the English. Thus, because both London and Washington interpreted the naval clause of the armistice in the same way (that is, in Mr. Welles's words, that it "threw the entire Fleet directly into German hands"), France's attempts to interest the United States in moderating British reactions were doomed to failure.[4]

In the week following June 22 both the British and French governments had made known their respective positions. Now the bitter dialogue was closed and an uneasy period of waiting began. The French Government, preoccupied with the immediate problems of restoring order to a shattered nation, with its projects for reorganizing the constitution along authoritarian lines the better to conform to the pattern of Hitler's New Order, and with setting up the apparatus by which the armistice would be carried out, was inclined to leave unresolved conflicts for the future to take care of. But in their somewhat sanguine view of what could be expected from across the Channel the French completely misjudged British character. They had forgotten that cold calculation and determined ferocity which the threat of defeat is capable of arousing in the Briton at bay.

# The Enigma
# of Admiral Darlan

THE one person who by virtue of his authoritative position as commander of the undefeated French fleet might have altered the course of French history—and with it the course of Anglo-French relations—was the enigmatic Admiral Darlan. As Churchill saw it, "Admiral Darlan had but to sail in any one of his ships to any port outside France to become the master of all French interests beyond German control." Unlike General de Gaulle, who brought with him no tangible assets,

he would have carried with him outside the German reach the fourth Navy in the world, whose officers and men were personally devoted to him. Acting thus, Darlan would have become the chief of the French Resistance with a mighty weapon in his hand. . . . The whole French Empire would have rallied to him. Nothing could have prevented him from being the Liberator of France.[1]

But whatever else may be true of him, one thing is certain: Darlan could not and did not see his place in history through the eyes of an Englishman.[2]

Up until mid-June Darlan had given every indication of being wholeheartedly opposed to an armistice and had not hesitated to express a salty contempt for Pétain and Weygand. On May 28, in a letter to Admiral Le Luc, he had stated that in case military events led to an armistice whose conditions were imposed by the Germans, and if these conditions included the surrender of the fleet, he did not intend to execute it. The fleet would instead receive the order to take refuge in British ports. This he repeated to Weygand on June 14. He had also told General d'Astier de la Vigerie on the 14th that if

329

necessary he would place the entire fleet under the British flag.[3] Darlan's most unequivocal statement, according to Reynaud and many others, was made to the socialist deputy Jules Moch (then a member of the Admiral's staff at Maintenon) on June 3; he was then reputed to have said: "If an armistice is asked for one day, I shall round off my career with an act of glorious indiscipline; I shall sail with the Fleet."[4] Even as late as June 15 Darlan was affirming the same intention to Édouard Herriot in the course of a conversation in which he also spoke of the desirability of the armed forces and government embarking for Algeria, where they could reorganize for the continuation of the war. On this occasion, he did not argue the impossibility of any large-scale evacuation; on the contrary, he claimed that the naval base of Toulon, the main port from which the transfer of men and goods to North Africa would take place, could successfully withstand a siege of several weeks.[5] Furthermore, early that same afternoon, to a member of Reynaud's military cabinet who had specifically asked for confirmation on this point, he had asserted his willingness, in the case of an armistice, to sail with the fleet for North Africa and later for America under the guise of conducting a personal rebellion.[6]

By refusing to consent to an armistice where the fleet was concerned, Darlan would, in effect, have made any armistice impossible, as France would then have continued in the coalition. Control of the fleet gave him an immense power, power which if used independently could have nullified the carefully laid plans of the defeatists. Conversely, the lack of his support could also nullify the plans of the colonial administrators who hoped to continue French resistance from North Africa. Why, then, after so many protestations as to the need for fighting on, did he not exercise his power to prevent an armistice? Reynaud believes that on June 11 he traded this power, which depended on an Allied victory to be worth anything, for Pétain's promise to make him "First Consul" in the new government when it came into being. In other words, Vichy was worth a mass. Whether it was on June 11 or, as Jules Moch believes, not until June 15 that Darlan changed his mind (if change it he did), by the crucial day—June 16—he was certainly in the pro-armistice camp.[7]

Adrienne Hytier, on the other hand, arguing from a somewhat different angle, believes that the Admiral's control over the fleet was not absolute and that Darlan was shrewd enough to realize that "any glorious indiscipline on his part might run head on into the proud obedience of the officers of the fleet and even of the sailors themselves." Even if followed by the entire fleet, Darlan would still have disposed of a force far inferior to Britain's and would of necessity have been relegated to a subordinate role; followed by only a few, Darlan would have been totally dependent on the British. "Darlan," she claims, "was sure that if he played his cards correctly there was political power within his reach and Darlan was an ambitious man." Throwing in his lot with the British offered no security, for not only was the loyalty of the French fleet in doubt, but he had no guarantee that England would not be defeated almost immediately. "In fact, he had thought that there was every chance that she would be and was anglophobe enough to relish the idea."[8]

Darlan's motives were no doubt mixed. Certainly he partook of the anti-British sentiment that was traditional in French naval circles even after the Entente Cordiale and that the Washington Naval Conference of 1921–22, the London Naval Conference of 1931, and the secret Anglo-German naval agreement of 1935 had done so much to confirm. Recent events at Dunkirk had done nothing to reduce this resentment,[9] while the treatment of Norway during that earlier disastrous campaign had only demonstrated the helplessness and humiliation of a defeated country vis-à-vis its still undefeated allies, foreshadowing the position France might expect to hold with respect to England if the French Government, like the Norwegian, chose to fight on after being chased out of its home territory. According to one of his biographers, this was the reason for Darlan's negative response to the British Government's last-minute offer of a Franco-British union: for "whatever its ultimate implications might be for the day after the war ended, its immediate result would be, in practical terms, the casting away of France like the classical peel of a squeezed orange and abandoning it to the Nazis, as Norway had been abandoned after her fleet, her gold hoard and all other easily movable goods had been taken abroad."[10]

British egoism, heartlessness, rapacity, and hypocrisy—all these themes permeated Darlan's thinking both before and after the Pétain cabinet came to power. The British ministers who came to Bordeaux on June 18 to discuss the fleet with him, he wrote his wife, "had the bearing of heirs who have come to assure themselves that the dying man has willed in their favor."[11] And to William C. Bullitt, after the American Ambassador had rejoined the French Government in Vichy, he gave as a reason for his unwillingness to send the French fleet to England under any conditions his belief that "the British would never return a single vessel of the fleet to France and that if

Great Britain should win the war the treatment which would be
accorded to France by Great Britain would be no more generous than
the treatment accorded by Germany." However, he did *not* believe in
England's lucky star; in fact, he was "certain that Great Britain
would be completely conquered by Germany within 5 weeks unless
Great Britain should surrender sooner." When Bullitt remarked on
this occasion (July 1) that "he seemed to regard this prospect with
considerable pleasure," Darlan had simply smiled and nodded agreement.[12] Therefore, as he had told Jules Moch on the morning of June
16, it was in France's interest to negotiate with Hitler before the
British did in order to obtain more advantageous terms.[13] Furthermore, the condition the British had attached to giving their assent to
a Franco-German armistice (that the French fleet be sent to British
ports before negotiations began) he thought nothing but a piece of
jesuitry, "because it was quite evident that the Germans would never
agree to grant an armistice if, while France was asking to negotiate,
she ordered the only part of her forces still capable of fighting to continue the war."[14]

But there were probably other motives besides ambition and Anglophobia for the course Darlan took. According to Rear Admiral
Belot, "If his temperament led Admiral Darlan to desire the continuation of the struggle, reason led him to the same conclusions as the
Marshal and Weygand: the armistice was a necessity but it was
essential to preserve the fleet and the empire." His son claims that
Darlan first began having second thoughts in the light of what Weygand had reported at Briare and the evident incapacity of the British
to participate further in the struggle on the continent. He was also
much shaken by Reynaud's huge demands on the French Admiralty
in mid-June, only a small proportion of which he believed the navy
could fulfill. Then too he had grave doubts as to whether the fleet
could even hang on to the ports—metropolitan or colonial—it would
need to continue the war in the face of the enemy's superior aviation.
And without the fleet the French Empire would rapidly fall prey to
the Axis powers. In these circumstances, again according to his son's
apologia, Darlan no longer felt he had the right to leave with the
fleet: it belonged to France, not to him, and this patrimony should be
used to alleviate France's martyrdom, not to exacerbate it. Just as the
British had the right to protect their own interests by conserving their
air force, the French had an identical right to use their fleet in the
service of France on condition that it did not directly harm their
British allies.[15] Darlan's approach may not have been this high-

minded, but certainly no Frenchman believed that he would ever consent to deliver the fleet to the Germans. Even General de Gaulle discounted that possibility; as he told Churchill on June 16, "A feudal lord does not surrender his fief." And Sir Ronald Campbell evidently felt heartened when Darlan told him late that same night: "So long as I can issue orders to it [the fleet] you have nothing to fear."[16]

Whether or not Darlan had ever seriously intended to sail in defiance of a capitulating government, he all but relinquished the idea upon becoming Minister of the Navy. From 17 June on, the notion was entertained only as an alternative to the fleet's surrender. Henceforth, he was to associate himself with the policy of the cabinet, which consisted in leaving France's naval forces where they were (or directing them to safe metropolitan or colonial ports) while awaiting the arrival of the armistice conditions, the acceptance of which would then not be prejudiced. In other words, Darlan would use the fleet as bait, as a means of obtaining more tolerable armistice terms from the Germans. Hereafter, in Reynaud's opinion, Darlan's threats to order the fleet to weigh anchor for the United States (as on June 22) can probably be better understood as an attempt to force Pétain's hand, as a bid to wrest the second most important post in the government away from his rival Laval.[17]

Before the two armistices came into effect Darlan ordered the fleet to pursue hostilities "with the fiercest energy," and, unlike the army, which for the most part had been completely demoralized by Pétain's speech to the nation on June 17, the navy gave the Germans a run for their money. In accordance with Darlan's order of June 18, which commanded, in case of a German threat to the Atlantic ports, the withdrawal to Africa of everything that floated and the scuttling or sabotaging of all vessels otherwise unable to get under way, most French ships of any importance in Cherbourg, Brest, Lorient, St.-Nazaire, and smaller harbors were successfully evacuated or destroyed before the arrival of the enemy on 18 and 19 June[18]—and this included the dramatic hairbreadth escapes of the French fleet's two superbattleships, the *Jean Bart* and the *Richelieu*. Thus by June 20 the only really important French naval forces still in metropolitan waters were the four 10,000-ton cruisers together with some destroyers and submarines anchored in the roads off Toulon; and this force, ready for action against the Italians, was capable of sailing anywhere at short notice.[19]

On June 20, in a general order ruling in advance the order of succession to be followed by the admirals called to replace him in the event that he was no longer able to exercise his command freely, Darlan emphasized that, whatever orders might be received, no warship was ever to be abandoned to the enemy intact. Specifying the course of action to be carried out once the armistice was effected, Darlan on June 22 ordered the organization of a resolute party on board each ship that would have as its mission the destruction of the armaments and the scuttling of the ship if the enemy or "any foreigner" attempted to utilize it for his own purposes. Then, on June 24, taking advantage of his last opportunity to transmit orders in code before the armistice entered into effect, Darlan laid bare his definitive thoughts on the subject in an important order of the day. The orders communicated were to remain valid whatever contrary orders were received subsequently—even if signed by the Admiral of the Fleet himself. Darlan ordered that:

(1) Demobilized warships must remain French, under French flag, with reduced French crews, and stationed in a French port, either metropolitan or colonial.

(2) Secret precautions for sabotage must be taken so that neither an enemy nor former ally seizing a ship by force can make use of it.

(3) If the Armistice Commission charged with interpreting the [armistice] text decides otherwise than in paragraph I, at the moment this new decision is executed, and without further orders, warships will either be conducted to the United States or scuttled if they cannot otherwise escape the enemy. In no case must they be left intact to the enemy.

(4) Warships thus taking refuge abroad must not be used in operations of war against Germany or Italy without orders from the Commander-in-Chief of French sea forces.

(5) In no case should the orders of a foreign admiralty be obeyed.[20]

Although Admiral Odend'hal of the French Naval Mission in London communicated a part of this order to the British on June 25, he did not mention paragraph (3), which thus escaped the attention of the Admiralty. In fact, on the basis of telegrammed instructions sent him on June 24, and according to the note he himself drew up for Admiral Pound the next day, Odend'hal conveyed only the information contained in paragraph (1)—which Darlan apparently considered the essence of the matter. And even this was vitiated by being coupled with Darlan's protest against the retention of French warships in United Kingdom ports.[21]

Yet the order was of utmost significance, for it not only demonstrated the determination of the French to prevent the fleet from falling into enemy hands and the lengths to which they were prepared to go to preclude this eventuality but it also suggested that Darlan, at heart, had scarcely more faith in the value of Hitler's promises than the British had. Had the degree of Darlan's skepticism vis-à-vis the Germans been plainer, it is just possible that the British would have been willing to place greater trust in the efficacy of his vigilance.[22] In its references to "former allies" and "foreign admiralties," however, it shows another dimension of Darlan's mind.

This note of hostility to Great Britain had been present in Darlan's messages since the Pétain government took over. As early as June 17 Darlan stopped sending French naval units to England and on June 18 began recalling some of those that had already found a refuge there. French ships participating in British convoys were also ordered to leave them. This probably accounts for Churchill's inaccurate and rather ungallant remark, when referring to this date (June 18–19), that "no more French warships moved beyond the reach of the swiftly approaching German power."[23] These orders of Darlan in fact countermanded his orders of June 14 and 15 (in response to prodding from Admiral Pound) that all warships, and especially the *Jean Bart* and *Richelieu,* were to be sailed to England in case of being threatened by the German advance. On June 21 Darlan ordered all French ships in British harbors to leave and protested to the French Naval Mission that the measures taken by the Admiralty with respect to French merchant shipping were "inadmissible." (The British had for the past few days been herding French merchant ships into their ports and would prevent the French men-of-war taking refuge in England from departing for North African or Mediterranean ports as directed.) Also on the same day Darlan ordered French warships sailing for North Africa to avoid provisioning at Gibraltar.[24]

The next day France signed the armistice with Germany. In his order of June 22, Darlan did not hesitate to blame the British for the reverses that had led to this pass; he also defended the policy of nonresistance in Africa by reference to the small support that could be expected from England, whose chances of success in the war he now rated as "problematical." That night Admiral Pound and Mr. Alexander appealed directly to Darlan, recalling in their telegrams that the condition for England's consent to an armistice had been the sending of the French fleet to British waters. They now asked if they could be assured, should the fleet cease to fight, that this condition would be fulfilled. Needless to add, Darlan, whose position all along (as Reynaud tells us) had been that he had "not created a fleet to offer it to the British," made no response to this call to order. On the contrary, deliberately ignoring the condition put by the British and setting aside his knowledge of the two telegrams redelivered by Sir Ronald Campbell on June 17, Darlan on June 23 set out to justify the armistice to his subordinate officers. Taking a leaf out of Baudouin's book, he insisted that on June 11 the British Prime Minister had declared his understanding of France's need to stop fighting and had bowed to it; Darlan therefore concluded that Churchhill did not now have the right to speak otherwise. At the same time he lashed out against the radio campaign launched by the British for the purpose of creating confusion and disunity among Frenchmen. If it succeeded, he warned, "it would result in putting the colonies and the French fleet at the disposal of the British Government for the defense of its interests alone." Therefore, each individual must "think only of the interests of France to the exclusion of any other"; the French fleet would remain French or perish.[25]

By June 24, fearful of surprise moves of a hostile nature, Darlan warned his officers to "beware of possible British attacks." At the same time he ordered an end to all liaison contact with British officers whether aboard French or British vessels. In fact, his general order of the day for June 25 expressed his anxiety lest the British, resentful over their failure to intern the French fleet in England, try to destroy or damage French warships, which, he stated, represented one of the essential elements in France's international position. Admiral Godfroy in Alexandria was ordered to use force to repel any British attempt to capture or sabotage his ships, while Admiral Odend'hal in London was also warned on the 25th that if the French naval squadron at Alexandria was not released from its detainment he might have to adopt a "solution extrême, catastrophique pour tous."[26]

On June 26 Darlan ordered the application of the armistice convention. In seeking to convince his officers that the two armistices contained in them nothing dishonorable he was no doubt precipitous in claiming that the French had succeeded in obtaining a softening of the terms on a number of points, for there was nothing *as yet* to indicate that French naval units would not be returning to their peacetime bases in France just as prescribed. As for the British, Darlan declared: "Our former allies must not be listened to. Let us think French, let us act French."[27]

Admiral Darlan had every reason to suspect the intentions of the British. It was not only his intense Anglophobia that had led him to believe in the possibility of conflict with France's former ally: hard facts definitely pointed that way. Yet, for all his awareness of impending danger, even Darlan did not attribute to the British the plan that was in fact taking shape. It was apparently inconceivable to him that the British in the last analysis would not trust his solemn word. To complicate matters, communication between France and England was close to a standstill. The departure of the British Naval Mission from Bordeaux on the night of June 22 had taken away the last direct means of liaison between the French and British admiralities. Then, since the 25th, in accordance with the terms of the armistice, French naval radio stations had been sealed, so that French Admiralty messages now took almost 35–40 hours to reach their destination by other means. Consequently, as Auphan and Mordal note, "communication between the French Admiralty and Admiral Odend'hal, its sole liaison with the British in London, took on many of the one-sided aspects of a dialogue between two deaf persons."[28]

Whether the French armistice commission negotiating in Wiesbaden might secure for French ships the right to be stationed in French ports not occupied by the enemy appeared to the French Naval Mission in London as an issue still capable of influencing the final plans of the British. On June 27 Admiral Odend'hal signaled Darlan that "before making up its mind definitively, the [British] Admiralty wished to know if our ships would be interned in metropolitan ports or in those of North Africa." He also informed Darlan that Admiral Pound still expressed his confidence that the French Admiralty would know how to maintain the fleet in North African ports, where it could escape the enemy. But, he added, "in its struggle to the death, Great Britain could not afford the risk that the French fleet, once interned in occupied ports or susceptible of being, might be captured by surprise and next used against England."[29] That very day, in a telegram that was not received until June 29, Darlan instructed Odend'hal to beg the British Admiralty to reserve its judgment until the conclusion of the armistice negotiations then in progress, which, he thought, very likely would result in French warships being immobilized in nonoccupied ports.[30]

In reporting his June 27 conversation with Pound, Admiral Odend'hal undoubtedly erred on the side of optimism and diplomacy. He had actually been handled quite roughly by the Naval Chief of Staff. As recorded in the War Cabinet Conclusions the next day, the

First Sea Lord had informed Odend'hal that the British "were by no means satisfied that the French ships would be permitted to remain in French colonial ports as the French seemed to think."[31] Pound's most recent information on the Italian terms in fact suggested quite the contrary. But (according to Pound's own note on the interview) it was necessary "to obtain at the earliest possible moment the exact terms of the armistice as it affected the French Fleet," about which the British up to the present had not received *any* information. Odend'hal had initially written Pound to convey Darlan's dissatisfaction with the continued detention of French ships in British ports, especially those at Alexandria. But in their interview Pound had impatiently brushed aside his sentimental references to Darlan's feeling of betrayal since June 18 as well as the plea that "crippled France . . . be treated not as an enemy but as a neutral Power." Instead, pointing out that Britain's one object was to win the war, which was as essential for France as it was for themselves, he had bluntly warned "That all trivialities such as questions of friendship and hurting people's feelings must be swept aside. That though there was not the slightest doubt that we should win the war it [was] essential that we should prevent, as far as possible, the scales being weighted any further against us at the present time." Therefore, Admiral Darlan should "remember this whenever anything occurred which seemed to him unfriendly." At the same time, in answer to Odend'hal's query, Pound also stated outright that if the French ships under British control at Alexandria attempted to leave port they would be fired on. But the exact tenor of this conversation was not conveyed to Darlan any more than Darlan's depth of displeasure was to Pound.[32]

In any event, no really new information regarding the final disposition of French warships was immediately available. As of June 28, it was Roger Cambon's understanding, as he reported to the Foreign Office, that all units of the French fleet would be required to proceed to French metropolitan ports in conformity with the armistice agreements—information seemingly confirmed by the terms of the Franco-Italian convention (signed on June 24), which Odend'hal sent the First Sea Lord the same day. Then, the following day, the War Cabinet learned that Darlan was instructing French admirals in various places to prepare to resist an attack by British ships—information somewhat at odds with Odend'hal's assurance on June 27 that it was "his foremost desire not to widen the gap between Great Britain and France."[33]

On June 30 the Italians authorized the stationing of the French fleet, with crews at half strength, at Toulon and in North Africa, but Darlan's message to this effect reached London in an incomplete form, so that on July 1 Odend'hal could only claim that he had "firm hopes" of such permission also being granted at Wiesbaden. It was rightly assumed by the French that whatever the Italians decided on this point the Germans would follow suit by virtue of their having agreed to accept the recommendations of Italy on all questions concerning the Mediterranean. However, it is unlikely that by July 1 this missing piece of information, for all its importance, could have made much difference to the War Cabinet, when in their eyes no location in the Mediterranean could be considered wholly secure, especially from a surprise German airborne attack. Certainly they did not judge it worthwhile to wait and find out. Mr. Churchill, for his part, had already decided that "any discussions as to the armistice conditions could not affect the real facts of the situation."[34] As proof that the British now considered the time for talk definitely over and done with, the French Naval Mission was told the same day that "henceforth their presence was no longer desirable."[35]

# British Planning
# and the French Fleet

IN 1807, menaced by the possibility of still another invasion and fearing lest Napoleon add to his strength by appropriating neutral Denmark's ships, the British had not hesitated to bombard Copenhagen and to seize the Danish fleet anchored there. Now in 1940, with somewhat more scruples but no less determination, the British War Cabinet resolved to crush the French fleet in one blow. As Churchill describes it, "This was a hateful decision, the most unnatural and painful in which I have ever been concerned. . . . the French had been only yesterday our dear allies, and our sympathy for the misery of France was sincere. On the other hand, the life of the State and the salvation of our cause were at stake. It was Greek tragedy. But no act was ever more necessary for the life of Britain and for all that depended upon it."[1]

The French Government's acceptance of naval clauses that were specious at best and extremely perilous at worst from the British point of view marked the most obvious milestone on the road to a final break between the two countries. It was, after all, at this point that formal diplomatic relations were abandoned by the British on the assumption that further negotiations with the Pétain government would be useless. Charles-Roux has stated that the British attack on the French fleet was the direct result of a fundamental divergence between the French and English interpretations of the naval clauses of the armistice, the English considering them as equivalent to a surrender, the French as not. And Admiral Auphan and Paul Baudouin have explained in detail why the British were particularly disturbed by the word "control" in Article 8, which in the English language means "the power of directing and restraining" or even "taking possession" but in the French language signifies merely "administrative verification, inspection, or censorship."[2]

This semantic divergence was real enough, and the British obviously were unwilling to test the accuracy or inaccuracy of the French interpretation. It is equally true that probably no clause the Germans could have put forth would have been acceptable to them. This is not the same thing, however, as saying with Adrienne Hytier, in *Two Years of French Foreign Policy,* that the British decision to destroy or seize the major part of the French fleet was not dictated by their alarm over the Franco-German armistice in general or over Article 8 in particular, as was long assumed because of Churchill's violent denunciations of both. She is on more solid ground in maintaining that "In reality, the British Government had considered the French fleet as a potential menace from the moment that the collapse of France had seemed possible." In fact, "as soon as the Reynaud Cabinet had resigned, and long before there had been any armistice with any alarming Article VIII to worry about, London had decided to eliminate the French fleet."[3] This should be amended to saying that from the very outset they were simply determined to prevent its being used against them, and, if this entailed elimination, so much the worse.

Precisely when this momentous decision was taken and how it was arrived at deserves to be set forth. Contingency planning for the day when France would no longer be in the war, as has been seen, got under way in England in late May. What would happen to the French fleet—and the need either to get hold of it or to render it harmless—immediately became a principal concern of the British Government from the moment the Battle of France was joined. The final decision may have been delayed for a month, and the tactics suggested variable, but there was never any question as to the goal. What is surprising in retrospect is that the French were not more aware of the policy taking shape virtually under their noses. The slightest familiarity with British history should have prepared them for the event.[4]

The thorniness of the issue was confronted squarely on June 7 when Lord Hankey, Sir Alexander Cadogan of the Foreign Office, and Admiral Pound met at the Admiralty "to discuss possible ways and means of preventing the French Fleet from falling into German hands in the event of the French being constrained to make a separate agreement with Germany." Because of their "assumption that the Germans would insist, as part of the terms of any armistice, that the French Fleet should be handed over to them intact, and that . . . they would continue to batter the French until the Fleet was delivered to them," they foresaw difficulties of two kinds: (1) either Admiral Darlan would refuse to order the fleet to British ports or even to allow it to cross the Atlantic to America; or (2), if the British did somehow acquire it, they might find themselves "in the intolerable position of having to stand by and see the continued devastation of French towns from the air," for which they would be held responsible so long as they held the fleet. But, because the First Sea Lord believed that the delivery of a fleet to an enemy was so deeply humiliating that any naval commander would do his utmost to avoid it, he thought that "the best result" for the British to aim at

would be that the Fleet should be sent to the bottom of the sea rather than surrendered. This could be effected in quite a short time and it was not at all unlikely that the responsible French authorities could be persuaded to take this course. Once the Fleet was at the bottom of the sea there was nothing the Germans could do to retrieve it. In the last resort, if the French would not sink their Fleet, we could perhaps do it for them.[5]

Their four options, as the Joint Planning Sub-committee summarized the matter on June 9, were: (1) to encourage steadfast elements in the French Navy to bring their ships over to join the British fleet; (2) to urge the French to intern their ships in a neutral country such as the United States; (3) to talk the French into scuttling their fleet; or (4) for the British themselves to sink such ships as intended to surrender. Two days later, the Chiefs of Staff reported that for all practical purposes these alternatives could be boiled down to two, but as they did not expect any efforts to persuade French ships to join their own to meet with much success this left pressing the French to sink the whole of their fleet as their principal policy recommendation. However, none of these options was ever wholly abandoned. Preventive measures had to be taken and pressure applied wherever, whenever, and however it was felt most suitable.[6]

By 14 June the First Sea Lord was suggesting to Admiral Sir Andrew Cunningham, Commander-in-Chief, Mediterranean—in view of the possibility of the French making a separate peace—that he arrange for French ships in the eastern Mediterranean to be with him at Alexandria so as to ensure that these ships were disposed of in accordance with British wishes. On the 14th and 15th Pound was trying to get Darlan to take immediate action regarding the transfer of the *Richelieu* and *Jean Bart* to the United Kingdom and the sailing of the Force de Raid for Gibraltar. At the same time, British naval liaison officers in major French ports were pointedly offering British assistance in connection with the demolition work to be undertaken before the Germans arrived. Churchill, who had not as yet discussed the matter of the fleet with the French Government, planned to do so as soon as it was established at Bordeaux; as it turned out, no opportunity for this consultation arose before Reynaud resigned and the reins of government passed to a hostile cabinet. In the meantime, Pound had insisted that while the French were contracting negotiations for an armistice their fleet should be away from France in harbors where the British could safeguard it. That this condition was ignored by the new French Government hardly came as a surprise to the British; they were not expecting compliance anyway. Already by June 17 more peremptory actions were under way.[7]

It was on the 17th that the Prime Minister ordered the detention in British harbors of all shipping and supplies destined for France or the French colonies. Simultaneously, the Admiralty instructed British naval and merchant vessels to direct all French ships met at sea to the nearest British port, an order that was extended on June 18 to neutral and allied shipping bound for France as well.[8] More to the point, Sir Dudley Pound telegraphed Admiral Cunningham on June 17: "If France made a separate peace every endeavour would be made to obtain control of the French Fleet beforehand, or failing that, to have it sunk." Also on the 17th Churchill approved Pound's and Alexander's decision to send the battle cruiser *Hood* and the aircraft carrier *Ark Royal* to join the *Resolution* at Gibraltar "to watch over the fate of the French fleet."[9] These ships formed the nucleus of Force H, which was to play the leading role in Britain's offensive action two weeks later.

Aggressive suggestions as to how to secure and utilize the French fleet were not wanting from the Foreign Office and other quarters.[10] On June 18 Lord Hankey suggested a series of raids on French Atlantic ports to destroy the oil supplies located there, but advised that nothing should be done before they were "sure about the French fleet." On the same date G. E. Millard came forward with the idea, "if the worst comes to the worst, of surprising the more important units of the French fleet with boarding parties," though he feared the notion was "rather wild." Legal justification for British designs was ingeniously set forth in a telegram from Lord Lothian, who had been told by a distinguished lawyer in America that if the French signed an armistice it was due to *force majeure* and therefore from that moment the British were entitled to capture or sink their fleet as having yielded to the enemy; because the French were in no position to act of their own free will, they could be considered virtually enemies of themselves. That the British were prepared to go beyond merely preventing the Germans from using the French fleet is shown by Millard's argument on June 21 that even if the French fleet joined their own the morale of the French crews would be sufficiently untrustworthy as to justify "seizing the ships and manning them, or as many of them as we can, with British naval reservists." "Indeed," he thought, "that might be the best course in any case, in order to ensure complete cohesion between the British and French fleets."[11]

As formal justification for their continuing to hold on to French vessels, about which Ambassador Corbin had complained on June 20, the British claimed they had evidence that the Germans were in possession of French naval codes with which they were transmitting false wireless signals ordering French warships to avoid British ports and to rally to French ports. There was thus the "suspicion that the orders now received by the Commander of the 'Emile Bertin' [a French cruiser carrying a cargo of gold then being detained in Halifax, Nova Scotia, which wanted to proceed to Martinique] might not be genuine." The ship broke out of Halifax on the 21st nonetheless.[12]

On the morning of June 22—before the armistice terms were yet known and despite the absent Prime Minister's conviction that the "policy of the French Government would be determined, not by any action which we might take, but by the terms offered by the Germans"—the War Cabinet agreed that "it was not desirable to run the risk of upsetting Admiral Darlan by making difficulties about the French warships leaving British ports." It therefore decided to allow French ships destined for French colonial ports *outside* the Mediterranean, though not those headed for neutral ports, to sail. Campbell, in a last conciliatory message that was a dead letter even before it was sent, was asked to inform Darlan that H.M. Government was now raising no objection to at least some French warships being moved in conformity with his orders.[13]

No immediate change in policy followed the signing of the Franco-German armistice; rather there was an escalation of the measures adopted and action foreseen. Although Churchill on the night of the 22nd was already belligerently talking of sinking France's two most modern battle cruisers, the War Cabinet merely agreed on the vital need for obtaining *control* of the French Navy. To this end they decided to make a final appeal to Admiral Darlan, another one to Admiral Esteva (French C-in-C in the Mediterranean), and for the Admiralty to prevent the *Jean Bart* and *Richelieu* from leaving Casablanca and Dakar. British policy, as defined on June 23, was to hold all French shipping wherever there was risk that it might comply with the armistice terms. The Admiralty ordered that French ships were not to be permitted to sail from any British port, but force was to be avoided unless an actual attempt to sail was made. However, H.M.S. *Dunedin* was ordered to seize the gold aboard the *Émile Bertin,* then en route to Martinique.[14]

It was not until June 24 that any large-scale aggressive action against the French fleet was actually discussed as a practical issue by the War Cabinet. By this time, as the First Sea Lord reported at midday, a British admiral had been orderd to see the French admiral commanding the Force de Raid at Oran "and also to obtain full information as to the berthing positions of the French ships, in case it might be necessary to take drastic action against them." Nevertheless, in the three cabinet sessions held that day no final decision on the matter was reached. Mr. Churchill was certainly the chief apostle of a policy of force, his argument being that so long as the position of the French warships was unsecured they could be used to blackmail the British and therefore that they must either be brought under British control or put out of the way for good. He did not blink at the possibility that Franco-British relations in the near future "might well approach very closely to those of two nations at war with each other." As far as British policy towards the French Government was concerned, he thought "the waverers would be influenced only by strong action on our part"; otherwise, "they would give way all along the line. . . . In these circumstances, it would be best to continue to express our sympathy and to avoid recriminations, but to act solely in accordance with the dictates of our own safety." At the very least, the British could not be expected to release ships, aircraft and gold, all of which would be afterwards turned against them by the enemy.[15]

Taking into consideration the fact that those ships the British already had under their control constituted the least valuable part of the French fleet and that it had now been established that the admiral commanding the Force de Raid was not prepared to disobey the orders of the legally constituted government of France,[16] the consensus of the War Cabinet by early evening was that two alternatives were open to them. "The first was to take immediate action to ensure that the main units of the French Fleet did not fall into the hands of the enemy. If necessary, we should not scruple to use force to secure this end. The second was that we should allow the ships of the French Fleet to go to the ports of rendez-vous laid down, and to watch events closely, being prepared to take action at once if we saw any risk that the ships would fall into German hands." The cabinet also contemplated sending an ultimatum to the French Government that would demand that the French scuttle their warships within a time to be specified, in default of which the British would be forced to take action against them. The Prime Minister and Foreign Secretary were asked to draft an ultimatum along such lines, while the First Lord of the Admiralty was to arrange for a naval staff appreciation of the action that would be involved if it became necessary to use force against the French warships not yet under British control. The cabinet's greatest concern was over the fate of the French Navy's four biggest ships, two of which were on the Atlantic coast of Africa, the two others at Oran. But for the moment, at least, the cabinet largely confined itself to confirming orders that had been activated a week earlier.[17]

The naval staff appreciation presented that night by the First Sea Lord was not at all optimistic as to the results that might be expected from an attempt to eliminate the French fleet. First of all, he reported, any attempt to seize or sink French ships would probably lead to the active hostility of other French naval units, thus reducing British chances of securing more than a small part of the fleet. If, however, the use of force did become necessary, they should concentrate on eliminating the capital ships in order to guard their position at both ends of the Mediterranean and to keep the Italian fleet bottled within it. The battle cruisers *Dunkerque* and *Strasbourg* were the most important units to be tackled; but an operation against the Force de Raid at Oran would be difficult. "The only real chance of success lay in a surprise attack carried out at dawn and without any form of prior notification" to French authorities. However, since the operation might well result in the loss or partial disablement of both the *Hood* and *Resolution,* they would then be badly handicapped in dealing with the *Richelieu* and *Jean Bart.* To Pound, "the probable loss of our 2 ships seemed a heavy price to pay for the elimination or partial elimination of the Force de Rade." Finally, because Admiral Darlan and other French admirals had consistently maintained that in no circumstances would the French fleet be surrendered, the First Sea Lord thought it more likely that the British would achieve their object by trusting in these assurances than by attempting to eliminate units of the French fleet by force. For these reasons, therefore, he could not recommend the proposed operation. A further point brought out in the cabinet discussion that followed was that "The decision to order the destruction of people who had only 48 hours before been Allies would be hard to make. If French sailors were to be killed in action with the British Fleet, the French and German Governments would declare that England was making war on France and the sympathy of the entire French Empire would probably be lost." With Churchill thus deprived of the support he needed, the cabinet deferred a decision on the action to be taken vis-à-vis French naval units generally until after the Franco-Italian armistice terms were known; and it also set aside the idea of making a formal communication to the French Government.[18]

With the news of the *Richelieu*'s breaking out of Dakar on June 25,[19] the War Cabinet that evening authorized the Admiralty to take whatever steps would be necessary to intercept and capture that ship or the *Jean Bart* if she too put to sea. The *Ark Royal* and *Hood,* as well as the cruiser *Dorsetshire,* were all detailed to this purpose. By June 27 the *Richelieu* was located and found to be returning to Dakar, but in the meantime the Chief of the Naval Staff, fearing that the *Dunkerque* and *Strasbourg* at Oran might attempt to sail for a French or Italian port on the north coast of the Mediterranean, had ordered two British submarines to prepare to take up stations outside Oran. The navy was thus proceeding on an ad hoc basis, acting in accordance with daily intelligence and with the firm intention of avoiding bloodshed if possible and of using no more force than was absolutely necessary. By its precautionary measures, French warships in British ports, in West Africa, and the eastern Mediterranean were to a large extent already under control. However, the bulk of the French fleet lay at Oran.[20]

Mr. Churchill was not the only one dissatisfied with the scope of these measures. Members of the Foreign Office were urging the use of *force majeure* against the French fleet (in short, the dispatch of British destroyers to Oran); otherwise, as Sir Robert Vansittart saw it, "if we let things drift on, the forces of inertia and despair will prevail and the 'Force de Rade' will simply set out for Toulon. What we want therefore is what the Germans call a 'dynamic' act." He thought it "might well be the spark which would set the whole of North Africa alight." Some members of the cabinet also believed that public opinion was demanding strong action—"on the lines of the measures taken at Copenhagen against the Danish Fleet." Thus on June 27, with any lingering confidence in Admiral Darlan's pledges sharply undercut by the *Richelieu* incident and both the CIGS and naval investigators reporting that there was now no hope of any French resistance in North Africa, the War Cabinet in principle approved of an operation to be undertaken against the French fleet at Oran (tentatively scheduled for July 3), which "might be combined with further operations in the Mediterranean, or with operations designed to secure the *Richelieu* and the *Jean Bart*." Planning of the operation was to begin at once under the supervision of the Chief of the Naval Staff; the same day Vice-Admiral Sir James Somerville was given command of Force H, then being assembled at Gibraltar, his initial assignment being "to secure the transfer, surrender or destruction of the French warships at Oran and Mers-el-Kébir so as to ensure that these ships could not fall into German or Italian hands."[21]

The report issued on June 29 by the Joint Planning Sub-committee on the implications of the naval action contemplated by the cabinet was as pessimistic as Pound's estimate of June 24 had been. Among the negative results that were thought possible were that the enemy would thereby acquire the warships (four light cruisers and four destroyers) then in metropolitan France; that other ships which the British failed to intercept might also reach French ports and subsequently become available to the enemy; that, because of the action, the Germans and Italians would be given every opportunity to establish their forces in North Africa without delay; and that the French fleet at Oran might receive reinforcements in submarines from elsewhere in French North Africa. The real question was how the French would react to the proposed naval action. "At the worst," the Joint Planners concluded, "the French reactions might be extremely serious and would then immensely complicate the already heavy task. If, therefore, there is a genuine danger that the action proposed would lead to the active hostility of France and of her colonial possessions, we do not consider that the destruction of these French ships by force would be justified."[22] This then was the considered opinion of the policy group that Mr. Churchill early in the war—with more verve than fairness—had already scathingly dubbed "that machinery of negation."[23] Their appreciation, however, was never to reach the cabinet.

Viewed from another angle, the essential and most immediate question ramained not how the French would react to *British* moves but rather how they would respond to German and Italian demands as laid down in the armistice conventions. And here the report of Captain E. Pleydell-Bouverie, head of the British Naval Mission in Bordeaux until the Embassy's withdrawal on June 22—with its pessimistic appraisal of the French Navy's outlook—must have been instrumental in determining the final direction of service advice. In a nutshell, the Captain reported, the French Government, of which Admiral Darlan was a member, was concerned solely with stopping the war; the navy and its commanders would in all circumstances obey Darlan's orders, including the recall of the fleet; but despite the almost mechanical repetition by high French naval authorities that the fleet would never be handed over to the Germans but would in the last resort be destroyed, he personally had never seen such orders and doubted that they had been issued other than to C-in-Cs. From these facts, Pleydell-Bouverie concluded that the French fleet would in all likelihood be ordered by Darlan to return to its home ports, there to be disarmed under the terms of the armistice, but that given the inability of the French to face up to unpleasant situations, insufficient preparation would have been made for the eventuality that was almost certain to happen. This, combined with the explanation offered by Captain C. S. Holland (Britain's former Naval Attaché in Paris) for Darlan's current conduct—that he was not a free agent, but rather "virtually a prisoner of the German Directorate"—must have removed the last underpinnings of Admiral Pound's faith in the French Chief of Naval Staff.[24] In this light—and considering that the War Cabinet had already reached a pretty firm decision on June 27— it was not surprising that the Chiefs of Staff should have bypassed the points made by the Joint Planners and arrived at their own quite different conclusions.

It was their contention that if the British extended the blockade to France, as the cabinet had decided to do on June 25, then it would be just a matter of time before the French became actively hostile in any event. Therefore, other considerations had to take priority. The first of these was the likelihood of French ships falling into the hands of Germany.

In the light of recent events [they reasoned], we can no longer place any faith in French assurances, nor could we be certain that any measures, which we were given to understand the French would take to render their ships unserviceable before reaching French metropolitan ports, would, in fact, be taken. Once the ships have reached French metropolitan ports we are under no illusions as to the certainty that, sooner or later, the Germans will employ them against us.

Second was the balance of strength in capital ships: if the two French battle cruisers fell into German hands, and if Britain's capital ship strength were then reduced by submarine or air attack, the situation would be extremely serious. Third was the home defense situation, which made it necessary to concentrate the maximum possible naval strength in English waters to meet the imminent threat of invasion. It was therefore "of paramount importance that the uncertainty regarding the French Fleet should be dissipated as soon as possible in order that the ships now shadowing the French Fleet can be released for operations elsewhere." Thus, "after balancing all the arguments both for and against such action," it was the recommendation of the Chiefs of Staff on June 30 that, "from the military point of view, Operation 'Catapult' should be carried out as soon as possible."[25]

Such was its military etiology. Politically, too, just as cogent reasons could be adduced in justification. Even if animated by the best will in the world and the most scrupulous sense of loyalty, there is no doubt that the French Navy in the hands of any government not determined to fight on did constitute a very real danger; and in the hands of an Anglophobe ministry it presented even more serious cause for alarm. Although it is clear that the Foreign Office had virtually no confidence in Pétain or his entourage from the outset, the basic question was not just what the present French administration in its present mood would do with the fleet but what this or another government in still harsher times, under increasing pressure from the enemy, might feel constrained to do. How, for instance, could the British be assured that Darlan's supposedly irrevocable orders, about which they were not at all clear to begin with, would be maintained if their author was superseded as Chief of the French Admiralty? As time went on, this or a successor ministry might well become completely collaborationist and for its own profit or survival enter the war on the side of Germany against Great Britain. Therefore, in a sense, the very fact that a government had been formed for the single purpose of treating with the Germans was enough to set in motion the elaborate precautions taken by the British from June 17 onwards.

In the ten days following Reynaud's fall every effort *was* made to gain control of the fleet, first by direct negotiations with the Pétain government, then by sub rosa activities in North Africa. It was France's refusal to accept the conditions posed by the British, not the armistice per se, that dictated British measures. But, because the signing of the armistice and its ultimate acceptance by the leaders of North Africa signaled the failure of Britain's efforts to secure the fleet by peaceful means, it can be said that the armistice did, in fact, trigger Britain's contingent plan. Article 8, inadmissible in itself and even more dangerous by virtue of its ambiguity, served as a convenient focus for righteous indignation and as formal justification for Operation Catapult.

As of the evening of June 30 it remained for the War Cabinet only to set the date, for Churchill to draft the communication that would be presented to the French admiral at Oran on behalf of His Majesty's Government, and for the Admiralty to prepare its final instructions to Force H. These were duly issued late the next night.[26]

# Operation Catapult

" 'OPERATION Catapult,' " in Winston Churchill's words, "comprised the simultaneous seizure, control, or effective disablement or destruction of all the accessible French Fleet."[1] "Accessible" meant principally those ships present in English waters and at Alexandria, Oran, and Dakar, with no action contemplated against French ships in Toulon, Algiers, or Casablanca, sites that were judged to be too strongly defended. The action commenced on July 3.

In the early hours of the morning all French vessels lying in Portsmouth, Plymouth, Falmouth, Southampton, Sheerness, and other British harbors were boarded and forcibly seized by English troops. The net haul included two old battleships (the *Paris* and the *Courbet*), two light cruisers, eight destroyers, six submarines, and some 200 lesser craft. The transfer to British control was peaceably achieved except on the destroyer *Mistral,* where sabotage was attempted, and the submarine *Surcouf,* where, all told, four were killed. The action was of necessity a complete surprise—only the evening before British officers had entertained their French colleagues—and to Churchill demonstrated the ease with which the Germans might have taken possession of any French warships lying in ports controlled by them. However, in that the attack took place in British harbors, where there was no chance of the French ships falling into enemy hands and where measures had already been taken to prevent their departure for France or Africa, the military justification for the operation was not strictly preventive. Already on June 29 the British had decided to use the destroyers captured, insofar as they could be manned, and the small craft in the harbors, especially since the latter were among the categories the Franco-German armistice permitted to be used against them. Nevertheless, the ships taken in British waters represented only a tenth of the French fleet in tonnage and far less in military value. The bulk of France's war fleet lay scattered in African ports.[2]

At Alexandria, where a French squadron including one battleship (the *Lorraine*), four cruisers, three destroyers, a submarine, and a number of smaller ships was stationed, tragedy was averted due to the good sense and gallantry of both the British and French commanders. Here the encounter had begun on June 24. Vice-Admiral René Godfroy was ordered by the French Admiralty to sail for Bizerte; Admiral Cunningham had received equally urgent orders to prevent the French force from leaving. This preliminary skirmish was settled on June 27 and 28 by a sort of gentleman's agreement: Godfroy gave his word not to try to sail without first warning his colleague, while Cunningham would appear to have engaged himself not to attempt to seize the French squadron "by surprise or by force"—although the British Admiralty specifically directed that "no such assurance was to be given." Neither government was satisfied with this arrangement. However, in partial deference to Cunningham's strong views on the matter, the orders sent to him by the Admiralty on July 1 with regard to Operation Catapult were less onerous than they might have been.

Thus on July 3 Godfroy was asked to choose between joining the British in a continuation of the struggle (entailing service under the British flag); immediately disarming his ships and reducing their complements to skeleton levels; or sinking his ships at sea. The French Admiral initially offered to accept scuttling in deep water as the only proposition that was consistent with naval honor, then was talked into putting his ships into a condition in which they could not put to sea. But upon later hearing of the British ultimatum at Mers-el-Kébir Godfroy discontinued the demilitarization measures already under way and refused to comply with any of Cunningham's alternatives under the implied threat of force. Nevertheless, in spite of frantic orders from the British Admiralty to force the French to start reducing their crews by dark[3] and from the French Admiralty to sail at any cost, both commanders continued to disobey their home governments and to maintain the status quo till the following day.

By July 4 London was insistent that Cunningham adopt one of three possible courses of action he had outlined to resolve the impasse: (1) send boarding parties to capture the French ships; (2) sink the ships at their moorings by gun and torpedo fire; or (3) confront

Godfroy with a demand either to surrender his ships or submit them
to internment, with the result that *he* would sink them. Cunningham
could only choose the third course as the lesser among evils. At 7
a.m., however, after learning of the fate of the French fleet at Oran,
Godfroy announced that he was resuming full liberty of action and
let it be understood that he would make a run for it, fighting his way
out of the harbor if necessary. Darlan by this time was urging him to
render an eye for an eye, a tooth for a tooth. The French ships were
now raising steam; the British ships in the meanwhile had taken up a
position of encirclement around the French squadron, their guns at
the ready. The scene was thus set for the one thing Admiral Cunningham wished above all to avoid—a costly battle or punitive self-
scuttling which would wreck the harbor and interfere with the traffic
of the port.

It was only after publicly appealing to the French officers and
crews, over the head of their commander, to avoid useless bloodshed,
and several more hours of patient negotiations during which the
French made no belligerent moves, that the crisis was finally settled
by compromise. Yielding to "overwhelming force," Godfroy that
evening agreed to immediately discharge his fuel oil and to demilitarize his ships to British satisfaction, though not under direct British
supervision—the breechblocks of guns and warheads of torpedoes
removed to be placed in the custody of the French Consulate at
Alexandria, in the presence of a British naval officer and the British
Consul-General. These measures were virtually complete by July 5.
Crews were to be reduced by 70 per cent within the next few days.
The remaining personnel, their pay assured by H.M. Government,
were pledged not to scuttle their ships, or to attempt any hostile act
against the British, or to leave port. In exchange, Cunningham guaranteed that no attempt would be made by the British to seize the
French ships by force so long as the Germans and Italians did not
break the armistice terms—in spite of the Prime Minister's strong
disapproval of this arrangement. A formal agreement embodying
these decisions was signed on July 7.[4]

Most of the French Atlantic squadron, comprising about a fifth of
the French fleet and including two modern battle cruisers (the *Dunkerque* and *Strasbourg*), two older battleships (the *Bretagne* and *Provence*), the seaplane carrier *Commandant Teste*, six superdestroyers,
seven smaller destroyers, and four submarines, was harbored at Mers-el-
Kébir and Oran in Algeria, and it was here that the British concentrated their energies. The exact layout of the fleet's principal units

was already known to them, and throughout July 3 naval air reconnaissance would keep the British abreast of all French moves and preparations. Being forbidden the use of their "eyes" by virtue of the armistice agreement, the French initially enjoyed no such advantage. The arrival off Mers-el-Kébir at 9:10 a.m. of a strong British force consisting of the battle cruiser *Hood,* the battleships *Valiant* and *Resolution,* two cruisers, eleven destroyers, and the aircraft carrier *Ark Royal* therefore took them completely by surprise. Their confusion was to be compounded by the fact that direct radio communications between the French Admiralty at Nérac and the fleet in North Africa had been suspended in keeping with Article 8, while the Admiralty itself on July 3 was in the midst of moving its headquarters from Nérac to Vichy. The French Government was in similar disarray, having been installed on the Allier only since July 1.[5]

Preceding the British battle squadron by nearly three hours, the destroyer *Foxhound* at 6:20 requested permission to enter the port, at the same time signaling that the British Admiralty was sending Captain Cedric Holland, formerly Naval Attaché in Paris and now Captain of the *Ark Royal,* to confer with Vice-Admiral Marcel Gensoul. A further signal at 7:09 announced the Royal Navy's general purpose. Anchored just outside the boom by 8 a.m., Holland was met by intermediaries from the flagship *Dunkerque* but was refused an interview with the French commander, who at 8:47 ordered the *Foxhound* to withdraw immediately. His mission frustrated, Holland nevertheless proceeded by motorboat and at 9:20 succeeded in transmitting to Gensoul's flag lieutenant the document addressed to the Admiral he had intended to present and to elaborate on himself.[6]

Prefaced by a recapitulation of British grievances, this set forth the alternatives the British Government now demanded the French squadron follow. Its third and most relevant paragraph stated:

It is impossible for us, your comrades up to now, to allow your fine ships to fall into the power of the German or Italian enemy. We are determined to fight on to the end, and if we win, as we think we shall, we shall never forget that France was our Ally, that our interests are the same as hers, and that our common enemy is Germany. Should we conquer, we solemnly declare that we shall restore the greatness and territory of France. For this purpose, we must make sure that the best ships of the French Navy are not used against us by the common foe. In these circumstances, His Majesty's Government have instructed me to demand that the French Fleet now at Mers-el-Kebir and Oran shall act in accordance with one of the following alternatives:

(a) Sail with us and continue to fight for victory against the Germans and Italians.

(b) Sail with reduced crews under our control to a British port. The reduced crews will be repatriated at the earliest moment.

If either of these courses is adopted by you, we will restore your ships to France at the conclusion of the war or pay full compensation, if they are damaged meanwhile.

(c) Alternatively, if you feel bound to stipulate that your ships should not be used against the Germans or Italians unless these break the Armistice, then sail them with us with reduced crews to some French port in the West Indies—Martinique, for instance—where they can be demilitarised to our satisfaction, or perhaps be entrusted to the United States and remain safe until the end of the war, the crews being repatriated.

If you refuse these fair offers, I must, with profound regret, require you to sink your ships within six hours.

Finally, failing the above, I have the orders of His Majesty's Government to use whatever force may be necessary to prevent your ships from falling into German or Italian hands.[7]


At 10 a.m. Admiral Gensoul's written reply arrived: the assurances he had given Admiral Sir Dudley North on June 24 remained valid, and in no case would his ships be allowed to fall intact into German or Italian hands. However, in view of the form and substance of the veritable ultimatum presented him, the French would defend themselves by force. Yet in spite of this unequivocal response, Holland and Flag Lieutenant Dufay guardedly hinted to each other that the disarmament of the fleet at Mers-el-Kébir might form the basis for a negotiated settlement. An hour later, after Dufay had again returned to the *Dunkerque,* this time bearing the typed notes Holland had hoped to use in his interview with Gensoul, Gensoul's Chief of Staff, Captain Danbé, brought back a second written message from the Admiral affirming his decision to defend himself by every means possible and drawing Admiral Somerville's attention to the fact that "the first shot fired against us would have the practical effect of aligning the entire French fleet against Great Britain—a result diametrically opposed to that which the British Government is seeking." At this point, sensing an impasse, Holland returned to the *Foxhound.* In the meantime, Admiral Gensoul had ordered his ships to raise steam and to prepare for action—activity British planes first observed at 8:35 and that Holland confirmed at 12:01 in a signal to

Somerville informing him that the French apparently intended to put to sea and to fight.[8]

Gensoul's intermediary had already been warned at 11:40 that Admiral Somerville would not allow the French squadron to leave port unless the British terms were accepted. To back up this threat, Somerville at 12:27 ordered magnetic mines laid in the entrance to the harbor at Mers-el-Kébir, which British seaplanes carried out at 1:30, thus bottling up the French squadron and increasing the odds against it. The French capital ships lay side by side, 150 yards apart, moored by their sterns to the breakwater, with their cannon facing land; in addition, their view of the British armada was obscured by a fortified promontory. So long as they remained in the harbor and were prevented from maneuvering or using their guns effectively, the British were in small danger, but this situation was subject to change from moment to moment. Seeing no alternative, Somerville informed the Admiralty that he was preparing to open fire at 1330, at the same time asking Holland if he knew of any reason to the contrary. Holland, however, believed that the French might yet be brought round and the use of force avoided, which encouraged Somerville to give the French until 1500 to make a decision. This signal was passed to the *Dunkerque* at 14:42.[9]

In the interim, Gensoul had signaled that he was still awaiting his government's reply, that he had no intention of sailing, and finally, at 14:40, that he was now ready to receive Somerville's delegate for "honourable discussion." Thus, in spite of the mounting tension and Somerville's justifiable fear that Gensoul was merely playing for time, negotiations that were on the point of being definitely severed once again resumed. It was only at the late hour of 16:15 that Captain Holland stepped aboard the *Dunkerque,* there to be told by Admiral Gensoul that "he had only consented to see me at this stage because should we open fire the first shot fired would not only alienate the whole French Navy but would be tantamount to a declaration of war between France and Great Britain . . . . We might sink his ships at Oran but we should [then] find the whole of the rest of the French Navy actively against us." With Holland, however, he was preaching to the already converted. More to the point, Gensoul produced his personal copy of Darlan's secret order of June 24, with its provisions for automatic scuttling or escape to America in the event that the armistice commissions did not agree to French warships remaining in French ports under French crews. Gensoul also personally guaranteed that if there were any danger of his ships falling into enemy hands he would take them to Martinique or the United States—but freely and not while under the threat of English guns. To Holland, this appeared so close to one of the British proposals offered that he thought he could eventually persuade the Admiral to accept it. Gensoul also mentioned the steps he had taken towards reducing his crews and, according to his own report but not Holland's, confirmed his readiness to accept the disarming of his ships at Mers-el-Kébir, though what he meant by this could hardly have been what Holland would have required. Somerville had been authorized to accept demilitarization *if volunteered* by the French and provided it could be carried out under British supervision within six hours and in such a way as to prevent the ships from being brought into service for at least a year, even at a fully equipped dockyard port. However, Gensoul's conciliatory comments, which did not conform to the conditions laid down in any case, only reached Somerville when it was too late.[10]

Time was of the essence and it was on the point of running out even before Gensoul and Holland started talking. Vice-Admiral Le Luc, at French naval headquarters at Nérac, had during the early afternoon ordered all French naval forces in the western Mediterranean (that is, the squadrons at Algiers and Toulon) to sail to the relief of the French squadron at Oran. In the first direct response he had had from the French Admiralty (though the message was sent four hours earlier), Gensoul was now ordered to inform the British of this move. Meanwhile, Somerville had been instructed by the British Admiralty in London (which had intercepted the French signal) to "settle matters quickly or you will have reinforcements to deal with." Upon receiving this, he immediately warned the French commander that if none of the British propositions was accepted before 17:30 BST—a mere quarter of an hour away by the time the signal reached its destination—it would be necessary for him to sink the French ships. At this point, both messages having arrived within minutes of each other, all hope for a peaceful settlement vanished. Admiral Gensoul could not accept this ultimatum. A sense of honor forbade him from obeying any injunction under the threat of force; besides which, he did not believe it within his competence to reject the obligations formally recognized by his superiors and government, especially when to have acepted any of the options offered by the British meant the probable abrogation of the armistice agreement by the Germans. Under the circumstances he felt he had no choice but to fight.[11]

Admiral Gensoul was determined not to fire the first shot, but for more than an hour all his ships had been in an advanced state of readiness for sea, with control positions manned, guns trained fore and aft, and tugs standing by the stern of each battleship. Meanwhile, the French had cleared an alternate channel so as to be able to bypass the mines clogging the harbor entrance. The fleet's shore batteries, which had been partially disarmed, and French fighter aircraft were also both prepared for action. By the time Captain Holland left the *Dunkerque* at 17:25, more than eleven hours had elapsed since he had first requested permission to see the French Admiral, and the final time limit had been vainly extended two hours beyond its projected expiry. The British opened fire at 17:54 with a bombardment that lasted ten or fifteen minutes—all that was necessary to make a shambles of at least three of their major targets. Within minutes, the battleship *Bretagne* had exploded and sunk, the *Dunkerque* was badly hit and adrift, while the *Provence* was beached and on fire. The destroyer *Mogador* also met with disaster. But by adroit maneuvering the *Strasbourg,* escorted by five destroyers and under cover of smoke, managed to escape and successfully to elude her pursuers in the oncoming darkness. Three days later Force H was to return to Mers-el-Kébir, at which time torpedo bombers from the *Ark Royal* put the *Dunkerque* completely out of commission. The French Navy's casualties from both days' action totaled 1,297 killed and 351 wounded. In terms of human lives lost, it was for France the most costly naval battle of the war.[12]

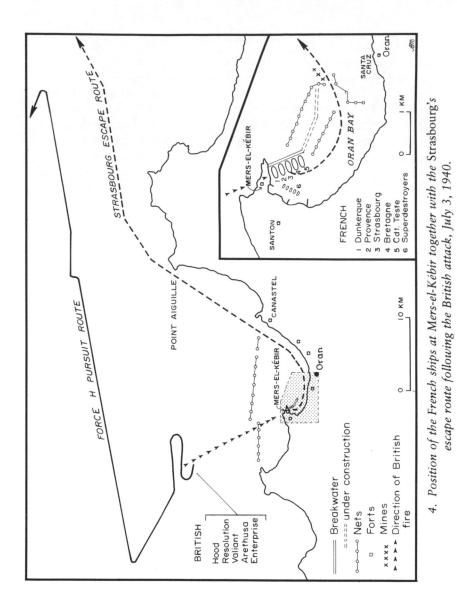

4. *Position of the French ships at Mers-el-Kébir together with the Strasbourg's escape route following the British attack, July 3, 1940.*

STRASBOURG ESCAPE ROUTE

FORCE H PURSUIT ROUTE

POINT AIGUILLE

CANASTEL

MERS-EL-KÉBIR

Oran

MERS-EL-KÉBIR

SANTON

SANTA CRUZ

Oran

ORAN BAY

1 KM

10 KM

FRENCH

1 Dunkerque
2 Provence
3 Strasbourg
4 Bretagne
5 Cdt. Teste
6 Superdestroyers

BRITISH

Hood
Resolution
Valiant
Arethusa
Enterprise

— Breakwater
==== under construction
Nets
Forts
xxxx Mines
Direction of British fire

# Mers-el-Kébir:
# Analysis and Aftermath

IT HAS often been suggested that the tragedy at Mers-el-Kébir could have been avoided. Admiral Gensoul in particular has been censured for not reporting the complete text of the British proposals to his superiors. At 9:45 a.m. (8:45 GMT) he had signaled to the French Admiralty only that he had been commanded to sink his ships within six hours, failing which the British would use force, and that his reply had been that the French would meet force with force. (Three and a half hours later he also made known the British offer to join them and mentioned the vague possibility of a forced disarmament.) Darlan, apprised of the situation by early afternoon, could on the basis of this scanty information hardly have done other than to approve Gensoul's answer and confirm Le Luc's orders, as did the French Council of Ministers when it was consulted at 3:30. But even after all the terms of the ultimatum were known by the Vichy government (and it was not until the afternoon of July 5 that the full text transmitted by the French Chargé d'Affaires in London was received or until July 9 that Gensoul himself submitted a detailed report to Darlan), Gensoul was never reproached for his laconic communication; though he had ignored the first three options, it was felt that he had stated the essentials and had been compelled to resist.[1]

Gensoul certainly felt, both then and later, that he *had* transmitted the essential part of the ultimatum and believed moreover that both the French Admiralty and the French Government would be of the same mind. He was confident that in acting as he did he was simply conforming to instructions previously received, that is, to have no relations with the British; to see that his ships did not fall into the hands of either the enemy or a former ally, and in no case to obey the orders of a foreign admiralty—Darlan's order of June 24; and, finally, to execute the terms of the armistice. In addition to which, and of overriding importance in his calculations, he knew that any ultimatum presented under the threat of force would be considered ipso facto unacceptable.[2]

In fact, Darlan's main criticism of Gensoul, as he later told his son, was that he lacked initiative and had not been aggressive enough. Darlan claimed that in the same circumstances he too would have played for time but would have put it to better use. For instance, at the expiry of the ultimatum he would have ordered the French ships to accede to the British demand to sail with them, *but,* once on the high seas, would have ordered them to break free and to fight if necessary. In this way, he thought, the French would merely have been responding "to a villainy with a ruse," and although the losses from that choice of action might have been as high, "at least they would have been in the course of combat and at sea rather than through letting themselves be massacred defenselessly at the bottom of a hole."[3] (Obviously, the conditions under which the British would have allowed the French out of the harbor would never have permitted the unfolding of this scenario.)

To have joined the British either as comrades in arms or as hostages in British ports would have been a direct violation of the armistice, bringing in its train the very consequences the French Government had hoped to avoid by signing the armistice. The alternative of scuttling, while under the threat of British cannons, would also have been dismissed by the government as dishonorable. Whether the choice of sailing the French squadron to French ports in the West Indies should have been accepted as a reasonable and honorable solution is the question most often discussed; but it is almost certain that the French Government would not have accepted this clause any more readily than the others, for internment in American waters was also contrary to the armistice conditions, which specified that ships must return to their peacetime ports. In the opinion of Charles-Roux, all alternatives would have been equally rejected by Vichy, because the only real question before the government was whether to respect or to violate the armistice, and on this point minds had been made up more than a week before.[4]

There is also the additional question of what the Germans would have done had Gensoul taken matters into his own hands by sailing to Martinique and allowing his ships to be demilitarized there to British satisfaction or entrusted to the United States. Certainly the

Germans, who intended to keep the fleet under their direct surveillance insofar as was possible, would then have been justified in breaking the armistice, but whether they would have felt it worthwhile to do so—considering that further severities at this time could well have sparked the dissidence in the French Empire and the reactivation of French naval forces that *they* wished to avoid—at least suggests that the proposition merited Gensoul's attention.[5]

To suggest that the Martinique "solution" perhaps contained unsuspected possibilities for the French, however, is not to say that the British themselves took it seriously. It is far more likely that this clause was simply the velvet glove over the fist of iron, a diplomatic flourish added to make the ultimatum appear less brutal on the off chance that Gensoul might balk at shedding blood. Admiral Somerville, at any rate, was under no illusion as to what he was *demanding* of the French: before the action he had told Admiral North in Gibraltar that he was "going to Oran to ask them to surrender or scuttle—or be sunk." Quite clearly the British had counted on the French to refuse any of the terms of an ultimatum backed by force. As proof, the British Admiralty was to admit later in July to Admiral North that their lordships had never doubted that the French fleet would fight in the last instance and that this fact had been taken fully into consideration beforehand. Furthermore, in discussing Gensoul's stance with Admiral Odend'hal on July 14, Admiral Pound, while refusing to answer the French officer's question as to whether he thought an English admiral would have behaved differently, nevertheless let it be known that he could hardly blame his French colleague for the position he had adopted. Captain Holland, for his part, had been even less ambiguous on this point during his negotiations with the French on July 3.[6]

Had the French accepted the Martinique alternative, the delays involved would have left the British open to attack both by Axis aircraft and submarines and by the French squadrons racing westwards from Algiers and Toulon. Furthermore, the British would not have wanted to risk a lengthy round trip to the West Indies when their own island's defense was under severe strain; indeed, one of the principal purposes of Catapult was to release British warships from the necessity of having to shadow the French fleet. Admiral Somerville had even expressed concern over the "considerable delay" that might be involved if the option of steaming their ships to a British port were accepted, which, however, he thought unlikely. That the British wished to be done with the deed by sundown at the latest is shown by the Admiralty's preliminary message to Somerville that "it was very important that the operation should be completed during [the] daylight hours of 3rd July," which was followed by more urgent orders in the course of the afternoon, as well as by the stipulation that if Gensoul offered to demilitarize his ships in the berths they then occupied he was to be given only six hours to do so and was to be hedged around by so many restrictions that the operation would have been virtually impossible to accomplish except by way of an immediate scuttling order. Certainly the War Cabinet was anxious not to have this latter possibility arise, as made clear both in its negative discussion of the issue on July 1 and in its last-minute refusal, on the morning or July 3, to signal Somerville that it might be included as an alternative—on the grounds that to allow this would look like weakening.[7]

In addition to the actions carried out on July 3–4, Operation Catapult included several other measures. On July 7 a British force off Dakar delivered its ultimatum to the commander of the battleship *Richelieu,* demanding that he either proceed under British control (with reduced crews and without ammunition) to a British port; sail with reduced crews for the French West Indies, where the ships could be demilitarized or perhaps entrusted to the USA; disarm at Dakar within twelve hours so that his ships would be incapable of taking further part in the war; or scuttle within six hours. Following the rejection of these terms, the *Richelieu* was seriously disabled by depth charges and a torpedo bombing attack launched from the aircraft carrier *Hermes* early on July 8. In the West Indies, following protracted discussions that began in early July, a French aircraft carrier, the *Béarn,* and two light cruisers were first restricted to the Caribbean and eventually immobilized by way of an agreement with the United States. French ships were also sunk, captured, or immobilized in Canada, off Crete, in the Suez Canal, and at Singapore during July.[8]

This most aggressive phase of British naval policy lasted only ten days, but during that time the object remained the same—to prevent units of the French fleet from falling into German hands; the methods prescribed for the high seas were to parallel those employed at Oran. The possibility of war was mitigated, however, by the stipulation that British ships were on no account to fire first (sufficient warning was to be given to enable less bloody alternatives to be considered) or to make contact at all with French warships unless British units were considerably superior in strength. By July 12, the government had decided that no further action was to be taken against French ships in North African or colonial ports. Thereafter, only French warships heading for ports under enemy control would be considered fair game.[9]

On July 4 a triumphant Churchill was able to announce to a cheering Commons that by virtue of Operation Catapult a large portion of the French fleet had either passed into British possession or been put out of action or otherwise withheld from the enemy.[10] Certainly from the standpoint of propaganda the operation was an unqualified success. By going on the offensive only a month after Dunkirk, the Prime Minister succeeded not only in dissipating the atmosphere of disaster which had enveloped the nation but, by reason of his infectious truculence, in rallying public opinion behind him personally.

If at home it stiffened morale still further, overseas it tended to diminish—if not altogether dispel—suspicions that Britain was on the brink of surrender or disposed to negotiate with the enemy in any way.[11] At least in Churchill's opinion, "The elimination of the French Navy as an important factor almost at a single stroke by violent action produced a profound impression in every country . . . . It was made plain that the British War Cabinet feared nothing and would stop at nothing."[12] Among neutrals, ever responsive to a show of force, England's stock was generally enhanced by Mers-el-Kébir, and nowhere more than in the United States, which reacted with a sigh of relief and where Roosevelt had given his prior approval to the operation in the belief that had there been but one chance in a hundred of France's warships falling into German hands the British attack would have been justified.[13]

Yet for all its propaganda value Catapult's success was far short of sensational. Sir Alexander Cadogan admitted as much when he wrote in his diary for July 4: "Result of naval operations yesterday not too good, but Winston was able to make a good enough showing in [the] House . . . . " That Somerville had "messed the job" was later revealed to Admiral North by the First Lord of the Admiralty, who thought that with such a powerful force at his disposal "he should have sunk all the French ships." The disconsolate Somerville, according to his personal diary, thought so too. It was true, as the First Lord, Mr. A. V. Alexander, was able to tell Parliament on July 9, that out of France's eight completed capital ships, seven had been rendered harmless by the operation—at least for a considerable time to come. However, the important, though unfinished, battleship *Jean Bart* at Casablanca (together with other warships there which left the port on July 4) was not touched any more than was the sizable French cruiser and destroyer squadron at Toulon; in addition, the six French cruisers from Algiers made their way to Toulon, as did the *Strasbourg* after its escape from Force H, followed by the five large destroyers from Mers-el-Kébir and eventually the *Commandant Teste;* all these remained practically unscathed.[14]

As of July 7, by the reckoning of the Chiefs of Staff, of the important units of the French fleet other than those in the capital ship category, many more were still at large than had been accounted for: 4 out of 7 eight-inch cruisers, 8 out of 11 six-inch cruisers, 24 out of 27 light cruisers, 19 out of 26 destroyers, and 67 out of 77 submarines. Thus, although the British had destroyed or immobilized about a third of the French Navy in tonnage, by far the largest portion of the French war fleet remained in Vichy hands. Furthermore, though Churchill avidly desired to make use of the big ships immobilized at Alexandria and to collect the French planes on Martinique, the only positive addition to British armed strength from the operation came from the generally decrepit or minor naval units seized in home waters. The immediate military costs to Britain of the attack on Oran were small—only five planes and slight damage to the *Hood.* Whether the gains from this exercise in violence could be said to have outweighed the overall losses was much more dubious.[15]

In his speech to the House on July 4 Churchill claimed that the government had been unanimous in its decision to attack the French fleet, that all members of the cabinet shared the same conviction, and that there had not been the least divergence of opinion among them. This may be so, but certainly the Prime Minister had spared no effort to bring his more cautious colleagues around to his point of view. In his capacity as Minister of Defence he was at any rate in a position to impose his thinking on others. He seldom consulted his three service ministers except on administrative questions, A. J. P. Taylor writes, while "the defense committee (operations) of the war cabinet, though nominally the constitutional authority, did little more than endorse Churchill's direction." J. R. M. Butler, the official historian of Britain's grand strategy during World War II, also informs us that when the Chiefs of Staff, together with the three Vice-Chiefs, finally reached their decision on June 30 as to the need for the operation, it was "without a dissentient voice." Yet the suspicion remains, in view of the quantum jump from negative to positive Admiral Pound would seem to have made between June 24 and June 30 and in view of the Joint Planners' continuing disapproval of the idea through the

29th, that the COS may have been under considerable pressure to produce this kind of helpful unanimity—and there seems little doubt whence such pressure would have come. Again as A. J. P. Taylor points out, with the reins of war now concentrated in the hands of the Defence Minister, including the power to appoint and to dismiss generals and admirals, the Chiefs of Staff Committee "could no longer claim autonomy nor doubt to whom it was subordinate." The suspicion is fueled by Cordell Hull's statement, based on what he was told by a British admiral accompanying Churchill to Washington in late 1941, that the Admiralty had been opposed to Catapult and, moreover, that there had been serious differences within the government over the question.[16]

There is little direct evidence of dissension between the government and the Admiralty—at least on the policy-making level—in late June. By June 27, when the cabinet made its decision to press forward with Catapult, the Chief of Naval Staff seemed as convinced as was Churchill of the need to prevent French ships from returning to stations in metropolitan France, and by the next day seemed satisfied that they would indeed be required to do just that. Nevertheless, his conversation with Odend'hal on the 27th suggests that he still believed at this time that North Africa would provide a sufficient margin of safety for the French warships—if only they could be induced to remain there—whereas Churchill made no such distinction between the northern and southern shores of the Mediterranean.

At the very least, one can assume some divergence between Dudley Pound and the Prime Minister as to the form and extent of Catapult. Pound, for instance, as he indicated to fellow officers on June 29, believed the situation at Alexandria already in hand *before* Catapult: he was content with the agreement reached by the two commanders. Churchill, on July 7, also wanted to extend the operation to Casablanca in order to destroy the *Jean Bart* and other ships in port there, though the Admiralty was able to deflect him from this course. Finally, it seems clear that Pound and Churchill did not see eye to eye on the terms to be offered the French at Mers-el-Kébir: not only did the original Admiralty instructions include demilitarization as one of the options, but at 11:30 on July 3, while negotiations were in progress, the First Sea Lord actually proposed signaling Somerville the authority to offer immediate demilitarization at Oran to the French Admiral—a proposal that was promptly scuttled by the cabinet. Pound was by no means averse to the use of force against the French; at the June 7 meeting which inaugurated discussions on the

French fleet he had even been the first to suggest sinking it as the most practical solution to the problem, though admittedly on this date he believed the French might cooperate in such a venture before suing for terms. His divergence from the cabinet concerned chiefly the degree of force that might prove necessary and the circumstances under which it would be judicious to employ it at all.[17]

In any event, the British naval officers most closely associated with Catapult, including Admirals North, Cunningham, and Somerville, as well as Captain Holland, had all opposed the use of force in the operation, feeling with Cunningham that an attack on their ally of the day before was "an act of sheer treachery which was as injudicious as it was unnecessary" and that the Oran decision "was almost inept in its unwisdom." Because they believed there was little danger of the French allowing their ships to fall into German or Italian hands, they had instead warned of the disastrous military and political consequences which could result from precipitous action. But Somerville's representations to this effect together with the alternate proposals he submitted to the Admiralty were rejected, it being "the firm intention of His Majesty's Government," as he was told July 1, "that if the French will not accept any of the alternatives which are being sent you their ships must be destroyed." In that they had already predicted that strong-arm methods would inevitably "alienate the French completely and transform them from a defeated ally into an active enemy," these naval officers must have agreed only too readily with Admiral North's judgment that Operation Catapult might more appropriately have been named Operation Boomerang.[18]

Certainly it boomeranged most effectively against General de Gaulle, whose embryonic campaign to build up a resistance movement in London received a setback and whose influence among potentially sympathetic but nationalistic Frenchmen both at home and abroad was thereby permanently undermined. In spite of his own grief and indignation, the General steeled himself to explain, if not wholly to condone, the act to his compatriots over the BBC on July 8; but the fact that British newspapers (at least in the eyes of sensitive Frenchmen) had seemed to glory in the operation, as if it were a great naval victory, rankled, and de Gaulle did not hesitate to blame the attack and its subsequent handling in the press for the immediate falling off in recruitment experienced by the Free French (who numbered only 7,000 by the end of July) as well as for the anti-Allied stance thereafter adopted by civilian and military authorities throughout the most important parts of the French Empire.[19]

# End of the Affair

NOT unnaturally, Catapult produced among the officer corps of the French Navy a lasting bitterness; its immediate effect was, as Gensoul had predicted, to line up almost the entire service behind the most extreme members of the Pétain government in resentment and hatred of Great Britain.[1] Britain's action was considered not only an unjustifiable aggression (after all, as Darlan asked ironically, did the gentlemen in London wish to be more French than the French?) but an affront to the honor of the navy and a betrayal of trust as well. Darlan was particularly outraged that the British should, in Robert Murphy's words, have "flaunted [sic] his honor by doubting his pledges." But it was the necessarily unchivalrous nature of the attack that quickly became Darlan's most effective weapon in the propaganda war. "The French Admiralty," he would state on July 5, "had the painful impression that France's misfortunes left England's leaders quite unmoved for the reason that they dreamt only of becoming masters of the French fleet . . . . In any case, the fleet hardly deserved being stabbed in the back by order of Mr. Churchill, who, only the previous winter, had begged the French Admiralty to assign [its] principal forces to the protection of the Canadian convoys, the British Admiralty itself not having sufficient means."[2] More melodramatically, as Vichy's propaganda commissar put it, to the epic of Dunkirk the British had replied by "assassinating" the *Dunkerque.* If there were a few within diplomatic circles sophisticated enough to appreciate the "hideous dilemma" that England had been faced with as well as some of the advantages to the French fleet resulting from the attack, at least in naval circles it was felt that from the moment the British had turned their guns on their former comrades the French need no longer entertain any scruples towards them.[3]

Less predictable than the emotional response of the French Navy was the enemy's reaction to the conflict between the former allies. On July 4, in recognition of Gensoul's determination to defend his ships against the British, the Germans agreed to suspend their demand for the disarmament of the French fleet and to grant the right of passage through Gibraltar to all French warships and merchant vessels; they also agreed to release the Navy Ministry's archives and several hundred officers and functionaries captured at Rochefort. Thus, while the French in effect regained their navy, the British and Americans in later actions of the war would have to contend with fully armed French naval units free to come and go as they pleased.[4]

Precisely how the Armistice Commission would finally have resolved the question as to where French units were to be stationed and disarmed had Mers-el-Kébir not intervened cannot be known. For all practical purposes, the choice lay only between French Mediterranean and French North African ports because, as Admiral Belot points out, the risks from British bombing attendant upon returning French warships to their Atlantic ports were so great that no one had even envisaged the move in actuality.[5] In any event, whether Article 8 was unrealistic or not, the Germans never relinquished any of their rights in theory, and for any relaxation of their original requirements would undoubtedly have demanded some quid pro quo. This they probably felt they had in the French Navy's newfound belligerency.

Would France's capital ships in North Africa have stayed put in the absence of Britain's preventive attack? It seems unlikely. Lieutenant-Commander Dufay, Gensoul's intermediary with Captain Holland, had admitted that the Atlantic fleet's port was still to be determined—and thus, indirectly, that it might be sent to Toulon.[6] Furthermore, Admiral Darlan had told Ambassador Bullitt on July 1—two days before Mers-el-Kébir—that he expected to send both the *Dunkerque* and the *Strasbourg* back to Toulon.[7] Therefore, it is misleading to blame Catapult for the return to Toulon of the bulk of the French fleet, as many French writers have, with the suggestion that otherwise it would have remained in North Africa, far from the immediate reach of the Germans.[8] Nevertheless, that said, it is quite true that with the ports of Mers-el-Kébir and Algiers open to further British attacks, many more of the French Navy's remaining large units were ordered—paradoxically, *after* the Germans had suspended their original stipulations—to take refuge under the powerful coastal batteries of Toulon, where, on November 27, 1942, they would meet an honorable but tragic and unnecessary end that could in no way aid the Allies.[9]

Operation Catapult's most serious consequence, as Bouthillier points out, was that henceforth French policy had to take into account the spirit of revenge animating the Admiral of the Fleet. Darlan's first reaction to Mers-el-Kébir had been to order French warships and aircraft to attack all English ships met. In addition, during the night of July 3–4, Darlan ordered the light cruiser squadron from Algiers along with the *Strasbourg* to the Balearics in preparation for an attack on Somerville's squadron as it returned to Gibraltar. Although these decisions were taken on his own initiative and rescinded either the next day or the day after before any damage could be done, Darlan in the next few days was nevertheless able to effect on his own authority or to persuade the Council of Ministers to adopt, at least in principle, several naval and military measures of a hostile nature. To begin with, a token air raid was carried out over Gibraltar early on July 5. More seriously, the fleet was ordered to stop and search British merchantmen; French warships escorting French commercial vessels were instructed to open fire at the least threat of British interference; and French authorities were ordered to forcibly prevent British ships and aircraft from approaching closer than 20 sea miles off the French coast. Darlan also proposed a combined Franco-Italian naval operation to relieve the French squadron blocked at Alexandria. (Pétain, for his part, agreed to examine the possibility of ceding air bases in Algeria to Italy so that Italian planes could protect the French fleet.) Then, in retaliation for the British action at Dakar, Darlan suggested an attack on Freetown in Sierra Leone. Darlan's pet project, however, remained a well-organized bombing raid of Somerville's Force H at Gibraltar. Although most of these projects were abandoned as inexpedient or, where collaboration with the enemy was involved, as dishonorable, the fact that they had ever come to light was proof enough of the dramatic shift that had taken place in French foreign policy. As the Ministry of Foreign Affairs' legal counselor pointed out, any of these measures, if carried out, would have created an immediate state of war.[10]

Although not every member of the cabinet shared Darlan's appetite for war against England or Laval's readiness for the collaborationist policy that would accompany it,[11] there can be no doubt that Mers-el-Kébir effectively destroyed any lingering sense of obligation to Britain and gave a powerful impetus to the political tendencies that Laval represented. Anglophobia was, after all, the touchstone of *rapprochement* wtih Germany. If Laval's assertion on the morrow of the disaster that "France has never had and never will have a more implacable foe than Great Britain" still fell short of full credibility, backed by the evidence of July 3 it easily assumed more resonance than would have seemed conceivable just two weeks before. Not recognizing any responsibility for what had transpired and still insisting on the loyalty France had maintained toward England, the French Government would from now on consider itself politically free to follow what Baudouin characterized as "a purely French policy," one dictated solely by French interests independent of ideology or passion.[12]

Given the reigning atmosphere in Vichy, a diplomatic rupture was unavoidable and was in a very real sense less alarming than many courses then under consideration. This was the course adopted by the Council of Ministers on July 4, almost in a spirit of compromise. Baudouin may have hoped that by making official the diplomatic break between England and France, which had existed in fact since June 22, he would, in Adrienne Hytier's words, be "manifesting France's anger without, however, involving irreparable consequences."[13] But, if his speech to the press that day reviewing Franco-British relations since the start of the war concluded on a moderate note, the rest seemed calculated to justify the worst British suspicions: for in it he talked of France's having entered the war "in the wake of England," publicly disparaged Britain's war effort, continuing egoism, and disloyalty, and, after admitting that a different French attitude with respect to the fleet might indeed have softened Germany's armistice terms, announced that Mers-el-Kébir could not fail to exercise "a profound influence on the orientation of [French] policy."[14] This public venting of spleen by the French Foreign Minister was no doubt intended less as an earnest of Baudouin's future intentions than as a sop to cabinet war hawks and German observers, but there can be no doubt that Mers-el-Kébir and the French Government's reaction to it did have irreparable consequences, so that, even as Baudouin looked to the future, events were in fact outstripping his control.

Roger Cambon, whose relationship to the chief architect of the Entente Cordiale made his position particularly difficult and who had served at the French Embassy since 1924, resigned in London even before receiving the instructions of his government. He had, of course, immediately and strenuously protested against the British action taken against the French fleet both in British ports and Oran, but then, on July 5, had submitted his resignation (to the Foreign Office, no less), fearing, as he told Lord Halifax, that "he might have to make a communication on behalf of his Government which, after having lived in this country for over twenty-five years, he would not wish to make."[15] This communication, formally breaking off diplomatic relations, was duly made by his replacement as chargé, the Marquis Boni de Castellane, on July 8.[16] Other than the Consul-General, Jacques Chartier, this left only Paul Morand of the French Commercial Mission as France's sole diplomatic representative in England; and, by a strange quirk, he too was to leave the country on his own initiative at the time the remaining personnel of the French Embassy departed.[17] Thus, after mid-July 1940, London and Vichy were destined to have no further *official* contact, though a shadowy, ambivalent relationship carried on in neutral capitals preserved a tenuous tie.

Mers-el-Kébir was in effect the end of an era—the bitter climax to eight weeks of mounting disaffection and distrust between England and France and the tragic proof that their friendship could not survive the defeat of the one or the threat of defeat hanging over the other. Within two weeks of the armistice of Compiègne, an alliance of thirty years lay in ruins. Alfred Fabre-Luce was undoubtedly premature in concluding from the physical solidarity of the European continent under Hitler that "Europe, against its will, was inexorably making itself."[18] But henceforth, as the two nations went their separate ways, the sundered alliance *would* be a frustrating reminder—as Churchill and General de Gaulle both agreed—that, "when all is said and done, Great Britain is an island; France, the cape of a continent; America another world."[19]

# *When All Is Said and Done*

*You fortunate people in your island! You can indulge in all your high-flown sentiments with security. You have the Channel and your Fleet to defeat all comers.*

Lord Mottistone quoting Marshal Foch, October 4, 1939, in *Parliamentary Debates, House of Lords*, 5th Series, Vol. CXIV, col. 1320.

*True, we rose to the very height of a great occasion. But we had a breathing space which was never accorded to France. It was given to us by the English Channel, to which, not for the first time, although very possibly for the last, our debt was great.*

Robert Boothby, *I Fight to Live* (London, 1947), p. 226.

# The Nature
# of the Problem

THE possibility of a complete French collapse was recognized as early as May 16, while after May 25 the outcome of the struggle in France was never seriously in doubt on either side of the Channel. Thus the question dominating Anglo-French relations from then on through June 16 was simply how the French Government would cope with its defeat. The only practical alternatives facing French statesmen were either to bring hostilities to an end on the basis of an armistice or to continue the war at the side of Great Britain either from London or from North Africa and other points in the French Empire. Neither course provided an easy solution; whether surrender or resistance was opted for, the road ahead would be hard and the final result uncertain.[1] A solution to the problem involved determining where France's best interests lay, but it was precisely this primordial question that proved such a stumbling block. If the outcome of the war itself has to some degree made the answer more obvious, by justifying retrospectively the dual, or schizophrenic, approach taken by Frenchmen, time and distance—notwithstanding the hindsight and insight they provide—have nevertheless not made the dilemma actually facing French decision makers in 1940 seem any the less trying.

The British, by contrast, recognized no such dilemma, though had they been able to see twenty years into the future, with the dissolution of Empire and the reduction of Britain to the position of an American satellite, their powers of perception and ability to act in 1940 might well have been as paralyzed as were those of the French. As it was, following Churchill's inspired lead, the overwhelming majority of Englishmen had a clear-cut conception of their national interest and this they believed was inextricably bound up with the prolongation of the war against Nazi Germany. The hesitations of Halifax and a few others notwithstanding, they were determined to pursue the struggle, no matter what the costs, and once having chosen this path naturally believed it to be in their interests that the French follow suit. A formal defection on the part of France, they were convinced, would adversely affect their own chances of victory. France's neutralization was not considered a viable possibility.

Thus arose the moral question, fiercely debated in 1940 and still at issue forty years later, as to the extent of French obligations to England in its hour of trial. Many in France doubted that they were altogether compelling because in their eyes the Anglo-French alliance itself seemed something of a sham. The brunt of the war, once it began in earnest, had, after all, fallen on France. It was French territory that had been invaded, French civilians who had been uprooted, and French soldiers who had suffered most of the casualties in battle. The British had contributed less than a tenth of the troops in France, and nine-tenths of these had departed at the time of Dunkirk. The evacuation itself was a source of particular resentment among the French. The British had begun preparing for a large-scale evacuation of the BEF as early as May 19 and had taken off considerable numbers from May 21 on; yet they did not inform the French of their arrangements or intentions until May 26, when Operation Dynamo was officially put into motion; even then the news did not filter through to those most affected until May 27 or 28. The fact that almost two-thirds of the soldiers rescued at Dunkirk were British only added to French indignation. Two British divisions had been sent back to the continent in mid-June, but no sooner had they landed than their commander began to urge London to withdraw them along with the remaining British troops in France in order to avoid a useless sacrifice in a hopeless situation. A second evacuation had begun immediately, so that by June 17, when Pétain called for an armistice, practically no British forces remained on French soil. Both evacuations could be justified from a military point of view, but the fact that they had been unilaterally decided on and put into operation without reference to the French High Command, under whose orders British troops were supposedly acting, could hardly calm French fears that they were being deserted.

Britain's steadfast refusal to part with a larger proportion of the RAF even during the height of the battle—though this was the one contribution it had the capacity to make—proved the biggest bone of contention. British strategic bombing at this early stage of the war was largely a wasted effort, only diverting from the bomber strength available to the Allied armies at the points where decisive results were being achieved. Furthermore, the British never provided France with more than a quarter of their home-based fighter squadrons and began to withdraw most of these starting May 20. They had of course intervened in strength at Dunkirk but then sent back only token support for the Battle of France. The British felt that they had a right to ensure their own defense and that even if they sent over the maximum amount of aid it would still not suffice to reverse the situation in France and would meanwhile only destroy their own chances of salvation.

The truth was that in their use of aircraft neither ally could be said to have respected the strategic principle of concentration. Nor had a joint plan for the employment of French and British aviation in France ever been agreed upon either before or during the war. Air cooperation for both, as students of the subject have concluded, was a means of furthering their own national strategies: initially, the British looked upon their air forces in France as a way of reducing the danger of air attack on Great Britain, while the French saw British support primarily as a means of redressing the imbalance between their own air force and that of Germany.[2] Whether, from the outset, a completely different strategic use of the British and French air forces combined, which would have enabled the Allies to meet the Luftwaffe over French skies in a ratio of 2:3 rather than the 1:2½ ratio later forced on the British alone, might have saved France in May 1940, and with it the coalition, remains an important question that has been insufficiently examined by objective observers.[3]

The posing of this question must of necessity go to the very heart of the matter: what was the nature of the alliance, was it of equal benefit to both partners, or did geography make it inevitable that competition rather than cooperation would be the keynote of a coalition based more on sentiment and political similarity than on a strict identity of strategic needs? Quite often it is simply argued, even by Frenchmen who in 1940 felt rather differently, that the British decision to save the bulk of their fighter squadrons for home defense was a providentially wise one, because it later enabled them to hold out against Hitler in the crucial Battle of Britain. At the time, however, it seemed to almost all Frenchmen not only exploitative but an actual miscalculation as to priorities if the British were, as they claimed, determined to pursue the war. So removed from the requirements of the situation did Britain's resolve to hoard its resources seem that

Marshal Pétain, among others, could only interpret it as a sign that the British were preparing to use them as a means of making a compromise peace with Germany.

This does not mean that had their positions been reversed the French would have reacted differently. On the contrary, the British had already determined back in April 1940, at the height of the Norwegian campaign, that in the event of the brunt of the German attack falling on Great Britain, France would not permit *its* aircraft to operate from British bases—for fear that the German air attack might be switched to France at short notice. In these circumstances, the French were prepared to provide air support from French bases, though not for action against targets that would bring retaliation on French industrial centers. They were, however, ready to send troops to England if that country were invaded and to give full naval support in the Mediterranean.[4] But, if where air support is concerned Britain and France were equal partners in selfishness, it should be remembered that France's air force was not in a class with Britain's, its bomber strength being practically nil, and that the contingency envisaged here was not seriously expected to materialize. The war that had been envisaged all along and for which the British had made commitments was the one that did in fact materialize, and although technically the British fulfilled their prewar promises to the French, their total contribution on land as in the air left many observers, British as well as French, with the impression of being considerably smaller than might have been expected in view of international developments since 1936.[5]

If, before the battle, British strategy, with its emphasis on maintaining the integrity of French soil along with access to cross-Channel Dutch and Belgian ports, had coincided with French needs, during the crisis all Britain's decisions appear to have been based on a different and ultimately isolationist conception of the war, in which France was once again relegated to the position of a buffer state.[6] In this strategy the fields of Flanders and northern France constituted but a first line of defense, the Channel the second and more vital bulwark, behind which they could regroup if the front line proved untenable. The French, however, had but one line and no contingency plan were this line driven in. In fact, the Allies had made no joint provisions for a really bad defeat. Most Frenchmen believed that the war's outcome would be decided by the battle being waged in France, just as it had been in World War I, and that if the British persisted in holding back their forces both countries would succumb, one after the other.

Once the "unthinkable" French collapse had occurred, the British quickly dropped their "European policy," of which the French alliance had been a cardinal feature. The war, they now believed, would be decided only after Hitler had hurled his air might against the British Isles and after the RAF had been given an opportunity to smash the Luftwaffe. If they could stave off a German invasion by retaining mastery of the seas and by keeping control of the air over Great Britain and the Channel, and Churchill had been told by his military advisers that they could do so only if they did not waste their air strength in France, then their success would prolong the war indefinitely, thus giving British sea power time to make itself felt and also proportionately increasing the chances of American intervention.

This "new" isolationism, from which the British in any event had only reluctantly parted in the recent past, was clearly and unsentimentally summed up by Lord Hankey in a note written soon after the collapse of France. After noting that France, "though supported by ten British divisions and large air forces, [had] only survived the German assault for a week or two longer than Poland," he concluded that if the British were going to survive it would be mainly by their own efforts, aided only by the Empire and the USA:

If we are successful we shall expose the fallacy of the glib statement that Great Britain is no longer an island. Assuming then . . . that we repel the expected attempt at invasion and the subsequent assaults on our economic position, we shall have disproved the strategical theories on which our policy has been based in recent years. There will be no strategical object in seeking alliance with France and other continental States that have proved so unreliable.[7]

This view had never lain far below the surface. Indeed it was a natural result of Britain's unhappy experience in the 1914–18 war, much as France's Maginot complex was of hers. But the British refusal even to contemplate fielding another mass army for service in France—until the last possible moment—coupled with their concentration on air defense at home, was hardly the best basis for an alliance.

Again, the British stance was to be vindicated, but to all but a few Frenchmen in 1940 it looked more like monumental arrogance. They could not believe that where the French had failed the British would succeed. It seemed almost a foregone conclusion that after France had fallen England too, in spite of the relative protection afforded by its superior "anti-tank ditch," would have its neck wrung like that of a chicken unless the government more wisely decided to avoid total defeat by suing for peace first. France's highest military leaders were disinclined in any case to see the conquest of France, to say nothing of the conquest of most of Europe, as merely one stage in a war that would expand. For them the loss of the Battle of France meant the loss of the war. The role of sacrificial lamb, which the British had apparently assigned them, was not a part they could readily accept.

Even had Pétain and Weygand believed that England was not completely finished, they would still have felt that France's withdrawal from the war was in order so as to enable the country to catch its breath and to avoid a second bloodletting after only twenty-two years. To have continued their participation in the coalition would in their view have involved disproportionate sacrifices by France primarily for England's benefit, and they felt that France had already expended far too much in this dubious cause. The disintegration of the French armies on the continent, they contended, was sufficient justification for France's terminating hostilities and they urged the government to seek an armistice before conditions grew even worse, while they still had assets that could be made to work for them. Strategically, this precluded looking upon the retreat of the French armies in France as a long delaying action that would serve to cover the transfer to Africa of a part of the armed forces together with the government as well as to delay the inevitable attack on an ill-prepared Britain. On the contrary, as Paul Kecskemeti points out, Pétain and Weygand "thought it urgent for France to surrender while she could obtain something for not using her residual capacity. To them, the chief value of the armistice lay in its being a *separate* arrangement, predicated upon the rupture of the coalition."[8] In short, the policy of collective security having failed, or rather never having been tried, a separate armistice would at least have the advantage of removing them from British tutelage and of allowing the French to devise a new policy which, however circumscribed, would be independent in the sense of being in their hands alone.[9] After twenty years of an ambitious policy that far exceeded their military capacities they could now try one less at variance with their modest means.

The defeatists argued that it was necessary to come to terms with the enemy in order to prevent the final destruction or capture of the French Army, the complete breakdown of civil and military order, and the invasion and occupation of the entire country. In other words, the suffering and destruction had to be stopped and French losses cut as far as possible. Inasmuch as they believed a universal armistice to be inevitable in any event, they felt the national interest would best be served by coming to terms immediately with the new masters of Europe, before England did it at their expense, and not by abandoning the people of France to the mercy of the invaders—to be Polandized—while the government pursued a hopeless struggle from ill-prepared bases in North Africa, where it would have been even more dependent on the good will and assistance of the British and Americans. Any other course, they feared, risked civil war or some sort of massive social dislocation in which French institutions and national traditions—political, social, legal, and economic—might be permanently altered or corrupted under the direct administration of the Nazis and their accomplices. In the arguments put forth by the defeatists France's relationship to Britain and the effect a French disengagement would have on their ally had no real place. It was simply accepted that England itself would shortly sue for peace, and that, in any case, England's contribution to the alliance had been so slight and so grudging that it had no right to hold France to the Anglo-French agreement or to make any further demands. In their view, France's demand for a separate peace was but the antidote to Britain's waging of a separate war.

Those who wished to continue resistance, such as Reynaud, Mandel, de Gaulle, and the leaders of the two assemblies, argued from a completely different vantage point. They contended that the fall of France constituted only the first phase of a much larger conflict and that coming to terms with the Germans could not be justified while France still had a huge colonial empire and a powerful and undefeated fleet with which to carry on the war. In their view the Anglo-French agreement played a vital role. And in Reynaud's case, as with a number of his colleagues, it was *the* dominant factor. An armistice might be thinkable; what was not thinkable was that France should fail to keep its word to an ally for the second time in two years, especially to an ally of Great Britain's standing.[10] France was bound by a solemn international undertaking not to conclude a separate armistice or peace and to break such an agreement would be both to dishonor themselves and to jeopardize French relations with the Anglo-Saxon world for all time. National interest dictated the continuance of the struggle at the side of Great Britain, for a future without the friendship and assistance of England and America was inconceivable. Coming to terms with the enemy at this stage of the war would be to rob France of the fruits of an ultimate Allied victory, such as a seat at the peace conference, with all the postwar power and influence that this implied.

It would mean sacrificing France's long-range interests for the sake of spurious advantages in the short run; and even such short-run advantages were not assured, because once France was disarmed, the Germans were free to act as harshly as they chose towards her despite any armistice agreement they might have signed. There were also more profound moral considerations. As Reynaud reminded his colleagues, Hitler was not to be confused with William I, the old gentleman who had simply absconded with Alsace-Lorraine—Hitler was Genghis Khan.[11]

The proresistance argument was premised on the requirement of loyalty to England and on the vague expectation that somehow or other, however farfetched it might look at the moment, Great Britain would be able to sustain herself. Understandably, it was powerful with those who had always supported the Entente and enthused over any tightening of the bonds with their cross-Channel neighbor. But it could hardly buttress the belligerents' case with those who, on the contrary, believed that French policy and interests had too often in the past been subordinated to those of England, who moreover did not believe that England would hold out, who if anything would have preferred that the argument to further resistance rest exclusively on appeals to French tradition and pride, and who in any event refused to admit that a decision to treat with the enemy could be defined as honorable or dishonorable according to whether the British approved of it or not.[12]

Both arguments—hawkish and doveish alike—contained valid points; both actually were based on a conception of France's interests that comprehended more than just the immediate present or the distant future; both reflected an ideal of national dignity—the one "romantically" slanted toward considerations of the state's untrammeled independence in the juridical sense, its prestige abroad and spiritual salvation at home, with hope of final victory as the goal that would more than justify any temporary sacrifices, the other more "realistically" grounded in a prudent regard for the permanence of the state, if not of the regime, for order, tradition, national recovery, and the material welfare of the greatest number;[13] both, moreover, amounted to a wager on who would be the ultimate victor in the war. In the summer of 1940, with Germany triumphant on the continent, the Soviet Union an unfriendly neutral, and the United States still strongly isolationist, a gamble on England to all but the most visionary obviously seemed the longer shot. Pierre Laval would later put it even more strongly: at the time, a man of good sense could hardly have imagined anything *but* the victory of Germany.[14] Yet, for all that it went unrecognized by the "practical" politicians and general public in France, the drama of France's choice lay precisely in the fact that the war was *not* over: the most appropriate response to the French dilemma demanded at least this much skepticism, failing which the most searching questions could not even be posed, the best or most honest answers never so much as adumbrated.

It was only after General Weygand had formally requested the government to conclude an armistice that these questions were first debated by the French Government sitting in full council. Even then the full implications of the various alternatives under discussion were never approached in anything but a polemical spirit. Minds tended to be made up on the basis of prewar foreign policy and ideological preferences, rather than by reference to some objective standard of feasibility. Until then there had also been no discussion with the British Government as to what precisely the French would do when the Battle of France was lost. The British were well aware that defeatist sentiment had steadily gathered force in France after May 25; yet in none of the Allied Supreme Councils that followed was there a really frank examination of the problems that were threatening the survival of the alliance.

In London on May 26, by unsuccessfully trying to embroil the British in a grand negotiation on the Munich model, which would have salvaged the alliance while simultaneously costing it the war, Reynaud had wasted an opportunity to explore privately with the War Cabinet Britain's demands on France in the likely event that the French Government did ultimately opt for a separate arrangement with Germany. Nor did the May 31 meeting in Paris, where Dunkirk was the principal concern, provide a forum for an exchange of ideas between allies whose needs were palpably diverging and who were fast drifting apart. Even at Briare on June 11, when the results of the struggle in France were already blindingly clear, and after the possibilities of holding out in the Breton redoubt or of conducting guerrilla warfare throughout the country had been dismissed from the debate as impractical, there was no further discussion of the continuation of French resistance from North Africa or of the naval contribution France could make to the war effort once hostilities ceased on metropolitan soil. On the contrary, Churchill, by his compassionate remarks, seemed to suggest that the British no longer expected the French to continue the struggle and would understand if they capitulated. He asked only to be consulted before the French Government took any decision that would govern its action in the second phase of the war.

The Supreme War Council held at Tours on June 13 proved little better at clarifying the situation. Reynaud, anxious that there be no falling-out between the French and British governments if he were overthrown by the pro-armistice faction in his cabinet, allowed the British to believe that this was virtually a foregone conclusion, when actually there was still fairly solid support among his colleagues for continued resistance. Confronted by the Premier's hypothetical arguments—in which the point of view of his political adversaries was expressed with rare understanding—the British were confused as to where Reynaud himself now stood. Churchill added to the confusion. When informed of Weygand's demand for an armistice, Churchill had at first indicated his hope that the French would continue fighting down to the sea and, if need be, from North Africa, and that France would remain in the war with its empire and fleet. When Reynaud asked him how the British Government would react if the French were forced to sue for an armistice, however, Churchill's reminder of France's obligations resulting from the Anglo-French agreement appears to have been overshadowed by his more sympathetic and impromptu allusions—which included a very rash promise of no reproaches or recriminations in any event—with the unfortunate consequence that the only two members of the French Government who had heard this statement of British policy were to varying degrees misled as to its implications.

Reynaud was later to be disabused of his misinterpretation, though not in time to sanction Churchill's presence at the Council of Ministers, where the British Prime Minister might conceivably have altered the course of events by encouraging the French Government to hold firm. But, even if he had not converted the French ministers to his own ardent faith, at the very least much Franco-British misunderstanding in the future could have been averted by a really open and searching discussion at this point. Baudouin, at any rate, was to go on insisting to the end that Churchill, backed by his colleagues, had implicitly released the French from their pledge and granted them the right to seek a separate armistice; and it was his version that was to be most widely credited.

The ironic upshot of this last formal meeting between the Allied governments was that the British were, perhaps unjustifiably, convinced by it that an armistice was unavoidable while the French received the erroneous impression that the British had no really strong objections. The only practical result was that the French Government agreed to postpone any action on the question of an armistice until after the Allies had received President Roosevelt's reply to their joint appeal for immediate American intervention. Churchill had indicated that there would be innumerable problems to examine at that time if the French Government then announced its resolve to treat separately; but once again the Allies had deferred any discussion on the essential issues. Neither North Africa nor the French fleet appear to have figured in the discussions, almost as if it had been tacitly recognized by both parties that an armistice was inevitable and that the only choice lay between sooner or later.

Whether Churchill refrained from raising these difficult subjects because he believed Reynaud would be able to hold on longer than he in fact did or because the nature of such talks could only have disheartened the French while embarrassing the British is unclear. What is evident is that the British were faced with a monumental dilemma. It was not in their interests to have the French abandon the struggle, for this would free the Germans to turn their full strength against them; whether from metropolitan territory or North Africa, and even if the outcome was unsuccessful, if the French continued to fight they would help retard any German invasion of the British Isles. On the other hand, if the French were to sacrifice themselves further, they would need tangible assistance—at a time when French demands for increased aid were already considered such a burden that the British were no longer prepared to support them except on a symbolic level. A French request for an armistice would relieve them of further obligations on this score; but, at the same time, it would immeasurably reduce their chances of acquiring the material resources they needed from the French. In short, by mid-June, the British were in the awkward position of wanting favors from their ally for which they were unable or unwilling to pay except by way of a promissory note that would not fall due for many years.[15]

Though Churchill's own feelings toward the French partook of all the ambivalence inherent in the situation, his policy throughout was to keep the French officially in the war.[16] Even reduced to the status of a government in exile operating out of London, the French would still constitute a propaganda plus; more to the point, the legal French Government would retain control over the military resources it was most necessary to deny the enemy. There can be no doubt that the principal reason for urging the French to fight on had to do with the fleet, because the British must have been aware, despite occasional signs to the contrary, that any government which came to terms with the Germans would never relinquish its principal asset. To sanction a separate armistice agreement, then, would be to acquiesce in the loss of the French fleet. Thus, it was essential either to hold the French to their treaty commitment or to release them on such conditions that the results, for all practical purposes, would amount to the same thing. In this way, under the guise of relaxing the letter of the law, the British could continue to demand their pound of flesh. In addition, this solution provided them with the legal justification for whatever actions might subsequently prove necessary.

Thus, forty-eight hours after the Tours meeting, when Reynaud, on behalf of his cabinet and after having first been pushed into a corner by the Chautemps maneuver and Roosevelt's negative reply, formally requested Britain's consent to inquire of the Germans what their terms for an armistice would be, the British decided that they had no choice but to attempt to rescue what they could by consenting to the French request on a conditional basis. In two messages sent to Reynaud on June 16, therefore, they stated their objections in principle to separate negotiations but nevertheless gave their permission to the French Government to ascertain what the terms of an armistice would be, *provided* the French fleet was sailed to British harbors pending negotiations. This conditional agreement, as Darlan later pointed out, was casuistical in the extreme but at least had the merit of presenting a frank and open claim on the one thing that really mattered to the British—the French fleet. Had the British never veered from this tack, the French could have been in no doubt as to what was expected of them, nor could they any longer have entertained the attractive notion that morally they had been released from their obligations to Great Britain. There is also little doubt, however, that this peremptory demand would have alienated them and been rejected by both pro- and anti-armistice factions as an unwarranted arrogation of French sovereignty. Astute British participants in the drama recognized this immediately.

As it turned out, the two telegrams setting forth the British point of view were never seen by any member of the Reynaud government but the Premier himself, for midway through the day the British suspended action on them and, in a last desperate bid to maintain the alliance, alternately proposed to the French Government an indissoluble political union of the two nations. But the offer of union, which had been concocted only to strengthen Reynaud's position and to keep the French fleet, the French Empire, and everything else of use to the British in the war, proved an instantaneous failure and instead paved the way for the fall of the Premier. The upshot was that the French Government, new and old alike, remained unaware of the British condition concerning the fleet and even of the fact that there had been a reply to Reynaud's specific request. Thus, the Pétain cabinet started down the path to an armistice without further thought being given the inconvenient question of France's obligations to the alliance.[17]

# Resolution
# and Inevitability

BEFORE the Pétain government came to power the dominant question had been what the French would do about their defeat. That question resolved, the new question immediately became what the British would do about the French armistice. They had in fact been preparing for this contingency for almost a month on the assumption that the French *would* eventually opt for an armistice. This advance planning, as it evolved from day to day, no doubt contributed to some of the confusion and ambiguity that marked British policy throughout the second and third weeks of June. In the British military's estimation of its own insolvency with respect to the aid it could afford to spare a faltering France, as well as in its pessimistic expectations regarding the final disposition of the French fleet, probably lies the explanation for Churchill's failure to raise the subjects of North Africa and the navy while the Reynaud government was still in power. Because the British were not relying implicitly on any French government's "doing the right thing," in the sense of according priority to their needs, they were preparing, should the worst come to the worst, to take the essentials regardless of the means necessary, and there was therefore a natural reluctance to showing their hand.

As has been seen, the British were prepared to accept France's withdrawal from the war, as its continued presence could have little practical effect, but they were unwilling to run the risk of seeing the French Navy fall into German hands. Therefore, from June 17 on the British concerned themselves almost exclusively with obtaining some sort of guarantee with regard to the French fleet. From the British point of view, the French fleet would be safe only if it were sent to British or American waters or if it were attached to a French government in

390

North Africa prepared to go on with the war. In the few days that elapsed before the arrival of the armistice terms the British did not, however, make their position crystal clear. By the possibly ambiguous action of the British Ambassador when he redelivered the two telegrams originally intended for the Reynaud government, the French Foreign Minister received the impression (or so he claimed) that the British demand contained in them was a dead letter. Furthermore, when the three British emissaries came to discuss the question of the fleet with Admiral Darlan, Baudouin, and Pétain, they did not demand unequivocally that the French fleet be sent to British harbors, and by all indications went away satisified with the arrangements the French had made to protect their warships. The fact that the British had been deliberately misled into thinking that the French Government would soon move to North Africa, where it it might then continue the war, had, of course, confused the issue at this point. But the French were at least temporarily convinced that their solemn and repeated declarations never to deliver the fleet to the enemy would be sufficient.

Had the members of the new French Government known for sure that, in British eyes, France was still bound by the agreement not to conclude a separate armistice because it had not yet fulfilled the one condition necessary for its release, however, this could not have altered the situation substantially. The one point that seems clear, in fact, is that under no circumstances would the French Government have sent its fleet into British control, for to have done so would undoubtedly have ruined any negotiations with the Germans beforehand by depriving the French of their principal bargaining weapon. By such a gesture they would have risked bringing to pass the very disasters they were hoping an armistice would prevent, for unless the French remained masters of this asset, it would hardly have been in the Germans' interest to offer an armistice. And if, as they expected, England were soon defeated, it would be a wasted effort in any case. French losses in casualties, prisoners, and territory between June 12, when the High Command had first demanded an armistice, and June 25, when it finally came into effect, must also have appeared to them as a sacrifice that could well be equated with the delaying operation the British had originally asked of their ally, and beyond which the French could not reasonably be expected to go (though it is doubtful that the armistice terms would have been much better even if they had been granted two weeks earlier). Therefore, Britain's attitude towards France at this juncture could not have weighed very heavily, even if misunderstandings had been avoided.

Whether the British had made it clear to the French or not, however, they were determined from the inception of the Pétain government to wrest control of the fleet, and indeed anything else they could obtain, away from those who were willing to make peace. Even before the armistice terms were known they had approached the colonial and naval authorities in North Africa with the purpose of inducing them to declare for continued resistance. And after June 23 their efforts to get proresistance elements to set up a dissident government in North Africa, to which the fleet would rally, were doubled. The failure of these attempts was in turn followed by the British Government's decision to destroy or capture as much of the French fleet as possible.

The naval clause of the armistice treaty was subsequently given as the justification for this operation. It is certain that the British would never willingly have allowed French ships of the line to return to occupied ports in metropolitan France, or even to ports in the so-called free zone, there to be disarmed under German or Italian control, as specified by Article 8; it is also clear that the British cabinet did not believe that any measures the French might take to prevent their ships from falling into enemy hands would be operable in an emergency. Some Royal Navy officers, possibly better attuned to French psychology than were their civilian superiors in London, were inclined to trust that the French would succeed in keeping control of their fleet; like the Germans, they believed that French honor and interest alike militated against the French ever relinquishing this essential trump or using it against Great Britain. It was precisely this faith—in French good will and in the ability of their ex-ally to interpret its interests in a neutral sense—that the British Government lacked. But how, for instance, *could* they be expected to trust people who not only predicted a British defeat but, in some cases, even actively desired it?[1]

Wishful thinking aside, it is difficult to see how relations between England and France during this period could have had a happier ending. Given the crushing defeat suffered by France, equivalent to the proverbial knockout blow, the strength of defeatist sentiment, the recrudescence of traditional Anglophobia, and the lack of preparations overseas, the military's advantage over civilian authority in a time of crisis in combination with the uncertain leadership provided by those theoretically committed to continuing the war made it almost inevitable that in one way or another the pro-armistice faction would win out.

Reynaud, despite his genuine loyalty to the Franco-British cause, was too deeply ambivalent and too subject to contradictory influences to pull it all together and save the alliance; but it is unlikely that any other Frenchman could have filled the breach either. Mandel—who more than any political figure on the French scene always appeared so solid and intransigent, so full of faith in the future, and to whom Churchill had looked as the possible savior of France—was, when all is said and done, not another Clemenceau, but merely an epigone, just as Weygand was of Foch; so that when his hour did at last strike, during the month-long crisis from May 16 to June 16, "everything passed," as Emmanuel Berl sadly notes, "as if he were not there." For all his lucidity, he was in the final analysis as subject to the debilitating sentiments, anxieties, failures, and errors in judgment as were his much weaker colleagues who also preached but did not successfully practice war to the bitter end.[2] Thus, one can only conclude, judging from the effect of national defeat on this most courageous and formidable of Frenchmen, that the general sense of abandon and prostration in France was far too profound for there to have been any realistic hope of the alliance continuing, let alone flourishing, in however minor a key. True, Mandel in principle was not averse to taking over the state, but to succeed he needed a following sufficient to oppose the defeatists and the support of determined politicians, and these he was convinced were just not there.[3]

Given the character of the new regime, the fact that the leading men in power had never been proponents of the Entente, and the fact that its decision to conclude an armistice amounted to a bet on the ultimate, or at least semipermanent, success of German arms, it was probably equally inevitable that the British should come to blows with the French Government. Those most securely entrenched in Bordeaux and Vichy were not the familiar Republican figures with whom the British were accustomed to working and wrangling over policy and procedures but a new breed whom it did not seem wise or even possible to trust, not only because they were by and large anti-English, and of course henceforth subject to German pressure, but also because the Pétain government was patently unstable and because its own members could not even trust each other—up to and including the supposedly universally venerated Marshal. Thus the British had ample justification for their fears, which of course were concentrated in their obsession with the fleet.

It has been suggested that a modus vivendi between British and French might have been reached had Admiral Darlan posed as a previous condition to any negotiations for an armistice that the French Navy be allowed to intern itself in an African port or in the French Antilles; that the Germans' desire for the neutralization of the French fleet, together with their desire to end operations towards the south, was so great that they would have accepted this; in short, that the Pétain government, either through poor judgment or fear, failed to take advantage of its master card in a way that would have satisfied both ally and enemy.[4] But even had the French known that there was some maneuverability in this area, or thought it worthwhile to be solicitous of the British, it is difficult to imagine that any locale agreeable to the Germans would have been acceptable to the British, or vice versa. The same fears would have come into play on both sides, leaving one of the parties, obviously the British, still dissatisfied once the Germans, as seems inevitable, had vetoed any ports potentially subject to British or American control. The truly significant point in this might-have-been scenario, however, is that not only did the possibility of demanding more from the Germans in the prenegotiating period not occur to the French, regardless of political complexion, it also never occurred to the British. In other words, both governments were as one in underestimating the initial strength of the French bargaining position with respect to the fleet as well as in their inability to appreciate German motives and needs. This lack of imagination in turn primed British readiness to look to desperate remedies.

The British had done all they could to induce the French to use their remaining resources in aid of the coalition, but France instead chose to use its residual strength to improve its negotiating position with the enemy—even if this was not accomplished with much skill. As the only great power among all the states that had been defeated by Hitler, France was in a unique position: unlike the smaller nations whose destinies had always been decided by others stronger than they and to whom it would not have been worthwhile for the Germans to grant an armistice,[5] France even at its weakest still possessed the power to inflict further damage by means of its fleet and empire and thus to command some respect. For better or worse, France was both too important and too well endowed either to leave its destiny to chance or to hostage it to an exaggerated sense of honor. That France hoped to exploit what remained of its international position to win a respectable place within the New Order organized by Germany, much as it had maneuvered after past defeats, therefore, should not really have surprised the British, despite the virulence with which they attacked the French defection. In the context of 1940 it was a reasonable thing to try to do.[6]

If it was true that this was a war quite unlike previous wars because Nazism represented a barbarism with which it was impossible to compromise, it was equally true that England had not recognized this until the eleventh hour, and then only after years of appeasing the same regime. Moreover, far into the phoney war period and again in late May and even beyond, talk of a compromise peace was still thinkable within British governing circles. It was neither an unnatural nor unreasonable thought to have had under the circumstances, and might easily have been entertained for the most patriotic motives—either because a pessimistic appraisal of the situation made a decisive defeat by Germany appear all too probable or, alternatively, because an optimistic evaluation of the future suggested that a temporary truce, which would have deferred Armageddon to a more distant day, held out more favorable possibilities for a British or Allied victory later on.

This was the point of view of Basil Liddell Hart (and others like him) who from March 1939—when the guarantee to Poland was given against the advice of the General Staff and before a Soviet alliance could be secured—had believed that strategically "the ground was not firm enough to stand on" and that "any sensible strategist does his utmost to postpone battle [when he has been outmaneuvered], and manoeuvres afresh with a view to regaining an advantageous position." Thus, in his opinion, a suspension of hostilities would have been justified because at the very least the time could be used to build up British strength, while, better still, it might provide "the necessary opportunity for Russia and Germany to rub against each other."[7] The short-lived Treaty of Amiens signed by Great Britain in 1802, as Lloyd George often reminded people, had not after all prevented the final overthrow of Napoleon.

Bowing to a Peace of Amiens was of course not in the Churchillian manner, but had Halifax or Chamberlain instead been prime minister, with all the influence that naturally accrues to this office, it is not inconceivable that the terrible risks of continuing the war at this very disquieting stage would have been found too great to sustain. The American Ambassador, for instance, had reported on May 27 that if the Germans made Britain, along with France, an offer of peace, there would be a row in the cabinet between the "do or die" group and the "group that want a settlement." Churchill and Attlee notwithstanding, Kennedy believed there were others who would feel that the "physical destruction of men and property in England will not be a proper offset to a loss [*sic*] of pride." After all, the Foreign Secretary (presumably the "my friend" of the telegram) had told Kennedy as early as May 16 that if the French cracked, he did not believe that England could fight on alone and that nothing could "save them from absolute defeat unless the President with some touch of genius and God's blessing can do it."[8]

Certainly Lord Halifax, as Oliver Harvey noted in his diary on June 2, was "anxiously exploring [the] possibility of peace proposals à la Lansdowne." On June 17, his parliamentary under-secretary, Mr. R. A. Butler, told the Swedish Minister in London that "no opportunity would be neglected for concluding a compromise peace if the chance offered on reasonable conditions" and that "the so-called diehards would not be allowed to stand in the way of negotiations." At the same time, Butler relayed a message from Halifax himself to the effect that "common sense and not bravado would dictate the British Government's policy."[9] His position had never been otherwise. The Foreign Secretary's preferred policy was simply the obvious alternative had Churchill's heroism brought on immediate disaster or proved untenable in the longer run.

Churchill's offer of a place in the War Cabinet to Lloyd George, a maverick but vocal defeatist since the start of the war, on May 28, the very day he had rejected further association with the French Government's bid for Italian mediation, suggests that at least privately the Prime Minister did not regard those of his colleagues who hoped for a compromise peace as irresponsible by that fact itself. As Halifax noted in his diary on June 6, Churchill "meant to put him [Lloyd George] through an inquisition first, as to whether he had the root of the matter in him. By this he means, so he explained to me, adopting a formula I suggested to him, that any peace terms now, as hereafter, offered must not be destructive of our independence." This proved unnecessary inasmuch as Lloyd George firmly rejected Churchill's initial invitation, as well as another made on June 19, to lend his name to Churchill's policies.[10] But one interpretation that can be put on the incident is that before the outcome of the Dunkirk operation was known and before Germany made its next move, Churchill genuinely feared (just as his opposite number, Reynaud, did) that he might soon be swept away by a current of adverse opinion from within the government or the Commons and was therefore making tentative preparations for an orderly transfer of power in this eventuality to those who would work towards a negotiated settlement.

Depressing as this unfolding of events would have been, such a course would have been understandable; thus, all the more so in that they *had* already been defeated and overrun, there was nothing intrinsically shocking in the French decision to come to terms. What A. J. P. Taylor describes as Churchill's refusal to admit that there might be some middle course between resistance and surrender or that other countries' interests could not necessarily be assimilated to the cause of England[11] can now be seen in a more nuanced light. The bulldog stance no doubt provided psychological strength at a critical hour; but though such ready nationalism lent itself to effective wartime propaganda, the propaganda itself can hardly serve as a permanent substitute for a realistic appraisal of the choices made by the French in 1940.

In his dealings with the United States, however, Churchill evidenced considerably greater understanding of the French predicament than he did in his public pronouncements. For instance, in a remarkable series of letters, the Prime Minister had warned President Roosevelt time and time again that if the British Isles were invaded and overrun, his own government might well be overthrown—just as Reynaud's had been—and replaced by an administration of pro-German or fascist tendencies prepared to seek terms. He was also aware that in case of defeat the British fleet would represent Britain's principal bargaining weapon with a triumphant enemy and as such would likely be used to ameliorate the country's situation rather than sent over to bolster the defenses of a lately awakening America. Churchill was also singularly resistant to making any precise commitments where the British fleet was concerned out of a desire to preserve their liberty of action.*

Thus, in spite of the genuine anger felt by the British towards the French for accepting the armistice, their reaction must be seen in perspective and judged for what it was: as going beyond disappointment, disapproval, or even fear (though these were all eminently present) to a kind of advance justification for the hostile moves they were preparing to take. The new ruthlessness toward France exhibited by the British Government, and especially by the Prime Minister, immediately following the armistice can also be seen as reflecting Churchill's desire to scotch any possibility that Britain too might succumb to a compromise peace, the attractions of which, as he well knew, exerted a powerful pull on at least a handful of key figures in the government. A month earlier, leading members of the British

---

*See Appendix L, Churchill, Roosevelt, and the British Fleet.

Union of Fascists had been arrested under regulation 18B, probably less for the danger they constituted than—as Oswald Mosley contends—because of the campaign for a negotiated peace they had waged.[12] Churchill's uncompromising speech to the House on June 25, much as Reynaud's to the French Chamber on the morrow of Belgium's defection, represented a decisive, and in his case successful, move against lingering appeasement in England, which would be capped a week later by the attack on the French fleet.

That Churchill was taking the matter in hand and had actually much less to fear from any "peace" group even by June 26 is shown by the letter he wrote on that date to the Foreign Secretary stating that he had been "strongly pressed in the House of Commons in the Secret Session to give assurances that the present Government and all its Members were resolved to fight on to the death." He had done so, "taking personal responsibility for the resolve of all" but warned that "any suspicion of lukewarmness in Butler" would subject them all to further annoyance. Replying the next day, Halifax was able to uphold the loyalty of Butler, who had written the Secretary of State on June 26 that he was ready to subscribe to the Prime Minister's courageous lead.[13] The internal dynamics of the British political scene in late June—if known or surmised by the French—may in fact account for the surprise occasioned by Mers-el-Kébir; they may well have dismissed the belligerent static in the air as propaganda alone.

British indignation and internal political needs notwithstanding, their French strategy was not motivated by malevolence or vindictiveness, however dangerous and dubious the personalities of the men of Bordeaux (or Vichy). To Churchill and his supporters it was simply the most realistic strategy available to a sea power fighting for its survival and intent on convincing the rest of the world that it had the capacity to succeed. The mistake of the French lay less in seeking an accommodation with Germany and in making do with a partial sovereignty than in imagining for a moment that by a stroke of the pen they could sign themselves into a convenient neutrality. However necessary the armistice was to a demoralized France in the summer of 1940—and few, whether politicians or historians, have disputed its initial popularity[14]—to the English it could only transform their late ally into a kind of enemy.

That there were profound moral issues at stake in the war is almost beside the point. Few countries, not excluding Britain and France, act primarily on behalf of moral principle unless, of course, their survival or well-being appear to depend on it. And this remains true even where moral considerations *have* played a lively part, as they did with Churchill and the men around him (and as they had in a more muddled way with the appeasers before them), and even where "survival" ultimately turns out to be considerably less than what its stubborn sponsors had hoped from it. From the point of view of his reputation in history, it was Mr. Churchill's good fortune that the survival of England *could* legitimately be linked to the survival of freedom, decency, and democratic institutions elsewhere. But the role of David to Hitler's Goliath was a role England might well have played regardless of the character of its formidable opponent.

It was in fact England's unique geographical position that had always enabled and encouraged it to play such a role. Balance of power calculations continued to dominate British thinking in the summer of 1940 just as they had in March of the previous year and throughout countless crises down the centuries. If strategically the picture had worsened dramatically since September 1939, causing some to question the wisdom of pursuing the gamble, diplomatically the threat and the need to counter that threat had become more imperative than ever. German hegemony over the European continent simply could not be countenanced without prejudicing Britain's continuing status as a great power or perhaps even its capacity to defend its national existence.[15] Thus British decisions in 1940 were supported by historical precedent. For the French Government to have decided other than it did would, in contrast, have involved embracing the unprecedented. What constitutes a nation's "best interests" can be debated ad inifinitum; but certainly at this point in European history the more abstract (to say nothing of mystical) components of national interest were not likely to have seemed terribly compelling to a beaten people. England, however, could afford—or thought it could—a last romantic fling. After the fall of France both British and French acted in accordance with their respective interpretations of the national interest. The immediate tragedy was that these were diametrically opposed, the greater that neither resignation nor defiance would be rewarded in the end but that both would be submerged in the overall eclipse of Europe that was the principal result of World War II.

# Appendices

# Leopold's Surrender

In view of Weygand's characterization of Leopold's decision to capitulate as an "act of desertion"; of Reynaud's claim that the Belgians had surrendered without warning, or even considering, the Allies who had risked their best armies to help them—and the French press's subsequent references to the Belgian monarch as the "felon king"; and of Churchill's abusive words to the Commons on June 4, it should be pointed out that Leopold's decision to ask terms of the Germans, which was activated at 5 p.m. on May 27, had been promptly communicated to the French and British missions at Belgian General Headquarters at 5:30, that it had been preceded by innumerable warnings, and that, in the upshot, the cease-fire order was not issued until 4 a.m. on May 28, while the Germans only resumed their attack on the British lines at 9:30 a.m. More to the point, as Gort's Chief of Staff admits, the Belgian surrender did not make for any immediate danger because the BEF's northern flank "was already pretty well catered for." Although it is true that no *formal* notification was given him before the armistice was requested, it is also true that Gort had virtually written off the Belgians as a lost cause at least seventy-two hours before and that he himself had earlier predicted their eventual surrender if a large-scale attack to the south was mounted. Therefore, his claim in the *Despatches* that the news of the surrender (learned from General Koeltz at 11 p.m. on May 27) was the "first intimation" he had received of the King's intention should not be accepted at face value. At 12:30 that day he had been sent, though he was not present to receive it, a message from Admiral Keyes stating that the moment was rapidly approaching when Belgian troops would no longer be able to fight and that the King wanted him to realize that he would be obliged to capitulate to avoid a débâcle. Anthony Eden makes it clear that the British were quite well informed about the situation in the north, chiefly through Sir Roger Keyes, the British War Cabinet's liaison officer with King Leopold. The Needham Mission dispatched the news of Leopold's forthcoming negotiations to the War Office at 5:54 p.m. and when Keyes telephoned the news to Churchill, as he points out, "the Prime Minister was not at all surprised."

The French were somewhat less well prepared. General Champon, Chief of the French Military Mission in Belgium, was unable to get through to Blanchard on May 27 but did succeed in informing Weygand by radio immediately after the King's decision was taken. Weygand claims that the news of the impending surrender fell like a thunderbolt; yet at noon on May 26 the Belgian Command had delivered a note to General Champon for Weygand to the effect that "the limits of [Belgian] resistance are close to being attained"; while Reynaud had been told the same day by the Belgian Foreign Minister, Paul-Henri Spaak, that the King had already formally expressed his intention to capitulate. Furthermore, as the American Ambassador to Belgium, John Cudahy, asserts, the French General Staff, like the British, had been kept fully advised in the few days preceding May 27 and knew that the Belgian King had no course but capitulation. General Champon, he says, "kept his superior officers in touch until the breaking off of communications."

As Sir Roger Keyes makes evident in his lengthy letter of 6 June to Lord Gort, and in the telegrams that accompanied it, he repeatedly warned both Gort and the government from May 20 onwards that King Leopold would be forced to capitulate if the British and Belgian armies became separated as the result of British participation in a southward drive. On May 25 Leopold himself informed Sir John Dill of the dangerous weakness in the Belgian lines and also wrote to George VI of England that Belgium's "means of resistance are now on the point of being totally destroyed." In this letter, he also set forth his intention of remaining in Belgium with his army and people after the capitulation, which he clearly adumbrated. That same night Keyes warned the Prime Minister that without further British support, particularly from the RAF, the Belgians would have to surrender in a day or so, a warning he repeated with even greater insistence the following night. Thus, it is safe to conclude that there was no real surprise on the part of either British or French when the long-foreseen Belgian surrender finally occurred, though General

Champon along with General Koeltz had rather foolishly misinterpreted their rude reception at Belgian headquarters and the warning the King's military adviser, General van Overstraeten, had conveyed to them during the afternoon of May 27.

If Leopold did not actually solicit the advice of his allies on this important question, it is equally true that the British did not inform him of their plans either. Gort did not tell Belgian headquarters of his decision on May 25 to retreat to the sea or of the evacuation orders he received from the War Office on the 26th. In fact, at the time of his decision to surrender—when Operation Dynamo was in full swing—Leopold had still not been officially informed of what was afoot, because Churchill's telegram to this effect (sent at 3 a.m. on May 27) reached Sir Roger Keyes only after his return to England on May 28 and consequently was never delivered to the King. Thus Leopold's unilateral decision to capitulate was preceded by the British cabinet's unilateral action by some twenty-four hours. See the loaded language, in reference to Leopold, used by *Paris Soir,* May 28, as transmitted by Ambassador Bullitt to Secretary Hull, May 28, in *FRUS,* 1940, I, p. 209; and selections quoted in Beau de Loménie, *La Mort de la Troisième République* (Paris, 1951), p. 266; the Gort-Keyes correspondence, together with Keyes's official messages, in Joseph P. Kennedy and James M. Landis, *The Surrender of King Leopold* (New York, 1950); also Cdt. Pierre Lyet, *La Bataille de France* (Paris, 1947), p. 108; H. R. Pownall, *Chief of Staff* (London, 1972), I, p. 365; WO 106/1731, Capitulation of Belgium, with a timetable of warnings given the British composed by G. M. D. Davy and an appreciation by J. G. Dill; also WO 106/1673, War Office Summary of Operations, May 10–31, 1940, for excerpts from Needham Mission dispatches; J. R. Colville, *Man of Valour* (London, 1972), p. 221; Gort, "Second Despatch," p. 5927; Anthony Eden, *Memoirs* (Boston, 1965), II, p. 128; J. Weygand, *The Role of General Weygand* (London, 1948), p. 75; Louis Thomas (ed.), *Documents sur la Guerre de 1939–1940* (Paris, 1941), pp. 192–93; General Koeltz's testimony and supporting documents, in *CE,* IX, pp. 2804–06, 2822–23; John Cudahy, *The Armies March* (New York, 1941), pp. 110–13; David Divine, *The Nine Days of Dunkirk* (New York, 1959), pp. 95–97, 239–40. Brian Bond's *France and Belgium, 1939–1940* (London, 1975), esp. pp. 144–56, is particularly good on the role of the Belgian Army and King Leopold.

# Churchill, Weygand, and the Breton Redoubt

Weygand had spoken out against this scheme repeatedly from the time it was first mooted on May 29. His argument was that, in the absence of advance planning, there would not be sufficient time or resources to organize a tolerable resistance along a 200-kilometer front, for which at least 15 divisions were essential. Whether, in spite of regarding the Breton redoubt as "a joke in very bad taste" and "no more than a phrase with nothing real at the back of it," Weygand actually "spared no effort to bring it into being" remains doubtful. See Maxime Weygand, *Recalled to Service* (London, 1952), pp. 148, 213–14; J. Weygand, *The Role of General Weygand* (London, 1948), pp. 88–89, 112; P.-A. Bourget, *De Beyrouth à Bordeaux* (Paris, 1946), pp. 81–82, 97–98; Paul Baudouin, *The Private Diaries of Paul Baudouin* (London, 1948), p. 94.

At any rate, Georges Mandel also opposed the idea of using Brittany as a governmental refuge, believing that no pretense could be made of governing France from a Breton port and that moreover all the military's efforts were needed to strengthen the line they had adopted. See Edward Spears, *Assignment to Catastrophe* (London, 1954), II, p. 98; Reynaud's testimony on Mandel's attitude, Dec. 12, 1950, in *CE*, VIII, p. 2400. On June 11 Reynaud's own military adviser, Lt.-Col. de Villelume, had actually ridiculed the idea of fighting on to the end in Brittany, telling him that it would be "very grand, very noble, very 'Götterdamerung' " but unfortunately a purely theatrical gesture. See his testimony, in *CE*, IX, pp. 2791–92. Admiral Darlan, according to Baudouin (p. 100), also thought Brittany indefensible. General de Gaulle, on the other hand, favored the Breton redoubt idea, not because he had illusions as to the possibility of holding out there, but because he felt the government's removal to Quimper would be "a stage on the way to decisions of energy." See Charles de Gaulle, *The Complete War Memoirs of Charles de Gaulle* (New York, 1964), p. 67.

It is also worth noting that none of the British except General Spears shared Churchill's enthusiasm for the Brittany project. Sir John Dill thought the peninsula too far from England to be adequately defended by the RAF (Spears, II, p. 129), while General Ismay, who described the plan as a fantasy, felt that it would only mean another evacuation. See Hastings Lionel Ismay, *The Memoirs of General Lord Ismay* (New York, 1960), p. 143. In fact, although requested by the Prime Minister on June 2 to develop a scheme for the maintenance of a bridgehead in Brittany, the Chiefs of Staff thought so little of the idea that they refused to refer the question to the Inter-Service Planning Staff. See COS (40) 419, June 2; COS (40) 436 (JP), also JP (40) 228, June 7. Yet in spite of the generally low esteem in which the plan was held, under pressure from Reynaud some halting steps were taken to construct a Breton redoubt and the idea lingered on till mid-June.

It again created difficulties between the Allies at the time General Brooke started pulling remaining British troops out of France instead of sending them to man the Brittany line in conformity with Weygand's orders. At this point, June 14, Churchill claimed that there was *no* agreement between the two governments on the Brittany scheme, whereas General Weygand seemed to think Reynaud and Churchill had reached just such an agreement on June 11. For the apparent reversal of Churchill's and Weygand's positions vis-à-vis the defense of Brittany three days after the Briare conference, see the somewhat tendentious "M. Churchill et le projet breton," in *Écrits de Paris* (March 1949), pp. 58–74, where the bad faith of Churchill and Dill in connection with the military decisions taken on June 14 is contrasted with Weygand's supposed loyalty. However, the anonymous author of this article nowhere alludes to the fact that on June 12 and 13 Weygand had asked his government to initiate armistice negotiations, a development which of necessity affected British attitudes on the 14th.

What seems to have happened is that at Briare Churchill suggested that the problem of an Atlantic bridgehead be studied jointly by the French and British staffs, though the idea could not have been taken seriously by Dill in view of the reservations General Weygand had expressed regarding the value of the redoubt. See the French *procès-verbal* of the June 11 meeting, submitted by General Weygand to the Committee of Inquiry, in *CE*, VI, p. 1896; and Spears, II, p. 158. In exoneration of the British, Spears furthermore notes (II, p. 208) that at Tours on June 13 Reynaud had stated that it was now too late to organize a defense of Brittany, although French troops were still being directed there. Weygand's argument rests on his claim that his orders to construct the Breton redoubt "had been confirmed by M. Reynaud in the presence of British Government representatives"; also that, from the confused discussions in the French Council of Ministers on June 13, he had "gathered that work there [Brittany] was to be continued"; and that he had Reynaud's note of the 13th reconfirming the plan of retreat on Brittany to which he had responded affirmatively only that day (June 14). See J. Weygand, *Role*, pp. 132, 136, 141; Bourget, p. 120; Louis Noguères, *Le Véritable Procès du Maréchal Pétain*, p. 96; and Weygand's testimony in *CE*, VI, p. 1815.

*C*

---

# *Mme Hélène de Portes*

Among the large army of diplomats, politicians, and journalists who have documented the last days of the French Republic Reynaud virtually alone fails to mention, or even to allude to, Mme de Portes in any of the memoirs (or court testimony) he has chosen to produce—perhaps the most fitting tribute to the formidable lady who played such a vital role in his life. Many, however, have seen in her the key to Reynaud's somewhat erratic behavior from mid-May to mid-June of 1940.

Camille Chautemps, perhaps the chief spokesman for this school of thought, hints broadly at the part played by Hélène de Portes when he writes: "In observing his [Reynaud's] reactions and those of his intimates at the moment of our first reverses, in analyzing his decisions, of which the least that can be said is that they did not measure up to events, we see born the psychological drama which, tragically, was going to dominate his life at the crucial moment and which no doubt will be for the historian the true key to the enigma of the armistice." See *Cahiers secrets de l'Armistice* (Paris, 1963), p. 93. In fact, virtually all the explanations offered by the ex-Vice-Premier for Reynaud's actions or inaction hark back to this *cherchez la femme* thesis. A less hostile critic than M. Chautemps, Jules Roy in *The Trial of Marshal Pétain* (New York, 1968), p. 63, sums up this position: "For M. Paul Reynaud, who was intelligence incarnate, the drama was being played out, not only on the national stage, but also in his heart. Mme de Portes was his courage. Isn't it reasonable to suppose that without her he weakened in his turn, despite de Gaulle?" Roy suggests that, inasmuch as unexpected results can issue from such extraofficial relations, the private lives of statesmen should be considered fair game for historical judgment.

409

Who was Hélène de Portes, and what were her politics and powers? According to the journalist Pierre Lazareff, throughout the 1930s she had shown a fondness for fascism and had even for a time flirted with royalism. She was an appeaser with a vengeance, as were most of her friends, with a particular interest in bringing about closer relations between Italy and France. Essentially, though, her political interests were impulsive and frivolous and certainly subordinate to her one overriding ambition, which was to advance the career of Paul Reynaud, with whom she had been openly allied for almost a decade. See *Deadline* (New York, 1942), pp. 210–15, 249–51.

Reynaud, at any rate, seems never to have been affected by her fashionable ideological enthusiasms, having been an opponent of Nazi aggression since 1935, a staunch supporter of alliances with both England and Russia, and a leading anti-Munichois. But this is not to say that she was without political influence. Principally, her influence was felt in the realm of appointments made by Reynaud and, especially during the débâcle, with respect to overtures made to Italy. By all accounts she can be credited with the ouster of Gaston Palewski, one of the intransigents around Reynaud, from his position as Reynaud's *chef de cabinet* as well as with the later addition—as Reynaud's staff military adviser—of Colonel de Villelume, who was considered something of a defeatist and right-wing opportunist; with the rapid rise to political prominence of Paul Baudouin, who conferred with her practically every day; with the dismissal of Alexis Léger from the Ministry of Foreign Affairs and his replacement by Charles-Roux; and with the June 5 cabinet appointments of Jean Prouvost and Yves Bouthillier. See, for instance, Lazareff, pp. 263–64, 272–74, 276, 280–81, 290–94; Elie J. Bois, *Truth on the Tragedy of France* (London, 1941), pp. 236–41, 294, 322–23, 355, 370, 372; Léon Guerdan, *Je les ai tous connus* (New York, 1942), pp. 46–48; Pertinax, *The Gravediggers of France* (Garden City, N.Y., 1944), pp. 189–90, 235, 237–38, 244, 246, 250, 255, 308; *The Diplomatic Diaries of Oliver Harvey, 1937–1940,* ed. by John Harvey (London, 1970), pp. 341, 373, 380.

But these successes were by no means the sum of her achievement. From a host of sources come accounts of her continuous on-stage interferences with the machinery of government at the very highest levels. Of these Vincent Sheean's, in *Between the Thunder and the Sun* (New York, 1943), p. 107, is probably the most comprehensive. He writes:

The whole story of Mme. de Portes almost defies belief. We are told that she presided over meetings of the General Staff, invaded the Supreme War Council, broke up cabinet sessions at will, prepared state papers for Reynaud, dismissed generals and reproved ambassadors in a way which even Mme. de Maintenon or Mme. de Pompadour would have found impossible. The evidence in this matter is overwhelming. If it were not so unanimous and so voluminous we might be inclined to doubt it, but there is no doubt possible. I have been told by persons in the highest positions (cabinet ministers, ambassadors and the like) that this woman behaved at times like a sovereign, at times like a fishwife, but at all times as if she had some vested right, whether constitutional or divine, in the government of the French Republic.

"In the end she will be shot," Ambassador Bullitt told President Roosevelt in a June 6 letter relating her most recent intrusions—at the same time observing that he thought the President "would like to know that there is still some continuity in French life, and that the mistress of the ruler again directs the State as she has since time immemorial." See *For the President, Personal and Secret,* ed. by Orville H. Bullitt (Boston, 1972), pp. 452–53. Other detailed references to her—which can be found in the pages of Jeanneney's *Journal Politique* (Paris, 1972), p. 68 and *passim;* General Spears's *Assignment to Catastrophe* (London, 1954), I, pp. 90–92; II, pp. 190, 195–96, 228, 280, 293; Lazareff; Pertinax; and Robert de Saint Jean, *France Speaking* (New York, 1941), pp. 271, 300, 309—merely confirm the picture. Among reporters, only Emmanuel Berl, in *La fin de la III<sup>e</sup> République* (Paris, 1968), pp. 54, 60, 68, 144, presents a more attractive portrait, but his vignettes unfortunately lack depth.

It is generally agreed that Mme de Portes was most industrious and influential following France's military reverses in May. We know that she was thoroughly defeatist by May 16, that she actively supported her friend Anatole de Monzie's intrigues vis-à-vis Italy, that she tried to sabotage de Gaulle's influence over Reynaud, that she pleaded constantly for an armistice, and that she became increasingly anti-British as France's position worsened. Sir Robert Vansittart, who rather unkindly refers to her as a "poisonous and promiscuous trull" who had always harmed Britain to the best of her abilities, in fact, accuses her of being "largely responsible for Reynaud's complete moral dégringolade." See FO 371/24311, C 7541, Note to Lord Halifax and Duff Cooper from R. V., June 28. And H. Freeman Matthews, First Secretary of the American Embassy, to whom Hélène de Portes openly applied on June 15 in an effort to get him to urge Reynaud to ask for an armistice, also classes her high among the strains and defeatist pressures under which Reynaud finally caved in. See William L. Langer, *Our Vichy Gamble* (New York, 1966), p. 35. Her influence is not assessed differently by Charles Pomaret (despite his fondness) in the pages he devotes to her relationship with Reynaud in *Le Dernier Témoin* (Paris, 1968), pp. 88–98.

A generally demoralizing effect on Reynaud, then, can certainly be inferred from her endless round of activity. What cannot be proven is the precise influence she wielded over the specific decisions taken by Reynaud, who was, after all, subject to a number of other powerful influences, not least of which was the influence of events themselves. There is no doubt that in making any assessment of Reynaud's character weight should be given Mme de Portes, but, however extraordinary a figure she cut and however convenient to turn to her for an explanation of his deepest motivations, it nevertheless must be conceded that equally valid explanations for Paul Reynaud's behavior can be found elsewhere. Therefore, the most one can say with certainty regarding Hélène de Portes's "influence on history" is that she probably contributed sizably to the ambivalence the Premier was already disposed to feel in a situation that was characterized above all by ambivalence.

Mme de Portes—ironically, as some see it—was killed instantly in an automobile accident on June 28, 1940, as she and Reynaud were driving through Languedoc near the Mediterranean town of Sète. By her premature death she has helped sustain one of the continuing mysteries of the period. Vincent Sheean's final words on her constitute a cruel but insightful epitaph: " . . . nobody seems to have found the lady attractive. She has been described . . . as a middle-aged woman, with a shrill voice and a clamorous, demanding manner, who chatted like a magpie and lost her temper with ease. She was not chic, she was not charming and she was not intelligent. Paul Reynaud was used to her, depended upon her, needed her: that was all." See p. 114.

# *Reynaud's Last Appeal to Roosevelt*

Reynaud's motives in making his last appeal to Roosevelt have been impugned by many critics, not all of whom can be considered his political enemies. But among the latter, Alfred Fabre-Luce sees in the maneuver simply a delaying tactic whereby Reynaud hoped to postpone what he knew to be inevitable, namely, "the brutal sundering, under the knife of events, of the two Siamese sisters: France—England." See *Journal de la France* (Ain, 1940), pp. 348–49. Reynaud himself would not deny that he was playing for time, but Camille Chautemps in addition suggests that he was playing for time precisely so as to *ensure* the failure of his war policy because the American response, which Chautemps claims was known in advance by the President of the Council, could only "underline the isolation of France and the chimerical character of her resistance." Because on June 13 Reynaud had nothing to fear from debate, Chautemps argues, to delay the government's decision until after Roosevelt's answer had been received was simply to play into the hands of the opposition, as the American refusal would furnish one more argument to the partisans of an armistice. See *Cahiers secrets de l'Armistice,* pp. 134–36.

The American Secretary of State, Cordell Hull, is hardly kinder. Basing his opinion on information received from Ambassador Bullitt, who was in turn influenced by the just-fired Alexis Léger, he concludes that Reynaud's final appeal "for an American declaration of war, without which France would fall" was made purely for the record. "We had made every effort to convince him of the impossibility of such a declaration by Congress at that time," writes Hull, "but he had determined to make the appeal just the same." As early as

May 18 Reynaud had wanted to make a dramatic appeal but had
been deflected by Bullitt's pointing out to him that such a statement
would be not only "without physical force" but "far worse than
useless." In the meantime he had contrived to send several lesser
appeals to Roosevelt, including an urgent request on May 28 that the
US Atlantic fleet be sent to the Mediterranean and the appeal on June
10 for the President to state publicly that the United States would
support the Allies by all means short of an expeditionary force. See
*The Memoirs of Cordell Hull* (New York, 1948), Vol. I, pp. 767–68,
773–74, 787–88; and Bullitt's dispatches to the Secretary of State,
May 18, 5 p.m. and 10 p.m.; May 28, 1 p.m. and 9 p.m.; June 10, 6
p.m., in *FRUS,* 1940, I (1959), pp. 227–30, 234, 236–37, 245–46.

Messrs. Langer and Gleason, however, feel that Hull's interpretation of Reynaud's efforts vis-à-vis Roosevelt (that he was simply
posturing for the sake of his reputation in history) is not quite fair
because Reynaud could not be expected to know the limits public
opinion imposed on the American President. See *The Challenge to
Isolation, 1937–1940* (New York, 1952), pp. 539–40. Reynaud
apparently rated Roosevelt's moral influence over Congress much
higher than it actually was, and he may not have known (or may
have chosen to forget) that Roosevelt had already told Daladier before him that any American entry into the war was out of the question before the presidential election of 1940. See Daladier's testimony, June 4, 1947, in *CE,* I, p. 66. Furthermore, he may have
expected that his own logic with respect to America's real interests
(that is, should France and England be defeated, "in the near future
the United States itself would be menaced as directly and completely
as France was today") would ultimately carry the day. It is at least
reasonable to give Reynaud the benefit of the doubt on this score. It
is also quite possible that, in spite of what he had been told, his inner
beliefs and hopes had something in common with those of the average Frenchman. Clare Boothe writes in this connection: "I never met
a single man on the street or a single man in high authority in France
who wasn't utterly convinced that if France ever should be on the
verge of defeat, Mr. Bullitt would prevail upon Mr. Roosevelt, and
then Mr. Roosevelt, their greatest and best American propagandist,
would bring a recalcitrant America quickly to heel and pour all its
enormous resources into the breach." The American Ambassador, as
Ms. Boothe points out, was at this time commonly considered the
most powerful man in France, a sort of gray eminence who was
believed to have made certain tacit commitments towards France on

behalf of Roosevelt, with whom he was very close. See *Europe in the Spring* (New York, 1940), pp. 123–24, 184. Under the circumstances, making the effort must certainly have seemed worthwhile to Reynaud no matter how slim the chances.

See also Lt.-Col. de Villelume's testimony in *CE,* IX, pp. 2791, 2793, for the origins of Reynaud's appeal, its dramatic language, and its possible uses in case of refusal (as a means of inducing the United States to play a mediating role); and Édouard Herriot, *Épisodes* (Paris, 1950), p. 65, for Jeanneney's warning of the danger in Reynaud's having declared that France must come to terms if the United States did not enter the war. For the final message, see Reynaud, *In the Thick of the Fight* (New York, 1955), pp. 508–09; and *FRUS,* 1940, I, pp. 252–54, transmitted by the Deputy Ambassador in France, Anthony J. Drexel Biddle, with commentaries, at noon on June 14.

Reynaud's public broadcast on the night of June 13, in which he called on the United States to give France a hope of common victory, is, however, more questionable, though Reynaud defended it on the grounds that it was necessary to prepare the French people for the transfer of the government overseas; and Mandel and Jeanneney had helped in outlining it. See Reynaud, p. 507; Jules Jeanneney, *Journal politique* (Paris, 1972), p. 66. See also Pierre Lazareff, *Deadline* (New York, 1942), pp. 301–02, for the newspaper world's, particularly the American correspondents', adverse reaction to Reynaud's pleas to America.

# The Possibility
# of a Coup in Bordeaux

Inasmuch as Reynaud does not marshal much hard, or legally impressive, evidence to justify such a fear, it is understandable that the instructions preceding the Pétain trial in 1945 and the Weygand case of 1946–47 should both have concluded that no military plot to overthrow the regime actually existed in 1940. However, their verdict does not absolve the military in general or Weygand in particular from responsibility in bringing about the armistice, which in turn paved the way for the French Republic's overthrow. It merely indicates that Weygand's behavior, in the words of Philip Bankwitz, represented "too complex a phenomenon to be explained on the simplistic grounds of plots or even of the quite special pressures of the hour alone." To the contrary, his acts in 1940 (his violent outbursts and partisan stance, his flagrant disobedience, his refusal to resign, his apparent avidity for bringing to a head the incipient clash between army and government—in sum, his rejection of any solution short of an armistice or his own destitution) were but the climax of a decade of political involvement in which he had repeatedly and successfully used techniques of intimidation to determine policy against a weakened civil authority that did not have the confidence to bring the Command to heel because it recognized that the preponderance of real power lay with France's armed forces. "Military pressure was indeed responsible for the demoralization and collapse of the Reynaud government," Bankwitz concludes, "but the soldiers did not have to put a plot into operation to achieve their aims. The elements of the problem itself made it certain that Weygand's strategical concepts would go virtually unchallenged. Because of this abnormal situation in which Weygand dominated the civil power and commanded the Army's support, Pétain could easily bring about the armistice that the General desired." On conspiracies, see Reynaud's testimony, Aug. 1, 1945, in *Procès Pétain,* p. 439; *La France a sauvé l' Europe* (Paris, 1947), II, pp. 443–46; and *Mémoires* (Paris, 1963), II, pp. 438–40; and for Weygand's concept of the civil-military relationship and his contributions to undermining the regime from 1919 to 1940, see Bankwitz's *Maxime Weygand and Civil-Military Relations in Modern France* (Cambridge, Mass., 1967), esp. pp. 32–33, 35, 62, 167, 292, 305, 312, 356–57.

That the potential for a coup existed and could not be overlooked by Reynaud or other cabinet members who opposed an armistice is emphasized by John M. Sherwood in *Georges Mandel and the Third Republic* (Stanford, Calif., 1970), pp. 247–48, 253. Weygand's supporters, he writes, "were aware of the revolutionary nature of his acts" and, in expectation that the government would retaliate by arresting him or Pétain, had "appealed for protection to the commanding general of the Bordeaux region, who complied by placing guards at strategic points around the city." At the same time, June 15, General Lafont made himself virtually military dictator of the region by applying the full provisions of a state of siege, which thus gave him absolute control over the police forces of the area—heretofore under the jurisdiction of the Minister of the Interior, Mandel, who consequently had no forces at his disposal even for the maintenance of order. Thus, Reynaud and Mandel were deprived of the necessary power with which to back up any radical measures they might decide to take, while General Lafont's first loyalty was to his friends, the Generalissimo and the Marshal, not to the government. What Weygand's next move would have been had Reynaud fired him outright cannot be known with certainty, but it is not generally believed that he would have retired quietly. Even in the absence of a proven plot, a prerevolutionary situation was certainly present in Bordeaux in mid-June 1940.

After the war it would be simple for Weygand to claim that Reynaud had only to throw him out in order to proceed with his policy and that if the Premier failed to do so it was because he was acting by default or because the government was "female," whereas he, Weygand, was "male." Yet in 1940 Weygand was deliberately daring the government to pit its constitutional authority, which was theoretically unlimited, against the actual power exercised by the military. Furthermore, the government was divided, largely through his efforts, which thus made it all the more imperative to arrive at decisions by time-consuming democratic methods. That Weygand had no need of a coup d'état is therefore no proof at all that it was not legitimately to be feared or that it might not have been mounted at a moment's notice had the need arisen. For the General's thoughts on Reynaud and the choices open to the government at this time, see his testimony, in *CE*, VI, pp. 1759, 1785, 1820, 1826–27, 1837–38, 1841, 1844, where his intemperance and antipathy to democratic functioning are amply illustrated.

# F

# *Behind the Chautemps Proposal*

Whether Chautemps was "sincere" in making his proposal, and what that sincerity might have consisted of, has been much disputed. Léon Blum's postwar acceptance of Chautemps's explanations was undoubtedly influenced by his knowledge of the effect of the maneuver on members of the government who had been active resisters up to that point and who were as a result won over to the idea that a demand for the enemy's conditions was necessary to arouse the nation, and that their inevitable harshness would actually facilitate the government's transfer and pursuit of the war. See Blum's testimony, July 27, 1945, in *Procès Pétain,* pp. 235–36, and July 30, 1947, in *CE,* I, p. 261. Blum's socialist colleague, Joseph Paul-Boncour, in any event was more dubious: he thought Chautemps and Frossard too well advised not to have known in advance what the final outcome of their maneuver would be. See *Entre Deux Guerres* (Paris, 1946), Vol. III, pp. 225–26.

Reynaud claims that in mid-June he still believed his vice-premier to be basically in agreement with him on the necessity of fighting on, even overseas—Chautemps had stated as much to both Reynaud and Mandel in late May—and assumed that he could count on his cooperation in a crisis. He therefore "put his change of face down to his weakness." See Reynaud, *In the Thick of the Fight* (New York, 1955), pp. 522–24; and Reynaud's testimony on this point, July 24, 1945, in *Procès Pétain,* pp. 62–63; and Dec. 12, 1950, in *CE,* VIII, p. 2401. However, it is difficult to believe that Reynaud could have been completely ignorant of Chautemps's part in promoting an armistice over the past three weeks, especially after his interpellation of

June 12, which Reynaud had not discouraged, and the obvious impatience with Reynaud's delaying tactics he had manifested on June 13.

Chautemps may well have been sincere in wanting to preserve the unity of the government and, with it, civilian control, but, considering his record as a pacifist at any price from the Rhineland crisis on and the fact that he had been one of the principal supporters of the Munich agreement, he was probably also sincere about wanting to come to terms with the Germans and evidently thought this could be done. General Spears, at any rate, gave no credence whatsoever to Chautemps's stated intentions, seeing him instead as a "subtle dialectician, who did not for a moment believe in the thesis he defended with so much eloquence" and concluding that "If ever a man knowingly and of malice aforethought sold his colleagues and his country it was Chautemps." See Edward Spears, *Assignment to Catastrophe* (London, 1954), II, p. 271. This judgment probably errs on the harsh side—Chautemps was at least not ideologically predisposed towards fascism or authoritarianism of any kind. To his credit, if not to his consistency, Chautemps during the following week would seem to have abandoned his thesis, in that from June 18 to 20 he strongly supported the government's removal to North Africa, even before a response from the Germans had been received. He also offered his resignation to Pétain on June 26. See also Elie Bois, *Truth on the Tragedy of France* (London, 1941), pp. 365–68, for an analysis of Chautemps's character; and the defense offered by his son, Jean Chautemps (who claims his father was anti-armistice), in Édouard Bonnefous, *Histoire Politique de la Troisième République,* VII (Paris, 1967), pp. 367–71.

# The Case
# of the Elusive Telegrams

Exactly when on June 16 the British Government's decision to release France conditionally from the no-separate-peace agreement was first conveyed to Reynaud remains a problem. Churchill in *The Second World War* (New York, 1961–62), II, pp. 175–77, writes that telegram No. 368 (on the French fleet) only repeated textually instructions that had been telephoned to the Ambassador in the morning and the substance of which Campbell had already transmitted to Reynaud orally. Bouthillier, in *Le Drame de Vichy* (Paris, 1950), I, pp. 83–84, Marin, in "Contribution à l'Étude des Prodromes de l'Armistice," *RHDGM* (June 1951), p. 15, and Reynaud himself in *La France*, II, pp. 347–49, and *In the Thick of the Fight*, pp. 534–35, all place this oral communication at about 12:30 (after the morning Council of Ministers) and the actual delivery of the telegram confirming the message sometime later in the afternoon. However, General Spears makes no allusion to any oral communication of this nature, though he reports in detail his and the Ambassador's conversations with Reynaud. The only morning conversation reported revolved around Britain's refusal to condone any separate negotiations. In fact, Spears notes his surprise and distress on receiving the message, as if this were his first knowledge of the cabinet's decision. It could be that he is simply telescoping into one event both the oral communication and the delivery of the telegram itself. A further complication is introduced by the fact that Spears claims that he and Campbell first consulted with the President of the Senate before approaching Reynaud with the British condition, whereas Jeanneney claims to have talked with the two men about Churchill's message at 3 p.m., at which time he implies he already knew Reynaud's reaction to it! See Spears, *Assignment to Catastrophe* (London, 1954), II, pp. 281–84; Jules Jeanneney, *Journal politique* (Paris, 1972), pp. 71–72.

As for the physical disposal of both London telegrams, Reynaud in his memoirs, p. 536, writes that an hour after the second telegram had been communicated to him the Ambassador and Spears came to ask him to return both messages, telling him that the British Government had changed its mind. Here he seems to be referring to the "message" sent to him at the Council mentioned by Spears (II, p. 294), though alternatively he may be referring to a preliminary oral communication followed by the Englishmen's personal delivery and withdrawal of the telegrams. In his testimony before the Commission of Inquiry in 1950, however, Reynaud specified that Campbell and Spears had withdrawn the telegrams at 4:15, half an hour after de Gaulle's telephone call and 45 minutes before the Council was to meet. Here, he places the delivery and withdrawal of both telegrams at the same time, saying that it was in the course of Campbell's *second* visit that afternoon. See *CE*, VIII, pp. 2428–29. If this sequence has any validity, and is not just the product of confusion, it may mean that there had been an oral communication of the contents of the first telegram in the late morning or a little after noon, a second oral communication in mid-afternoon of the contents of the second telegram, and the actual delivery and withdrawal of both telegrams around 4, sometime in the hour before the Council met. Moreover, it is not inconsistent with the timing of the telephoned suspension order (3:10) relating to the first telegram (No. 368), which the Ambassador and Spears may have known before seeing Reynaud a bit after 4, and it would not be inconsistent with some sort of message cancelling both telegrams having been sent round to Reynaud at the Council, or immediately before it, even though both telegrams had been physically withdrawn already. This sequence of events is much less simple than that given by Spears, who speaks only of two communications in the course of two afternoon visits (the second placed at 4:05) and who says nothing at all as to the material withdrawal of the documents. However, Spears's account does not conform with what either Churchill or Jeanneney (indirectly) say concerning the dissemination of the British Government's first message. Sir Ronald Campbell is even less helpful in his Final Report: he mentions that he received the telegrams in the afternoon and that he and General Spears delivered the messages as soon as they were deciphered; however, he refers to only one meeting in the afternoon (during which de Gaulle called). See FO 371/24311, C 7541, paras. 32–33; also C 7294/G, No. 428 DIPP from Campbell by telephone, 7 p.m., June 16. The exact chronology of successive events on June 16 resists precision, and the full story of the disappearing telegrams must remain one of the more intriguing mysteries connected with that historic day.

# Reynaud's Cabinet:
# Rundown on the Armistice

Whether or not a majority in favor of an armistice existed in the Council of Ministers on the night of June 16 has been the subject of protracted and heated controversy. Pertinax states that at this point 13 ministers (not counting Baudouin, an undersecretary) supported the Chautemps proposal, while 11 opposed it, but gives no rundown on which ministers actually favored an armistice per se. Baudouin and Bouthillier in their books claim only that a strong majority favored the Chautemps resolution, the greater number of ministers not wishing to embark for North Africa before knowing whether the armistice conditions would be acceptable or not. But under questioning by the Commission of Inquiry Baudouin subsequently admitted that at least 10 ministers were opposed to an armistice: Reynaud, Marin, Delbos, Campinchi, Rio, Monnet, Dautry, Julien, Mandel, and Sérol; 2 (Laurent-Eynac and Rollin) he thought "neutral," though not pro-armistice; 1 (Queuille) was hesitant but leaning against; 1 (Pernot) was hesitant but leaning in favor; while there was still another (Tellier) about whom he could say nothing. Thus, with 13 ministers who can be assigned to the anti-armistice columns, Baudouin's majority disappears. Frossard in 1941 also stated that if a vote had been taken the pro-armistice forces would have received a majority of votes, yet mentions only 12, including Baudouin, who were either for or leaning towards an armistice.

Louis Marin, however, contests that at this point there was a majority for anything, because the question before the ministers was quite different from what it had been the evening before. A strong majority had favored the Chautemps proposal on June 15, but now Reynaud had indicated that the British cabinet refused to consent to

France's demanding the conditions of an armistice. Therefore, without expressly consulting each minister, it was impossible to infer that the majority of the previous evening still existed for the act of asking Germany's armistice conditions without England's agreement. According to Charles Pomaret, Minister of Labor, who was himself in favor of an armistice, at the moment of Reynaud's resignation a majority actually existed against an armistice. Ranked definitely against an armistice by Pomaret are Reynaud, Marin, Mandel, Campinchi, Delbos, Rollin, Laurent-Eynac, Jullien, Rio, Thellier, Dautry, and Monnet—12; for, Pétain, Chautemps, Ybarnegaray, Bouthillier, Prouvost, Frossard, Pomaret, and Baudouin—8; hesitant, but rather against an armistice, Sérol, Queuille, and Pernot—3; hesitant, but more in favor of an armistice, Rivière and Chichery—2; in other words, a total of 15 against and 10 for. But, as Marin points out, Baudouin, as Under-Secretary of State to the Presidency of the Council, should be subtracted from the total as he did not attend Council meetings as a minister but merely in his capacity as secretary. Furthermore, on the basis of personal conversations, Marin ranks Sérol, Queuille, and Pernot as strongly opposed to an armistice.

Alphonse Rio's count is virtually identical with that made by Pomaret; subtracting only Pernot, whom he thought undecided, from the anti-armistice group, he arrives at the figure 14 against as opposed to 10 for. Georges Monnet thought Rio's figures technically correct as far as a vote strictly for or against an armistice or a vote on a question of confidence were concerned, but believed there was an intermediate level of ministers who while not for an armistice nevertheless did not exclude the possibility of entering into negotiations. Laurent-Eynac's and Dautry's counts pretty much conform with those made by Marin and Pomaret, though Dautry's sweeping qualifications tend to moot the whole question. Of those who opposed an armistice, only Louis Rollin, apart from Reynaud, saw the cabinet as more or less equally divided on the issue; he counted 10 against the armistice (but forgot to mention Campinchi); did not know about Queuille or Delbos; and considered Pernot undecided. He mentions 12 who supported an armistice, among them Sérol, but also includes 2 (Baudouin and Février) who should be discounted.

According to Albert Kammerer, who adds both Queuille and Pernot to the pro-armistice group, the figure tallies at 13 against and 11 for an armistice if the count is limited only to ministers, but if Baudouin is counted then the figure drops to 13 opposed and 12 for, a slim majority of one against an armistice. But outside the Council of

Ministers were the two presidents of the assemblies, Jeanneney and Herriot, and the President of the Republic, Albert Lebrun, all of whom opposed an armistice. Kammerer therefore concludes that inasmuch as the partisans of an armistice always remained in the minority they were able to carry the day only because of the dominant ascendancy of the military element—the tremendous prestige enjoyed by Weygand and Pétain.

Although Reynaud apparently believed at the time that he had been beaten and was in the minority, he subsequently testified at the Pétain trial in 1945 and before the Commission of Inquiry in 1950 that the question of whether a majority existed or not was not the essential one. What *was* important was that a new government had become a necessity because a president of the Council who, on a vital issue, has against him his two vice-presidents and a large number of ministers can no longer govern even *with* a majority and therefore *must* resign. The Chautemps proposal had, in effect, put him in an untenable position. Raoul Dautry certainly agreed that he could not have continued with such a divided government and that it was necessary for him to resign, while Rollin bluntly stated that in the circumstances, with both vice-presidents and all the military chiefs against him, it was morally and materially impossible for Reynaud to have remained at the head of the government.

Chautemps thus seems more than a little disingenuous in claiming that the anti-armistice forces would have won a clear victory if the Council had been able to vote directly on the problem of the armistice and if, in addition, Reynaud had placed before his colleagues the question of confidence and made known to them that what was at stake was the survival or dislocation of the French Government. It is debatable first of all whether President Lebrun would have permitted this—given his personal predilection for the Chautemps proposal together with the fact that it had been raised first and accepted by a majority—and second of all whether it would have been possible to cast aside Pétain and Chautemps (or Weygand from his post) even had Reynaud emerged with that 15-9 majority Marin insists he had on the basic question. Their activity outside the Council—backed by the military and an increasingly hostile public opinion—might well have made any real government impossible and shortly brought about that very dissolution which Reynaud sensed had already occurred by June 15–16.

On this question, see Pertinax, *The Gravediggers of France* (Garden City, N.Y., 1944), p. 306; *The Private Diaries of Paul Bau-*

*douin* (London, 1948), p. 117; Yves Bouthillier, *Le Drame de Vichy* (Paris, 1950), I, pp. 88–89; Baudouin's testimony, July 12, 1949, in *CE,* VII, p. 2068; Paul Reynaud, *In the Thick of the Fight* (New York, 1955), p. 543 (for Frossard); Louis Marin, "Contribution à l'Étude des Prodromes de l'Armistice," *RHDGM* (June 1951), pp. 19, 22–23; Pomaret, *Le Dernier Témoin* (Paris, 1968), pp. 61–65; Lebrun's testimony, June 17, 1948, *CE,* IV, pp. 1088–89; M.-M. Tony-Révillon, *Mes Carnets* (Paris, 1945), pp. 21–22 (for Mandel's 14–10 anti-armistice count on the night of June 15); Rio's testimony, Dec. 16, 1948, *CE,* V, p. 1321; Monnet's testimony, Feb. 3, 1949, *CE,* V, pp. 1425, 1428–29; Laurent-Eynac's testimony, Feb. 8, 1949, *CE,* V, pp. 1453–54; Dautry's testimony, Jan. 18, 1949, *CE,* VII, pp. 2028–32, 2034; Rollin's testimony, Jan. 20, 1949, *CE,* V, pp. 1394, 1397, 1402–03; Kammerer, *La Vérité sur l'Armistice* (Paris, 1945), pp. 209–12; Jules Roy, *The Trial of Marshal Pétain* (New York, 1968), p. 58; Louis Noguères, *Le Véritable Procès du Maréchal Pétain* (Paris, 1955), p. 114; Reynaud's testimony, July 24 and 26, 1945, in *Procès Pétain,* pp. 67, 226; and Dec. 12, 1950, in *CE,* VIII, pp. 2421–22 (including Marin's interpellations); Camille Chautemps, *Cahiers secrets de l'Armistice* (Paris, 1963), p. 171. As for Pernot's final position, he admitted to Jules Jeanneney on July 5, 1940, that though he had originally been for resistance *à outrance,* once the armistice question had been put to a voice vote at Bordeaux he had resigned himself to it—out of consideration for France's demographic weakness. See Jeanneney, *Journal politique* (Paris, 1972), p. 90.

# *Reynaud's Resignation*

A number of Reynaud's colleagues were surprised, and even outraged, by his unorthodox method of stepping down, as they had thought the final decision would be made only after the Council reassembled at 10. Some had resolved to demand a vote at that time and even to refuse to hand in their resignations if this was denied. See Blum's testimony, July 27, 1945, in *Procès Pétain*, p. 236; also the evidence given by various members of Reynaud's cabinet before the Commission of Inquiry: Rio, *CE*, V, pp. 1321–22; Rollin, V, pp. 1403–04; Monnet, V, pp. 1428–29; Laurent-Eynac, V, pp. 1456–57; Dautry, VII, pp. 1973, 2033; and Marin, in the course of Lebrun's testimony, IV, pp. 1080, 1082–83, and in the course of Reynaud's testimony, VIII, pp. 2424–25; also Marin, "Contribution à l'Étude des Prodromes de l' Armistice," *RHDGM* (June 1951), pp. 18 and 21–22; and Pomaret, *Le Dernier Témoin* (Paris, 1968), p. 81.

Reynaud himself has taken different positions on different occasions as to what actually occurred, on July 24, 1945, claiming to have stated to his colleagues that they would reunite at 10 for the express purpose of resigning, but in his memoirs emphasizing rather his desire for a suspension of the session so that he could discuss the matter with President Lebrun with a view to obtaining the latter's permission to reshuffle his cabinet once more. See Reynaud's testimony in *Procès Pétain*, p. 67; Reynaud, *In the Thick of the Fight* (New York, 1955), pp. 543, 545, 553; *La France a sauvé l'Europe* (Paris, 1947), II, p. 355; and *Mémoires* (Paris, 1963), II, p. 432.

Baudouin (p. 117) and Bouthillier (I, p. 90) both claim that the government had in effect resigned by 7, though they were later forced to back down from this bald position before the Commission of Inquiry and to qualify their stands somewhat (see Baudouin's testimony in *CE,* VII, pp. 2128–29; Bouthillier's, VIII, pp. 2488–90, 2497); while Frossard, in 1941, wrote that " 'on leaving the Presidency each Minister knew that the Council had met for the last time' and that it was 'without surprise' that they learned two hours later that the Pétain Administration had been formed" (quoted in Reynaud, *Fight,* p. 543). Lebrun in *Témoignage* (Paris, 1945), p. 84, and repeatedly in his testimony before the Commission of Inquiry in 1948 insisted that Reynaud declared at the end of the Council that the cabinet had resigned; yet at the same time Lebrun admitted that Reynaud had asked his ministers to be on hand at 10 "under the impression that he would be given office again, and that he would need several of his former colleagues to reconstitute his Government." See Lebrun's testimony, in *CE,* IV, pp. 1081–86; Reynaud, *Fight,* p. 553.

Apparently, much of the confusion over this particular incident derives from the fact that President Lebrun openly begged the President of the Council not to resign, after Reynaud had announced his intention of doing so, at the same time stating his belief that some sort of arrangement would result from their conferring alone. That there was little question that Reynaud *would* resign if he failed to obtain Lebrun's support seems fairly clear. Immediately following the afternoon Council of Ministers he had told Ambassador Biddle that cabinet pressure to ask for armistice terms was "too strong to be held down," and from his "state of fatigue and despondency" Biddle felt it quite probable that Reynaud would tender his resignation later that evening when the "final decision" was scheduled to take place and that any more positive outcome could be considered "remote." See Biddle's dispatch of June 16, 9 p.m., in *FRUS,* 1940, I, pp. 260–61. The only real question involves the exact point at which Reynaud decided that reconvening the Council was unnecessary.

# Reynaud
# and the American Embassy

When on June 18 Pétain asked Reynaud to accept the ambassadorial post in Washington, Reynaud did not reject the offer outright but asked to defer his final answer until after the armistice terms were known. If the French Government accepted humiliating conditions, he stated, he would have to refuse the post. Reynaud claims that he did not at this point wish to precipitate a break with Pétain, because in the eventuality of his being recalled to office for the purpose of continuing the war in North Africa he would need to make use of Pétain in metropolitan France as a go-between with the occupying authorities. The possibility of calling Reynaud back to power was also President Lebrun's motive for refusing to sign the decree of appointment that Pétain had sent him before the question was settled. See Reynaud, *Au Cœur de la Mêlée* (Paris, 1951), pp. 883–85; Reynaud's testimony, July 24, 1945, in *Procès Pétain,* p. 69; and Lebrun, *Témoignage* (Paris, 1945), p. 90.

Baudouin, on the other hand, claims that Reynaud on June 19 asked him to get Lebrun to sign the decree in advance even before he had made up his mind. He also claims that Reynaud definitely decided to accept the post on June 21, that in fact he asked Pétain to make the appointment, but that by this time, with the French plenipotentiaries face to face with the Germans, the Marshal had changed *his* mind about the appropriateness of the nomination. See *The Private Diaries of Paul Baudouin* (London, 1948), pp. 125, 127–28, 132; also Bouthillier, *Le Drame de Vichy* (Paris, 1950), I, pp. 113–14; Bouthillier's testimony in *CE,* VIII, pp. 2511–13, 2519–20; and Pomaret, *Le Dernier Témoin* (Paris, 1968), pp. 95–96. In response, Reynaud says only that after a momentary decision in favor of accepting he freely rejected the offer on June 23 because he felt that it was morally impossible for him to become the ambassador of Pétain. See Reynaud, *Au Cœur de la Mêlée* (Paris, 1951), p. 890; and his testimony in *Procès Pétain,* p. 71. However, Jeanneney writes that Reynaud confessed to him and Herriot on June 23 that he had accepted the post the day before, in spite of their disapproval, and that by midday there was as yet no thought of refusing it. See his *Journal politique* (Paris, 1972), p. 84.

# *The Republic's Three Presidents*

To what extent the two parliamentary leaders and President Lebrun can be charged with negligence, or an overemphasis on form at the expense of substance that amounted to dereliction of duty, is another question with some bearing on Anglo-French relations in the third week of June. Henri Becquart writes that MM. Herriot and Jeanneney had legal powers they never used to prevent the general *débandade* then in course. For instance, they could have convoked the chambers, whose session had not yet closed, for the purpose of approving or rejecting the pro-armistice policy of the Pétain government; and it was Becquart's impression from a meeting of deputies he had attended on June 18 that the majority still favored continued resistance. Paul-Boncour also believed that Parliament could have played a more positive role: instead of feeling useless and in the way, sensing themselves the target of the public's need for a scapegoat, had the nation's elected representatives been publicly reunited in a body and encouraged by firm leadership, he thought, they might well have gotten a grip on themselves and rejected the counsels of despair and abandon to which as isolated and fearful individuals they were prey.

Though these men were not alone in wishing to see Parliament convoked, others, including Jeanneney, either feared the result or were content to leave the responsibility for making major decisions to the government. In short, few believed that the situation could be turned around by this means, and many were losing faith in the institution itself. Besides which, Herriot and Jeanneney, interpreting their constitutional role in a limited sense and believing moreover that the power to conclude an armistice legitimately belonged to the government, and to it alone, apparently had no stomach for opening up a conflict between Parliament and the new government or for the national dissensions that would in this way have been laid bare. When Vincent Auriol told Herriot that he ought to call Parliament, claiming that it was the business of the assemblies to decide between an armistice and national resistance, Herriot's immediate reaction was: "Great God! What on earth for? What a fine spectacle they would afford the country." Moreover, he thought it useless, because the armistice request was already in Hitler's hands. Lebrun likewise thought "it would be a disaster" if Parliament were reunited. They were probably right in their pessimistic appraisals as to what would have happened had Parliament played a more active role after Pétain came to power. The total and abject abdication to which the National Assembly lent itself on July 10, Herriot's and Jeanneney's own mild weaknesses during those early July days, together with Lebrun's lassitude before the constitutional project whose most notable accomplishment would be the eclipse of his own office, not to speak of the death of the Republic, hardly encourage one to think otherwise.

The fact remains that, outside of their efforts to assure the security of the public powers, these three men did not try very hard to gather support for the idea of continued resistance or to avail themselves of whatever democratic sentiment still held sway in parliamentary circles. If they had not given up already before the onslaughts of the Lavalian whirlwind, they seem almost to have been counting on the harshness of Hitler's terms to provide that patriotic shot in the arm which they themselves felt incapable of injecting—except for the influence they could bring to bear on a restricted few. But it may also be that, like many others, they instinctively realized that the Republic was for all intents and purposes dead—even before the formal coup de grâce administered July 10—that it had in fact entered its terminal death throes on June 16 and that there was little actually to be done other than to supply some degree of dignity and decorum as they presided over the obsequies.

See Becquart, *Au Temps du Silence* (Paris, 1945), pp. 63–65; Joseph Paul-Boncour, *Entre Deux Guerres* (Paris, 1946), III, pp. 221–23, 270; Jacques Chastenet, *Histoire de la Troisième République*, Vol. VII, *Le Drame Final (1938–1940)* (Paris, 1963), p. 220; Charles Pomaret, *Le Dernier Témoin* (Paris, 1968), pp. 195–96; Henri Amouroux, *Le 18 Juin* (Paris, 1964), p. 202; Vincent Auriol, *Hier . . . Demain* (Paris, 1945), pp. 77–78; Jeanneney's testimony, July 26, 1945, in *Procès Pétain*, pp. 185–86, 191; Baudouin's testimony in *CE,* VII, pp. 2133–34; Joel Colton, *Léon Blum* (New York, 1966), pp. 375, 382, 384; Emmanuel Berl, *La Fin de la III<sup>e</sup> République* (Paris, 1968), pp. 10, 107, 210–11, 218, 220; and Louis-Dominique Girard, *Montoire* (Paris, 1948), pp. 55–57 and 94, on the responsibility of Messrs. Herriot, Jeanneney, and Lebrun; and Peter J. Larmour, *The French Radical Party in the 1930's* (Stanford, Calif., 1964), pp. 250–55, on Parliament's abdication in the preceding peacetime years.

# Churchill, Roosevelt, and the British Fleet

Churchill's correspondence with Roosevelt and others regarding the fate of the British fleet in case of a German victory is instructive for the light it casts on the French Government's behavior in June as well as for what it inadvertently reveals about the likenesses between the two allies, other things being equal. American concern for the safety of the British fleet seems to have been sparked originally by Ambassador Bullitt's fear that, in the event of Britain's defeat and the installation there of a collaborationist government, "the British Navy would be against us." He therefore advised the President on May 16, "by way of a conversation with Mackenzie King or some direct arrangement wth the officers of the British fleet . . . to try to make certain that in case the war goes as badly as it may, the British fleet would base itself on Canada for the defense of the dominion which might become the refuge of the British crown." See No. 706 in *For the President, Personal and Secret,* ed. by Orville H. Bullitt (Boston, 1972), pp. 427–28. Bullitt's hypothesis was in turn used by the British Prime Minister. For instance, in a letter to the President on May 20, emphasizing the dangers facing Great Britain and the urgent need for American assistance in fighters and destroyers, Churchill indicated that if England were overrun his own administration would likely go down in the process as others "came in to parley amid the ruins": in this case, he warned, "the sole remaining bargaining counter with Germany would be the Fleet, and, if this country was left by the United States to its fate, no one would have the right to blame those then responsible if they made the best terms they could for the surviving inhabitants." He and his colleagues would fight on to the end, but he could not answer for his successors, "who in utter despair and helplessness might well have to accommodate themselves to the German will." See Winston S. Churchill, *Their Finest Hour,* Vol. II of *The Second World War* (Bantam edition, 1962), p. 50; also *FRUS: Diplomatic Papers,* 1940, Vol. III (1958), p. 51.

Roosevelt's response to what the Prime Minister considered a "nightmare" possibility was that if the time ever came "when a British Government found it necessary to ask for peace terms from Germany, all ships under construction in the British Isles should be destroyed and all merchant ships in British ports should leave immediately for safe Empire ports." See *Memoirs of Cordell Hull* (New York, 1948), Vol. I, p. 772. But lest the Americans view too complacently the prospect of a British collapse, "out of which they would get the British Fleet and the guardianship of the British Empire," Churchill on June 5 pointed out to Prime Minister Mackenzie King of Canada, who had been in contact with the US Government regarding the British fleet, that such a sequence of events might be natural if America were in the war, but, if not, he could not predict "what policy might be adopted by a pro-German administration such as would undoubtedly be set up" if Britain were overpowered. See Churchill, II, p. 125.

As Mr. King interpreted Churchill's message, this meant that while the Prime Minister would never consider surrendering on any terms, if a strong division of opinion arose within Britain concerning the desirability of making peace, and if he "felt that he and his Government were in the minority, the only way in which he would bow to the will of the majority would be to go to the King, tender his resignation and ask the King to call on whoever was the leader of the surrender party, to form a Government to negotiate terms of surrender. To Mr. Churchill's way of thinking such a government would be pro-German." See Laurence Thompson, *1940* (New York, 1966), pp. 183–84; William L. Langer and S. Everett Gleason, *The Challenge to Isolation, 1937–1940* (New York, 1952), p. 514. This interpretation was seconded on June 11 by the British Ambassador in Washington, Lord Lothian, who told Secretary of State Hull that "Churchill did not remotely contemplate Germany's getting the British fleet so far as his Government was concerned. The only danger in this respect would arise in connection with some successor government of the Mosley (British Fascist) or Communist type." See Hull, I, p. 797; also Ambassador Kennedy's dispatch to the Secretary of State, June 10, and Hull's memorandum of his conversation with Lord Lothian, June 11, in *FRUS,* 1940, III, pp. 35–36.

Again, on June 15, as the British were preparing to demand that the French fleet be sent for safekeeping to British ports, Churchill directly renewed his warning to the President:

Although the present Government and I personally would never fail to send the Fleet across the Atlantic if resistance was beaten down here, a point may be reached in the struggle where the present Ministers no longer have control of affairs and when very easy terms could be obtained for the British island by their becoming a vassal state of the Hitler Empire. A pro-German Government would certainly be called into being to make peace, and might present to a shattered or a starving nation an almost irresistible case for entire submission to the Nazi will. The fate of the British Fleet, as I have already mentioned to you, would be decisive on the future of the United States, because if it were joined to the fleets of Japan, France, and Italy and the great resources of German industry, overwhelming sea power would be in Hitler's hands.

See Churchill, II, p. 162; FO 371/24311, C 7294/G, No. 1146 to Lord Lothian, dis. June 17, 6:20 a.m.; *FRUS,* 1940, III, p. 53.

Finally, on June 28, in response to American suggestions that preparations be made for transferring the British fleet across the Atlantic—and five days after denouncing the Pétain government for refusing to part with the French fleet for England's benefit—Churchill cabled Lord Lothian that "if this country were successfully invaded and largely occupied after heavy fighting, some Quisling Government would be formed to make peace on the basis of our becoming a German Protectorate. In this case the British Fleet would be the solid contribution with which this Peace Government would buy terms. Feeling in England against [the] United States would [then] be similar to French bitterness against us now." See Churchill, II, pp. 194–96.

All this requires little comment: the analogies fairly leap to mind. Granted that Churchill was deliberately using scare tactics on the Americans to wrest from them essential aid and that he was envisaging (and no doubt exaggerating) contingencies that he never expected to come to pass, still the scenario for how the British might have handled a defeat such as was visited upon the French is there in outline. Like M. Reynaud, "the fighting spirit," Mr. Churchill would fight on to the end; he personally would not fail to send the fleet to American shores (as Paul Reynaud [according to Langer and Gleason, p. 541] on the morning of June 16 had promised Biddle to do); however, he might lose control of events if defeatist sentiment carried the day, in which case he would feel obliged to resign. Then a successor government (in all likelihood one formed by Halifax, as in late May he had not been loath to consider negotiations leading to a peace settlement, and not one by Mosley, who in any case had been interned since May 23)—rather than enriching a hitherto indifferent America with its undefeated resources—would use the fleet to bargain for the best terms it could get.

In the upshot, Roosevelt continued to ask for assurance that if Britain were overrun the fleet would neither be surrendered nor sunk but instead sent across the Atlantic, while Churchill, for his part, despite the need to clinch the destroyers for bases deal, consistently refused a specific declaration to this effect, or even to allow discussion of the possibility of the fleet's transference by his military staff, on the grounds that to do so would be to compromise their liberty of action. See a note by Churchill to the Foreign Secretary on Aug. 7, and a telegram to Lord Lothian on the same date in Churchill, II, pp. 347–48. In the light of this, how much value ought to be attached to "Churchill's personal promise to send the fleet to Canada in the event England was defeated" or to the cagily worded telegrams for public consumption worked out by the two Former Naval Persons—which Roosevelt wrested from the Prime Minister before the end of August, when full agreement between the Anglo-Saxon powers was finally reached—is anybody's guess. See Richard J. Whalen, *The Founding Father: The Story of Joseph P. Kennedy* (New York, 1966), p. 301; and Churchill, II, p. 355.

For further discussions between the British and Americans on the public handling of this touchy topic, see a memo by President Roosevelt, Aug. 2; letter from Lord Lothian to Sumner Welles, Aug. 8; message from Roosevelt to Churchill, Aug. 13; reply from the PM to President, Aug. 15; Ambassador Kennnedy's pessimistic appraisal of the future value of any "personal" promise, Aug. 15; Churchill's insistence on a "general declaration," Aug. 22; and the final notes on the subject exchanged by Secretary Hull and the British Ambassador on Aug. 29 and Sept. 2, in *FRUS, 1940, III*, pp. 47, 58–59, 64, 65–66, 67, 68, 69. For more on Lothian's role in the destroyer deal, see Elizabeth Langhorne, *Nancy Astor and Her Friends* (New York, 1974), pp. 217–22. See also Norman Longmate, *If Britain Had Fallen* (New York, 1974), pp. 50–51 and 259, for further suggestive analogies (1) between British and French thinking (in conditions of defeat) and (2) between Great Britain and the United States regarding their egoistic motives for continental involvement.

# Notes
# and References

COMINCIA LA COMMEDIA

## The Separate Slide Over the Precipice

[1]For two sympathetic analyses of British Government attitudes during the last days of peace, see Correlli Barnett, *The Collapse of British Power* (London, 1972), pp. 570–74; and Sidney Aster, *1939: The Making of the Second World War* (London, 1973), pp. 331, 335, 348–49, 364. For further light on the attitudes of Halifax and Chamberlain as shed by Ambassador Joseph P. Kennedy's dispatches of Aug. 23 and 30 (5 p.m. and 8 p.m.), consult also *Foreign Relations of the United States (FRUS): Diplomatic Papers, 1939*, Vol. I (Washington, D.C., 1956), pp. 355, 386–87, and 392.

[2]British guarantee to Poland, Mar. 31, 1939, and Anglo-Polish Mutual Assistance Treaty, signed Aug. 25, 1939; Franco-Polish Treaties of Feb. 19, 1921 and Oct. 16, 1925, and military convention of May 19, 1939.

[3]For Halifax's secret efforts to get Mussolini to play a mediating role, see Gordon Waterfield, *Professional Diplomat: Sir Percy Loraine of Kirkhale Bt., 1880–1961* (London, 1973), pp. 239, 241, 243–44; and for Loraine's personal role, *Documents on German Foreign Policy, 1918–1945*, Series D (1937–1945), Vol. VII, *The Last Days of Peace, August 9–September 3, 1939* (Washington, 1956), Nos. 220, 320, 349; for the French Foreign Ministry's efforts, see *Carnets Secrets de Jean Zay (De Munich à la Guerre)*, edited by Philippe Henriot (Paris, 1942), pp. 75, 79; and Anthony Adamthwaite, *France and the Coming of the Second World War, 1936–1939* (London, 1977), p. 343. That British and French efforts in this direction were independent of each other is brought out by Martin Gilbert and Richard Gott in *The Appeasers* (London, 1963), pp. 265, 268.

[4]*The Ciano Diaries, 1939–1943*, ed. by Hugh Gibson (New York, 1946), p. 134; *Documents on British Foreign Policy, 1919–1939*, ed. by E. L. Woodward and Rohan Butler, 3rd Ser., Vol. VII (London, 1954), Nos. 580,

584, 590, 646, 649, 682, 693; *French Yellow Book: Diplomatic Documents (1938–1939)* (New York, 1940), Nos. 306, 327, 335, 337, 344, 345, and Appendix III, pp. 413–17; Zay, pp. 79–82, 85–86; Philippe Henriot, *Comment Mourut la Paix* (Paris, 1941), pp. 36, 39, 46–47; Georges Bonnet, *De Munich à la Guerre: Défense de la Paix* (Paris, 1967), pp. 485, 488–89, 495; Pierre-Étienne Flandin, *Politique française, 1919–1940* (Paris, 1947), pp. 325–28; L. B. Namier, *Diplomatic Prelude, 1938–1939* (London, 1948), pp. 384–87, 390; *The Diplomatic Diaries of Oliver Harvey, 1937–1940,* ed. by John Harvey (London, 1970), p. 313; Gilbert and Gott, pp. 300, 302.

[5]Ciano *(Diaries)*, pp. 136–37; *DGFP,* Ser. D, VII, Nos. 535, 539, 541; *DBFP,* 3rd Ser., VII, No. 709 (Minute by Sir P. Loraine of Conversation with Count Ciano, Sept. 2); No. 710 (Minute by Mr. Harvey on Telephone Conversation between Count Ciano and Lord Halifax, 2:30 p.m., Sept. 2); *French Yellow Book,* No. 360 (François-Poncet to M. Bonnet on Conversation with Count Ciano at 2 p.m.); Appendix III (Communication telephoned by Count Ciano to M. Bonnet, 2:15 p.m., Sept. 2), pp. 417–18; Harvey, p. 313.

[6]Viscount Templewood (Sir Samuel Hoare), *Nine Troubled Years* (London, 1954), pp. 393–94; Viscount John Simon, *Retrospect* (London, 1952), p. 252; *DBFP,* 3rd Ser., VII, No. 700 (Lord Halifax to Sir E. Phipps, 12:30 p.m.); No. 708 (Phipps to Halifax, 1:30 p.m.); No. 718 (Record of Telephone Conversation between Sir A. Cadogan and M. Bonnet, 5 p.m.); No. 727 (Minute by Cadogan of Telephone Conversation between Halifax and Phipps, 6 p.m.); *French Yellow Book,* No. 354 (Corbin to Bonnet, 2:30 p.m., Sept. 2); Bonnet, *De Munich à la Guerre,* pp. 492, 498–500, 503; Harvey, p. 314; and for Ambassador William C. Bullitt's variable views on the French situation on Sept. 2, see his dispatches from Paris of 11 a.m., 2 p.m., and 8 p.m., in *FRUS,* 1939, I, pp. 409–10, 411–12, and 413.

[7]Ian Colvin, *The Chamberlain Cabinet* (New York, 1971), pp. 249–53; Gilbert and Gott, Chap. 21, esp. pp. 303–05; Henriot, pp. 47–49; and for more personal accounts of the crisis, *The Diaries of Sir Alexander Cadogan, 1938–1945,* ed. by David Dilks (London, 1971), p. 212; Harvey, p. 315; Major-General Sir Edward L. Spears, *Assignment to Catastrophe,* Vol. I, *Prelude to Dunkirk, July 1939–May 1940* (London, 1954), pp. 20–22; L. S. Amery, *My Political Life,* Vol. III, *The Unforgiving Years, 1929–1940* (London, 1955), pp. 323–25; Harold Nicolson, *Diaries and Letters, 1930–1939,* ed. by Nigel Nicolson (New York, 1966), p. 419; *DGFP,* Ser. D, VII, No. 558, for Sir Horace Wilson's statement to German Embassy officials; and *Parliamentary Debates, House of Commons,* 5th Ser., Vol. 351, cols. 280–86, Sept. 2, for the actual scene on the floor of the Commons. For the hour-by-hour developments between French and British on Sept. 2, see Louis Thomas (ed.), *Documents sur la Guerre de 1939–1940* (Paris, 1941), pp. 142–47, 149–53 (containing Ambassador Corbin's report of Sept. 7).

⁸Thomas, p. 153; Henriot, pp. 49–50; Namier, p. 395. According to Hugh Dalton, whose source was Brendan Bracken, Churchill had told Corbin that "if France failed again and ratted on the Poles, as she had ratted on the Czechs, he, who had always been a friend of France, would be utterly indifferent to her fate." Whether Churchill on this occasion really treated Corbin "as though he were an old washerwoman" cannot be known (Corbin's report does not mention it), but all are agreed that he expressed himself vehemently. See *The Fateful Years: Memoirs, 1931–1945* (London, 1957), p. 271; also Spears, I, p. 18, for the same incident; and Jean Montigny, *La Défaite: Heures Tragiques de 1940* (Paris, 1941), p. 159, who claims that Corbin did protest against the angry reproaches of Churchill when the latter, leading a parliamentary delegation, invaded the Ambassador's office.

⁹*DBFP*, 3rd Ser., VII, No. 740 (Minute by Cadogan of Telephone Conversation between Chamberlain and Daladier, 9:50 p.m.); No. 741 (Minute by Cadogan of Telephone Conversation between Halifax and Bonnet, 10:30 p.m.); Bonnet, *De Munich à la Guerre*, pp. 505, 507–12; Anatole de Monzie, *Ci-Devant* (Paris, 1941), pp. 157–58; Ciano (*Diaries*), p. 137; *DGFP*, Ser. D, Vol. VIII, *The War Years, September 4, 1939–March 18, 1940* (Washington, 1954), No. 176 (Conversation between the Führer and Count Ciano, Oct. 1, 1939, regarding Bonnet); *French Yellow Book*, Nos. 365 and 366; Namier, p. 389.

¹⁰*French Yellow Book*, No. 367 (Coulondre to Bonnet, 5:50 p.m., Sept. 3).

## The Reluctant Allies

¹Yvon Delbos, quoted in John E. Dreifort, *Yvon Delbos at the Quai d'Orsay: French Foreign Policy during the Popular Front, 1936–1938* (Lawrence, Kan., 1973), p. 194.

²On the Entente's origins, see Samuel R. Williamson, Jr., *The Politics of Grand Strategy: Britain and France Prepare for War, 1904–1914* (Cambridge, Mass., 1969), esp. pp. 353, 367.

³On the deficiencies of the Peace Treaty, see Correlli Barnett, *The Collapse of British Power* (London, 1972), pp. 309–10, 313, 331–32; and Arnold Toynbee, ed., *Survey of International Affairs, 1939–1946* (London, 1958), pp. 254–55.

⁴See Arnold Wolfers, *Britain and France between Two Wars: Conflicting Strategies of Peace from Versailles to World War II* (New York, 1966; originally published 1940), pp. 380–83.

⁵*Ibid.*, pp. 233, 240.

⁶Barnett, pp. 319, 325–27.

⁷*Ibid.*, pp. 334–36.

⁸*Ibid.*, pp. 277, 294, 333, 338–44.

⁹Bullitt to the President, Nov. 23, 1937, in Orville H. Bullitt (ed.), *For the President, Personal and Secret: Correspondence Between Franklin D. Roosevelt and William C. Bullitt* (Boston, 1972), p. 237.

[10] See W. M. Jordan, *Great Britain, France, and the German Problem, 1918–1939: A Study of Anglo-French Relations in the Making and Maintenance of the Versailles Settlement* (London, 1943), p. 197; and J. Néré, *The Foreign Policy of France from 1914 to 1945* (London, 1975), p. 197.

[11] Barnett, p. 415; Sir Charles Webster and Noble Frankland, *The Strategic Air Offensive Against Germany, 1939–1945,* Vol. I, *Preparation* (London, 1961), pp. 74–76, 87, 91–92, 101.

[12] Webster and Frankland, I, pp. 87–88, 101; Michael Howard, *The Continental Commitment: The Dilemma of British Defence Policy in the Era of the Two World Wars* (London, 1972), pp. 117, 120.

[13] For the warning conveyed to Georges Bonnet on May 22, 1938, and repeated in September, see Anthony Adamthwaite, *France and the Coming of the Second World War, 1936–1939* (London, 1977), pp. 190, 207.

[14] Howard, p. 127 (quoting Chiefs of Staff European Appreciation, Feb. 20, 1939).

[15] See Wolfers, pp. 69, 241. The French Foreign Minister in March 1936, Flandin, had embraced this position following the reoccupation of the Rhineland. He then warned the British that this meant "a fundamental reorientation of French policy" and that, by virtue of the strategic loss suffered, France would "now have to make the best terms with Germany" she could get, "and leave the rest of Europe to her fate." Quoted in Robert Boothby, *I Fight to Live* (London, 1947), p. 137.

[16] See D. C. Watt, *Too Serious a Business: European Armed Forces and the Approach to the Second World War* (Berkeley, Calif., 1975), pp. 130–31; Howard, pp. 119, 122; Barnett, p. 555.

[17] Barnett, p. 558; Néré, pp. 235, 242; Watt, p. 122.

## Slouching into War: Poland

[1] J. R. M. Butler (ed.), *Grand Strategy,* Vol. II, *September 1939–June 1941* (London, 1957), p. 166; and *FRUS,* 1939, I, pp. 547–48, and *French Yellow Book,* No. 369, for the Allies' full statement regarding bombing policy; Amery, III, pp. 328–29.

[2] See *Parl. Deb., H. of C.,* 5th Ser., Vol. 351, col. 582, for PM's statement on war situation, Sept. 7.

[3] Amery, III, p. 330; Spears, I, pp. 31–32. See also Wood's response to Hugh Dalton in Dalton, p. 276.

[4] See Sir Charles Webster and Noble Frankland, *The Strategic Air Offensive Against Germany, 1939–1945,* Vol. I, *Preparation* (London, 1961), pp. 104–05, 130, 134–35; Butler, II, pp. 56–57.

[5] See dispatches by Kennedy to the Secretary of State, Sept. 15 and Sept. 18, in *FRUS,* 1939, I, pp. 427 and 441. Up to September 12, Gamelin even had the gall to maintain that two-thirds of the German air force was concen-

trated on the western front rather than in Poland. British air inactivity served as a convenient excuse for the C-in-C and possibly for Daladier as well.

[6]See Jon Kimche, *The Unfought Battle* (London, 1968), especially pp. 1–2, 91–93, 142, for the best analysis of French and German strength on the western front during successive weeks in September 1939. It is his thesis that while Germany was preoccupied in Poland the Allies, enjoying overwhelming superiority on land, in the air, and at sea, could have delivered a knockout blow to the Germans by attacking them on their virtually undefended western flank. See pp. 87, 94–95, 142, 145.

[7]See *Diplomat in Paris, 1936–1939: Papers and Memoirs of Juliusz Lukasiewicz, Ambassador of Poland,* ed. by Wacław Jędrzejewicz (New York, 1970), pp. 217, 290, 297, 313; General Gamelin's testimony in *Les Événements survenus en France de 1933 à 1945: Témoignages et Documents Recueillis par la Commission d'Enquête Parlementaire* (hereafter cited as CE), Vol. II, pp. 395–96, 415, 459; Bonnet, *Quai d'Orsay* (Isle of Man, 1965), pp. 272–73; Spears, I, note to p. 30; Cadogan, p. 214; Colonel Raphael de Bardies, *La Campagne 39–40* (Paris, 1947), pp. 37–40, 44; Guy Rossi-Landi, *La Drôle de guerre: la vie politique en France 2 septembre 1939–10 mai 1940* (Paris, 1971), pp. 11, 170.

[8]Harvey, p. 318 (entry for Sept. 11).

[9]Maurice Gustave Gamelin, *Servir,* Vol. III, *La Guerre (Septembre 1939–19 Mai 1940)* (Paris, 1947), pp. 47–48; Aster, pp. 87, 96, 106, 117, 144, 146; Sir John Slessor, *The Central Blue: The Autobiography of Sir John Slessor, Marshal of the RAF* (New York, 1957), pp. 214, 229, 231, 239–40; Butler, II, p. 12; Kimche, pp. 44–45, 48, 67, 71–72.

## The Politics of Pessimism

[1]André Beaufre, *1940: The Fall of France* (London, 1967), p. 154. Jean Cocteau also saw it as a play—which had failed to open on time: "The tragedy of the war has been painstakingly mounted; the public is favorable; all the conditions for its success are joined. However, the play refuses to get off the ground." Quoted in Alfred Fabre-Luce, *Journal de la France: Mars 1939–Juillet 1940* (Paris, 1940), p. 169.

[2]See Laurence Lafore, *The End of Glory: An Interpretation of the Origins of World War II* (Philadelphia, 1970), p. 229. Hitler contributed to this limbolike state of affairs even at sea by forbidding any offensive operations against the French Navy and mercantile marine during the first weeks of the war. This ban was lifted only at the end of September. See Jacques Mordal, *La Marine à l'Épreuve: De l'Armistice de 1940 au Procès Auphan* (Paris, 1956), p. 18; DGFP, Ser. D., VII, No. 576, for Hitler's Directive No. 2 of Sept. 3, 1939; and "Fuehrer Conferences on Naval Affairs, 1939–1945," in *Brassey's Naval Annual 1948* (New York, 1948), pp. 40–41, for his decisions of Sept. 7 and 23.

³Beaufre, p. 155.

⁴Janet Flanner, Letter from Paris, Sept. 10, 1939, reprinted in *The New Yorker Book of War Pieces* (New York, 1947), p. 6.

⁵The press reported the unanimity of the vote, which was taken by a show of hands, but there were probably anywhere from 30–40 to 100 in the Chamber who opposed the bill and whose opinion was not solicited. See Rossi-Landi, pp. 19–20; and Beau de Loménie, *La Mort de la Troisième République* (Paris, 1951), pp. 133–36. The larger historical controversy revolves around whether the vote for war credits was equivalent to a declaration of war (the preponderant view in 1939) or whether it should be interpreted merely as support for the mobilization measures taken by the government (the Vichy thesis). For arguments justifying the propriety of the government's moves, see Bonnet, *De Munich à la Guerre*, pp. 466–67, 492–93, 499, 501–02; Jules Jeanneney, *Journal politique (septembre 1939–juillet 1942)* (Paris, 1972), ed. and annotated by Jean-Noël Jeanneney, pp. 360–62, n. 14; Albert Lebrun, *Témoignage* (Paris, 1945), p. 32; Lebrun's testimony, *CE*, IV, p. 972; and Joseph Paul-Boncour, *Entre Deux Guerres: Souvenirs sur la III^e République* (Paris, 1946), Vol. III, *Sur les chemins de la défaite, 1935–1940*, pp. 160–61. For the "unconstitutionality of the war" thesis, see Laval's testimony before the High Court, Aug. 3, 1945, in *Procès Pétain*, p. 513; and Flandin, pp. 322, 332–36. For a maverick view, see Henri de Kerillis, *Français, Voici la Vérité* (New York, 1942), p. 224.

⁶On the French political scene, see Pierre Renouvin, *World War II and Its Origins: International Relations, 1929–1945* (New York, 1968), pp. 188–89; Rossi-Landi, pp. 113, 119–20, 192; Fabre-Luce, pp. 146–47; François Fonvieille-Alquier, *The French and the Phoney War, 1939–1940* (London, 1973), pp. 111–12; Elie J. Bois, *Truth on the Tragedy in France* (London, 1941), pp. 70–71, 122; André Simone, *J'Accuse!* (New York, 1940), pp. 320–21; and Louis Lévy, *The Truth about France* (Harmondsworth, Middlesex, England, 1941), p. 143.

⁷General Paul Armengaud, *Batailles Politiques et Militaires sur l'Europe: Témoignages (1932–1940)* (Paris, 1948), pp. 169–70, 173.

⁸See Flandin, pp. 351–53. French opinion was further confused in October when the Communist Party, making a 180° turn, suddenly inaugurated its own peace offensive, in this way embarrassing and inhibiting those who had previously advocated a compromise agreement. Thereafter, pacifism would take on some of the coloring of treason, as a result of which the defeatists were forced to play a waiting game and to employ less direct methods of agitation. See Rossi-Landi, pp. 115, 188–89.

⁹Gordon Wright, "Ambassador Bullitt and the Fall of France," *World Politics,* Vol. X, No. 1 (October 1957), p. 79.

¹⁰*Parl. Deb., H. of C.,* 5th Ser., Vol. 352, col. 567, Oct. 12, Chamberlain quoting from Daladier's broadcast speech, in the course of giving the British

reply to the German peace proposals. See also Henri Michel, *La Drôle de Guerre* (Paris, 1971), p. 132.

[11]Fonvieille-Alquier, p. 112. It was, as de Monzie (p. 173) saw it, the policy of continuing the war because of the political impossibility of ending it. In other words, the time was not ripe; there had been no reverse; thus war had become easier than peace. See Fabre-Luce, pp. 147, 149. Daladier himself, at least on the basis of what he told Elie Bois, saw his policy as one of calculated ambiguity, undertaken to disconcert his enemies both within and without. Inwardly resolved to pursue the war, but believing for military reasons in the necessity of playing a waiting game, "it was in order to leave the enemy in ignorance of his resolves that he put aside any public action calculated to awaken Hitler and Ribbentrop from their dream of driving a wedge between the Allies." "I allowed *them* to imagine that one day or other *they* might be able to come to some arrangement with me," he told Bois in June. And to the American Ambassador he described a similar maneuver involving peace proposals emanating from Goering. His pretense of readiness to consider such proposals he believed to be "the main factor in keeping the Germans from attacking" throughout the autumn. See Bois, pp. 170–71, 327, based on interviews with Daladier on Oct. 26, 1939, and June 6, 1940; and Bullitt to President Roosevelt, Dec. 11, 1939, in *For the President, Personal and Secret,* ed. by Orville H. Bullitt (Boston, 1972), pp. 389–91. For a less favorable comment on Daladier's stance, see Léon Guerdan, *Je les ai tous connus* (New York, 1942), p. 106, where he is described as "before the opening of hostilities, in turn, both for and against Munich, and, after, for a total war and for an indefinite defensive, for an absolute alliance with England, implying the destruction of Nazism, and for flirtations with Germany in view of a compromise peace, for concessions to Italy and for ringing *nevers,* and so on." This judgment is closer to that rendered by Jules Jeanneney, who in October 1939 saw Daladier as a man "without a compass, buffeted between those whom he consulted, showing at short intervals quite opposite tendencies, concluding often in the sense of the last heard," in short a man "embarrassed by his irresolution" whom it was necessary to protect from electoral influences and from "ceding too much to the noisy currents of parliamentary opinion, to the detriment of courageous solutions." See *Journal Politique,* p. 20 (entry for Oct. 21). For the Polish Ambassador, Daladier was a moody man who "often went from determination to doubt and depression, which repeatedly ruined already-made decisions and plans." See Łukasiewicz, p. 268.

[12]Harold Nicolson, *The War Years, 1939–1945,* Vol. II of *Diaries and Letters,* ed. by Nigel Nicolson (New York, 1967), p. 31; Keith Feiling, *The Life of Neville Chamberlain* (London, 1946), p. 424; Amery, III, p. 333; Kennedy's dispatches of Sept. 11, Sept. 15, and Oct. 4, in *FRUS,* 1939, I, pp. 421–24, 426–27, and 502.

[13]Nicolson, II, p. 35; Harold Macmillan, *The Blast of War, 1939–1945*

(London, 1967), p. 10; *Parl. Deb., H. of C.*, 5th Ser., Vol. 351, cols. 1870–74, for Lloyd George statement, Oct. 3. See also Sir Samuel Hoare's comment on Lloyd George's speech in a letter to Lord Lothian, Oct. 7, in Templewood, p. 406; and Chamberlain's reaction in a letter to his sister, Oct. 8, in Iain Macleod, *Neville Chamberlain* (London, 1961), pp. 278–79. For Lloyd George's arguments (in favor of a negotiated peace) before a parliamentary study group, Sept. 27, and in private conversation with Robert Boothby, Sept. 28, see Boothby's *I Fight to Live* (London, 1947), pp. 195–97.

[14]*Parl. Deb., H. of. C.*, 5th Ser., Vol. 351, cols. 1855–61, Prime Minister's statement, Oct. 3.

[15]Cadogan, p. 223 (entry for Oct. 12).

[16]For Butler's statement, see *DGFP*, Ser. D, VIII, No. 285, German Ambassador in Soviet Union to Reichs Foreign Ministry, Oct. 20, 1939, p. 325; and skeptical interpretation by Gilbert and Gott, pp. 334–35.

[17]For British contacts with the Germans, see Cadogan, pp. 220, 224, 226, 228, 236, 249, 255; Harvey, pp. 324, 327–28; dispatches from Ambassadors Kennedy, Sept. 25 and Oct. 16, and Bullitt, Oct. 23, in *FRUS, 1939*, I, pp. 454, 516, and 519–20; Brian Bond (ed.), *Chief of Staff: The Diaries of Lieutenant-General Sir Henry Pownall* (hereafter cited as Pownall), Vol. I, *1933–1940* (London, 1972), p. 271; FO 800/318, H/XV/370, Letter from Sir Francis D'Arcy Osborne of the British Legation to the Holy See concerning German officers' peace plot, Feb. 7; H/XV/373, Halifax's answer to Osborne, Feb. 17; *The Von Hassell Diaries, 1938–1944: The Story of the Forces Against Hitler Inside Germany* (Garden City, N.Y., 1947), pp. 115–18, 133–34, for Ulrich von Hassell's contacts with an agent of Halifax; and Harold C. Deutsch, *The Conspiracy Against Hitler in the Twilight War* (Minneapolis, 1968), esp. pp. 138, 158–60, 166, 168, 171, 194, 257, 289, 294, for the most complete account of the various chains operating between London and Berlin. For Sumner Welles's account of the kind of peace that leading French and British statesmen might have found acceptable, as of February and March 1940, see Report by the Under Secretary of State on His Special Mission to Europe, in *FRUS*, 1940, I (1959), pp. 21–117. From his interviews it is clear that the real sticking point was that practically no one in a position of leadership in either France or England had any confidence whatsoever in the word or good faith of the Nazi regime, even if, under certain circumstances, they might have agreed to do business with them; furthermore, Chamberlain thought that no British government which entered into negotiations with Hitler could survive politically.

[18]For Chamberlain's formal reply to Hitler's "peace proposal," see *Parl. Deb., H. of C.*, 5th Ser., Vol. 352, cols. 565, 567.

[19]Cadogan, p. 228; Nicolson, II, p. 58. The cabinet would have been still less pleased had it known of Baron de Ropp's secret contacts with an agent

of Rosenberg's (mid-August through late October) on behalf of the Air Ministry, for which see *DGFP*, Ser. D, VII, Nos. 74 and 151; VIII, Nos. 134, 203, 235, and 318.

[20]*Parl. Deb., H. of L.*, 5th Ser., Vol. CXIV, col. 1402.

[21]Dalton, pp. 278–79; Colvin, p. 255; Churchill, I, p. 402.

## Disparities, Divisions, and the Search for Diversions

[1]A. J. Liebling, Paris Postscript, August 3/10, 1940, reprinted in *The New Yorker Book of War Pieces*, p. 40.

[2]Lafore, pp. 229, 260; Renouvin, p. 190; Beaufre, pp. 153, 157–58, 160; Bois, pp. 93, 170, 327; Harvey, pp. 321–22; Barnett, pp. 569, 573, 575–76; General Sir Edmund Ironside, *The Ironside Diaries, 1937–1940*, ed. by Col. Roderick Macleod and Denis Kelly (London, 1962), pp. 173–74; Gamelin, III, p. 206; and Feiling, pp. 418, 428; Macleod, p. 281; Amery, III, pp. 328–29; Lord Boothby, *My Yesterday, Your Tomorrow* (London, 1962), p. 127; and Ambassador Kennedy's dispatches of Sept. 18 and Nov. 8, in *FRUS, 1939*, I, pp. 440–41 and 527, for Chamberlain's hopes of a collapse of the German home front; and Fabre-Luce, pp. 126, 139, 171, for French hopes of a German revolution.

[3]Churchill quoted in Basil Liddell Hart's article in *Churchill Revised: A Critical Assessment* (New York, 1969), p. 206. As for British optimism regarding the French Army, General Sir Harold E. Franklyn writes: "When we arrived back in England after Dunkirk, many people declared that they had known that the French Army was rotten: yet before May 1940 I only heard one person make this criticism." He was referring to General Alan Brooke; and Brooke, as the BEF's Chief of Staff points out, had been a bit of a defeatist all along. See Franklyn's *The Story of One Green Howard in the Dunkirk Campaign* (Richmond, Yorkshire, 1966), p. 13; Pownall, I, p. 243 (entry for Oct. 12, 1939). D. C. Watt, in *Too Serious a Business: European Armed Forces and the Approach to the Second World War* (Berkeley, Calif., 1975), p. 132, observes that the confidence in the French Army was so great that even those who witnessed the slow collapse of French morale at all levels would not believe it.

[4]Butler, II, pp. 32–33; Ironside, pp. 104, 113, 126; Slessor, p. 282; R. J. Minney, *The Private Papers of Hore-Belisha* (London, 1960), pp. 235, 245, 250; *Parl. Deb., H. of C.*, 5th Ser., Vol. 352, col. 342, statement by Mr. Hore-Belisha, Oct. 11; Feiling, p. 425; Anthony Eden, *The Memoirs of Anthony Eden, Earl of Avon*, Vol. II, *The Reckoning* (Boston, 1965), p. 89.

[5]Feiling, p. 405; Templewood, p. 335.

[6]For a comparison of casualties, see Clare Boothe, *Europe in the Spring* (New York, 1940), pp. 144, 168; and Boothby, *I Fight to Live*, p. 202.

[7]Feiling, p. 433; "Cato," *Guilty Men* (New York, 1940), pp. 120–21; *Parl. Deb., H. of. C.*, 5th Ser., Vol. 353, col. 1280, statement by Mr.

Lawson, Nov. 22; also col. 1368 for table circulated Nov. 23 by Mr. Ernest Brown, Minister of Labour, showing 1,231,692 unemployed on Aug. 14, 1,430,638 unemployed on Oct. 16; Vol. 360, col. 1105, for statement by Sir Archibald Sinclair, May 7.

[8]FO 371/24309, C 4522, Mar. 25; FO 371/24310, C 6306, Apr. 18, Memo from G. M. Warr.

[9]Ironside, pp. 162–64. Just the same, the disparity was still on Daladier's mind a month later, when at the Inter-Allied Council meeting of December 19 he claimed that in France one man in seven had been mobilized. See SWC (39/40), 4th meeting.

[10]FO 800/326, H/XL/16, FO Circular Letter, May 4, 1940; Pertinax, *The Gravediggers of France: Gamelin, Daladier, Reynaud, Pétain, and Laval* (Garden City, N.Y., 1944), pp. 129–30; testimony of Raoul Dautry, in *CE,* VII, pp. 1953, 1963, 1981–82; André Maurois, *Tragedy in France* (New York, 1940), p. 49; and *Survey of International Affairs, 1939–1946. The Eve of War, 1939,* ed. by Arnold Toynbee and Veronica M. Toynbee (London, 1958), p. 711.

[11]FO 371/24296, C 501/9/17, Report on Anglo-French Propaganda, Jan. 1, 1940. If the French bourgeoisie was not deprived or seriously inconvenienced by the war, the sacrifices demanded of the working class were disproportionately stiff. Defense workers now saw their eight-hour day extended to twelve (or the work week lengthened to seventy-two hours), a 40 per cent withholding placed on all wages from overtime, and their hard-won paid vacations postponed for the duration. By contrast, no new taxes were imposed on profits from armaments. British journalists and trade unionists criticized these harsh measures, but then, as they were sometimes told in no uncertain terms, their country's own small contribution in effectives to the North-East front had in large part made them necessary. See Rossi-Landi, pp. 130–31 and 173; Simone, pp. 249–51, 288, 324; Raoul Dautry's testimony, in *CE,* VII, pp. 1963–64; and Somerset Maugham's account of his interview with Dautry and tour of French munitions factories in *France at War (1940)* (London, 1940), pp. 36, 46.

[12]See Alexander Werth, *The Last Days of Paris: A Journalist's Diary* (London, 1940), pp. 139, 252; André Simone, *J'Accuse!: The Men Who Betrayed France* (New York, 1940), p. 330; Henri de Kerillis, *Français, Voici la Vérité* (New York, 1942), p. 122. According to Alfred Fabre-Luce, "La conscience populaire conserve l'image d'un Anglais aristocrate, combattant peu pressé, largement payé, pourvu d'un imperméable, qui, dans les ports où il s'attarde, séduit à coup de shillings la femme du Français mobilisé." See p. 287. French soldiers were not always susceptible; yet André Maurois, who had been a liaison officer in the First World War, found German propaganda in 1939 "insistent, insinuating, sarcastic, tenacious and ingenious" in sowing distrust and in exploiting the smallest difficulties between the British soldiers and the

French civilians among whom they were billeted. See his *Memoirs, 1885–1967* (New York, 1970), pp. 230–31.

[13]FO 800/325, H/XXXIX/32. On Oct. 12, to the embarrassment of the government, Mr. S. O. Davies aired this awkward question when he asked whether Parliament could be told whether the British Government, which had repeatedly claimed that perfect accord existed between itself and France, approved "the horrible and tragic step which was taken recently in France in proscribing over 70 members of the French Chamber and disfranchising thousands of electors." No answer was forthcoming, however, as Davies was promptly ruled out of order. See *Parl. Deb., H. of. C.,* 5th Ser., Vol. 352, cols. 648–49. However, Hugh Dalton and a party of Labour MPs had no trouble accepting the explanations offered by French Socialists as to the anti-Communist measures taken in France. See Dalton, pp. 291–92. Léon Blum, for instance, though troubled by the French Government's repressive measures against the Communists, believing them to be "morally wrong and politically ill-advised," nevertheless did not withhold his or his party's support from the government when it came to a vote on disqualifying the Communist deputies in January. As he explained it to the British Labour Party in May, stringent measures against the Communists were necessary for reasons of national security, and it would have been impossible to discuss the conduct of the war in secret session so long as the Communists were present in Parliament. See Joel Colton, *Léon Blum: Humanist in Politics* (New York, 1966), pp. 337–40, 347; also Blum's *Populaire* articles on the French Communists, reprinted in *L'Oeuvre de Léon Blum,* IV, ii (1937–1940) (Paris, 1965), pp. 324–25 and 331–32.

[14]Fonvieille-Alquier, pp. 134–38; Pertinax, pp. 134–35; Rossi-Landi, pp. 37–38, 40–41, 136–57; Jacques Chastenet, *Histoire de la Troisième République,* Vol. VII, *Le Drame Final, 1938–1940* (Paris, 1963), pp. 119–21, 124; Paul-Marie de la Gorce, *The French Army: A Military-Political History* (New York, 1963), pp. 284–85; FO 371/24310, C 5582, Minute by G. M. Warr, Apr. 11, on French measures against Communists; C 6545, May 4, Brochure on Communist Question; FO 371/24309, C 4865, No. 373 from Sir Ronald Campbell, March (?) 30. The French Government's anti-Communist campaign, and more specifically the dissolution of the Communist Party, it should be emphasized, *preceded* rather than followed the Party's reversal of policy towards the war. Two French historians, Rossi-Landi, pp. 139, 144, 160–65, and Henri Michel, *Drôle de Guerre,* p. 199, disagree as to whether the government's sanctions provoked the about-face in the first place. See also Daladier's defense of this policy, June 4, 1947, before the postwar Commission of Inquiry in *CE,* I, pp. 68–70.

[15]FO 371/24310, No. 287 from Campbell to FO, Apr. 11; dispatch by Bullitt on Daladier's motives, Jan. 11, in *FRUS,* 1940, I, pp. 589–90; Fonvieille-Alquier, pp. 147, 185; Rossi-Landi, p. 152; Spears, I, p. 113; Werth, *Last Days of Paris,* pp. 40, 103, 250; FO 371/24309, C 5294/65/17, No. 448 from

Campbell to FO, June 7; John M. Sherwood, *Georges Mandel and the Third Republic* (Stanford, Calif., 1970), pp. 233–35; Heinz Pol, *Suicide of a Democracy* (New York, 1940), pp. 157, 172; and Émile Kahn's evocation of the roundup of anti-Hitler Germans, against which a parliamentary delegation protested to Reynaud on May 16, 1940, in *CE*, IX, p. 2865 (during the course of Reynaud's testimony, Apr. 26, 1951). See Arthur Koestler's *Scum of the Earth* (London, 1968, first published 1941) and Pol's *Suicide* for a description of the workings and composition of French concentration camps. When all category B Germans and Austrians resident in Great Britain were interned in May and June 1940, a similar dilemma stood revealed in that most internees proved to be either Jewish refugees or otherwise politically opposed to the Nazis. However, the internment camps in Britain, notwithstanding parliamentary criticism, bore no relationship to their counterparts in France. Furthermore, of British subjects interned for security reasons, a substantial number had belonged to Oswald Mosley's British Union of Fascists. See A. J. P. Taylor, *English History, 1914–1945* (London, 1965), pp. 491–92 and n. 1, 492; and, for the government's evolving policy towards aliens, see the Duke of Devonshire's statements, May 23 and June 12, 1940, in *Parl. Deb., H. of. L.,* 5th Ser., Vol. 116, cols. 423–33 and 557–67.

[16]Fonvieille-Alquier, pp. 86–88; Rossi-Landi, pp. 89, 96, 99, 180–85; Pertinax, pp. 91–92; Pol, pp. 281–86; Werth, *Last Days of Paris,* pp. 29, 117; also Leo Lania, *The Darkest Hour* (Boston, 1941), pp. 102–05, and André Simone, *J'Accuse!,* pp. 345–47, on the French Propaganda Department. The British had their traitor, William Joyce (better known as Lord Haw Haw), to whom they too listened, though less for the information he was purveying than for the purpose of amusing themselves. Shades of Joyce can be discerned in one of the pivotal characters of Nancy Mitford's satirical novel of English life during the phoney war, *Pigeon Pie* (1940), as well as in the lyrics to one of Mr. Noel Coward's songs of the period: "Where is the H. M. S. *Disgusting?*" (an oblique reference to the *Ark Royal,* which the Germans mistakenly believed they had sunk). His harmlessness is suggested by the purely rhetorical question posed by Mr. Samuel in the House of Commons, Dec. 13: "Is there any truth in the suggestion that the German broadcaster known as Lord Hee-Haw—[Hon. Members: "Haw-Haw."]—of Zeesen is being paid by the British Government to broadcast fantastic and demonstrably untrue assertions, so as to bring the Nazi Government and propaganda machine into ridicule and disrepute?" See *Parl. Deb., H. of C.,* 5th Ser., Vol. 355, col. 1189. This did not mean that the British were satisfied either with the quantity or quality of news they were receiving from official sources. The new Ministry of Information, in fact, was the most criticized department in the government, being variously labeled in Parliament and elsewhere as the Ministry of Misinformation, Ministry of Irritation, Ministry of Repression, Ministry of Obfuscation, etc. However, embarrassing as all this not too unfriendly chiding was (the Marquess of Dufferin

and Ava on December 12 claimed that jokes at the expense of this "National Aunt Sally" had got them through the first three months of the war), it compared favorably with the reputation enjoyed by the French Ministry of Information, which, Arthur Koestler reports, was known familiarly to the press as "The Brothel" and whose military personnel, according to another critic, were "papa's boys, happier to expose their elegant uniforms in the corridors of the Hotel Continental than in the mud of the trenches." See Cadogan, p. 221; *Parl. Deb., H. of L.*, 5th Ser., Vol. CXIV, for Lord Macmillan's statement, Sept. 14, col. 1070; CXV, for the Marquess of Dufferin and Ava's remark, col. 212; Koestler, p. 161; and Léon Guerdan, *Je les ai tous connus* (New York, 1942), p. 122.

[17]Alexander Werth, *France, 1940–1955* (Boston, 1966, first published 1956), p. 188; *Last Days of Paris*, p. 255; Gamelin, III, pp. 190, 205; Pertinax, pp. 141–42; Fabre-Luce, pp. 161–62; Harvey, p. 332.

[18]Simone, p. 323.

[19]On September 26, Mr. Vyvyan Adams criticized *The Times* in the House of Commons for its defeatist views and pro-German past. It now "seemed bent on involving us in a war against Russia as well as against Germany.... It did not seem to have occurred to this paper that Russia may indeed have been engaged in roping Germany off from the Ukraine and the Balkans. We shall not lose the war," he stated, "but that will not be the fault of the 'Times'." See *Parl. Deb., H. of C.*, 5th Ser., Vol. 351, cols. 1273–74; also John Evelyn Wrench, *Geoffrey Dawson and Our Times* (London, 1955), pp. 362 and 376, for Dawson's prewar view of Nazi Germany as "a barrier to the spread of Communism in the West"; and pp. 401 and 404 for his more ambiguous position following Soviet moves in Poland and Finland.

[20]Macmillan, pp. 23–24; Gorce, p. 285; Wrench, p. 406. "Altogether," commented Arthur Koestler cynically, "the French attitude to the Finnish War reminded one of the voyeur who gets his thrills out of watching other people's manly exploits." See *Scum of the Earth* (London, 1968), p. 162. Alfred Fabre-Luce analyzed French opinion likewise, at the same time exposing its ideological basis. "It was sweet to love from afar and to act by proxy. The Mannerheim Army assumed the defense of civilization. Through her [Finland], that half of the French nation which wished to make war, not against Hitler but against Stalin, satisfied its desires platonically." See p. 235.

[21]Gorce, p. 286; Gamelin, III, pp. 194, 199; Beaufre, pp. 168–69; Fabre-Luce, pp. 163, 237; Macmillan, p. 24. See also Ironside's comments, p. 188, and de Monzie's, pp. 189–90.

[22]Feiling, pp. 427–28.

[23]Cadogan, p. 235 (diary entry for Dec. 6 and minute of same date).

[24]FO 800/309, H/V/4, Summary of a meeting held in Lord Halifax's room, Dec. 14, 1939; see also Prime Minister's statement on Finland, Dec. 14, in *Parl. Deb., H. of C.*, 5th Ser., Vol. 355, cols. 1337–40. Russia was expelled

from the League on December 14 by a resolution that was largely the work of Daladier. See Pertinax, p. 154; de Monzie, p. 189; Fabre-Luce, p. 163; and dispatch by Bullitt, Dec. 14, in *FRUS, 1939,* I, pp. 534–35. But, except for a greater emphasis on the need to expel the USSR, French policy at Geneva, as represented by Paul-Boncour and as previously shaped by people like Jules Jeanneney and Champetier de Ribes, was not substantially different from that of the Foreign Office. *They,* at least, did not want a break with the Soviets or to turn Russia into Enemy No. 1. See Jeanneney's *Journal Politique,* pp. 24–25 (entries for Dec. 9 and 20); and Paul-Boncour, *Entre Deux Guerres,* III, pp. 183–89.

²⁵FO 800/310, H/XIII/247, Note from Halifax to Chamberlain, Feb. 10, 1940.

²⁶*Parl. Deb., H. of C.,* 5th Ser., Vol. 351, cols. 995–98 (Mr. Boothby); col. 1016 (Mr. Price); see also cols. 992–93 for statement by Sir Archibald Sinclair the same day, Sept. 20. For other favorable comments on Russia, see Vol. 352, Oct. 12, cols. 595–96, 614, and 620 (Col. Wedgewood, Mr. Emmott, and Mr. Lipson); Oct. 26, cols. 1570–71 (Chamberlain), and Nov. 2, col. 2156 (Chamberlain). For the Foreign Office's appraisal of Russia's intentions, as reported by the American Ambassador, see Kennedy's dispatch of Sept. 30, in *FRUS, 1939,* I, pp. 461–62.

²⁷Fonvieille-Alquier, p. 104; Churchill, I, pp. 398–99. It was on October 1 that Churchill characterized Russian action, in the since celebrated phrase, as "a riddle wrapped in a mystery inside an enigma." The key to it, he thought, lay in Russian national interest, which could hardly be served by Germany's planting herself on the shores of the Black Sea or overrunning the Balkan states. Privately Chamberlain agreed with him.

²⁸Churchill, I, Appendix, pp. 659–60, Minute by First Lord to First Sea Lord, Oct. 27, 1939, for circulation to the cabinet.

²⁹Ironside, p. 182, as his military assistant, Col. Macleod, points out.

³⁰Sir Llewellyn Woodward, *British Foreign Policy in the Second World War,* Vol. I (London, 1970), pp. 104–05 (from a Chiefs of Staff memo, Mar. 27). As Sir John Slessor, air member of the Joint Planning Committee, puts it, "we viewed the prospect [of war with Russia] with serious misgivings, especially in relation to our weakness in India; and the Chiefs of Staff recommended accepting the very grave risks involved solely on the assumption that to run these risks in connexion with support to Finland would give us a real chance of winning the war quickly by cutting off the Swedish iron-ore." See Slessor, *The Central Blue,* p. 270.

³¹Fonvieille-Alquier, p. 146; Pertinax, pp. 143, 152–54; Bois, p. 177; Gamelin, III, pp. 112, 152, 199, 205, 211, 216; Gamelin's testimony, *CE,* II, pp. 417, 538.

³²Beaufre, p. 169; B. H. Liddell Hart, *History of the Second World War* (London, 1970), p. 34 (although in the 1930s Liddell Hart had advocated

this very kind of fringe maritime venture as the "British way in warfare," as Correlli Barnett, p. 503, has observed). A. J. P. Taylor's comment on the Finnish project is that "the only charitable conclusion is to assume that the British and French governments had taken leave of their senses." See *English History,* p. 469, n. 1.

[33]Pownall, I, pp. 281, 283, 288, 296; Slessor, p. 269; and Fabre-Luce, p. 320, for Hitler's pronouncement. See also Lt.-Col. de Villelume's reasoned defense of these "proxy battles" in distant lands, which he justifies not for their capacity to create new fronts—from which, generally speaking, only the most powerful adversary would benefit—but for their capacity to create liabilities for the enemy where it was weakest, i.e., in overseas transport and supply. Thus, he claims, the primary justification given by General Gamelin for the Norwegian affair was the very factor that should, on the contrary, have dissuaded him from undertaking it. See his testimony, in *CE,* IX, pp. 2757–58.

### Finland: The Alliance Makes Its Debut

[1]SWC (39/40), 2nd meeting, Sept. 22; Cadogan, pp. 218, 226–27; Woodward, I, pp. 22–23, 28–29; Butler, II, pp. 65–66, 69–70; Gamelin, III, pp. 110–11, 206–13; Commandant J. Weygand, *The Role of General Weygand: Conversations With His Son* (London, 1948), pp. 33–36; Gen. Weygand's testimony in *CE,* VI, pp. 1548–50; Maxime Weygand, *Recalled to Service* (London, 1952), pp. 10, 13, 24–29; Col. P.-A. Bourget, *De Beyrouth à Bordeaux: La Guerre 1939–40 vue du P.C. Weygand* (Paris, 1946), Ch. I; Ironside, pp. 169–71; Pownall, I, pp. 268–70; Harvey, pp. 317, 321, 327; and CAB 85, Anglo-French Liaison, MR (40), 31st meeting, Feb. 2 (Balkan Policy).

[2]See General Bergeret's revelation of this strategy to Paul Stehlin in Stehlin's *Témoignage Pour L'Histoire* (Paris, 1964), pp. 215, 234; also Édouard Bonnefous, *Histoire Politique de la Troisième République,* Vol. 7, *La Course vers l'Abîme: La fin de la IIIᵉ République (1938–1940)* (Paris, 1967), p. 157; Fonvieille-Alquier, pp. 150, 152–53; Simone, p. 329. The Munichois, pacifists, defeatists—in short, the opposition—as Fabre-Luce suggests, additionally hoped that by enlarging the bloodbath they would end by drowning the "warmongers." See pp. 161–62.

[3]Churchill, I, p. 485.

[4]Paul Reynaud, *In the Thick of the Fight, 1930–1945* (New York, 1955), p. 254; SWC (39/40), 4th meeting, Dec. 19; Butler, II, pp. 95, 100; Woodward, I, p. 38; Gamelin, III, p. 195.

[5]Gamelin, III, pp. 198–200; Butler, II, pp. 106–07; Ironside, pp. 213–14; Woodward, I, pp. 78–79; COS (40) 220, Jan. 28; CAB 85, MR (40), 30th meeting, Jan. 30. And for the opinion of the French Secretary-General, Alexis Léger, that "the British were entirely idiotic in believing that they could detach the Russians from the Germans and that they could finally

obtain the support of the Soviet Union against Germany," see Ambassador Bullitt's dispatch, Jan. 15, 1940, in *FRUS, 1940,* I, pp. 276–77.

[6]Cadogan, p. 253; Woodward, I, pp. 79–80; Ironside, p. 215; Reynaud, p. 256; Gamelin, III, p. 201; Butler, II, pp. 107–08; Liddell Hart, p. 55; Churchill, I, pp. 499–500; SWC (39/40), 5th meeting, Feb. 5, 1940; Pownall, I, pp. 280–82. As to winning the cooperation of the Scandinavian governments, Sir John Slessor writes: "Why anyone should have imagined that there was the remotest chance of any such thing, it is difficult to think. It seemed more probable that in the face of pressure from us Norway and Sweden would voluntarily accept the 'protection' of Germany—they would certainly have preferred that to domination by Russia and, if we won the war, could count on regaining their independence. It was, however, not long before the exercise of *force majeure* on Norway and Sweden was being seriously considered." See Slessor, pp. 264, 271–72.

[7]Churchill, I, p. 517; Reynaud, p. 256; Butler, II, pp. 111–12; Woodward, I, pp. 86–87, 94; Ironside, pp. 219, 222–25 (diary entries for Feb. 19, 24, and 25, Mar. 2 and 4); Slessor, p. 275.

[8]Woodward, I, p. 90.

[9]Ironside, p. 226; Max Jakobson, *The Diplomacy of the Winter War: An Account of the Russo-Finnish War, 1939–1940* (Cambridge, Mass., 1961), pp. 240–44; Väinö Tanner, *The Winter War: Finland Against Russia, 1939–1940* (Stanford, Calif., 1957), pp. 195–201, 210–13; Cadogan, pp. 257–58; Macmillan, pp. 52, 54; Woodward, I, pp. 92–93.

[10]Cadogan, pp. 259–62; Woodward, I, pp. 95–97, 99; Churchill, I, p. 512; Butler, II, p. 113; Ironside, pp. 226–28; *Parl. Deb., H. of C.,* 5th Ser., Vol. 358, col. 836; Eden, II, p. 107; Macmillan, p. 23.

[11]Jeanneney, p. 35; Harvey, p. 340; Pertinax, pp. 156–60; Fabre-Luce, pp. 248–52; Bois, pp. 184–87; Chastenet, p. 132; Rossi-Landi, pp. 49, 52.

[12]Reynaud, p. 257, n. 1; FO 800/312, Viscount Halifax Private Papers, H/XIV/410, Letter from Campbell to Halifax, Mar. 23.

[13]Eden, II, pp. 108–09.

[14]Woodward, I, p. 100. For instance, in the days immediately after Daladier's fall when the ex-Premier was expected at any moment to return to power, Oliver Harvey wrote that "The bad men, Laval (whose attack on Daladier in the Senate started the landslide), Flandin (very anxious now to display his patriotism), and Bonnet (always double-crossing) are raising their heads and will become a danger if there is a prolonged Government crisis coupled with a peace offensive." Harvey, p. 341 (entry for Mar. 25).

[15]See, for instance, Daladier's telegram of March 14 to Ambassador Corbin (Nos. 863–72) on the need for an immediate British decision regarding (1) the extension of Allied control to Norwegian territorial waters and (2) the occupation of certain ports in Norway that would be required if the Germans reacted to the Allies' interception of their Swedish iron supply. In

*Les Événements survenus en France de 1933 à 1945: Rapport de M. Charles Serre, Deputé, au nom de la Commission d'Enquête Parlementaire* (hereafter called *Rapport*), Tome II, *Documents sur la période 1936–1945*, Part III, pp. 349–50. The note presented the following day by Corbin in accordance with these instructions remained unanswered by the British for almost two weeks.

## Dress Rehearsal in Norway

[1]See FO 800/312, Halifax Private Papers, H/XIV/405, 421, 422, and 425, Campbell to Halifax, Feb. 12, Apr. 29 (2), and May 1; Reynaud, pp. 260–61; Churchill, I, pp. 513–14; Spears, I, p. 88; FO 371/24309, C 4658/65/17, Minute by F. K. Roberts, Mar. 29, on a telegram from Sir Ronald Campbell analyzing Daladier's fall.

[2]Reynaud, pp. 258–59, 261–63; Jeanneney, pp. 38–39 (entry for Mar. 24); Thomas, pp. 159–77; Pertinax, pp. 169–71; Bois, pp. 211–12; Rossi-Landi, pp. 50, 53, 55, 62.

[3]Communication de M. Paul Reynaud au Gouvernement britannique, 25 mars 1940, in *Rapport*, Tome II, *Documents*, Part III, pp. 351–54; WP (40) 109, Mar. 26, 1940, Translation of a Note from M. Reynaud, Mar. 25; Woodward, I, p. 102; Butler, II, p. 120. Reynaud's ideas, as embodied in this document, appear to derive ultimately from ideas that his liaison with the High Command, Lt.-Col. de Villelume, had first submitted to Alexis Léger in mid-March and that the Ministry of Foreign Affairs had subsequently adopted as its own and formalized in a note drawn up by M. Hoppenot, Under-Secretary at the Quai d'Orsay. Villelume's own note to Reynaud on the general conduct of the war dated only from March 27, but its outlines were already known to the new Premier through departmental channels. Villelume's dominating thought was that in default of help from a third power (America) it was vain to hope for a military victory in the west; therefore, the Allies must carry the war onto the only terrain where they were superior to the enemy, i.e., the sea, by attacking Germany where it was most vulnerable, namely its economy. To this end he urged an intensification of the blockade that would be directed to depriving the Germans of their most vital strategic resources—Swedish iron and Russian oil—by means of operations that could be undertaken in Scandinavia, the Black Sea, and the Caucasus. See Villelume's testimony, together with information supplied by M. Dhers, in *CE*, IX, pp. 2753–54, 2758, 2774–77. Yet Alexis Léger, Secretary-General of the French Ministry of Foreign Affairs, had made it clear to the American Ambassador as early as January 15 that the French Government had already proposed to the British Government that the British and French fleets should enter the Black Sea for the purpose of bombarding Batum and that they should also send airplanes to bomb Baku. The British at this time had promptly vetoed any Black Sea venture just as they did the French proposal for an expedition against Petsamo—and for the same

reason: the refusal to undertake any action "which could be construed by the Bolsheviks as a hostile British act against the Soviet Union." Léger also admitted at this time that the Turks were opposed to letting the French and British fleets into the Black Sea to bombard the Russian coast. See Bullitt's dispatch, Jan. 15, 1940, in *FRUS, 1940,* I, pp. 276–77.

[4]Ironside, pp. 234–37; also Gamelin, III, pp. 295–96, and 199, 216, 311, 337, 361, for French interest in the Caucasus project; Weygand's testimony on the affair, in *CE,* VI, pp. 1551, 1611; and Reynaud's embarrassed and rather faulty recollection of his interest in the anti-Russian operation, under the close questioning of M. Dhers, Dec. 7, 1950, in *CE,* VIII, pp. 2383–84.

[5]Woodward, I, pp. 108–09 (from COS Report, Mar. 8, on Implications of War with Russia).

[6]WP (40) 111, Mar. 26, also COS (40) 270; WP (40) 103, Mar. 23, Grand Strategy of Allies. This point of view was perfectly expressed by Oliver Harvey on the morrow of the Russo-Finnish peace. Like Cadogan, he too was relieved at the collapse of the Scandinavian expedition because "our resources are not adequate and we should have risked another Dardanelles campaign, possibly prolonging the war an extra year." The only solution was to "go slow until our resources in men and material are far greater, this means staying on the defensive the whole of this year. Next year we should have air superiority and then we can allow ourselves the luxury of attack. To have gone into Finland across a reluctant and possibly obstructive Norway and Sweden with two divisions and lines of communication stretching across the North Sea, always seemed to me madness." Harvey, pp. 339–40 (entry for Mar. 14). However, there were rival strains at work.

[7]Cadogan, pp. 264–65; Butler, II, pp. 120–21; WP (40) 107, Mar. 26, Policy To Be Adopted Towards Norway and Sweden; Aide-mémoire du Gouvernement britannique, 27 mars 1940 (actually a response to Corbin's démarche of Mar. 15, not to Reynaud's note of Mar. 25), in *Rapport,* Tome II, *Documents,* Part III, 354–57.

[8]Woodward, I, pp. 102–03; Butler, II, p. 114; Churchill, I, p. 512; Spears, I, pp. 70–73; Cadogan, p. 262; Jeanneney, *Journal politique,* p. 35; WM (40) 61st, Mar. 6, CA, min. 7; ADM 116/4239 and 4240, Royal Marine, containing notes to First Lord regarding French objections to the operation; letters, Churchill to Daladier, Mar. 11, and Churchill to Gamelin, Mar. 16; telegram, Campbell to Halifax, Mar. 13.

[9]WM 76 (40), Mar. 27, 11 a.m.; Woodward, I, pp. 110–12; Churchill, I, pp. 514–16; Reynaud, pp. 266–68; SWC (39/40), 6th meeting, Mar. 28; Butler, II, pp. 121–22; Denis Richards, *Royal Air Force, 1939–1945,* Vol. I, *The Fight at Odds* (London, 1953), p. 78; Ironside, pp. 237–38; Cadogan, p. 265; Gamelin, III, pp. 297–98.

[10]Ironside, pp. 243–44, 246; Harvey, p. 346. Concerning Daladier's role in scotching the fluvial mines project, the British Ambassador wrote: "Still

more reprehensible was his action in putting it about that Reynaud had agreed in London to an operation which was dangerous to France." Campbell thought the "circumstantial evidence that the leakage originated with Daladier, or a member of his entourage . . . very strong" and claimed that "The Royal Marine operation is now freely talked of." As for the personal rivalry between Reynaud and Daladier, the Ambassador thought it "deplorable" in the circumstances but was "afraid no reconciliation would ever be permanent. No doubt the influence of the ladies makes matters worse," he concluded in reference to the rival mistresses of the two gentlemen. "It is all very sordid and tragic." See FO 800/312, Viscount Halifax Private Papers, H/XIV/418, Letter from Sir Ronald Campbell to Lord Halifax, Apr. 7. Reynaud's "problem" stemmed from the fact that his position in the Chamber was so shaky that in forming his government he had felt compelled to offer Daladier the key post of Minister of Defense in order even to survive his first vote. Thereafter, as Pertinax writes, Daladier's "conduct was not unlike 'non-belligerency,' as the Italians understood it." Considering his slim majority of one—and that, on the evidence of Herriot, possibly not quite legitimate—Georges Mandel had prophetically remarked to the new Premier: "And now, you have only to govern." Reynaud was to remain "a passenger in his own Government," as General Spears phrased it, until May 19, when he turned over Foreign Affairs to Daladier and himself took over Defense. See Pertinax, p. 167; *The Complete War Memoirs of Charles de Gaulle* (New York, 1964), p. 31; Werth, *Last Days of Paris*, p. 256; Rossi-Landi, pp. 62–63; Marcel Peyrouton, *Du Service Public à la Prison Commune* (Paris, 1950), p. 87; Spears, I, p. 97. See also Jeanneney's unfavorable comments on Daladier's spiteful and hostile behavior towards Reynaud and on his indiscretion in the fluvial mines matter, in *Journal Politique*, pp. 38, 40, 42; and WM (40) 84th, Apr. 8, CA, min. 5.

[11]FO 800/312, Halifax Private Papers, H/XIV, 414, Note by Prime Minister, Mar. 31; WM 78 (40), Apr. 1, 11:30 a.m.; Cadogan, pp. 266–67 (entries for Apr. 1 and 2); ADM 116/4240, C 4892/G, Tel. No. 734 to Sir R. Campbell, Apr. 2, based on R. M. Makins's minute of Cadogan's discussion with Ambassador Corbin, Apr. 2; Spears, I, pp. 96–97; Churchill, I, p. 519; Harvey, pp. 346–47 (entry for Apr. 4); Gamelin, III, pp. 218–20, 300; Reynaud's testimony, Dec. 7, 1950, in *CE*, VIII, pp. 2378, 2379.

[12]ADM 116/4240, FO minute by Vernon, Apr. 4, and Tels. Nos. 87 and 88 DIPP from Sir R. Campbell, rec'd 1 a.m. and 5:45 a.m., Apr. 5, regarding Churchill's trip; Memo from Churchill to Cabinet on R.M., Apr. 7; WM 82 (40), Apr. 5, 11:30 a.m.; Spears, I, pp. 97–101; Churchill, I, p. 520; FO 800/312, H/XIV/419, Note by Churchill on Royal Marine, Apr. 7. Royal Marine was eventually put into operation the evening of May 10, but, not surprisingly, got lost in the crush of events and in any case gave rather unimpressive results. See Cadogan, p. 281; Ironside, p. 302; Gamelin, III, p. 220; and ADM 116/4240, Report on Results of Operation R.M. (10 May–

31 May), June 6, 1940, and an air reconnaissance report, June 8, which come to somewhat more positive conclusions. Albert Lebrun, in his testimony in *CE,* IV, pp. 1001–02, points out that the Chief of the Air Staff, General Vuillemin, the Minister for Air, Laurent-Eynac, and Minister of the Navy, César Campinchi, had all been highly critical of the venture, believing that the small results that could be anticipated were not worth the large risks involved.

[13]Ironside, p. 245; Woodward, I, p. 112; Butler, II, p. 123.

[14]SWC (39/40), 7th meeting, Apr. 9; Gamelin, III, pp. 318–19; Butler, II, pp. 128–29; Churchill, I, pp. 534–35.

[15]See Churchill, I, pp. 528, 542, 547, 549–51, 554, 556, 558; Reynaud, pp. 277–80; Slessor, pp. 278–79; and Ironside, pp. 245–98, for the mishaps and bungling that plagued the campaign, and T. K. Derry, *The Campaign in Norway* (London, 1952), Chaps. V and XV, for the official historian's assessment of the strategy and the machinery for implementing it that led to the failure in Norway.

[16]Churchill, I, pp. 558–63, 571; Cadogan, p. 272; Macmillan, pp. 63–64; SWC (39/40), 8th meeting, Apr. 22 and 23; Butler, II, pp. 136–38; Woodward, I, pp. 123–25; Ironside, pp. 262–64, 269–71, 279–81; Gamelin, III, pp. 337, 354, 360–61.

[17]Gamelin, III, pp. 365–69; SWC (39/40), 9th meeting, Apr. 26; SWC (39/40), 10th meeting, Apr. 27; Reynaud, pp. 280–81; *The Private Diaries (March 1940 to January 1941) of Paul Baudouin* (London, 1948), pp. 19, 22; Bois, pp. 225–26; Woodward, I, pp. 126–27; Butler, II, pp. 139–40; Ironside, pp. 284–87; Cadogan, pp. 273–74.

[18]Ironside, p. 285; Bullitt to President, in *For the President, Personal and Secret,* p. 411; FO 800/312, H/XIV/430, Sir Ronald Campbell to Lord Halifax, May 13. Two months later, Admiral Darlan would tell Ambassador Bullitt that "he had spent a month trying to discover who was responsible for the fiasco of the Norwegian expedition and he was unable to pin the responsiblity on any single Englishman since the board of directors had taken the responsibility collectively." And this board "could never make up their minds about anything until it was too late." See Bullitt's dispatch to the Secretary of State, July 1, in *FRUS,* II, p. 465. Hitler, however, had no such trouble in assigning responsibility for the Anglo-French failure. Writing to the Duce on April 26 regarding Allied documents captured by the Germans in Norway, he stated that "the English operations themselves bear the visible stamp of Churchill's work" and that "from the military point of view it can only be described as frivolous dilettantism." See *DGFP,* Ser. D, IX, No. 168, p. 239.

[19]Reynaud, p. 266; de Monzie, p. 209; Baudouin, p. 22.

[20]Reynaud, pp. 269, 284–87; *CE,* VIII, pp. 2375–76, 2380, 2385; Gamelin, III, pp. 314, 382–83; Baudouin, pp. 9, 23–26; de Monzie, p. 218;

Gordon Wright, *World Politics* (October 1957), p. 78; Richard D. Challener, "The Third Republic and the Generals," in *Total War and Cold War: Problems in Civilian Control of the Military,* ed. by Harry L. Coles (Columbus, O., 1962), p. 96; Jacques Bardoux, *Journal d'un Témoin de la Troisième: 1ᵉʳ septembre 1939–15 juillet 1940* (Paris, 1957), p. 295; William L. Langer and S. Everett Gleason, *The Challenge to Isolation, 1937–1940* (New York, 1952), p. 445; Spears, I, pp. 135–36; FO 371/24310, C 6660/G, Campbell to FO, Nos. 178 and 179, May 9 and 10; Harvey, p. 355 (entry for May 10); Jeanneney, pp. 45–46; Bois, pp. 262–63. See also other reminiscences of the May 9 Cabinet Council in *CE:* Lebrun, IV, pp. 972–73; Rio, V, p. 1315; Rollin, V, p. 1404; Monnet, V, pp. 1432–33; Laurent-Eynac, V, p. 1440; Héraud, VI, pp. 1501–04; Dautry, VII, pp. 1964, 2019; and Villelume, IX, pp. 2758–60, 2769–70, for the document he had prepared for Reynaud to read at this session as well as for the Colonel's role in the affair.

[21]Wright, p. 78.

[22]Churchill, I, pp. 521–22, 588; Amery, III, p. 355; Macmillan, pp. 60–61. There were, of course, rude catcalls of "Hitler missed the bus" thrown back at the Prime Minister several times in the course of his long statement—mostly from the back benches. But Chamberlain's unfortunate phrase, and the facile optimism that inspired it, provided the leitmotif for the responsible Opposition's whole attack. See *Parl. Deb., H. of C.,* 5th Ser., Vol. 360, cols. 1081–82, for PM's statement, May 7; and col. 1093, for Attlee's statement.

[23]A. J. P. Taylor, on the basis of a rundown of the division lists, shows that the negative voters included 33 Conservatives and 8 other usual government supporters, with about 60 Conservative members abstaining. See *English History,* p. 473, n. 1; also *Parl. Deb., H. of C.,* 5th Ser., Vol. 360, cols. 1141, 1145–46, for Leo Amery's celebrated statement, May 7; and cols. 1326–28, for Commander Bower's interesting (but retrospectively ironic) words, May 8. Good, detailed accounts of the two-day debate can be found in Amery, III, pp. 358–69; Macmillan, pp. 67–75; and especially Spears, I, pp. 117–30.

[24]Spears, I, p. 129; Amery, III, p. 368; Cadogan, p. 277; Wrench, p. 414.

### All Quiet on the Western Front

[1]For the many considerations involved in the adoption of "Plan D," see Brian Bond, *France and Belgium, 1939–1940* (London, 1975), pp. 43–62; Churchill, I, pp. 428–30, 497; Ironside, pp. 108, Ch. VII, 150–52, 157, 206; Minney, p. 248; Pownall, I, pp. 236, 245, 250, 253, 255–56, 360; Slessor, pp. 250–53; Butler, II, pp. 159–63; SWC (39/40), 3rd meeting, Nov. 17; Gamelin, *Servir,* Vol. I, *Les Armées Françaises de 1940* (Paris, 1946), pp. 82–94, 103–04, 106; III, pp. 142–47, 358–60; Gamelin's testimony, in *CE,* II, pp. 408–11, 465–66, 536; Daladier's deposition, June 4, 1947, in *CE,* I, p. 72; Reynaud, p. 247; WP (40) 132, Apr. 19, also COS

(40) 298 (S); WP (40) 136, SWC Resolutions of April 23. For a brief summary of how (and why) the Dyle plan evolved, see Lieutenant-Colonel Lugand, "Les Forces en présence au 10 mai, 1940," *Revue d'Histoire de la Deuxième Guerre Mondiale,* Vol. III (June 1953), pp. 19–27. And for the active role of the British in Gamelin's decision to advance to the Antwerp-Namur line (Dyle-Meuse) and in supposedly deflecting Gamelin from his original hostility (May 1939) to a Belgian expedition, see the testimony of Col. de Villelume, in *CE,* IX, pp. 2760–65. For General Armengaud's strictures against the Belgian maneuver, unless carried out preventively and offensively before mid-October, while the Germans were still in the east, see his *Batailles Politiques et Militaires,* pp. 193–94, 214, 318, 322.

²SWC (39/40), 1st meeting, Sept. 12; SWC (39/40), 3rd meeting, Nov. 17; Gamelin, III, p. 145; Cadogan, p. 231; Harvey, pp. 329, 330; Butler, II, p. 169; Slessor, pp. 233, 239, 246, 248–49, 250–53; Webster and Frankland, I, pp. 136–37.

³Butler, II, pp. 17, 165–68; Slessor, p. 238; Ironside, p. 156; Gamelin, III, p. 144; Pownall, I, pp. 248, 297, 300.

⁴WP (40) 132, Apr. 19, also COS (40) 298 (S), Air Action To Be Taken in Event of German Invasion of Lowlands; Woodward, I, p. 146; SWC (39/40), 8th meeting, Apr. 22 and 23; Cadogan, p. 272; Butler, II, p. 165; Ironside, p. 279; Slessor, p. 254; Webster and Frankland, I, p. 143; WP (40) 136, SWC Resolutions, April 23. However, what the Chiefs of Staff had pushed for in the way of air action and what Chamberlain had asked Reynaud to accept was not quite in keeping with the advice tendered by the Military Co-ordinating Committee on April 12. This group, chaired by Winston Churchill, had concluded that "in the event of a major land attack on the Western Front the primary task of the heavy bombers of the Metropolitan Air Force will be to intervene in the land battle, which may be decisive. It will be for the French High Command to indicate the targets which they require to be attacked, and the order of priority for such attack; and it will be for the Air Staff to decide the allocation of the available bomber force between these various objectives." See WP (40) 128, Apr. 12, Memo by Military Co-ordinating Committee.

⁵Templewood, p. 429.

### The Allied Balance Sheet

¹See Sir Archibald Sinclair's comment, Mar. 19, 1940, *Parl. Deb., H. of C.,* 5th Ser., Vol. 358, col. 1859; also Maurois, *Memoirs,* p. 239; and for Mandel's prophecy, Fabre-Luce, p. 294; Robert de Saint-Jean, *France Speaking* (New York, 1941), p. 244; Pierre Lazareff, *Deadline: The Behind-the-Scenes Story of the Last Decade in France* (New York, 1942), p. 306; Guerdan, p. 59.

²From Reynaud's September 10 radio broadcast and February poster campaign. See Reynaud, p. 241; Spears, I, p. 79.

³Concerning the blockade there is conflicting evidence from the Germans

themselves. On March 10 von Ribbentrop told Mussolini that the blockade had been ineffective and that the supply of foodstuffs and raw materials didn't cause Germany any anxiety, not even in the event of a long war. However, on March 18 Hitler told the Duce that the situation of Germany, "which can at any moment be cut off from its sources of essential raw materials, is in the long run an untenable one." See *Ciano's Diplomatic Papers,* ed. by Malcolm Muggeridge (London, 1948), pp. 347, 363; *DGFP,* Ser. D, VIII, No. 665, p. 891; IX, No. 1, p. 6. Fear of the blockade's ultimate effectiveness had in fact been one of Hitler's motives for invading Norway.

[4]Michel, *Drôle de Guerre,* pp. 275–76; and John McVickar Haight, Jr., *American Aid to France, 1938–1940* (New York, 1970), pp. 228–32; message from Secretary of State Hull to Ambassador Bullitt, Dec. 22, 1939, in *FRUS,* 1939, II (1956), pp. 527–28; and Guy La Chambre's testimony, November 1947, in *CE,* II, pp. 321–22, 334–35, on French purchases in America.

[5]WP (40) 111, Mar. 26, also COS (40) 270.

[6]Gorce, p. 292; Gamelin, I, pp. 87–88; III, pp. 217, 315, 319, 384–85; Reynaud, p. 264, 282–84; *CE,* I, pp. 111–12; VIII, p. 2376; Villelume, *CE,* IX, pp. 2761–62.

[7]Ironside, pp. 203–04, 241, 388; WP (40) 145, also COS (40) 320, May 4, Review of Strategical Situation on Assumption That Germany Has Decided to Seek a Decision in 1940. According to Sir Samuel Hoare, Chamberlain was shattered not by the fall of his government or by the apparent failure of his policy but by the unexpected collapse of the French Army, which caused the disruption of Britain's whole strategy. See Templewood, pp. 432–33.

[8]Henri Michel, *Drôle de Guerre,* p. 184; Adamthwaite, p. 333.

[9]On economic unity, see statements in the House of Commons by the Under-Secretary of State for Foreign Affairs, Mr. Butler (Nov. 30); by Mr. R. S. Hudson (Dec. 6); and, on the financial agreement, by Sir John Simon, Chancellor of the Exchequer (Dec. 12), in *Parl. Deb., H. of C.,* 5th Ser., Vol. 355, cols. 306, 670, 1028–30; also Michel, p. 185; and Haight, *American Aid to France,* esp. pp. 160, 162, 185, 187, 198, note 21, 257–58, for the workings of the Allied Purchasing Commission. For the diplomatic record of French efforts to realize their aviation needs in the United States, consult also *FRUS,* 1939, II, esp. pp. 518–28; and for joint British and French efforts to the same purpose, I, esp. pp. 566–71. For Dautry's testimony, see *CE,* VII, p. 1952. For Anglo-French unity a generation earlier, see Jean Baptiste Duroselle, "Strategic and Economic Relations During the First World War," pp. 40–66 of Neville Waites (ed.), *Troubled Neighbours: Franco-British Relations in the Twentieth Century* (London, 1971).

[10]See, for instance, FO 800/318, H/XV/378, Mar. 6, letter by Halifax concerning propaganda for Germany; FO 371/24299, C 5614, Apr. 16, Anglo-French Collaboration: Quotes from Speeches.

## Tightening the Knot

[1]Spears, I, p. 44; Cadogan, p. 222; Eden, II, p. 83; Templewood, pp. 413–14.

[2]See FO 800/325, H/XL/15, letter from Halifax to Lord Lothian, Nov. 21, 1939; Pownall, I, p. 271 (entry in Pownall's diary for Dec. 17); Woodward, I, pp. 284–86.

[3]See *Parl. Deb., H. of C.,* 5th Ser., Vol. 352, cols. 2, 585–86; Vol. 355, cols. 294 and 360.

[4]Fonvieille-Alquier, p. 106.

[5]Spears, I, pp. 43, 64–65.

[6]Bois, pp. 110, 136–37, 168–69, also 170–71.

[7]See FO 800/309, Halifax Papers, H/V/4, meeting held in Lord Halifax's room, FO, Dec. 14, 1939.

[8]Gamelin, III, p. 152; Woodward, I, p. 287; SWC (39/40), 4th meeting, Dec. 19; Elizabeth R. Cameron, "Alexis Saint-Léger Léger," in Vol. II, *The Thirties,* of *The Diplomats,* ed. by Gordon A. Craig and Felix Gilbert (New York, 1967), p. 400; Pertinax, p. 108, n. 1; Cadogan, p. 238; FO 371/24297, C 2051; C 2051/9/17, Sir A. Cadogan to Sir R. Campbell, Feb. 21. See Bois, pp. 170–74, for Daladier's views on the proposed declaration.

[9]FO 371/24297, C 2986, Feb. 27, Sir R. Campbell to Sir A. Cadogan. Mandel's "faith" in Daladier, as explained to General Spears, rested on a somewhat ironic basis. He thought "Daladier was fundamentally weak, but could be relied on not to make a separate peace, for such an act of cowardice would require courage of a kind, and even that debased kind of pluck was beyond him." Spears, I, p. 59. From a different vantage point, Alfred Fabre-Luce rated Daladier in the same way. "To cross into Belgium [in a preventive move regardless of Belgian neutrality] or to treat with Hitler required a Hercules; to continue the *drôle de guerre* a bull from the Camargue sufficed." See pp. 148–49.

[10]FO 371/24298, C 3894/G, also WP (G) (40) 86, Mar. 19. Some within the Foreign Office, Orme Sargent in particular, had even more ambitious ideas as to what the Anglo-French agreement should involve. On March 25 he told Oliver Harvey that the idea was to make a declaration at the next Supreme War Council "about our joint intention of continuing after the war our existing arrangement. This declaration would be followed . . . by a regular treaty covering customs union, military unified command, common finance and foreign policy, etc. . . ." Sargent was already thinking, Harvey wrote, "on the lines of a common Anglo-French nationality and of the perpetuation of the Supreme Council as the organ of the dual Anglo-French State." See Harvey, p. 342 (entry for Mar. 26).

[11]FO 371/24299, C 5939, Apr. 22, re Last Meeting of SWC, March 28. According to Reynaud's military adviser, Lt.-Col. de Villelume, the first

paragraph of the declaration was dictated by the British, the second and third by the French; the Colonel himself claimed credit for the addition of the "security" paragraph, while, according to M. Dhers, a member of the Parliamentary Commission of Inquiry, it was Reynaud who introduced the word "armistice" into the agreement. See Villelume's testimony before the Parliamentary Commission, Apr. 17, 1951, in *CE,* IX, pp. 2755, 2796–97.

[12]Woodward, I, p. 288.

[13]Evidence given by M. Louis Marin before the High Court, July 26, 1945, in *Procès Pétain,* pp. 210–11.

[14]Vice-Admiral Docteur, *La Vérité sur les Amiraux* (Paris, 1949), p. 16, n. 1.

[15]FO 371/24298, C 4679, Campbell to FO, Mar. 29.

[16]Baudouin, p. 6; Chastenet, VII, p. 139; Fabre-Luce, p. 264. For instance, many years after the fact, Georges Bonnet would write in connection with the March 28 agreement: "Its weakness was that it put us completely into the hands of the British and gave us nothing in return. At the beginning of the war, when I was still at the Quai, there had been some talk of such an agreement and while I did not reject it a priori, I did demand that it should be *accompanied by a military convention specifying the military and air support* that Britain would be obliged to furnish. . . . It was taking a risk to agree vis-à-vis an ally not to conclude an agreement without being assured that that ally would give us the maximum of support to the very last." See Bonnet, *Quai,* p. 283. It is unlikely that this argument would have weighed heavily with Reynaud in late March of 1940. His own liaison with GHQ, Lt.-Col. de Villelume, had advised him, before his departure for London, not to accept the British proposal on the grounds that such a resolution would only encourage their ally's military laziness and also because it made no sense if they were not previously in agreement on what kind of peace they wanted and on how the war was to be conducted. Reynaud was influenced only to the extent of insisting on the introduction of a general clause relating to postwar security. Ironically, de Villelume's objections to the March 28 agreement and the arguments he used against it were the very ones the British had employed against the Russians in the summer of 1939 when the latter had suggested a no-separate-peace clause as part of the Anglo-French-Russian pact then being considered. See his testimony, Apr. 12, 1951, in *CE,* IX, pp. 2748, 2755–56.

[17]Reynaud's testimony, Dec. 7, 1950, before the Parliamentary Commission of Inquiry, in *CE,* VIII, p. 2373. Ironically, similar motivation was attributed to him by some of his most hostile wartime critics. See, for instance, the article by M. R. de Marmande, reprinted in Thomas, *Documents sur la Guerre de 1939–1940,* esp. p. 171, where it is claimed that to prolong the life of his cabinet Reynaud had signed the London accord, which "in advance delivered France to British sovereignty in case of failure," also that

he secretly agreed that the French Government would leave French soil for London to unite itself with Britain if his more aggressive war policy were to meet with disaster. For a less partisan allusion to Anglo-French planning for a London-based French resistance government in case of a French military collapse (with Mandel as the centerpiece), see Maurice Martin du Gard, *La Chronique de Vichy, 1940–1944* (Paris, 1948), p. 23, n. 1.

[18]Harvey, p. 346 (entry for Apr. 4). Anatole de Monzie, pp. 206–07, suggests otherwise; according to his diary entry for March 29, Daladier was depressed for purely patriotic reasons by what Reynaud had accomplished in London on the 28th: " 'He has done everything that they have wanted,' he told me, 'and everything that I have not wanted. Monzie, I am terrified to think of all that such a man is capable of consenting to to the detriment of our country.' " However, Daladier may well have been referring to the fluvial mines scheme.

[19]See Laurent-Eynac's testimony, Feb. 8, 1949, in *CE*, V, p. 1439; Dautry's testimony, Jan. 11, 1949, in *CE*, VII, p. 1959; Reynaud's testimony, Dec. 7, 1950, in *CE*, VIII, pp. 2373–74; also Gamelin, III, p. 356; Pertinax, p. 185. Paul Baudouin's position on the March 28 agreement (which was to fuel Vichy propaganda), as he explained it to the Commission of Inquiry in 1949, was that it was merely a personal engagement made by Reynaud concerning which he had not previously consulted the Council of Ministers and which, on his return, had never specifically (or formally) been ratified by the Council, the chambers, or the President of the Republic. But his memory of the reception given the agreement does not accord with that of his colleagues, and his criticism that the Supreme War Council deliberated no more than five minutes on the question is proof not, as Baudouin claims, that the project had not been sufficiently studied, but rather that it had been so well prepared that lengthy discussion was subsequently felt to be unnecessary. See Baudouin's testimony, in *CE*, VII, pp. 2044, 2046. See also Pierre Dhers's disposal of the Vichy argument on the March 28 agreement (in his critique of Jacques Benoist-Méchin as an historian) in *Regards Nouveaux sur les Années Quarante* (Paris, 1958), pp. 39–41. Édouard Bonnefous also writes that the accord was accepted as a matter of course, Parliament being unanimous in thinking that there could be no separate negotiations, though it would have preferred "that the guarantees to be taken after victory (notably the occupation of the left bank of the Rhine), in short, Allied war aims, had been more clearly defined." Thus, he concludes, "if the legal authority of the London accord is debatable, its moral validity regarding an armistice and negotiations with the enemy was not. Our honor was engaged. No one, at the time it was signed, would have put forth the hypothesis that it concerned only Paul Reynaud himself." See his *Histoire Politique de la Troisième République,* Vol. 7, *La Course vers L'Abîme: La fin de la III^e République (1938–1940)* (Paris, 1967), p. 156.

[20]Louis Marin, testifying July 26, 1945, in *Procès Pétain,* p. 211.

[21]Monnet's testimony, Feb. 3, 1949, in *CE*, V, pp. 1436–37. Fabre-Luce, p. 269, denies that Reynaud's parliamentary support was increasing at this time and explains the unanimous vote given him April 19 in a wholly negative sense. "Reynaud," he writes, "wished to be able to say at the end of the debate that his majority had increased. But the opposition refused him this pleasure. Since circumstances did not permit his overthrow, they would accord him a unanimous vote. In moments of crisis, this was the hypocritical formula for a disavowal." See also André Maurois, *Tragedy in France* (New York, 1940), p. 79. Yet, machiavellian plots notwithstanding, it must be remembered that in mid-April the Norwegian campaign was considered a naval success, the prestige of which inevitably rubbed off onto Reynaud. At any rate, the Chamber's vote assured his government's survival, while the thunderous applause accorded by the Senate could hardly have been simulated.

[22]Sub-Committee Report on The Military Needs of the Empire, July 24, 1909, quoted in Samuel R. Williamson, Jr., *The Politics of Grand Strategy: Britain and France Prepare for War, 1904–1914* (Cambridge, Mass., 1969), p. 110.

## I Trial By Fire in the North (May 10–June 4)

### Breakthrough on the Meuse

[1]General Georges's estimate, found in *Les Événements Survenus en France de 1933 à 1945: Témoignages et Documents Recueillis par la Commission d'Enquête Parlementaire* (*CE*), Vol. III, pp. 628, 683. Among the best general accounts of the events covered in Chapter I are Theodore Draper, *The Six Weeks' War: France, May 10–June 25, 1940* (New York, 1944); Commandant Pierre Lyet, *La Bataille de France (Mai–Juin 1940)* (Paris, 1947); Colonel Raphael de Bardies, *La Campagne 39–40* (Paris, 1947); Colonel A. Goutard, *The Battle of France, 1940* (New York, 1959); Telford Taylor, *The March of Conquest: The German Victories in Western Europe, 1940* (New York, 1958); John Williams, *The Ides of May: The Defeat of France, May–June, 1940* (New York, 1968); Guy Chapman, *Why France Collapsed* (London, 1968); Alistair Horne, *To Lose a Battle: France 1940* (Boston, 1969); and Brian Bond, *France and Belgium, 1939–1940* (London, 1975).

[2]For General Georges's and General Giraud's criticisms of Gamelin's plan, particularly its Dutch aspect, see Lt.-Col. Lugand, "Les Forces en Présence au 10 mai 1940," *Revue d'Histoire de la Deuxième Guerre Mondiale*, Vol. III (June 1953), pp. 25–27; for Georges's reservations on the Belgian maneuver because of his suspicion that a German attack on this terrain might be only a diversion, see his testimony before the Parliamentary Commission of Inquiry, Feb. 12, 1948, in *CE*, III, p. 685.

[3]For a detailed study of the gradual transformation of the German plan (*Fall Gelb*) from October through its final definition by Brauchitsch and

Halder on Feb. 20, see General L. Koeltz, *Comment s'est joué notre destin: Hitler et l'offensive du 10 mai 1940* (Paris, 1957); also comments by the plan's originator, in Field-Marshal Erich von Manstein, *Lost Victories* (Chicago, 1958), pp. 104–05, 111, 122–23. This shifted the original center of gravity of the German attack from Army Group B (von Bock) in the north to Army Group A (von Rundstedt) farther south, the latter ultimately being assigned 3 armies (45 divisions), as opposed to Bock's 2 (29 divisions), and 7 out of Germany's 10 armored divisions. Army Group C (von Leeb), facing the Rhine and Maginot Line, was to have only 1 army (19 divisions).

[4]See General Maurice Gamelin, *Servir* (Paris, 1946 and 1947), Vol. I, *Les Armées Françaises de 1940*, pp. 336, 346; Vol. III, *La Guerre (Septembre 1939–19 Mai 1940*, pp. 392, 400, 401, 409, 410, n. 1, 411, 418, 422.

## The Battle for Air Support

[1]See Daladier's testimony, May 29 and June 4, 1947, before the Parliamentary Commission of Inquiry, in *CE,* I, pp. 56, 66. Here he evidently forgot Chamberlain's caveat, which was the impossibility of foreseeing where the attack would develop and thus the necessity of "disposing of the maximum possible combat planes and antiaircraft to defend Great Britain." See Jean Lecuir and Patrick Fridenson, "L'Organisation de la coopération aérienne Franco-britannique (1935–mai 1940)," *Revue d'Histoire de la Deuxième Guerre Mondiale* (January 1969), p. 66.

[2]Most figures extrapolated from a summary given by Goutard in *The Battle of France*, pp. 32–33. The German Air Force in May, according to H. A. Jacobsen, had a total of 3,226 aircraft: 1,016 fighters; 1,120 bombers; 248 medium bombers; 342 Stukas; and 500 reconnaissance planes. The French, according to Colonel de Cossé-Brissac, had 1,279 planes: 743 fighters; 144 bombers; and 392 reconnaissance planes. The RAF, according to J. R. M. Butler (ed.), *Grand Strategy,* Vol. II, *September 1939–June 1941* (London, 1957), p. 33, in September 1939 had a Metropolitan Air Force of some 1,460 first-line aircraft: 608 fighters; 536 bombers; 96 army cooperation planes; 216 coastal reconnaissance planes; and some 2,000 reserves. For varying postwar appreciations of the relative strengths of the three air forces in May 1940, see *Revue de Défense Nationale:* Paquier, Postel, Lyet, and Cossé-Brissac, "Combien d'avions allemands contre combien d'avions français le 10 mai 1940?" (June 1948), pp. 741–59; Lt.-Col. Rogé, "Les Aviations allemande, française et anglaise du 10 mai au 25 juin 1940" (February 1951), pp. 162–76; Col. M. de Lesquen, "L'Armée de l'Air Française en 1940" (January 1952), pp. 74–84. At the Riom trial in 1942, Generals Gamelin, Vuillemin (C-in-C, French Air Force), and d'Harcourt (C-in-C, Fighter Command), respectively, gave as the strength of French fighters on May 10, 1940, the figures 483, 580, and 418. See *Survey of International Affairs, 1939–1946. The Eve of War, 1939*, ed. by Arnold Toynbee and Veronica M. Toynbee (London, 1958), p. 724, n. 6. See also

the testimony of Guy La Chambre (Air Minister, 1938–40), in *CE,* II, pp. 342–43.

[3]See Butler, *Grand Strategy,* II, pp. 58, 165, 168–70; Denis Richards, *Royal Air Force, 1939–1945,* Vol. I, *The Fight at Odds* (London, 1953), pp. 110–12; J. R. Colville, *Man of Valour: The Life of Field-Marshal The Viscount Gort* (London, 1972), pp. 174–75; General Sir Edmund Ironside, *The Ironside Diaries, 1937–1940,* ed. by Col. Roderick Macleod and Denis Kelly (London, 1962), Ch. IX; Brian Bond, ed., *Chief of Staff: The Diaries of Lieutenant-General Sir Henry Pownall,* Vol. I, *1933–1940* (London, 1972), pp. 241, 244, 248, 253, 258, 297, 300, 305 (hereafter cited as Pownall); and Sir John Slessor, *The Central Blue: The Autobiography of Sir John Slessor, Marshal of the RAF* (New York, 1957), pp. 254–56.

[4]Butler, II, p. 154; Colville, pp. 200–01; Richards, I, p. 109.

[5]Richards, I, pp. 119–20, 127; Winston S. Churchill, *The Second World War,* Vol. II, *Their Finest Hour* (New York, Bantam, 1962; originally published 1949), pp. 35–37.

[6]Churchill, II, p. 37. This assessment credited by Churchill to Dowding was subsequently to cause the latter no little embarrassment when it was repeated in Mr. Churchill's memoirs because it so grossly misrepresented his views of that time. See Robert Wright, *The Man Who Won the Battle of Britain* (New York, 1969), pp. 118–19.

[7]Richards, I, pp. 123–24.

[8]Churchill, II, p. 37.

[9]See Gamelin, I, p. 342; III, p. 399; WM (40) 123, min. 2, CA, May 15. What Dowding had done to convince this group was to place before Churchill a graph showing that if the ten fighter squadrons demanded by Reynaud were sent to France and the current rate of wastage continued, within a fortnight there would not be a single Hurricane left in either France *or* England. See Richards, I, p. 123; and Basil Collier, *The Defence of the United Kingdom* (London, 1957), p. 109. And for the argument that Churchill remained unconvinced by Dowding's reasoning on May 15, rescinding the decision shortly thereafter, see Robert Wright, pp. 101–07; and A. J. P. Taylor, *Beaverbrook* (New York, 1972), pp. 435–36.

[10]Note by VCIGS on Situation as Seen at Paris, 1900/16 May, WO 106/1751, Operations I: French Front, North-East, March–June 1940.

[11]Paul Reynaud, *In the Thick of the Fight* (New York, 1955), p. 326, n. 1. Not that there was "none," as Churchill was later to write (*supra,* p. 41). For the paucity of French reserves ready to intervene in the battle, General Gamelin's eccentric use of the 7th (Giraud) Army in Holland and the over-manning of the Maginot Line are generally held responsible.

[12]Churchill, II, p. 43.

[13]SWC (39/40) 11th meeting, May 16, 5:30 p.m.

[14]WM (40) 124, min. 1, CA, May 16.

[15]It is difficult to know how Churchill arrived at the figure of 25, or precisely what significance the number 39 had for him—considering that 53 squadrons for home use was the long-established goal of Fighter Command, with 46 having been accepted by Dowding in September as a minimum figure for the island's main scheme of air defense. See Basil Collier, *The Defence of the United Kingdom* (London, 1957), pp. 88, 90, 108, 110; also Collier's *Leader of the Few: The Authorised Biography of Air Chief Marshal the Lord Dowding of Bentley Priory* (London, 1957), pp. 160, 177, 183–84, 186, 188, 192; and Butler, II, pp. 36–37, 185. The explanation may lie in the fact that by September 1939 Fighter Command had mobilized 39 squadrons (out of the planned 53), 26 of which were armed with Spitfires and Hurricanes. Churchill was apparently not familiar with Air Staff estimates.

[16]Reynaud, pp. 325–26. That aircraft *could* be used to fight tanks, guns, men, railways, and other targets on the ground had already been proved by the Luftwaffe in Poland and Norway and was in process of being proved again—even more stunningly—in France. However, the German doctrine of close support as between army and air force was alien to the RAF, which, in any case, lacking dive-bombers, did not have the instrument best equipped to do this job.

As to what constituted "essential targets," Churchill on this issue—the Ruhr—had the entire weight of army brass against him. Lord Gort, who since October 1939 had strongly opposed the Ruhr strategy, on April 24 claimed that it was "a target which can have no immediate effect on the danger threatening the Allied Armies in the field," while the Deputy CIGS, Sir John Dill, writing to the C-in-C on the very eve of the operation, complained: "When one thinks what bombing has done to make the German's advance difficult and costly, I cannot see how anyone could suggest taking any available bombers off targets on his communications and installations." Both Ironside and Eden—newly installed at the War Office and believing that the battle in progress *was* the decisive one—had also opposed bombing the Ruhr for the present, preferring instead to see "every bomb dropped where it would tell most for the battle in France" rather than on oil targets, "which could not conceivably affect the actual fighting." All had been overruled by the Air Staff and Prime Minister. According to Pownall, the army had lost its battle with the Air Ministry *and* Winston Churchill as to the proper employment of the heavy bomber force by May 11—or even as early as May 4, Churchill evidently having gone back on what the Co-ordination Committee had formally recommended only three weeks before in favor of the Ruhr policy which the RAF had been pleading for all along. In any event, the RAF's first attacks on the Ruhr on the night of May 15–16 and again the following night proved woefully inadequate, in General Fuller's estimation doing minimal damage, "equivalent to dropping peas on the great pyramid." After this, pressured both by Eden and the French, the British compromised by ordering their bomber force dispersed over a variety of targets. See Colville, pp. 174–75, 197; Anthony Eden, *The Memoirs of Anthony Eden, Earl of Avon*, Vol. II, *The Reckoning* (Boston, 1965), p. 120; Pownall, I, pp. 305, 310; and Major-General J. F. C. Fuller, *The Decisive Battles of the Western World and Their Influence Upon History*, Vol. III (London, 1956), p. 398, n. 2.

[17]Churchill, II, pp. 44–45.

[18]Churchill, II, p. 45; Richards, I, pp. 124–26; Robert Wright, pp. 116–17; A. J. P. Taylor, *Beaverbrook*, p. 436; Colville, pp. 197–98; Collier, *Defence of U.K.*, p. 111; and Collier, *Leader of the Few*, pp. 192, 194.

## The Looming Contingency

[1]Churchill, II, p. 48; Ironside, p. 314.

[2]Notes on Situation as Believed at War Office to Exist at 0900/17 May, WO 106/1751.

[3]Gamelin, I, pp. 319–20; Georges's testimony in *CE*, III, pp. 679–80; Pownall, I, pp. 313–14. It was precisely this type of dual authority that the British wished to avoid. See Ironside's letter, Feb. 17, 1940, to Gamelin on this point, WO 106/1655, Correspondence with Major-General Sir Richard G. Howard-Vyse, No. 1 British Military Mission, Jan. 1–Mar. 3, 1940; also Brian Bond, *France and Belgium, 1939–1940* (London, 1975), p. 81.

[4]Ironside, p. 322. "Here were possibilities of trouble," noted General Bernard Montgomery, "and they descended on the North-Eastern front in full measure." *The Memoirs of Field-Marshal the Viscount Montgomery of Alamein, K.G.* (Cleveland and New York, 1958), p. 51.

[5]See Pownall, I, pp. 316–19; Colville, pp. 195–96, 202. Compare also General Pownall's conclusions at the end of the campaign, where he writes (p. 367): "Of the French generals I saw, only Laurencie was worth a damn. The others, in various degrees, were unfitted for command."

[6]See Weygand's testimony in *CE*, VI, pp. 1691, 1707.

[7]Even more surprising, Gamelin's headquarters at Vincennes was not equipped with wireless. Colonel de Bardies, for his part, likened it to a "submarine without periscope." See p. 188.

[8]Montgomery, p. 53.

[9]Colville, p. 202; Lord Gort's "Despatches," *Supplement to the London Gazette of Friday, the 10th of October, 1941*, Oct. 17, 1941, p. 5915.

[10]Gort, p. 5915.

[11]*Ibid.*

[12]Pownall, I, pp. 322–23, 327–28.

[13]Arthur Bryant, *The Turn of the Tide 1939–1943: A Study Based on the Diaries and Autobiographical Notes of Field-Marshal The Viscount Alanbrooke* (London, 1965), p. 94.

[14]Churchill, II, p. 55; A. V. Alexander Papers, File 5/4, Notes on a meeting attended by First Lord, First Sea Lord, and VCNS, 1730/19 May, in Churchill College Archives, Cambridge.

[15]Admiral Sir Bertram Ramsay, "The Evacuation of the Allied Armies from Dunkirk and Neighbouring Beaches," *Supplement to the London Gazette of Tuesday, the 15th of July, 1947,* July 17, 1947, p. 3299.

[16]WM (40) 130, min. 1, CA, May 19. Of the Defence Committee meeting that night which confirmed this decision, J. R. M. Butler writes that "some at least of those present . . . were convinced that the proposed action was quite impracticable, and, further, that it was 'dangerous . . . to try and command the British Expeditionary Force from London.' " One of these was Sir John Slessor, instructed to accompany Ironside to France to arrange for the disposition of the Air Component, who wondered whether the War Cabinet was in any position to direct the BEF's operations considering that it did not really know the latest situation. But Churchill was adamant. At any rate, Dill, while encouraging the French the next day, simultaneously warned them that the BEF might possibly have no choice but to make its way to the Channel ports. See DO (40) 4th, May 19, 8:15 p.m.; Butler, II, p. 188; Slessor, p. 287; Major L. F. Ellis, *The War in France and Flanders, 1939–1940* (London, 1953), p. 104.

[17]Gamelin, I, pp. 4, 9; III, pp. 431–32.

[18]Gort, p. 5916; Slessor, pp. 288–89.

[19]Gort, p. 5916; Slessor, p. 289.

[20]Ironside, pp. 321–22; Gort, p. 5916; Pownall, I, pp. 323–24; de Bardies, p. 208.

[21]Churchill, II, pp. 54–55; Ellis, pp. 104–06; Pownall, I, p. 323; Gort, pp. 5916–17.

[22]For the instructions issued by Gort on May 20 and Franklyn's subsequent misunderstanding with General René Altmayer as to the scope of the operation, see General Sir Harold E. Franklyn, *The Story of One Green Howard in the Dunkirk Campaign* (Richmond, Yorkshire, 1966), pp. 14–17; and for additional light on liaison between the French and British on May 20 and 21, see the account of Commandant Vautrin, in Paul Reynaud, *Au Cœur de la Mêlée, 1930–1945* (Paris, 1951), pp. 555–59. For Martel's account of the Arras action, see his *An Outspoken Soldier: His Views and Memoirs* (London, 1949), pp. 156–58; and, for two French accounts which sometimes differ substantially from British, see General A. Doumenc, *Dunkerque et la Campagne de Flandre* (Paris, 1947), pp. 181–82, 187–90, 194–97, 199, 201–02; and Cdt. Lyet, *La Bataille de France,* pp. 85–86, 88, 90, 93–94. The impression made on the Germans is indicated by the fact that Rommel estimated the strength of his attackers at five divisions. But beyond its material results, it encouraged the German High Command to believe that it was merely a preliminary to the big flank attack they most feared. See

B. H. Liddell Hart (ed.), *The Rommel Papers* (New York, 1953), pp. 33–34; Goutard, pp. 216–17; and Horne, pp. 501, 508.

## Paper Tiger: The Counterattack Manqué

[1]General Maurice Gamelin, *Servir,* I, pp. 3–5, 11–15; III, pp. 430, 432, 436, 445; Doumenc, pp. 177, 184; Georges's testimony in *CE,* III, pp. 689, 725, 730–31; Weygand's in *CE,* VI, pp. 1680, 1690, 1705. Gamelin implies that the change in command detracted from Allied chances of counterattacking earlier, but his retrospective opinion in this matter need not be taken too seriously. See his testimony in *CE,* II, pp. 433–34. General Georges apparently told Col. de Villelume that Gamelin knew very well that the maneuver he had defined on May 19 was unrealizable. See Villelume's testimony, *CE,* IX, p. 2771. General Paul Armengaud concludes that for the maneuver to have had any chance of success it would have had to be mounted no later than May 15. See his *Batailles Politiques et Militaires sur l'Europe: Témoignages (1932–1940)* (Paris, 1948), p. 212; also Pierre Lyet, "Témoignages et Documents, 1939–1940," *Revue Historique de l'Armée,* XVII (March 1961), pp. 96–97, 100–02, for even more damning criticism of Gamelin's lack of realism, together with the argument that the change in command occasioned no loss of time in the execution of Gamelin's suggestions (at least their substance) because (1) they represented both Georges's and Weygand's ideas and (2) preparations for the disengagement maneuver outlined demanded several days' delay in any case.

[2]For the Ypres conference, see Commandant J. Weygand, *The Role of General Weygand: Conversations With His Son* (London, 1948), pp. 51–52, 54–58; Weygand's testimony in *CE,* VI, pp. 1553–54, 1680, 1682, 1686, 1705; Joseph P. Kennedy and James M. Landis, *The Surrender of King Leopold,* with an appendix containing the Keyes-Gort Correspondence (New York, 1950), pp. 42–44 (from Sir Roger Keyes's letter to Lord Gort, June 6, 1940); and Bryant, *Turn of the Tide,* p. 99.

[3]Kennedy and Landis, pp. 17–19, 43; Pownall, I, pp. 328–30; Bryant, p. 98; also John Cudahy, *The Armies March: A Personal Report* (New York, 1941), pp. 102–04.

[4]See Divine, pp. 45–46; Colville, p. 213.

[5]See J. Weygand, *Role,* pp. 60–61; Weygand's testimony in *CE,* VI, pp. 1687–88 (the French *procès-verbal* of the May 22 SWC meeting), 1553–54, 1686, 1710; General Maxime Weygand, *Recalled to Service* (London, 1952), pp. 67–68; Reynaud, pp. 365–67; Kennedy and Landis, p. 17; and Guy Chapman, *Why France Collapsed* (London, 1968), p. 197, for the probably garbled account of the final arrangements made at Ypres transmitted to Weygand by General Champon. (In fact, the Belgians would later write Champon in no uncertain terms that at Ypres they had announced their determination *not* to retreat on the Yser by virtue of the dislocation that would result for their army from such a move. See memo by General Michi-

els to the Chief of the French Mission, May 26, 1940, in *CE,* IX, p. 2822.) General Champon also played a key role early on May 22, following Billotte's accident, in relaying to Blanchard and Gort, neither of whom had conferred personally with Weygand, what the General had decided at Ypres. See Doumenc, p. 196; de Bardies, p. 219. For the *procès-verbal* of this morning meeting at British headquarters, see Weygand's testimony, *CE,* VI, pp. 1917–18; also Commandant Vautrin's account of the arrangements made, in Reynaud, *Au Cœur de la Mêlée,* pp. 559–60.

⁶Churchill, II, p. 57; Reynaud, p. 367.

⁷Weygand, p. 69; J. Weygand, *Role,* pp. 61–62; Weygand's testimony in *CE,* VI, pp. 1554–55, 1689 (based on the French *procès-verbal*).

⁸Churchill, II, p. 57; Reynaud, pp. 367–68; Weygand's testimony in *CE,* VI, pp. 1686–87, 1690–91. For Weygand's Operational Order No. 1, in which the plan was formally embodied, see *Rapport de M. Charles Serre, Deputé, au nom de la Commission d'Enquête Parlementaire,* Tome II, *Documents sur la période 1936–1945,* Part III, p. 364. This does not specify the number of divisions to be used but seems to assume seven or eight.

⁹Pownall, I, p. 333.

¹⁰Gort, pp. 5920–21; also Pownall, I, p. 334. If Commandant Vautrin's chronology is more correct than Gort's and Pownall's, it is possible that this meeting took place on the 22nd rather than the 23rd. See Reynaud, *Au Cœur de la Mêlée,* pp. 559–60.

¹¹Gort, p. 5920; WO 106/1682, C-in-C to Gen. Dill, May 23, dispatched 12:58.

¹²Kennedy and Landis, p. 44, from Keyes's letter to Gort, June 6, 1940.

¹³Colville, p. 211.

## A Chill Descends

¹Churchill, II, p. 60.

²Reynaud, p. 369.

³For the possibilities open to the 7th Army, May 23–25, see Commandant Vial, "Une Semaine décisive sur la Somme, 18–25 mai 1940," *Revue Historique de l' Armée,* V (December 1949), pp. 45–58; VI (March 1950), pp. 46–60. This suggests optimistically that Frère might productively have used the forces at his disposal (including 9 infantry divisions, 3 light cavalry divisions, 2 armored divisions, and the British 1st Armoured Division) against the 6 infantry divisions left by the Germans on the Somme had his (and Georges's) primary concern not always been defensive, i.e., to bar the routes to Paris.

⁴Ironside, p. 331; Eden, II, p. 125; Gort, p. 5920; WO 106/1698, Personal Telegrams from the Secretary of State.

⁵WO 106/1697, Personal Telegrams from CIGS, May 22–June 16, 1940, CIGS to Col. Redman, dis. 0430/May 24, containing PM's message to Rey-

naud for Weygand; Churchill, II, p. 60; Spears, I, pp. 167–68; WO 106/1682, C-in-C to Sec. of State, May 23, dis. 19:55; J. Weygand, *Role*, p. 67.

⁶Reynaud, pp. 370–71.

⁷See Paul Baudouin, *The Private Diaries of Paul Baudouin (March 1940 to January 1941)* (London, 1948), p. 43.

⁸Reynaud, p. 371; also WO 106/1697, Ironside to Gort, dis. 0430/May 25, containing Reynaud's telegram to Churchill. Weygand more accurately speaks of a withdrawal of 25 km in J. Weygand, *Role*, p. 67. What he does not mention, as Brian Bond points out, is the fact that Arras by this time was not even in the British sector, but in the French, and that the withdrawal was not in the direction of the ports, but to the Canal Line. See *France and Belgium*, p. 130.

⁹Ellis, p. 143; Weygand's testimony, *CE*, VI, p. 1708.

¹⁰Reynaud, pp. 371–73; Churchill, II, pp. 63–64.

¹¹Reynaud, pp. 373–74; J. Weygand, *Role*, pp. 71–72; Weygand's testimony, in *CE*, VI, pp. 1556, 1681, 1708, 1710; Weygand, pp. 77–78 (Weygand's principal orders and telegrams up to June 23 can be found in *Rapport, Tome II, Documents, Part III*, pp. 364–81); also Spears, I, pp. 180, 185–96, for the discussion leading up to these decisions. An interesting light is thrown on this episode by Hervé Cras, who obtained significant background details from Fauvelle and Blanchard in 1948. According to his account, Commandant Fauvelle's journey to Paris was the direct result of a meeting between him (Fauvelle was chief of the Operations Section at the 3ᵉ Bureau of Army Group I) and Major Archdale, Gort's chief liaison officer attached to Billotte's general staff, at midnight on May 23. Archdale then told his French colleague that, although the decision was still very secret, the BEF was leaving and that he had therefore come to say goodbye. This news Fauvelle imparted to Blanchard early the next morning at Attiches. When Blanchard tried to confirm it at Gort's headquarters, however, Pownall denied that there was any question of the British reembarking, although Blanchard thought he detected a certain reticence in the Chief of Staff's attitude. As a result of his suspicions, Blanchard sent Fauvelle to report to Weygand in Paris, where he was received by the Commander-in-Chief at 9 a.m. on May 25 and later by the War Committee. Fauvelle's stark presentation of the situation in the north, which he asserted meant the loss of the battle of France, had several immediate consequences: Blanchard was given permission to abandon the offensive, General Koeltz was sent north the next day to coordinate efforts to establish a large bridgehead, and Admiral Darlan was forced to start thinking in terms of an eventual large-scale evacuation. The more far-reaching consequences of Fauvelle's exposition will be taken up in the next chapter. Consult Hervé Cras, *Dunkerque* (Paris, 1960), pp. 163–74. For a comparison of Blanchard's and Fauvelle's impressions with those of

General Pownall on May 24 (though the Chief of Staff doesn't refer to this morning meeting in his diary), see Pownall, I, pp. 336–37; also note 6, *Giving Up the Ghost.*

[12]Marc Bloch, *Strange Defeat* (London, 1949), pp. 74–75.

[13]See ADM 205/6, Operations Conducted by FOC Dover, 10–25 May 1940, on Dutch, Belgian and French Coasts; WO 106/1697, Ironside to Brig. Nicholson, May 24; Churchill, II, pp. 71–72; Divine, pp. 78–81; Airey Neave, *The Flames of Calais* (London, 1972), pp. 16–18, 91, 101–05, 109, 111, 202; Heinz Guderian, *Panzer Leader* (London, 1952), p. 118.

## Giving Up the Ghost

[1]Telford Taylor, *March of Conquest,* pp. 240–41, 246–47, 255; WO 106/1673, MO 4 War Diary, War Office Summary of Operations, May 10–31, 1940.

[2]Gort, pp. 5922–23; WO 106/1682, Gen. Dill to Prime Minister and Secretary of State, May 25, dispatched 8:10.

[3]Churchill, II, p. 73.

[4]Franklyn, p. 28; Pownall, I, pp. 340 and 342.

[5]Colville, p. 213.

[6]Pownall, I, pp. 336–37. Both the general drift and the tentative nature of British thinking as of May 24 are well summed up by Pownall's philosophical comment: "Our spirits rise and fall—sometimes, most of the time, the position seems perfectly hopeless and we are of course working out plans for withdrawal north-west; then the clouds lift a little and there seems just a chance of seeing it through."

[7]Bryant, p. 107.

[8]Gort, pp. 5923–24; Pownall, I, pp. 342–43, 364. Commandant Vautrin, who witnessed the meeting, says that a "final withdrawal in the direction of Dunkirk was envisaged." See Reynaud, *Au Cœur de la Mêlée,* p. 562.

[9]Consult DO (40) 8th; DO (40) 9th; Spears, I, p. 192; WM (40) 139, min. 1, CA, May 26.

[10]Gort, p. 5924; WO 106/1698, No. 72157, Secretary of State to C-in-C, May 26, dispatched 0410.

[11]Gort, p. 5924; WO 106/1698, May 26, dispatched 1747.

[12]Churchill, II, p. 76.

[13]WM (40) 140, CA, May 26; Eden, II, p. 128.

[14]General Pownall's impression, after discussing Anglo-French difficulties at Dunkirk with Churchill on May 30 (immediately following his return from France), was that "the French and British Governments were none too well *d'accord* over the business [of evacuation] and had not indeed got a common policy which the French Government could explain to the Admiral at Dunkirk." See Pownall, I, pp. 356–57. This too suggests that Churchill,

or possibly Reynaud, may have deliberately refrained from articulating British policy to the relevant French authorities on May 26. See also note 8, *Dunkirk.*

[15]WM (40) 139, min. 1, CA, May 26.

[16]Weygand, p. 80.

[17]Churchill, II, p. 76; Gort, p. 5927; WO 106/1698, dispatched 1300.

[18]See Ellis, pp. 197–98; and General Koeltz's testimony regarding his mission to the north in *CE,* IX, pp. 2803, 2806–08. Yet Commandant Vautrin claims that after learning late on May 26 that the British Command was preparing evacuation plans he had warned 1st Army headquarters of the fact. See Reynaud, *Au Cœur de la Mêlée,* p. 563.

[19]See Cras, pp. 173–74; Ellis, p. 174; Bourget, p. 53. Gamelin had ordered Admiral Darlan as early as May 19 to investigate the possibility of evacuating certain French units by sea. Like the first directive issued the same day by the British War Cabinet, Gamelin's instructions were couched in purely contingent terms. Darlan, in any case, thought that enemy air superiority would render any attempt at evacuation impossible and concerned himself chiefly with plans for supplying the northern French armies, which would enable them to conduct a prolonged defense of any bridgehead established in the Dunkirk area. This supply operation had been set in motion on May 22. See David Divine, *The Nine Days of Dunkirk* (New York, 1959), pp. 46, 57; also Jacques Mordal, *La Marine à l'Épreuve: De l'Armistice de 1940 au Procès Auphan* (Paris, 1956), p. 23.

[20]See Weygand's testimony, *CE,* VI, p. 1556.

[21]Gort, p. 5927; also Pownall, I, pp. 347–50; and de Bardies, pp. 240–41. General Prioux was captured at Steenwerck at midday on May 29.

[22]Cras, pp. 192–93; Chapman, pp. 222–23.

[23]Gort, p. 5929; Bourget, p. 54.

[24]Bourget, p. 60; WO 106/1673, Summary of Operations, May 10–31, Report from Swayne Mission.

[25]In recognition of their gallant stand, these five divisions (General Weygand always speaks of eight) under General Molinié were allowed by the Germans to surrender with the full honors of war. The usefulness of their doomed struggle is more debatable. General Weygand claims that it "kept away from Dunkirk six enemy divisions," thus implying that the escape of the BEF was made at the expense of this French sacrifice. David Divine, however, argues that "by the night of May 29th the maps show thirteen [enemy] divisions in contact with the sides of the narrowing pocket, nine moving against it or in reserve. It would have been scarcely possible to deploy six more divisions against that shrinking front." See Weygand, p. 89; Divine, p. 108. Also relevant to the same debate is General Pownall's somewhat bitter comment written shortly after the close of the campaign: "Never

let it be said that the French protected the British withdrawal; it was we that guarded their flanks for many days, the frontal pressure was practically nil." On the contrary, he argues, "the French commanders had not of themselves the moral strength even to make an effort [to reach the coast]. It was due to British persuasion that some 120,000 Frenchmen escaped the fate of becoming prisoners of war." Elsewhere, however, Pownall admits that the British did not have to bear the same weight and violence of attack that fell on others, including the French 1st Army. See Pownall, I, pp. 341, 352, 360, 365–66.

## Dunkirk

[1]Weygand's testimony, *CE*, VI, pp. 1557, 1684.

[2]Gort, p. 5929; WO 106/1682, telephone message from C-in-C to CIGS, May 29, dispatched 1715; also Pownall, I, pp. 353–55.

[3]Rear Admiral Paul Auphan and Jacques Mordal, *The French Navy in World War II* (Annapolis, Md., 1959), pp. 72–73. The way in which the British dealt with the forthcoming evacuation of Narvik in northern Norway tends to support these claims. The War Cabinet did not formally agree until May 30 to its evacuation, but it is clear that the decision in principle had been taken a week earlier and was deliberately withheld from the French and Norwegians. On May 21 the Joint Planning Sub-Committee recommended a complete Allied withdrawal from Norway, advice seconded by the Chiefs of Staff the next day—provided that Narvik was first captured. And on 23 May the War Cabinet commenced planning for this contingency: the Ministry of Shipping, in consultation with the Admiralty, was instructed to prepare plans to obtain the largest possible amount of Norwegian shipping in case Norway decided to leave the war and to withdraw its ships from British service after the British evacuated their country; while at the same time it was agreed "that the utmost secrecy should be observed in regard to any suggestion that we might withdraw from Narvik." The decision was activated May 24 when the Admiralty signaled the Flag Officer, Narvik, that Allied forces were to be withdrawn from northern Norway at the earliest moment but that evacuation would be facilitated if enemy forces were first destroyed or captured and the town of Narvik taken. Narvik fell into Allied hands at 10 p.m. on May 28, but on May 29 the Chiefs of Staff reported that the French High Command had not yet been told officially (although General Béthouart, in command of the French and Polish contingent, had been informed on the 26th) that the British were planning to evacuate. Nor had the Norwegian Government, and it was only that day that the cabinet considered the question whether they should be so informed before the very last minute. However, because both Norway and Sweden had already accused the British of having abandoned the Norwegian Army without warning at Andalsnes and Namsos and because of the importance of maintaining control over Norwegian shipping, it was recommended that the problem of evacuating be handled with

consideration for Norwegian interests. In the meantime, the British decision was communicated to the French High Command through the Allied Military Committee, and Reynaud, who had been privately told by Churchill on May 25 of British intentions, formally agreed to the immediate evacuation of the Narvik area at the Supreme War Council, May 31. Only then was the decision to be conveyed to the Norwegian Government—on June 2. The evacuation of Narvik's 27,000 Allied troops duly commenced on June 3 and was completed in good order on June 8. See Churchill, I, pp. 544, 581–82; Richards, I, p. 95; JP (40) 185, May 21, also COS (40) 372 (JP); Butler, II, pp. 145–46; WM (40) 135, min. 9, CA, May 23; DO (40) 7th, May 24, 5 p.m.; COS (40) 157th, May 29, 10 a.m.; WP (40) 181, May 29, Question of Informing Norwegian Government of British Intention to Evacuate Narvik; JP (40) 205, May 29; COS (40) 149th, May 25, 3:30 p.m.; SWC (39/40), 13th meeting, May 31, 2:30 p.m.; WP (40) 188, June 1, Resolutions of 10th meeting of SWC; JP (40) 214, also COS (40) 419 (JP), June 2. See also General Béthouart's note on the conduct of operations in Norway in Édouard Bonnefous, *Histoire Politique de la Troisième République,* Vol. 7, *La Course vers l'Abîme: La fin de la IIIᵉ République (1938–1940)* (Paris, 1967), pp. 342–43; and Lord Cork's dispatch on the Norway campaign in *Supplement to the London Gazette of Tuesday, the 8th of July, 1947,* pp. 3167–96.

[4]See WO 106/1613, May 29. Pownall also emphasized to Churchill the next day in London "that so long as the French did not produce resources of their own for embarkation this meant that every Frenchman embarked meant one more Englishman lost"—an "inconvenient truth which he [the Prime Minister] did not gladly hear. . . ." See Pownall, I, p. 356.

[5]Churchill, II, pp. 92–93; Sir Edward L. Spears, *Assignment to Catastrophe,* Vol. I, *Prelude to Dunkirk* (London, 1954), p. 278; WO 106/1697, CIGS to C-in-C, May 29, dis. 1830.

[6]See WO 106/1618; Ramsay, p. 3306; WO 106/1613; Pownall, I, p. 358.

[7]Reynaud, pp. 449–50; Spears, I, pp. 296–97. The most detailed record of this conference is to be found in Spears, I, pp. 294–317.

[8]WO 106/1697, CIGS to General Weygand, May 30, dis. 2035. An undated *draft* telegram from the Prime Minister to M. Reynaud, possibly written on May 26 and apparently not communicated, contains the identical information and phrasing, with slight variations, now used by Dill in his message to Weygand. The failure to transmit, at an earlier date and to the person most directly concerned, the crucial information contained herein ("Policy must therefore be to evacuate and orders to this effect have been given to Lord Gort") may actually account for much of the muddle between British and French over policy in the north which existed between May 27 and May 31. See WO 106/1699, Personal Telegrams from the Prime Minister.

[9]It was a question of five, not eight, divisions and it was, in any event, too late to save them regardless of how long Dunkirk remained open because their escape route to the bridgehead had been cut off three days before when the German pincers closed.

[10]SWC (39/40) 13th, May 31, 2:30 p.m.; also Churchill, II, pp. 96–97. During the period of the evacuation, British fighters flew an average of 300 sorties per day, an effort that led Dowding to warn as early as the third day of the nine-day operation that his forces were "almost at cracking point." See Collier, *Defence of U.K.,* pp. 115–16. In fact, so passionately concerned was Dowding for the survival of Fighter Command that he even went so far as to tell Sir Frederick Pile, head of Anti-Aircraft Command, that "the best service the British Army could now render to its country was to lay down its arms and let such of the Air Force as could be salved return to this country for the ensuing battle." See Robert Wright, *The Man Who Won the Battle of Britain,* p. 122.

[11]See Gort, p. 5930; Ellis, p. 234.

[12]The original plan called for lifting the final contingents of the BEF (some 4,000) off the beaches between 1:30 and 3 a.m. on June 1. This was altered during the early evening of May 31. See Ramsay, pp. 3307–08.

[13]See Harold Alexander, Field-Marshal Earl Alexander of Tunis, *The Alexander Memoirs, 1940–1945* (London, 1962), pp. 78–79; Gort, Appendix, p. 5934; DO (40) 13th, May 31, 7:45 p.m.; WO 106/1697, WO to Madelon, June 1, containing cabinet instructions to Alexander, sent 2300, May 31; Divine, pp. 192, 204. The most complete account of Alexander's confusing interview with the French commanders and its immediate aftermath is to be found in Cras, pp. 326–31. For some of the tactical considerations prompting Alexander's decision, see Ellis, pp. 239–40; for the orders issued Alexander, see Nigel Nicolson, *Alex: The Life of Field Marshal Earl Alexander of Tunis* (London, 1973), pp. 102–14.

[14]Weygand, p. 89.

[15]Churchill, II, pp. 98–99. Two other messages urging completion of evacuation that night were sent Weygand on June 1—by the VCIGS at 1131 and by the CIGS at 1410, for which see WO 106/1697, Personal Telegrams from CIGS, May 22–June 16, 1940. These were based on Alexander's view that the number of effectives available for manning the perimeter was not sufficient to withstand the serious infiltration attacks already being pressed. However, the CIGS signaled Alexander at 1841: "We do not order any fixed moment for evacuation. You are to hold on as long as possible in order that the maximum number of French and British may be evacuated. Impossible from here to judge local situation. In close co-operation with Admiral Abrial you must act in this matter on your own judgement." See COS (40) 162nd, June 1, 3:30 p.m.; Ramsay, p. 3309.

[16]Reynaud, p. 452; Major-General Sir Edward L. Spears, *Assignment to*

*Catastrophe* (London, 1954), Vol. II, *The Fall of France, June 1940,* pp. 6, 18–19.

[17]Baudouin, p. 75.

[18]Albert Kammerer, *La Vérité sur l'Armistice* (Paris, 1945), p. 400; Jacques Benoist-Méchin, *Sixty Days That Shook the West: The Fall of France: 1940* (New York, 1963), p. 214.

[19]See Alexander, p. 79; Divine, pp. 215–16, 219–21, 224–25.

[20]Ramsay, pp. 3309, 3310, 3311; WO 106/1613, Evacuation from Dunkirk; ADM 199/360, Dover Command: War Diaries.

[21]Auphan and Mordal, pp. 80–81; Robert Merle, *Week-end at Zuydcoote* (London, 1950).

[22]British shipping losses included 6 destroyers, 6 personnel carriers, 5 minesweepers, 1 hospital ship, 1 gunboat, 10 trawlers, 4 drifters, 3 special service vessels, and far more than 100 lesser craft sunk, and damage to at least as many vessels, including 23 destroyers and 1 cruiser. Over a somewhat longer period, the French lost 2 destroyers, 5 torpedo boats, 30 armed trawlers, 5 tugs, 3 oil tankers, 12 cargo boats, and 1 Channel steamer—or about a fifth of the units that had been engaged in Holland and Flanders. In addition, the RAF lost 177 aircraft during the course of Dynamo, between May 26 and June 3. See Ramsay, pp. 3314–16; Ellis, p. 246; Auphan and Mordal, p. 82.

[23]Major Ellis explains the higher number of British embarked by the fact that after the start of Operation Dynamo, 58,583 British troops (but only 814 Allied soldiers) were taken off before General Weygand authorized the progressive evacuation of French troops and before the British Government ordered facilities to be shared. Thereafter, he claims, the numbers evacuated were practically equal—139,732 British and 139,097 French. In addition, even before Operation Dynamo got under way on May 26, the British had embarked 26,402 British soldiers and 1,534 Allied personnel. Thus, the grand total of troops evacuated from Dunkirk was actually 366,162. Of this number, 224,320 were members of the BEF. See Ellis, pp. 246–48. However, Admiral Ramsay, who commanded the naval operation from Dover, gives 123,095 as the number of Frenchmen rescued, in contrast to 186,587 British, while Lord Gort states that 112,546 Allied soldiers were embarked as opposed to 224,585 British. See Ramsay, p. 3318; Gort, p. 5930. It is generally held that twice as many British as French escaped from Dunkirk, but in the light of Ellis's more carefully broken-down figures, which have the virtue of tallying, this would seem to be an exaggeration.

[24]This figure, given by Rear Admiral R. de Belot in *La Marine Française pendant la Campagne 1939–1940* (Paris, 1954), p. 136, is considerably lower than the estimated 200 or even 300 French units cited by Auphan and Mordal (pp. 73 and 82) as having been committed to the operation, or the 336 ships mentioned by Hervé Cras (p. 493), but would seem to be more likely in that rival French statistics pertain to the entire naval campaign in

the north, not just to the week during which the French participated in the Dunkirk evacuation.

[25]Admiral Ramsay lists only 20,525 as having been lifted by French vessels, while the official historian Stephen Roskill attributes 29,338 to the efforts of Allied ships. Auphan, on the other hand, claims a total of 48,288 for the French Navy for the six-day period May 29–June 3, 44,352 having been landed in England, with another 3,936 evacuated directly to Havre or Cherbourg. Part of the discrepancy is due to the fact that Frenchmen landed in French ports do not figure in Ramsay's statistics at all, while 11,347 men transported by three French steamers serving under his orders were counted as having been rescued by British means. It should also be remembered that French ships too picked up British personnel. See Ramsay, p. 3318; Captain S. W. Roskill, *The War at Sea, 1939–1945,* Vol. I, *The Defensive* (London, 1954), p. 227; Auphan and Mordal, pp. 78, 81; Cras, pp. 497–99.

[26]Baudouin, p. 76.

[27]A more acerbic comment is offered by General Montgomery, commander of the BEF's 3rd Division: "The fact that the B.E.F. had escaped through Dunkirk was considered by many to be a great victory for British arms. I remember the disgust of many like myself when we saw British soldiers walking about in London and elsewhere with a colored embroidered flash on their sleeve with the title 'Dunkirk.' They thought they were heroes and the civilian public thought so too. It was not understood that the British Army had suffered a crushing defeat at Dunkirk and that our island home was now in grave danger." Sir Edward Bridges, Secretary of the Cabinet, disposed of the general ecstasy then prevailing even more cynically by remarking that "evacuation is becoming our greatest national industry." See Montgomery, p. 63; Colville, p. 225.

[28]See Gen. Weygand (July 31, 1945) in *Procès Pétain,* p. 385, and his testimony in *CE,* VI, p. 1647, for French losses.

[29]Divine, p. 271; COS (40) 418 (JP), 1 June; Richards, I, p. 145; Collier, p. 120.

[30]Ellis, p. 274.

## II  THE GROWING RIFT BETWEEN THE ALLIES (MAY 15–JUNE 12)

### *"A Certain Eventuality"*

[1]For Clement Attlee's appreciation of Churchill's acceptance of professional advice, see Francis Williams, *A Prime Minister Remembers* (London, 1961), pp. 45–46.

[2]COS (40) 133rd, May 15, 10 a.m.

[3]COS (40) 133rd, May 15, 10 a.m.; Basil Collier, *Leader of the Few* (London, 1957), pp. 192–94; Robert Wright, *The Man Who Won the Battle of Britain* (New York, 1969), pp. 111–12; WP (40) 159, May 18.

[4]COS (40) 134th, May 16, 10:15 a.m.

[5]Paul Baudouin, *The Private Diaries of Paul Baudouin (March 1940 to January 1941)* (London, 1948), p. 33.

[6]In fact, Lord Halifax remembers asking Churchill about this time "whether he could ever imagine circumstances in which he might think it right to recommend the King and Government to move to Canada." The Prime Minister's emphatic response was that "he could conceive no such circumstances; that every man ought to fight to the death on his own soil." See The Earl of Halifax, *Fulness of Days* (London, 1957), p. 221. However, he had told Ambassador Kennedy on May 14—in the course of assuring him that England would never give up so long as he remained in power—that if England were burnt to the ground, the government *would* move to Canada, taking the fleet with them. See dispatch by Ambassador Kennedy to Secretary of State Hull, May 15, 2 a.m., in *FRUS*, 1940, III (1958), p. 30; also Richard J. Whalen, *The Founding Father: The Story of Joseph P. Kennedy* (New York, 1966), p. 285.

[7]Winston S. Churchill, *The Second World War,* Vol. II, *Their Finest Hour* (New York, 1962, Bantam ed.; first published Boston, 1949), p. 48; WM (40) 128, min. 1, CA, May 18.

[8]*The Diaries of Sir Alexander Cadogan, 1938–1945,* ed. by David Dilks (London, 1971), p. 285. Discussed at this meeting were the measures outlined by Lord Hankey that might be taken either to remove or to destroy certain valuable French assets that would otherwise fall into enemy hands: gold reserves, oil stocks, ports, munitions factories, aircraft, merchant and naval shipping. The Foreign Office did not deem it advisable as yet to approach the French Government on most of these questions. See Sir Llewellyn Woodward, *British Foreign Policy in the Second World War* (London, 1970), Vol. I, p. 196; and Stephen Roskill, *Hankey: Man of Secrets,* III (London, 1974), pp. 469–70.

[9]*The Ironside Diaries, 1937–1940,* ed. by Colonel Roderick Mcleod and Denis Kelly (London, 1962), pp. 316–17.

[10]Churchill, II, p. 49.

[11]WP (40) 159, May 18.

[12]Basil Collier, *The Defence of the United Kingdom* (London, 1957), p. 111; WM (40) 131, min. 10, CA, May 20. Churchill informed Reynaud of this decision on May 19, telling him that "It would be shortsighted to squander bit by bit and day by day the fighter squadrons which are in effect our Maginot Line" and reminding him that the additional squadrons recently sent to France were "over and above the numbers agreed before the war." See J. R. Colville, *Man of Valour: The Life of Field-Marshal The Viscount Gort* (London, 1972), p. 204.

[13]DO (40) 7th, May 24, 5 p.m.

[14]COS (40) 417, May 31; Collier, *Defence of U.K.,* p.124.

[15]WP (40) 168; also COS (40) 390, May 25.

[16]*Ibid.;* also Sir John Slessor, *The Central Blue: The Autobiography of Sir John Slessor, Marshal of the RAF* (New York, 1957), p. 298.

[17]WP (40) 169; also COS (40) 397, May 26.

[18]David Divine, *The Nine Days of Dunkirk* (New York, 1959), p. 280. Yet one of the Joint Planners, whose thoughts fed into these somber productions of the COS, writes that the gist of their feelings "at that horrible time" was "that we felt in our bones that we could not be defeated, but it was extremely difficult to see how we were going to win." See Slessor, p. 299.

[19]Keith Feiling, *The Life of Neville Chamberlain* (London, 1946), p. 444.

## The French Temptation

[1]Paul Reynaud, *In the Thick of the Fight* (New York, 1955), p. 323. General Gamelin denies that he said to Reynaud on May 19 (or, presumably, earlier): "Either demand an armistice" or "plan on a withdrawal to the empire." Gamelin believed that if the maneuver suggested in his last instruction did not succeed it would indeed be difficult to defend metropolitan France for long, but declined to warn the government of this eventuality on the grounds that if he raised that hypothesis before his plan was attempted he would be accused of pessimism and of having lost the game in advance. See General Maurice Gamelin, *Servir,* Vol. I, *Les Armées Françaises de 1940* (Paris, 1946), p. 260; Vol. III, *La Guerre (Septembre 1939–19 Mai 1940)* (Paris, 1947), pp. 427, 430–31; also Gamelin's testimony in *CE,* II, pp. 531–32. Like many French memoirs of this period, Gamelin's seem in large part a defense of himself against "crimes" that in May 1940 had not yet been defined as such.

[2]Pertinax, *The Gravediggers of France: Gamelin, Daladier, Reynaud, Pétain, and Laval* (Garden City, N.Y., 1944), p. 74; Alistair Horne, *To Lose a Battle: France 1940* (Boston, 1969), pp. 380–81; dispatch by Bullitt to the Secretary of State, May 16, 11 a.m., in *FRUS,* 1940, I (1959), pp. 200–01; and No. 736, May 18, noon, for Roosevelt in *For the President, Personal and Secret,* ed. by Orville H. Bullitt (Boston, 1972), p. 426.

[3]*The Diplomatic Diaries of Oliver Harvey, 1937–1940,* ed. by John Harvey (London, 1970), p. 362.

[4]See Elizabeth R. Cameron, "Alexis Saint-Léger Léger," in *The Diplomats, 1919–1939,* Vol. II, *The Thirties,* ed. by Gordon A. Craig and Felix Gilbert (New York, 1967), pp. 400–02; Jacques Chastenet, *Histoire de la Troisième République,* Vol. VII, *Le Drame Final (1938–1940)* (Paris, 1963), p. 137. See also Pertinax, pp. 243–50; Pierre Lazareff, *Deadline* (New York, 1942), pp. 290–94; and Elie J. Bois, *Truth on the Tragedy of France* (London, 1941), pp. 230–35, 294–300, for the machinations surrounding Léger's dismissal.

[5]FO 371/24309, C 4369/65/17, Letter from Lord Perth to Gladwyn Jebb, May 20, 1940.

[6]Reynaud's Deputy Prime Minister, Camille Chautemps—along with many others—would subsequently accuse him of having anticipated the need for an armistice when he nominated Pétain and Weygand; that is, the two older men would provide cover for such a momentous decision. De Gaulle, Chautemps suggests, would have infused new blood and vigor into the campaign and would have better conformed to Reynaud's public image. See his *Cahiers secrets de l'Armistice (1939–40)* (Paris, 1963), pp. 89–90. At the time, however, both Parliament and the French press hailed Reynaud's action as a positive and unifying move. And given the dearth of inspiring French leaders, Reynaud's choice of Pétain hardly needs justification. Reynaud had asked him to join his government in late April, three weeks before the crisis was upon France. Furthermore, Daladier had hoped to add the Marshal's luster to *his* jaded cabinet back in September at the very start of the war. See Gamelin, I, p. 7; Pertinax, pp. 112, including n. 4, 191–92; Bois, pp. 84–86; testimony of Messrs. Reynaud, Daladier, and Lebrun, July 23, 24, and 25, 1945, before the High Court, in *Procès Pétain*, pp. 48–50, 120, 151; and Reynaud's testimony, in *CE*, I, p. 114; VIII, 2387, 2389–90, 2395–96; IX, 2863–64.

[7]For evidence on Weygand's appraisal of the situation, May 16–19, see Pertinax, pp. 198–99; Gabriel Puaux, *Deux Années au Levant: Souvenirs de Syrie et du Liban, 1939–1940* (Paris, 1952), pp. 190–91; Gamelin, I, p. 12; III, p. 435; Commandant J. Weygand, *The Role of General Weygand: Conversations With His Son* (London, 1948), pp. 40–42, 45; also P.-A. Bourget, *De Beyrouth à Bordeaux: La Guerre 1939–40 vue du P.C. Weygand* (Paris, 1946), pp. 25–26. For Pétain's attitude on May 16, see Louis Noguères, *Le Véritable Procès du Maréchal Pétain* (Paris, 1955), p. 33.

[8]Baudouin, pp. 43, 45, 76, 83. That French anti-British feelings might easily be paralleled by British anti-American feelings in the near future was perspicaciously recognized by Ambassador Kennedy in his usual pessimistic way. "If things go badly for Great Britain," he reported on June 10, "everyone here is going to look around for somebody to blame." He could visualize Britain's "possible eventual acceptance of a German victory, but [he believed] they will never forgive us for not having come to their aid." In fact, he thought Americans were already well on their way "to becoming the 'patsys.'" See Kennedy to Secretary of State, in *FRUS*, 1940, III, pp. 34–35; Whalen, pp. 290–91.

[9]See Clare Boothe, *Europe in the Spring* (New York, 1940), p. 265; Harold Nicolson, *The War Years, 1939–1945,* Vol. II of *Diaries and Letters,* ed. by Nigel Nicolson (New York, 1967), pp. 89, 91; *Diplomatic Diaries of Oliver Harvey,* p. 359; Cadogan, pp. 285, 288, 293, 294; J. R. Colville, *Man of Valour: The Life of Field-Marshal The Viscount Gort* (London, 1972), p. 229; WM (40) 151, June 1, 11:30 a.m.

[10]Alfred Fabre-Luce, *Journal de la France, mars 1939-juillet 1940* (Paris, 1940), p. 349.

[11]Baudouin, p. 47; Villelume's testimony in *CE,* IX, p. 2786.

[12]See Gordon Wright, "Ambassador Bullitt and the Fall of France," *World Politics,* Vol. X, No. 1 (October 1957), p. 82; Bullitt's dispatch to the Secretary of State, May 18, 10 p.m., in *FRUS,* 1940, I, p. 229.

[13]Reynaud, pp. 382–83; also Reynaud's testimony on this point, July 23 and Aug. 1, 1945, in *Procès Pétain,* pp. 52–53, 55, 434–35; and in *CE,* I, p. 115; VIII, pp. 2398–99. Weygand said to Baudouin on May 26 that if the government wished to preserve intact the morale of the army and to avoid the growth of a revolutionary movement in Paris, it ought to remain in the capital, "even at the risk of being taken by the enemy." It was a matter of the preservation of power. "Let us remember that when we entered Rome— and we were the barbarians in those days—we found the senators sitting in their curule chairs." See Baudouin, p. 56. And with Rollin, Minister for the Colonies, he used similar language on or about this date—language that when reported to the President of the Republic the latter characterized as "insane." See Rollin's testimony, in *CE,* VII, p. 2136. After the war Weygand himself would dismiss this idea of the government's remaining in Paris as a "sottise." See Weygand's testimony, in *CE,* VI, pp. 1780–81. That Daladier shared Weygand's reasoning is made clear in the message Ambassador Bullitt sent Roosevelt on May 27. See No. 899 in *For the President,* p. 432.

[14]Reynaud, p. 382. At the Pétain trial in 1945 General Weygand hotly denied that there had been any conspiracy or collusion between himself and Marshal Pétain in favor of an armistice. However, meetings between the two became far more frequent and assumed an undeniable momentum from June 11. See Michel Clemenceau's testimony on this point, July 28, and General Weygand's, July 31, in *Procès Pétain,* pp. 281, 284–85, and 379–80.

[15]Albert Kammerer, *La Vérité sur l'Armistice* (Paris, 1945), pp. 53–54.

[16]Reynaud, pp. 383–85, 388.

## The Problem Posed

[1]See Hervé Cras, *Dunkerque* (Paris, 1960), pp. 168–72. Baudouin, pp. 48–49; Reynaud, p. 374, n. 2; General Maxime Weygand, *Recalled to Service* (London, 1952), pp. 79–81; and Major-General Sir Edward L. Spears, *Assignment to Catastrophe,* Vol. I, *Prelude to Dunkirk* (London, 1954), pp. 188–96, also deal with this episode, but only Cras contains the common-sense analysis made by Fauvelle. The French witnesses may have had some reason for suppressing the alternatives presented by Fauvelle, while General Spears, according to Cras, distorted Fauvelle's recital and the nature of his "defeatism" in his own account out of pique at being contradicted by the major. Fauvelle, incidentally, would seem to be the origin of the Breton redoubt scheme that Reynaud soon took up as his own.

[2]For the factors affecting General Weygand's decision, see his testimony in *CE,* VI, pp. 1558–59. The May 26 order itself appears in *Rapport,* Tome II, *Documents,* Part III, pp. 370–71; and Weygand, pp. 97–98.

[3]Philip C. F. Bankwitz, "Maxime Weygand and the Fall of France: A Study in Civil-Military Relations," *The Journal of Modern History,* Vol. XXXI, No. 3 (September 1959), pp. 230–32.

[4]The German plan for the second phase of the campaign (*Fall Rot*) called for the employment of some 140 divisions, of which 137 actually participated. See Major L.F. Ellis, *The War in France and Flanders, 1939–1940* (London, 1953), p. 274. The number of French divisions available by the time the battle began, according to informed estimates, was between 62 and 66. But on May 25 Weygand envisaged only 60 by June 15. See Baudouin, pp. 52, 92. Elsewhere, Weygand speaks of the losses in the north amounting to 30 per cent, not 80 per cent, of their armored forces. See his testimony in *CE,* VI, p. 1647; but for his statement at the May 25 meeting, see p. 1694.

[5]Albert Lebrun, *Témoignage* (Paris, 1945), p. 72; Reynaud, p. 389. Reynaud's question *at precisely this point* together with General Weygand's answer do not figure in the *procès-verbal* of the meeting, but the existence of such an exchange alone renders intelligible the remark by Reynaud immediately following, which out of context makes little sense.

[6]Kammerer, p. 50. This is most likely what Reynaud did say at the moment, although the phrase was later expunged (by his hand) from the first draft of the *procès-verbal* and did not appear in Baudouin's final version, for which see Baudouin, p. 53. Reynaud always contested this *first* reference to an armistice, of which Weygand was subsequently to make much capital, but in context it is hardly damaging. Of great help in reconstructing this meeting would be precise knowledge of when Reynaud made his corrections of the first draft, or *projet,* of the *procès-verbal.* His own tortured exegesis of the passage, pp. 391–94, *In the Thick of the Fight,* casts little light on the matter. But cf. Reynaud's testimony, July 31, 1945, in *Procès Pétain,* p. 420. For the original draft of the minutes of the May 25 meeting, complete with insertions and deletions in the handwriting of M. Reynaud, see *CE,* VI, pp. 1711–16; for Weygand's commentaries on this document, a photocopy of which he had submitted to the Commission of Inquiry, see his testimony, VI, pp. 1693–98, as well as pp. 1559, 1767, and 1769–71 for further tendentious discussion of the May 25 meeting. For Baudouin's explanations concerning the differences between his first draft and the final draft and the subsequent history of these documents, see his testimony, July 12, 1949, in *CE,* VII, pp. 2037–40.

[7]*Procès-verbal* of the War Committee meeting, May 25, in *CE,* VI, p. 1714; Baudoin, p. 52; Lebrun, p. 72; Reynaud, p. 390; Pierre Dhers, "Le Comité de Guerre du 25 mai 1940," *Revue d'Histoire de la Deuxième Guerre Mondiale* (June 1953), pp. 172–73; Kammerer, p. 51; Louis Noguères, *Le Véritable Procès du Maréchal Pétain* (Paris, 1955), p. 71.

[8]*Procès-verbal,* CE, VI, p. 1714; Baudouin, pp. 53–54; J. Weygand, *Role,* pp. 83–84; Lebrun's testimony, in CE, IV, p. 994; Dhers, "Comité de Guerre," p. 182. Before the postwar Commission of Inquiry, Laurent-Eynac stressed the hypothetical, or conditional, nature of this discussion, but it is unlikely that it was quite so hypothetical as the Air Minister believed. See his testimony, Feb. 8, 1949, in CE, V, pp. 1442–43.

[9]See Jules Jeanneney, *Journal politique (septembre 1939–juillet 1942)* (Paris, 1972), pp. 55–56, for these revealing conversations, which clearly show that on this date the four highest personages of the French Republic experienced no difficulty in entertaining the possibility of a French withdrawal from the war; it was largely a question of how the situation was to be controlled and of whether the unstable assemblies could be trusted to reject dishonorable conditions.

[10]Baudouin, p. 54; Laurent-Eynac, CE, V, p. 1443.

[11]CE, VI, p. 1715; Baudouin, *Neuf mois au gouvernement (Avril-Décembre 1940)* (Paris, 1948), p. 87; J. Weygand, *Role,* pp. 84–85. Reynaud, Rollin, and Laurent-Eynac all later denied that Campinchi could have made this last remark, on the grounds that its cynicism was inconsistent both with his beliefs (he was a long-term supporter of the entente with England) and his subsequent behavior (as an opponent of the armistice). Campinchi's former *directeur de cabinet,* Matteo Connet, furthermore pointed out to the Commission of Inquiry the internal contradiction in the words lent Campinchi by Baudouin. But Baudouin, when questioned, refused to back down from his version of the May 25 meeting: he saw no contradiction in Campinchi's thought because at the time—indeed from May 16 on—he often heard similar proposals from many people. Mention of peace or armistice terms on May 25 was quite natural, he thought, because in the panicky atmosphere in which the War Committee had been convoked there was every expectation that a question of a capitulation or an armistice might arise in the near future. See CE, Vol. VII, testimony by Baudouin, July 12, 1949, pp. 2041, 2044–45, 2047–48, 2053; Rollin, July 28, 1949, pp. 2135–36; Laurent-Eynac, Nov. 29, 1949, pp. 2164–66; Connet, Jan. 12, 1950, pp. 2186, 2189–90; VIII, Reynaud, Dec. 12, 1950, p. 2397. See also Reynaud, pp. 394–97; and Dhers, "Comité de Guerre," pp. 174, 180–81.

[12]M. Charles Serre questioning President Lebrun, June 8, 1948, in CE, IV, p. 993; William L. Langer, *Our Vichy Gamble* (New York, 1947), p. 17. Ambassador Bullitt cabled the American Secretary of State on May 22 that Reynaud had learned from Italian and Swedish sources that if the Germans were spectacularly successful in the battle then raging in northern France, Hitler intended to offer France a generous, but separate, peace. Reynaud told Bullitt that if such a proposal were made at a moment of great discouragement "there was an enormous danger that the French public would be disposed to accept it." The Premier himself thought acceptance would be "suicidal." See Hull, I, pp. 768–69. To Baudouin Reynaud expressed the same

thought on May 24; he wondered if "in the event of a peace offer by Germany on moderate terms the state of public opinion would permit of it being rejected." In such a case, Reynaud vowed to resign. Baudouin, p. 47.

[13]Baudouin, p. 54.

[14]*CE*, VI, pp. 1715–16; J. Weygand, *Role*, pp. 85–86; Dhers, "Comité de Guerre," p. 175; Baudouin, pp. 55–56; Baudouin's testimony, in *CE*, VII, pp. 2047, 2123; comment by M. Dhers in the course of Col. de Villelume's testimony, in *CE*, IX, p. 2787.

## May 26: The Crisis Contained

[1]Churchill, II, p. 106.

[2]Langer, *Our Vichy Gamble*, p. 17.

[3]Reynaud, p. 405.

[4]WM (40) 140, CA, May 26, 2 p.m. It appears that on May 20 Reynaud was approached by the Swedish Consul-General, Raoul Nordling, with a semiofficial offer from Goering of "reasonable conditions" if he would consent to ask for an armistice. Reynaud had refused even to consider the prospect and had asked Nordling not to speak of this message to anyone. See Pierre Dhers, *Regards Nouveaux sur les Années Quarante* (Paris, 1958), p. 59. But, rumors to this effect notwithstanding, the Germans never did make an explicit offer, and the suspicion remains that Hitler was simply using a clever psychological technique to soften up the French. Having anticipated a proposal for so long, and with it a certain power to answer either "yes" or "no," the French in their disappointment would be ripe for the plucking when the time came, eager in fact to solicit an armistice themselves.

[5]WM (40) 140, CA, May 26, 2 p.m.

[6]Baudouin, p. 58. The full passage is worth quoting: "I asked M. Paul Reynaud, 'What did you say of the necessity in which we may shortly find ourselves of breaking off the fight? In what conditions will the English free us from our promise?' 'I was not able to put the question,' he replied. I told him that he had done wrong; that he had not fulfilled the mission with which the War Committee had entrusted him; and that the longer this problem was postponed the more difficult it would be of solution." *Had* Reynaud posed the question, however, Churchill was prepared to place on the French several stiff and probably unacceptable conditions.

[7]DO (40) 9th, May 25, 10 p.m.

[8]The COS memo comprised four categories: (1) arguments to deter the French from capitulating, in which appeals to honor and realism were combined with a variety of threats; (2) arguments to strengthen the French will to fight on—a notably slim section; (3) measures to press on the French if Reynaud was determined to surrender; and (4) measures the French should agree to after they capitulated—the last two relating primarily to France's obligation to extricate the BEF and British air forces then serving in France

and the need to prevent French military, naval, and economic resources from falling into the hands of the enemy. COS (40) 391, May 26.

[9]Woodward, I, p. 198.

[10]See Reynaud's testimony, Dec. 12, 1950, in *CE,* VIII, pp. 2398, 2404. However, in his memoirs, Reynaud is less reticent regarding Lord Halifax's proposals and intentions. See Reynaud, p. 405.

[11]See Villelume's testimony, in *CE,* IX, pp. 2785, 2787. Interestingly enough, Reynaud had told Sumner Welles on March 9, 1940, that he was not in principle opposed to negotiations between the Allies and Germany if only some practical scheme could be devised whereby "France could obtain security and insure herself against a repetition of German aggression." Such a negotiation, he believed, would be "infinitely more in the interests of the French people than the continuation of the present war, with the probable economic and social havoc and ruin which would result, quite apart from the inevitable losses in life and property." This exchange, to be sure, took place deep in the phoney war period, when the circumstances were entirely different, and before Reynaud had become Premier. Five days later he also told Welles that "Mr. Churchill's point of view was utterly intransigent" and that "his mind had lost its elasticity." "He felt that Mr. Churchill could conceive of no possibility other than war to the finish—whether that resulted in utter chaos and destruction or not. That he felt sure was not true statesmanship." See Report by the Under Secretary of State (Welles) on His Special Mission to Europe, in *FRUS,* 1940, I, pp. 71 and 92.

[12]WM (40) 140, CA, May 26, 2 p.m.

[13]See WM (40) 139, min. 1, CA, May 26; COS (40) 150th, May 26, 8 a.m.

[14]WM (40) 140, CA, May 26, 2 p.m.

[15]Woodward, I, pp. 197–98; WM (40) 139, min. 1, CA, May 26; Reynaud, p. 405; and *FRUS,* 1940, II (1957), pp. 709–11, for the British exchanges with the American State Department. The real purpose of the Secretary of State's conversation with the Italian Ambassador on May 25 is made clear in the following extracts from a letter sent by Lord Halifax to the British Ambassador in Rome, Sir Percy Loraine, following his interview that afternoon:

. . . His Excellency asked me whether he might inform his Government [Italy] that His Majesty's Government considered it opportune now to examine the questions at issue between our two countries within the larger framework of a European settlement.

I said that I had always thought, if any discussions were to be held with a view to solving European questions and building a peaceful Europe, that matters which caused anxiety to Italy must certainly be discussed as part of the general European settlement.

Whether or not it might be possible to bring matters, which caused anxiety to Italy, to solution while the war was still in progress would no doubt depend upon the nature of the issues raised, and upon the course which any discussions might take.

Signor Bastianini then said that he would like to know whether His Majesty's Government would consider it possible to discuss general questions involving not only

Great Britain and Italy, but other countries. On my saying that it was difficult to visualise such wide discussions while the war was still proceeding, the Ambassador replied that once such a discussion were begun, war would be pointless.

After Bastianini had stated that Mussolini was interested in European questions, Poland, for instance, and in a settlement that would be more than an armistice, Lord Halifax had concluded by stating that his government "would never be unwilling to consider any proposal made with authority that gave promise of the establishment of a secure and peaceful Europe." This, he added, was also the attitude of the French Government. See WP (40) 170, Halifax to Sir P. Loraine, May 25. But, in spite of the attempt, Sir Alexander Cadogan wrote in his diary that night that, according to Gladwyn Jebb, the Halifax-Bastianini conversation "had raté [misfired] completely." Apparently the Ambassador had expected some concrete proposals and was consequently disappointed. See Cadogan, pp. 289–90. Ciano's response to the initiative was not known till 28 May.

[16]Woodward, I, p. 198.

[17]WP (40) 170, May 26, Suggested Approach to Signor Mussolini, Memo by Secretary of State along lines of Reynaud's proposal; Woodward, I, p. 200.

[18]Reynaud, p. 404. The impetus for this plan seems to have come from the French Ambassador in Italy, André François-Poncet, although it was also strongly supported by the Italophile members of Reynaud's government and by those in whom the desire for appeasement sprang eternal. But the impetus for the larger scheme—a peace conference via Italian mediation—may have come from Reynaud himself, backed by Col. de Villelume and Baudouin, and, if known in advance at all, was probably not discouraged by many others. It accorded entirely with Lord Halifax's view of the necessities of the moment.

[19]Reynaud, p. 405. A suggestion pretty much along these lines was in fact sent off to Mussolini that very afternoon by President Roosevelt at the prompting of the Foreign Office.

[20]Churchill, II, p. 107.

[21]Baudouin, pp. 57–58. This conforms with what he had told Col. de Villelume and Roland de Margerie immediately after leaving the British: that he had obtained nothing, although Halifax appeared disposed to make concessions to Italy, but that Churchill remained immovable. See Villelume's testimony, in *CE,* IX, p. 2785.

[22]Chautemps, p. 101; Oliver Harvey, *Diplomatic Diaries,* p. 369.

[23]WM (40) 140, CA, May 26, 2 p.m.

[24]*Ibid.*

[25]J. R. M. Butler (ed.), *Grand Strategy,* Vol. II, *September 1939–June 1941* (London, 1957), pp. 211–12; WM (40) 141, min. 9, CA, May 27.

[26]The Earl of Birkenhead, *Halifax: The Life of Lord Halifax* (Boston, 1966), p. 458.

[27]WM (40) 142, CA, May 27, 4:30 p.m.; Woodward, I, p. 203.

[28]WM (40) 142, CA, May 27, 4:30 p.m.; Woodward, I, pp. 203–04.

[29]Woodward, I, pp. 202–04; WM (40) 142, CA, May 27, 4:30 p.m.

[30]Woodward, I, p. 202.

[31]François Charles-Roux, *Cinq mois tragiques aux affaires étrangères (21 mai–1$^{er}$ novembre 1940)* (Paris, 1949), pp. 10–12; Reynaud, pp. 411–12; and Reynaud's testimony, together with a deposition by Charles-Roux, July 24, 1945, in *Procès Pétain,* pp. 105–08. Anatole de Monzie was less interested in making precise offers to the Italians than simply in entering into direct conversations with Rome. He insisted to Daladier that his thesis was "that of Halifax." However, with or without England, he favored some sort of Franco-Italian entente. As he saw it, "The engagement not to treat separately concerned only Germany, the only enemy at the moment when Paul Reynaud pledged our word to England." See *Ci-Devant* (Paris, 1941), pp. 236–38, 241. For Reynaud's report to Jeanneney on the May 27 Council, see Jeanneney, *Journal politique,* pp. 59–60 (entries for May 30 and 31). With respect to the French offers themselves, they represented an advance over what Daladier had told Sumner Welles on March 7 that he was willing to concede to Mussolini if a general peace settlement could be reached. See Welles's Report, in *FRUS,* 1940, I, pp. 61, 67.

[32]Hugh Dalton, *The Fateful Years: Memoirs, 1931–1945* (London, 1957), pp. 335–36. This also accords with Churchill's recollection of the event, although his account is much less explicit with respect to the options he presented; cf. Churchill, II, p. 87. This episode would seem to be just the kind that Lord Hankey most feared at the time Churchill first took over the reins of government. He had then written: "God help the country which, at the beginning of the supreme crisis of its fate . . . commits its future existence to the hands of a dictator whose past achievements, even though inspired by a certain amount of imagination, have never achieved success." He thought the only hope for such an administration lay in "the solid core of Churchill, Chamberlain and Halifax, but whether the wise old elephants will ever be able to hold the Rogue Elephant, I doubt." They could not, apparently, on May 28. See letter from Hankey to Sir Samuel Hoare, May 12, 1940, in Hankey Papers, File 4/32, Churchill College Archives, Cambridge. This doesn't mean that Hankey would have been willing to accept a peace offer made by Hitler, however. He had certainly opposed Hitler's October offer.

[33]Churchill, II, pp. 107–09; Reynaud, pp. 412–13. For the British Ambassador's urgent approach to the American Secretary of State and to President Roosevelt, May 25; for the suggested contents of the President's offer to Mussolini (May 26); for the President's actual message sent that very afternoon; and for Ambassador Phillips's reply, May 27, see *FRUS,* 1940, II

(1957), pp. 709–12. See also Hull, *Memoirs*, I, pp. 782–84; *Ciano's Diplomatic Papers*, ed. by Malcolm Muggeridge (London, 1948), p. 369; and for Roosevelt's speech at the University of Virginia, June 10, summarizing his offer, see *Documents on American Foreign Relations: July 1939–June 1940*, ed. by S. Shepard Jones and Denys P. Myers (Boston, 1940), pp. 80–81. Lord Halifax's suggestion to Bastianini was not even considered, the British Ambassador, Sir Percy Loraine, being told on May 28 that all talk of negotiations was useless because they (the Italians) were on the brink of war. This was anticipated when the War Cabinet made its decision. See *The Ciano Diaries, 1939–1943*, ed. by Hugh Gibson (Garden City, N.Y., 1946), pp. 255, 256; Gordon Waterfield, *Professional Diplomat: Sir Percy Loraine of Kirkhale Bt., 1880–1961* (London, 1973), p. 270; and *Documents on German Foreign Policy, 1919–1945*, Series D (1937–1945), Vol. IX, *The War Years, March 18–June 22, 1940* (Washington, 1956), Nos. 339 and 342, Ambassador Mackensen in Italy to Foreign Ministry, May 29, pp. 461 and 463–64.

[34]However, in the bosom of the War Cabinet Halifax remained unconvinced that any attempt at mediation would be worthless and reminded his colleagues that they stood a better chance of being offered acceptable terms before France capitulated and before their own aircraft industry was bombed than in three months' time. Chamberlain, while not anxious to become embroiled in another Munich-style conference, showed himself cautious and realistic. See WM (40) 145, min. 1, CA, May 28, 4 p.m.

[35]See de Monzie, pp. 239–41; Baudouin, pp. 59, 63, 66–67.

[36]Paul Reynaud, *La France a sauvé l'Europe* (Paris, 1947), Vol. II, p. 219; Charles-Roux, p. 15. For Oliver Harvey's and General Spears's diverse impressions of Charles-Roux, see Harvey, p. 371, and Spears, I, p. 267.

[37]Baudouin, p. 67.

[38]According to Oliver Harvey's diary entry for May 31, Hoppenot, the Quai d'Orsay's Under-Secretary, was sorry that Daladier's last attempt to buy off Mussolini was not stopped by the British. In his opinion, it was still "a manoeuvre by certain *milieux politiques* [meaning Monzie] to start up conversations having as their objective negotiations with Germany for a separate peace." See Harvey, p. 375.

[39]Baudouin, p. 75. Count Ciano, as he reported to the German Ambassador, had told François-Poncet on the evening of May 27 that "even if he served him up Tunis, Algiers, Corsica, and Nice on a platter, he could only say no, because there was only one thing for Italy now and that was war." See *DGFP*, Ser. D, IX, No. 340, Mackensen to Foreign Minister, May 29, p. 462; also *FRUS*, 1940, II, p. 716.

[40]Fabre-Luce, p. 313.

## Stiffening the French

[1]Cadogan, pp. 290, 293.

[2]Spears, I, pp. 235, 238, 245.

[3]Churchill, II, p. 95; FO 800/311, H/XIV/319, Sir Eric Phipps to Neville Chamberlain, Nov. 4, 1938; Pierre Varillon, *Mers-el-Kébir* (Paris, 1949), pp. 40–41; and see also John C. Cairns, "Great Britain and the Fall of France: A Study in Allied Disunity," *Journal of Modern History,* XXVII (December 1955), pp. 379, 397–400, for some incisive comments on Spears's contributions to Allied ill-will. Spears's remarks to Sir Eric Phipps, who had taken over the Paris Embassy in April 1937, must have been all the more galling in that during the Czechoslovak crisis of 1938 the Ambassador had cabled London on September 24—in a report later to become famous—that "All that is best in France is against war, almost at any price," the only exception to his mind being a "small, but noisy and corrupt, war group." This lost him the confidence of the Foreign Office, though he was not retired until the following year, when Sir Ronald Campbell replaced him as Ambassador to France starting October 24, 1939. For the Phipps-Halifax correspondence, Sept. 24–28, 1938, esp. telegrams 292, 302, and 320, see PHPP, 1/20, in Churchill College Archives, Cambridge.

[4]Chautemps, p. 104.

[5]Langer and Gleason, p. 489.

[6]Baudouin, p. 63.

[7]Col. de Villelume explains Reynaud's ambivalence, or changeability, by his inclination to weigh men more than the counsel they offered: unconsciously he placed a premium on their presence so that often whoever was speaking to him at the moment would have one leg up on everyone else. It is worth noting in this regard that by late May de Villelume had ceased for a time to speak on behalf of an armistice to Reynaud because he believed, after the failure of the northern armies' attempt to break out, that the French no longer had any cards to bargain with. However, he would resume his pressuring in mid-June. See his testimony, *CE,* IX, pp. 2767, 2785.

[8]FO 800/312, H/XIV/439, Campbell to Halifax, May 30; FO 371/24383, C 7074/G, Campbell to Halifax, June 4.

[9]Baudouin, pp. 64–65, 80, 84, 88–89.

[10]See Spears, I, pp. 258–59; Joseph P. Kennedy and James M. Landis, *The Surrender of King Leopold* (New York, 1950), p. 2, n. 4, for French pressure exerted on Churchill, including a telegram from the British Ambassador, May 29, "saying that the French did not wish the British Prime Minister to suspend judgment on Leopold but wanted him to join in Reynaud's denunciation of the surrender as an act of treachery"; and FO 371/24310, C 6913/65/17, Minute by R. L. Speaight, May 31, on the original Foreign Office instructions to the media. See also Alexander Werth, *The Last Days*

*of Paris* (London, 1940), p. 99, for the Chamber's stiff-upper-lip reaction to Reynaud's speech condemning Leopold's defection.

[11]Spears, I, pp. 267–68; FO 371/24310, C 6913/65/17, No. 296 from Sir Ronald Campbell, May 28, 11:30 p.m.; also comment by Speaight of the Foreign Office, May 31 (on telegram from Campbell sent May 29), as to the usefulness of King Leopold as a "safety valve"; Boothe, p. 267; Werth, *Last Days of Paris,* pp. 103–04. Admiral Keyes continued to think it "damnably unfair to throw all the blame on the Belgians, and [to] try to make their King a French and British scapegoat." His criticism of Churchill's policy is contained in the long letter he wrote on June 6 to Lord Gort, whom he also accused of joining in the anti-Belgian fever. See Kennedy and Landis, pp. 39–40, 49–50.

[12]Reynaud, pp. 442–43; Weygand, pp. 106–07.

[13]Reynaud, pp. 444–45; Weygand's testimony, *CE,* VI, pp. 1559–60, 1809.

[14]The War Committee had already decided unanimously on 25 May to evacuate the government to Bordeaux in case of necessity. See Baudouin, pp. 50, 55. However, Reynaud kept the question open for nearly three more weeks.

[15]Weygand, p. 110; Baudouin, p. 74.

[16]Spears, I, pp. 313–14.

[17]Baudouin, p. 73.

[18]Churchill, II, p. 98; Spears, I, p. 316.

## Always Hungry, Always Asking for More

[1]Reynaud, p. 464.

[2]See Pierre Cot, *Triumph of Treason* (Chicago and New York, 1944), pp. 59–60, 210; also Cot's testimony, Aug. 1, 1947, in *CE,* I, pp. 265–66; and Guy La Chambre's testimony, *CE,* II, p. 344.

[3]Baudouin, pp. 67, 76–77; Senator Jacques Bardoux, *Journal d'un Témoin de la Troisième: 1ᵉʳ septembre 1939–15 juillet 1940* (Paris, 1957), p. 348; Laurent-Eynac's testimony, Feb. 8, 1949, before the Parliamentary Commission of Inquiry, in *CE,* V, p. 1446; and Vuillemin's statement, July 29, 1940, quoted by La Chambre, *CE,* II, p. 343. See also Bourget, pp. 68–69, for air statistics.

[4]Baudouin, p. 67; Collier, *Defence of U.K.,* p. 120; Denis Richards, *Royal Air Force, 1939–1945,* Vol. I, *The Fight at Odds* (London, 1953), p. 156; WM (40) 154, min. 1, CA, June 4, 11:30 a.m.

[5]Collier, *Defence of U.K.,* p. 139. Up to June 12, when BAFF prepared to pull out, a total of 959 British aircraft, in addition to nearly 300 fighter pilots, had been lost in the campaign. See Richards, I, pp. 147, 150, 156.

[6]Colonel A. Goutard, *The Battle of France, 1940* (New York, 1959), p.

38; Telford Taylor, *The Breaking Wave: The Second World War in the Summer of 1940* (New York, 1967), p. 24; and statement by Sir Kingsley Wood, Mar. 7, 1940, in *Parl. Deb., H. of C.,* 5th Ser., Vol. 358, col. 603.

[7]Baudouin, p. 71.

[8]Major-General Sir Edward L. Spears, *Assignment to Catastrophe,* Vol. II, *The Fall of France: June 1940* (London, 1954), p. 3; also testimony of Pierre Cot, *CE,* I, p. 266, for total French losses in May and June.

[9]Spears, II, pp. 15–16.

[10]Reynaud, pp. 464–66; Spears, II, pp. 51–52.

[11]Cadogan, p. 294; WM (40) 153, min. 10, CA, June 3; Ironside, p. 351.

[12]WP (40) 189, also COS (40) 421, 3rd June; JP (40) 211, also COS (40) 418 (JP), 1st June.

[13]Spears, II, p. 53.

[14]Baudouin, p. 78.

[15]Reynaud, pp. 466–67. In his note of May 31, which had been forwarded to London and later seconded by Weygand on June 4, Vuillemin had asked that the entirety of Britain's fighter force be detailed to take part in the coming battle, half of which should be based in France—thus, as General Spears points out, leaving nothing for the protection of Great Britain. Spears, II, p. 60; Bourget, pp. 85–86.

[16]As reported by Reynaud to the British Ambassador. See Oliver Harvey, *Diplomatic Diaries,* p. 379 (entry for June 5).

[17]Pétain's suspicions were shared by Ambassador Bullitt, who as early as May 16 started warning Roosevelt that "in order to escape from the ultimate consequences of absolute defeat, the British may install a government of Oswald Mosley and the union of British fascists which would cooperate fully with Hitler." His anger and willingness to give credence to Anglophobic informants was based largely on Britain's refusal to send over the bulk of its fighter planes to France. As late as June 5 and 6, in spite of the British Ambassador's explanations, Bullitt still suspected that the British, while encouraging the French to fight to the bitter end, were conserving their fleet and air force as possible bargaining counters in future negotiations with Germany. See No. 706, May 16, 6 p.m., from Bullitt in *For the President,* p. 427, and Gordon Wright, "Ambassador Bullitt and the Fall of France," *World Politics,* Vol. X, No. 1 (October 1957), pp. 82–83; Bullitt's dispatches of June 5, midnight, and June 6, 5 p.m., to the President, in *FRUS,* 1940, I, pp. 240–42; William W. Kaufmann, "Two American Ambassadors: Bullitt and Kennedy," in *The Diplomats, 1919–1939,* Vol. II, *The Thirties,* ed. by Gordon A. Craig and Felix Gilbert (New York, 1967), p. 676; Hull, *Memoirs,* I, p. 774; Langer, *Our Vichy Gamble,* pp. 18–19.

[18]See No. 1022 to President Roosevelt from Bullitt, June 4, 4 p.m., in *FRUS,* 1940, I, p. 239, and *For the President,* pp. 450–51.

[19]Baudouin, pp. 45, 79–82, 83–84.

[20]Baudouin, p. 81; Bardoux, p. 326; Bois, pp. 320–21, 323; Reynaud's testimony, Dec. 12, 1950, in *CE,* VIII, pp. 2404–05; and Jeanneney's reactions to this Laval-instigated maneuver, in his *Journal politique,* pp. 54–55.

[21]*The Complete War Memoirs of Charles de Gaulle* (New York, 1964), pp. 54, 56.

[22]See Bois, p. 329; Werth, *Last Days of Paris,* p. 134; FO 371/24310, C 7125/65/17, No. 354 from Campbell, June 6, 11:20 a.m.; No. 442 Saving from Campbell, June 6, received 6:50 p.m. For Reynaud's quite reasonable explanations as to the June 5 cabinet changes, see his testimony, Dec. 12, 1950, in *CE,* VIII, pp. 2407–08; also Marcel Héraud's comments, Feb. 17, 1949, in *CE,* VI, pp. 1505–06. For Rio's defense of Reynaud's personnel changes generally and comments on Baudouin and Bouthillier specifically, see his testimony, Dec. 16, 1948, in *CE,* V, pp. 1316–17; also Laurent-Eynac's testimony, Feb. 8, 1949, in *CE,* V, p. 1445; and President Lebrun's defense of Reynaud, June 8, 1948, in *CE,* IV, pp. 992, 1006. Bullitt's gossipy reactions to the cabinet changes ("strange things are still going on at the top") can be found in his June 6 letter to President Roosevelt, in *For the President,* pp. 452–53.

[23]Jeanneney, *Journal politique,* pp. 59, 61.

[24]Spears, II, p. 66; Reynaud, p. 467.

[25]So Spears (II, pp. 46–47) had reported. However, Hervé Cras claims that of the 94,725 French troops from the north who had been returned to Brest or Cherbourg by June 9, almost half were able to join the battle before the campaign in France ended. See *Dunkerque,* pp. 496–97.

[26]Spears, II, pp. 67–68; Reynaud, pp. 467–68.

[27]Spears, II, pp. 74–78, 93–94; Reynaud, p. 471.

[28]Spears, II, p. 92; Reynaud, p. 471.

[29]Woodward, I, pp. 220–21.

[30]Reynaud, p. 473; Spears, II, p. 107. This support was consistent with what the Joint Planning Sub-committee had stated on June 1 to be the maximum fighter effort that could be made available once it was certain that the German Air Force was being concentrated on the Somme-Aisne front. JP (40) 211.

[31]Reynaud, p. 474.

[32]As with the May 25 decision to order Gort to march to the coast, Churchill was the last to come round, and it is interesting to note that his argument at this Defence Committee meeting was cast in much the same terms as those used by Sir John Dill at that other fateful meeting. See DO (40) 14th, June 8, 5:15 p.m. It also depended heavily on the arguments Sir Cyril Newall had used in his paper "The Air Defence of Great Britain," prepared on May 16.

³³Baudouin, pp. 90–91; also de Gaulle, pp. 58–59, for the account of his trip, June 9.

³⁴Spears, II, p. 120.

## The Battle Lost

¹Reynaud, p. 472; Villelume's testimony, *CE*, IX, p. 2794; Ellis, p. 275.

²Churchill, II, pp. 128–29; Ellis, pp. 282, 292–93; Desmond Young, *Rommel The Desert Fox* (New York, 1957), pp. 64–66; WO 106/1697, Lt.-Gen. Marshall-Cornwall to CIGS, June 8, dis. 0800; WO 106/1774, Operations on Western Front, Marshall-Cornwall's Summary of Operations of BEF in France from 1st to 18th June, 1940, dated June 20; tel. from SNO, Havre, to C-in-C, Portsmouth, 0810/June 13; and Admiral Sir W. M. James, *The Portsmouth Letters* (London, 1946), pp. 59–62, 68.

³Reynaud, pp. 475–76; Weygand, pp. 138–39.

⁴See Charles Reibel, *Pourquoi et comment fut décidée la demande d'armistice (10–17 Juin 1940)* (Paris, 1940), pp. 13, 17; Joseph Paul-Boncour, *Entre Deux Guerres*, Vol. III, *Sur les chemins de la défaite, 1935–1940* (Paris, 1946), p. 218.

⁵Spears, II, pp. 136–37; Churchill, II, p. 130; de Gaulle, p. 63; also Weygand, *En Lisant les Mémoires de Guerre du Général de Gaulle* (Paris, 1955), pp. 54–56.

⁶Spears, II, p. 140; JP (40) 235, June 11.

⁷Reynaud, p. 484. Reynaud reprints the complete *procès-verbal* of the Briare conference in *Au Cœur de la Mêlée*, pp. 747–57; Weygand, in *CE*, VI, pp. 1891–96.

⁸Weygand, pp. 149–50; Spears, II, pp. 141–44; Reynaud, *Au Cœur de la Mêlée*, pp. 748–50.

⁹Reynaud, p. 485; Spears, II, pp. 145–46.

¹⁰Spears, II, pp. 147–48, 151; Churchill, II, p. 132.

¹¹Churchill, II, p. 133; Spears, II, pp. 149, 152–53; Reynaud, *Au Cœur de la Mêlée*, pp. 753–54.

¹²Spears, II, pp. 153–54; Reynaud, p. 486; J. Weygand, *Role*, p. 123; SWC (39/40) 14th, June 11, 7 p.m.

¹³Spears, II, pp. 154–55; Reynaud, *Au Cœur de la Mêlée*, p. 755.

¹⁴Reynaud, p. 486; also Spears, II, pp. 155–56.

¹⁵Reynaud, p. 487; Spears, II, pp. 156–57.

¹⁶SWC (39/40), 13th meeting, May 31, and 10th meeting, Apr. 27; Spears, II, pp. 139–40, 162–63, 167–68; Ismay, pp. 140–41. However, a successful aeronaval operation *was* launched by the French against the Italian coast on the night of June 13–14. The French Admiralty was not at all pleased by the intitial delay. See French Admiralty messages on the subject in *Rapport, Tome II, Documents*, Part III, pp. 404–06.

[17]Reynaud, p. 488; Weygand's testimony, July 31, 1945, in *Procès Pétain,* p. 388; his note to Reynaud of June 10 and his order of June 12 in *Rapport,* Tome II, *Documents,* Part III, pp. 377–79; and his testimony in *CE,* VI, pp. 1562–63, 1884–86; also Roger Langeron, *Paris Juin 1940* (Paris, 1946), pp. 23, 25, and Léon Blum's testimony on the abandonment of Paris in *CE,* I, p. 260.

[18]On this one question Spears argues sympathetically that Reynaud could not have done otherwise. To have fought in Paris "would have been a stupendous undertaking even with the full and enthusiastic backing of Pétain and Weygand, the only two military leaders France recognised. In the face of their opposition he would, in the view of his compatriots, merely have proclaimed himself to be a lunatic, for to allow the destruction of Paris would be to tear a shrine out of the heart of every Frenchman. . . ." Spears, II, pp. 122, 134, 135, 136.

[19]Churchill, II, p. 136.

[20]Weygand, p. 153; Churchill, II, p. 137.

[21]Churchill, II, pp. 137–38; Spears, II, p. 171.

[22]J. Weygand, *Role,* p. 130; Reynaud, p. 489.

[23]De Gaulle, p. 59.

## III   CRISIS OVER THE ARMISTICE (JUNE 12–JUNE 16)

### *The Opening Phase: June 12*

[1]Major-General Sir Edward L. Spears, *Assignment to Catastrophe* (London, 1954), Vol. II, *The Fall of France: June 1940,* pp.174–76.

[2]Whether this colorful expression so often attributed to General Weygand was ever actually used by him is of little consequence: it represented his thought at the time. For Reynaud's attribution of the expression to Weygand in his testimony before the High Court, July 24, 1945, and General Weygand's formal denial of the embarrassing words, July 31, see *Procès Pétain,* pp. 67 and 408; also Paul Reynaud, *In the Thick of the Fight, 1930–1945* (New York, 1955), pp. 582–83; and Weygand's *En Lisant les Mémoires de Guerre du Général de Gaulle* (Paris, 1955), pp. 35–36.

[3]Gamelin's testimony before the Parliamentary Commission, in *CE,* II, p. 533; Paul Reynaud, pp. 571 and 584–85; also his *Mémoires,* Vol. II, *Envers et Contre Tous: 7 Mars 1936–16 Juin 1940* (Paris, 1963), p. 439.

[4]See Paul-Marie de la Gorce, *The French Army: A Military-Political History* (New York, 1963), pp. 296, 304.

[5]Spears, II, pp. 193–95, 223–26; Commandant J. Weygand, *The Role of General Weygand: Conversations With His Son* (London, 1948), pp. 129–30; P.-A. Bourget, *De Beyrouth à Bordeaux: La Guerre 1939–40 vue du P. C. Weygand* (Paris, 1946), pp. 113–14; Yves Bouthillier, *Le Drame de Vichy* (Paris, 1950), Vol. I, *Face à l'Ennemi, Face à l'Allié,* p. 58; Paul Baudouin,

*The Private Diaries of Paul Baudouin (March 1940 to January 1941)* (London, 1948), p. 98; Reynaud, *In the Thick of the Fight,* pp. 490–93; Louis Noguères, *Le Véritable Procès du Maréchal Pétain* (Paris, 1955), pp. 83–88.

[6]Reynaud, p. 493; Maxime Weygand, *Recalled to Service* (Garden City, N.Y., 1952), pp. 158–59; Louis Rollin's testimony before the Commission of Inquiry, Jan. 20, 1949, in *CE,* V, p. 1398.

[7]Following the Council's meeting Reynaud was first talked out of the move by Baudouin, then talked back into it later that night by General de Gaulle. The final decision against seems to have been made by Reynaud together with Mandel, Jeanneney, and Herriot on the morning of June 13, though the possibility was again discussed by the Council that evening. See Baudouin, pp. 100–01; *The Complete War Memoirs of Charles de Gaulle* (New York, 1964), pp. 66–67; Reynaud, p. 494; and Jeanneney's *Journal politique (septembre 1939–juillet 1942)* (Paris, 1972), p. 66.

[8]Weygand's testimony, in *CE,* VI, p. 1781.

[9]Camille Chautemps, *Cahiers secrets de l'Armistice (1939–1940)* (Paris, 1963), pp. 127–28.

[10]Chautemps's pro-armistice position from May 26 on is well documented by Baudouin, pp. 57, 88, 95. As for precisely when Chautemps thought the government should act, Baudouin notes on June 10: "He is not in favour of a request for an armistice, as public opinion is not prepared, but he thinks that the fall of Paris would justify such a request."

[11]See Pierre Lazareff, *Deadline: The Behind-the-Scenes Story of the Last Decade in France* (New York, 1942), p. 328, for Prouvost's contributions to this Council meeting. Jean Prouvost, owner and director of *Paris-Midi* and *Paris-Soir,* was, according to Lazareff, who worked for him, an intellectual lightweight and opportunist who frequently changed his mind, rather anti-British on the whole. Lazareff claims that in early June Prouvost was sent by Reynaud to London on a secret mission to explore with Lord Beaverbrook (also a press lord and former appeaser) and Churchill the possibilities of a joint Franco-British request for an armistice and negotiated peace. The English response had been wholly negative; instead they had counseled the French to fight a delaying action before retiring to the colonies. See pp. 307–08.

[12]Pertinax, *The Gravediggers of France* (Garden City, N.Y., 1944), pp. 265–66. Pertinax appears to have gotten this account from Louis Marin, who overheard part of a private conversation between Reynaud and Chautemps. See Marin's testimony, July 26, 1945, in *Procès Pétain,* p. 209, where he claims that Chautemps had requested Reynaud to ask Churchill "if the British Government would be likely to release us from our word"; also Louis Marin, "Contribution à l'Étude des Prodromes de l'Armistice" (hereafter cited as "Contribution"), *Revue d'Histoire de la Deuxième Guerre Mondiale* (June 1951), p. 5; and Marin's interpellations during Lebrun's deposition,

June 8, 1948, in *CE,* IV, pp. 1007–08. For a confrontation between M. Marin, a member of the postwar Parliamentary Commission of Inquiry, and M. Reynaud, in which Reynaud denied that Chautemps had intervened in this sense on June 12 but admitted that the purpose behind his wanting Churchill to be heard by the Council tended in the same direction, see Reynaud's testimony, Dec. 12, 1950, in *CE,* VIII, pp. 2411–12. For Rollin's memory of the incident, see *CE,* V, p. 1399.

[13]Chautemps, p. 120. But then Chautemps's motives are perhaps even less capable of withstanding examination.

[14]De Gaulle, pp. 63–64, 65. Without naming any names, Weygand at the Pétain trial suggested that it was Huntziger who was reluctant to take over the task rather than the government which failed to pursue him. See Weygand's deposition, July 31, 1945, *Procès Pétain,* p. 390. According to Henri Massis, a staff officer attached to Huntziger to whom the latter confided on June 15, de Gaulle on 11 June discussed only the Cotentin peninsula and Breton redoubt strategies with him, North Africa not having figured in their conversation at all. See his article "Huntziger, Weygand, de Gaulle," in *Hommes et Mondes* (December 1954), pp. 9–10; also Weygand's *En Lisant de Gaulle,* pp. 56–58, which makes use of this memoir. However, though Huntziger most probably did disapprove of the Atlantic bridgehead idea, it is still not clear that he rejected the offer made him.

### Paul Reynaud at Tours: June 13

[1]See Henri Amouroux, *Le 18 Juin 1940* (Paris, 1964), p. 36.

[2]Emmanuel Berl, *La fin de la III^e République* (Paris, 1968), pp. 54–56.

[3]See, for instance, Weygand's deposition, July 31, 1945, in *Procès Pétain,* p. 400; Philip C. F. Bankwitz, "Maxime Weygand and the Fall of France: A Study in Civil-Military Relations," *The Journal of Modern History,* Vol. XXXI, No. 3 (September 1959), pp. 233–34; Chautemps, pp. 175–76; Alfred Fabre-Luce, *Journal de la France, mars 1939–juillet 1940* (Paris, 1940), p. 362; and Col. de Villelume's testimony in *CE,* IX, p. 2787, where he claims that Reynaud "was convinced in his innermost heart of the necessity for stopping operations" but at the same time "was prisoner of the attitude he had upheld for so long before public opinion" and "from which moreover he did not want to be swayed."

[4]De Gaulle, p. 78. Yet the General subsequently told Elie Bois that "the Prime Minister, his nerves completely frayed, his powers of resistance broken, had probably regarded the decision to surrender as a deliverance." See Elie J. Bois, *Truth on the Tragedy of France* (London, 1941), p. 386. Vincent Auriol and Léon Blum also believed that "Reynaud gave way because he was overcome by strain and fatigue and found himself surrounded by defeatist ministers and military commanders whom he had himself appointed." See Joel Colton, *Léon Blum: Humanist in Politics* (New York, 1966), p. 358.

[5]Spears, II, pp. 310–11. Churchill, however, would have his moments of doubt. But for General Gamelin, who certainly had no reason to be charitable to Reynaud, "In the eyes of history he would remain incontestably the leader who refused to despair and to abandon our British allies." See Gamelin, *Servir,* I, *Les Armées Françaises de 1940* (Paris, 1946), p. 8.

[6]General Weygand's testimony, *CE,* VI, pp. 1778–79, 1805–06, 1814–15; De Gaulle, pp. 67–68; Jeanneney, p. 66.

[7]Churchill himself explains that throughout the Briare conference he was haunted by the grief that Great Britain had not contributed more to the land war against Germany and that "so far nine-tenths of the slaughter and ninety-nine-hundredths of the suffering had fallen upon France and upon France alone." See Winston S. Churchill, *The Second World War,* Vol. II, *Their Finest Hour* (New York, 1962; first published 1949), pp. 133–34.

[8]Reynaud, pp. 495–96.

[9]Churchill, II, pp. 154–55.

[10] Spears, II, p. 202.

[11]Reynaud, p. 496; and his explanations in *CE,* VIII, pp. 2410–11. The French Premier (so he told General de Gaulle on June 6) had used this questionable technique both on May 26 and May 31 with the British in the hopes of gaining from them greater assistance. But by June 13, de Gaulle could not accept Reynaud's tactics as valid. See De Gaulle, pp. 54 and 70. That he was "forcing the note of despair" to get the maximum aid possible from the English, however, proved an acceptable explanation to Elie Bois (not always a friendly critic), who had also inquired whether Reynaud was capitulating. See Bois, p. 356. At any rate, the despairing note had already been used by Churchill with Roosevelt—and for the same purpose—as early as May 20; while Reynaud's predecessor, Daladier, in order to put through the purchase of 10,000 planes in America, had in the fall of 1939 "threatened to resign if sufficient planes could not be obtained from the United States and to turn the government over to 'Bonnet or Flandin, either one of whom would make an early compromise peace with Germany.' " See John McVickar Haight, Jr., *American Aid to France, 1938–1940* (New York, 1970), p. 158, based on a dispatch from Ambassador Bullitt to the Secretary of State, Nov. 23, 1939, for which see *FRUS,* 1939, II (1956), pp. 520–22.

[12]Churchill, II, pp. 155–56; Spears, II, p. 203.

[13]Churchill, II, p. 156.

[14]Spears, II, p. 207.

[15]Spears, II, p. 208. Spears's rendering of Reynaud's long question conforms substantially with that made by de Margerie in the French *procès-verbal,* reprinted in Reynaud's *Au Cœur de la Mêlée* (Paris, 1951), pp. 770–74. See especially p. 771.

[16]Reynaud, pp. 496, 499.

[17]Baudouin, pp. 102–03; Albert Kammerer, *La Vérité sur l'Armistice: Ephéméride de ce qui s'est Réellement Passé au Moment du Désastre* (2nd ed.; Paris, 1945), pp. 118–19, also 525 and 535 (reprints of notes dictated by Paul Baudouin in 1944 and 1945).

[18]See, for instance, WM (40) 165, June 13, 10:15 p.m.; FO 371/24311, C 7541, Campbell's Final Report, para. 16; Hastings Lionel Ismay, *The Memoirs of General Lord Ismay* (New York, 1960), pp. 145–46; *The Diaries of Sir Alexander Cadogan, 1938–1945*, ed. by David Dilks (London, 1971), p. 298; The Earl of Birkenhead, *Halifax: The Life of Lord Halifax* (Boston, 1966), p. 459; A. J. P. Taylor, *Beaverbrook* (New York, 1972), p. 437. Only Spears, who thought that Reynaud might be playing the part of devil's advocate to see how Churchill would react, accepts the "hypothetical" nature of the Premier's inquiry and accompanying remarks; and even he sensed a trap in this rather strange exercise in ventriloquism. See Spears, II, pp. 209, 214. However, Lord Halifax—possibly for tactical reasons—would state to the French Ambassador the next day that he "had gained the impression that M. Reynaud had put this question [the possibility of England's releasing France from its obligations] in the hope that H. M. Government would give a negative reply and thus strengthen his hand." FO 371/24310, C 7263/65/17, Foreign Office Minute by Lord Halifax, June 14.

[19]Churchill, II, p. 157; Spears, II, pp. 209–10; SWC (39/40) 16th, June 13, 3:30 p.m.; Reynaud, *Au Cœur de la Mêlée*, pp. 771–72; C 7541, Campbell's Final Report, para. 16; WM (40) 165, June 13, 10:15 p.m.

[20]Spears, II, pp. 211–13; Reynaud, *Au Cœur de la Mêlée*, p. 772; Baudouin, p. 104.

[21]Reynaud, *Au Cœur de la Mêlée*, p. 773; Spears, II, p. 214.

[22]Beaverbrook bluntly advised Churchill to stall for time and to say or discuss nothing more until the French had first sorted themselves out. But his impressions of French intentions were bad enough to inspire him to say that night after returning to England: "We are all Splended Isolationists now." See A. J. P. Taylor, *Beaverbrook,* p. 437; also Spears, II, p. 215.

[23]Spears, II, pp. 216–17.

[24]Churchill, II, p. 157.

[25]See SWC (39/40) 16th, June 13, 3:30 p.m. The French *procès-verbal* is similar, but rather closer at this point to Spears's rendering.

[26]For a discussion on this point, see Kammerer, pp. 119–22. For Reynaud's testimony, see *Procès Pétain. Compte rendu in extenso* (Paris, 1945), pp. 16, 148.

[27]Reynaud, pp. 496–97; cf. Paul Reynaud, *La France a sauvé l'Europe* (Paris, 1947), Vol. II, p. 320. By the time *Au Cœur de la Mêlée* (1951) appeared, de Margerie's *procès-verbal,* after a sojourn of many years in America, had also been published—for the first time in *Le Figaro,* May 30, 1949.

²⁸See Albert Lebrun, *Témoignage* (Paris, 1945), pp. 77–78; also Lebrun's testimony in *CE*, IV, pp. 975, 1004–05, 1028. And Laurent-Eynac's memory of what Reynaud said on this date is substantially the same; he too mentioned the personal character of the Churchillian declaration. See his testimony in *CE*, V, p. 1451. Jeanneney, who was briefed by Reynaud during the conference's intermission and who also heard Churchill himself a few minutes later, seems to have perceived the situation more accurately—namely that the gist of the Prime Minister's response to Reynaud's question was simply that Roosevelt's reply must be awaited. He also understood that it was *this* that the PM's colleagues were confirming. Otherwise, the generous sentiments attributed to Churchill are the same as in other versions. See *Journal politique,* pp. 67–68.

²⁹Baudouin, pp. 103–05; Kammerer, pp. 120–21, 535–36.

³⁰See Baudouin's testimony in *CE*, VII, pp. 2061–62, 2071.

³¹For instance, Henri Becquart, Deputé du Nord and a sober and fair-minded analyst of the period, writes that he was under the impression that Churchill had released France from its engagements on June 13 but that overnight the British cabinet had refused to confirm this response for fear of destroying for all time the value of international pacts. See *Au Temps du Silence: De Bordeaux à Vichy* (Paris, 1945), p. 21.

³²See *The Diplomatic Diaries of Oliver Harvey* (London, 1970), p. 389. This argument was not apparently used by Weygand, however helpful it was to his cause, and at the Pétain trial he readily admitted that Churchill had "never authorized France to ask for an armistice"—virtually the one point on which he and the former Premier found themselves in agreement. See dialogue between Reynaud and Weygand, with a contribution from the Marshal, hearing of July 31, 1945, in *Procès Pétain*, p. 425.

³³Reynaud, *La France*, II, p. 321; and testifying Dec. 12, 1950, in *CE*, VIII, p. 2411.

³⁴De Gaulle, p. 69.

³⁵Baudouin, p. 159; Kammerer, pp. 122–23, n. 3; Jean Montigny, *Toute la Vérité sur un Mois Dramatique de Notre Histoire: De l'Armistice à l'Assemblée Nationale, 15 juin–15 juillet 1940* (Clermont-Ferrand, 1941), p. 49. Yet on July 21, 1949, Baudouin told the Parliamentary Commission of Inquiry that "at no moment during the Supreme Council of June 13 had M. Churchill posed the question of the fleet, at no moment had the word 'fleet' been pronounced." See *CE*, VII, p. 2073.

³⁶Kammerer, pp. 123–24.

³⁷In this connection, Spears's comment on Churchill's ten-minute visit with the French parliamentary leaders—during which the General, who frequently acted as a watchdog, was otherwise occupied—could be significant. He writes: "I very soon had reason to regret not having been there, for within

the next few days statements which I am sure Churchill never made during that interview were attributed to him." Spears, II, p. 218.

[38]Spears, II, pp. 217–18; SWC (39/40) 16th, June 13, 3:30 p.m.

[39]See COS (40) 456 (JP), also JP (40) 240, June 13. See also below for details of Churchill's reaction to Roosevelt's message.

[40]Spears, II, pp. 218–20; Churchill, II, pp. 159–60; Churchill's message also in *FRUS, 1940,* I (1959), pp. 250–51, transmitted by Ambassador Kennedy at 3 a.m., June 14. Likewise, in a circular telegram (No. 108) sent to United Kingdom high commissioners in the dominions on the night of June 13–14, the Prime Minister stated, in reference to the Tours meeting, that the British could not consent to a separate peace. See FO 800/310, H/IX/153, sent at 5 a.m., June 14.

## Cangé II: June 13

[1]For the opening of this meeting, see Weygand, pp. 160–61, 222–23; J. Weygand, *Role,* pp. 131, 134; Marin, "Contribution," p. 8; Bouthillier, I, pp. 66–67; Baudouin, pp. 106–07; Reynaud, p. 501; Lebrun, pp. 77–79; Chautemps, pp. 130–34; and testimony in *CE* by Lebrun, IV, pp. 1007, 1011; by Rollin, Monnet, and Laurent-Eynac, V, pp. 1401, 1420–21, and 1451; by Bouthillier, VIII, pp. 2451–52, 2465, 2486. Before the Parliamentary Commission of Inquiry, however, Reynaud gave still another explanation as to why he had failed to invite Churchill to Cangé: it was that he did not wish the British leader to be exposed to the demoralizing spectacle of a French cabinet in course of dissolution. See *CE,* VIII, p. 2411 (testimony of Dec. 12, 1950).

[2]Spears, II, p. 226 (based on Spears's conversation with Mandel that night); Weygand, p. 161; Weygand, in *Procès Pétain,* pp. 395, 422–23; and Weygand's testimony in *CE,* VI, pp. 1564–65; Charles Pomaret, *Le Dernier Témoin* (Paris, 1968), pp. 212–13; Baudouin, p. 107; Bouthillier, I, pp. 96–97. See Marin, "Contribution," pp. 9–10, for both denials and confirmation that Weygand took this position; Marin's collection of testimony on this point in *Rapport de M. Serre,* Tome II, *Documents,* Part III, pp. 413–15; also Marin's discussion with Baudouin on this point, in *CE,* VII, pp. 2097–99; and with Weygand, in *CE,* VI, pp. 1763–67. In this latter exchange, Weygand suggested a reason why Marin, Campinchi, and Monnet might have opposed his proposition concerning the fleet (which Marin always denied he had made): this was that the government could not be deprived of the fleet so long as it intended to leave for North Africa and required it to protect its departure as well as to transport troops there.

[3]Langeron, pp. 34–37; Spears, II, p. 222; testimony of Louis Marin, July 26, 1945, in *Procès Pétain,* p. 221; testimony before the Commission of Inquiry in *CE,* IV, by Lebrun, pp. 1008–09; V, by Rio, p. 1319, by Rollin, pp. 1399–1400, by Monnet, p. 1421, by Laurent-Eynac, pp. 1451–52; VII,

by Dautry, p. 1971, by Marin, pp. 1988, 2101, and 2192; Weygand, p. 162; Bourget, p. 119; Bois, pp. 358–60. Explaining this incident before the High Court, July 31, 1945, Weygand claimed that the false message, taken over the telephone by his aide-de-camp, emanated from a low-ranking functionary within the Ministry of Marine who did not specify the origins of the information. See *Procès Pétain,* p. 396. This answer was not very satisfying, then or later, and the suspicion of a plot persists, especially in the light of testimony given Jan. 12, 1950, before the Parliamentary Commission by Campinchi's former chief of staff, M. Matteo Connet. Connet claimed that Weygand did not just learn this "news" via a staff officer during the course of the Council, as he later testified, but that on the contrary Pétain (together with Weygand) had been propagating this scare story among certain ministers in the hour before the Council began, while they were all awaiting Reynaud's return from Tours. See *CE,* VII, pp. 2187, 2191–93. In fairness to Weygand, it should be pointed out that the General was not alone in fearing a Communist uprising in the Paris region. Reynaud and Mandel both shared his uneasiness, to some degree. According to Weygand, the Minister of the Interior had on May 28 requested that three infantry regiments be put at his disposal to meet the risks of any disturbance breaking out in the capital. See Weygand, p. 118; Bourget, pp. 58–59. This is corroborated by a dispatch sent on the same date by Ambassador Bullitt, in which he claimed that Reynaud and Mandel feared that the Communists would seize power and cause butcheries once the government had departed. See Gordon Wright, "Ambassador Bullitt and the Fall of France," *World Politics,* Vol. X, No. 1 (October 1957), p. 85; also *FRUS,* 1940, II (1957), p. 453, for Bullitt's May 28 telegram; and *For the President, Personal and Secret,* ed. Orville H. Bullitt (Boston, 1972), pp. 441 and 479, for Bullitt's May 30 letter to Roosevelt and July 31 Memorandum for the Secretary of State detailing French fears of a Communist uprising.

[4]Weygand, p. 163; J. Weygand, *Role,* p. 133; Weygand's testimony, *CE,* VI, pp. 1780-81; Reynaud, pp. 502–04; Spears, II, pp. 222–23; Reynaud's testimony before the High Court, Aug. 1, 1945, in *Procès Pétain,* p. 435; testimony of Lebrun before the Commission of Inquiry, *CE,* IV, pp. 996, 1011; and of Rollin and Monnet, V, pp. 1400 and 1422, 1424.

[5]Reynaud, pp. 505–06; Bouthillier, I, p. 69.

[6]Reynaud, pp. 506–07.

[7]Baudouin, pp. 108–09.

[8]Many ministers considered Bouthillier's turncoat performance on June 13 a shocking betrayal of his chief, whose patronage he had enjoyed in the Ministry of Finance and who had only recently brought him into the cabinet to support his policy of resistance. In that they were protégés of Mme de Portes, Baudouin's and Bouthillier's views should have been well known to Reynaud, but their unwillingness to follow him was perhaps just beginning

to be unveiled at Cangé and Bordeaux. See testimony of Monnet in *CE,* V, p. 1423; Laurent-Eynac, V, p. 1451; Dautry, VII, p. 1971; also an anecdote in Louis Lévy, *The Truth About France* (Harmondsworth, Middlesex, 1941), p. 161, which focuses on Baudouin but should, more accurately, be applied to Bouthillier. Pomaret, Minister of Labor, was a leftover from many past cabinets who had been a long-term pacifist, while Ybarnégaray, though a former Croix de Feu member and champion in Parliament of Colonel de la Rocque, had been brought into the cabinet on May 10 (along with Louis Marin) in the belief that he was a die-hard—by virtue of his consistent opposition to German expansionism and support for collective security. See Alexander Werth, *The Twilight of France, 1933–1940* (New York, 1942), pp. 146–47.

⁹"Mandel's conclusion," as reported later that night to General Spears, "was that, although a vote for continuing the war would probably have been obtained yesterday, today, had one been taken, it would in all probability have been in favour of surrender." See Spears, II, p. 227. Mandel's estimate was undoubtedly exaggerated for the date in question, but it was the trend that counted.

¹⁰Spears, II, p. 232.

¹¹Spears, II, p. 234.

### June 14: Dangerous Moves

¹Arthur Bryant, *The Turn of the Tide, 1939–1943: A Study Based on the Diaries and Autobiographical Notes of Field-Marshal The Viscount Alan-brooke* (London, 1965), pp. 139–41; General Alan Brooke, "Operations of the British Expeditionary Force, France from 12th June, 1940 to 19th June, 1940," *Supplement to the London Gazette of Tuesday, the 21st of May, 1946,* May 22, 1946, pp. 2433–34, 2437; Weygand, p. 167; WO 106/1774, Operations on Western Front, Phase 3, Last Battle in France from Appointment of General Brooke as C-in-C to Final Evacuation of BEF, Brooke to CIGS, June 14, sent 1330, rec'd 1515; Barratt, BAFF, to Air Ministry, June 14, sent 1220; and telephone conversation between CIGS and General Brooke at 1815, June 16; also WO 106/1744, Telegrams to CIGS, June 10–19; Major L. F. Ellis, *The War in France and Flanders, 1939–1940* (London, 1953), pp. 298–300.

²Bryant, pp. 141–45; Brooke, pp. 2434–39; WO 106/1774, WO to HQ, L of C Area, for GOC-in-C, BEF, June 14, 1525; Secretary of State to General Brooke, June 14, 2220; Sec. of State to Brooke, June 15, 1235; and June 16, 1229; telephone conversations between CIGS and Brooke, 1815 hours, June 16; and 1030 hours, June 17; Sec. of State to Brooke, June 17, 1520, releasing Normanforce for evacuation; Lt.-Gen. Marshall-Cornwall's Summary of Operations of BEF in France from 1st to 18th June, 1940 (June 20). See also DO (40) 16th, June 14, 6:30 p.m.; WO 106/1698, Personal Telegrams from the Secretary of State; WO 106/1743, Operational Telegrams,

June 10-16; WO 106/1609, Evacuation of British Troops from France, June 15–29. In all, 144,171 British troops from south of the Somme plus 47,699 Allied personnel (French, Polish, Czech, and Belgian) were safely evacuated to England by the Royal Navy, most before June 25, when such operations officially ended. See Ellis, pp. 301, 305.

³WO 106/1697, Personal Telegrams from CIGS, May 22–June 16, 1940, CIGS to General Weygand, June 15, dis. 0230; CIGS to Weygand, June 16, dis. 2110, containing extract from message to Reynaud; and, for the reactions of Generals Doumenc and Weygand to the British decision, WO 106/1774, Howard-Vyse to CIGS, June 15, 0830; H-V to CIGS, June 16, 1200; and WM (40) 167, June 15, 10 a.m. See also WO 106/1743, Operational Telegrams, June 10–16; WO 106/1744, Telegrams Out, June 10–19; Bryant, pp. 146, 148–49; Weygand, pp. 170, n. 1, 172–74; J. Weygand, *Role,* pp. 139–41; Reynaud, p. 514, n. 1; Bourget, pp. 135–37.

⁴Reynaud, pp. 509, 512; Churchill, II, pp. 160–61, 172; Spears, II, pp. 240–43.

⁵In answer to de Gaulle's question as to whether he was resolved to pursue the war from Algiers, Reynaud had stated that he was and had even told the General that following his trip to England he should rejoin the head of government in Algiers. See De Gaulle, p. 71.

⁶From Churchill's message to Reynaud, sent late June 13, in Churchill, II, p. 160.

⁷See WM (40) 165, June 13, 10:15 p.m.; WM (40) 165, min. 1, CA, June 13, 10:15 p.m.; also Harvey, p. 389; William L. Langer and S. Everett Gleason, *The Challenge to Isolation, 1937–1940* (New York, 1952), pp. 531–32. Ambassador Joseph P. Kennedy had duly reported on June 12 the growing British assumption that it would take very little to bring the United States into the war. Churchill had in fact stated to him that he expected the United States to "be in right after the election." See Kennedy's dispatch to the Secretary of State, June 12, 2 p.m., in *FRUS,* 1940, III (1958), p. 37; also Richard J. Whalen, *The Founding Father: The Story of Joseph P. Kennedy* (New York, 1966), p. 292. Both Kennedy and Roosevelt attempted to disabuse Churchill of this facile optimism on June 14 and to convey that their primary concern was the future disposition of the French fleet. See Kennedy's message to the President, June 14, noon; and the President's to Churchill, June 14, 3 p.m., in *FRUS,* 1940, I, pp. 251–52 and 254–55.

⁸FO 371/24310, C 7263/G, Campbell to Foreign Office, dispatched 3:45 a.m., June 15; also FO 371/24311, C 7541, Campbell's Final Report, para. 23. Spears had already wired the Prime Minister the previous night that "extremely pernicious rumours [were being] spread at Tours that Britain would liberate France from her engagements should America not declare war." Mandel had privately advised him that "it would be most desirable to make it clear in documents that must be placed before [the] French Cabinet

that in no case will England do this; he suggests you should state bluntly that [the] joint declaration was made to meet just such a case as has arisen and . . . emphasises that the documents should be received by the French Government today." See FO 371/24383, C 7182/G, No. 405, dispatched 3:15 a.m., June 14, received 7:55 a.m. This does not appear to have been done, but in an afternoon message to Campbell, the Foreign Office instructed the Ambassador to invite M. Reynaud to help in scotching the rumors that were doing the damage. C 7182/G, No. 356 DIPP, dispatched 4:22 p.m., June 14.

### The Slide Downhill: June 15

[1]Before the Commission of Inquiry in 1950, Reynaud categorically denied that he had said this to the Ambassador, and he may be right, but it *was* the way Sir Ronald had understood him and the mood of the French cabinet. See *CE*, VIII, pp. 2414–15; FO 371/24311, C 7541, Campbell's Final Report, paras. 23 and 28; C 7263/G, No. 409 DIPP from Campbell, dis. June 15, 4 p.m. The origin of this plan, if such it was, can probably be traced to Col. de Villelume, whose thought contains both Pétainist and Gaullist elements. See his testimony, in *CE*, IX, pp. 2788–89.

[2]Reynaud's testimony on Darlan, in *CE*, VIII, p. 2409.

[3]See comments by Messrs. Serre and Dhers in the course of Weygand's testimony before the Commission of Inquiry, in *CE*, VI, pp. 1850–51, 1854–55; their further comments during Baudouin's testimony, in *CE*, VII, pp. 2063–66; and Bouthillier's explanation of this reunion, under fire from Messrs. Dhers and Marin, in VIII, pp. 2467–72; also Georges Monnet on the Marshal's "premeditated" and "concerted" interventions, in V, p. 1426.

[4]FO 371/24310, C 7263/G, Nos. 407, 406, 409, and 413 DIPP from Campbell, all dispatched during the afternoon of June 15; FO 371/24311, C 7541, Campbell's Final Report, paras. 25–29; Spears, II, pp. 253, 257–58.

[5]François Charles-Roux, *Cinq mois tragiques aux affaires étrangères (21 mai–1$^{er}$ novembre 1940)* (Paris, 1949), p. 36; also testimony of Charles-Roux, July 27, 1945, in *Procès Pétain*, p. 249. Before the Parliamentary Commission of Inquiry, Reynaud denied that the Ambassador had made this démarche on the 15th. His position was always that the question of the fleet had not been raised before June 16. See his testimony, Dec. 12, 1950, in *CE*, VIII, p. 2415. But Churchill confirms Charles-Roux on this point.

[6]Spears, II, pp. 245, 257, 259.

[7]Reynaud, pp. 515–16; Weygand, p. 169; J. Weygand, *Role*, pp. 137–38. See also p. 162, *Role*, pp. 401–03 of Weygand's testimony in *Procès Pétain*, and pp. 1760, 1852–53 of Weygand's testimony before the Parliamentary Commission, *CE*, VI, for the General's reasoned arguments against a capitulation (or cease-fire), as opposed to an armistice. General Georges held identical views regarding the advantages of an armistice over a capitulation and

the shame attaching to the latter. See his testimony, Aug. 1, 1945, in *Procès Pétain*, pp. 461, 464. But political considerations could not have been absent from the minds of any of the army's top leadership. Obviously, a capitulation would tend to place the blame for the defeat squarely on the army, while an armistice would make the government, and indeed the whole Republican regime, look responsible.

[8]Col. de Villelume claims that in 1940 Reynaud never used the expression "cease-fire," that it was always simply a question of a (government-ordered) capitulation, and that Reynaud only adopted the more appealing term on his return from Germany. See his testimony, in *CE*, IX, pp. 2785, 2790–91. General Weygand, on the other hand, told the Commission of Inquiry in 1949 that Reynaud had "never dared to pronounce the word capitulation" (though he recanted on this point later in his testimony); while in his deposition for the Supreme Court at Riom in August 1940 he claimed that Reynaud had tried to win his adhesion to an "armistice affecting only the army." See Weygand's testimony in *CE*, VI, pp. 1823–26, 1842–43, 1872. The precise words used by Reynaud on June 15, however, have only a semantic interest, because the conflict between the two men was not over words but over their sharply divergent appreciations of what constituted the best course to follow. In later years, rather in the manner of the White Queen, each would seek to castigate the other's chosen course as a "capitulation" or "surrender."

[9]Except for Denmark, which was possibly too tiny to take account of. Halifax had stated to the War Cabinet on the night of 13 June that he thought it still possible "to get the French to play the part of Holland, rather than of Denmark." WM (40) 165. The cease-fire solution urged by Reynaud on Weygand was obviously what the British were now pushing for, as made clear in the Foreign Office's message to Campbell on the afternoon of June 15: "Though situation may arise in which military comander finds himself compelled to ask for armistice, that is entirely different from Government formally consenting to negotiate a peace or surrender. We have the example, in Holland, of army surrendering while Government yet survives and provides rallying point for national life of Holland and of her Overseas Empire." In this same telegram, it was suggested that the French Government be invited to seek asylum in the United Kingdom. FO 371/24310, C 7263/G, No. 362 DIPP, June 15, dispatched 2:45 p.m.

[10]Five years later, during the Pétain trial, Weygand denied both that the Marshal had attempted to influence him or that Reynaud had offered to give him authorization for a cease-fire. He was forced to retreat from this position after the aged Pétain, in one of his rare interventions, admitted discussing the question with the General, though he was unable to remember whether they had reached agreement or not. See *Procès Pétain*, hearing of July 31, pp. 401, 421–22; also Reynaud's testimony, July 23, on the Council of June 15, pp. 61–62.

[11]Churchill, II, p. 174.

[12]Reynaud, p. 518. Reynaud's understanding of the Chautemps proposition—especially that it involved an inquiry concerning Germany's *armistice* conditions—was shared by and large by Lebrun, Rollin, Monnet, Laurent-Eynac, Dautry, and Bouthillier, at least according to their testimony before the Commission of Inquiry, but tenaciously disputed by Louis Marin, who insisted that the proposal had only to do with the enemy's *peace* terms. See *CE*, IV, pp. 1018–19 (Lebrun); V, p. 1393 (Rollin), pp. 1426–27 (Monnet), p. 1452 (Laurent-Eynac); VII, p. 2027 (Dautry); VIII, p. 2416 (Reynaud), pp. 2475–76, 2480 (Bouthillier and Marin).

[13]Pertinax, *Gravediggers of France,* p. 267; Chautemps, p. 155. Chautemps, incidentally, on p. 141, claims to have formulated his proposition on the morning of June 16, not the evening of June 15, but on this score he is contradicted by most other witnesses—Baudouin, Bouthillier, Reynaud, Pomaret, Lebrun, and Spears, for instance.

[14]Reynaud, p. 520. In addition to the 9 ministers known definitely to have favored an armistice Reynaud had listed Queuille, Julien, Laurent-Eynac, and Thellier as among those who supported the Chautemps proposal. But this count has been disputed. For instance, Mandel told Campbell and Spears later that night that at least 8 ministers besides Reynaud had strongly opposed the idea. These were Rio, Marin, Monnet, Sérol, Dautry, Campinchi, Thellier, and Mandel himself. See Spears, II, p. 271; and Jules Moch, *Rencontres Avec . . . Darlan: Eisenhower* (Paris, 1968), pp. 140–41, for a different list of 9 given by Mandel to the author. Rollin, who years later claimed to have spoken out against the proposal, also listed 9 who opposed it: Reynaud, Rio, Mandel, Marin, Thellier, Julien, Laurent-Eynac, Dautry, and himself; 12 who favored it, of which 2 however were under-secretaries; 1 who was hesitant (Pernot); and 1 whose opinion was unknown to him (Queuille). See his testimony, Jan. 20, 1949, in *CE*, V, pp. 1393–94. Rollin thus strikingly contradicts Reynaud with respect to at least three out of the four men the Premier believed had been won over to the Chautemps proposal, if not to an armistice itself. However, none of the tallies made by anti-armistice ministers questions the fact that Chautemps had garnered a majority. Bouthillier, for his part, claims that three-fourths of the ministers were favorable; but then, as was subsequently brought out, his conception of the Chautemps proposal was that it emphasized getting England's authorization before the inquiry vis-à-vis Germany was undertaken. See Bouthillier, I, p. 77; and his testimony, Dec. 19, 1950, in *CE*, VIII, pp. 2477–80. For further testimony on this point by Rio and Marin, see Louis Noguères, *Le Véritable Procès du Maréchal Pétain* (Paris, 1955), p. 104.

[15]Churchill, II, pp. 174–75. This was precisely the same reasoning Churchill had used in late May to oppose an approach to Mussolini, which both Reynaud and Lord Halifax had then thought opportune. Halifax's argument as to the harmlessness of such a procedure was essentially similar to that

now advanced by Chautemps. See also Léon Blum's similar but retrospective analysis of the Chautemps proposal's effect in his testimony before the High Court, July 27, 1945, in *Procès Pétain,* p. 236; and before the Parliamentary Commission, July 30, 1947, in *CE,* I, p. 261.

[16]See especially Reynaud's testimony, *CE,* VIII, pp. 2416–17, for these retrospective critical perceptions. However, Reynaud himself was not quite so clear-headed about the Chautemps proposal at the time. Emmanuel Berl is even more cynical in his analysis: not only was it successful *because* of its very lack of clarity, which, he asserts, was precisely the one thing the Council (except for Mandel) was unanimous in wishing to avoid, but he also claims that no one was fooled by it in that each minister knew that it represented a big gain for Weygand and a corresponding loss for Reynaud. See Berl, pp. 96–97, 105. However, as anxious as most Council members were to stave off an open rupture necessitating the resignation of one faction or another, the various interpretations of the proposal given by ministers of all persuasions both in 1940 and in later years suggest that in a good many instances their confusion was real and their naiveté before subtlety quite genuine. They were united only by a desire to avoid the irreparable—both governmentally and nationally.

[17]See Marin's recollection of the June 15 Council, sent to Jeanneney and appended to the latter's *Journal politique,* pp. 73–74; Reynaud, pp. 520–21; and Reynaud's testimony, in *CE,* I, p. 116; VIII, pp. 2417–18.

[18]Spears, II, pp. 265–67; FO 371/24310, C 7263/G, No. 419 DIPP, dispatched 1:05 a.m., June 16; No. 420 DIPP, telephoned 1:20 a.m., June 16; No. 422 DIPP, telephoned 4 a.m., June 16; FO 371/24311, C 7541, Campbell's Final Report, paras. 30–31.

[19] Campbell's Final Report, para. 31; Spears, II, pp. 267–68.

[20]Jeanneney, *Journal politique,* pp. 73–74 (entry for June 16).

[21]Langer and Gleason, p. 545; Biddle to Secretary of State, June 16, 1 a.m., in *FRUS,* 1940, I, pp. 258–59.

[22]The Secretary-General of the Polish Ministry of Foreign Affairs, on the basis of what Reynaud supposedly said to the Foreign Minister of the exiled Polish Government on June 15, infers that Reynaud was virtually converted to the idea of an armistice by the afternoon of that date and was moreover inviting Poland to join France in demanding one. See Jan Ciechanowski, *Defeat in Victory* (Garden City, N.Y., 1947), pp. 10–12.

### June 16: Britain's Conditional Acceptance

[1]Mandel had spoken with Campbell and Spears immediately after they had talked with Reynaud. See Spears, II, pp. 272, 278; C 7263/G, No. 422 DIPP, by telephone, 4 a.m., June 16. Mandel was one of the few who opposed an armistice even if Britain's acquiescence had been forthcoming. If he was so pro-English, Emmanuel Berl explains, it was because "he saw in England the

predestined savior of France." And if in March he had helped unhorse Daladier it was because "he believed Reynaud more capable of aiding Churchill against his Munichite opponents." See Berl, p. 63.

[2]See FO 800/312, H/XIV/447, Record of Phone Calls between Hopkinson and Campbell; C 7263/G, No. 362 DIPP, dispatched 2:45 p.m., June 15.

[3]Deposition of Jules Jeanneney before the High Court, July 26, 1945, in *Procès Pétain,* pp. 186–87; Jeanneney, *Journal politique,* p. 71.

[4]Baudouin, p. 115.

[5]Spears, II, pp. 278–79. They apparently also discussed a prospective meeting between the two prime ministers at this time because in an 11 a.m. telephone conversation between Campbell and London, the Ambassador reported that Reynaud welcomed the idea of a visit by Mr. Churchill.

[6]Baudouin, p. 115. Baudouin's further paraphrasing of Reynaud's announcement to the Council is debatable when he writes: "That morning Sir Ronald Campbell had told him that the British Cabinet had not endorsed the point of view expressed by Mr. Churchill at the last meeting of the Supreme Council at Tours"; or when he claims that "M. Paul Reynaud, embarrassed and sad, replied that these three members of the British Cabinet had not committed the whole of that body, and that in consequence no other course was open to us but to bow to its decisions." See Baudouin, pp. 114–15. It is impossible that the British Ambassador could have made such a statement because he was aware that Churchill's point of view on the binding nature of France's treaty obligations in no way differed from that of the cabinet. Not only that but Campbell had actually asked Baudouin on the morning of June 15 "if he could throw any light on the source of rumours to the effect that Churchill had said Britain would consent to France suing for an armistice," upon which "Baudouin had declared that this was indeed strange, for he knew the Prime Minister had said nothing of the sort, and he himself was prepared to say so explicitly." Spears, II, p. 264. It also seems unlikely (though not impossible) that Reynaud on the 16th would have drawn a distinction between the position taken by Churchill and his colleagues at Tours and that of the British cabinet; for only the previous evening, in the course of a discussion with Campbell and Spears on the precise words used by Churchill on June 13, he had checked his own not very reliable recollections of that meeting with de Margerie's official *procès-verbal;* it was no doubt this refreshing of his memory that had prompted his announcement to the Council to begin with, especially since his own summary of the Tours conference to his colleagues on June 13 had bypassed the most essential points. (At the Pétain trial, Reynaud himself claimed that he had responded to Baudouin's remark by stating that at Tours Mr. Churchill had by no means authorized a demand for an armistice—a point not mentioned by Baudouin or others. See Reynaud's testimony, July 31, 1945, in *Procès Pétain,* p. 425.) Yet, in support of Baudouin's version, Bouthillier, Prouvost,

Lebrun, and even Marin and Monnet attribute to Reynaud similar words, words he may never have spoken, but words they later assumed he had used either because they were convinced that Baudouin's account of the Inter-Allied conference at Tours, which had it that Churchill had implicitly released the French from their agreement, was the correct one or because his own account on the 13th had been misleading. See Bouthillier, I, pp. 82, 122; Kammerer, pp. 188–89; Lebrun, p. 83; Marin's remarks and Monnet's testimony before the Commission of Inquiry, in *CE*, V, pp. 1401–02, 1427. Reynaud and Lebrun, it must be noted, both place this conversation in the afternoon session of the Council (see Reynaud, p. 542; Lebrun, p. 83), but Baudouin and Bouthillier attribute it to the morning, which seems more likely for two reasons: (1) Bouthillier indicates that the communication made by Reynaud on behalf of the British was a preliminary one and was expected to be followed by a definitive response to their request of the night before; and (2) it was closer to the time when Reynaud had had his memory refreshed by Campbell and Spears.

[7]FO 371/24310, C 7263/G, No. 368 DIPP, by telephone.

[8]WM (40) 168, min. 1, CA, June 16, 10:15 a.m. The input of the Chiefs of Staff respecting this decision was in the form of an *aide-mémoire* drawn up the previous day. They had written: "If it is clear that the French are on the point of making terms, it is vital that they should move their Fleet to British ports *before discussing terms with Germany*. Otherwise the Germans will insist on its surrender. In the last resort they must scuttle their Fleet rather than surrender it." COS (40) 466, June 15.

[9]Spears, II, pp. 284–85; Reynaud, p. 534.

[10]See Fabre-Luce, p. 230; Chautemps, pp. 168–69; Spears, II, p. 283; Jeanneney, pp. 71–72.

[11]Spears, II, pp. 282, 284–85.

[12]FO 371/24310, C 7263/G, No. 369, by telephone; also Churchill, II, p. 177.

## June 16: The Proposal of Union

[1]Although Reynaud in his testimony before the Commission of Inquiry (1950) implicitly denied, and in his memoirs (1963) actually denied, that the two Englishmen were with him at the time of *this* call, in 1964 he personally confirmed to Henri Amouroux that Spears had been present when de Gaulle telephoned in the late afternoon. See *CE*, VIII, p. 2429; Reynaud, *Mémoires*, II, p. 428; Amouroux, *Le 18 Juin*, p. 61, n. 1; Spears, II, p. 291.

[2]FO 371/24311, No. 375 to Sir R. Campbell, by telephone, dispatched 8 p.m., June 16; also Churchill, II, p. 179.

[3]Churchill, II, p. 176.

[4]On the history of the proposal, see FO 371/24298, C 3894/G; C 4092; FO 371/24299, C 5162; C 5614; and, for more on its antecedents, see Léon

Noël, "Le Projet d'Union Franco-Britannique de Juin 1940," *Revue d'Histoire de la Deuxième Guerre Mondiale* (January 1956), pp. 34–37.

[5]Churchill, II, p. 176.

[6]See WM (40) 167, min. 6, CA, June 15, 10 a.m.; Avi Shlaim, "Prelude to Downfall: the British Offer of Union to France, June 1940," *Journal of Contemporary History,* Vol. 9, No. 3 (July 1974), pp. 43–44; Harold Macmillan, *The Blast of War, 1939–1945* (New York, 1967), p. 150; de Gaulle, pp. 76–77.

[7]See René Pleven's account, dated June 22, 1940, in J.-R. Tournoux, *Pétain and De Gaulle* (Paris, 1964), pp. 426–27; Noël, "Le Projet d'Union Franco-Britannique," pp. 22–23; Reynaud, pp. 537, 540; de Gaulle, p. 77; and Max Beloff, "The Anglo-French Union Project of June 1940," in *The Intellectual in Politics and Other Essays* (London, 1970), p. 190, n. 63.

[8]Churchill, II, pp. 178, 181; Noël, p. 23; FO 371/24311, C 7294/G, No. 374, Halifax to Campbell, dispatched 8 p.m., June 16. With respect to the suspension order, two telegrams were involved, one sent *en clair* at 3:10 regarding 368, the other at 4:45 regarding 369.

[9]Pleven, pp. 427–28; Noël, p. 24; Churchill, II, pp. 178–80, 181; Reynaud, p. 539; Spears, II, p. 293; WM (40) 169, June 16, 3 p.m.

[10]Spears, II, pp. 291, 293–94; Campbell's Final Report, para. 33; Reynaud, p. 536.

[11]Churchill, II, p. 180. The British "line" on the uninterrupted validity of the telegrams was, of course, challenged in the days to come, and remained a point at issue even after the war. But that it was the British Government's *official* policy all along seems clear from a Foreign Office message sent to Lord Lothian on the evening of June 16, even before the final results of the French cabinet crisis were known in London. In this Halifax wrote: "After [a] message was sent to Reynaud in reply to his request for permission from us to make [an] enquiry about [an] armistice, we received information from responsible French quarters that [a] decision of [the] French Government to continue [the] war might still be secured, if we would agree immediately to a declaration . . . . This has been conveyed to Reynaud and our earlier reply on the armistice proposal has been suspended, pending further consideration of [the] position by [the] French Government in [the] light of [the] declaration contained in Paragraph 2 above. If [the] French Government decide to continue [the] war on [the] strength of this, the armistice proposal and our reply to it will of course lapse. Alternatively, if they decide to pursue [an] armistice proposal, the declaration will not be proceeded with." See FO 371/24311, C 7294/G, No. 1143 from Halifax to Lothian, sent June 16 at 7:16 p.m.

[12]See FO 371/24310, C 7263/G, Nos. 370 and 371, Foreign Office to Campbell, telephoned 3:10 and 4:45 p.m., respectively; Spears, II, p. 294; FO 371/24311, C 7294/G, No. 428 DIPP from Campbell to Foreign Office by telephone, 7 p.m., June 16; Churchill, II, p. 180.

[13]For instance, Reynaud seems always to have believed that the telegrams were withdrawn because *he* had found them unacceptable. Putting aside the question of *why* he found them objectionable and why he "maneuvered" to have them withdrawn, his perception as to British motives for the later offer was evidently shared by General Spears. According to Jeanneney, Spears explained to him that evening "that an understanding not appearing possible on the conditions by which Churchill would admit overtures for a separate peace, the British Cabinet had deliberated again" and come up with "a new formula." See Jeanneney, *Journal politique,* p. 72. And Spears himself writes that he had originally feared that Churchill's first message would both encourage the defeatists, by its consent to an inquiry, while insulting all Frenchmen, by the conditions concerning the fleet it had laid down. See Spears, II, pp. 282–83.

[14]Reynaud, pp. 536–37; Spears, II, p. 290; Jeanneney, p. 74.

## The Government's Collapse

[1]Just when Reynaud communicated Roosevelt's reply to the Council remains somewhat uncertain. It is clear from Spears's account that Reynaud received the President's answer by telegram the night before while he was with the two Englishmen, but from this it does not necessarily follow that he communicated its contents at the earliest opportunity, namely, at the Council's morning session. Baudouin, Bouthillier, Chautemps, and Marin all claim that he read the President's message at the morning Council. But Reynaud, who moreover claims that he only received Roosevelt's telegram *after* this meeting, and Lebrun both say that it was read in the afternoon. Because Reynaud wished to make known the American and British replies at one and the same time, it is possible that though he later lied about the time he had received Roosevelt's telegram he is correct about the time he actually read it out. See Spears, II, pp. 265–66; Reynaud, pp. 535, 540; Baudouin, p. 144; Bouthillier, I, p. 81; Chautemps, p. 157; Lebrun, p. 82; Marin, "Contribution," p. 14; Kammerer, pp. 175–76. Ambassador Biddle claims to have delivered Roosevelt's message at 7 p.m. on June 15. See *FRUS,* 1940, I, pp. 255–56, for the President's message, and p. 258 for Biddle's telegram of June 16, 1 a.m.

[2]Reynaud, p. 540; Reynaud's testimony, July 24, 1945, in *Procès Pétain,* pp. 94–95; Reynaud's testimony before the Parliamentary Commission, in *CE,* I, p. 116; VIII, p. 2417; Kammerer, pp. 183–84; Marin, "Contribution," p. 17; Pomaret, p. 80. Albert Lebrun, in his deposition before the Commission of Inquiry in 1948, had no precise memory of the allusion supposedly made by Reynaud to Britain's condition regarding the French war fleet, but stated categorically that it was not presented under the form of a withdrawal to British ports. As for the telegrams, they were not read out, and he personally had heard nothing about them. See *CE,* IV, pp. 1029–31. Baudouin in 1949 confirmed that the telegrams had not been communicated

to the Council on the evening of June 16 and stated—with M. Marin's approval—that the question of Britain's conditions had never been raised by the Premier with his Council. See his testimony in *CE,* VII, p. 2074. On the other hand, Rollin claimed that Reynaud had indicated that the British had first given their consent to an armistice inquiry on condition that the French fleet rally in English ports but had then retracted this, declaring that they could not release France from its obligations. Rio also stated that Reynaud had spoken of a telegram concerning the fleet. See their testimony in *CE,* V, pp. 1397, 1407 (Rollin); p. 1322 (Rio). But their memories are highly suspect on this score, especially inasmuch as Reynaud told the British Ambassador that night (June 16) that he had not mentioned the two telegrams. There may have been some discussion regarding the possibility of sending the fleet to England at the Council's morning session (Dautry affirms that there was), in anticipation of British demands, but if so it was not in the context of a condition formally presented by the British Government. See Dautry's testimony in *CE,* VII, p. 2027; and Monnet's, V, p. 1432.

[3]See Chautemps, p. 160; Lebrun, p. 83.

[4]President Lebrun later claimed that he too had upheld the project. Rio, for his part, believed that he was the only one to speak in its behalf (though he actually spoke against an armistice), while Reynaud writes that he was quite alone in defending Churchill's offer and that nobody else expressed adherence. Pomaret agrees: no one approved, he writes; everyone remained silent. See Lebrun, p. 84; Rio's testimony, Dec. 16, 1948, in *CE,* V, p. 1320; Reynaud, p. 541; Pomaret, pp. 85–86. Marin claims that both he and Mandel supported the idea, but then goes on to say that Mandel only spoke for the first time in the Council at a later point. See Marin, "Contribution," pp. 17–18.

[5]See Churchill, II, pp. 182–83; Kammerer, p. 190; testimony of Lebrun, in *CE,* IV, pp. 976, 1016; of Rollin, Monnet, and Laurent-Eynac, V, pp. 1402, 1427, 1455; and of Dautry, VII, pp. 1972–73; also Pomaret, p. 87; and Louis-Dominique Girard, *Montoire: Verdun Diplomatique* (Paris, 1948), pp. 49, 61, 66. The unkindest cut of all was administered later by Admiral Darlan: "Mr. Churchill is like Siegfried and France like Brunnehilde. Only, instead of killing the dragon first, the hero asks her to marry him at once and make him her heir, in case the dragon should swallow her up after all." See Alec de Montmorency, *The Enigma of Admiral Darlan* (New York, 1943), p. 90.

Not all the unfavorable comments on the proposal emanated from the French, however. When first informed of it by Jean Monnet, General Ismay, for instance, felt that the project was "so divorced from reality" that he could hardly believe Monnet was serious. See Ismay, p. 146. Lord Hankey, who actually headed a committee on Anglo-French postwar unity but who had not been consulted concerning the offer of union, was even more outspoken in his condemnation of the project—and of the French. A few of the passages from the letter he wrote Lord Halifax on June 22 expressing his shock and indignation are worth quoting as a counterpoint to the vehement reaction of some Frenchmen:

I was greatly shocked [he wrote] when I first read the draft 'Declaration of Indissoluble Union,' but I was somewhat reassured when the Lord President [Chamberlain] told me that it was intended to apply only to the period of the war, for I would swallow a good deal to prevent the French fleet falling into the power of the Germans .... I should not rule out the possibility of closer relations with France, but I should resist to the uttermost in my power any sacrifice of our nationality or any permanent fusion with France. To my mind the French are more responsible for our present troubles than anyone else. They have been our evil genius from the time of the Paris Peace Conference until today.... In the war the French have brought us nothing but disaster.... In any event it is surely inconceivable that we should rush into such an epoch-making measure without any serious examination or exploration at all—and, incidentally, I would remark that the work of the Committee over which you asked me to preside ... does not encourage the belief that these half-baked ideas would be workable. But I hope you can reassure me to the extent that —(a) the plan is only for the war; or, better still, (b) That it is dead.

On both these points Lord Halifax was able to reassure him the next day. The whole exchange merely underscores the expedient nature of the offer and the context in which it was seen by the British. See FO 371/24298, C 4442/9/17; FO 800/312, H/XIV/455 and 456.

[6]See, for instance, the analyses given by Kammerer, p. 183; Marin, "Contribution," p. 17; and Noël, pp. 30, 31. The proposal did not come as a *complete* surprise to everyone. At least five ministers had heard of it from Reynaud before the Council met—and word undoubtedly spread fast. Spears (II, p. 293), noting that Mme de Portes—who as usual was performing prodigies of ubiquity—had actually hovered over Reynaud's secretary while he was typing up the historic document, traces the leak of the British bombshell to her. Mme de Portes, in a vain attempt to prejudice Reynaud against the offer of union, reportedly laid on his desk just prior to the Council meeting a message reading: "I hope you will not be an Isabel of Bavaria"—in allusion to the 15th-century consort of Charles VI who had disinherited her son in favor of Henry V of England. See Pertinax, p. 308; Pomaret, p. 91.

[7]De Gaulle, p. 75. Jeanneney's appreciation was similar. See *Journal politique,* pp. 72–73.

[8]Noël, pp. 32–33; Charles-Roux, pp. 46–47; Charles-Roux's testimony, July 27, 1945, in *Procès Pétain,* p. 251; Chautemps, p. 161; Bouthillier, I, pp. 86–87; Baudouin, p. 116.

[9]Spears, II, pp. 300, 315.

[10]Lebrun, p. 83; Lebrun's testimony, July 25, 1945, in *Procès Pétain,* p. 156; Reynaud, pp. 545–46; Reynaud's testimony in *CE,* IX, p. 2849.

[11]Reynaud, pp. 542–43, 545; also Reynaud's testimony in *CE,* VIII, p. 2428; Bouthillier, I, pp. 87–88; Marin, "Contribution," p. 18; Marin's testimony, July 26, 1945, in *Procès Pétain,* p. 210; Spears, II, p. 315.

[12]Reynaud, pp. 544–45; Dautry's testimony, Jan 18, 1949, before the Commission of Inquiry, in *CE*, VII, pp. 2028–29, 2031–32, 2034–35.

[13]See Churchill, II, pp. 181–82; FO 371/24311, C 7294/G, No. 431 from Campbell, received by telephone 10:10 p.m., June 16. Yet the Foreign Office had rung up Sir Alexander Cadogan at 8:50 to say that the trip was off. At 9:30 he was told it was on again but, arriving at the station, found it was off. He was then told to stand by. Instead he decided to "lie by"—in bed. See Cadogan, p. 303. A previous telegram from Campbell, who sensed trouble, had urged a change of venue for the next day's meeting, so this may be why the trip was aborted in time. See C 7294/G, No. 427 DIPP, by telephone, 6:15 p.m.

[14]Spears, II, pp. 300–01. Jeanneney's account of this meeting (for which, see *Journal politique*, pp. 72–73) is quite different, being limited to an exposé of the Franco-British Union project, which was shown him at this time and which he apparently believed had not yet been submitted to the Council of Ministers. He makes no mention at all of the attempt by Campbell and Spears to influence him, though in their eyes this was the main purpose of their visit. Spears also writes that they had told him of the results of the Council's last session. M. Jeanneney's grandson and editor seems to feel that the Spears account has therefore misrepresented the nature of the démarche (see his note 123, pp. 412–13), even though he quotes Churchill, II, pp. 183–84, which should explain the matter. Yet Sir Ronald Campbell, in a telegram sent to his government later that night, describes it in exactly the same light: "After seeing M. Mandel for a moment we then called for [the] second time today on [the] President of [the] Senate in [the] hope of his being able to influence [the] President of the Republic to insist on M. Reynaud forming [a] new government." The confusion may be explained by the following paragraph: "We begged him to make it very clear to [the] President that [the] offer contained in [the] Prime Minister's message would not be extended to a Government which entered into negotiation with [the] enemy." In other words, Campbell and Spears still had hopes of the offer being accepted—but only by a reorganized government under the direction of Reynaud or Mandel. See FO 371/24311, No. 432 DIPP from Campbell to FO, received by telephone, 4:05 a.m., June 17.

[15]Becquart, pp. 24–25.

[16]See Jeanneney's *Journal politique*, p. 8; Pertinax, *Gravediggers*, pp. 164–65.

[17]See Reynaud's testimony on Lebrun, July 24, in *Procès Pétain*, pp. 64, 67; and Dec. 12, 1950, in *CE*, VIII, pp. 2416, 2423–24, 2427; and Reynaud, pp. 545, 547, 552; also Lebrun's testimony, July 25, in *Procès Pétain*, regarding his conception of his role as arbiter (p. 181), his anti-armistice position (pp. 181–82), his attitude towards the March 28 convention (pp. 179–81), and his strong belief that a majority had crystallized (pp. 156–

57). The most interesting point made by the former President had to do with Churchill's words at Tours to the effect that whatever happened England would not waste time in reproaches and recriminations. Lebrun thought this could only refer to an armistice—otherwise, the statement was meaningless. Thus, he tended to feel at the time that although the Anglo-French agreement had not been abrogated, there was a sense in which it could be considered as no longer in force. Lebrun also testified before the Parliamentary Commission on the meaning and value of the Anglo-French agreement, *CE,* IV, pp. 1003–05, and on the question of the majority, pp. 976, 1081, 1084, 1087.

[18]Reynaud, of course, stresses his retention of power on the night of June 15 as a means of thwarting those advocating an armistice. As we have seen, the picture was actually a lot more complex. He certainly made no attempt with Lebrun to disguise the fact that he was in the minority. But, for Reynaud's explanations of the motives involved in this first meeting with Lebrun on the evening of June 16, see Reynaud, pp. 547–48; Reynaud's testimony, July 24, 1945, in *Procès Pétain,* pp. 67–68; and Dec. 12, 1950, in *CE,* VIII, pp. 2423, 2425, 2426–27. For Baudouin's insinuations, see his testimony, July 1949, in *CE,* VII, pp. 2076, 2128–29; and Lebrun's lame and unenlightening explanations in 1948, in IV, pp. 976, 1086.

[19]See Reynaud, pp. 551–52; Édouard Herriot, *Épisodes* (Paris, 1950), p. 74; Jeanneney, pp. 73–75; also depositions of Jeanneney and Herriot before the High Court, July 26 and July 30, 1945, in *Procès Pétain,* pp. 187 and 339–40. The picture of this conference given by Jeanneney, some of whose impressions have been included here, is radically different from that given by Reynaud or Herriot and is of considerable importance for the light it sheds on the Premier's state of mind at this juncture. It is especially significant in that it comes from a man who had always had warm feelings for Reynaud. For instance, it shows that Reynaud was at least half won over to the Chautemps proposition himself (though subsequently he sought always to conceal this) in that he now thought it necessary for the "abscess to be drained" before the hesitants could return to their senses. This is certainly consistent with others' impressions of Reynaud as a man who was tired and quite willing, even eager, to be done with the whole business.

However, M. Jeanneney additionally suggests that the political situation at this point was even more in the air than previous eyewitness accounts have allowed us to believe. He even paraphrases Reynaud as saying about Churchill's offer of union that "he is going to submit it to the Council"—although Reynaud had already done this several hours earlier and although there was no question as to its overwhelming rejection. In fact, much of Reynaud's exposé of the situation, as given in Jeanneney's journal, has to do with the Council of Ministers that took place during the evening of the 15th, though Reynaud had seen the presidents of the assemblies the following morning and presumably would have had a chance at that time to catch them up on the latest developments. Therefore, it is difficult to accept Jeanneney's account as a completely accurate *compte-rendu* of what Reynaud actually said at 9 p.m. on June 16.

First of all, Reynaud would not seem to have had any motivation for presenting his colleagues' point of view as so uncertain, not only as regards the Chautemps proposal but also as regards the proposed Franco-British union—and still less motivation if it is true that he was now ready to throw in the sponge. Second, other hypotheses explain matters better: (1) that at least part of this conversation took place earlier in the day, before the Council at 5, most likely by telephone, and was later mistakenly transcribed together with the 9 p.m. interview (there is, for example, a hint elsewhere in the journal that Jeanneney was in touch with Reynaud's position on the first British proposal, though no discussion with Reynaud on this subject is recorded in the journal); alternatively (2) that Jeanneney simply misinterpreted what Reynaud was saying either because he had misunderstood what Campbell and Spears had previously told him about the outcome of the afternoon Council of Ministers and the reception accorded the second British proposal (the offer of union) or because *they* had misled him as to the future chances of this proposal in their zeal to win his support for it. These conjectures are contrary to the conclusions reached by Jean-Noël Jeanneney, the annotater of his grandfather's journal (see notes 123, p. 413; 128, pp. 413–14; and 130, pp. 414–17), but they do make sense.

This is not to exonerate Reynaud from whatever responsibility he shares with President Lebrun for not having done more to combat the Chautemps proposal and for not having seen more clearly its true deadliness or that it was not "tactical" to go through with it (although they were by no means the only anti-armistice members of the Council to have made this fundamental error of judgment); but it does suggest that other elements of appreciation must be brought to bear on this particular interview. M. J.-N. Jeanneney is quite correct in saying that Reynaud's decision to resign did not flow directly from this meeting of the four presidents: it flowed not only from his earlier meeting with M. Lebrun but more fundamentally from all that had transpired in the Council—the refusal of ministers to go to Africa, the rejection of or indifference to closer ties with England, the impossible position in which the Chautemps proposal had placed him, in short, all those considerations which to a large degree rendered irrelevant the actual number of those for or against an armistice per se. Messrs. Jeanneney's and Herriot's advice was, of course, impeccable, but was probably also irrelevant at this point.

20See Georges Bonnet, *Quai d'Orsay* (Isle of Man, 1965), p. 290.

21See Reynaud, pp. 521, n. 1, 550, 553; also Marin's questioning of Reynaud, Dec. 12, 1950, in *CE,* VIII, p. 2424.

22See Marin, "Contribution," pp. 23–24.

23See Rollin's testimony, Jan. 20, 1949, in *CE,* V, pp. 1391, 1395–96, 1406; Monnet's testimony, Feb. 3, 1949, V, p. 1425; Dautry's testimony,

Jan. 11 and 18, 1949, VII, pp. 1972, 2031–32, 2035–36; Matteo Connet's testimony, Jan. 12, 1950, VII, p. 2189.

[24]See FO 371/24311, C 7294/G, Campbell to Foreign Office, No. 432 DIPP, received by telephone 4:05 a.m., June 17; also C 7541, Campbell's Final Report, para. 34.

[25]Reynaud, p. 554; Reynaud, *La France a sauvé l'Europe*, II, p. 366; Spears, II, p. 310. Reynaud's perceptions of Lebrun's intentions were correct. Lebrun reserved to himself the right to call once more on Reynaud if the armistice negotiations broke down and the government was forced to install itself in Africa. See Lebrun, p. 90; Becquart, p. 25. It is worth noting that Georges Mandel at first also believed that the German terms would be so harsh that no French government could accept them. He expected that Pétain would be forced to resign, after which Reynaud would be reinvested for the purpose of carrying on the war from North Africa. He was less sanguine as to this scenario after his own arbitrary (though short-term) arrest on June 17. See John M. Sherwood, *Georges Mandel and the Third Republic* (Stanford, Calif., 1970), p. 254; also Bois, pp. 385, 392.

[26]See Marin, "Contribution," p. 20.

## IV THE QUESTION OF THE FRENCH FLEET (JUNE 17–JUNE 22)

### *The Telegrams Resurface*

[1]Baudouin was to tell the American Ambassador late that night that as a guarantee that the French fleet would never be surrendered to Germany, Admiral Darlan, whose views were well known on the subject, had been named Minister of the Navy. Nevertheless, Biddle, who felt that the appointment was largely for the purpose of reassuring the British and Americans, cabled Washington on the 17th: "The Admiral's new Government associates hardly inspire complete confidence that the French Fleet will remain a bulwark against Nazi aggression." See William L. Langer, *Our Vichy Gamble* (New York, 1947), pp. 42, 44; Biddle's dispatch of 2 a.m. on June 17, in *FRUS*, 1940, II (1957), p. 455. The British found Darlan's inclusion a rather more hopeful sign.

[2]Prouvost would join the new administration as High Commissioner for Information within the next three days, while Robert Schuman and André Février, under-secretaries in the Reynaud cabinet, also stayed on.

[3]Paul Baudouin, *The Private Diaries of Paul Baudouin* (London, 1948), p. 118; Maxime Weygand, *Recalled to Service* (Garden City, N.Y., 1952), pp. 178, 229; Commandant J. Weygand, *The Role of General Weygand: Conversations With His Son* (London, 1948), p. 143; François Charles-Roux, *Cinq mois tragiques aux affaires étrangères (21 mai–1$^{er}$ novembre 1940)* (Paris, 1949), pp. 50–51; Charles-Roux's and Laval's depositions before the High Court, July 27 and Aug. 3, 1945, in *Procès Pétain*, pp. 252–53 and 511.

[4]Albert Lebrun, *Témoignage* (Paris, 1945), p. 85; Lebrun's testimony, 1948, in *CE*, IV, p. 1020; Charles-Roux, p. 49; Baudouin's testimony, 1949, in *CE*, VII, p. 2075; William L. Langer and S. Everett Gleason, *The Challenge to Isolation, 1937–1940* (New York, 1952), p. 546.

[5]See Baudouin's testimony on this Council of Ministers before the postwar Commission of Inquiry, in *CE*, VII, pp. 2070, 2124; and Weygand's in VI, p. 1850. Bouthillier, in his testimony, VIII, pp. 2477–78 and 2498–99, gives a somewhat more anodyne impression of what the government was up to, as does Lebrun, IV, pp. 1018–19, when he claims that the Council's decision *was* consistent with the sense of the Chautemps proposal, furthermore that the Pétain cabinet's first session was merely the conclusion of the debates that had agitated the preceding Council of Ministers. Jules Jeanneney described it more accurately, in his deposition before the Commission of Inquiry of the High Court of Justice in 1945, when he said: "It appeared forthwith that the Pétain cabinet was not limiting itself to sounding Hitler on his conditions for an armistice, but [instead] solicited an armistice itself, and that it was inclined to submit to this whatever its terms." Published as Annex VII of Jeanneney's *Journal politique (septembre 1939–juillet 1942)* (Paris, 1972), p. 347.

[6]*Documents on German Foreign Policy, 1918–1945,* Ser. D (1937–1945), Vol. IX, *The War Years, March 18–June 22, 1940,* No. 459, German Ambassador in Spain to Foreign Ministry, June 17, p. 590. Baudouin and Charles-Roux (as well as Bouthillier) subsequently denied that this was the nature of the request, but the evidence of Lequerica, including the note drawn up by Baudouin, clearly contradicts them; besides which, similar words were used with the Holy See the next day as well as in the radio speech Baudouin made at 9:30 p.m. on June 17. Equally to the point, four days later the French armistice delegation also inquired as to the enemy's peace conditions, though on instructions from the Marshal, not from the Foreign Minister. See Baudouin, p. 121; and Baudouin's testimony in *CE*, VII, p. 2122; Charles-Roux, p. 53, n.1; Bouthillier's testimony, together with information supplied by M. Dhers, in *CE*, VIII, pp. 2477–78; Jacques Benoist-Méchin, *Sixty Days That Shook the West: The Fall of France: 1940* (New York, 1963), pp. 381, 385–86; FO 371/24311, C 7541, Campbell's Final Report, para. 38; Col. Adolphe Goutard, "Pourquoi et Comment l'Armistice a-t-il été 'Accordé' par Hitler?," *La Revue de Paris,* Vol. LXVII (October 1960), pp. 86–87; Albert Kammerer, *La Vérité sur l'Armistice* (Paris, 1945), pp. 230, 232, 235; Léon Noël, *Le Diktat de Rethondes et l'Armistice Franco-Italien de Juin 1940* (Paris, 1945), pp. 18, 25–26; and Noël's testimony in *CE*, IV, p. 1138; Henri Michel, *Vichy: Année 40* (Paris, 1966), pp. 40–41. As an addendum, see also Pétain's speech, July 11, 1940, in which the Marshal clearly states: "It is necessary for it [the government] to negotiate and conclude peace." Reprinted in Emmanuel Berl's *La fin de la III<sup>e</sup> République* (Paris, 1968), p. 279.

[7]Yves Bouthillier, *Le Drame de Vichy* (Paris, 1950), Vol. I, *Face à l'Ennemi, Face à l'Allié*, p. 95; Charles-Roux, p. 53; Baudouin, p. 119.

[8]FO 371/24311, C 7294/G, No. 433 from Campbell, dispatched by telephone, 4:40 a.m., June 17; C 7541, Campbell's Final Report, paras. 35–36; see also C 7301/G, No. 438 DIPP, dis. 1 p.m., June 17, rec'd 4 p.m.

[9]Baudouin, p. 119.

[10]Campbell's Final Report, para. 130.

[11]Nevertheless, it is unlikely that the flavor of Anglo-French relations during this period would have been substantially different even if the British Ambassador had been more like the "amiable Mr. Biddle" (see Baudouin, p. 119) or the gossipy, outspoken Mr. Bullitt, about whom Secretary of the Interior Harold Ickes once wrote: "Bullitt practically sleeps with the French cabinet." Ickes quoted in Gordon Wright, "Ambassador Bullitt and the Fall of France," *World Politics,* Vol. X, No. 1 (October 1957), p. 66.

[12]FO 371/24311, C 7301/G, No. 411 DIPP from Campbell, by telephone at 6:45 p.m., June 17.

[13]C 7294/G, Nos. 379 and 380 DIPP from Halifax to Campbell, dispatched at 11 a.m. and 1 p.m., respectively, June 17. See also WM (40) 170, June 17, 11 a.m., for the Prime Minister's suggestion that a further telegram should be sent "pointing out that if the French Government sought an armistice without fulfilling this condition, our consent would not be forthcoming."

[14]C 7301/G, No. 437 DIPP, by wireless, received 4:25 p.m., June 17; Campbell's Final Report, paras. 40–42; see also *The Diplomatic Diaries of Oliver Harvey, 1937–1940,* ed. by John Harvey (London, 1970), p. 392.

[15]C 7301/G, No. 385 from Halifax to Campbell, dis. 5:45 p.m., June 17.

[16]C 7301/G, No. 444 DIPP, Campbell to Foreign Office, dis. 11:45 p.m., June 17, rec. 2:10 a.m., June 18; Campbell's Final Report, para. 46. Pertinax is even more explicit on this point. He claims that Campbell asked Charles-Roux to have *copies* of the English notes distributed to every minister. See *The Gravediggers of France* (Garden City, N.Y., 1944), p. 436, n. 2. Kammerer, p. 311, writes that Campbell also distributed copies of the two telegrams among certain parliamentarians so that they would know that France was not free of its engagements. They are not corroborated by any British source, however.

[17]Baudouin's testimony, July 1949, in *CE,* VII, p. 2078.

[18]Charles-Roux, pp. 56–57.

[19]Bouthillier, I, p. 96.

[20]*The Diaries of Sir Alexander Cadogan, 1938–1945,* ed. by David Dilks (London, 1971), p. 304; Winston S. Churchill, *The Second World War,* Vol. II, *Their Finest Hour* (New York, 1962), p. 186; C 7301/G, FO No. 397, sent 4 a.m., June 18.

[21]See Corbin's telegram, sent on June 18 at 4:09 a.m., received on June 18 at 12:30 p.m., in *Rapport de M. Charles Serre, Deputé, au nom de la Commission d'Enquête Parlementaire*, Tome II, *Documents sur la période 1936-1945*, Part III, p. 432. Sir Alexander Cadogan says of the interview only that at 11 p.m. on the 17th he found the PM "storming at Corbin—who was singing in chorus." See Cadogan, p. 304.

[22]Baudouin, p. 123; and Baudouin's testimony in *CE*, VII, p. 2079; also Charles-Roux's testimony, July 27, 1945, in *Procès Pétain*, p. 256.

[23]Baudouin, p. 124; Baudouin's testimony in *CE*, VII, pp. 2079, 2081; Bouthillier, I, pp. 96, 99; Kammerer, pp. 237 and 539 (reprint of Baudouin's *À Propos* of 1945); Charles-Roux, p. 59. However, Weygand testified at the Pétain trial in 1945 that he had learned on 17 June of the redelivery of the telegrams, though in 1949 he claimed that he knew of the telegrams' existence only after the war. See his testimony in *Procès Pétain*, p. 398; and in *CE*, VI, pp. 1566, 1865–67. In 1950 Bouthillier told the Commission of Inquiry that he too had been shown the telegrams by Baudouin on June 17. See his testimony, *CE*, VIII, p. 2516.

[24]L. B. Namier, *Europe in Decay* (London, 1950), p. 93.

[25]Baudouin, p. 124, n. 1; and Baudouin's testimony in *CE*, VII, pp. 2077, 2079–80. His conclusions were incorporated in a note on the history of the telegram affair and its repercussions drawn up by Charles-Roux on August 14, 1940. For the Foreign Office document which inspired this exculpatory effort on the part of Charles-Roux and Baudouin, see FO 371/24301, C 7492/9/17, Memo from Lord Halifax for the French Embassy, July 12, 1940, which is also self-serving. But there was an *earlier* telegram from the Marquis de Castellane to the French Ministry of Foreign Affairs (No. 2896–2903, sent on July 10 at 2:15 and received in sections by the Department, July 10 and 11) translating a communication he had just received from Lord Halifax in which the latter recalled "that British acceptance of the French government's demand to be released from its engagement not to seek a separate armistice was given only on condition that the French fleet take itself to British ports during negotiations." See *Rapport*, Tome II, *Documents*, Part III, pp. 432-34; and for Castellane's denial that the French Government knew of the British condition or that it had even been expressed by the British Ambassador, see FO 371/24301, C 7700/9/17, Note to Lord Halifax from French Government, July 15.

[26]Charles-Roux, p. 60.

[27]FO 371/24310, C 7263/G, Minute by R.V., June 22.

[28]Consult FO 371/24311, C 7301/G, No. 440 DIPP, rec. 8:10 p.m., June 17; Campbell's Final Report, para. 45.

### Promises, Promises

[1]Cordell Hull, *The Memoirs of Cordell Hull* (New York, 1948), Vol. I, p. 792; Langer, *Our Vichy Gamble*, p. 45; Secretary of State's dispatch, June

17, 5 p.m., in *FRUS,* 1940, II, p. 456. That this message was instigated by
the British is shown by a telegram from the British Ambassador in Washington indicating that the "President agreed to telegraph at once to Pétain
expressing this hope in [the] strongest terms and saying that the surrender or
sinking [of the fleet] would produce [a] deplorable effect on American opinion and would greatly weaken the possibility of [the] eventual freedom of
France." See C 7301/G, No. 1017 from Lord Lothian, sent 11:49 p.m., June
17, rec. 7:30 a.m., June 18. Not surprisingly, the President's communication
infuriated the French Government, which "regarded it as an intolerable interference from a neutral country," especially inasmuch as the United States
had failed to come up to French expectations. See Campbell's Final Report,
para. 60.

It was not the first warning concerning the French fleet that had come
from America. As early as May 26 President Roosevelt had warned Reynaud
and Daladier against letting their fleet "get caught bottled up in the Mediterranean." He had suggested that French warships in the eastern Mediterranean should be in a position to exit through the Suez Canal, while those in
the western Mediterranean should be able to pass Gibraltar and, if the worst
came, to retire to the West Indies or to safe ports in French West Africa.
Adumbrating the thrust of the June 18 message, Roosevelt had referred to
the "retention of the French fleet . . . as vital to the reconstitution of France
and of the French colonies and to the ultimate control of the Atlantic and
other oceans and as a vital influence towards getting less harsh terms of
peace." Secretary of State to Bullitt, May 26, in *FRUS,* 1940, II, pp. 452–53;
Langer, *Our Vichy Gamble,* pp. 13–14; Hull, I, p. 771. American anxiety
for the safety of the French fleet never relaxed, and in the days following
Reynaud's fall Ambassador Biddle was "authorized to promise almost anything—short of involving the United States directly in the war—which
would take the French fleet beyond any possible German control." See
Robert Murphy, *Diplomat Among Warriors* (New York, 1965), p. 65.

2Pétain, in fact, was so affected by the threatening tone of the message that
he immediately appealed to Paul Reynaud, whose credit was high in the
United States, to accept the Washington embassy.*

3Baudouin, pp. 123–24; Bouthillier, I, p. 97; Weygand, p. 183.

4FO 371/24311, C 7301/G, No. 399 DIPP for Campbell, dispatched 4
a.m., June 18; No. 449 DIPP from Campbell, dis. by telephone at 3 p.m.,
June 18; Campbell's Final Report, paras. 51–53.

5See Baudouin, p. 124 plus n. 1; Baudouin's testimony, in *CE,* VII, p.
2079.

6Campbell's Final Report, paras. 54–56; C 7301/G, No. 450 DIPP from
Campbell, dis. 1:50 p.m., June 18; No. 453 DIPP from Campbell, rec. 3:45
p.m., June 18.

---

*See Appendix J, Reynaud and the American Embassy.

[7]Harvey, *Diplomatic Diaries,* p. 394.

[8]See Langer, *Our Vichy Gamble,* p. 46; Hull, I, p. 793; Biddle to Secretary of State, noon, June 18, in *FRUS,* 1940, II, p. 457.

[9]For instance, this would seem to be the case with respect to one phrase in the ultimatum presented to Admiral Gensoul at Mers-el-Kébir three weeks later, in which the British Government would claim: "The Council of Ministers declared on 18th June that, before capitulating on land, the French Fleet would join up with the British or sink itself." See J. R. M. Butler, *Grand Strategy* (London, 1957), II, p. 223, for the full text of the ultimatum. Lord Halifax too would later allude to the French Foreign Minister's words in his July 12 memorandum, saying that when Campbell spoke with Baudouin on the morning of June 18, the decision (by which was meant a decision to send the French fleet to British ports) had been taken, and only remained to be confirmed by the Council of Ministers. FO 371/24301, C 7492/9/17, Memorandum of July 12 from Lord Halifax to French Embassy. At least in this document the meaning assigned to Baudouin's words conforms with Campbell's understanding of them (however faulty) at the time they were spoken, whereas in the ultimatum they appear to have been rather cavalierly wrenched from their original context.

[10]Kammerer, pp. 253–54; Charles-Roux, p. 75.

[11]*Parliamentary Debates, House of Commons,* 5th Series, Vol. 362, cols. 51–61.

[12]See message from Churchill to Roosevelt, June 15, 9 p.m., in *FRUS,* 1940, III (1958), p. 54; Langer and Gleason, *Challenge,* p. 549; Adrienne Doris Hytier, *Two Years of French Foreign Policy: Vichy, 1940–1942* (Paris, 1958), pp. 38–39.

[13]In fact, so pessimistic had General Weygand become, according to his sometime spokesman, Senator Charles Reibel, that he did not feel sure that even in several years' time would Anglo-American air power be greater than Germany's, especially when the present German superiority in production would in the meantime have been further augmented by the resources of French industry. See Reibel's *Pourquoi et comment fut décidée la demande d'armistice (10–17 Juin 1940)* (Paris, 1940), p. 22.

[14]See Emmanuel Berl, *La fin de la III^e République,* p. 45, for the statement of this equation.

[15]As put by Robert Mengin, in *No Laurels for de Gaulle* (New York, 1966), p. 62.

## To Leave or Not to Leave

[1]Jules Jeanneney, *Journal politique,* p. 78; and Jeanneney's testimony, July 26, 1945, in *Procès Pétain,* pp. 188–89, 200; Édouard Herriot, *Épisodes, 1940–1944* (Paris, 1950), pp. 84–85, also 92, 99, 104; Lebrun, pp. 88–89; and Lebrun's testimony in *CE,* IV, p. 1015. See also Charles Pomaret, *Le*

*Dernier Témoin* (Paris, 1968), p. 165; Kammerer, pp. 255–56; and Louis Noguères, *Le Véritable Procès du Maréchal Pétain* (Paris, 1955), p. 123.

[2]Henry Lémery, *D'une République à l'autre* (Paris, 1964), pp. 235–36; Jean Montigny, *Toute la Vérité sur un Mois Dramatique de Notre Histoire: De l'Armistice à l'Assemblée Nationale, 15 juin–15 juillet 1940* (Clermont-Ferrand, 1940), p. 17; Baudouin, pp. 125–26.

[3]Baudoin, p. 126; also Bouthillier, I, p. 102; Lebrun, p. 89; Pomaret, pp. 169–71; Noël, *Diktat*, p. 23; *DGFP,* Ser. D, IX, No. 489, p. 621.

[4]*DGFP,* Ser. D, IX, No. 490, June 19, p. 622.

[5]See Hull, I, p. 794; Langer, *Our Vichy Gamble,* p. 51; also *DGFP,* Ser. D, IX, No. 496, p. 629, for the substance of Baudouin's and Pétain's warnings to the Spanish Ambassador.

[6]See Kammerer, p. 273; Baudouin, p. 132; Charles-Roux, p. 86; Noël, pp. 50, 70. For instance, the armistice delegation was instructed on June 20 to try to get the Germans to agree to stopping their advance on Bordeaux before negotiations commenced. But for the considerable differences between Ambassador Léon Noël and Paul Baudouin respecting the French delegation's instructions, powers, and accomplishments, cf. Noël's *Diktat de Rethondes* and Baudouin's testimony in *CE,* VII, pp. 2084, 2087, 2089, 2122.

[7]See Camille Chautemps, *Cahiers secrets de l'Armistice (1939–1940)* (Paris, 1963), pp. 192–93; Bouthillier, I, pp. 102–03; Kammerer, pp. 263, 265.

[8]See Chautemps, pp. 194–95, 198–200.

[9]Baudouin, pp. 129–30.

[10]The *Massilia* actually set sail at 1:30 p.m. the next day. That the government was providing more than just a service in making the *Massilia* available to parliamentarians is shown by the orders signed by Admiral Darlan on June 19 and 20 and by the notices he had posted. These officially *ordered* senators and deputies to leave for Le Verdon at 5:30 p.m. on the 20th in cars that were to be procured for this purpose by the government. See Herriot, pp. 90–98; Jeanneney, pp. 79–80; Henri Becquart, *Au Temps du Silence; De Bordeaux à Vichy* (Paris, 1945), pp. 94–95, 97; Noguères, pp. 124–25, 128, 130–31; Robert Aron, *The Vichy Regime, 1940–44* (Boston, 1969), pp. 46–47. Nevertheless, the vast majority of parliamentarians stayed put in Bordeaux, not wishing to leave in case the government decided to remain after all. For what happened to the *Massilia* passengers in the next few days, see Chapter V. See also Kammerer, pp. 262, n. 1, 270–73; Jean Zay, *Souvenirs et Solitude* (Paris, 1945), Annexes, pp. 433–71 (L'Affaire Jean Zay); Pomaret, pp. 162–200; Édouard Barthe, *La Ténébreuse Affaire du "Massilia": Une Page d'Histoire (18 Juin 1940–Octobre 1940)* (Paris, 1945); and Joel Colton, *Léon Blum: Humanist in Politics* (New York, 1966), p. 363, on the *Massilia* "plot," as well as the more nuanced conclusions of Joseph Paul-Boncour on the affair in *Entre Deux Guerres: Souvenirs sur la III^e*

*République* (Paris, 1946), Vol. III, *Sur les chemins de la défaite, 1935–1940,* pp. 228, 242, and of Emmanuel Berl, pp. 149–50, 157, 237–38.

[11]See Chautemps, p. 204. Ambassador Noël, for his part, thought the point of unconditional capitulation had been reached as early as June 17, when Pétain thoughtlessly broadcast the words "il faut cesser le combat." This formula, he claimed, gravely compromised the French armistice delegation's bargaining position because it encouraged the Germans to believe that the Pétain government was resigned to accepting whatever conditions were offered. See Noël's deposition, Aug. 2, 1945, before the High Court, in *Procès Pétain,* pp. 472–73; and Noël's testimony, June 24, 1948, in *CE, IV,* pp. 1138–39.

[12]Weygand's testimony, in *CE,* VI, pp. 1860–61, 1933; Kammerer, p. 273; Lebrun, p. 91; Barthe, pp. 19–20. See J. C. Fernand-Laurent, *Un peuple ressuscite* (New York, 1943), pp. 87–91, and the same author's *Gallic Charter: Foundations of Tomorrow's France* (Boston, 1944), pp. 177–83, for the confession Alibert made to him in 1942 in Clermont-Ferrand concerning the lie and forgery which, he claimed, had "made Pétain." See also Noguères, pp. 134–35; Aron, pp. 47–49.

[13]Harvey, p. 397.

[14]At least when Baudouin asked Pétain on June 21 what attitude he would adopt towards Lebrun if the latter insisted on leaving, the Marshal had answered: "That is very simple, I would have him arrested." See Baudouin, *Neuf Mois au Gouvernement (Avril-Décembre 1940)* (Paris, 1948), p. 195.

[15]See, on this incident, Lebrun, pp. 91–93; testimony of Messrs. Lebrun (July 25) and Laval (Aug. 3), in *Procès Pétain,* pp. 161 and 512; and in *Procès Laval,* pp. 77–79, and 210–12; testimony of Héraud, in *CE,* VI, pp. 1512–13; Barthe, pp. 24–26; and especially Montigny, *Toute la Vérité,* pp. 25–30, for a blow-by-blow account of the Laval-Lebrun confrontation. Laval's ideas, briefly summarized, were that by the "subterfuge" of departing for Africa the President would be depriving the ministers who remained of the credit and authority necessary to negotiate; that it was not by leaving France that one could serve it; that if Lebrun left the country he would never set foot on French soil again; and that the abandoned French people would themselves constitute the true government of France. Marquet, the Mayor of Bordeaux, Georges Bonnet, and Gaston Bergery were among the participants in this parliamentary delegation.

[16]Baudouin, pp. 131–32.

## The Bordeaux Conversations

[1]See FO 371/24311, C 7301/G, Minute by O. G. Sargent, June 17; FO 371/24310, C 6950/G, No. 1156, Halifax to Campbell, June 19; C 7301/G, No. 445 DIPP, Campbell to Foreign Office, dis. June 17, rec. 5:30 a.m., June 18; C 7541, Campbell's Final Report, para. 49; FO 371/24310, C 7263/G,

No. 383 to Sir Samuel Hoare, dis. noon, June 18; FO 371/24311, C 7301 S (1), FO Minute, June 18.

²The date of this meeting is frequently given as June 19, but, inasmuch as Admiral Pound arrived by air in the vicinity of Bordeaux at 1 p.m. on June 18 and left that very night (at 1 a.m., June 19), no other date is possible. A certain amount of confusion derives from the fact that the First Lord of the Admiralty, Alexander, stayed on through the 19th till about 10 p.m., while Lord Lloyd only *arrived* at 5:30 p.m. on June 19 and remained till the next day. In addition, Admiral Auphan had mistakenly remembered the date as the 19th. See Rear Admiral Paul Auphan and Jacques Mordal, *The French Navy in World War II* (Annapolis, Md., 1959), p. 109, n. 7; Harvey, p. 396; Colin Forbes Adam, *Life of Lord Lloyd* (London, 1948), p. 299; Campbell's Final Report, paras. 57, 64, 69; Alain Darlan, *L'Amiral Darlan Parle* (Paris, 1952), p. 67.

³Admiral Paul Auphan, *Les Grimaces de l'Histoire* (Paris, 1951), p. 256 (from Chap. VIII, "Histoire de mes 'Trahisons' ou La Marine au Service des Français"); also quoted in Bouthillier, I, pp. 98–99. Commenting on tendentious accounts of this meeting, Reynaud always claimed that the question of the fleet's sailing for British waters *must* have come up because Darlan on December 4, 1942, wrote to Churchill, in reference to this interview: "If I did not consent to authorize the French Fleet to proceed to British ports, it was because I knew that such a decision would bring about the total occupation of metropolitan France as well as North Africa." Quoted in Paul Reynaud, *In the Thick of the Fight* (New York, 1955), p. 564; also in Churchill, II, p. 198. We now know that Reynaud was correct, though the subject came up in a somewhat different context. But, even if it had not, Darlan would have assumed that the question was one of the principal purposes of the British mission because for the past few days, Pound—whether directly or through the French naval and military missions in London—had been appealing to Darlan to send the French fleet to English ports before the armistice was concluded.

⁴ADM 205/4, First Sea Lord's Records, 1939–1945, Record of Conversation Held at Bordeaux on 18th June, 1940, Between First Lord, First Sea Lord and Admiral Darlan.

⁵Harvey, pp. 394–95; FO 371/24311, C 7301/G, No. 459 from Campbell, containing message for PM from First Sea Lord, dis. 2 a.m., June 19; C 7352/G, War Cabinet Minutes, June 19; Campbell's Final Report, para. 57.

⁶Baudouin, pp. 127–28; FO 371/24311, C 7301/G, No. 474 DIPP from Campbell, by wireless, rec. 6:50 a.m., June 20; Campbell's Final Report, para. 65; WM 173 (40), June 20, 12 noon.

⁷Baudouin, pp. 129–30.

⁸From Charles Corbin's deposition at the Baudouin trial, referred to in Baudouin's testimony in *CE,* VII, p. 2080.

[9]Adam, *Life of Lord Lloyd,* pp. 299–300. Lord Lloyd was not inspired by his meetings with France's two elderly statesmen. In a letter dated June 22, he describes Lebrun as having been "tearful as usual and quite fragile" and Pétain as "vain, ramolli, and dangerously ga-ga." Caught in the heavy bombing of Bordeaux on the night of June 19, he felt that the Germans were making a psychological mistake in trying to bomb the President's house. "They did not realise how much it would have strengthened France if they had succeeded in bombing both old Brown and Pétain!" Campbell also thought that President Lebrun was "in a pitiable condition," "in a state bordering on collapse," and found Pétain ever vague and indefinite, to say nothing of stubborn to the point of mulishness. See Campbell's Final Report, paras. 64 and 123; No. 474 DIPP, dis. by wireless, rec. 6:50 a.m., June 20; C 7352/G, No. 506 DIPP, dis. 8:25 p.m., June 21, rec. 5 a.m., June 23.

[10]From Baudouin's *À Propos d'un Nouveau Livre de M. Kammerer* (1945), reprinted in Kammerer, p. 540. See also Baudouin's testimony, in *CE,* VII, pp. 2080, 2082–83.

[11]FO 800/323, H/XXXIV/30.

[12]As early as June 14 the First Sea Lord had telegrammed Admiral Darlan concerning the urgent need to send the two biggest battleships, the *Richelieu* and *Jean Bart,* to England. See COS (40) 182, June 15, 3 p.m.

[13]In addition to shipping facilities, which to avoid delay were to be directed to French Atlantic ports, Lloyd was authorized to offer planes, for the use of French pilots evacuated to Africa, and the collaboration of the British Mediterranean fleet and air force for the defense of North Africa. See FO 371/24321, C 7342/G, Lord Lloyd's Offer to the French Government; WM 172 (40), June 19, 12:30 p.m.; and WO 106/1774, Operations on Western Front, Phase 3, for Admiralty message to Marseilles, 2011/June 19, regarding the offer of British shipping assistance from southern French ports for the purpose of evacuation to North Africa.

[14]FO 371/24321, C 7342/G; Harvey, p. 396. Lord Lloyd may have overplayed his hand on this score. While urging Baudouin on the night of June 19 to join the ministers who were preparing to leave for North Africa the following day, he had said: "Understand that the interests of France and those of England are identical, and you will have your reward." M. Baudouin, who did not see things in quite the same light, had replied: "How wonderful to be able to declare with such certainty that the service of England will have its reward in Heaven." The conversation had gone no further. Baudouin, *Neuf Mois,* p. 190.

[15]WM (40) 173, June 20, 12 noon; No. 474 DIPP from Campbell, by wireless, rec. 6:50 a.m., June 20. For the part played by Jean Monnet and René Pleven in inspiring and supplementing Lord Lloyd's mission, see Pleven's "Témoignage sur l'Histoire d'une Tentative Pour Mettre le Gouvernement de la République à l'Abri des Pressions de l'Ennemi," in J.-R.

Tournoux, *Pétain et De Gaulle* (Paris, 1964), pp. 429–41. They too seem to have received rather too rosy an impression of the French Government's intentions. For instance, they were encouraged by Baudouin's claim that it was on *his* suggestion that the Council of Ministers had decided that the three presidents and certain ministers would depart for Algeria under written order from the Marshal, as well as by his claim that the British offer of union had not actually been rejected and would now be studied with care!

[16]FO 371/24311, C 7301/G, No. 460 DIPP, by wireless, rec. 5:50 a.m., June 19; No. 467 DIPP, by wireless, rec. 3:20 p.m., June 19; Harvey, p. 395; C 7352/G, No. 468 DIPP, rec. 5:45 p.m., June 19; C 7301/G, No. 474 DIPP, dis. by wireless, rec. 6:50 a.m., June 20; C 7352/G, No. 480 DIPP, by wireless, rec. 3:15 p.m., June 20; also No. 477 DIPP, dis. 4:20 p.m., June 20; C 7352/G, No. 483 DIPP, rec. 2:16 p.m., June 20; No. 485 DIPP, dis. 2:20 a.m., June 21, rec. 4:13 a.m., June 21; C 7541, Campbell's Final Report, paras. 59, 62–63, 66, 72, 75–76.

## Hitler's Terms

[1]Campbell's Final Report, paras. 78–79; C 7352/G, No. 496 DIPP, dis. 11:05 a.m., June 21, rec. 2:20 a.m., June 22; Charles-Roux, p. 81. According to Baudouin, when Campbell wrote his note, he apparently believed the armistice terms had already arrived for "he expressed his great astonishment that he had not been told" them. Baudouin, p. 131.

[2]C 7352/G, No. 495 DIPP, dis. 10:32 a.m., June 21, rec. 10:05 a.m., June 22; Campbell's Final Report, para. 78.

[3]C 7352/G, No. 498 DIPP, dis. 5 p.m., June 21; Campbell's Final Report, para. 80.

[4]C 7352/G, No. 499 DIPP, dis. 4 p.m., June 21, rec. 8 p.m.; No. 500, dis. 5 p.m., June 21, rec. 10 p.m.; Campbell's Final Report, paras. 81–82; Harvey, p. 399.

[5]C 7352/G, No. 503 DIPP, dis. 6:43 p.m., June 21, rec. 2:25 p.m., June 22; No. 505 DIPP, dis. 8:25 p.m., June 21, rec. 8:20 a.m., June 23; Campbell's Final Report, paras. 83–84.

[6]No. 508 DIPP, sent 2:15 a.m., June 22.

[7]See Paul Kecskemeti, *Strategic Surrender: The Politics of Victory and Defeat* (New York, 1964), pp. 47, 53–55; Henri Amouroux, *Le 18 Juin 1940* (Paris, 1964), pp. 287–88; Col. A. Goutard, "Pourquoi et Comment l'Armistice a-t-il été 'Accordé' par Hitler?," *La Revue de Paris,* LXVII (October 1960), pp. 81–85, 90–93; Langer, *Our Vichy Gamble,* pp. 47–49; and *DGFP,* Ser. D, IX, No. 479, Partial Record of Conversation Between the Führer and Duce, June 18, pp. 608–11. This is essentially what Hitler told Mussolini on June 18–19 when the two met in Munich to discuss the armistice terms that should be offered the French. On this occasion Count Ciano was especially impressed by Hitler's moderation and sense of statesmanship.

Noting the Führer's desire to offer lenient terms in order "to avoid an uprising of the French Navy in favor of the English," Ciano thought it clear that he wanted "to act quickly to end it all. Hitler is now the gambler who has made a big scoop and would like to get up from the table, risking nothing more. Today he speaks with a reserve and a perspicacity which, after such a victory, are really astonishing." Before this meeting Mussolini had been prepared to impose very stiff conditions, for instance, the occupation of France east of the Rhône, of Corsica, Tunis, and Djibouti as well as the surrender of the French fleet. But after hearing that "it was the Fuehrer's intention to avoid offering conditions to the French such as would give [them] a pretext to refuse to conclude the negotiation" and after reading Germany's terms on June 21, he decided to defer his own territorial claims so as not to provoke a rift with Berlin. Three weeks later Hitler would tell Ciano how much Italian moderation, and especially the clause which left to the French their disarmed fleet, had contributed to the success of the agreement. See *The Ciano Diaries,* ed. by Hugh Gibson (Garden City, N.Y., 1946), pp. 265–67; *DGFP,* Ser. D, IX, No. 525, Memo by State Secretary on Letter from Mussolini to Hitler, June 22, pp. 679–80; *Ciano's Diplomatic Papers,* ed. by Malcolm Muggeridge (London, 1948), pp. 372–76 (Conversation with von Ribbentrop, June 19; Conversation with Hitler, July 7). See also FO 371/24312, C 9959/65/17, Minute by W. H. B. Mack, Sept. 8, 1940, for a late British appreciation of the Germans' interest in maintaining a constitutional French government on unoccupied territory, that is, because it provided a basis of allegiance both for the empire and the French army, navy, and administration.

[8]See J. R. M. Butler (ed.), *Grand Strategy,* II, p. 218; COS (40) 462 (JP), June 14.

[9]Berl, pp. 91–92.

[10]Baudouin, p. 144; Weygand, pp. 218–19; J. Weygand, *Role,* pp. 154–55; Weygand's testimony, July 31, 1945, in *Procès Pétain,* pp. 405–07; and in *CE,* VI, pp. 1572, 1760–61, 1877. The Italians would soon authorize a 127,000-man army for North Africa.

[11]Weygand's testimony in *CE,* VI, p. 1760; Noël's testimony in *CE,* IV, pp. 1144–45.

[12]Charles-Roux's testimony, in *Procès Pétain,* p. 259. To Senator Jacques Bardoux on June 23, Charles-Roux wondered whether the armistice did not entail all the inconveniences of a total occupation without any of the advantages that an outright refusal to negotiate might have left them. Bardoux, after reading the convention himself, went even further: he did not see how an enemy could demand more, and concluded that in accepting such terms France became a second Czechoslovakia. See his *Journal d'un Témoin de la Troisième: 1<sup>er</sup> septembre 1939–15 juillet 1940* (Paris, 1957), pp. 375–76, 378.

[13]See Baudouin, pp. 133, 135; Pomaret, p. 219; Lebrun's testimony in *CE,* IV, pp. 1027–28.

[14]See *Politique française, 1919–1940* (Paris, 1947), pp. 431–32.

[15]From Kammerer, pp. 442–46; Weygand, pp. 189–95; *DGFP,* Ser. D, IX, No. 523, German-French Armistice Treaty, pp. 671–76.

[16]See *DGFP,* Ser. D, IX, No. 512, Memorandum on Armistice Negotiations at Compiègne, June 21, pp. 646–47; and No. 513, Record of Telephone Conversation Between Generals Huntziger and Weygand, Evening of June 21, pp. 652–53; Noël, p. 26; Weygand's testimony on Huntziger's explications, in *CE,* VI, p. 1858; Goutard, "Pourquoi et Comment l'Armistice a-t-il été 'Accordé' par Hitler?", pp. 88–89; Ulrich von Hassell, *The Von Hassell Diaries, 1938–1944* (Garden City, N.Y., 1947), p. 139. For Italy's territorial claims, such as they were understood by the German Ambassador in Rome, July 17, see *DGFP,* Ser. D, X (Washington, 1957), p. 252.

## Sir Ronald's Vigil: Diplomatic Confusion

[1]Baudouin, pp. 133–34; Charles-Roux, p. 85; Pomaret, p. 220.

[2]Aron, pp. 58–59; Baudouin, p. 133.

[3]Baudouin, pp. 134–37.

[4]Charles-Roux, pp. 86–88. As will be seen, Charles-Roux's account contains a number of errors and misapprehensions that might easily have been avoided had either he or the British Ambassador been more forthright in their dealings with each other. But from this account particularly (Baudouin being under something of a cloud in postwar France), it is easy to see why Robert Aron could have concluded that, contrary to promises made, the armistice conditions were not communicated to Campbell, even orally, except after a delay of more than half a day—and only after the French armistice delegation was practically through its negotiations. See *The Vichy Regime,* pp. 57–60. But Lord Halifax certainly encouraged such a conclusion in the summer of 1940 by writing in his July 12 memorandum that, although Sir Ronald Campbell had been assured by M. Baudouin that he would be consulted once the armistice terms were known,

he experienced difficulty even in obtaining the text of the German conditions before the despatch of the French Government's reply. Nor was he afforded any adequate opportunity of discussing the terms of the reply of which also he had difficulty in obtaining a copy. Finally, he was only informed of the nature of the German rejoinder to the French Government's reply after the armistice delegation had been instructed to sign. Not only was it thus impossible for His Majesty's Government to take any of these documents into consideration, but His Majesty's Ambassador was in effect denied the opportunity of making, save in the most cursory manner, such observations as he might have thought that His Majesty's Government would desire to offer.

See FO 371/24301, C 7492/9/17, Memo of July 12 from Lord Halifax for the French Embassy, in reply to a recent memo by M. Baudouin presented July 1 by the French Chargé d'Affaires. Though most of this is technically true, it nevertheless leaves a somewhat misleading impression as to what actually happened on June 22.

[5]FO 371/24348, C 7375/G, Nos. 512, 513, and 516 DIPP.

[6]Campbell's Final Report, para. 85.

[7]FO 371/24348, C 7375/G, No. 514 DIPP, dis. by wireless 12:45 p.m., June 22; C 7541, Campbell's Final Report, para. 86. According to Pertinax, pp. 441–42, Baudouin, after giving a summary of the naval clauses, told the Ambassador that the rest did not concern him and sought to break off the conversation, whereupon Campbell attempted to extract the document from him by force. This unseemly scene apparently had its witnesses, the dénouement not.

[8]See Berl, pp. 171, 174, 196–97, 198.

## Diplomatic Conclusions

[1]FO 371/24348, C 7375/G, No. 515 DIPP, dis. by wireless, rec. 3:30 p.m., June 22; also Campbell's Final Report, para. 88.

[2]FO 371/24348, C 7375/G, No. 517 DIPP, dis. via Admiralty, rec. 6:10 p.m., June 22, plus separate section sent 2:30 p.m., rec. 4:45 p.m.; Campbell's Final Report, paras. 89–93.

[3]Campbell's Final Report, para. 95; also FO 371/24348, C 7375/G, No. 518, dis. 2:20 p.m., rec. 4:45 p.m., June 22.

[4]Harvey, p. 399. This passage implies two meetings between Campbell and the Secretary-General in the morning, neither of which is mentioned by Campbell or Charles-Roux. In fact, in his account Charles-Roux seems to have telescoped into one his multiple meetings with the British Ambassador on June 22.

[5]FO 371/24348, C 7375/G, No. 519 DIPP, dis. 5:20 p.m., June 22, rec. 3:15 a.m., June 23; also Campbell's Final Report, paras. 96–97.

[6]C 7375/G, No. 519 DIPP and Campbell's Final Report, para. 97–98. Apparently the same arguments and counterarguments had been used earlier between Campbell and Charles-Roux. See Harvey, p. 400; Charles-Roux, p. 89.

[7]C 7375/G, No. 519 DIPP, dis. 5:20 p.m., June 22, rec. 3:15 a.m., June 23; also Campbell's Final Report, para. 99. Campbell's belief that he was being kept "at arm's length," that he was becoming the "object of hostile looks," and that there was an "organised conspiracy" to keep the facts from him was not paranoid. The American Ambassador, referring to the rising tide of Anglophobia, expressed his belief that the British over the past few weeks had not been kept "au courant of the hourly changing temperature and plans of the French Government and its leaders to the extent for example that we are: in fact they are being deliberately kept in the dark." See Biddle's dispatch of 4 p.m., June 21, in *FRUS, 1940*, I, p. 264.

[8]Campbell's Final Report, para. 127.

[9]Campbell's Final Report, paras. 100–01; FO 371/24348, C 7375/G, No. 521 DIPP, rec. 9:55 p.m., June 22; No. 524 DIPP, dis. 8:01 p.m., June 22, rec. 3:15 a.m., June 23; No. 525 DIPP, dis. 8 p.m., June 22, rec. 3:15 a.m., June 23. See also C 7375/G, No. 458, FO to Campbell, dis. 1 p.m., June 22; FO No. 460 DIPP, dis. 4:50 p.m., June 22; FO No. 461, dis. 5:50 p.m., June 22.

[10]Campbell's Final Report, para. 102; FO 371/24348, C 7375/G, No. 527 DIPP, rec. 11:40 p.m., June 22. According to Kammerer, General Keitel had pointed out to the French negotiators that the stipulation according to which French warships were to return to their home ports was not an absolute obligation; the German text allowed for further discussion on the point by members of the commission charged with implementing the terms of the convention. See Kammerer, p. 434; also Charles-Roux, p. 87; and J. Weygand, *Role,* p. 148. William L. Langer claims that the Germans at this time agreed that ships normally based on Brest might report instead to Toulon. See *Our Vichy Gamble,* p. 55. What exactly the Germans were prepared to permit at this early stage, however, was not especially clear. For instance, Baudouin told Ambassador Biddle that the Germans had agreed to allow the withdrawal of the fleet to African ports, but, when pinned down, admitted that the fleet would first be required to return to ports in metropolitan France for disarmament under German control. Based on a telegram from Biddle dispatched on June 22, quoted by Langer, pp. 56–57. According to Léon Noël, the Germans refused four out of the six amendments proposed by the French (including the amendment concerning the fleet); but they did agree that military aviation, instead of being surrendered, could be disarmed and stocked under German supervision. In addition, the Germans refused even to discuss Marshal Pétain's previous demand that Bordeaux be freed from the threat of enemy operations—French concern in the matter being used simply as an inducement to the delegates to sign the convention as quickly as possible. See Noël, pp. 70, 81, 118–19; depositions by Noël and General Bergeret, Aug. 2 and Aug. 8, 1945, before the High Court, in *Procès Pétain,* pp. 470 and 711; Bourget, pp. 162–64, 167; Kammerer, pp. 292, 439. The French proposals for amendments, together with the German responses to each request, are set forth systematically in *DGFP,* Ser. D, IX, No. 521 (Record of Telephone Conversation Between General Huntziger and Colonel Bourget, Weygand's Adjutant, at 10 a.m., June 22), pp. 662–64; No. 522 (Record of Second Day's Negotiations at Compiègne, June 22), pp. 664–71; and No. 524 (German Explanatory Notes to Armistice Treaty), pp. 676–79.

[11]Campbell's Final Report, para. 103; FO 371/24348, C 7375/G, No. 529 DIPP, dis. 11:30 p.m., June 22, rec. 2:30 a.m., June 23.

[12]Charles-Roux, pp. 89–90; Kammerer, pp. 302–03, 305; also Kammerer, *La Passion de la Flotte Française: De Mers El-Kébir à Toulon* (Paris, 1951), pp. 105–09.

[13]Quoted in Kammerer, p. 303. See also Charles-Roux, pp. 88–89.

[14]Campbell's Final Report, para. 104; Kammerer, *Passion*, p. 110. See also No. 531 DIPP, dis. W/T, rec. 11:40 p.m., June 22, for Campbell's explanations of what he had done.

[15]Baudouin, p. 136; Baudouin's testimony, *CE*, VII, pp. 2086–88; Bouthillier, I, p. 110; Weygand, p. 200; Weygand's testimony, *CE*, VI, pp. 1568, 1858–59; P.-A. Bourget, *De Beyrouth à Bordeaux* (Paris, 1946), pp. 164–65; Kammerer, p. 440; Charles-Roux, p. 90; Noël, pp. 82–84; Lebrun's testimony, *CE*, IV, pp. 998, 1024–25. In the light of this, and of General Keitel's ultimatum to the French delegation 20 minutes before the document was signed, Baudouin's persistence in claiming that the French had never accepted the Germans' naval clause seems a bit wide of the mark. See p. 2084 of his testimony, in *CE*, VII.

[16]Harvey, p. 400; FO 371/24348, C 7375/G, No. 532 DIPP, dis. 10:25 p.m., June 22, rec. 5:55 a.m., June 23; Campbell's Final Report, para. 108. The only instructions relevant to this that Campbell had received were to avoid falling into the hands of the Germans. On July 4 this was the official reason invoked for his departure. See Charles-Roux, p. 91; Baudouin, p. 137, n. 1; Kammerer, p. 312. The reasons Oliver Harvey cites for the Ambassador's decision are: (1) that they were no longer safe from the German advance; (2) that henceforth it would be *infra dig.* to remain; and (3) that the danger to the British cruiser which had been patrolling off Arcachon since June 20 was increasing. Early in the morning of June 23 Campbell and Harvey embarked at Arcachon in an open sardine boat for the *Galatea,* which was then found to have departed for the safer and more southerly port of St. Jean de Luz. Picked up after several hours by the Canadian destroyer *Fraser,* they arrived at St. Jean at 6 p.m., and sailed aboard the cruiser *Galatea* at midnight. They reached Plymouth by 9 p.m. on June 24. See Harvey, pp. 400–01; also Campbell's Final Report, paras. 109 and 114; and ADM 199/379, where somewhat different timings are given. The British Consular staff together with the Naval Control Office, the remainder of the War Cabinet Secretariat, No. 1 Military Mission, and the staffs of the Canadian and South African legations had already left Bordeaux on the afternoon of June 19. At this time the Consulate was handed over to the safekeeping of Mr. Biddle, arrangements having been made for the British Ambassador and his staff to remain in occupancy for as long as they wished. More expendable members of the Embassy staff had left even earlier—on June 17. See Campbell's Final Report, paras. 40 and 70.

[17]Charles-Roux, p. 91; Baudouin, p. 137; Bouthillier, I, p. 112; Campbell's Final Report, para. 127.

[18]Campbell's Final Report, para. 116; Kammerer, p. 306.

[19]WM (40) 176, June 22, 9:30 p.m.; Woodward, pp. 313–14, 323. Baudouin, p. 138, writes that Churchill's statement was delivered on the night of

June 22 and claims to have received a text of it first thing the next morning. Charles-Roux, pp. 96, 99; Reynaud, p. 563; Auphan and Mordal, p. 117; and Kammerer, pp. 306–07, also assign the radio speech to the night of June 22.

[20]De Gaulle, if anything, went even further than Churchill in castigating the armistice not only as a capitulation but as an enslavement whose conditions (so he claimed) demanded the surrender of all French arms and the total occupation of French territory. At the same time he also blamed "a bad military system" and "faults committed in the conduct of operations" for France's defeat, a gratuitous (if well founded) insult that must have made it all the simpler for Weygand on 23 June to strip the General of his rank and to have him struck from the rolls of the officer corps for indiscipline. See Édouard Bonnefous, *Histoire Politique de la Troisième République,* VII (Paris, 1967), pp. 253, 381–82.

## V  TOWARDS A FINAL BREAK (JUNE 17–JULY 4)

### The Politics of Intimidation

[1]Corbin quoted in Albert Kammerer, *La Vérité sur l'Armistice* (Paris, 1945), p. 314. See also Paul Baudouin, *The Private Diaries of Paul Baudouin* (London, 1948), p. 142.

[2]For Pétain's speech, see Emmanuel Berl, *La fin de le III^e République* (Paris, 1968), pp. 275–76; and Édouard Bonnefous, *Histoire Politique de la Troisième République,* Vol. VII, *La Course vers l'Abîme: La fin de la III^eRépublique (1938–1940)* (Paris, 1967), p. 378.

[3]See Baudouin's telegram in *Rapport de M. Charles Serre, Deputé, au nom de la Commission d'Enquête Parlementaire,* Tome II, *Documents sur la période 1936–1945,* Part III, pp. 434–35; Baudouin, pp. 139–40; and Baudouin's testimony in *CE,* VII, pp. 2090–91. See also François Charles–Roux, *Cinq mois tragiques aux affaires étrangères* (Paris, 1949), p. 96.

[4]See Paul Reynaud, *In the Thick of the Fight* (New York, 1955), pp. 563–64; Deputy Ambassador Biddle's dispatch of June 24, 7 p.m., in *FRUS,* 1940, I (1959), pp. 266–67; and WM (40) 178, June 24, 12 noon.

[5]Albert Lebrun, *Témoignage* (Paris, 1945), p. 98; Kammerer, p. 316. This telegram (No. 464 to Campbell) had originally been sent on June 22 at 8:40 p.m., but did not reach Sir Ronald in time to be delivered before his departure. On June 24 the King was advised not to respond to any reply he might receive. See FO 371/24348, C 7375/G. The British would naturally have supported the stationing of French warships in North Africa had a French government prepared to resist been established there.

[6]Jacques Benoist-Méchin, *Sixty Days That Shook the West* (New York, 1963), pp. 458–59.

[7]WM (40) 177, June 23, 10 a.m.

[8]See Sir Llewellyn Woodward, *British Foreign Policy in the Second World War,* Vol. I (London, 1970), pp. 325–26; WM (40) 178, June 24, 12 noon; also FO 800/312, H/XIV/460, Record of Conversation between Lord Halifax and French Ambassador, June 24. That some within the Foreign Office agreed with this estimate is suggested by J. G. Ward's comment two days later that "Gen. de Gaulle will always appear tarred with the British brush in *this* country." FO 371/24321, C 7342/G, Minute by J. G. Ward, June 26.

[9]Kammerer, pp. 321–22.

[10]Viscount Caldecote (formerly Sir Thomas Inskip), speaking in the House of Lords for the government at the same time, more bluntly stated that it would be both distasteful and dangerous for there to be British representatives in unoccupied France, "the French submission [having] made the severance of formal relations between France and Great Britain, for the time being, almost inevitable." See *Parliamentary Debates, House of Lords,* June 25, 1940, 5th Ser., Vol. 116, col. 657.

[11]*Parliamentary Debates, House of Commons,* 5th Series, Vol. 362, cols. 301–05; also Winston S. Churchill, *Blood, Sweat and Tears* (New York, 1941), pp. 317–19.

[12]Winston S. Churchill, *The Second World War,* Vol. II, *Their Finest Hour* (New York, 1962, Bantam ed.), p. 200.

## North Africa: Its Role in British Policy

[1]Churchill, II, pp. 190–91.

[2]Maxime Weygand, *Recalled to Service* (Garden City, N.Y., 1952), pp. 215–18. See also his arguments in *Procès Pétain* (July 31, 1945), pp. 402–05; in Commandant J. Weygand, *The Role of General Weygand: Conversations With His Son* (London, 1948), pp. 156–59; in testimony before the Commission of Inquiry, in *CE,* VI, pp. 1760, 1784–85, 1811–13, 1853–54, 1876–77; and in Weygand's *En Lisant les Mémoires de Guerre du Général de Gaulle* (Paris, 1955), pp. 80–93. For a similar retrospective defense of Vichy's wisdom in neutralizing French North Africa, see Pierre-Étienne Flandin, *Politique française, 1919–1940* (Paris, 1947), pp. 422–28. In support of his argument, Weygand quotes a June 24 note from Darlan to the effect that the prolongation of the struggle in Africa would lead to the loss of that territory because the British, threatened at home, would be unable to give any substantial aid for many months, by which time Africa would no longer have any ports. See Weygand, p. 217, n. 4; also Darlan's order, No. 5139–40, to this effect issued on June 24, in Vice-Admiral Docteur, *La Vérité sur les Amiraux* (Paris, 1949), p. 42; and *Rapport,* II, pp. 465–66.

[3]Testimony in *CE,* V, pp. 1322–23 (Rio); p. 1450 (Laurent-Eynac); VII, pp. 1970–71, 2026 (Dautry); p. 2195 (Connet). On June 13 Raoul Dautry had submitted to Reynaud a short paper clearly outlining the choices before the government and the steps that would have to be taken immediately in

consequence of its decision. Dautry advocated the continuation of the war overseas, notwithstanding his realistic appraisal of the sufferings France would be subjected to in the meantime and the length of time it would take the Allies to go over to the offensive. He predicted that the Allies would only attain industrial superiority over the Germans in two or three years and that a reconquest of France would take even longer. He believed moreover that whatever decision the Council took it should be unanimous so as to fully engage the energies of the entire nation. See "Note Remise par M. Dautry, Ministre de l'Armement, à M. Paul Reynaud, Président du Conseil (13 juin 1940)," *Revue d'Histoire de la Deuxième Guerre Mondiale,* No. 3 (June 1951), pp. 56–58.

[4]See, for instance, Major-General J. F. C. Fuller, *The Decisive Battles of the Western World and Their Influence Upon History,* Vol. III (London, 1956), pp. 407–08; Paul Kecskemeti, *Strategic Surrender: The Politics of Victory and Defeat* (New York, 1964), pp. 54–55, 57; Guy Chapman, *Why France Collapsed* (London, 1968), p. 292; William L. Langer and S. Everett Gleason, *The Challenge to Isolation, 1937–1940* (New York, 1952), pp. 558–59; William L. Langer, *Our Vichy Gamble* (New York, 1966, originally published 1947), pp. 64–65; and Robert Murphy, *Diplomat Among Warriors* (New York, 1964), p. 103.

[5]See André Truchet, *L'Armistice de 1940 et l'Afrique du Nord* (Paris, 1955), for the best-documented and sustained argument that French North Africa had the wherewithal to wage war successfully in 1940 and that such a decision could reasonably have been reached on the basis of technical information available to the French Government at the time. (Truchet was a colonel and a militant follower of General de Gaulle in late June 1940.) A partial summary of this thesis can be found in *Revue d'Histoire de la Deuxième Guerre Mondiale* (June 1951), pp. 27–50. See also General Paul Armengaud, *Batailles Politiques et Militaires sur l'Europe: Témoignages (1932–1940)* (Paris, 1948), pp. 233, 237–39, for a more sophisticated, more realistic version of the Churchillian view.

[6]WP (40) 168, also COS (40) 390, May 25; COS (40) 391, May 26, Aide-Mémoire for PM on Occasion of M. Reynaud's Visit.

[7]COS (40) 466, June 15, Aide-Mémoire on British Requirements from the French. The French Ministry of Armaments, it should be pointed out, had tried to do the same thing in Belgium from May 10 on: to export as many men, factories, manufactured products, and raw materials as possible. See Raoul Dautry's testimony, *CE,* VII, p. 1964.

[8]See FO 371/24383, C 7074/G, Lord Hankey to Lord Halifax, May 27; Minutes by Cadogan and Strang, May 30.

[9]FO 371/24383, C 7074/G, Letter from Cadogan to Campbell, June 3; Letter from Campbell to Cadogan, June 4.

[10]WP (40) 189, also COS (40) 421, June 3.

[11]JP (40) 230, also COS (40) 440 (JP), June 9; FO 371/24383, C 7074/G, Campbell to Cadogan, June 5.

[12]WP (40) 201, also COS (40) 444, June 11; COS (40) 455 (JP), also JP (40) 239, June 13; FO 371/24311, June 15, Circular Telegram to Consular Representatives.

[13]COS (40) 462 (JP), also JP (40) 234, June 14. The French were not psychologically prepared for this strategy or the total lack of sentimentality underpinning it. In a conversation with Lord Halifax on June 14, Ambassador Corbin had suggested that the British ought to receive 2–3 million of the 6–7 million war refugees then in southern France and "had not taken kindly to the reply that from the blockade point of view, it was more advantageous to us that these millions should be where they were." See FO 371/24310, C 7263/65/17, FO Minute by Lord Halifax, June 14.

[14]WP (40) 207, also COS (40) 465, June 15. British policy in French West Africa, as spelled out by the Joint Planners on June 22, had a slightly different cast. Here, the possibility of a British takeover was at least contemplated. For instance, Lt.-Gen. G. J. Giffard, the new GOC, West Africa, was told that his job was first to try to get the local French administrations to continue as active allies and to maintain their forces for the defense of their own territories, but that, failing this, he should endeavor to persuade the French military authorities to assume control, and, if they refused, to have the British take over the administration themselves. See JP (40) 270, also COS (40) 480 (JP), June 22, Defence of British Interests in West Africa.

[15]General Bertrand, who was General Noguès's *chef de cabinet* in 1940, saw Britain's policy as one of wanting to see North Africa become "an artificial abscess which would attract German troops," but this is perhaps to attribute too positive a character to what was essentially an exercise in solipsism. See Bertrand's testimony in *CE,* VI, p. 1799. Surprisingly, the British do not seem to have given any real thought to the Germans' embarking on such an eccentric movement or to the effect this would have had on their own position in Africa. The defense of England took priority over every other consideration.

[16]FO 371/24311, C 7278/G, No. 393, FO to Campbell, June 17, sent 10:40 p.m.; Kammerer, p. 337; Truchet, p. 49.

[17]FO 371/24311, C 7278/G, Draft Telegram on Possible Action by H.M. Government in the Event of France Capitulating, June 14; C 7278/G, Circular Telegram No. 18 to H.M. Consular Officers in French Possessions, sent June 17, 5:45 p.m.; Circular Telegram No. 21, sent June 17, 11:45 p.m.

[18]See, for instance, FO 371/24327, C 7343/G, Circular Tel. No. 23, June 19, 11:20 p.m.; COS (40) 476, June 19; Truchet, pp. 81–82; and C 7343/7327/17, for a June 20 minute by G. E. Millard of the Foreign Office in which he writes: "It should not be impossible to bribe French colonial governors, and the (black) colonial troops will fight for whoever pays them."

[19]FO 371/24311, C 7316/G, No. 461 from Campbell, dispatched June 19, 4 a.m., received 7:45 a.m.; No. 432, Halifax to Campbell, sent June 19, 9 p.m.

[20]Not only were there assurances to the British representatives in Bordeaux regarding the French Government's intention to leave for Algiers but on June 21 an order instructing colonial governors to carry on independently of the home government was under discussion in the cabinet. See FO 371/24311, C 7352/G, No. 499 DIPP from Campbell, dis. June 21, 4 p.m., rec. 8 p.m.

[21]FO 371/24327, C 7343/G, Tel. to Mr. Knight, No. 20, June 21, 11:10 p.m.; and C 7380/G, Circular No. 30 from FO to H.M. Consular Officers, June 22, 2:15 p.m.

## North Africa: The French View

[1]See, for instance, C 7343, Tel. No. 12 from H.M. Consul, Jibuti, dis. 12:14 a.m., June 20; Tel. No. 27 from Mr. Knight in Tunis, dis. 12:50 a.m., June 20.

[2]FO 371/24311, C 7316/G, No. 420 from FO to Campbell, June 19, 1 p.m., Canvass of French Colonial Territories; Truchet, pp. 73, 87; Gabriel Puaux, *Deux Années au Levant: Souvenirs de Syrie et du Liban, 1939–1940* (Paris, 1952), pp. 200–01.

[3]Truchet, pp. 72, 80–83; Jacques Soustelle, *Envers et contre tout, De Londres à Alger (1940–1942)* (Paris, 1947), pp. 60, 96–99. Peyrouton was apparently anti-British even before the British Consul-General tried to talk him into defying his government.

[4]For the telegrams exchanged between Noguès in North Africa and Weygand and Baudouin in Bordeaux from June 17 to the end of the month, see *Rapport,* II, pp. 416–29.

[5]Weygand, p. 251, n. 1; Truchet, pp. 94–95. On June 29, to three of the parliamentarians who had sailed on the *Massilia* and who were then in Algiers, General Noguès—the decision behind him—made an even stronger argument in favor of North Africa's capacity for carrying on the war successfully. See M.-M. Tony-Révillon, *Mes Carnets* (Paris, 1945), pp. 96–100.

[6]Consult Weygand, pp. 109, 249–50, 251–52; Weygand's *En Lisant de Gaulle,* pp. 85–86, 209–19; Bourget, *De Beyrouth à Bordeaux* (Paris, 1946), pp. 133, 146; Charles Reibel, *Pourquoi et comment fut décidée la demande d'armistice (10–17 Juin 1940)* (Paris, 1940), p. 22.

[7]Truchet, pp. 13, 28–29, 90, 108–09, 111–12, 115, 137, 174, 198–99, 254, 341; Tony-Révillon, p. 44; Commandant Pierre Lyet, *La Bataille de France (Mai-Juin 1940)* (Paris, 1947), p. 169; account by Captain Loiret of Noguès's staff of his mission to metropolitan France, June 23–24, in *Rapport,* II, pp. 429–31; John McVickar Haight, Jr., *American Aid to France, 1938–1940* (New York, 1970), pp. 235, 257–58.

[8]Charles-Roux's testimony, *Procès Pétain,* p. 259.

[9]Tony-Révillon, p. 98; Kammerer, p. 346; General Koeltz's testimony before the Commission of Inquiry, in *CE,* IX, pp. 2811–14.

[10]Even *whether* he reported in person is in question. Weygand, p. 251, Baudouin, p. 140, Yves Bouthillier, *Le Drame de Vichy* (Paris, 1950), Vol. I, *Face à l'Ennemi, Face à l'Allié,* p. 108, and Charles Pomaret, *Le Dernier Témoin* (Paris, 1968), p. 197, all claim that he did, but Koeltz himself testified in 1951 that he was not present at the Council of Ministers on June 23, categorically rejecting Baudouin's assertion to the contrary. Furthermore, the General formally denied having told Weygand that North Africa could not resist. See Koeltz's testimony on his mission to Algiers, in *CE,* IX, pp. 2810–16; Truchet, pp. 365–68; also Charles-Roux's testimony on this point, July 27, 1945, in *Procès Pétain,* pp. 271–72.

[11]Baudouin, pp. 135–36, 141; Bouthillier, I, pp. 107–08. Weygand's selective interpretation of Noguès is illustrated to some extent by his testimony in *CE,* VI, pp. 1782–84.

## Caution Cast Off

[1]FO 371/24327, C 7380/7327/17, FO Circular No. 32 to H. M. Representatives in Leading French Colonial Cities, dis. 3:15 a.m., June 23; also Kammerer, pp. 339–40.

[2]FO 371/24383, C 7366/G, Tel. from CIGS to General Dillon, June 21; Viscount Eric Dillon, *Memories of Three Wars* (London, 1951), pp. 138–39.

[3]See, for instance, C 7366/G, Tel. No. 70 from Mr. Gascoigne, Tangier, June 20; and FO 371/24327, C 7396/7327/17, Tel. from Mr. Parr, Marrakesh, June 24, 9:30 p.m., for the suggestion sent to the PM by Mr. Black Hawkins, a local Lawrence of Arabia, that the British take over the French army in Morocco if its Commander-in-Chief refused to fight on.

[4]CAB 107/10, Co-ordination of Department Action in Respect of French Colonial Possessions, meeting of June 21.

[5]For instance, see FO 371/24383, C 7366/G, Minutes by J. G. Ward, June 23 and 24; Letter to R. M. Makins from R. H.(?), June 24; and one on July 2 by Ward (FO 371/24327, C 7478/7327/17) predicting that "As we can apparently *do* nothing we shall have an Axis Morocco in a month."

[6]FO 371/24327, C 7388/7327/17, No. 36 from Mr. Knight in Tunis, dis. 2:25 p.m., June 24; C 7394, Nos. 34, 35, and 38 from Mr. Knight, dis. 7 p.m., June 23, 1:30 p.m., June 24, and 2 p.m., June 25, respectively; C 7392/7327/17, Nos. 35, 37, and 39 from Mr. Lowdon in Algiers, dis. 6 p.m., June 24, 1:30 a.m., June 25, and 1:15 p.m., June 26, respectively. See also Marcel Peyrouton, *Du Service Public à la Prison Commune* (Paris, 1950), p. 76, for the Resident-General's comments on British attempts at corrupting French functionaries.

[7]Truchet, p. 59; Tony-Révillon, p. 104, paraphrasing what Noguès had told deputy Paul Bastid on July 1; Bastid himself giving evidence before the

Commission of Inquiry in 1949, *CE,* VI, p. 1780; also Daladier's account of a discussion with Noguès in late June, in *CE,* I, p. 80; and General Bertrand's testimony, 1949, on all the factors weighing on Noguès up to June 24–25, in *CE,* VI, pp. 1789–94, 1800–01, esp. pp. 1791–92.

[8]Dillon also claims that Noguès was saying *"La Marine ne marche pas"* as early as June 15, but this clearly contradicts what he claims were Noguès's thoughts on the subject on June 24—i.e., that Darlan's *défaillance* began only on June 23 with Laval's entry into the government. See Dillon, pp. 138–39, 141.

[9]In this telegram (dispatched at 11 p.m. on June 25), he claimed that the government, finding itself in an atmosphere of rout, was unable to appreciate the strength and moral element represented by North Africa, which with the navy and air force could hold out against the attrition of the enemy. It would regret its decision bitterly. "Personally," he wrote, "I will remain at my post so long as there is danger, to carry out a mission of sacrifice which covers my face with shame, so as not to cut France in two. But as soon as I believe calm is assured, I shall ask you to relieve me of my command." See Truchet, pp. 98–99; Lebrun, p. 115. Noguès was in fact relieved of his operational command of French forces in North Africa but not of his civil post in Morocco, where he remained, loyal to the armistice and to Vichy, until after the American landings in November 1942. For his later career, see Fernand-Laurent, *Un peuple ressuscite* (New York, 1943), pp. 195–217.

[10]Weygand's telegram, dispatched June 25, 22:55, in *Rapport,* II, pp. 424–25; also Truchet, pp. 57, 97–98; Tony-Révillon, p. 99.

[11]See FO 371/24327, E 2200/2170/89, No. 20 from Mr. Havard in Beirut, dis. 5 p.m., June 27; also Truchet, pp. 75–78; Kammerer, pp. 341–42. At Djibouti, General Legentilhomme would hold out until July 22. Despite a willingness to continue some sort of cooperation with the British even after hostilities ended, Puaux distrusted British ambitions in the Levant and particularly feared opening the door of the mandated states to British forces, as he believed any kind of Franco-British condominium in Damascus and Beirut could only be the prelude to France's ultimate eviction from the Middle East. In fact, it was British interests in this part of the world, he claims, that decided him finally to adopt a position of *attentisme.* His position differed from that of the French governors in North Africa in that it was based on a fear of too much, rather than too little, British "aid" and also in that his *attentisme* was genuine, not after the fact. See Puaux, pp. 200, 202–05, 208, 214.

[12]FO 371/24301, C 7492/9/17, Record of Conversation with M. Cambon, June 24; Notes by William Strang on Cambon's Visit, June 24; Strang's Reply to Cambon, June 28. Roger Cambon had delivered the protest because Ambassador Corbin, who had retired the day before, was unwilling to make

this sort of communication. Cambon himself told Strang that he "doubted whether, if there were many such communications to make, he would be able to continue to come to us with them."

[13]WM (40) 180, June 24, 10:30 p.m.

[14]From Campbell's Final Report, para. 123, FO 371/24311, C 7541.

[15]For the *Massilia* story, consult Daladier's testimony, July 25, 1945, in *Procès Pétain*, pp. 126–27; and his testimony before the Parliamentary Commission, June 4, 1947, in *CE*, I, pp. 79–80, in both of which there appears to be some confusion regarding dates; Marin, July 26, 1945, in *Procès Pétain*, pp. 217–18; Jean Zay, *Souvenirs et Solitude* (Paris, 1945), pp. 87–88, Annexes, pp. 441–48, 451; Tony-Révillon, pp. 66, 78–85, 105, 127–29, 131–32, 139–42; Pierre Mendès-France, *The Pursuit of Freedom* (London, 1956), pp. 41–49; Truchet, pp. 51–54; Kammerer, pp. 342–43; Churchill, II, p. 188; John M. Sherwood, *Georges Mandel and The Third Republic* (Stanford, Calif., 1970), pp. 256–60, 262–69; extracts from the report of the *Massilia*'s commander, submitted July 8, 1940, in *Rapport*, II, pp. 474–75 and FO 371/24321, C 7342/G, Tel. No. 32 from Consul-General, Rabat, to Gibraltar, dis. June 24, 6:50 p.m., regarding the French ministers' intention to go on to England barring a French declaration to resist in Morocco and North Africa coming within the next 24 hours. See C 7342/G for further telegrams from Mr. Bond in Casablanca (early July) and Mr. Gascoigne in Tangier (late July) relating to Daladier's desire to escape to England and the negative reaction of the Foreign Office and War Cabinet to this possibility. Attempts (unsuccessful) were nevertheless made to rescue Daladier and some of his collaborators from Casablanca between July 27 and 30.

The treatment of a number of those who had sailed on the *Massilia* marked the beginning of Vichy's program of political persecution directed against leading figures of the Third Republic, more especially if they happened also to be Jewish. In mid-July Mandel was charged with plotting against the security of the state and later brought before the military tribunal at Meknès, though the case was ultimately dismissed for lack of evidence; on August 16 and 31, respectively, Jean Zay and Pierre Mendès-France, both members of the armed forces—the one charged with a liaison mission, the other serving with a unit in North Africa—were arrested in Rabat on trumped-up charges of desertion; while in September Reynaud, Gamelin, Blum, Daladier and Mandel (both now back in France) were imprisoned, prior to their planned appearance before the Supreme Court in Riom, the first of many trials and prisons to which each would be subjected.

[16]See FO 371/24327, C 7396/7327/17, No. 35 from Mr. Hurst, Rabat, dis. 10:45 a.m., June 25; Alfred Duff Cooper, *Old Men Forget: The Autobiography of Duff Cooper (Viscount Norwich)* (New York, 1954), pp. 282–84; Dillon, pp. 141–44; Kammerer, pp. 344–45.

[17]See WP (40) 226, June 28, Memo by the Minister of Information on the Situation in Algeria and Morocco; COS (40) 508, July 1; COS (40) 202, July 1, 10:15 a.m.; COS (40) 205, July 3, 10:15 a.m.; Churchill, II, Appendix, pp. 547–48, Minute of PM to Secretary of State, July 3.

## Straws in the Wind

[1]FO 371/24327, C 7392/7327/17, Nos. 37 and 46 from Mr. Lowdon in Algiers, dis. 1:30 a.m., June 25 and 6 p.m., June 28, respectively; FO 371/24383, C 7366/G, Tel. from Mr. Lowdon for Air Ministry, dis. 7 p.m., June 27; also Dillon, p. 144. For General Weygand's telegram, dispatched June 24, at 15:15, officially ending the British Mission with General Noguès, see *Rapport,* II, p. 424. The British consuls in Tunis, Algiers, Rabat, Casablanca, and Dakar were finally required to leave in early July. See FO 371/24301, C 8234, Aug. 10, 1940, Summary of Anglo-French Relations since June 23.

[2]On French Foreign Ministry policy in the last week of June, see Baudouin, pp. 145, 150–51; telegram from Baudouin to the French Embassy in London, June 27, dispatched 18:45, in *Rapport,* II, pp. 435–36; Lebrun, pp. 98–99; Charles-Roux, p. 99; and his testimony, July 27, 1945, in *Procès Pétain,* p. 263; L. B. Namier, *Europe in Decay, 1936–1940* (London, 1950), p. 95; Kammerer, pp. 347–48, 369–70. See also FO 371/24301, C 7492/9/17, Translation of a Memo by M. Baudouin on Recent Anglo-French Relations, submitted by the French Chargé d'Affaires, July 1. At Baudouin's trial after the war, M. Hoppenot, formerly Deputy Director for European Affairs at the Ministry of Foreign Affairs, testified that on June 22 Baudouin had told him that England was beaten and that he had just received reliable information that Churchill would leave office on July 15, to be replaced by Halifax, who would treat immediately with the Axis. Before the Commission of Inquiry in 1949 Baudouin denied that he had ever said this to Hoppenot, but did admit that during the summer of 1940 he had feared that a strong German attack against England would be fatal for her. See his testimony, in *CE,* VII, pp. 2114–15. The belief in a short war, or compromise peace, was quasi-universal in Bordeaux and Vichy, and certainly no less strong among Baudouin, Weygand, and Pétain than with Darlan and Pierre Laval. For the thoughts of Lebrun, Pétain, and Darlan on England's chances of holding out and on the possible duration of the war, see Ambassador Bullitt's report of July 1, in *FRUS,* 1940, II, pp. 462–68.

[3]See Baudouin, pp. 148–49; Charles-Roux, p. 95. Pierre Bressy had formerly been Georges Bonnet's *chef de cabinet* and was then Under-Director of Europe in the Ministry of Foreign Affairs, while Jacques Chastenet was managing director of *Le Temps* (Vol. VII of his *Histoire de la Troisième République,* published in 1963, is a reference for this period). For the colorful details surrounding this incident, see FO 371/24301, C 7539/G, Minute by William Strang, July 3; Note from Vansittart to Secretary of State, July 1;

Tel. No. 33 to Sir W. Selby (the British Ambassador) in Lisbon, June 29; Tel. No. 370 from Selby, July 4; Note from David Eccles in Lisbon, July 3.

[4]Charles-Roux, pp. 92, 104–07, 122; WM (40) 186, June 28, 5:30 p.m.; Cordell Hull, *The Memoirs of Cordell Hull* (New York, 1948), Vol. I, p. 796; Langer and Gleason, p. 564; Memorandum of Conversation by the Under Secretary of State (Welles) with the French Ambassador, June 24, and Memorandum of the Secretary of State's Conversation with Count de Saint-Quentin, June 27, in *FRUS*, 1940, II, pp. 460–62.

## The Enigma of Admiral Darlan

[1]Churchill, II, p. 197.

[2]As Churchill would later discover in connection with that other proud and prickly Gaul, whose Cross of Lorraine he claimed was the heaviest he had had to bear during the war and about whom he was thinking in December 1942 when he stated to the Commons: "The Almighty in his wisdom did not see fit to create Frenchmen in the image of Englishmen." Quoted by Keith Sainsbury, in "The Second Wartime Alliance," pp. 228–58 of Neville Waites (ed.), *Troubled Neighbours: Franco-British Relations in the Twentieth Century* (London, 1971).

[3]Pierre Varillon, *Mers-el-Kébir* (Paris, 1949), pp. 31–32; Rear Admiral R. de Belot, *La Marine Française pendant la Campagne 1939–1940* (Paris, 1954), pp. 202–03; Henri Amouroux, *Le 18 Juin 1940* (Paris, 1964), pp. 240–41; Albert Kammerer, *La Passion de la Flotte Française: De Mers El-Kébir à Toulon* (Paris, 1951), pp. 58–59, 66–67.

[4]Reynaud, pp. 574–75; Albert Kammerer, *La Tragédie de Mers-el Kébir: L'Angleterre et la Flotte Française* (Paris, 1945), p. 56. This phrase, or slight variations thereof, became very widely known. However, in Jules Moch's *Rencontres Avec . . . Darlan: Eisenhower* (Paris, 1968), p. 138, Darlan's words ("Alors, je terminerai ma carrière par un acte de splendide indiscipline: je prendrai le commandement de la flotte et nous rallierons l'Angleterre") appear in a somewhat more ambiguous context. Moch had asked him what he would do if the government asked for an armistice and the *delivery of the fleet* was one of the conditions posed. However, since it was generally believed that this *would* be a condition, Darlan's answer can be accepted as an earnest of his intentions at that time.

[5]Édouard Herriot, *Épisodes, 1940–1944* (Paris, 1950), pp. 64–65; Kammerer, *Passion*, pp. 67–68; Paul-Marie de la Gorce, *The French Army: A Military-Political History* (New York, 1963), p. 307; Fernand-Laurent, *Un peuple ressuscite*, p. 220. Thirty-six hours later, after the resignation of Reynaud, when Herriot asked him if he were preparing the departure of the government, Darlan's reply was: "A government which leaves never returns." Herriot's comment on this: "This admiral certainly knows how to swim." See Herriot, p. 75.

[6]Col. de Villelume's testimony in *CE*, IX, pp. 2789–90, 2793–94; Kammerer, *Passion*, pp. 68–69. Col. de Villelume had taken it upon himself, without Reynaud's authorization, to send a naval officer to Darlan to make this inquiry. Villelume's thoughts on North Africa's possibilities can be found on pp. 2782–84 of *CE*, IX.

[7]Reynaud, pp. 578–82; Reynaud's testimony, July 24, 1945, in *Procès Pétain*, pp. 81–82; Moch, pp. 144–51. On the basis of what Darlan said either to him or to others between June 3 and June 16, Jules Moch has pinpointed the Admiral's conversion to a pro-armistice position to the afternoon or evening of June 15—the motive being the role he had been promised in the new government. This is in keeping with the testimony given to the postwar Commission of Inquiry by Matteo Connet (Campinchi's *directeur de cabinet*) and Louis Rollin (Reynaud's Minister for the Colonies) concerning conversations they had with Darlan on 14 and 15 June respectively. See *CE*, V, p. 1393 (Rollin); VII, pp. 2188, 2193 (Connet). See also Bouthillier, I, p. 26, and his testimony in *CE*, VIII, pp. 2458, 2474–75, on Darlan's *crise de conscience* in mid-June. An alternative motive for it, suggested by M. Dhers of the Parliamentary Commission, is that it resulted from what Baudouin had told him that afternoon—at the quasi-clandestine meeting called by Pétain—regarding the comprehensive position Churchill had taken at Tours, i.e., his supposed pledge of solidarity with France notwithstanding a French request for an armistice. Thus, with the English alliance secured, Darlan would, according to this theory, have felt safe in passing over to a pro-armistice stance. See Dhers's comments, in the course of Weygand's testimony, in *CE*, VI, pp. 1855–56.

[8]Adrienne Doris Hytier, *Two Years of French Foreign Policy: Vichy, 1940–1942* (Paris, 1958), pp. 46–48. Others have had even fewer doubts as to the refusal of French naval forces to follow a Darlan not in rapport with the regularly constituted government. See, for instance, Jacques Mordal, *La Marine à l'Épreuve: De l'Armistice de 1940 au Procès Auphan* (Paris, 1956), p. 30. Captain E. Pleydell-Bouverie, head of the British Naval Mission in France until the signing of the armistice, thought that the fleet would be utterly loyal to Darlan's orders but observed that there was "considerable fear amongst the Officers and men of the Fleet of the effect upon their families of any failure on their part to obey the terms of the Armistice and the recall of the Fleet." See his Report on the Situation Regarding the French Fleet (undated) in ADM 205/4, First Sea Lord's Records, 1939–1945.

[9]See, for instance, a letter to his wife on May 31, where he says "The British lion appears to have wings when it is a question of regaining the sea"; also a letter from Admiral Odend'hal on June 5, in which Odend'hal has to remind Darlan that "it is not with the English (but) with the Boche that we are at war." See Alain Darlan, *L'Amiral Darlan Parle* (Paris, 1952), p. 56; Amouroux, p. 240.

[10]Alec de Montmorency, *The Enigma of Admiral Darlan* (New York,

1943), p. 89. Montmorency goes on to explain what the Norwegian experience meant to Darlan: "In the short period between the invasion of Norway and that of France, Admiral Darlan had had time to ponder over the inconvenience of a Government-in-exile, and he had become convinced that the position of such a government was bound to become one of complete subordination to the wishes of the hosts, however friendly the latter may be." See pp. 93–94.

[11]Darlan, pp. 67–68, also Kammerer, p. 265, n.1.

[12]From Bullitt's long report of July 1, in *FRUS,* 1940, II, pp. 465–66. See also Langer, *Our Vichy Gamble,* p. 63; and Hull, I, pp. 799–800.

[13]See Moch, p. 145.

[14]Darlan, p. 66.

[15]Belot, pp. 207–08; Darlan, pp. 50, 59, 60–61, 65; also Varillon, p. 73.

[16]Charles de Gaulle, *The Complete War Memoirs of Charles de Gaulle* (New York, 1964), p. 76; FO 371/24311, C 7294/G, No. 435 DIPP from Campbell by telephone, 4:50 a.m., June 17.

[17]Varillon, p. 65; Charles-Roux, p. 61; Reynaud, p. 581.

[18]Rear Admiral Paul Auphan and Jacques Mordal, *The French Navy in World War II* (Annapolis, Md., 1959), p. 108; Varillon, pp. 79–80. See especially Darlan's orders No. 8413 (June 17) and Nos. 5025–26 (June 18) in *Rapport,* II, pp. 442, 446. Admiral Belot's rundown on French naval losses throughout the whole campaign of France is as follows: warships—12 destroyed by the enemy, 11 scuttled, 10 captured in port, 65 interned in England; ships of the auxiliary fleet—26 destroyed by the enemy, 7 sunk, 95 captured, 154 interned in England; commercial ships of some size—30 destroyed by the enemy, 6 sunk, 56 captured, and 86 interned in British possessions. Belot, p. 168.

[19]Rear Admiral William Jameson, *Ark Royal, 1939–1941* (London, 1957), p. 150.

[20]For Darlan's orders of June 20, 22, and 24 (Nos. 5057–59, 5098–5101, and 5143–45), see *Rapport,* II, pp. 454, 459, and 466.

[21]For Odend'hal's note to Pound, June 25, see ADM 205/4, File 4, French Fleet at the time of French Armistice—1940; and for the French Admiralty's message to Odend'hal (No. 5147–5150), sent June 24 at 13:56, see *Rapport,* II, p. 466. For the British Admiralty's ignorance of certain basic facts, see also J. R. M. Butler, ed., *Grand Strategy,* Vol. II, *September 1939–June 1941* (London, 1957), p. 220; and Major-General I. S. O. Playfair, *The Mediterranean and Middle East,* Vol. I, *The Early Successes against Italy* (London, 1954), pp. 137–38.

[22]Alain Darlan, p. 71, claims that neither his father "nor any other member of the French government entertained the least illusion on the value of the guarantee offered by a 'solemn engagement' of the Nazis." That is why,

he says, the disposition of the fleet as specified by the armistice was inconceivable: "The units would have been practically at the mercy of a German seizure whose rapidity would perhaps have prevented even their sinking"; and why Darlan on June 22 had ordered the greater part of the fleet to bases in North Africa.

²³Kammerer, *Passion,* pp. 93–94; Hytier, p. 49; Churchill, II, p. 186. The COS résumé of events for the week June 13–20 reads: "All French naval ships which could steam have left Brest, St. Nazaire and Cherbourg for either British ports or Dakar and Casablanca. *Richelieu* sailed for Dakar on the 18th, *Jean Bart* for Casablanca on the 19th." WP (40) 212, also COS (40) 483, issued June 21. See also WO 106/1619 and ADM 199/361, War Diary, Home Fleet, for Admiralty messages of June 18, 20, and 21 confirming the clearing of French Atlantic ports; and Admiral Darlan's June 20 message to the French Naval Mission to the same effect, in *Rapport,* II, p. 453.

²⁴For Darlan's orders of June 14 and 15, see Varillon, p. 51, Auphan and Mordal, p. 87, and *Rapport,* II, p. 439. For Pound's prodding, see COS (40) 182nd, June 15, 3 p.m. For Darlan's orders of June 21 (Nos. 5070, 5073, 5077, 3088), see *Rapport,* II, pp. 455–56; Auphan and Mordal, pp. 87, 116–17; Docteur, *Vérité,* p. 37.

²⁵For Darlan's orders of June 22 and 23 (Nos. 5098 and 5124–27), see Docteur, *Vérité,* pp. 37, 39; Belot, pp. 218–20; and *Rapport,* II, p. 464. For Pound's message to Darlan, sent 0124/23 June, see ADM 205/4. See also Kammerer, p. 319; Reynaud, p. 559, n.1.

²⁶For Darlan's orders of June 24 and 25, see *Rapport,* II, pp. 465, 469–70; Docteur, *Vérité,* pp. 41 and 43 (Nos. 5136 and 5159); Kammerer, *Passion,* p. 132 (No. 5156); and René Godfroy, *L'Aventure de la Force X à Alexandrie (1940–1943)* (Paris, 1953), p. 43.

²⁷Kammerer, *Passion,* p. 121 (Nos. 5168–75); Belot, p. 222; *Rapport,* II, p. 471 (No. 3158).

²⁸Auphan and Mordal, pp. 117–18.

²⁹Kammerer, pp. 335, 378; Varillon, pp. 85–86. As regards Pound's confidence in his French opposite number, Vansittart in a Foreign Office minute on 26 June had chided: "Admiral Darlan has turned crook like the rest. I hope this will be put in its true light to Admiral Pound, who has a deal too much confidence in old friends and sailors of other races." See FO 371/24348, C 7375/G, Minute by R V, June 26.

³⁰Varillon, p. 85, for No. 5185–86, French Admiralty to French Naval Mission in London, sent June 27, at 16:05; also *Rapport,* II, p. 472.

³¹WM (40) 185, min. 7, CA, June 28, 12 noon.

³²For Odend'hal's memo to Pound, June 27, and Pound's note on his interview with Odend'hal the same day, see ADM 205/4, First Sea Lord's Records, 1939–1945. In the War Cabinet minutes, June 28, Pound's warn-

ing was politely transmuted into: "Admiral Darlan should realise that the only hope of France's resurrection lay in a British victory, and he should not allow any niceties of procedure at this time to jeopardise the success of our efforts." See also FO 371/24321/C 7553/G for Sir Alexander Cadogan's note (June 28) on Cambon's shocked reaction to the possibility of force being used against the French ships in Alexandria. In this version, Pound was quoted as saying that "the only hope of the French Empire was that we sh[d] win the war: that was the main thing, & he mustn't fuss about trifles like this." The formal British reply—in far more diplomatic language—to the French Embassy protest against the policy adopted towards the French squadron at Alexandria (lodged on June 28) was made on June 30, but in essence it was simply a flowery replay of Pound's more direct and pungent phrasing. See ADM 1/10321, French Warships at Oran and Alexandria on the Surrender of France, FO Reply, June 30, to French Embassy Aide-Mémoire of June 28.

[33]FO 371/24321, C 7483/839/17, Memo from Cambon to Strang, June 28; ADM 205/4; WM (40) 187, min. 8, CA, June 29, 10 a.m.

[34]Kammerer, *Passion*, p. 134 (No. 5202 to French Naval Mission, sent June 30, 14:30, arrived July 1); Butler, II, p. 220; Playfair, I, p. 137; Auphan and Mordal, pp. 120–21; WM (40) 190, min. 1, CA, July 1, 6 p.m.

[35]Kammerer, *Passion*, p. 138.

### British Planning and the French Fleet

[1]Churchill, II, p. 200.

[2]Charles-Roux, p. 119; Auphan and Mordal, p. 115; Baudouin's testimony, in *CE*, VII, p. 2084; Varillon, p. 77. The word is rendered as "supervision" in the English translation of Article 8 appearing in *DGFP*, Ser. D, IX, No. 523.

[3]Hytier, pp. 41–42.

[4]Even in the very recent past, the rather irrepressible General Dillon, promised by certain French admirals in Algiers that their ships would never fight against the British, had admitted that he "was not in a position to give a corresponding undertaking, as the Germans, having scuttled their own Fleet [at Scapa Flow, after World War I], would take good care that the French did not follow their example." See Dillon, p. 140.

[5]FO 371/24383, C 7074/G, Letter from Cadogan to Campbell, June 8.

[6]COS (40) 440 (JP), June 9, Plans to Meet a Certain Eventuality; WP (40) 201, also COS (40) 444, June 11.

[7]WO 106/1774, Naval Cypher 1930/June 14, First Sea Lord to C-in-C, Mediterranean; Interdepartmental Cypher 1608/June 14, First Sea Lord to Admiral Darlan; and Naval Cyphers 0200 and 0237/June 15, First Sea Lord to BNLO Moliere; COS (40) 182nd, June 15, 3 p.m.; FO 371/24310, C

7263/G, FO No. 363 DIPP to Campbell, June 15, 5:25 p.m.; WM (40) 167, min. 6, CA, June 15, 10 a.m.; WM (40) 168, min. l, CA, June 16, 10:15 a.m.

[8]WM (40) 171, June 18, 12:30 p.m.; ADM 199/361, War Diary, Home Fleet, June 17, Admiralty's 1940; June 18, Admiralty's 1314; *The Diaries of Sir Alexander Cadogan, 1938–1945,* ed. by David Dilks (London, 1971), p. 304. Also proposed on June 18, rather as a preview of coming attractions, was the seizure of four Swedish destroyers en route from Eire to the Faeroe Islands, an action that was authorized by the War Cabinet on June 19 and completed by June 21. See WM (40) 171, June 18, 12:30 p.m.; WM (40) 172, June 19, 12:30 p.m.; WM (40) 174, June 21, 12 noon.

[9]Cunningham of Hyndhope, *A Sailor's Odyssey* (London, 1951), p. 240; Note on a meeting attended by PM, First Lord, First Sea Lord, and VCNS, June 17, in Alexander Papers, File 5/4, Churchill College Archives, Cambridge; ADM 199/1930, First Lord's Records, May-August 1940, WSC Memo to First Lord, June 17; Churchill, II, Appendix, p. 545; Jameson, *Ark Royal,* pp. 143, 154; Auphan and Mordal, p. 122.

[10]Among the less likely of these schemes was the suggestion by Lord Lloyd, Mr. Alexander, and Mr. Greenwood on June 17 that the French fleet be purchased at once. This was quashed on June 19 by Sir Alexander Cadogan, who thought that "If the French Government have it in mind to buy some measure of mercy for their people by handing over the fleet, they will hardly be more ready to sell it than to transfer it to us." "Probably in the end," he reasoned, "scuttling would be the only solution in the event of a French capitulation." The urgency of the need, however, had not prevented some members of the Foreign Office from proposing that "discussions [as to the purchase] should begin *well below* £100 m.," even though the cost of the French Navy was estimated at £200 m. See FO 371/24311, C 7352/G, Note by Cadogan, June 19.

[11]COS (40) 185th, June 18, 10:30 a.m.; FO 371/24311, C 7278/G, Minute by G. E. Millard, June 18; FO 371/24301, C 7350, Tel. No. 1034 from the Marquess of Lothian in Washington, dis. June 19, 12:49 a.m.; FO 371/24301, C 7350, Note by G. E Millard, June 21.

[12]FO 371/24311, C 7373/65/17, No. 1158, Halifax to Campbell, June 21, on Corbin's visit; C 7455/G, Note by Cadogan on Corbin's visit, June 20; C 7352, War Cabinet Conclusions 174 (40), June 21; FO 371/24327, C 7387/7327/17, FO Circular No. 31 to H.M. Consuls, June 22, dis. 2 a.m.; C 7352/G, Note by Cadogan on *Émile Bertin,* June 21; see also Amouroux, p. 233. If the Germans *were* transmitting false signals, they were not the only ones to play this game. A wireless signal of June 24—an hour after the armistice with Italy had been signed—ordering French warships to continue the fight by all means "with our English allies" and to rally to British bases could only have emanated from a British source. See Docteur, *Vérité,* p. 41.

[13]For Churchill's conviction, see FO 371/24311, C 7352/G, War Cabinet

Conclusions, June 21, WM (40) 174; WM (40) 175, June 22, 10 a.m.; FO 371/24348, C 7375/G, FO No. 462 to Campbell, dis. 7:45 p.m., June 22.

[14]WM (40) 176, min. 5, CA, June 22, 9:30 p.m.; WM (40) 177, June 23, 10 a.m.; ADM 199/1052, Admiralty's 1929, June 23.

[15]WM (40) 178, June 24, 12 noon, and CA, min. 6; WM (40) 179, min. 3, June 24, 6 p.m.

[16]This was known as the result of the interview Admiral North (FOC, North Atlantic) had had that day with Admiral Gensoul at Oran. Among other things, Gensoul had stated that "As long as there was a Government, he would obey it"; "that France was utterly defeated and that the French Fleet was all that was left to bargain with"; and that he would not turn his ships over to the British: "if they were going to be used for fighting, they would be used by him or not at all." However, he had also made clear "his determination to obey Admiral Darlan's orders that under no circumstances would the ships be handed over intact to the enemy," and North reported that he had reason to believe that a scuttling organization existed for this purpose. See Noel Monks, *That Day at Gibraltar* (London, 1957), pp. 19–21. See also WO 106/1609, Message to Admiralty from FOC, North Atlantic, sent 1400, June 24.

[17]WM (40) 179, min. 3, CA, June 24, 6 p.m.; WM (40) 179, June 24, 6 p.m. An expedition to the Gironde to "cut out" British and Allied merchant vessels still located there was also authorized.

[18]WM (40) 180, June 24, 10:30 p.m.

[19]News of the *Richelieu*'s sailing was as much of a shock to Admiral Darlan as it was to the British, and it is clear from his message to the ship's commander at 7:45 on June 26 that Darlan believed that the *Richelieu* was about to place itself at the disposal of the English, probably as the result of phoney emissions emanating from this source. The *Richelieu* was promptly ordered back to Dakar. See *Rapport*, II, p. 470. Yet, according to Pound's report to the War Cabinet on June 27, the *Richelieu* did not alter course for Dakar until 3 p.m. on the 26th. See WM (40) 184.

[20]WM (40) 182, min. 2, CA, June 25, 6 p.m.; WM (40) 184, min. 5, CA, June 27, 12 noon; WM (40) 183, min. 5, CA, June 26, 11:30 a.m.; also ADM 199/361, War Diary, Home Fleet, June 27, 0016; Jameson, *Ark Royal,* pp. 157–58.

[21]FO 371/24321, C 7483/839/17, Minute by Vansittart to Cadogan, June 26; also C 7388, Minute by Orme Sargent, June 26; Minute by W. Strang, June 26; Minutes by Cadogan and Halifax, June 26; WM (40) 184, June 27, 12 noon; WM (40) 184, min. 5, CA, June 27, 12 noon; ADM 199/391, Report of Proceedings, Force H, June 28–July 4, 1940, submitted to Admiralty, July 26, by Admiral Somerville (hereafter cited as Somerville's Report, July 26), para. 2.

[22]COS (40) 505 (JP), also JP (40) 295, June 29, Implications of Action Contemplated in Respect of Certain French Ships.

[23]See Sir John Slessor, *The Central Blue: The Autobiography of Sir John Slessor, Marshal of the RAF* (New York, 1957), pp. 261, 299. Slessor, who participated in this decision, would later write about Catapult:

It seemed to some of us an act which would be worthwhile only if we could be certain of complete success—which was by no means a certainty and which we did not achieve. I personally did not (and still do not) think it was worth it. We submitted our view that even the successful destruction of the French ships would not be justified if it carried with it the genuine danger of resulting in the active hostility of France and her colonial possessions. That perhaps was not a very real danger, but the day after the action at Mers-el-Kebir the Joint Planners found themselves faced with the necessity of producing a fresh series of papers—this time on the implications of French hostility.

[24]See Preliminary Report on the Situation Regarding the French Fleet (undated) by Capt. E. Pleydell-Bouverie; and Review of the Situation: Attitude of Senior Officers at Casablanca (undated) by Capt. C. S. Holland, in ADM 205/4, First Sea Lord's Records, 1939–1945. In *his* review of the situation at Mers-el-Kébir, Commander Collett, recently liaison officer with Admiral Gensoul, also remarked significantly that though when he left the fleet he was convinced that the ships would never be turned over intact to the Germans or Italians, and though orders for scuttling and for wrecking the ships had been issued, he was unable to judge whether this state had been modified in view of the threatening attitude adopted by the British. Thus, regardless of whether these officers themselves opposed the use of force—and they did—the intelligence being transmitted by them all tended to point in but one direction.

[25]COS (40) 510, June 30, Implications of Action Contemplated in Respect of Certain French Ships. For the blockade decision, see Hugh Dalton, *The Fateful Years: Memoirs, 1931–1945* (London, 1957), p. 349. On July 13, it was decided to extend the blockade to French North Africa. Admiral Pound's position, revealing the influences at work on him since June 24, is set forth in the minutes of a meeting held at the Admiralty, 10:15, June 29 (see ADM 205/4):

By the terms of the Italian Armistice [he stated], the ships were to return to French metropolitan ports, and therefore in this case they would come under German and Italian supervision entirely. . . . the French had said they would sink their ships, but this would be impossible once they were under German and Italian control. In addition, in connection with the blockade of France which had been announced, the Germans would say to the French that Great Britain was now the enemy and would work on the French to declare war on us, in which case the French Fleet would be brought into operation against us. It was, therefore, essential that we should get control of the French ships or sink them.

[26]WM (40) 188, min. 1, CA, June 30, 7 p.m.; WM (40) 190, min. 1, CA, July 1, 6 p.m.; WM (40) 191, July 2, 12 noon; ADM 199/391, Somerville's Report, July 26, para. 18, re Admiralty's 0103, July 2 (preliminary instructions had been sent the night of June 30–July 1, for which see para. 14); Playfair, I, pp. 131–32.

## Operation Catapult

[1]Churchill, II, p. 201.

[2]Kammerer, *Mers-el-Kébir*, pp. 150–52; Docteur, *Vérité*, p. 47; Churchill, II, pp. 200, 202; Auphan and Mordal, pp. 116, n.1, 124–26; ADM 199/822, Final Orders to Adm. M. E. Dunbar-Nasmith, C-in-C, Western Approaches, July 2; also Report on Seizure of French Warships at Plymouth, Dartmouth, and Falmouth, July 3; Admiral Sir W. M. James, *The Portsmouth Letters* (London, 1946), pp. 65–67; Varillon, p. 164; ADM 205/4, First Sea Lord's Records, Minutes of a Planning Meeting held at Admiralty, June 29, 10:15.

[3]Cunningham, p. 250, has described this order as "a perfect example of the type of signal which should never be made." Aside from its unhelpfulness, it was impossible to implement, sunset having already occurred in Alexandria before the message was even sent from London. That Churchill had intruded himself into this matter is suggested by Cunningham's further autobiographical comment: "At the time I did not believe that signal emanated in the Admiralty, and do not believe it now." But cf. Arthur J. Marder's arguments on Churchill's role in operational matters in *From the Dardanelles to Oran: Studies of the Royal Navy in War and Peace, 1915–1940* (London, 1974), pp. 111 and 177.

[4]For the whole Alexandria episode, see Cunningham, pp. 234, 243–57; Godfroy, pp. 21, 40–74; Kammerer, *Mers-el-Kébir*, pp. 142–48; Auphan and Mordal, pp. 135–37; Darlan's orders of June 24 and 27 to Godfroy in *Rapport*, II, pp. 467 and 472; Playfair, I, pp. 138–41; Hytier, pp. 58–60; Robert L. Melka, "Darlan between Britain and Germany, 1940–41," *Journal of Contemporary History*, Vol. 8, No. 2 (April 1973), p. 61; WM (40) 193, min. 8, July 4, 11:30 a.m.; WP (40) 262, also COS (40) 545, Weekly Résumé for July 4–11, issued July 12; ADM 1/10321, Admiralty Diary of Events at Alexandria, July 3 and 4; ADM 199/386, War Diary, C-in-C, Mediterranean, July 4 and 5. For Cunningham's agreement with Godfroy as transmitted July 7, see ADM 116/4413, Force X; for the First Sea Lord's instructions to Cunningham, July 1, showing that Pound approved in advance of the agreement's being tied to the Germans' and Italians' willingness to respect the armistice, see ADM 1/10321, French Warships at Oran and Alexandria on the Surrender of France; for progress reports by Cunningham, July 6, 9, and 14, and for the flurry of minutes among Churchill, Alexander, and Pound regarding the C-in-C's undertaking to the French Admiral, consult ADM 199/1930, First Lord's Records: May–August 1940, sections 14 and 32. It is possible that Admiral Godfroy was in a sense "inviting" the use of overwhelming force against his squadron when he spoke to the British Consul-General in Alexandria on June 28 of the "demoralised readiness" of the French Navy to obey the Pétain government. As Sir Miles Lampson, the British Ambassador, reported to the Foreign Office, Godfroy had "expressed his conviction that in nearly every instance the French commanders would take steps not to let their ships fall intact into enemy hands but seemed

nevertheless to think that units of the French fleet unless prevented would sail to [the] ports indicated under [the] Armistice." FO 371/24327, C 7536, No. 637 from Sir M. Lampson in Cairo, June 30; also ADM 1/10321.

⁵Captain S. W. Roskill, *The War at Sea, 1939–1945,* Vol. I, *The Defensive* (London, 1954), p. 241; Auphan and Mordal, p. 127; Kammerer, *Mers-el-Kébir,* pp. 107–08; Cunningham, p. 243.

⁶ADM 199/391, Somerville's Report, July 26, paras. 28–31, 34, plus Enclosure No. 4, containing Capt. C. S. Holland's Narrative of Events, July 3. British Summer Time is used throughout British reports on the Oran action, and will be used here. GMT is employed in French accounts.

⁷Churchill, II, pp. 202–03.

⁸ADM 199/391, Somerville's Report, July 26, paras. 32, 35–38, 41, Holland's Report, and Enclosure No. 7, Vice-Admiral, Aircraft Carriers' Report, July 4; Admiral Gensoul's Official Report to Admiral Darlan, July 9, 1940, in Kammerer, *Passion,* pp. 509–11; Belot, pp. 271–72; Auphan and Mordal, p. 129; Kammerer, *Mers-el-Kébir,* pp. 110–11; Monks, p. 20; Varillon, pp. 98, 129; Warren Tute, *The Deadly Stroke* (London, 1973), pp. 100, 110, 124, 137.

⁹ADM 199/391, Sommerville's Report, July 26, paras. 39, 41–43, and Holland's Report; Gensoul's Report, July 9, in Kammerer, *Passion,* p. 111; Auphan and Mordal, pp. 127, 129; Jameson, *Ark Royal,* pp. 163, 167.

¹⁰ADM 199/391, Somerville's Report, July 26, paras. 45–46, 48, 50, Holland's Report, and Enclosure No. 1 (Admiralty instructions to Somerville); Gensoul's Report, July 9, in Kammerer, *Passion,* pp. 512–13 (and 169); also Belot, pp. 274–75; Auphan and Mordal, p. 130; Kammerer, *Mers-el-Kébir,* pp. 111–12; Varillon, pp. 131–34; Charles-Roux, pp. 121, 123.

¹¹Varillon, pp. 123–24; Docteur, *Vérité,* pp. 64–65; Auphan and Mordal, pp. 129–30; ADM 199/391, Somerville's Report, July 26, paras. 49–50, and Holland's Report; Belot, p. 276; Charles-Roux, p. 142; Kammerer, *Passion,* pp. 164–65, 177; Gensoul's testimony, in *CE,* VI, pp. 1898–99, 1900, 1903, 1905.

¹²Auphan and Mordal, pp. 131–35; Gensoul's Report, July 9, in Kammerer, *Passion,* pp. 511–12, 513–15; ADM 199/391, Somerville's Report, July 26, paras. 46, 51–70, and Holland's Report; Somerville's Report of July 29, paras. 12–15; Playfair, I, pp. 136–37; WP (40) 262, also COS (40) 545, Weekly Résumé for July 4–11, issued July 12; Charles-Roux, p. 118.

## *Mers-el-Kébir: Analysis and Aftermath*

¹Kammerer, *Passion,* pp. 164–65, 167, 178–79, 193; Jameson, pp. 163–64; Varillon, p. 124; Baudouin, p. 156; Charles-Roux, pp. 118–20, 137–38; Gensoul's testimony, *CE,* VI, p. 1905; Hytier, pp. 54–55. As for when the full text of the ultimatum was *first* known, Gensoul claims that the French Admiralty had knowledge of it by the morning of July 4—through monitor-

ing British radio broadcasts. See his testimony, *CE,* VI, pp. 1899–1900. Yet the disorganization of the government in early July, with part of it in Vichy, another part still in Clermont-Ferrand—as General Weygand suggests—may have kept members of the cabinet in ignorance. See his testimony, in *CE,* VI, pp. 1919–20.

[2]Admiral Gensoul's testimony, June 28, 1949, before the Commission of Inquiry, in *CE,* VI, pp. 1897–1901, 1910–12.

[3]Darlan, pp. 76–78. Gensoul *was* relieved of his command on August 10 and never received another one, though he continued to exercise the purely honorary function of Inspector of Maritime Forces. Gensoul believed that his fall from grace was the result not of having lost his ships but of having parleyed too extensively with the British instead of breaking with them definitively. For instance, Gensoul had twice signaled Somerville *after* the battle in an attempt to prevent a resumption of British fire or the return of the British another day. See Kammerer, *Passion,* pp. 172, 176; Admiral Gensoul's testimony, in *CE,* VI, pp. 1903, 1906.

[4]Hytier, p. 56; Auphan and Mordal, pp. 128–29; Charles-Roux, pp. 121, 139, 142, 162.

[5]Henri Michel, *Vichy: Année 40* (Paris, 1966), p. 235; Kammerer, *Passion,* pp. 161–62. Weygand, p. 257, oddly enough, thought that some accommodation on this basis might have been reached.

[6]Monks, pp. 22, 28, for North's information; Kammerer, *Passion,* pp. 140–41; Varillon, p. 118, based on Lieut. Dufay's *compte rendu* of his negotiations with Holland. Admiral Somerville, however, originally thought otherwise. When first assigned his task on June 27, he was of the opinion that "the French collapse was so complete and the will to fight so entirely extinguished, that it seemed highly improbable that the French would, in the last resort, resist by force the British demands." He became less sure of the probable French reaction in the course of conferring with other senior officers at Gibraltar. See ADM 199/391, Somerville's Report, July 26, paras. 3–4, 12, 15–17.

[7]Hytier, p. 57; ADM 199/391, Somerville's Report, July 26, paras. 6, 27, 49, and Enclosure No. 1 (containing Admiralty message 0103/2nd July: Final Instructions on Alternatives to be given French); WM (40) 190, min. 1., CA, July 1, 6 p.m.; WM (40) 192, min. 5, CA, July 3, 11:30 a.m.; ADM 1/10321, Admiralty Diary of Events for Force H, July 3 and 4; Roskill, I, p. 243; Playfair, I, p. 132; Cunningham, p. 243. However, demilitarization had figured as an alternative in the initial orders issued the night of June 30–July 1; later, the Martinique clause was substituted. Stranger still, the Admiralty had actually informed Somerville "that the French had a scheme for demilitarisation at two hours' notice." Captain Holland was to question them on this "should necessity arise." See ADM 1/10321, First Sea Lord to Flag Officer, Force H, June 30 (alternatives to be given French); ADM 199/391, Somerville's Report, July 26, para. 25.

[8]ADM 199/826, Operations at Dakar, including Admiralty signals 0344 and 0345 of July 7 to *Hermes* (containing instructions to Rear Admiral and terms to be given French naval authorities at Dakar) and Report No. 95/6/007 submitted July 9 by Rear Admiral Richard Onslow; WM (40) 196, min. 1, CA, July 7, 7 p.m.; WM (40) 197, min. 4, CA, July 8, 11:30 a.m.; WM (40) 198, min. 2, CA, July 9, 12 noon; *Parl. Deb., H. of C.,* July 9, 1940, Vol. 362, cols. 1088–90; Kammerer, *Mers-el-Kébir,* pp. 153, 157–58, 163–64; Charles-Roux, pp. 149–50; Admiral Georges Robert, *La France aux Antilles de 1939 à 1943* (Paris, 1950), pp. 56, 79–81; Commander C. Alphonso Smith, "Martinique in World War II," *United States Naval Institute Proceedings,* Vol. 81, No. 2 (February 1955), pp. 170–71; and *FRUS,* 1940, II, pp. 505–16, for Franco-American negotiations leading up to the agreement of Aug. 7.

[9]For the development of British naval policy in the days immediately following Mers-el-Kébir, see DO (40) 19th, July 3, 11 p.m., for the Defence Committee's recognition that "there was a strong likelihood that the French Government would in the very near future declare war against us"; JP (40) 309, July 4, Note by Joint Planning Sub-committee for COS on Implications of French Hostility; WM (40) 193, min. 8, CA, July 4, 11:30 a.m.; WM (40) 195, min. 3, CA, July 6, 10 a.m.; and Admiralty messages 2300/3rd July, 2005/9th July, and 0241/12th July, in File 7/25, Somerville Papers, Churchill College Archives, Cambridge, and in Monks, pp. 19, 30–32, and 79–80. For the enunciation to the French of its naval policy, at the close of this hostile phase, see Pound to Vice-Admiral J. E. Odend'hal, c/o French Embassy, July 14, in ADM 205/4, First Sea Lord's Records, and in Kammerer, *Passion,* pp. 140–43; for Vichy's reception of the news on July 15, see Charles-Roux, p. 162.

[10]*Parl. Deb., H. of C.,* July 4, 1940, 5th Ser., Vol. 362, cols. 1043–51; also Churchill, II, p. 205. For Parliament's reaction to Churchill's speech, see Dalton, in *The Fateful Years,* p. 349, who writes that Churchill received a louder and longer ovation "than he, or Chamberlain or anyone else, had yet had during the war"; and Harold Nicolson, *The War Years, 1939–1945,* Vol. II of *Diaries and Letters,* ed. by Nigel Nicolson (New York, 1967), p. 100, who recorded: "The House is at first saddened by this odious attack but is fortified by Winston's speech. The grand finale ends in an ovation, with Winston sitting there with the tears pouring down his cheeks." Churchill's emotion on this occasion was no doubt genuine, but the precise psychological components of this emotion are harder to determine. Lord Beaverbrook claims that "Nothing in his life could have grieved him more deeply than his decision to attack the French fleet at Oran" and that the act "left him profoundly shaken." See Lord Beaverbrook, "Two War Leaders. Lloyd George and Churchill," *History Today,* Vol. XXIII, No. 8 (August 1973), pp. 551–52. Yet in view of the insistence with which Churchill had long urged this course and the ruthlessness with which he overrode all conflicting

advice from commanders in the field and from the Joint Planners, it is probably more likely that his emotion and shaken condition immediately before and after the event were motivated less by sorrow than by fear of not being vindicated.

[11]For instance, in December 1941 Churchill told Cordell Hull, who himself thought of the attack on Mers-el-Kébir as "a tragic blunder," that "since many people throughout the world believed that Britain was about ready to surrender, he had wanted by this action to show that she still meant to fight." See Hull, I, p. 799, and cf. Admiral Gensoul's appraisal of Mers-el-Kébir as "essentially an operation of internal policy"—rammed down the throats of a reluctant British Admiralty by Mr. Churchill and the War Cabinet, in his testimony, in *CE*, VI, pp. 1914–15.

[12]Churchill, II, p. 205.

[13]Though the US Chargé d'Affaires in Vichy, Robert Murphy, may have been able to "say to French officials with complete truth that the American Government had no prior knowledge of the British naval attack, and deplored it," it is obvious that he was kept ignorant of the true story. See Murphy's *Diplomat Among Warriors*, p. 70. This is made clear in a telegram sent by the British Ambassador from Washington on July 2. In response to a suggestion by the President, Lord Lothian had asked Roosevelt "whether that meant that American opinion would support [the] forcible seizure of these ships. He said certainly. They would expect them to be seized rather than that they should fall into German hands and that he would do everything in his power to help this solution." FO 371/24321, C 7553, Tel. No. 1206 from Lord Lothian, dis. 12 a.m., July 2, rec. 10:10 a.m., July 2; also WM (40) 192, min. 5, CA, July 3, 11:30 a.m. Further, on July 4, Lothian sent a note to Roosevelt saying: "You will see that Winston Churchill has taken the action in regard to the French Fleet which we discussed and you approved." After the event, Roosevelt was quite frank about his feelings even with the French, for he told Ambassador St. Quentin that "Even if there was only an extremely remote possibility that your Fleet would pass into German hands, the British Government had good reason to act as it did. I would not have acted otherwise." See Langer and Gleason, *Challenge,* pp. 573–74; Charles-Roux, pp. 130–31; Kammerer, *Mers-el-Kébir,* p. 133.

[14]Cadogan, p. 310; Monks, p. 73; July 3 entry in Somerville's 1940 Collins' Pocket Diary, File 1/31, Somerville Papers, Churchill College Archives, Cambridge; WM (40) 198, min. 2, CA, July 9, 12 noon; *Parl. Deb., H. of C.,* July 9, 1940, 5th Ser., Vol. 362, cols. 1087–92; also Alexander's July 9 Appreciation for PM of Action Against French Capital Ships, File 5/4, Alexander Papers, Churchill College Archives; FO 371/24301, C 7636/G, Tel. No. 1119 from H.M. Consul-General at Tangier, July 5; Gensoul's Official Report to Admiral Darlan, July 9, 1940, in Kammerer, *Passion,* pp. 514–15; Varillon, p. 92, n.2; Hytier, p. 69.

[15]WP (40) 256, also COS (40) 543, July 16; ADM 199/1930, First Lord's Records: May–August 1940, File 32, Memo from WSC to First Lord and First Sea Lord, July 5; File 8, Memo from WSC to First Lord, June 29; File 4, Weekly Report to COS on Progress and Condition of Allied Naval Contingents, July 13; ADM 199/391, Somerville's Report, July 26, paras. 56 and 76.

[16]*Parl. Deb., H. of C.,* July 4, 1940, 5th Ser., Vol. 362, cols. 1043–51; Taylor, *Beaverbrook* (New York, 1972), p. 444; Butler, II, p. 222; Taylor, *English History, 1914–1945* (London, 1965), pp. 479, 481–83; Hull, I, p. 798.

[17]See Minutes of a Meeting Held at Admiralty, 10:15, June 29, in ADM 205/4, First Sea Lord's Records, 1939–1945; Prime Minister to First Lord and First Sea Lord, July 7, 1940, File 12, Correspondence with PM, April to December 1940, ADM 205/6, First Sea Lord's Records; Admiralty Diary of Events, Force H, July 3, 1940, ADM 1/10321; Minutes of a Meeting Held in First Sea Lord's Room at Admiralty, 1830, June 7, ADM 205/4.

[18]Cunningham, pp. 244–45; ADM 199/391, Somerville's Report, July 26, paras. 8, 9, 13, 15, 16; ADM 1/19178, Operation Catapult: Notes on the Discussions Which Preceded the Operation, Vice-Admiral, Force H, to Admiralty, July 1, sent 1220, rec'd 1705; ADM 1/10321, Admiralty to Vice-Admiral, Force H, July 1, sent 1820; Churchill, II, p. 202; Monks, pp. 22–29. It boomeranged most dramatically on Admiral North himself, who several months later was removed from his command at Gibraltar, ostensibly for having allowed a French cruiser squadron to pass the straits on September 11, just twelve days before the disastrous Anglo-Gaullist attempt on Dakar, but ultimately for his stance at the time of Oran, which had caused the Admiralty to lose confidence in him. North had not only advised Somerville that force should be avoided at all costs, even if it meant the withdrawal of Force H from Mers-el-Kébir, mission unaccomplished, but had made the crucial tactical error of giving the Admiralty the benefit of his thoughts on the subject *after* the July 3 attack. For this he was severely admonished by the Admiralty. Ironically, the later decision that wrecked his career was taken in strict conformity with standing orders, which the Admiralty had simply failed to update in the light of the coming expedition to Dakar. See Monks, pp. 24–29, 70, 141–42, 161–62. For a fellow professional's appraisal of the government's responsibility in this matter, see Rear Admiral H. G. Thursfield, "Pour Encourager les Autres," *The National Review,* Vol. CXXXI (October 1948), pp. 343–53. For Admiral North's negative appreciation of Operation Catapult, sent to the Admiralty on July 4; for Their Lordships' reprimand, July 17; for A. V. Alexander's and Churchill's opinion of North, showing that they (but not Pound) wished to replace him in mid-July; and for North's August 6 letter exonerating himself, see ADM 1/19177, Admiral Sir Dudley North: Correspondence between First Lord of Admiralty and Prime Minister; and ADM 1/19178, Operation Catapult:

Notes on the Discussions Which Preceded Operation. For his final interviews with Pound and Alexander following his dismissal, see Somerville Papers, File 7/25, Churchill College Archives, Cambridge; and for North's explanation of the Gibraltar affair, Dec. 8, 1940, see Alexander Papers, File 5/4, together with additional material on the North *cause célèbre,* as it continued into the 1950's, in Files 5/5, 5/16, and 5/17, Churchill College Archives.

[19]De Gaulle, *Memoirs,* pp. 91–93, 106; Major-General Sir Edward Spears, *Two Men Who Saved France: Pétain and De Gaulle* (London, 1966), p. 165; Murphy, pp. 68–69. For de Gaulle's speech, see *Discours aux Français: 18 Juin 1940–2 Janvier 1944* (n.d.), pp. 19–20. Emmanuel Berl, p. 197, summarizes the paradoxical reactions aroused by Mers-el-Kébir: It was as if "the Free French could admit that the government of Vichy was a government of 'traitors,' but not that England could legitimately fear from France a betrayal." As for its effect on colonial administrators, Gabriel Puaux, who as High Commissioner in the Levant had adopted a policy of benevolent neutrality towards England, told Mr. Havard, the British Consul-General, after the event: "My attitude will not change; you can always count on me, but [hereafter] it will be by virtue of reason and duty. My heart will no longer be in it." See Puaux, pp. 207–08.

## End of the Affair

[1]There had been many reports of fairly intense anti-British sentiment in naval circles at least a week before Mers-el-Kébir. See, for instance, FO 371/24383, C 7497/G, Tel. No. 96 from Consul-General, Tangier, dis. 2:30 p.m., June 28.

[2]Docteur, *Vérité,* p. 75, from Darlan's order of the day, July 5; Murphy, p. 78; Kammerer, *Passion,* p. 198, from a July 5 radio address by Darlan, published July 6.

[3]Kammerer, *Passion,* p. 206, press declaration by Jean Prouvost, July 7; also pp. 187, 214; Charles-Roux, pp. 122–23; Auphan and Mordal, p. 138.

[4]Kammerer, *Passion,* pp. 213–14; Docteur, *Vérité,* pp. 78–79; and an exchange between M. Serre and Admiral Gensoul in the course of the latter's testimony, in *CE,* VI, pp. 1908–09. For the French delegation's negotiations with the German Armistice Commission at Wiesbaden leading to these results, see *La Délégation Française auprés de la Commission Allemande d'Armistice,* Vol. I (Paris, 1947), pp. 34, 38–42. For the German decision to suspend Articles 8 and 12 (regarding disarmament of French air forces) of the armistice agreement, see also *Documents on German Foreign Policy, 1918–1945,* Ser. D, Vol. X (Washington, 1957), pp. 124 and 127 (documents 111 and 115). For André Gide's perceptive response to these "gifts," see *The Journals of André Gide,* ed. and trans. by Justin O'Brien (New York, 1956), Vol. II, *1924–1949,* pp. 256–57.

[5]Belot, p. 211.

⁶Varillon, p. 116, based on Dufay's *compte rendu*. As far as the merchant marine was concerned, it had already been recalled to its home ports in accordance with the armistice provisions, and Ambassador Biddle reported on June 27 that the docks at Bordeaux were filled. See *FRUS*, 1940, II, p. 461.

⁷See Bullitt's dispatch of July 1 from La Bourboule (Vichy), in *FRUS*, 1940, II, p. 466.

⁸See, for instance, Auphan and Mordal, p. 139; Darlan, pp. 81–82; Docteur, *Vérité*, p. 73.

⁹Auphan and Mordal, p. 139; Varillon, p. 216. The self-scuttling of the French fleet at Toulon when the Germans were practically upon the quays is invariably seen by most Frenchmen as the ultimate proof that Darlan's secret orders were not only workable but that they would be obeyed no matter what the circumstances—even when Darlan himself was ordering French warships at Toulon to rally to Africa. See Charles-Roux, p. 121; Kammerer, *Mers-el-Kébir*, p. 141. The handing over of French ships and naval installations at Bizerte on December 8, 1942, when the Germans threatened to annihilate the French garrison if there were any attempt at resistance or sabotage, on the other hand, is seen by skeptics as complete justification for Britain's action at Oran. See, for instance, Major-General Sir Edward Spears, *Two Men Who Saved France*, pp. 165–66. For the circumstances surrounding this incident, see Docteur, *Vérité*, pp. 161–71; Albert Kammerer, *Du Débarquement Africain au meurtre de Darlan* (Paris, 1949), pp. 568–72.

¹⁰Bouthillier, I, pp. 150–53; Auphan and Mordal, p. 134; ADM 199/391, Somerville's Report, July 29, para. 4; WM (40) 195, min. 3, CA, July 6, 10 a.m.; Baudouin, pp. 157, 161–64, 168–70, 172, 184; Charles-Roux, pp. 132–35; Kammerer, *Mers-el-Kébir*, pp. 115–16, 118; Kammerer, *Passion*, pp. 184–85, 188–89, 196, 199, 207–09. The French did eventually carry out two heavy air raids over Gibraltar, but not until September 24 and 25— in retaliation for the unsuccessful British-Free French attack on Dakar. By this time Weygand had rallied to Darlan's Gibraltar scheme, though in early July he was opposed to the bombardment. See Monks, pp. 38–39; Weygand's testimony, *CE*, VI, pp. 1920–21.

¹¹The two chief American observers in Vichy at the time of the British attack give a vivid, if somewhat partial, view of how leading members of the French Government reacted. According to Robert Murphy, "Baudouin was so angry and humiliated that he even hinted the French Navy might cooperate with the Germans." As for Darlan, he "was more outraged than anybody else, and his resentment surpassed all reasonable bounds. . . . At that moment he would have thrown in his lot with Hitler if he had not been even more anti-Nazi than he was anti-British." All in all, Murphy felt that the Pétain government probably would not declare war against England, and would keep its pledge to the United States regarding the fleet. See Murphy,

pp. 68, 78. Ambassador Bullitt, for his part, reported on July 5 that Pétain was the only one keeping his head: while the reaction of other French leaders (including Baudouin) to Oran was "violent in the extreme," to the point of openly favoring "immediate acts of war against England," the Marshal, who was "sincerely desirous of a British victory," was ready to write off that tragic incident "by attributing it to Churchill's personal lack of balance." See *FRUS, 1940,* II, pp. 470–71; also Gordon Wright, "Ambassador Bullitt and the Fall of France," *World Politics,* Vol. X, No. 1 (October 1957), p. 87. However, Pétain's exemplary statesmanship was less apparent to those closest to him. According to Baudouin, who is backed up on this by Weygand, it was only with considerable difficulty and after frequent representations that he was able to convince the Marshal not to allow Darlan to carry out the heavy bombardment of Gibraltar which the cabinet in principle had agreed upon on July 8 and which was scheduled to take place on July 16. See Baudouin, pp. 157, 161–63, 168–69, 170, 172; Weygand, p. 256. As for Laval, always considered the most anti-British member of the Pétain administration and who did indeed favor a policy of collaboration with the Germans, his bark was still probably worse than his bite. For many reasons, it is unlikely that even he truly wanted a shooting war with England—one proof being his supposed retort to Darlan when the latter suggested punitive military operations against the British: "Is not one defeat enough for you?" See Berl, p. 202; Geoffrey Warner, *Pierre Laval and the Eclipse of France* (London, 1968), p. 196; Hytier, p. 62. See also Laval's testimony on his political goals, which excluded a reversal of alliances, in *Procès Laval,* pp. 89–90.

[12]Charles-Roux, pp. 123–24; and Charles-Roux's testimony, July 27, 1945, in *Procès Pétain,* p. 264; Laval, speaking on July 5, quoted by Michel, p. 226, and Bonnefous, VII, p. 274; Hytier, p. 63, quoting Baudouin.

[13]Charles-Roux, pp. 127–28; Lebrun, p. 103; Baudouin, pp. 157–58; also Baudouin's explanations of his policy decisions July 4, in *CE,* VII, pp. 2090, 2092, 2095, 2113, 2117; and Hytier, p. 62.

[14]See Baudouin's July 4 statement in Jean Montigny, *Toute la Vérité sur un Mois Dramatique de Notre Histoire: De l'Armistice à l'Assemblée Nationale, 15 juin–15 juillet 1940* (Clermont-Ferrand, 1941), pp. 47–50. Baudouin himself prints only a portion of this statement, the less rancorous part, in his diaries. See pp. 159–60.

[15]WM (40) 193, July 4, 11:30 a.m.; WM (40) 194, July 5, 12 noon. For Cambon's first protest, see Cadogan, p. 309; also Kammerer, *Passion,* pp. 181–83, 186–87. In the protest he submitted to Halifax on July 4 Cambon had stated that the communication made to Admiral Gensoul at Oran constituted "a demand which no officer responsible for the command of a fleet could accept. The refusal which was finally returned by the French Admiral was therefore to be expected, as were also the consequences of this refusal." This second protest was in execution of instructions sent by the Ministry of

Foreign Affairs on July 3. See FO 371/24321, C 7483/839/17, Cambon to Lord Halifax, July 4; also Kammerer, pp. 314–15; Charles-Roux, pp. 125–26. Vichy's view of the British ultimatum could hardly have caused surprise because, as we have seen, it was virtually the same as the British Admiralty's.

[16]WM (40) 196, July 7, 7 p.m.; FO 371/24301, C 7652/G, July 7, and C 7700/9/17, July 8, Notes on Castellane's Resignation; Charles-Roux, p. 128.

[17]Baudouin, pp. 158, 185–86; WM (40) 200, July 11, 11 a.m.; C 7652/G, July 12; Charles-Roux, pp. 144, 155–56, 161; Kammerer, p. 315.

[18]Alfred Fabre-Luce, *Journal de la France, mars 1939–juillet 1940* (Paris, 1940), p. 361.

[19]De Gaulle, *Memoirs,* p. 104.

## WHEN ALL IS SAID AND DONE

### The Nature of the Problem

[1]For a summary of the alternatives open to French statesmen and of the arguments used to support pro- or anti-armistice positions, see Paul Farmer, *Vichy: Political Dilemma* (New York, 1955), pp. 93–99, 120–22.

[2]For the development of, and limitations on, Allied air cooperation, see Lecuir and Fridenson, "L'Organisation de la coopération aérienne Franco-britannique (1935–mai 1940)," *Revue d'Histoire de la Deuxième Guerre Mondiale* (January 1969), pp. 43–74.

[3]See Pierre Cot, *Triumph of Treason* (Chicago and New York, 1944), pp. 279–83, 287, for an interesting argument to this effect; also Col. A. Goutard, *The Battle of France* (London, 1958), p. 33.

[4]See CAB 85, Vol. 4, Meetings of Allied Military Committee, MR (40) 22, April 19, Probable French Reactions to Development of Scandinavian Operations as Major Phase of War.

[5]FO 371/24302, C 10700/G, Provisional Note by E. L. Woodward on Fulfillment of Our Undertakings to French in Present War, Oct. 1, 1940. Ambassador Charles Corbin told André Maurois on June 12: "They have punctiliously kept the engagements that they made. The dates were fixed for the formation of the British divisions; these dates have been met. The fault was not to ask our allies for as many divisions as in 1914. . . ." See Maurois, *Memoirs, 1885–1967* (New York, 1970), pp. 203, 257; also Reynaud's testimony on this point, July 31, 1945, in *Procès Pétain, Compte rendu in extenso,* p. 146, cols. 2–3.

[6]See Arnold Wolfers, *Britain and France Between Two Wars: Conflicting Strategies of Peace from Versailles to World War II* (New York, 1966, originally published 1940), pp. 235–36.

[7]See Hankey Papers, Churchill College Archives, Cambridge, File 10/7, Rough Preliminary Note on Postwar Settlement, Written in 1940.

[8]Paul Kecskemeti, *Strategic Surrender: The Politics of Victory and Defeat* (New York, 1964), p. 57.

[9]D. C. Watt, in *Too Serious a Business* (Berkeley, Calif., 1975), p. 152, points to the paradox that the doctrine of the Vichy army, of *La France seule*, eventually came to be shared by de Gaulle and was embodied in the foreign policy of the Fifth Republic.

[10]See testimony on the role of the March 28 agreement, and the fear of betrayal it evoked, in *CE*, V, by Georges Monnet, pp. 1418, 1420; VII, by Raoul Dautry, p. 2019; and by Matteo Connet (quoting César Campinchi), p. 2186.

[11]Farmer, p. 98; Paul Reynaud, *In the Thick of the Fight, 1930–1945* (New York, 1955), p. 492.

[12]See Emmanuel Berl, *La fin de la IIIᵉ République* (Paris, 1968), pp. 98, 106, 166, for the suggestion that Reynaud actually weakened his position—if his position truly was to fight on—by his constant references to France's obligations to England under the March 28 agreement through the unflattering impression this left of his being tied to Churchill's apron strings.

[13]See Pierre Renouvin, *World War II and Its Origins: International Relations, 1929–1945* (New York, 1968), p. 224; also David Thomson, *Two Frenchmen: Pierre Laval and Charles de Gaulle* (London, 1951), especially pp. 120–24, for an interesting comparison between the defeatist and resistant viewpoints as represented by their two leading spokesmen. Laval diverged from Pétain and Weygand in not caring a whit for tradition or for anything that smacked of moral reformism, while de Gaulle converged with France's military notables in his penchant for authoritarianism and a quasi-religious mystique. See also Berl, *Fin de la IIIᵉ*, pp. 120, 138, 202, for some of the more striking and amusing differences between Laval and the devotees of the National Revolution at Vichy.

[14]Testifying Aug. 3, 1945, before the High Court, in *Procès Pétain*, p. 539.

[15]Significantly, Britain's former Prime Minister, David Lloyd George, had stated before the House of Commons on May 8 that "Our promissory notes are now rubbish on the market." See *Parl. Deb., H. of C.*, 5th Ser., Vol. 360, col. 1281.

[16]Churchill's thoughts on this subject appear more than a little ambivalent, though perhaps "compartmentalized" would be the better term. It will be remembered that as early as May 26 the Prime Minister had momentarily expressed the opinion that the British would be better off if France pulled out of the war, allowing them to concentrate on their own defenses; nevertheless, until the position became really hopeless, as it did in the second week of June, he was in the forefront of those demanding more aid for the French in order to keep them in, though undoubtedly more for political reasons than for any military good he thought it would do. But by June 17, at

least to some of his colleagues, he had reverted to his earlier thought that "we should do better without the French than with them." See *The Diaries of Sir Alexander Cadogan, 1938–1945,* ed. by David Dilks (London, 1971), p. 290; The Earl of Birkenhead, *Halifax: The Life of Lord Halifax* (Boston, 1966), p. 459.

Others quite openly viewed France as a heavy burden, which it was necessary to slough off, and gave full vent to their feelings after the French defeat. Chamberlain, for instance, spoke with relief of being "at any rate free of our obligations to the French, who have been nothing but a liability to us," even going so far as to claim: "It would have been far better if they [the French] had been neutral from the beginning." See Keith Feiling, *The Life of Neville Chamberlain* (London, 1946), p. 449. Lord Hankey, Chancellor of the Duchy of Lancaster, also felt that France had been "a debit rather than an asset in the present war" and found it "almost a relief to be thrown back on the resources of the Empire and of America." Quotes from letters to Lord Halifax, July 11, and Sir Samuel Hoare, July 19, Files 5/4 and 4/32 of Hankey Papers, Churchill College Archives. Air Marshal Dowding, who had jealously guarded his fighter squadrons throughout the Battle of France, went farthest of all. At the end of this agony, he actually said to Halifax: "I don't mind telling you that when I heard of the French collapse I went on my knees and thanked God." See Cadogan, p. 299, quoting from Lord Halifax's diary, Feb. 8, 1941; also The Earl of Halifax, *Fulness of Days* (London, 1957), p. 223; Robert Wright, *The Man Who Won the Battle of Britain* (New York, 1969), p. 129. Even King George, in a letter to his mother after the fall of France, claimed to "feel happier now that we have no allies to be polite to and to pamper." See Laurence Thompson, *1940* (New York, 1966), p. 138. There can be no doubt that the French request for an armistice was a boon insofar as it relieved the British of any further obligations to a needy and querulous ally. Nevertheless, higher state interests dictated a different policy. It was up to Churchill to balance not only the priorities of one service against another but also the needs of defense against the needs of diplomacy, all of which made for a rather tortured and frequently mystifying relationship.

[17]See Adrienne Doris Hytier, *Two Years of French Foreign Policy: Vichy, 1940–1942* (Paris, 1958), pp. 22–24.

## Resolution and Inevitability

[1]For instance, Ambassador Bullitt's impression of Vichy psychology as of July 1 was that "So as to have as many companions in misery as possible, they hoped England would be rapidly and completely defeated by Germany and [that] the Italians would suffer the same fate." See Cordell Hull, *The Memoirs of Cordell Hull* (New York, 1948), Vol. I, p. 799; Gordon Wright, "Ambassador Bullitt and the Fall of France," *World Politics,* Vol. X, No. 1 (October 1957), p. 87; *FRUS, 1940,* II, p. 462.

[2]See Berl, *Fin de la III^e*, pp. 62–66, for an excellent analysis of Mandel's character and ultimate ineffectuality. The most striking point made by Emmanuel Berl in his brilliant psychological reconstruction of the collapse of the French Republic is the closeness of views entertained by both proponents and opponents of the armistice. On the most crucial questions—for instance, whether England would survive, whether the French Empire could continue the struggle, whether a policy of national sacrifice should be demanded of the French—he finds a remarkable degree of unanimity in the France of June 1940. As he remembers it, all questions revolved around one basic fact: "that almost all citizens saw no other alternative but the cessation of the war or its continuation on the national soil." Thus, he concludes, "there were not then in Touraine or Bordeaux 'those who wish to fight and those who do not want to' [Mandel's famous phrase, spoken at Reynaud's last Council of Ministers on the evening of June 16]—the stout-hearted on one side, the cowards, if not traitors, on the other—but rather simply partisans of an armistice and partisans of a capitulation, two forms of the same abandon." In short, it was not a question of whether France would or would not remain in the war, but simply a question as to the means and timing whereby she would get out of it. For what people were feeling, thinking, and arguing *at the time* on issues affecting Anglo-French relations, see esp. pp. 42–43, 45–47, and 95–96. Anthony Adamthwaite makes much the same point about attitudes in French governmental circles during the Munich period, in *France and the Coming of the Second World War, 1936–1939* (London, 1977).

[3]See Mandel's conversation with the Polish Foreign Minister, June 15, as reported by Jan Ciechanowski in *Defeat in Victory* (Garden City, N.Y., 1947), pp. 12–13.

[4]See Édouard Bonnefous, *Histoire Politique de la Troisième République*, Vol. 7, *La Course vers l'Abîme: La fin da la III^e République (1938–1940)* (Paris, 1967), pp. 265, 313–14, for this line of reasoning.

[5]For instance, the Belgian government in exile, before leaving unoccupied France for England, unsuccessfully tried to contact the Reich in the hope of obtaining an armistice agreement and being included in the Wiesbaden negotiations. This was in late June and early July, the Pierlot government having decided to follow France's example (and to abandon its original inclination to go to England) the day after the Pétain cabinet was installed. Only in late August, after being consistently ignored by the Germans, did a strong nucleus of the Belgian Government opt for the Allied side. This government was officially reconstituted in London on October 31. Consult FO 800/309, Halifax Private Papers, H/III, 19 and 20, Record of Conversations between Secretary of State and Belgian Ambassador, June 20 and June 25, 1940; testimony of Yves Bouthillier before the Commission of Inquiry, in *CE,* VIII, pp. 2459, 2532; J. Gérard-Libois and José Gotovich, *L'An 40: La Belgique occupée* (Brussels, 1973), pp. 202, 240–59; Thomas J. Knight, "Belgium Leaves the War, 1940," *Journal of Modern History,* Vol. 41, No. 1 (March

1969), pp. 46–67; and *Survey of International Affairs, 1939–1946. The Initial Triumph of the Axis,* ed. by Arnold Toynbee and Veronica M. Toynbee (London, 1958), pp. 167–68.

[6]For instance, Alfred Fabre-Luce, remembering that France had always better exploited her defeats than her victories, wrote that "Talleyrand would today adhere to the Axis just as in 1815 he adhered to the Holy Alliance." See *Journal de la France, mars 1939-juillet 1940* (Paris, 1940), p. 389. Backhanded evidence of the "reasonableness" of the French Government's position can be deduced from Lady Spears's description of General de Gaulle (who on June 17 left France with Major-General Sir Edward Spears) and his followers as "a very small company of magnificent madmen." "There was no sense in what they were trying to do," she continues. "Reason should have convinced them that they had no chance of succeeding. Repeated disappointments should have proved to them that their project was doomed. But they were inspired by something more powerful than logic." See Mary Borden, *Journey Down a Blind Alley* (New York, 1946), p. 134. Likewise General Armengaud, who thought the armistice both a military error and a political fault, found it understandable that practical men should have judged the situation otherwise as they contemplated the slender resources of North Africa and the desperate state of British defenses. His conclusion: "It was necessary to close one's eyes to the material situation, to call on all one's moral force, all one's faith, to hope even as one despaired, to remember Joan of Arc, from Domrémy to the stake; to listen to General de Gaulle." See *Batailles Politiques et Militaires sur l'Europe: Témoignages (1932–1940)* (Paris, 1948), pp. 239, 242.

[7]For Liddell Hart's views on the disadvantages of entering the war and on the advantages of negotiating out of it, see B. H. Liddell Hart, *The Memoirs of Captain Liddell Hart,* Vol. II (London, 1965), pp. 220–21, 254–55; and A. J. Sylvester, *Life with Lloyd George,* ed. by Colin Cross (London, 1975), pp. 238–39.

[8]See Kennedy's dispatches of May 16, 6 p.m., and May 27, 9 p.m., in *FRUS,* 1940, I, pp. 224–25 and 233; also Richard J. Whalen, *The Founding Father: The Story of Joseph P. Kennedy* (New York, 1966), pp. 285–86; and William L. Langer and S. Everett Gleason, *The Challenge to Isolation, 1937–1940* (New York, 1952), p. 491.

[9]*The Diplomatic Diaries of Oliver Harvey, 1937–1940* (New York, 1970), p. 377; Sir Llewelyn Woodward, *British Foreign Policy in the Second World War,* I (London, 1970), p. 204, n. 1.

[10]See Frank Owen, *Tempestuous Journey: Lloyd George, His Life and Times* (New York, 1955), pp. 748–50; Keith Feiling, *The Life of Neville Chamberlain* (London, 1946), pp. 447–48; Thomas Jones, *A Diary with Letters, 1931–1950* (London, 1954), pp. 464–65; The Earl of Birkenhead, *Halifax: The Life of Lord Halifax* (Boston, 1966), p. 459; Paul Addison,

"Lloyd George and Compromise Peace in the Second World War," pp. 361–84 of *Lloyd George: Twelve Essays,* ed. by A. J. P. Taylor (New York, 1971); Sylvester, *Life with Lloyd George,* pp. 262–64, 267–70.

[11]See A. J. P. Taylor's article in *Churchill Revised: A Critical Assessment* (New York, 1969), p. 45.

[12]Sir Oswald Mosley, *My Life* (New Rochelle, N.Y., 1968), p. 402.

[13]See FO 800/322, H/XXXII/42, 43, and 44.

[14]Pierre-Étienne Flandin states bluntly that at the time he never heard a Frenchman in France contest the armistice, which, he insists, was accepted by the populace, not with amazement, as a tendentious literature would have it, but with an immense relief and an almost unanimous consent. And Paul-Boncour, though himself opposed to the armistice, agrees that it was accepted easily, the shock of defeat having been equivalent to a knockout blow. Paul Reynaud also implied as much in his testimony at the Pétain trial when he asserted that in the days immediately following the armistice, had a referendum been held, the majority of Frenchmen would have voted for the Marshal—whose policy it was; while Laval, in his testimony, claimed that on July 10, the day the National Assembly voted full powers to Pétain, "there was not at any moment, under any form, direct or indirect, the least reservation or the least protest made against the armistice which had been signed by the Marshal." President Lebrun was to echo Laval's observations in his testimony before the Commission of Inquiry in 1948. See Pierre-Étienne Flandin, *Politique française, 1919–1940* (Paris, 1947), pp. 409, 411; Joseph Paul-Boncour, *Entre Deux Guerres* (Paris, 1946), Vol. III, pp. 210, 244; Reynaud's testimony, July 24, 1945, and Laval's testimony, Aug. 3, 1945, in *Procès Pétain,* pp. 103 and 524; also Laval's testimony in *Procès Laval,* pp. 67–68, 72, 147; Lebrun's testimony in *CE,* IV, p. 1092. For further comments on this state of mind, see, among others, Kecskemeti, p. 65; Alexander Werth, *France, 1940–1955* (Boston, 1966, first published 1956), p. 27; Robert O. Paxton, *Vichy France: Old Guard and New Order, 1940–1944* (New York, 1972), pp. 11, 14.

[15]See Birdsall Scrymser Viault, "Les Démarches pour le rétablissement de la paix (septembre 1939-août 1940)," *Revue d'Histoire de la Deuxième Guerre Mondiale,* No. 67 (July 1967), p. 29; Laurence Lafore, *The End of Glory: An Interpretation of the Origins of World War II* (Philadelphia, 1970), p. 232; Correlli Barnett, *The Collapse of British Power* (London, 1972), pp. 558, 567, 573, 586–88.

# *Bibliography*

## Unpublished Documents in the Public Record Office, London

*War Cabinet Minutes,* 1939 and 1940: CAB 65 (WM Series)/ 1, 2, 5, 6, 7, 8

*Confidential Annexes* to War Cabinet Minutes, 1939 and 1940: CAB 65/ 3, 4, 11, 12, 13, 14

*War Cabinet Memoranda,* 1940: CAB 66 (WP Series)/ 6, 7, 8, 9; CAB 67 (WP (G) Series)/ 5, 6, 7; CAB 68 (WP (R) Series)/ 6

*Defence Committee* (Operations), 1940: CAB 69 (DO Series)/ 1

*Chiefs of Staff Committee:* Minutes, CAB 79/4, 5; Memoranda, CAB 80/ 11, 12, 13, 14

*Deputy Chiefs of Staff Committee:* Minutes, CAB 82/2; Papers, CAB 82/5

*Joint Planning Sub-Committee:* Minutes, CAB 84/2; Memoranda, CAB 84/14, 15

*Anglo-French Liaison,* 1940: Allied Military Committee Minutes and Papers: MR, MR (P), MR (S), and MR (J) (S) Series, CAB 85/ 3, 4, 5, 9– 12, 16

*Supreme War Council,* 1939–1940: Meetings, CAB 99/3

*Co-ordination of Departmental Action in Event of War with Certain Countries:* CAB 107/1, 10

*Foreign Office:* General Correspondence (Political), FO 371/24231, 24296– 304, 24307–15, 24321, 24327, 24348, 24358, 24360, 24370, 24383; Cadogan Private Papers, FO 800/294; Halifax Private Papers, FO 800/309–12, 316–26, 328

*War Office:* Directorate of Military Operations, WO 106/1607–09, 1613, 1618–19, 1655, 1673, 1676, 1680, 1682, 1684, 1688, 1697–99, 1713, 1716–17, 1731, 1742–46, 1751, 1754, 1757, 1759, 1771, 1774; Military Headquarters Papers, British Expeditionary Force, WO 197/18, 97, 123

*Admiralty:* Admiralty and Secretariat Papers, ADM 1/10321, 11328, 19177, 19178; Admiralty and Secretariat Cases, ADM 116/4239–40, 4413; War History Cases, First Lord's Records, ADM 199/360–61, 370–71, 379, 386–87, 391–93, 445–47, 786–87, 803, 822, 824, 826–27, 1052, 1928–30, 1940–41, 1959–60; First Sea Lord's Papers, ADM 205/4, 5, 6

## Unpublished Documents in
## Churchill College Archives, Cambridge

*A. V. Alexander,* Files 5/4, 5/5, 5/16, 5/17, 12/9, 12/10, 13/2, 13/3, 13/4, 13/5

*Lord Maurice Hankey,* Files 4/31, 4/32, 5/1, 5/4, 5/5, 8/32–33, 10/1, 10/2, 10/3, 10/4, 10/5, 10/7, 10/8, 11/1, 11/2

*Sir Roger Keyes,* File 13/12

*Sir Eric Phipps,* Files 1/20, 1/21, 1/22, 1/23, 2/1, 2/20, 3/2, 3/3, 3/4, 3/5, 4/3, 5/8; Phipps II, Files 4/1, 5/1–4, 5/3, 5/4, 5/5, 5/7, 5/7–8

*Admiral James F. Somerville,* Files 1/31, 7/1, 7/2, 7/3, 7/19, 7/25, 7/26, 7/27, 7/28, 7/29

## Published Documentary Material

*Ciano's Diplomatic Papers.* Edited by Malcolm Muggeridge. Translated by Stuart Hood. London: Odhams Press, 1948.

Dautry, Raoul. "Note remise par M. Dautry, Ministre de l'Armement, à M. Paul Reynaud, Président du Conseil (13 juin 1940)." *Revue d'Histoire de la Deuxième Guerre Mondiale,* No. 3 (June 1951), pp. 56–58.

France. Assemblée Nationale. *Les Événements Survenus en France de 1933 à 1945: Rapport de M. Charles Serre, Deputé, au nom de la Commission d'Enquête Parlementaire.* 2 vols.; *Annexes (Dépositions): Témoignages et Documents Recueillis par la Commission d'Enquête Parlementaire.* 9 vols. Paris: Presses Universitaires de France, 1947–51.

———. Haute Cour de Justice. *Procès du Maréchal Pétain: Compte rendu in extenso des audiences transmis par le Secrétariat général de la Haute Cour.* Paris: Imprimerie des Journaux Officiels, 1945.

———. *La Délégation Française auprès de la Commission Allemande d'Armistice: Recueil de Documents publié par le Gouvernement Français.* Vol. I, *29 Juin 1940–29 Septembre 1940.* Paris: Alfred Costes, Imprimerie Nationale, 1947.

———. Ministry for Foreign Affairs. *The French Yellow Book: Diplomatic Documents (1938–1939).* New York: Reynal & Hitchcock, 1940.

"Fuehrer Conferences on Naval Affairs, 1939–1945." In *Brassey's Naval Annual 1948.* New York: The Macmillan Company, 1948.

Great Britain. Foreign Office. *The British War Blue Book: Documents concerning German-Polish Relations and the Outbreak of Hostilities between Great Britain and Germany on September 3, 1939.* New York: Farrar & Rinehart, 1939.

Great Britain. Foreign Office. *Documents on British Foreign Policy, 1919–1939.* Edited by E. L. Woodward and Rohan Butler. 3rd Series (1938–1939): Vol. VII. London: H. M. S. O., 1954.

———. *Parliamentary Debates, House of Commons.* 5th Series: Vols. 351–62 (comprising period from 24 August 1939 to 11 July 1940). London: H. M. S. O.

———. *Parliamentary Debates, House of Lords.* 5th Series: Vols. CXIV–CXVI (comprising period from 11 July 1939 to 25 July 1940). London: H. M. S. O.

Hoover Institution on War, Revolution, and Peace. *France During the German Occupation, 1940–1944: A Collection of 292 Statements on the Government of Maréchal Pétain and Pierre Laval.* 3 vols. Translated by Philip W. Whitcomb. Stanford, Calif.: Hoover Institution on War, Revolution, and Peace, 1958.

*Le Procès du Maréchal Pétain.* Compte Rendu Sténographique. 2 vols. Paris: Éditions Albin Michel, 1945.

*Le Procès Laval.* Compte Rendu Sténographique. Paris: Éditions Albin Michel, 1946.

"Un Document Historique: Le Procès-Verbal Français du Conseil Suprême de Tours établi en 1940." *Le Figaro,* May 30, 1949, pp. 1 and 6.

United States. Department of State. *Documents on German Foreign Policy, 1918–1945.* Series D (1937–1945): Vol. VII, *The Last Days of Peace, August 9–September 3, 1939;* Vol. VIII, *The War Years, September 4, 1939–March 18, 1940;* Vol. IX, *March 18–June 22, 1940;* Vol. X, *June 23–August 31, 1940.* Washington: G. P. O., 1954–57.

United States. Department of State. *Foreign Relations of the United States: Diplomatic Papers, 1939:* Vol. I, General; Vol. II, General, British Commonwealth, and Europe (Washington: G. P. O., 1956); 1940: Vol. I, General (1959); Vol. II, General and Europe (1957); Vol. III, British Commonwealth, Soviet Union, Near East, and Africa (1958).

World Peace Foundation. *Documents on American Foreign Relations: July 1939–June 1940.* Edited by S. Shepard Jones and Denys P. Myers. Boston: World Peace Foundation, 1940.

### OFFICIAL MILITARY DISPATCHES

Brooke, Lieutenant-General Sir Alan. "Operations of the British Expeditionary Force, France, from 12th June, 1940 to 19th June, 1940." *Supplement to the London Gazette of Tuesday, the 21st of May, 1946,* May 22, 1946, pp. 2433–39.

Cork and Orrery, Admiral of the Fleet the Earl of. "Norway Campaign, 1940," with Appendix A, "Report on Operations in Northern Norway, 14th April to 13th May, 1940" (submitted by Major-General P. J. Mackesy), and Appendix B, "Report on Operations in Northern Norway, 13th May to 8th June, 1940" (submitted by Lieutenant-General C. J. E. Auchinleck). *Supplement to the London Gazette of Tuesday, the 8th of July, 1947,* July 10, 1947, pp. 3167–96.

"First and Second Battles of Narvik on 10th and 13th April 1940 Respectively." *Supplement to the London Gazette of Tuesday, the 1st of July, 1947,* July 3, 1947, pp. 3047–56.

Gort, Viscount. "First Despatch (Covering the Period from 3rd September, 1939, to 31st January, 1940)" and "Second Despatch (Covering the Period from 1st February, 1940, to 31st May, 1940, with an Appendix Covering Operations of 1st Corps from 6 P.M. 31st May, to Midnight 2nd/3rd June)." *Supplement to the London Gazette of Friday, the 10th of October, 1941,* October 17, 1941, pp. 5899–934.

Massy, Lieutenant-General H. R. S. "Operations in Central Norway, 1940." *Supplement to the London Gazette of Tuesday, the 28th of May, 1946,* May 29, 1946, pp. 2597–612.

Ramsay, Vice-Admiral Sir Bertram H. "The Evacuation of the Allied Armies from Dunkirk and Neighbouring Beaches." *Supplement to the London Gazette of Tuesday, the 15th of July, 1947,* July 17, 1947, pp. 3295–318.

Wavell, General Sir Archibald P. "Operations in the Middle East from August, 1939 to November, 1940." *Third Supplement to the London Gazette of Tuesday the 11th of June, 1946,* June 13, 1946, pp. 2997–3006.

———. "Operations in the Somaliland Protectorate, 1939–1940." *Supplement to the London Gazette of Tuesday, the 4th of June, 1946,* June 5, 1946, pp. 2719–27.

## MEMOIRS, DIARIES, PERSONAL AND JOURNALISTIC ACCOUNTS

Alexander, Harold, Field-Marshal Earl Alexander of Tunis. *The Alexander Memoirs, 1940–1945.* Edited by John North. London: Cassell, 1962.

Amery, L. S. *My Political Life.* Vol. III, *The Unforgiving Years, 1929–1940.* London: Hutchinson & Co., 1955.

Arenstam, Arved. *Tapestry of a Debacle: From Paris to Vichy.* Translated by E. Neville Hart. London: Constable & Co., 1942.

Armengaud, General Paul. *Batailles Politiques et Militaires sur l'Europe: Témoignages (1932–1940).* Paris: Éditions du Myrte, 1948.

Attlee, C. R. *As It Happened.* New York: The Viking Press, 1954.

Auriol, Vincent. *Hier . . . Demain.* 2 vols. Paris: Éditions E. Charlot, 1945.

Bardoux, Jacques. *Journal d'un Témoin de la Troisième: 1$^{er}$ septembre 1939–15 juillet 1940.* Paris: Librairie Arthème Fayard, 1957.

Barlone, D. *A French Officer's Diary (23 August 1939–1 October 1940).* Translated by L. V. Cass. London: Cambridge University Press, 1942.

Barthe, Édouard. *La Ténébreuse Affaire du "Massilia": Une Page d' Histoire (18 Juin 1940–Octobre 1940).* Paris: Imprimerie Paul Dupont, 1945.

Baudouin, Paul. *Neuf mois au gouvernement, avril-décembre 1940.* Paris: La Table Ronde, 1948.

———. *The Private Diaries of Paul Baudouin (March 1940 to January 1941).* Translated by Sir Charles Petrie. Foreword by Malcolm Muggeridge. London: Eyre & Spottiswoode, 1948.

Beauvoir, Simone de. *The Prime of Life.* Translated by Peter Green. New York: Lancer Books, 1962.

Becquart, Henri. *Au Temps du Silence: De Bordeaux à Vichy.* Paris: Éditions Iris, 1945.

Blum, Léon. *For All Mankind.* Translated by W. Pickles. New York: The Viking Press, 1946.

———. *L'Oeuvre de Léon Blum.* Vol. IV, ii (1937–1940). Paris: Éditions Albin Michel, 1965.

Bois, Elie J. *Truth on the Tragedy of France.* Translated by N. Scarlyn Wilson. London: Hodder and Stoughton, 1941.

Bonnet, Georges. *De Munich à la Guerre: Défense de la Paix.* Paris: Plon, 1967.

Boothby, Robert. *I Fight to Live.* London: Victor Gollancz Ltd, 1947.

———. *My Yesterday, Your Tomorrow.* London: Hutchinson & Co. Ltd, 1962.

Boothe, Clare. *Europe in the Spring.* New York: Alfred A. Knopf, 1940.

Borden, Mary. *Journey Down a Blind Alley.* New York: Harper & Brothers Publishers, 1946.

Bouthillier, Yves. *Le Drame de Vichy.* Vol. I, *Face à l'Ennemi, Face à l'Allié.* Paris, Plon, 1950.

Bryant, Sir Arthur. *The Turn of the Tide, 1939–1943: A Study Based on the Diaries and Autobiographical Notes of Field-Marshal the Viscount Alanbrooke.* London: Fontana Books, 1965; first published by Collins, 1957.

Bullitt, William C. *For the President, Personal and Secret: Correspondence Between Franklin D. Roosevelt and William C. Bullitt.* Edited by Orville H. Bullitt. Boston: Houghton Mifflin Company, 1972.

Butler, R. A. *The Art of the Possible: The Memoirs of Lord Butler.* London: Hamish Hamilton, 1972.

Cadogan, Alexander. *The Diaries of Sir Alexander Cadogan, 1938–1945.* Edited by David Dilks. London: Cassell, 1971.

Carton de Wiart, Sir Adrian. *Happy Odyssey.* London: Jonathan Cape, 1950.

Chambrun, René de. *I Saw France Fall; Will She Rise Again?* New York: William Morrow & Company, 1940.

Charles-Roux, François. *Cinq Mois Tragiques aux Affaires Étrangères (21 Mai–1ᵉʳ Novembre 1940).* Paris: Plon, 1949.

Chautemps, Camille. *Cahiers secrets de l'Armistice (1939–1940).* Paris: Plon, 1963.

Churchill, Winston S. *The Second World War.* 6 vols. New York: Bantam Books, 1961–62; originally published Boston: Houghton Mifflin Company, 1948–53.

Ciano, Count Galeazzo. *The Ciano Diaries, 1939–1943: The Complete, Unabridged Diaries of Count Galeazzo Ciano, Italian Minister for Foreign Affairs, 1936–1943.* Edited by Hugh Gibson. Introduction by Sumner Welles. Garden City, N. Y.: Doubleday & Company, 1946.

Ciechanowski, Jan. *Defeat in Victory.* Garden City, N.Y.: Doubleday & Company, Inc., 1947.

Cooper, Lady Diana. *The Light of Common Day.* London: Rupert Hart-Davis, 1959.

Cudahy, John. *The Armies March: A Personal Report.* New York: Charles Scribner's Sons, 1941.

Cunningham, Andrew Browne. *A Sailor's Odyssey: The Autobiography of Admiral of the Fleet Viscount Cunningham of Hyndhope.* London: Hutchinson & Co., 1951.

Dalton, Hugh. *The Fateful Years: Memoirs, 1931–1945.* London: Frederick Muller, 1957.

Dillon, Viscount Eric. *Memories of Three Wars.* London: Allan Wingate, 1951.

Duff Cooper, Alfred. *Old Men Forget: The Autobiography of Duff Cooper (Viscount Norwich).* London: Rupert Hart-Davis, 1954.

Eden, Anthony. *The Memoirs of Anthony Eden, Earl of Avon.* Vol. II, *The Reckoning.* Boston: Houghton Mifflin Company, 1965.

Fernand-Laurent, J. C. *Gallic Charter: Foundations of Tomorrow's France.* Boston: Little, Brown and Company, 1944.

———. *Un Peuple ressuscite.* New York: Brentano's, 1943.

Flandin, Pierre-Étienne. *Politique française, 1919–1940.* Paris: Les Éditions Nouvelles, 1947.

Flanner, Janet. *An American in Paris.* New York: Simon and Schuster, 1940.

———. *Paris Was Yesterday (1925–1939).* Edited by Irving Drutman. New York: Popular Library, 1973; originally published by The Viking Press, 1970.

François-Poncet, André. *Au Palais Farnèse: Souvenirs d'un ambassade à Rome, 1938–1940.* Paris: Librairie Arthème Fayard, 1961.

———. *The Fateful Years: Memoirs of a French Ambassador in Berlin, 1931–1938.* Translated by Jacques Le Clercq. New York: Harcourt, Brace and Company, 1949.

Franklyn, General Sir Harold E. *The Story of One Green Howard in the Dunkirk Campaign.* Richmond, Yorkshire: 1966.

Freeman, C. Denis, and Cooper, Douglas. *The Road to Bordeaux.* New York and London: Harper and Brothers, 1941.

Gamelin, General Maurice Gustave. *Servir.* 3 vols. Vol. I, *Les Armées Françaises de 1940;* Vol. III, *La Guerre (Septembre 1939–19 Mai 1940).* Paris: Librairie Plon, 1946–47.

Gaulle, General Charles de. *The Complete War Memoirs of Charles de Gaulle.* 3 vols. in 1. Translated by Jonathan Griffin and Richard Howard. New York: Simon and Schuster, 1964.

Gide, André. *The Journals of André Gide.* Edited, translated, and abridged by Justin O'Brien. Vol. II, *1924–1949.* New York: Vintage Books, 1956.

Godfroy, Vice-Admiral René. *L'Aventure de la Force X à Alexandrie (1940–1943).* Paris: Librairie Plon, 1953.

Greenwall, H. J. *When France Fell.* London: Allan Wingate, 1958.

Guderian, General Heinz. *Panzer Leader.* Translated by Constantine Fitzgibbon. Foreword by Captain B. H. Liddell Hart. London: Michael Joseph, 1952.

Guerdan, Léon. *Je les ai tous connus.* New York: Brentano's, 1942.

Halifax, [Edward Wood], The Earl of. *Fulness of Days.* London: Collins, 1957.

Harvey, Oliver. *The Diplomatic Diaries of Oliver Harvey, 1937–1940.* Edited by John Harvey. London: Collins, 1970.

Hassell, Ulrich von. *The Von Hassell Diaries, 1938–1944: The Story of the Forces Against Hitler Inside Germany.* Introduction by Allen Welsh Dulles. Garden City, N.Y.: Doubleday & Company, 1947.

Herriot, Édouard. *Épisodes, 1940–1944.* Paris: Flammarion, 1950.

Hoare, Sir Samuel. *Ambassador on Special Mission.* London: Collins, 1946.

———. (Viscount Templewood). *Nine Troubled Years.* London: Collins, 1954.

Huddleston, Sisley. *France: The Tragic Years 1939–1947: An Eyewitness Account of War, Occupation and Liberation.* New York: The Devin-Adair Company, 1955.

Hull, Cordell. *The Memoirs of Cordell Hull.* 2 vols. New York: The Macmillan Company, 1948.

Ironside, Sir Edmund. *The Ironside Diaries, 1937–1940.* Edited by Roderick Macleod and Denis Kelly. London: Constable and Company, 1962.

Ismay, Hastings Lionel. *The Memoirs of General Lord Ismay.* New York: The Viking Press, 1960.

James, Admiral Sir W. M. *The Portsmouth Letters.* London: Macmillan & Co., 1946.

Jeanneney, Jules. *Journal politique (septembre 1939–juillet 1942)*. Edited and annotated by Jean-Noël Jeanneney. Paris: Librairie Armand Colin, 1972.

Jebb, Gladwyn. *The Memoirs of Lord Gladwyn*. London: Weidenfeld and Nicolson, 1972.

Jones, Thomas. *A Diary with Letters, 1931–1950*. London: Oxford University Press, 1954.

Keitel, Wilhelm. *The Memoirs of Field-Marshal Keitel*. Edited by Walter Gorlitz. Translated by David Irving. New York: Stein and Day, 1966.

Kirkpatrick, Ivone. *The Inner Circle: Memoirs of Ivone Kirkpatrick*. London: Macmillan & Co., 1959.

Koestler, Arthur. *Scum of the Earth*. Danube Edition. London: Hutchinson & Co., 1968; originally published by Cape, 1941.

Langeron, Roger. *Paris Juin 40*. Paris: Ernest Flammarion, 1946.

Lania, Leo. *The Darkest Hour: Adventures and Escapes*. Introduction by Edgar Ansel Mowrer. Boston: Houghton Mifflin Company, 1941.

Laval, Pierre. *The Diary of Pierre Laval*. Preface by Josée Laval. New York: Charles Scribner's Sons, 1948.

Lazareff, Pierre. *Deadline: The Behind-the-Scenes Story of the Last Decade in France*. Translated by David Partridge. New York: Random House, 1942.

Leahy, Admiral William D. *I Was There: The Personal Story of the Chief of Staff to Presidents Roosevelt and Truman*. New York: Whittlesey House, McGraw-Hill Book Company, 1950.

Lebrun, Albert. *Témoignage*. Paris: Plon, 1945.

Lémery, Henry. *D'une République à l'autre: Souvenirs de la Mêlée Politique 1894–1944*. Paris: La Table Ronde, 1964.

Leutze, James. Editor. *The London Journal of General Raymond E. Lee*. Boston: Little, Brown and Company, 1971.

Liddell Hart, B. H. *The Memoirs of Captain Liddell Hart*. Vol. II. London: Cassell, 1965.

————. Editor. *The Rommel Papers*. Translated by Paul Findlay. New York: Harcourt, Brace and Company, 1953.

Liebling, A. J. Editor. *The Republic of Silence*. New York: Harcourt, Brace and Company, 1947.

Listowel, Judith, Countess of. *This I Have Seen*. London: Faber and Faber, 1943.

Łukasiewicz, Juliusz. *Diplomat in Paris, 1936–1939: Papers and Memoirs of Juliusz Łukasiewicz, Ambassador of Poland*. Edited by Wacław Jędrzejewicz. New York: Columbia University Press, 1970.

Macmillan, Harold. *The Blast of War, 1939–1945*. New York and Evanston: Harper & Row, Publishers, 1967.

Malaquais, Jean. *War Diary*. Translated by Peter Grant. Garden City, N.Y.: Doubleday, Doran and Co., 1944.

Manstein, Field-Marshal Erich von. *Lost Victories*. Edited and translated by Anthony G. Powell. Foreword by Captain B. H. Liddell Hart. Chicago: Henry Regnery Company, 1958.

Maritain, Jacques. *France My Country Through the Disaster*. New York and Toronto: Longmans, Green and Co., 1941.

Martel, Lieutenant-General Sir Giffard. *An Outspoken Soldier: His Views and Memoirs*. London: Sifton Praed & Co., 1949.

Martin du Gard, Maurice. *La Chronique de Vichy, 1940–1944*. Paris: Flammarion, 1948.

Maugham, W. Somerset. *France at War*. London: William Heinemann, 1940.

Maurois, André. *The Battle of France*. Translated by F. R. Ludman. London: John Lane, The Bodley Head, 1940.

———. *Memoirs, 1885–1967*. Translated by Denver Lindley. New York: Harper & Row, 1970.

———. *Tragedy in France*. Translated by Denver Lindley. New York and London: Harper & Brothers, 1940.

Mendès-France, Pierre. *The Pursuit of Freedom*. London: Longmans, Green and Co., 1956.

Middleton, Drew. *Our Share of Night*. New York: The Viking Press, 1946.

Minney, R. J. *The Private Papers of Hore-Belisha*. London: Collins, 1960.

Montgomery, Bernard Law. *The Memoirs of Field-Marshal the Viscount Montgomery of Alamein*. Cleveland and New York: The World Publishing Company, 1958.

Montigny, Jean. *Toute la Vérité sur un Mois Dramatique de Notre Histoire: De l'Armistice à l'Assemblée Nationale, 15 juin–15 juillet 1940*. Clermont-Ferrand: Éditions Mont-Louis, 1940.

Monzie, Anatole de. *Ci-Devant*. Paris: Flammarion, 1941.

Morize, André. *France Été 1940*. New York: Éditions de la Maison Française, 1941.

Mosley, Sir Oswald. *My Life*. New Rochelle, N.Y.: Arlington House, 1968.

Muggeridge, Malcolm. *Chronicles of Wasted Time: The Infernal Grove*. New York: William Morrow & Company, 1974.

Murphy, Robert. *Diplomat Among Warriors*. New York: Pyramid Books, 1965; originally published by Doubleday & Company, 1964.

*The New Yorker Book of War Pieces*. New York: Reynal & Hitchcock, 1947.

Nicolson, Harold. *Diaries and Letters*. Vol. I, *1930–1939;* Vol. II, *The War Years, 1939–1945*. Edited by Nigel Nicolson. New York: Atheneum, 1966–67.

Panter-Downes, Mollie. *Letter from England.* Boston: Little, Brown and Company, 1940.

———. *London War Notes, 1939–1945.* Edited by William Shawn. New York: Farrar, Straus and Giroux, 1971.

Paul, Oscar. *Farewell, France! An Eye-Witness Account of Her Tragedy.* London: Victor Gollancz, 1941.

Paul-Boncour, Joseph. *Entre Deux Guerres: Souvenirs sur la III<sup>e</sup> République.* Vol. III, *Sur les chemins de la défaite, 1935–1940.* Paris: Librairie Plon, 1946.

Peyrouton, Marcel. *Du Service Public à la Prison Commune.* Paris: Librairie Plon, 1950.

Pol, Heinz. *Suicide of a Democracy.* Translated by Heinz and Ruth Norden. New York: Reynal & Hitchcock, 1940.

Pomaret, Charles. *Le Dernier Témoin.* Paris: Presses de la Cité, 1968.

Porter, Roy P. *Uncensored France: An Eyewitness Account of France under the Occupation.* New York: The Dial Press, 1942.

Pownall, H. R. *Chief of Staff: The Diaries of Lieutenant-General Sir Henry Pownall.* Vol. I, *1933–1940.* Edited by Brian Bond. London: Leo Cooper, 1972.

Puaux, Gabriel. *Deux Années au Levant: Souvenirs de Syrie et du Liban, 1939–1940.* Paris: Hachette, 1952.

Reynaud, Paul. *Au Cœur de la Mêlée: 1930–1945.* Paris: Flammarion, 1951.

———. *In the Thick of the Fight, 1930–1945* (abridged English version of *Au Cœur de la Mêlée*). Translated by James D. Lambert. New York: Simon and Schuster, 1955.

———. *La France a sauvé l'Europe.* 2 vols. Paris: Flammarion, 1947.

———. *Mémoires.* Vol. II, *Envers et Contre Tous: 7 Mars 1936–16 Juin 1940.* Paris: Flammarion, 1963.

Robert, Admiral Georges. *La France aux Antilles de 1939 à 1943.* Paris: Plon, 1950.

Romains, Jules. *Seven Mysteries of Europe.* Translated by Germaine Brée. New York: Alfred A. Knopf, 1940.

Rowse, A. L. *All Souls and Appeasement.* London: Macmillan & Co., 1961.

Saint-Jean, Robert de. *France Speaking.* Translated by Anne Green. New York: E. P. Dutton & Co., 1941.

Schmidt, Paul. *Hitler's Interpreter.* Edited by R. H. C. Steed. New York: The Macmillan Company, 1951.

Selby, Sir Walford. *Diplomatic Twilight, 1930–1940.* London: John Murray, 1953.

Sheean, Vincent. *Between the Thunder and the Sun.* New York: Random House, 1943.

Shirer, William L. *Berlin Diary: The Journal of a Foreign Correspondent, 1934–1941.* New York: Alfred A. Knopf, 1941.

Simon, John. *Retrospect: The Memoirs of the Rt. Hon. Viscount Simon.* London: Hutchinson & Co., 1952.

Slessor, Sir John. *The Central Blue: The Autobiography of Sir John Slessor, Marshal of the RAF.* New York: Frederick A. Praeger, 1957.

Soustelle, Jacques. *Envers et contre tout.* Vol. I, *De Londres à Alger: Souvenirs et Documents sur la France Libre, 1940–1942.* Paris: Robert Laffont, 1947.

Spears, Major-General Sir Edward Louis. *Assignment to Catastrophe.* 2 vols. London: William Heinemann, 1954.

Stehlin, Paul. *Témoignage Pour l'Histoire.* Paris: Robert Laffont, 1964.

Strang, Lord William. *Home and Abroad.* London: André Deutsch, 1956.

Tabouis, Geneviève. *They Called Me Cassandra.* New York: Charles Scribner's Sons, 1942.

Tanner, Väinö. *The Winter War: Finland Against Russia, 1939–1940.* Stanford, Calif.: Stanford University Press, 1957.

Tony-Révillon, M.-M. *Mes Carnets (Juin–Octobre 1940): Documents et Témoignages pour Servir à l'Histoire.* Paris: Odette Lieutier, 1945.

Vansittart, Lord [Robert]. *The Mist Procession: The Autobiography of Lord Vansittart.* London: Hutchinson & Co. Ltd, 1958.

Warlimont, Walter. *Inside Hitler's Headquarters, 1939–1945.* Translated by R. H. Barry. London: Weidenfeld and Nicolson Ltd, 1964.

Welles, Sumner. *The Time for Decision.* New York and London: Harper & Brothers Publishers, 1944.

Werth, Alexander. *The Last Days of Paris: A Journalist's Diary.* London: Hamish Hamilton, 1940.

Weygand, Maxime. *En Lisant les Mémoires de Guerre du Général de Gaulle.* Paris: Flammarion, 1955.

———. *Recalled to Service: The Memoirs of General Maxime Weygand.* Translated by E. W. Dickes. London: William Heinemann, 1952.

Zay, Jean. *Carnets secrets de Jean Zay (De Munich à la Guerre).* Edited by Philippe Henriot. Paris: Les Éditions de France, 1942.

———. *Souvenirs et Solitude.* Preface by Jean Casson. Paris: René Julliard, 1945.

## BIOGRAPHICAL STUDIES AND INTERVIEWS

Adam, Colin Forbes. *Life of Lord Lloyd.* London: Macmillan & Co., 1948.

Bankwitz, Philip Charles Farwell. *Maxime Weygand and Civil-Military Relations in Modern France.* Cambridge, Mass.: Harvard University Press, 1967.

Berlin, Isaiah. *Mr. Churchill in 1940.* Boston: Houghton Mifflin Company, 1964.

Birkenhead, The Earl of. *Halifax: The Life of Lord Halifax.* Boston: Houghton Mifflin Company, 1966.

Bolton, Glorney. *Pétain.* London: Allen & Unwin, 1957.

Churchill, Randolph S. *The Rise and Fall of Sir Anthony Eden.* London: MacGibbon & Kee, 1959.

Cole, Hubert. *Laval: A Biography.* New York: G. P. Putnam's Sons, 1963.

Collier, Basil. *Leader of the Few: The Authorised Biography of Air Chief Marshal the Lord Dowding of Bentley Priory.* London: Jarrolds, 1957.

Colton, Joel. *Léon Blum: Humanist in Politics.* New York: Alfred A. Knopf, 1966.

Colville, J. R. *Man of Valour: The Life of Field-Marshal the Viscount Gort.* London: Collins, 1972.

Darlan, Alain. *L'Amiral Darlan Parle.* Paris: Amiot Dumont, 1952.

Docteur, Admiral Jules Théophile. *Darlan: La Grande Énigme de la Guerre.* Paris: Éditions de la Couronne, 1949.

Eade, Charles. Editor. *Churchill By His Contemporaries.* London: Hutchinson & Co., 1953.

Feiling, Keith. *The Life of Neville Chamberlain.* London: Macmillan & Co., 1946.

Flanner, Janet. *Pétain: The Old Man of France.* New York: Simon and Schuster, 1944.

Gardner, Brian. *Churchill In His Time: A Study in Reputation, 1939–1945.* London: Methuen & Co., 1968.

Griffiths, Richard. *Marshal Pétain.* London: Constable & Company, 1970.

Guedella, Philip. *The Two Marshals: Bazaine, Pétain.* New York: Reynal & Hitchcock, 1943.

James, Robert Rhodes. *Churchill: A Study in Failure, 1900–1939.* London: Weidenfeld and Nicolson, 1970.

Langhorne, Elizabeth. *Nancy Astor and Her Friends.* New York: Praeger Publishers, 1974.

Leasor, James. *War at the Top: Based on the Experiences of General Sir Leslie Hollis.* London: Michael Joseph, 1959.

Macleod, Iain. *Neville Chamberlain.* London: Frederick Muller Limited, 1961.

Martel, Francis. *Pétain, Verdun to Vichy.* New York: E. P. Dutton & Company, 1943.

Mengin, Robert. *No Laurels for de Gaulle.* Translated by Jay Allen. New York: Farrar, Straus and Giroux, 1966.

Moch, Jules. *Rencontres Avec . . . Darlan: Eisenhower.* Paris: Plon, 1968.

Montmorency, Alec de. *The Enigma of Admiral Darlan.* New York: E. P. Dutton & Co., 1943.

Nicolson, Nigel. *Alex: The Life of Field Marshal Earl Alexander of Tunis.* London: Weidenfeld and Nicolson, 1973.

Owen, Frank. *Tempestuous Journey: Lloyd George, His Life and Times.* New York: McGraw-Hill Book Company, 1955.

Roskill, Stephen. *Hankey: Man of Secrets.* Vol. III, *1931–1963.* London: Collins, 1974.

Sherwood, John M. *Georges Mandel and the Third Republic.* Stanford, Calif.: Stanford University Press, 1970.

Spears, Major-General Sir Edward. *Two Men Who Saved France: Pétain and De Gaulle.* London: Eyre & Spottiswoode, 1966.

Sylvester, A. J. *Life with Lloyd George: The Diary of A. J. Sylvester, 1931–45.* Edited by Colin Cross. London: Macmillan London Ltd, 1975.

Taylor, A. J. P. *Beaverbrook.* New York: Simon and Schuster, 1972.

Taylor, A. J. P.; James, Robert Rhodes; Plumb, J. H.; Liddell Hart, Basil; and Storr, Anthony. *Churchill Revised: A Critical Assessment.* New York: The Dial Press, 1969.

Thomson, David. *Two Frenchmen: Pierre Laval and Charles de Gaulle.* London: The Cresset Press, 1951.

Tournoux, J.-R. *Pétain et De Gaulle.* Paris: Plon, 1964.

Warner, Geoffrey. *Pierre Laval and the Eclipse of France.* London: Eyre & Spottiswoode, 1968.

Waterfield, Gordon. *Professional Diplomat: Sir Percy Loraine of Kirkhale Bt., 1880–1961.* London: John Murray, 1973.

Werth, Alexander. *De Gaulle: A Political Biography.* Harmondsworth, Middlesex: Penguin Books, 1965.

Weygand, Commandant Jacques. *The Role of General Weygand: Conversations with His Son.* Translated by J. H. F. McEwen. Introduction by Cyril Falls. London: Eyre & Spottiswoode, 1948.

Whalen, Richard J. *The Founding Father: The Story of Joseph P. Kennedy.* New York: New American Library, Signet, 1966.

Williams, Francis. *A Prime Minister Remembers: The War and Post-War Memoirs of The Rt. Hon. Earl Attlee Based on his Private Papers and on a Series of Recorded Conversations.* London: Heinemann, 1961.

Wrench, John Evelyn. *Geoffrey Dawson and Our Times.* London: Hutchinson & Co., 1955.

Wright, Robert. *The Man Who Won the Battle of Britain.* New York: Charles Scribner's Sons, 1969.

Young, Desmond. *Rommel: The Desert Fox.* New York: Berkley Publishing Corp., 1957; first published by Harper & Brothers, 1950.

## History of the Second World War, United Kingdom Military Series: General Editor, J. R. M. Butler

Butler, J. R. M. Editor. *Grand Strategy.* Vol. II, *September 1939–June 1941.* London: H. M. S. O., 1957.

Collier, Basil. *The Defence of the United Kingdom.* London: H. M. S. O., 1957.

Derry, T. K. *The Campaign in Norway.* London: H. M. S. O., 1952.

Ellis, Major L. F. *The War in France and Flanders, 1939–1940.* London: H. M. S. O., 1953.

Playfair, Major-General I. S. O. *The Mediterranean and Middle East.* Vol. I, *The Early Successes Against Italy.* London: H. M. S. O., 1954.

Richards, Denis. *Royal Air Force, 1939–1945.* Vol. I, *The Fight at Odds.* London: H. M. S. O., 1953.

Roskill, Captain S. W. *The War at Sea, 1939–1945.* Vol. I, *The Defensive.* London: H. M. S. O., 1954.

Webster, Sir Charles, and Frankland, Noble. *The Strategic Air Offensive Against Germany, 1939–1945.* Vol. I, *Preparation.* London: H. M. S. O., 1961.

Woodward, Sir Llewellyn. *British Foreign Policy in the Second World War.* Vol. I. London: H. M. S. O., 1970.


## Studies

Adamthwaite, Anthony. *France and the Coming of the Second World War, 1936–1939.* London: Frank Cass, 1977.

Albert-Sorel, Jean. *Histoire de France et d'Angleterre: La Rivalité, L'Entente, L'Alliance.* Amsterdam: Les Éditions Françaises d'Amsterdam, 1950.

Amouroux, Henri. *Le 18 Juin 1940.* Paris: Fayard, 1964.

————. *La Vie des Français sous l'Occupation.* Paris: Librairie Arthème Fayard, 1961.

Armstrong, Hamilton Fish. *Chronology of Failure: The Last Days of the French Republic.* New York: The Macmillan Company, 1940.

Aron, Robert. *The Vichy Regime: 1940–44.* In collaboration with Georgette Elgey. Translated by Humphrey Hare. Boston: Beacon Press, 1969; English version first published in London by Putnam & Co., 1958.

Aster, Sidney. *1939: The Making of the Second World War.* London: André Deutsch, 1973.

Auphan, Admiral Paul. *Les Grimaces de l'Histoire.* Paris: Librairie Plon, 1951.

Auphan, Rear Admiral Paul, and Mordal, Jacques. *The French Navy in World War II.* Translated by A. C. J. Sabalot. Annapolis, Md.: United States Naval Institute, 1959.

Azéma, Jean-Pierre and Winock, Michel. *La III<sup>e</sup> République (1870–1940)*. Paris: Calmann-Lévy, 1970.

Baldwin, Hanson W. *Battles Lost and Won*. New York: Avon Books, 1968; originally published by Harper & Row, Publishers, 1966.

Barber, Noel. *The Week France Fell*. New York: Stein and Day, Publishers, 1976.

Bardies, Colonel Raphael de. *La Campagne 39–40*. Paris: Librairie Arthème Fayard, 1947.

Barnett, Correlli. *The Collapse of British Power*. London: Eyre Methuen, 1972.

Beau de Loménie, E. *La Mort de la Troisième République*. Paris: Éditions du Conquistador, 1951.

Beaufre, General André. *1940: The Fall of France*. Translated by Desmond Flower. Preface by Basil Liddell Hart. London: Cassell, 1967.

Beckles, Gordon. *Dunkirk—and After, May 10th–June 17th, 1940*. London: Hutchinson & Co., n.d.

Beer, Max. *La Guerre N'a Pas Eu Lieu*. New York: Editions de la Maison Française, 1941.

Bell, P. M. H. *A Certain Eventuality: Britain and the Fall of France*. London: Saxon House, 1974.

Belot, Rear-Admiral Raymond de. *La Marine Française pendant la Campagne 1939–1940*. Paris: Librairie Plon, 1954.

———. *The Struggle for the Mediterranean, 1939–1945*. Translated by James A. Field, Jr. Princeton, N.J.: Princeton University Press, 1951.

Benoist-Méchin, Jacques. *Sixty Days That Shook the West: The Fall of France, 1940*. Edited by Cyril Falls. Translated by Peter Wiles. New York: G. P. Putnam's Sons, 1963.

Berl, Emmanuel. *La fin de la III<sup>e</sup> République: 10 Juillet 1940*. Paris: Gallimard, 1968.

Bloch, Marc. *Strange Defeat: A Statement of Evidence Written in 1940*. Translated by Gerard Hopkins. Introduction by Sir Maurice Powicke. London, New York: Oxford University Press, 1949.

Bond, Brian. *France and Belgium 1939–1940*. London: Davis-Poynter, 1975.

Bonnefous, Édouard. *Histoire Politique de la Troisième République*. Vol. 7, *La Course vers l'Abîme: La fin de la III<sup>e</sup> République (1938–1940)*. Paris: Presses Universitaires de France, 1967.

Bonnet, Georges. *Quai d'Orsay*. Isle of Man: Times Press and Anthony Gibbs & Phillips, 1965.

Bourget, Colonel P.-A. *De Beyrouth à Bordeaux: La guerre de 1939–40 vue du P. C. Weygand*. Paris: Éditions Berger-Levrault, 1946.

Carr, E. H. *International Relations Between the Two World Wars, 1919–1939.* New York: Harper Torchbooks, 1966; first published under present title by St. Martin's Press, 1947.

"Cato." *Guilty Men.* New York: Frederick A. Stokes Company, 1940.

Chapman, Guy. *Why France Collapsed.* London: Cassell, 1968.

Chastenet, Jacques. *Histoire de la Troisième République.* Vol. VII, *Le Drame Final (1938–1940).* Paris: Hachette, 1963.

Cherdevon, Maurice. *Les Causes Morales de l'Affaissement de la France en 1940 et du gâchis actuel.* Paris: Les Éditions du Scorpion, 1960.

Collier, Richard. *The Sands of Dunkirk.* New York: Dell Publishing Co., 1962; first published by E. P. Dutton & Co., 1961.

Colvin, Ian. *The Chamberlain Cabinet.* New York: Taplinger Publishing Company, 1971.

———. *Vansittart in Office: An Historical Survey of the Origins of the Second World War Based on the Papers of Sir Robert Vansittart.* London: Victor Gollancz, 1965.

Connell, John [pseud.]. *The 'Office': The Story of the British Foreign Office, 1919–1951.* New York: St. Martin's Press, 1958.

Cot, Pierre. *Triumph of Treason.* Translated by Sybille and Milton Crane. Chicago and New York: Ziff-Davis Publishing Company, 1944.

Cras, Hervé. *Dunkerque.* Paris: Éditions France-Empire, 1960.

De Jong, Louis. *The German Fifth Column in the Second World War.* Translated from the Dutch by C. M. Geyl. Chicago: The University of Chicago Press, 1956.

De Launay, Jacques. *Secret Diplomacy of World War II.* Translated by Edouard Nadier. New York: Simmons-Boardman, 1963.

Deutsch, Harold C. *The Conspiracy Against Hitler in the Twilight War.* Minneapolis: The University of Minnesota Press, 1968.

Dhers, Pierre. *Regards Nouveaux sur les Années Quarante.* Paris: Flammarion, 1958.

Divine, David. *The Nine Days of Dunkirk.* New York: W.W. Norton & Company, 1959.

Docteur, Vice-Admiral Jules Théophile. *La Vérité sur les Amiraux.* Paris: Éditions de la Couronne, 1949.

Doumenc, General A. *Dunkerque et la Campagne de Flandre.* Paris: B. Arthaud, 1947.

Draper, Theodore. *The Six Weeks' War: France, May 10–June 25, 1940.* New York: Book Find Club, 1944.

Dreifort, John E. *Yvon Delbos at the Quai d'Orsay: French Foreign Policy during the Popular Front, 1936–1938.* Lawrence, Kan.: The University Press of Kansas, 1973.

Ducloux, Louis. *From Blackmail to Treason: Political Crime and Corruption in France, 1920–1940.* Translated by Ronald Matthews. London: André Deutsch, 1958.

Duroselle, J.-B. *Histoire Diplomatique de 1919 à nos jours.* Paris: Dalloz, 1971.

Dutourd, Jean. *The Taxis of the Marne.* Translated by Harold King. New York: Simon and Schuster, 1957.

Earle, Edward Mead. Editor. *Modern France: Problems of the Third and Fourth Republics.* Princeton, N.J.; Princeton University Press, 1951.

Fabre-Luce, Alfred. *Journal de la France, mars 1939–juillet 1940.* Ain: Imprimerie de Trévoux, 1940.

Farmer, Paul. *Vichy: Political Dilemma.* New York: Columbia University Press, 1955.

Fonvieille-Alquier, François. *The French and the Phoney War, 1939–40.* Translated and introduced by Edward Ashcroft. London: Tom Stacey, 1973.

Freiden, Seymour, and Richardson, William. Editors. *The Fatal Decisions.* Translated by Constantine Fitzgibbon. New York: Berkley Medallion Books, 1966; originally published by William Sloane Associates, 1956.

Fuller, Major-General J. F. C. *The Decisive Battles of the Western World and Their Influence Upon History.* Vol. III. London: Eyre & Spottiswoode, 1956.

Furnia, Arthur. *The Diplomacy of Appeasement: Anglo-French Relations and the Prelude to World War II, 1931–1938.* Preface by James Fitzgerald Brewer. Washington, D.C.: The University Press, 1960.

Gannon, Franklin Reid. *The British Press and Germany, 1936–1939.* Oxford: Clarendon Press, 1971.

Gérard-Libois, J. and Gotovitch, José. *L'An 40: La Belgique occupée.* Brussels: Crisp, 1973.

Gilbert, Martin, and Gott, Richard. *The Appeasers.* London: Weidenfeld and Nicolson, 1963.

Girard, Louis-Dominique. *Montoire: Verdun Diplomatique.* Paris: Éditions André Bonne, 1948.

Gorce, Paul-Marie de la. *The French Army: A Military-Political History.* Translated by Kenneth Douglas. New York: George Braziller, 1963.

Goutard, Colonel Adolphe. *The Battle of France, 1940.* Translated by Captain A. R. P. Burgess. Foreword by Captain B. H. Liddell Hart. London: Frederick Muller, 1958.

Graves, Robert, and Hodge, Alan. *The Long Week-end: A Social History of Great Britain, 1918–1939.* London: Faber and Faber Limited, 1940.

Greene, Nathanael. *Crisis and Decline: The French Socialist Party in the Popular Front Era.* Ithaca, N.Y.: Cornell University Press, 1969.

Gretton, Vice-Admiral Sir Peter. *Former Naval Person: Winston Churchill and the Royal Navy.* London: Cassell, 1968.

Haight, John McVickar, Jr. *American Aid to France, 1938–1940.* New York: Atheneum, 1970.

Henriot, Philippe. *Comment Mourut la Paix.* Paris: Les Éditions de France, 1941.

Hoffmann, Stanley, *et al. In Search of France.* Cambridge, Mass.: Harvard University Press, 1963.

Horne, Alistair. *To Lose a Battle: France 1940.* Boston: Little, Brown and Company, 1969.

Howard, Michael. *The Continental Commitment: The Dilemma of British Defence Policy in the Era of the Two World Wars.* London: Temple Smith, 1972.

Hytier, Adrienne Doris. *Two Years of French Foreign Policy: Vichy, 1940–1942.* Paris: Librairie Minard, 1958.

Jacobsen, H. A., and Rohwer, J. Editors. *Decisive Battles of World War II: The German View.* Translated by Edward Fitzgerald. New York: G. P. Putnam's Sons, 1965.

Jakobson, Max. *The Diplomacy of the Winter War: An Account of the Russo-Finnish War, 1939–1940.* Cambridge, Mass.: Harvard University Press, 1961.

James, Admiral Sir W. M. *The British Navies in the Second World War.* London: Longmans, Green and Co., 1946.

Jameson, Rear Admiral William. *Ark Royal, 1939–1941.* London: Rupert Hart-Davis, 1957.

Joll, James. Editor. *The Decline of the Third Republic.* London: Chatto & Windus, 1959.

Jordan, W. M. *Great Britain, France, and the German Problem, 1918–1939: A Study of Anglo-French Relations in the Making and Maintenance of the Versailles Settlement.* London: Oxford University Press, 1943.

Kammerer, Albert. *Du Débarquement Africain au Meurtre de Darlan.* Paris: Flammarion, 1949.

———. *La Passion de la Flotte Française: De Mers El-Kébir à Toulon.* Paris: Librairie Arthème Fayard, 1951.

———. *La Tragédie de Mers-el Kébir: L'Angleterre et la Flotte Française.* Paris: Éditions Médicis, 1945.

———. *La Vérité sur l'Armistice: Ephéméride de ce qui s'est Réellement Passé au Moment du Désastre.* 2nd ed. Paris: Éditions Médicis, 1945.

Kecskemeti, Paul. *Strategic Surrender: The Politics of Victory and Defeat.* New York: Atheneum, 1964.

Kennedy, Joseph P., and Landis, James M. *The Surrender of King Leopold.* New York: 1950.

Kerillis, Henri de. *Français, Voici la Vérité!* New York: Éditions de la Maison Française, 1942.

Kimche, Jon. *The Unfought Battle.* London: Weidenfeld and Nicolson, 1968.

Koeltz, General L. *Comment s'est joué Notre Destin: Hitler et l'Offensive du 10 Mai 1940.* Paris: Hachette, 1957.

Lafore, Laurence. *The End of Glory: An Interpretation of the Origins of World War II.* Philadelphia and New York: J. B. Lippincott Company, 1970.

Langer, William L. *Our Vichy Gamble.* New York: W. W. Norton & Company, 1966; first published by Alfred A. Knopf, 1947.

Langer, William L., and Gleason, S. Everett. *The Challenge to Isolation, 1937–1940.* New York: Harper & Brothers Publishers, 1952.

Larmour, Peter J. *The French Radical Party in the 1930's.* Stanford, Calif.: Stanford University Press, 1964.

Lash, Joseph P. *Roosevelt and Churchill, 1939–1941: The Partnership That Saved the West.* New York: W. W. Norton, 1976.

Levy, Louis. *The Truth About France.* Translated by W. Pickles. Harmondsworth, Middlesex: Penguin Books, 1941.

Liddell Hart, B. H. *The German Generals Talk.* New York: William Morrow & Co., Apollo Editions, 1965; first published 1948.

———. *History of the Second World War.* London: Cassell, 1970.

Longmate, Norman. *If Britain Had Fallen.* New York: Stein and Day, 1974.

Luethy, Herbert. *France Against Herself; A Perceptive Study of France's Past, Her Politics, and Her Unending Crises.* Translated by Eric Mosbacher. New York: Frederick A. Praeger, 1955.

Lyet, Commandant Pierre. *La Bataille de France (Mai-Juin 1940).* Paris: Payot, 1947.

Marchal, Léon. *Vichy: Two Years of Deception.* New York: The Macmillan Company, 1943.

Marder, Arthur J. *From the Dardanelles to Oran: Studies of the Royal Navy in War and Peace, 1915–1940.* London: Oxford University Press, 1974.

———. *Operation 'Menace': The Dakar Expedition and the Dudley North Affair.* London: Oxford University Press, 1976.

McCallum, R. B. *England and France, 1939–1943.* London: Hamish Hamilton, 1944.

Medlicott, W. N. *British Foreign Policy Since Versailles.* London: Methuen & Co., 1940.

Micaud, Charles A. *The French Right and Nazi Germany, 1933–1939: A Study of Public Opinion.* Durham, N.C.: Duke University Press, 1943.

Michel, Henri. *La Drôle de Guerre.* Paris: Hachette, 1971.

————. *La Seconde Guerre Mondiale.* Vol. I, *Les Succès de l'Axe (septembre 1939–janvier 1943).* Paris: Presses Universitaires de France, 1968.

————. *The Shadow War: Resistance in Europe, 1939–1945.* Translated by Richard Barry. London: André Deutsch, 1972.

————. *Vichy: Année 40.* Paris: Robert Laffont, 1966.

Monks, Noel. *That Day at Gibraltar.* London: Frederick Muller, 1957.

Montigny, Jean. *La Défaite: Heures Tragiques de 1940.* Paris: Éditons Bernard Grasset, 1941.

Mordal, Jacques. *La Marine à l'Épreuve: De l'Armistice de 1940 au Procès Auphan.* Paris: Librairie Plon, 1956.

Mowat, Charles Loch. *Britain Between the Wars, 1918–1940.* Chicago: The University of Chicago Press, 1955.

Muggeridge, Malcolm. *The Thirties in Great Britain: 1930–1940.* London: Collins, Fontana Books, 1971; first published by Hamish Hamilton, 1940.

Namier, L. B. *Diplomatic Prelude, 1938–1939.* London: Macmillan & Co., 1948.

————. *Europe in Decay: A Study in Disintegration, 1936–1940.* London: Macmillan & Co., 1950.

————. *In the Nazi Era.* London: Macmillan & Co., 1952.

Neave, Airey. *The Flames of Calais: A Soldier's Battle, 1940.* London: Hodder and Stoughton, 1972.

Néré, J. *The Foreign Policy of France from 1914 to 1945.* Translated by Translance. London: Routledge & Kegan Paul, 1975.

Newhouse, John. *De Gaulle and the Anglo-Saxons.* New York: The Viking Press, 1970.

[Noël, Léon]. *Le Diktat de Rethondes et L'Armistice Franco-Italien de Juin 1940.* Paris: Flammarion, 1945.

Noguères, Louis. *La Haute Cour de la Libération (1944–1949).* Paris: Les Éditions de Minuit, 1965.

————. *Le Véritable Procès du Maréchal Pétain.* Paris: Librairie Arthème Fayard, 1955.

Osgood, Samuel M. *French Royalism Under the Third and Fourth Republics.* The Hague: Martinus Nijhoff, 1960.

Parkinson, Roger. *Blood, Toil, Tears and Sweat.* New York: David McKay Company, 1973.

————. *Peace for Our Time: Munich to Dunkirk—the Inside Story.* New York: David McKay Company, 1972.

Paxton, Robert O. *Vichy France: Old Guard and New Order, 1940–1944.* New York: Alfred A. Knopf, 1972.

Pertinax [André Géraud]. *The Gravediggers of France: Gamelin, Daladier,*

*Reynaud, Pétain and Laval.* Garden City, N.Y.: Doubleday, Doran & Company, 1944.

Pickles, Dorothy M. *France Between the Republics.* London and Redhill: Love & Malcomson, 1946.

Reibel, Charles. *Pourquoi et comment fut décidée la demande d'armistice (10–17 Juin 1940).* Vanves (Seine): Imprimerie Kapp, 1940.

Renouvin, Pierre. *World War II and Its Origins: International Relations, 1929–1945.* Translated by Rémy Inglis Hall. New York, Evanston, and London: Harper & Row, Publishers, 1968.

Rossi-Landi, Guy. *La Drôle de Guerre: la vie politique en France, 2 septembre 1939–10 mai 1940.* Paris: Armand Colin, 1971.

Roy, Jules. *The Trial of Marshal Pétain.* Translated by Robert Baldick. New York and Evanston: Harper & Row, Publishers, 1968.

Shirer, William L. *The Collapse of the Third Republic: An Inquiry into the Fall of France in 1940.* New York: Simon and Schuster, 1969.

Simon, Yves R. *The Road to Vichy, 1918–1938.* Translated by James A. Corbett and George J. McMorrow. New York: Sheed & Ward, 1942.

Simone, André. *J'accuse!: The Men Who Betrayed France.* New York: The Dial Press, 1940.

Stevenson, William. *A Man Called Intrepid: The Secret War.* New York: Ballantine Books, 1977; originally published by Harcourt Brace Jovanovich, 1976.

Tannenbaum, Edward R. *The Action Française: Die-hard Reactionaries in Twentieth-Century France.* New York: John Wiley and Sons, 1962.

Taylor, A. J. P. *English History, 1914–1945.* London: Oxford University Press, 1965.

———. *The Origins of the Second World War.* New York: Premier Books, Fawcett World Library, 1963; originally published by Atheneum, 1961.

Taylor, A. J. P. Editor. *Lloyd George: Twelve Essays.* New York: Atheneum, 1971.

Taylor, Telford. *The Breaking Wave: The Second World War in the Summer of 1940.* New York: Simon and Schuster, 1967.

———. *The March of Conquest: The German Victories in Western Europe, 1940.* New York: Simon and Schuster, 1958.

Thomas, Louis. Editor. *Documents sur la Guerre de 1939–1940.* Paris: Aux Armes de France, 1941.

Thompson, Laurence. *1940.* New York: William Morrow & Company, 1966.

Thompson, Neville. *The Anti-Appeasers: Conservative Opposition to Appeasement in the 1930s.* Oxford: Clarendon Press, 1971.

Thompson, R. W. *Generalissimo Churchill.* London: Hodder and Stoughton, 1973.

Tissier, Lieutenant-Colonel Pierre. *The Riom Trial.* Foreword by General Charles de Gaulle. London: George G. Harrap & Co., 1942.

Tompkins, Peter. *The Murder of Admiral Darlan: A Study in Conspiracy.* New York: Simon and Schuster, 1965.

Toynbee, Arnold, and Toynbee, Veronica M. Editors. *Survey of International Affairs 1939–1946: Hitler's Europe.* Royal Institute of International Affairs, London: Oxford University Press, 1954.

———. *Survey of International Affairs, 1939–1946. The Eve of War, 1939.* London: Oxford University Press, 1958.

———. *Survey of International Affairs 1939–1946: The Initial Triumph of the Axis.* Royal Institute of International Affairs, London: Oxford University Press, 1958.

Truchet, André. *L'Armistice de 1940 et l'Afrique du Nord.* Paris: Presses Universitaires de France, 1955.

Tute, Warren, *The Deadly Stroke.* London: Collins, 1973.

Varillon, Pierre. *Mers-el-Kébir.* Paris: Amiot-Dumont, 1949.

Waites, Neville. Editor. *Troubled Neighbours: Franco-British Relations in the Twentieth Century.* London: Weidenfeld and Nicolson, 1971.

Waterfield, Gordon. *What Happened to France.* London: John Murray, 1940.

Watt, D. C. *Personalities and Policies: Studies in the Formulation of British Foreign Policy in the Twentieth Century.* London: Longmans, Green and Co., 1965.

Watt, Donald Cameron. *Too Serious a Business: European Armed Forces and the Approach to the Second World War.* Berkeley, Calif.: University of California Press, 1975.

Werth, Alexander. *France, 1940–1955.* Boston: Beacon Press, 1966; first published by Robert Hale, 1956.

———. *The Twilight of France, 1933–1940.* Edited with an Introduction by D. W. Brogan. New York: Harper & Brothers Publishers, 1942.

Wheeler-Bennett, John W. *Munich: Prologue to Tragedy.* New York: The Viking Press, Compass Books, 1964; originally published by Duell, Sloan & Pearce, 1948.

Williams, Douglas. *Retreat from Dunkirk.* New York: Brentano's, 1941.

Williams, John. *France: Summer 1940.* New York: Ballantine Books, 1970.

———. *The Ides of May: The Defeat of France, May–June, 1940.* New York: Alfred A. Knopf, 1968.

Williamson, Samuel R., Jr. *The Politics of Grand Strategy: Britain and France Prepare for War, 1904–1914.* Cambridge, Mass.: Harvard University Press, 1969.

Winterbotham, F. W. *The Ultra Secret.* New York: Dell Publishing Co., 1975; first published by Harper & Row, 1974.

Wiskemann, Elizabeth. *The Rome-Berlin Axis: A History of the Relations Between Hitler and Mussolini.* London: Oxford University Press, 1949.

Wolfers, Arnold. *Britain and France between Two Wars: Conflicting Strategies of Peace from Versailles to World War II.* New York: W. W. Norton & Company, 1966; reprinted from Harcourt, Brace and Company, 1940.

## ARTICLES

Aron, Raymond. "On Treason." *Confluence,* Vol. 3, No. 3 (1954), pp. 280–94.

Auphan, Rear Admiral Paul. "The French Navy Enters World War II." *United States Naval Institute Proceedings,* Vol. 82, No. 6 (June 1956), pp. 592–601.

Bankwitz, Philip C. F. "Maxime Weygand and the Fall of France: A Study in Civil-Military Relations." *Journal of Modern History,* Vol. XXXI, No. 3 (September 1959), pp. 225–42.

Bardoux, Jacques. "La Rupture Franco-Britannique." *Revue des Deux Mondes,* LVIII (July 15, 1940), pp. 54–63.

Baumont, Maurice. "French Critics and Apologists Debate Munich." *Foreign Affairs,* Vol. 25, No. 4 (July 1947), pp. 685–90.

Beauman, Brigadier A. B. "France: May–June 1940: Operations on the British Lines of Communications." *Army Quarterly,* August 1943, pp. 184–90; October 1943, pp. 51–56; January 1944, pp. 170–76; April 1944, pp. 37–43.

Beaverbrook, Lord [William Maxwell Aitken]. "Two War Leaders: Lloyd George and Churchill." *History Today,* Vol. XXIII, No. 8 (August 1973), pp. 546–53.

Bell, P. M. H. "Note sur le Blocus Britannique de la France non-occupée." *Revue d'Histoire de la Deuxième Guerre Mondiale* (October 1957), pp. 91–94.

———. "Prologue de Mers-el-Kébir." *Revue d'Histoire de la Deuxième Guerre Mondiale,* Vol. IX, No. 33 (January 1959), pp. 15–36.

Beloff, Max. "The Anglo-French Union Project of June 1940," pp. 172–99 of *The Intellectual in Politics and Other Essays.* London: Weidenfeld and Nicolson, 1970.

Boucherie, General Marcel. "Les Causes politiques et morales d'un désastre: 1940." *Revue de Défense Nationale,* Vol. XIV (March 1958), pp. 409–16.

Brooks, Russell. "The Unknown Darlan." *United States Naval Institute Proceedings,* Vol. 81, No. 8 (August 1955), pp. 879–92.

Butterworth, Susan Bindoff. "Daladier and the Munich Crisis: A Reappraisal." *Journal of Contemporary History,* Vol. 9, No. 3 (July 1974), pp. 191–216.

Cailloux, Colonel. "Campagne de France, 1940: La Contre-Attaque Qui

N'Eut Jamais Lieu, 19–25 Mai." *Revue Historique de l'Armée,* 1966, No. 3, pp. 133–47.

Cairns, John C. "Along the Road Back to France, 1940." *American Historical Review,* Vol. LXIV, No. 3 (April 1959), pp. 583–603.

———. "A Nation of Shopkeepers in Search of a Suitable France, 1919–1940." *American Historical Review,* Vol. 79, No. 3 (June 1974), pp. 710–43.

———. "Great Britain and the Fall of France: A Study in Allied Disunity." *Journal of Modern History,* Vol. XXVII (December 1955), pp. 365–409.

———. "Some Recent Historians and the 'Strange Defeat' of 1940." *Journal of Modern History,* Vol. 46, No. 1 (March 1974), pp. 60–85.

Cameron, Elizabeth R. "Alexis Saint-Léger Léger." In *The Diplomats, 1919–1939,* Vol. II, *The Thirties,* pp. 378–405. Edited by Gordon A. Craig and Felix Gilbert. New York: Atheneum, 1967; originally published by Princeton University Press, 1953.

Castex, Admiral Raoul. "L'Afrique et la stratégie française." *Revue de Défense Nationale,* Vol. XIV (May 1952), pp. 523–34.

Challener, Richard D. "The Third Republic and the Generals." In *Total War and Cold War: Problems in Civilian Control of the Military,* pp. 91–107. Edited by Harry L. Coles. Columbus: The Ohio State University Press, 1962.

Champoux, Richard J. "The Massilia Affair." *Journal of Contemporary History,* Vol. 10, No. 2 (April 1975), pp. 283–300.

Chapman, Guy. "The French Army and Politics." In *Soldiers and Governments: Nine Studies in Civil-Military Relations,* pp. 53–72. Edited by Michael Howard. London: Eyre & Spottiswoode, 1957.

Chautemps, Camille. "Lettre d'un condamné." *Écrits de Paris,* June 1947, pp. 117–22.

Conquet, General Alfred. "À propos de la thèse: nous pouvions vaincre en 1940." *Écrits de Paris,* No. 168 (March 1958), pp. 55–66; No. 169 (April 1958), pp. 56–64; No. 170 (May 1958), pp. 71–85.

Cossé-Brissac, Colonel Charles de. "L'Armée allemande dans la campagne de France de 1940." *Revue d'Histoire de la Deuxième Guerre Mondiale,* Vol. XIV, No. 53 (January 1964), pp. 3–28.

Craig, Gordon A. "High Tide of Appeasement: The Road to Munich, 1937–38." *Political Science Quarterly,* Vol. LXV, No. 1 (March 1950), pp. 20–37.

Dhers, Pierre. "Le Comité de Guerre du 25 Mai 1940." *Revue d'Histoire de la Deuxième Guerre Mondiale,* Vol. III, No. 10–11 (June 1953), pp. 165–83.

———. "Du 7 mars 1936 à l'Ile d'Yeu." *Revue d'Histoire de la Deuxième Guerre Mondiale,* Vol. II, No. 5 (January 1952), pp. 17–26.

d'Hoop, Jean-Marie. "La Politique française du réarmement." *Revue d'Histoire de la Deuxième Guerre Mondiale,* Vol. IV, No. 14 (April 1954), pp. 1–26.

Dufieux, General J. "1940: La Guerre des occasions perdues (À propos du livre du Colonel Goutard)." *Revue d'Histoire Diplomatique,* LXX (1956), pp. 362–74.

Eatwell, Roger. "Munich, Public Opinion, and Popular Front." *Journal of Contemporary History,* Vol. 6, No. 4 (1971), pp. 122–39.

Ely, General Paul. "La leçon qu'il faut tirer des opérations de 1940." *Revue de Défense Nationale,* Vol. IX (December 1953), pp. 563–82.

Evans, Major-General R. "The 1st Armoured Division in France." *Army Quarterly,* November 1942, pp. 55–69; February 1943, pp. 179–87; May 1943, pp. 46–54.

Finer, Herman. "The British Cabinet, the House of Commons and the War." *Political Science Quarterly,* Vol. LVI, No. 3 (September 1941), pp. 321–60.

Funk, Arthur L. "Negotiating the 'Deal with Darlan'." *Journal of Contemporary History,* Vol. 8, No. 2 (April 1973), pp. 81–117.

Gadrat, F., and Renouvin, P. "Les Documents diplomatiques français." *Revue d'Histoire de la Deuxième Guerre Mondiale,* No. 71 (July 1968), pp. 1–11.

Géraud, André. "Riom." *Foreign Affairs,* Vol. 20, No. 4 (July 1942), pp. 679–93.

Gibbs, Norman. "Winston Churchill and the British War Cabinet." In *Total War and Cold War: Problems in Civilian Control of the Military,* pp. 27–41. Edited by Harry L. Coles. Columbus: The Ohio State University Press, 1962.

Gottschalk, Louis. "Our Vichy Fumble." *Journal of Modern History,* Vol. XX, No. 1 (March 1948), pp. 47–56.

Goutard, Colonel Adolphe. "Pourquoi et comment l'Armistice a-t-il été 'accordé' par Hitler?" *Revue de Paris,* LXVII (October 1960), pp. 79–95.

Haight, John McVickar, Jr. "France, the United States, and the Munich Crisis." *Journal of Modern History,* Vol. 32, No. 4 (December 1960), pp. 340–58.

———. "Les Négociations relatives aux achats d'avions américains par la France pendant la période qui précéda immédiatement la guerre." *Revue d'Histoire de la Deuxième Guerre Mondiale,* No. 58 (April 1965), pp. 1–34.

Hoffmann, Stanley. "After the Fall (review of Robert Paxton's *Vichy France*)." *New York Review of Books,* Vol XX, No. 1 (February 8, 1973), pp. 19–20.

————. "Collaborationism in France during World War II." *Journal of Modern History,* Vol. 40, No. 3 (September 1968), pp. 375–95.

Johnson, D. W. J. "Britain and France in 1940." *Transactions of the Royal Historical Society,* 5th Series, Vol. 22 (London, 1972), pp. 141–57.

Kaufmann, William W. "Two American Ambassadors: Bullitt and Kennedy." In *The Diplomats, 1919–1939,* Vol. II, *The Thirties,* pp. 649–81. Edited by Gordon A. Craig and Felix Gilbert. New York: Atheneum, 1967; originally published by Princeton University Press, 1953.

Kelly, George Armstrong. "The French Army Re-enters Politics, 1940–1955." *Political Science Quarterly,* Vol. LXXVI, No. 3 (September 1961), pp. 367–92.

Knight, Thomas J. "Belgium Leaves the War, 1940." *Journal of Modern History,* Vol. 41, No. 1 (March 1969), pp. 46–67.

Kovacs, A. F. "Military Origins of the Fall of France." *Military Affairs,* Vol. VII (Spring 1943), pp. 25–40.

La Baume, R. de. "L'Espagne 'non-belligérante' (1940)." *Revue d'Histoire Diplomatique,* April–June 1955, pp. 126–29.

Lammers, Donald. "Fascism, Communism, and the Foreign Office, 1937–39." *Journal of Contemporary History,* Vol. 6, No. 3 (1971), pp. 66–86.

Lecuir, Jean, and Fridenson, Patrick. "L'organisation de la coopération aérienne Franco-britannique (1935-mai 1940)." *Revue d'Histoire de la Deuxième Guerre Mondiale,* No. 73 (January 1969), pp. 43–74.

Le Goyet, Lieutenant-Colonel. "La Percée de Sedan (10-15 mai 1940)." *Revue d'Histoire de la Deuxième Guerre Mondiale,* No. 59 (July 1965), pp. 25–52.

Lesquen, Colonel M. de. "L'Armée de l'air française en 1940." *Revue de Défense Nationale,* January 1952, pp. 74–84.

Lestien, General. "La Commission d'enquête parlementaire et les événements militaires du 10 mai au 11 juin 1940." *Revue d'Histoire de la Deuxième Guerre Mondiale,* Vol. III, No. 10–11 (June 1953), pp. 184–91.

Leutze, James. "The Secret of the Churchill-Roosevelt Correspondence: September 1939–May 1940." *Journal of Contemporary History,* Vol. 10, No. 3 (July 1975), pp. 465–91.

Lugand, Lieutenant-Colonel. "Les Forces en présence au 10 mai 1940." *Revue d'Histoire de la Deuxième Guerre Mondiale,* Vol. III, No. 10–11 (June 1953), pp. 5–48.

Lyet, Colonel Pierre. "À propos de Sedan, 1940." *Revue Historique de l'Armée,* 1962, No. 4, pp. 89–109.

————. "Documents militaires sur l'Armistice, juin 1940." *Revue Historique de l'Armée,* January–March 1947, No. 1, pp. 45–64.

————. "Témoignages et documents, 1939–1940." *Revue Historique de l'Armée,* Vol. XVI (February 1960), pp. 139–54; XVII (March 1961), pp. 81–105.

Manne, Robert. "The British Decision for Alliance with Russia, May 1939." *Journal of Contemporary History,* Vol. 9, No. 3 (July 1974), pp. 3–26.

Marin, Louis. "Contribution à l'Étude des Prodromes de l'Armistice." *Revue d'Histoire de la Deuxième Guerre Mondiale,* Vol. I, No. 3 (June 1951), pp. 1–26.

————"Gouvernement et commandement (conflits, différends, immixtions qui ont pesé sur l'Armistice de juin 1940)." *Revue d'Histoire de la Deuxième Guerre Mondiale,* Vol. II, No. 8 (October 1952), pp. 1–28; Vol. III, No. 9 (January 1953), pp. 1–14.

Massis, Henri. "Huntziger, Weygand, De Gaulle." *Hommes et Mondes,* December 1954, pp. 1–12.

"M. Churchill et le projet breton." *Écrits de Paris,* March 1949, pp. 58–74.

Medlicott, W. N. "The Coming of War in 1939." In *From Metternich to Hitler: Aspects of British and Foreign History, 1814–1939,* pp. 231–56. Edited by Medlicott. London: Routledge and Kegan Paul, 1963.

Melka, Robert L. "Darlan between Britain and Germany, 1940–41." *Journal of Contemporary History,* Vol. 8, No. 2 (April 1973), pp. 57–80.

Michel, Henri. "L'Oeuvre de la Commission parlementaire chargée d'enquêter sur les événements survenus en France de 1933 à 1945." *Revue d'Histoire de la Deuxième Guerre Mondiale,* Vol. I, No. 3 (June 1951), pp. 94–96.

Morvan, Jean. "Encore le Réduit Breton." *Écrits de Paris,* October 1955, pp. 79–83.

Noël, Léon. "Le Projet d'union franco-britannique de juin 1940." *Revue d'Histoire de la Deuxième Guerre Mondiale,* Vol. VI, No. 21 (January 1956), pp. 22–37.

Padover, Saul K. "France in Defeat: Causes and Consequences." *World Politics,* Vol. II, No. 3 (April 1950), pp. 305–37.

Paquier, Col. Pierre, Lyet, Cdt. Pierre, and Cossé-Brissac, Lt.-Col. Charles de. "Combien d'avions allemands contre combien d'avions français le 10 mai 1940?" *Revue de Défense Nationale* (June 1948), pp. 741–59.

Parker, R. A. C. "Economics, Rearmament and Foreign Policy: The United Kingdom before 1939—A Preliminary Study." *Journal of Contemporary History,* Vol. 10, No. 4 (October 1975), pp. 637–47.

Philibert, Colonel J. "Les Forces françaises d'Afrique du Nord, septembre 1939–juin 1940." *Revue Historique de l'Armée,* IX (December 1953), pp. 105–10.

Powers, Richard Howard. "Winston Churchill's Parliamentary Commentary on British Foreign Policy, 1935–1938." *Journal of Modern History,* Vol. XXVI, No. 2 (June 1954), pp. 179–82.

Reussner, André. "La Réorganisation du Haut Commandement au mois de mai 1940." *Revue d'Histoire de la Deuxième Guerre Mondiale,* Vol. III, No. 10–11 (June 1953), pp. 49–59.

Robert, Fernand. "Il Était déjà trop tard: les travaux de la Commission Jacquet sur les événements de 1933–1945 en France." *Revue Socialiste,* Vol. 98 (June 1956), pp. 34–48.

Rogé, Lieutenant-Colonel. "Les Aviations allemande, française et anglaise du 10 mai 1940 au 25 juin 1940." *Revue de Défense Nationale,* February 1951, pp. 162–76.

————"La Campagne de France vue par le Général Guderian." *Revue Historique de l'Armée,* III (March 1947), pp. 109–19.

Saunders, Commander M. G. "L'Évacuation par Dunkerque." *Revue d'Histoire de la Deuxième Guerre Mondiale,* Vol. III (June 1953), pp. 119–34.

Scherer, André. "Les Mémoires du Général Weygand." *Revue d'Histoire de la Deuxième Guerre Mondiale,* Vol. IX, No. 33 (January 1959), pp. 67–71.

"Scrutator." "Le Gendre de Pierre Laval au secours de l'Angleterre." *Écrits de Paris,* August 1949, pp. 104–13.

Shlaim, Avi. "Prelude to Downfall: The British Offer of Union to France, June 1940." *Journal of Contemporary History,* Vol. 9, No. 3 (July 1974), pp. 27–63.

Smith, Commander C. Alphonso. "Martinique in World War II." *United States Naval Institute Proceedings,* Vol. 81, No. 2 (February 1955), pp. 168–74.

Soucy, Robert J. "The Nature of Fascism in France." *Journal of Contemporary History,* Vol. I, No. 1 (1966), pp. 27–55.

Taylor, A. J. P. "Daddy, What was Winston Churchill?" *New York Times Magazine,* April 28, 1974, pp. 30–31, 80–84, 92.

Thursfield, Rear Admiral H. G. "Pour Encourager les Autres." *The National Review,* Vol. CXXXI (October 1948), pp. 343–53.

Truchet, André. "L'Armistice de Juin 1940 et l'Afrique du Nord." *Revue d'Histoire de la Deuxième Guerre Mondiale,* Vol. I, No. 3 (June 1951), pp. 27–50.

Vial, Lieutenant-Colonel Jean. "Une Semaine décisive sur la Somme, 18–25 mai 1940." *Revue Historique de l'Armée,* Vol. V (December 1949), pp. 45–58; VI (March 1950), pp. 46–60.

Viault, Birdsall Scrymser. "Les Démarches pour le rétablissement de la paix (septembre 1939–août 1940)." *Revue d'Histoire de la Deuxième Guerre Mondiale,* No. 67 (July 1967), pp. 13–30.

Villate, Colonel Robert. "Le Changement de commandement de mai 1940:

Étude critique de témoignages." *Revue d'Histoire de la Deuxième Guerre Mondiale,* Vol. II, No. 5 (January 1952), pp. 27–36.

Wright, Gordon. "Ambassador Bullitt and the Fall of France." *World Politics,* Vol. X, No. 1 (October 1957), pp. 63–90.

Young, Robert J. "The Aftermath of Munich: The Course of French Diplomacy, October 1938 to March 1939." *French Historical Studies,* Vol. VIII, No. 7 (1973), pp. 305–22.

———. "The Strategic Dream: French Air Doctrine in the Inter-War Period, 1919–39." *Journal of Contemporary History,* Vol. 9, No. 4 (October 1974), pp. 57–76.

### SPEECHES

Churchill, Winston S. *Blood, Sweat and Tears.* Preface and Notes by Randolph S. Churchill. New York: G. P. Putnam's Sons, 1941.

———. *Into Battle: Speeches by the Right Hon. Winston S. Churchill.* Compiled by Randolph S. Churchill. London, 1941.

———. *Secret Session Speeches.* Compiled by Charles Eade. London: Cassell and Company, 1946.

Gaulle, Charles de. *Discours aux Français: 18 Juin 1940–Janvier 1944.* Algiers: n.d.

Pétain, Henri Philippe. *Quatre années au pouvoir.* Paris: La Couronne Littéraire, 1949.

### FICTION AND BELLES-LETTRES

Brée, Germaine and Bernauer, George. Editors. *Defeat and Beyond: An Anthology of French Wartime Writing, 1940–45.* New York: Pantheon Books, 1970.

Céline, Louis-Ferdinand. *Castle to Castle.* Translated by Ralph Manheim. New York: Delacorte Press, 1968.

Dutourd, Jean. *The Best Butter.* Translated by Robin Chancellor. New York: Simon and Schuster, 1955.

Ehrenburg, Ilya. *The Fall of Paris.* Translated by Gerard Shelley. New York: Alfred A. Knopf, 1943.

Merle, Robert. *Week-end at Zuydcoote.* Translated by K. Rebillon-Lambley. London: John Lehmann, 1950.

Mitford, Nancy. *Pigeon Pie.* Harmondsworth, Middlesex: Penguin Books, 1965; first published by Hamish Hamilton, 1940.

Peyrefitte, Roger. *Diplomatic Conclusions.* Translated by Edward Hyams. London, New York: Thames and Hudson, 1954.

Powell, Anthony. *The Valley of Bones.* Boston: Little, Brown and Company, 1964.

Saint-Exupéry, Antoine de. *Flight to Arras.* Translated by Lewis Galantière. Harmondsworth, Middlesex: Penguin Books, 1961; earlier published in English by Heinemann, 1942.

Sartre, Jean-Paul. *The Reprieve.* Translated by Eric Sutton. New York: Bantam Books, 1960; earlier published in English by Alfred A. Knopf, 1947.

————. *Troubled Sleep.* Translated by Gerard Hopkins. New York: Bantam Books, 1961; earlier published in English by Alfred A. Knopf, 1950.

Simenon. *The Premier* and *The Train.* Translated by Daphne Woodward. New York: Harcourt, Brace & World, 1966.

Waugh, Evelyn. *Men at Arms* and *Officers and Gentlemen.* New York: Dell Publishing Co., 1961; originally published by Little, Brown and Company, 1952 and 1955.

## MISCELLANEOUS

*Annuaire Diplomatique et Consulaire de la République Française.* 1947 edition. Paris: Imprimerie Nationale, 1947.

*Brassey's Naval Annual.* 1940 and 1941 editions. Edited by Rear Admiral H. G. Thursfield. London: William Clowes, 1940, 1941. 1948 edition. New York: The Macmillan Company, 1948.

*Dictionnaire biographique français contemporain.* Paris: Pharos, 1950.

*Dictionnaire de parlementaires français: notices biographiques sur les ministres, senateurs et députés français de 1889 à 1940.* Paris: Presses Universitaires de France, 1966.

*Foreign Office List and Diplomatic and Consular Yearbook* (1940). London: Harrison and Sons, 1940.

# Index